# ADOPTION AND ASSISTED REPRODUCTION: FAMILIES UNDER CONSTRUCTION

ASPEN PUBLISHERS

# *ADOPTION AND ASSISTED REPRODUCTION: FAMILIES UNDER CONSTRUCTION*

**Susan Frelich Appleton**
*Washington University in St. Louis*

**D. Kelly Weisberg**
*University of California*
*Hastings College of Law*

Wolters Kluwer
Law & Business

AUSTIN    BOSTON    CHICAGO    NEW YORK    THE NETHERLANDS

Aspen Publishers
Attn: Permissions Department
76 Ninth Avenue, 7th Floor
New York, NY 10011-5201

To contact Customer Care, e-mail customer.care@aspenpublishers.com, call 1-800-234-1660, fax 1-800-901-9075, or mail correspondence to:

Aspen Publishers
Attn: Order Department
PO Box 990
Frederick, MD 21705

Printed in the United States of America.

1 2 3 4 5 6 7 8 9 0

ISBN 978-0-7355-7813-5

**Library of Congress Cataloging-in-Publication Data**

Appleton, Susan Frelich, 1948-
    Adoption and assisted reproduction: families under construction / Susan Frelich Appleton, D. Kelly Weisberg.
        p. cm.
    Includes bibliographical references and index.
    ISBN-13: 978-0-7355-7813-5
    ISBN-10: 0-7355-7813-3
1. Adoption—Law and legislation—United States. 2. Human reproductive technology—Law and legislation—United States. I. Weisberg, D. Kelly. II. Title.

    KF545.A97 2009
    346.7301'78–dc22

                                                                            2009002848

# About Wolters Kluwer Law & Business

Wolters Kluwer Law & Business is a leading provider of research information and workflow solutions in key specialty areas. The strengths of the individual brands of Aspen Publishers, CCH, Kluwer Law International and Loislaw are aligned within Wolters Kluwer Law & Business to provide comprehensive, in-depth solutions and expert-authored content for the legal, professional and education markets.

**CCH** was founded in 1913 and has served more than four generations of business professionals and their clients. The CCH products in the Wolters Kluwer Law & Business group are highly regarded electronic and print resources for legal, securities, antitrust and trade regulation, government contracting, banking, pension, payroll, employment and labor, and healthcare reimbursement and compliance professionals.

**Aspen Publishers** is a leading information provider for attorneys, business professionals and law students. Written by preeminent authorities, Aspen products offer analytical and practical information in a range of specialty practice areas from securities law and intellectual property to mergers and acquisitions and pension/benefits. Aspen's trusted legal education resources provide professors and students with high-quality, up-to-date and effective resources for successful instruction and study in all areas of the law.

**Kluwer Law International** supplies the global business community with comprehensive English-language international legal information. Legal practitioners, corporate counsel and business executives around the world rely on the Kluwer Law International journals, loose-leafs, books and electronic products for authoritative information in many areas of international legal practice.

**Loislaw** is a premier provider of digitized legal content to small law firm practitioners of various specializations. Loislaw provides attorneys with the ability to quickly and efficiently find the necessary legal information they need, when and where they need it, by facilitating access to primary law as well as state-specific law, records, forms and treatises.

Wolters Kluwer Law & Business, a unit of Wolters Kluwer, is headquartered in New York and Riverwoods, Illinois. Wolters Kluwer is a leading multinational publisher and information services company.

# SUMMARY OF CONTENTS

# CONTENTS

# *ACKNOWLEDGMENTS*

We would like to thank the publishers and copyright holders listed here for their permission to reprint the various excerpts indicated.

Andrews, Lori, Between Strangers: Surrogate Mothers, Expectant Father and Brave New Babies (Harper & Row 1989). Copyright © 1989 by Lori B. Andrews. Reprinted by permission.

Bartholet, Elizabeth, Where Do Black Children Belong? The Politics of Race Matching in Adoption, 139 University of Pennsylvania Law Review 1163 (1991). Copyright © 1991 by the University of Pennsylvania. Reprinted by permission.

Berebitsky, Julie, Like Our Very Own: Adoptions and the Changing Culture of Motherhood, 1851-1950 (University Press of Kansas 2000). Copyright © 2000 by University Press of Kansas. Reprinted by permission.

Fessler, Ann, THE GIRLS WHO WENT AWAY (The Penguin Press 2006). Copyright © 2006 by Ann Fessler. Used by permission of The Penguin Press, a division of Penguin Group (USA) Inc.

Golden, Daniel, When Adoption Doesn't Work . . . , The Boston Globe, June 11, 1989, Magazine Section, at 16. Copyright © 1989 by the Globe Newspaper Company. Reprinted by permission.

Orenstein, Peggy, The Other Mother, New York Times, July 25, 2004, Section 6 (Magazine), at 24. Copyright © 2004 by The New York Times. All rights reserved. Used by permission and protected by the Copyright Laws of the United States. The printing, copying, redistribution, or retransmission of the Material without expression written permission is prohibited.

Perry, Twila L., Transracial and International Adoption: Mothers, Hierarchy, Race, and Feminist Legal Theory, 10 Yale Journal of Law & Feminism 101 (1998). Copyright © 1998 by the Yale Journal of Law & Feminism. Reprinted by permission.

Presser, Stephen, The Historical Background of the American Law of Adoption, 11 Journal of Family Law 443 (1971). Copyright © 1971 by University of Louisville, Louis D. Brandeis School of Law. Reprinted by permission of Stephen Presser.

# INTRODUCTION

Today, family law attorneys and students work in a time of exhilarating change. They must grapple with upheavals in longstanding principles and challenges to the traditional understanding of the family itself. Among the many important shifts that are remaking family law, certain transformations in the fundamental concept of parentage stand out. No longer can one unequivocally answer questions as basic as: Who is a child's parent? On what basis does the law recognize the rights and impose the responsibilities that parental status entails? How many parents may a given child have?

Once, parentage rules relied on biology, marriage to the child's mother, and adoption. Now, such familiar connections merely provide a starting point for more expansive and often more contested approaches that look to behaviors, functions, and intentions. These new approaches also defy conventional assumptions reflected in gendered terms such as "mother" and "father."

Scientific developments, such as more accurate genetic testing and assisted reproductive technologies (or ARTs), account for some of the ongoing changes in the law of parentage. Social developments have also played an important role, including high divorce and remarriage rates, the increasing emergence of families headed by gay men and lesbians, a decreasing number of white infants available for placement, a growing number of older children with special needs without permanent homes, the rise of adoptions across earlier racial and geographic boundaries, and a burgeoning market for infertility treatments.

Against the background of the changing landscape of parentage, this book explores adoption and ARTs. As ordinarily understood, adoption ends an existing parent-child relationship and replaces it with a new one. Hence, an examination of adoption must consider how the law begins such relationships, what legal consequences follow from such relationships, and how the law terminates such relationships.

Today, a study of adoption would remain incomplete without a study of ARTs, too. Millions of babies now have been born as a result of such medical interventions. Two principal ARTs, alternative insemination (once called "artificial insemination") and in vitro fertilization (commonly called "IVF") permit a range of collaborations, including use of donated genetic material or gestational services. Such arrangements require rethinking traditional parentage rules and also complicate the concept of adoption.

Investigating adoption and ARTs together highlights several important themes and tensions. First, the juxtaposition of these topics recognizes that for many persons who face reproductive challenges (from infertility, perhaps, or the absence of a heterosexual partner) adoption, increasingly, has become only one option among many.

Second, the laws governing adoption and ARTs are entwined because the resolution of legal problems in one context often provides models for issues arising in the other, although not without controversy. The law's familiarity with adoption has provided one ready guidepost for addressing novel problems presented by ARTs. Indeed, popular locutions, such as "embryo adoption," illustrate the pervasiveness of this analogical reasoning.

Third, adoption and ARTs both exemplify a more far-reaching tension between privacy and state intervention in family decisionmaking. Some children become available for adoption after state child-protective efforts result in termination of parental rights. Further, although the right to privacy protects sexual reproduction, child welfare remains a centerpiece of American adoption law, with "best interests" as the test, even in contemporary variations such as stepparent and second-parent adoptions. Hence, the state closely regulates adoption — from the acquisition of the original parents' consent to the criteria for child placement. Increased use of independent placements, in which birth parents select adoptive parents, however, reveals a movement toward greater autonomy and private ordering. This tension surfaces in a number of particular contexts, including the ongoing debate over the disclosure of the identities of birth and genetic parents, in which both proponents and opponents of secrecy invoke privacy principles.

If sexual reproduction and adoption mark the ends of a continuum that runs from protected privacy, on the one hand, to state regulation, on the other, then each particular arrangement permitted by ARTs (for example, donor insemination, "surrogacy" agreements, and "embryo adoption") occupies a contested place along this continuum. More specifically, these alternatives to adoption raise the question whether reproductive autonomy includes protection for medical interventions that facilitate procreation. This question, in turn, implicates issues of gender equality, morality, religion, race, class, market freedom, and the role of the state in health care.

Fourth, a study of the parentage rules and procedures applicable to adoption and ARTs emphasizes how the law constructs our understanding of the family. These rules and procedures accord official recognition to certain relationships while making others legally irrelevant. The new Uniform Parentage Act, promulgated in 2000 and revised in 2002, provides one model for such construction. Although observers often point out that modern family law attempts to reflect the realities of family life, the process is a dynamic one because the constructions imposed by the law necessarily shape lived experience.

Finally, this book's topics and themes — which raise issues of identity, ancestral roots, and family secrets — touch deep emotions. Hence, one can find many relevant works in literature, popular culture, and nonlegal scholarship. This book reaches beyond the law to include contributions from such other sources, which help to bring the legal materials to life and to evoke a deeper understanding of them.

Teaching Notes

Before the semester begins, instructors might wish to assign to each student a relevant book or film (from those summarized throughout this book or from a much longer list that one might compile). Inviting each student to introduce his or her book or film to the other members of the class on the first day provides a stimulating point of departure for the course; returning to the "student experts" on particular topics (based on the earlier assigned book or film), as different issues arise during the semester, helps to enrich the discussion.

Editorial Matters

Cases and excerpts have all been edited, often quite extensively. Most deletions are indicated by ellipses, with some exceptions: Some concurring and dissenting opinions have been eliminated; citations have been modified or eliminated; some footnotes and references have been omitted; and paragraphs have been modified, and sometimes combined, to save space and to make the selections more coherent. Brackets are used at times to indicate substantial deletions. Original footnotes in cases and excerpts are reprinted nonconsecutively throughout the book. The editors' textual footnotes are numbered consecutively in each chapter and appear in brackets to differentiate them from original footnotes. We have relied on A Uniform System of Citation (18th ed. 2005), except when that style conflicts with the publisher's style. In addition, statutory citations were checked on Lexis or Westlaw, with the date in each citation showing the year appearing on the database.

Acknowledgments

This project grows out of our earlier efforts on our casebook, Modern Family Law: Cases and Materials. Here, the authors acknowledge the outstanding research assistance of Elizabeth McDonald of Washington University School of Law (class of 2009). In addition, students in Washington University School of Law's seminar in Adoption and Assisted Reproduction (in 2006 and 2007) and in Hastings College of the Law's seminar in Advanced Family Law: Adoption and Assisted Reproduction (in 2007) helped "test drive" these materials, improving them in the process. Janice Houf provided invaluable administrative assistance. We appreciate the excellent suggestions from reviews of the manuscript by Professors Elizabeth Bartholet of Harvard Law School, Anita Bernstein of Brooklyn Law School, and an anonymous reader.

We also thank those at Aspen who supported our work, specifically Eric Holt, Lynn Churchill, John Devins, and Emily Bender. Although many individuals contributed to this project, the authors take responsibility for any remaining errors or shortcomings.

Susan Frelich Appleton
D. Kelly Weisberg

January, 2009

# ADOPTION AND ASSISTED REPRODUCTION: FAMILIES UNDER CONSTRUCTION

# PART I

# ADOPTION

Some historians describe adoption as the creation of a legal fiction because adoption establishes by law a parent-child relationship as if there were a biological tie. Beneath this understanding of adoption lie several important questions explored in this part. How does the law conceptualize and construct the original parent-child relationship, which adoption replaces? To what extent is this original parent-child relationship based on biology versus other criteria? What principles and values govern the ending of this original relationship and the selection of adoptive parents? What specific consequences follow from the legal fiction?

In examining these questions, this part considers adoption's history and the traditional practice of adoption, as well as adoption's place in nontraditional family arrangements. For example, adoption today is often "open," instead of relying on secrecy, and adoption no longer always seeks to "imitate nature," with transracial adoptions and adoptions by same-sex parents notably on the rise. Such multiple expressions of adoption have produced a variety of legal responses among the states and across national boundaries, so this part also considers questions of jurisdiction, choice of law, and recognition of adoption decrees.

# CHAPTER 1

# ORIGINS

## A. ADOPTION'S HISTORY AND PURPOSE

Where does adoption, as we know it today, come from? What is its purpose? Is it designed to serve primarily adults' interests, those of children, or both? In an ideal world, would adoption exist at all?

STEPHEN B. PRESSER, THE HISTORICAL BACKGROUND OF
THE AMERICAN LAW OF ADOPTION

11 J. Fam. L. 443, 446-489 (1971)

We can document the practice of adoption among the ancient Babylonians, Egyptians, and Hebrews, as well as the Greeks, but the most advanced early law on adoption which we have is from the Romans. In contrast with current adoption law, which has as its purpose the "best interests" of the child, it appears that ancient adoption law, and particularly the Roman example, was clearly designed to benefit the *adopter*, and any benefits to the adoptee were secondary. There were two broad purposes that Roman adoption law served: (1) to avoid extinction of the family, and (2) to perpetuate rites of family religious worship. . . .

[Adoption was not known at common law.] The usual explanation for the absence of a legal recognition of adoption in the English common law is the inordinately high regard for blood lineage of the English. [Another possible reason was xenophobia.]

The purpose of the American adoption statutes passed in the middle of the nineteenth century was to provide for the welfare of dependent children, a purpose quite different from that of the old Roman laws. [On the other hand, in England] there were mechanisms for the care of children, dependent and otherwise, that made adoption for social welfare purposes unnecessary. These mechanisms, which were instituted early and which were very well developed by the seventeenth century, were the institutions of "putting out" and "apprenticeship." In a very real sense these institutions were a form of "adoption," although the purpose was neither inheritance nor the perpetuation of the adopter's family, but the temporary training of the child. [T]he customs of "apprenticeship" and "service" were brought to America by the New England Puritans. . . .

The first comprehensive adoption statute was passed in 1851 in Massachusetts. Among its key provisions were requirements 1) that written consent be given by the natural parents . . . ; 2) that the child himself must consent if he is fourteen years of age or older; 3) that the adopter's [spouse] must join in the petition for adoption; 4) that the probate judge . . . must be satisfied that the petitioner(s) were "of sufficient ability to bring up the child . . . and that it is fit and proper that such adoption should take effect" . . . ; 5) that once the adoption was approved by the probate court, the adopted child would become "to all intents and purposes" the legal child of the petitioner(s); [and] 6) that the natural parents would be deprived by the decree of adoption of all legal rights and obligations respecting the adopted child. . . .

[The purpose of the Massachusetts law and others like it remains unclear. One theory says that an increase in adoptions arranged by foundling societies prompted these statutes.] It is naive to attribute the passage of adoption statutes in so many states solely to the activities of "foundling societies." The activity of these societies *is* demonstrative of a larger movement for child welfare of which the passage of the adoption statutes also represents a part. This movement came about as a result of the economic changes which made the stop-gap institutions of apprenticeship, service, and indenture quite unable to cope with the great numbers of children who had been neglected by their families and also were neglected, until about the middle of the nineteenth century in most cases, by the society and the state. In order to understand better the motives that lay behind the passage of the adoption statutes, it is important to understand some of these other developments in child welfare work. . . .

[F]rom philanthropic motives most probably inspired by the continuing plight of dependent children in the hands of public authorities, private agencies for the care of such children were founded. . . . In the first half of the nineteenth century, at least seventy-seven such agencies were founded. . . . After 1850 the increase in the number of such agencies was even more rapid. . . . Before 1850, the private agencies sought to teach their charges to read and write. . . . Prior to the establishment of the public school systems and compulsory attendance, the agencies felt their primary service should be to give to their children the rudiments of an education before they were placed out in indenture or service.

Around 1850, however, private agencies began to be founded with the avowed purpose of placing younger children in a suitable family atmosphere. The work of some of the "infant's hospitals," "foundling asylums," and "maternity hospitals" in New York and Boston stands out in this regard, as does the work of the Children's Aid Societies started in those cities in 1853 and 1865, respectively. . . . The Children's Aid Societies made efforts to place children in suitable homes, usually homes far from the city, in the expanding states and territories of the West. [T]he Children's Aid Society of New York [ ] placed over twenty thousand children in homes out of New York City in the twenty years after it was founded. . . .

[Many of] the children placed by such agencies as the New York Children's Aid Society found themselves in situations which not only resembled "adoption" as we know it today but which was called by the same name. As the phenomenon of children in adopted homes became more common, there was increased pressure not only to pass laws regulating and insuring the legal relations between adopted children and their natural and adoptive parents, but to guarantee that some benefits of heirship were conferred on the adopted child. This pressure, which originated with the activities of the charitable associations working in child welfare, led to passage of the general adoption statutes in the third quarter of the nineteenth century. . . .

## NOTES AND QUESTIONS

1. *Adoption's roots.* Professor Presser offers several reasons why English law did not develop adoption before it emerged in the United States. Not only did the British hostility reflect xenophobia and strict adherence to a common law of inheritance based on blood ties, but the British practices of indenture, placing out, and apprenticeship (both voluntary and involuntary) offered ways to provide care for children who could not remain in their birth parents' homes. Similarly, traditional Jewish law does not recognize formal adoption because of the importance of biological lineage, although informal arrangements to care for orphans and to facilitate inheritance appear as far back as the Bible. See Pamela Laufer-Ukeles, Gestation: Work for Hire or the Essence of Motherhood? A Comparative Legal Analysis, 9 Duke J. Gender L. & Pol'y 91, 122-123 (2002). See generally Daniel Pollack et al., Classical Religious Perspectives on Adoption, 79 Notre Dame L. Rev. 693 (2004) (examining adoption in Jewish law, Canon law, and Islamic law).

In colonial America, care for children who could not remain at home was regarded as a community responsibility necessary to produce good citizens for the future. See Elaine Tyler May, Barren in the Promised Land: Childless Americans and the Pursuit of Happiness 24-31 (1997); Mary Ann Mason, From Father's Property to Children's Rights: A History of Child Custody in the United States 73 (1994). This notion of community responsibility for developing future citizens underlies the public school system, an understanding that persists today. See, e.g., Brown v. Board of Educ., 347 U.S. 483, 493 (1954); David Tyack, Preserving the Republic by Educating Republicans, in Diversity and its Discontents: Cultural Conflict and Common Ground in Contemporary America 63 (Neil J. Smelser & Jeffrey C. Alexander eds., 1999). By contrast, family law now treats childrearing outside of school as an almost exclusively private endeavor. Why? See, e.g., Katharine K. Baker, Bargaining or Biology? The History and Future of Paternity Law and Parental Status, 14 Cornell J.L. & Pub. Pol'y 1 (2004); Laura A. Rosenbury, Between Home and School, 155 U. Pa. L. Rev. 833 (2007). Can you envision a return today to an understanding of childrearing as a community responsibility, at least for some children?

2. *Early adoption statutes.* Because adoption remained unknown at common law, it is a purely statutory institution. Although many statutes enacted in the mid-nineteenth century reflected the old civil law of adoption,

the Massachusetts statute transformed the earlier understanding by making adoption "a legal procedure" and "creat[ing] a means of establishing an artificial bond between a parent and child that closely approximated the legal ideal of republican domestic relations." Michael Grossberg, Governing the Hearth: Law and the Family in Nineteenth Century America 271 (1985). See generally Jamil S. Zainaldin, The Emergence of a Modern American Family Law: Child Custody, Adoption, and the Courts, 1796-1851, 73 Nw. U. L. Rev. 1038 (1979). More significantly, however, the Massachusetts statute and others modeled on it portrayed adoption as a child-welfare measure, in contrast to the emphasis on adult interests reflected in earlier approaches. Grossberg, supra, at 271-272.

3. *Adoption in the Progressive Era.* The child-centered understanding of adoption gained strength in the Progressive Era of the late nineteenth and early twentieth century. During this period, a broad reformist movement embraced child welfare and provided a focus for the then-new profession of social work; the resulting "childsaving" project saw adoption as the goal for children removed from their homes because of poverty, neglect, and abuse. See Grossberg, supra, at 278-280; Mason, supra, at 87-92, 189. See Chapter 3, section A. Despite the primary emphasis on "adoption as rescue" during this time, the practice served to achieve other objectives as well. Based on an examination of California "trial court records, orphanage reports, appellate court decisions, and other sources," Professors Chris Guthrie and Joanna Grossman discern three types of adoptions from this period:

> *Family preservation* adoption, which reflected a tie to past, informal "adoption" practices, enabled adopters to keep already-established families and family money together.
>
> *Family creation* adoption, which emerged as the dominant type of adoption in the late nineteenth and early twentieth centuries, gave childless couples a way to approximate the biological parent-child relationship.
>
> And *family re-creation* adoption, a precursor to the modal practice of adoption in the mid-to-late twentieth century, enabled stepfathers to remake families previously disrupted by divorce or death.

Chris Guthrie & Joanna L. Grossman, Adoption in the Progressive Era: Preserving, Creating, and Re-Creating Families, 43 Am. J. Legal Hist. 235, 236 (1999). They find that family creation adoptions accounted for approximately two-thirds of the adoptions obtained during this period. Id. at 245.

4. *Orphan trains.* The Progressive Era's childsaving initiatives included "orphan trains," developed by Charles Loring Brace (founder of the New York Children's Aid Society in 1853) to send poor children from large East Coast urban areas, where they might land in almshouses or other institutional settings, to live and work in Midwest farm families. Despite the nomenclature, the practice was not limited to orphans. Although Brace's supporters lauded his child-welfare motives, critics claim that the shipment of child labor westward constituted exploitation, removed children from parental care without valid consent, and disregarded the best-interests-of-the-child principle. See generally Marilyn Irvin Holt, The Orphan Trains: Placing Out in

America (1992); Stephen O'Connor, Orphan Trains: The Story of Charles Loring Brace and the Children He Saved and Failed (2001). The sharply contrasting views of the orphan trains evoke questions about the Progressive Era's child-centered understanding of adoption and presage more modern controversies, including debates about transracial and international adoptions. See Chapter 3, section A1; Chapter 5, section C.

---

### Depictions in Popular Culture: John Irving, The Cider House Rules (1985)

In this novel, a sprawling Dickensian tale that begins during the Progressive Era at St. Cloud's, a remote Maine orphanage, Dr. Wilbur Larch provides to his many clients facing unwanted pregnancies a choice: to give birth to an orphan (to await adoption) or have an abortion (illegal at the time). As the story progresses, Homer Wells, an orphan who returns to St. Cloud's after several foster placements fail, grows up there—emerging as the protagonist who struggles with the moral issues posed by abortion, by his love for Candy who is betrothed to a close friend serving far away in World War II, and by his obligations to St. Cloud's mission after Dr. Larch's demise. When Candy and Homer secretly have a child, they present him as an orphan whom Homer has adopted.

What reflections of the way we think about adoption and its purposes appear in *The Cider House Rules*? How is adoption regarded at St. Cloud's? Consider the verbal ritual, after each adoptive placement, in which Dr. Larch informs the orphans that one of their number "has found a family" and he urges them "to be happy" for the child. Consider also Homer's preference for staying at the orphanage, rather than joining an adoptive family. What can one learn about the secrecy traditionally associated with adoption from Candy's and Homer's secret (which turns on its head the traditional practice of presenting adopted children as if they had been born to the family)? What insights come from Dr. Larch's even-handed willingness to offer women with unwanted pregnancies the choice of the delivery of an orphan, on the one hand, or an abortion, on the other?

More generally, what is the relationship between abortion and adoption? Several observers agree that the number of white infants available for adoption dramatically declined with the legalization of abortion in Roe v. Wade, 410 U.S. 113 (1973). Note, too, that many opponents of abortion advocate adoption instead, although *Roe*—in listing the postbirth detriments suffered by women who were denied legal abortions—implied that relinquishing a child for adoption does not sufficiently avoid such detriments. See id. at 153. Why? What reasoning underlies the Court's rejection of adoption as an adequate way for a woman to extricate herself at least from the problems that she would face after the child's birth? What

> burdens might continued pregnancy and adoption relinquishment impose that legally permissible abortion might avoid? What other considerations should inform an analysis of the connections between adoption and abortion law? See Chapter 2, section B1.

5. *Adoption as a legal fiction.* As noted, some historians describe adoption as creating a legal fiction, establishing a parent-child relationship as if there were a biological tie. See, e.g., Presser, supra, at 445. To what extent does the legal understanding of parentage make a biological tie necessary? Sufficient? Critiquing the assumption that parentage rests on nature rather than law, Professor James Dwyer points out that the state assigns parents to children, even when it chooses to rely on biological criteria. James G. Dwyer, The Relationship Rights of Children 26, 135 (2006). If only a biological tie determines a "real" parent-child relationship, what does this tie entail? A genetic link? Gestation? Consider the role and meaning of biological ties in the following sections on parentage.

# B. ESTABLISHING, RECOGNIZING, AND LIMITING PARENTAL RIGHTS

## 1. WHO IS A PARENT (ORIGINALLY)?

Because adoption replaces one parent-child relationship with another, the practice presupposes a determination of a child's original parents. Historically, the law regarded a child born out of wedlock as "filius nullius" (a child of no one) without a father and in some jurisdictions with questionable maternal ties, too. See, e.g., Michael Grossberg, Governing the Hearth: Law and the Family in Nineteenth Century America 197, 207 (1985). Beginning in the late 1960s, the United States Supreme Court struck down many laws discriminating against such children as an "illogical and unjust" means of deterring adults' extramarital sexual conduct. See, e.g., Weber v. Aetna Casualty & Surety Co., 406 U.S. 164, 175 (1972). These rulings, extending the rights of nonmarital children under the Fourteenth Amendment's Equal Protection Clause, raised two related issues: how the law determines the parents, especially the father, of such children and whether the prevailing inequalities violate the constitutional rights not only of the children but also of the unmarried adults themselves.

Some significant contextual factors require emphasis in an examination of the law's evolving treatment of parentage. First, the move toward equal treatment of nonmarital children began before the advent of today's sophisticated and largely accurate methods of genetic testing. Second, sex outside of marriage violated not only social norms but also criminal laws against fornication and adultery. Third, a double standard and gender stereotypes prevailed, so that women typically bore the brunt of the stigma of nonmarital pregnancy and birth while the notion of fatherhood, especially outside marriage, included no expectation that a man would perform a parental role. A racial and class-based hierarchy prevailed as well, so that nonmarital childbearing in poor minority communities was understood as the predictable deviancy of an entire population; among middle- and upper-class white women, however, it was a sign of personal and scandalous transgression. See, e.g., Rickie Solinger, Beggars and Choosers: How the Politics of Choice Shapes Adoption, Abortion, and Welfare in the United States 69-70 (2001).

## a. Constructing Legal Fatherhood

STANLEY V. ILLINOIS

405 U.S. 645 (1972)

Mr. Justice WHITE delivered the opinion of the Court.

Joan Stanley lived with Peter Stanley intermittently for 18 years during which time they had three children. When Joan Stanley died, Peter Stanley lost not only her but also his children. Under Illinois law the children of unwed fathers become wards of the State upon the death of the mother. Accordingly, upon Joan Stanley's death, in a dependency proceeding instituted by the State of Illinois, Stanley's children were declared wards of the State and placed with court-appointed guardians. Stanley appealed, claiming that he had never been shown to be an unfit parent and that since married fathers and unwed mothers could not be deprived of their children without such a showing, he had been deprived of the equal protection of the laws guaranteed him by the Fourteenth Amendment. . . .

Stanley presses his equal protection claim here. The State continues to respond that unwed fathers are presumed unfit to raise their children. . . . We granted certiorari to determine whether this method of procedure by presumption could be allowed to stand in light of the fact that Illinois allows married fathers — whether divorced, widowed, or separated — and mothers — even if unwed — the benefit of the presumption that they are fit to raise their children.

We must [examine this question]: Is a presumption that distinguishes and burdens all unwed fathers constitutionally repugnant? We conclude that, as a matter of due process of law, Stanley was entitled to a hearing on his fitness as a parent before his children were taken from him and that by denying him a hearing and extending it to all other parents whose custody of their children is challenged, the State denied Stanley the equal protection of the laws guaranteed by the Fourteenth Amendment.

Illinois has two principal methods of removing nondelinquent children from the homes of their parents. In a dependency proceeding it may demonstrate that the children are wards of the State because they have no surviving parent or guardian. Ill. Rev. Stat., c. 37, §§702-1, 702-5. In a neglect proceeding it may show that children should be wards of the State because the present parent(s) or guardian does not provide suitable care. Ill. Rev. Stat., c. 37, §§702-1, 702-4.

The State's right—indeed duty—to protect minor children through a judicial determination of their interests in a neglect proceeding is not challenged here. Rather, we are faced with a dependency statute that empowers state officials to circumvent neglect proceedings on the theory that an unwed father is not a "parent" whose existing relationship with his children must be considered. "Parents," says the State, "means the father and mother of a legitimate child, or the survivor of them, or the natural mother of an illegitimate child, and includes any adoptive parent," Ill. Rev. Stat., c. 37, §701-14, but the term does not include unwed fathers.

Under Illinois law, therefore, while the children of all parents can be taken from them in neglect proceedings, that is only after notice, hearing, and proof of such unfitness as a parent as amounts to neglect, an unwed father is uniquely subject to the more simplistic dependency proceeding. By use of this proceeding, the State, on showing that the father was not married to the mother, need not prove unfitness in fact, because it is presumed at law. Thus, the unwed father's claim of parental qualification is avoided as "irrelevant."

In considering this procedure under the Due Process Clause, we recognize, as we have in other cases, that due process of law does not require a hearing "in every conceivable case of government impairment of private interest." Cafeteria Workers v. McElroy, 367 U.S. 886 (1961). [That case] firmly established that "what procedures due process may require under any given set of circumstances must begin with a determination of the precise nature of the government function involved as well as of the private interest that has been affected by governmental action." . . .

The private interest here, that of a man in the children he has sired and raised, undeniably warrants deference and, absent a powerful countervailing interest, protection. . . . The Court has frequently emphasized the importance of the family. The rights to conceive and to raise one's children have been deemed "essential," Meyer v. Nebraska, 262 U.S. 390, 399 (1923), "basic civil rights of man," Skinner v. Oklahoma, 316 U.S. 535, 541 (1942), and "[r]ights far more precious . . . than property rights," May v. Anderson, 345 U.S. 528, 533 (1953). . . .

Nor has the law refused to recognize those family relationships unlegitimized by a marriage ceremony. The Court has declared unconstitutional a state statute denying natural, but illegitimate, children a wrongful-death action for the death of their mother, emphasizing that such children cannot be denied the right of other children because familial bonds in such cases were often as warm, enduring, and important as those arising within a more formally organized family unit. Levy v. Louisiana, 391 U.S. 68, 71-72 (1968). "To say that the test of equal protection should be the 'legal' rather than the biological relationship is to avoid the issue. For the Equal Protection Clause necessarily limits the authority of a State to draw such 'legal' lines as it chooses." Glona v. American Guarantee Co., 391 U.S. 73, 75-76 (1968). These authorities make it clear that, at the least, Stanley's interest in retaining custody of his children is cognizable and substantial.

For its part, the State has made its interest quite plain: Illinois has declared that the aim of the Juvenile Court Act is to protect "the moral, emotional, mental, and physical welfare of the minor and the best interests of the community" and to "strengthen the minor's family ties whenever possible, removing him from the custody of his parents only when his welfare or safety or the protection of the public cannot be adequately safeguarded without removal. . . ." Ill. Rev. Stat., c. 37, §701-2. These are legitimate interests well within the power of the State to implement. We do not question the assertion that neglectful parents may be separated from their children.

But we are here not asked to evaluate the legitimacy of the state ends, rather, to determine whether the means used to achieve these ends are constitutionally defensible. What is the state interest in separating children from fathers without a hearing designed to determine whether the father is unfit in a particular disputed case? We observe that the State registers no gain towards its declared goals when it separates children from the custody of fit parents. Indeed, if Stanley is a fit father, the State spites its own articulated goals when it needlessly separates him from his family. . . .

It may be, as the State insists, that most unmarried fathers are unsuitable and neglectful parents. It may also be that Stanley is such a parent and that his children should be placed in other hands. But all unmarried fathers are not in this category; some are wholly suited to have custody of their children. This much the State readily concedes, and nothing in this record indicates that Stanley is or has been a neglectful father who has not cared for his children. Given the opportunity to make his case, Stanley may have been seen to be deserving of custody of his offspring. Had this been so, the State's statutory policy would have been furthered by leaving custody in him. . . .

It may be argued that unmarried fathers are so seldom fit that Illinois need not undergo the administrative inconvenience of inquiry in any case, including Stanley's. . . . But the Constitution recognizes higher values than speed and efficiency. . . . Procedure by presumption is always cheaper and easier than individualized determination. But when, as here, the procedure forecloses the determinative issues of competence and care, when it explicitly disdains present realities in deference to past formalities, it needlessly risks running roughshod over the important interests of both parent and child. It therefore cannot stand.

. . . The State's interest in caring for Stanley's children is *de minimis* if Stanley is shown to be a fit father. It insists on presuming rather than proving Stanley's unfitness solely because it is more convenient to presume than to prove. Under the Due Process Clause that advantage is insufficient to justify refusing a father a hearing when the issue at stake is the dismemberment of his family.

The State of Illinois assumes custody of the children of married parents, divorced parents, and unmarried mothers only after a hearing and proof of neglect. The children of unmarried fathers, however, are declared dependent children without a hearing on parental fitness and without proof of neglect. Stanley's claim in the state courts and here is that failure to afford him a hearing on his parental qualifications while extending it to other parents denied him equal protection of the laws. We have concluded that all Illinois parents are constitutionally entitled to a hearing on their fitness before their children are removed from their custody. It follows that denying such a hearing to Stanley and those like him while granting it to other Illinois parents is inescapably contrary to the Equal Protection Clause. . . .

## MICHAEL H. v. GERALD D.

491 U.S. 110 (1989)

Justice SCALIA announced the judgment of the Court and delivered an opinion, in which THE CHIEF JUSTICE joins, and in all but note 6 of which Justice O'CONNOR and Justice KENNEDY join.

Under California law, a child born to a married woman living with her husband is presumed to be a child of the marriage. Cal. Evid. Code Ann. §621 (West Supp. 1989). The presumption of legitimacy may be rebutted only by the husband or wife, and then only in limited circumstances. The instant appeal presents the claim that this presumption infringes upon the due process rights of a man who wishes to establish his paternity of a child born to the wife of another man, and the claim that it infringes upon the constitutional right of the child to maintain a relationship with her natural father.

The facts of this case are, we must hope, extraordinary. On May 9, 1976, in Las Vegas, Nevada, Carole D., an international model, and Gerald D., a top executive in a French oil company, were married. The couple established a home in Playa del Rey, California, in which they resided as husband and wife when one or the other was not out of the country on business. In the summer of 1978, Carole became involved in an adulterous affair with a neighbor, Michael H. In September 1980, she conceived a child, Victoria D., who was born on May 11, 1981. Gerald was listed as father on the birth certificate and has always held Victoria out to the world as his daughter. Soon after delivery of the child, however, Carole informed Michael that she believed he might be the father.

In the first three years of her life, Victoria remained always with Carole, but found herself within a variety of quasi-family units. In October 1981, Gerald moved to New York City to pursue his business interests, but Carole chose to remain in California. At the end of that month, Carole and Michael had blood tests of themselves and Victoria, which showed a 98.07% probability that Michael was Victoria's father. In January 1982, Carole visited Michael in St. Thomas, where his primary business interests were based. There Michael held Victoria out as his child. In March, however, Carole left Michael and returned to California, where she took up residence with yet another man, Scott K. Later that spring, and again in the summer, Carole and Victoria spent time with Gerald in New York City, as well as on vacation in Europe. In the fall, they returned to Scott in California.

In November 1982, rebuffed in his attempts to visit Victoria, Michael filed a filiation action in California Superior Court to establish his paternity and right to visitation. In March 1983, the court appointed an attorney and guardian ad litem to represent Victoria's interests. Victoria then filed a cross-complaint asserting that if she had more than one psychological or de facto father, she was entitled to maintain her filial relationship, with all of the attendant rights, duties, and obligations, with both. In May 1983, Carole filed a motion for summary judgment. During this period, from March through July 1983, Carole was again living with Gerald in New York. In August, however, she returned to California, became involved once again with Michael, and instructed her attorneys to remove the summary judgment motion from the calendar.

For the ensuing eight months, when Michael was not in St. Thomas he lived with Carole and Victoria in Carole's apartment in Los Angeles and held Victoria out as his daughter. In April 1984, Carole and Michael signed a stipulation that Michael was Victoria's natural father. Carole left Michael the next month, however, and instructed her attorneys not to file the stipulation. In June 1984, Carole reconciled with Gerald and joined him in New York, where they now live with Victoria and two other children since born into the marriage.

In May 1984, Michael and Victoria, through her guardian ad litem, sought visitation rights for Michael *pendente lite*. To assist in determining whether visitation would be in Victoria's best interests, the Superior Court appointed a psychologist to evaluate Victoria, Gerald, Michael, and Carole. The psychologist recommended that Carole retain sole custody, but that Michael be allowed continued contact with Victoria pursuant to a restricted visitation schedule. The court concurred and ordered that Michael be provided with limited visitation privileges *pendente lite*.

On October 19, 1984, Gerald, who had intervened in the action, moved for summary judgment on the ground that under Cal. Evid. Code §621 there were no triable issues of fact as to Victoria's paternity. This law provides that "the issue of a wife cohabiting with her husband, who is not impotent or sterile, is conclusively presumed to be a child of the marriage." The presumption may be rebutted by blood tests, but only if a motion for such tests is made, within two years from the date of the child's birth, either by the husband or, if the natural father has filed an affidavit acknowledging paternity, by the wife.

On January 28, 1985, having found that affidavits submitted by Carole and Gerald sufficed to demonstrate that the two were cohabiting at conception and birth and that Gerald was neither sterile nor impotent, the Superior Court granted Gerald's motion for summary judgment, rejecting Michael's and Victoria's challenges to the constitutionality of §621. The court also denied their motions for continued visitation pending the appeal under Cal. Civ. Code §4601, which provides that a court may, in its discretion, grant "reasonable visitation rights . . . to any . . . person having an interest in the welfare of the child." Cal. Civ. Code Ann. §4601 (West Supp. 1989). It found that allowing such visitation would "violate the intention of the Legislature by impugning the integrity of the family unit." [Michael and Victoria appeal.]

Before us, Michael and Victoria both raise [constitutional] challenges. . . . We address first the [due process] claims of Michael. At the outset, it is necessary to clarify what he sought and what he was denied. California law, like nature itself, makes no provision for dual fatherhood. Michael was seeking to be declared the father of Victoria. The immediate benefit he evidently sought to obtain from that status was visitation rights. But if Michael were successful in being declared the father, other rights would follow — most importantly, the right to be considered as the parent who should have custody. . . . All parental rights, including visitation, were automatically denied by denying Michael status as the father. . . .

Michael contends as a matter of substantive due process that, because he has established a parental relationship with Victoria, protection of Gerald's and Carole's marital union is an insufficient state interest to support termination of that relationship. This argument is, of course, predicated on the assertion that Michael has a constitutionally protected liberty interest in his relationship with Victoria. . . .

In an attempt to limit and guide interpretation of the [Due Process] Clause, we have insisted not merely that the interest denominated as a "liberty" be "fundamental" (a concept that, in isolation, is hard to objectify), but also that it be an interest traditionally protected by our society. . . . This insistence that the asserted liberty interest be rooted in history and tradition is evident, as elsewhere, in our cases according constitutional protection to certain parental rights. Michael reads the landmark case of Stanley v. Illinois, 405 U.S. 645 (1972), and the subsequent cases of Quilloin v. Walcott, 434 U.S. 246 (1978), Caban v. Mohammed, 441 U.S. 380 (1979), and Lehr v. Robertson, 463 U.S. 248 (1983), as establishing that a liberty interest is created by biological fatherhood plus an established parental relationship — factors that exist in the present case as well. We think that distorts the rationale of those cases. As we view them, they rest not upon such isolated factors but upon the historic respect — indeed, sanctity would not be too strong a term — traditionally accorded to the relationships that develop within the unitary family.[3] . . .

Thus, the legal issue in the present case reduces to whether the relationship between persons in the situation of Michael and Victoria has been treated as a protected family unit under the historic practices of our society, or whether on any other basis it has been accorded special protection. We think it impossible to find that it has. In fact, quite to the contrary, our traditions have protected the marital family (Gerald, Carole, and the child they acknowledge to be theirs) against the sort of claim Michael asserts.[4]

The presumption of legitimacy was a fundamental principle of the common law. H. Nicholas, Adulturine Bastardy 1 (1836). Traditionally, that presumption could be rebutted only by proof that a husband was incapable of procreation or had had no access to his wife during the relevant period.

---

3. Justice Brennan asserts that only "a pinched conception of 'the family'" would exclude Michael, Carole, and Victoria from protection. We disagree. The family unit accorded traditional respect in our society, which we have referred to as the "unitary family," is typified, of course, by the marital family, but also includes the household of unmarried parents and their children. Perhaps the concept can be expanded even beyond this, but it will bear no resemblance to traditionally respected relationships — and will thus cease to have any constitutional significance — if it is stretched so far as to include the relationship established between a married woman, her lover, and their child, during a 3-month sojourn in St. Thomas, or during a subsequent 8-month period when, if he happened to be in Los Angeles, he stayed with her and the child.

4. Justice Brennan insists that in determining whether a liberty interest exists we must look at Michael's relationship with Victoria in isolation, without reference to the circumstance that Victoria's mother was married to someone else when the child was conceived, and that that woman and her husband wish to raise the child as their own. We cannot imagine what compels this strange procedure of looking at the act which is assertedly the subject of a liberty interest in isolation from its effect upon other people — rather like inquiring whether there is a liberty interest in firing a gun where the case at hand happens to involve its discharge into another person's body. The logic of Justice Brennan's position leads to the conclusion that if Michael had begotten Victoria by rape, that fact would in no way affect his possession of a liberty interest in his relationship with her.

As explained by Blackstone, nonaccess could only be proved "if the husband be out of the kingdom of England (or, as the law somewhat loosely phrases it, *extra quatuor maria* [beyond the four seas]) for above nine months. . . ." 1 Blackstone's Commentaries 456 (J. Chitty ed. 1826). And, under the common law both in England and here, [neither parent could testify to bastardize the child]. The primary policy rationale underlying the common law's severe restrictions on rebuttal of the presumption appears to have been an aversion to declaring children illegitimate, thereby depriving them of rights of inheritance and succession, and likely making them wards of the state. A secondary policy concern was the interest in promoting the "peace and tranquillity of States and families," a goal that is obviously impaired by facilitating suits against husband and wife asserting that their children are illegitimate. . . .

We have found nothing in the older sources, nor in the older cases, addressing specifically the power of the natural father to assert parental rights over a child born into a woman's existing marriage with another man. Since it is Michael's burden to establish that such a power (at least where the natural father has established a relationship with the child) is so deeply embedded within our traditions as to be a fundamental right, the lack of evidence alone might defeat his case. But the evidence shows that even in modern times — when, as we have noted, the rigid protection of the marital family has in other respects been relaxed — the ability of a person in Michael's position to claim paternity has not been generally acknowledged. . . .

Moreover, even if it were clear that one in Michael's position generally possesses, and has generally always possessed, standing to challenge the marital child's legitimacy, that would still not establish Michael's case. As noted earlier, what is at issue here is not entitlement to a state pronouncement that Victoria was begotten by Michael. It is no conceivable denial of constitutional right for a State to decline to declare facts unless some legal consequence hinges upon the requested declaration. What Michael asserts here is a right to have himself declared the natural father and *thereby to obtain parental prerogatives*. What he must establish, therefore, is not that our society has traditionally allowed a natural father in his circumstances to establish paternity, but that it has traditionally accorded such a father parental rights, or at least has not traditionally denied them. . . . What counts is whether the States in fact award substantive parental rights to the natural father of a child conceived within, and born into, an extant marital union that wishes to embrace the child. We are not aware of a single case, old or new, that has done so. This is not the stuff of which fundamental rights qualifying as liberty interests are made.[6] . . .

---

6. Justice Brennan criticizes our methodology in using historical traditions specifically relating to the rights of an adulterous natural father, rather than inquiring more generally "whether parenthood is an interest that historically has received our attention and protection." . . .

We do not understand why, having rejected our focus upon the societal tradition regarding the natural father's rights vis-à-vis a child whose mother is married to another man, Justice Brennan would choose to focus instead upon "parenthood." Why should the relevant category not be even more general — perhaps "family relationships"; or "personal relationships"; or even "emotional attachments in general"? Though the dissent has no basis for the level of generality it would select, we do: We refer to the most specific level at which a relevant tradition protecting, or denying

We do not accept Justice Brennan's criticism that this result "squashes" the liberty that consists of "the freedom not to conform." It seems to us that reflects the erroneous view that there is only one side to this controversy — that one disposition can expand a "liberty" of sorts without contracting an equivalent "liberty" on the other side. Such a happy choice is rarely available. Here, to provide protection to an adulterous natural father is to deny protection to a marital father, and vice versa. If Michael has a "freedom not to conform" (whatever that means), Gerald must equivalently have a "freedom to conform." One of them will pay a price for asserting that "freedom." . . . Our disposition does not choose between these two "freedoms," but leaves that to the people of California. Justice Brennan's approach chooses one of them as the constitutional imperative, on no apparent basis except that the unconventional is to be preferred.

We have never had occasion to decide whether a child has a liberty interest, symmetrical with that of her parent, in maintaining her filial relationship. We need not do so here because, even assuming that such a right exists, Victoria's claim must fail. Victoria's due process challenge is, if anything, weaker than Michael's. Her basic claim is not that California has erred in preventing her from establishing that Michael, not Gerald, should stand as her legal father. Rather, she claims a due process right to maintain filial relationships with both Michael and Gerald. This assertion merits little discussion, for, whatever the merits of the guardian ad litem's belief that such an arrangement can be of great psychological benefit to a child, the claim that a State must recognize multiple fatherhood has no support in the history or traditions of this country. Moreover, even if we were to construe Victoria's argument as forwarding the lesser proposition that, whatever her status vis-à-vis Gerald, she has a liberty interest in maintaining a filial relationship with her natural father, Michael, we find that, at best, her claim is the obverse of Michael's and fails for the same reasons.

Victoria claims in addition that her equal protection rights have been violated because, unlike her mother and presumed father, she had no opportunity to rebut the presumption of her legitimacy. We find this argument wholly without merit. We reject, at the outset, Victoria's suggestion that her equal protection challenge must be assessed under a standard of strict scrutiny because, in denying her the right to maintain a filial relationship with Michael, the State is discriminating against her on the basis of her illegitimacy. See Gomez v. Perez, 409 U.S. 535, 538 (1973). Illegitimacy is a legal construct, not a natural trait. Under California law, Victoria is not illegitimate, and she is treated in the same manner as all other legitimate children: she is entitled to maintain a filial relationship with her legal parents. . . . Since it pursues a legitimate end [protecting the integrity of the marital family] by rational means,

---

protection to, the asserted right can be identified. If, for example, there were no societal tradition, either way, regarding the rights of the natural father of a child adulterously conceived, we would have to consult, and (if possible) reason from, the traditions regarding natural fathers in general. But there is such a more specific tradition, and it unqualifiedly denies protection to such a parent. . . .

California's decision to treat Victoria differently from her parents is not a denial of equal protection. . . .

Justice O'CONNOR, with whom Justice KENNEDY joins, concurring in part.

I concur in all but footnote 6 of Justice Scalia's opinion. This footnote sketches a mode of historical analysis to be used when identifying liberty interests protected by the Due Process Clause of the Fourteenth Amendment that may be somewhat inconsistent with our past decisions in this area. See Griswold v. Connecticut, 381 U.S. 479 (1965); Eisenstadt v. Baird, 405 U.S. 438 (1972) [(protecting right to use and have access to birth control)]. On occasion the Court has characterized relevant traditions protecting asserted rights at levels of generality that might not be "the most specific level" available [(as specified in the plurality's footnote 6)]. See Loving v. Virginia, 388 U.S. 1, 12 (1967) [(holding unconstitutional ban on interracial marriage)]. I would not foreclose the unanticipated by the prior imposition of a single mode of historical analysis.

Justice STEVENS, concurring in the judgment.

. . . I do not agree with Justice Scalia's analysis. He seems to reject the possibility that a natural father might ever have a constitutionally protected interest in his relationship with a child whose mother was married to, and cohabiting with, another man at the time of the child's conception and birth. I think cases like Stanley v. Illinois, 405 U.S. 645 (1972), and Caban v. Mohammed, 441 U.S. 380 (1979), demonstrate that enduring "family" relationships may develop in unconventional settings. I therefore would not foreclose the possibility that a constitutionally protected relationship between a natural father and his child might exist in a case like this. Indeed, I am willing to assume for the purpose of deciding this case that Michael's relationship with Victoria is strong enough to give him a constitutional right to try to convince a trial judge that Victoria's best interest would be served by granting him visitation rights. I am satisfied, however, that the California statute, as applied in this case, gave him that opportunity.

Section 4601 of the California Civil Code Annotated (West Supp. 1989) provides:

> "[R]easonable visitation rights [shall be awarded] to a parent unless it is shown that the visitation would be detrimental to the best interests of the child. In the discretion of the court, reasonable visitation rights may be granted *to any other person having an interest in the welfare of the child.*" (Emphasis added.)

The presumption established by §621 denied Michael the benefit of the first sentence of §4601 because, as a matter of law, he is not a "parent." It does not, however, prevent him from proving that he is an "other person having an interest in the welfare of the child." On its face, therefore, the statute plainly gave the trial judge the authority to grant Michael "reasonable visitation rights." . . .

Under the circumstances of the case before us, Michael was given a fair opportunity to show that he is Victoria's natural father, that he had developed a relationship with her, and that her interests would be served by granting him visitation rights. On the other hand, the record also shows that after its rather shaky start, the marriage between Carole and Gerald developed a stability that now provides Victoria with a loving and harmonious family home. In the circumstances of this case, I find nothing fundamentally unfair about the exercise of a judge's discretion that, in the end, allows the mother to decide whether her child's best interests would be served by allowing the natural father visitation privileges. . . . I am satisfied that the California statutory scheme is consistent with the Due Process Clause of the Fourteenth Amendment. . . .

Justice Brennan, with whom Justice Marshall and Justice Blackmun join, dissenting. . . .

Today's plurality . . . does not ask whether parenthood is an interest that historically has received our attention and protection; the answer to that question is too clear for dispute. Instead, the plurality asks whether the specific variety of parenthood under consideration — a natural father's relationship with a child whose mother is married to another man — has enjoyed such protection. . . .

In construing the Fourteenth Amendment to offer shelter only to those interests specifically protected by historical practice, moreover, the plurality ignores the kind of society in which our Constitution exists. We are not an assimilative, homogeneous society, but a facilitative, pluralistic one, in which we must be willing to abide someone else's unfamiliar or even repellant practice because the same tolerant impulse protects our own idiosyncracies. Even if we can agree, therefore, that "family" and "parenthood" are part of the good life, it is absurd to assume that we can agree on the content of those terms and destructive to pretend that we do. In a community such as ours, "liberty" must include the freedom not to conform. The plurality today squashes this freedom by requiring specific approval from history before protecting anything in the name of liberty. . . . [Here,] we confront an interest — that of a parent and child in their relationship with each other — that was among the first that this Court acknowledged in its cases defining the "liberty" protected by the Constitution. . . .

The evidence is undisputed that Michael, Victoria, and Carole did live together as a family; that is, they shared the same household, Victoria called Michael "Daddy," Michael contributed to Victoria's support, and he is eager to continue his relationship with her. Yet they are not, in the plurality's view, a "unitary family," whereas Gerald, Carole, and Victoria do compose such a family. The only difference between these two sets of relationships, however, is the fact of marriage. . . . However, the very premise of *Stanley* and the cases following it is that marriage is not decisive in answering the question whether the Constitution protects the parental relationship under consideration. . . .

The plurality's exclusive rather than inclusive definition of the "unitary family" is out of step with other decisions as well. This pinched conception of "the family," crucial as it is in rejecting Michael's and Victoria's claims of a liberty interest, is jarring in light of our many cases preventing the States from denying important interests or statuses to those whose situations do not fit the government's narrow view of the family. From Loving v. Virginia, 388 U.S. 1 (1967), to Levy v. Louisiana, 391 U.S. 68 (1968), and Glona v. American Guarantee & Liability Ins. Co., 391 U.S. 73 (1968), and from Gomez v. Perez, 409 U.S. 535 (1973), to Moore v. East Cleveland, 431 U.S. 494 (1977), we have declined to respect a State's notion, as manifested in its allocation of privileges and burdens, of what the family should be. Today's rhapsody on the "unitary family" is out of tune with such decisions. . . .

## NOTES AND QUESTIONS ON *STANLEY* AND *MICHAEL H.*

1. Stanley's *basis*. Why did the Court invoke the Due Process Clause to resolve a claim that Stanley pressed under the Equal Protection Clause? What classifications did the Illinois law reflect? Why might the Court have avoided a broad holding based on equal protection? The Court's emphasis on due process to resolve claims of discrimination surfaced in several cases decided contemporaneously and became known as the "irrebuttable presumption doctrine." See, e.g., Cleveland Bd. of Educ. v. LaFleur, 414 U.S. 632 (1974); Note, The Irrebuttable Presumption Doctrine in the Supreme Court, 87 Harv. L. Rev. 1534 (1974).

To what extent does *Stanley* recognize substantive, as distinguished from procedural, rights for unwed fathers? Whose rights are being vindicated? The father's? The children's?

2. *State interests in* Stanley. Today, the legal regime challenged in *Stanley* seems surprising, if not perverse. As Professor Nancy Polikoff writes:

> The rule disregarding as a parent the father of children born outside marriage was consistent with centuries of law that such children were not legally his, but it was clearly not good for these children. . . . The outcome . . . may seem obvious today — how could it possibly be in children's best interests to lose their father after they have lost their mother? But it was extraordinary in 1972. The Supreme Court found that Peter Stanley's right to raise his children had been violated, and the decision required *every* state to revise its laws.

Nancy D. Polikoff, Beyond (Straight and Gay) Marriage: Valuing All Families Under the Law 130 (2008).

Why did Illinois enact the statute challenged in *Stanley*? Consider and evaluate the following possibilities: (a) The state assumed that unmarried fathers, unlike unmarried mothers and married fathers, have no interest in a relationship with their children. On the constitutionality of sex-based classifications that rest on gender stereotypes, see, e.g., United States v. Virginia, 518 U.S. 515 (1996). See also infra at 21-23 (Note 7). (b) The state sought to facilitate adoptions of children born to and relinquished by unmarried mothers, and requiring unmarried fathers to consent would slow down or thwart the process. See Chapter 2, section B2b. (c) The state sought to encourage marriage by making it a precondition for men to acquire parental rights over children conceived by sexual intercourse.

3. Stanley's *scope*. *Stanley* suggests that not all genetic fathers are entitled to the protections afforded to those men, like Stanley, who have both "sired and raised" their children. Precisely what degree of involvement is necessary to trigger constitutional protection? If *Stanley* guarantees only notice and a hearing, how can a particular man's involvement with his child be assessed *before* the hearing?

How do the following facts, presented in an omitted dissenting opinion, affect the understanding of Stanley's involvement with the children and the scope of the holding?

> The position that Stanley took at the dependency proceeding was not without ambiguity. Shortly after the mother's death, he placed the children in the care of Mr. and Mrs. Ness, who took the children into their home. The record is silent as to whether the Ness household was an approved foster home. Through Stanley's act, then, the Nesses were already the actual custodians of the children. At the dependency proceeding, he resisted only the court's designation of the Nesses as the legal custodians; he did not challenge their suitability for that role, nor did he seek for himself either that role or any other role that would have imposed legal responsibility upon him. Had he prevailed, of course, the status quo would have obtained: the Nesses would have continued to play the role of actual custodians until either they or Stanley acted to alter the informal arrangement, and there would still have been no living adult with any legally enforceable obligation for the care and support of the infant children.

405 U.S. at 663 n.2 (Burger, C.J., dissenting).

4. *"Biology plus."* In later cases, a majority of the Court elaborated on the requirement of paternal involvement, sometimes finding a father's conduct sufficient to trigger constitutional protection (e.g., Caban v. Mohammed, 441 U.S. 380 (1979)) and sometimes finding it insufficient (e.g., Quilloin v. Walcott, 434 U.S. 246 (1978); Lehr v. Robertson, 463 U.S. 248 (1983)). As the Court summarized in one of these cases:

> The significance of the biological connection is that it offers the natural father an opportunity that no other male possesses to develop a relationship with his offspring. If he grasps that opportunity and accepts some measure of responsibility for the child's future, he may enjoy the blessings of the parent-child relationship and make uniquely valuable contributions to the child's development.

*Lehr*, 463 U.S. at 262. Commentators have discerned in this approach a "biology plus" test. E.g., Melanie B. Jacobs, My Two Dads: Disaggregating Biological and Social Paternity, 38 Ariz. St. L.J. 809, 827-828 (2006); Daniel C. Zinman, Note, Father Knows Best: The Unwed Father's Right to Raise His Infant Surrendered for Adoption, 60 Fordham L. Rev. 971, 975, 980 (1992). In an omitted dissent in *Michael H.*, Justice White refers to the quoted summary from *Lehr*: "It is as if this passage was addressed to Michael. Yet the plurality today recants." 491 U.S. at 163. Do you agree that the *Michael H.* plurality conflicts with this reading of the earlier cases? Can you reconcile them? What role do the children's interests play in the cases?

Notwithstanding the plurality opinion, does a majority in *Michael H.* reject the "biology plus" test? Note that a sharply divided Court decided the case. In an omitted portion of the dissenting opinion, Justice Brennan (joined by Justices Marshall and Blackmun) highlights the divisions, pointing out that five Justices refuse to foreclose the possibility that a natural father in Michael's position might ever have a constitutionally protected interest, four Justices agree that Michael has a liberty interest, and five Justices believe that the flaw is procedural. Indeed, a majority of the Justices agree that Michael is entitled to some procedural protections; however, Justice Stevens, providing the fifth vote on this point, concurs in the result because he finds that Michael received the process that was due.

5. *Relationship to the mother.* Professor Janet L. Dolgin sees familial relationships as the determinative variables in the cases:

> [T]he unwed father cases, from *Stanley* through *Michael H.*, delineate three factors that make an unwed man a father. These are the man's biological relation to the child, his social relation to the child, and his relation to the child's mother. . . . In this regard, *Michael H.* clarifies the earlier cases. A biological father does protect his paternity by developing a social relationship with his child, but this step demands the creation of a family, a step itself depending upon an appropriate relationship between the man and his child's mother.

Janet L. Dolgin, Just A Gene: Judicial Assumptions About Parenthood, 40 UCLA L. Rev. 637, 671 (1993). According to Professor Gary Spitko, the mother's consent is critical, and biological paternity becomes important to the extent that it usually signals "the implicit consent of the biological mother to allow the biological father to co-parent her child." E. Gary Spitko, The Constitutional Function of Biological Paternity: Evidence of the Biological Mother's Consent to the Biological Father's Co-Parenting of Her Child, 48 Ariz. L. Rev. 97, 100 (2006).

6. *Definitions.* In Moore v. City of East Cleveland, 431 U.S. 494 (1997), the Court overturned the city zoning law's definition of "family" because it prohibited a grandmother from living with her two grandsons, who were cousins, not brothers. A plurality condemned the law for "slicing deeply into the family itself," thereby suggesting a constitutionally protected definition of family that exists apart from any legislative definition; this plurality found that the law thus violated Inez Moore's substantive due process rights. See id. at 498 (plurality opinion). Like *Moore*, *Stanley* and *Michael H.* test the government's power to write its own definition of certain terms: "parent" in *Stanley* and "father" in *Michael H.* Can you reconcile the *Michael H.* plurality's approach to the definitional question with the approach of the two earlier cases? Is footnote 3 in the *Michael H.* plurality opinion persuasive?

7. *Interplay of parentage rules and sex equality doctrine.* The Supreme Court began to transform family law in the 1970s from a field constructed from traditional gender-based role assignments to a site committed to equal treatment for women and men. See, e.g., Orr v. Orr, 440 U.S. 268 (1979) (striking down gender-based alimony statute); Stanton v. Stanton, 421 U.S. 7 (1975) (invalidating gender-based differences for age of majority); Weinberger v. Wiesenfeld, 420 U.S. 636 (1975) (invalidating unequal Social Security benefits for survivors of female and male workers). In such cases, the Court explicitly rejected reliance on gender stereotypes. See, e.g., Reed v. Reed, 404 U.S. 71 (1971) (rejecting such stereotypes in striking down a statutory preference for

men over women to administer decedents' estates). The Court announced that, to pass constitutional scrutiny, gender-based classifications must meet an intermediate standard of review, which requires that the classification must serve important governmental objectives and must have a substantial relationship to achieving such objectives. See Craig v. Boren, 429 U.S. 190 (1976). See also United States v. Virginia, 518 U.S. 515, 531 (1996) (requiring an "exceedingly persuasive justification" for gender classifications).

At the same time, however, the Court has indicated that gender-based classifications reflecting "real differences" would survive constitutional review. For example, the Court has upheld a statutory rape law applicable only to male perpetrators because only females can become pregnant; thus, the statute, purportedly designed to combat teen pregnancy, "realistically reflects the fact that the sexes are not similarly situated." Michael M. v. Superior Ct., 450 U.S. 464, 469 (1981) (plurality opinion).

Do parentage laws like those examined in *Stanley*, *Michael H.*, and the intervening cases rest on "real differences," given the distinct roles of women and men in reproduction, or on gender stereotypes, particularly contrasting gender norms and expectations for family care work? See, e.g., Nevada Dept. of Hum. Resources v. Hibbs, 538 U.S. 721 (2003). The Justices have not answered this question with one voice. For example, in Nguyen v. INS, 533 U.S. 321 (2001), a divided Supreme Court rejected a claim that different requirements for a nonmarital child's acquisition of citizenship, depending on the gender of the citizen-parent, violate equal protection. According to INS regulations, nonmarital children born abroad to citizen mothers become citizens based on a short residency requirement for the mother. However, additional requirements exist for nonmarital children born abroad to citizen fathers: The father must act affirmatively to establish paternity before the child reaches the age of 18. The petitioners had unsuccessfully argued that the statutory distinction rested on problems of paternity establishment now obviated by the reliability of DNA testing. The majority reasoned that the distinction satisfied the important governmental interest in assuring that children have a biological and social attachment to their citizen parent; while attachment to the mother is established by the pregnancy and birth, only a father's affirmative act can show attachment. According to the four dissenters, however, the "idea that a mother's presence at birth supplies adequate assurance of an opportunity to develop a relationship while a father's presence at birth does not would appear to rest only on an overbroad sex-based generalization." 533 U.S. at 86 (O'Connor, J., dissenting).

Do you see a "real difference" or a gender stereotype — or both? Note that in *Nguyen* the gender-based stereotypes invoked by the majority are belied by the facts: The child's Vietnamese mother abandoned the child soon after birth, but the American father brought him to the United States. See generally Comment, Caroline Rogus, Conflating Women's Biological and Social Roles: The Ideal of Motherhood, Equal Protection, and the Implications of the Nguyen v. INS Opinion, 5 U. Pa. J. Const. L. 803 (2003); Laura Weinrib, Protecting Sex: Sexual Disincentives and Sex-Based Discrimination in Nguyen v. INS, 12 Colum. J. Gender & L. 222 (2003).

Finally, some men have unsuccessfully invoked gender equality and a woman's right to terminate an unwanted pregnancy to argue for a right to reject unwanted parentage, especially when the mother allegedly deceived the father about her use of contraception. Courts have concluded that paternity laws do not violate equal protection, that women choosing abortions are not similarly situated to fathers seeking to disclaim financial obligations, and that children have an interest in paternal support, regardless of maternal deception. See, e.g., Dubay v. Wells, 506 F.3d 422 (6th Cir. 2007); Wallis v. Smith, 22 P.3d 682 (N.M. Ct. App. 2001); In re L. Pamela P. v. Frank S., 449 N.E.2d 713 (N.Y. 1983).

---

## Depictions in Popular Culture: Evelyn (2002)

This film tells the story of Desmond Doyle, an unemployed housepainter with three children, whose wife deserts him for another man, prompting the National Society for the Prevention of Cruelty to Children to take custody of his children, daughter Evelyn and her two younger brothers. Ireland's Children Act of 1908 authorizes a judge to send a child under the age of 15 who is destitute to an industrial school. A subsequent amendment (the Children Act of 1941 §10) mandates the consent of both parents for the child's detention unless the child is an orphan. Additional exceptions to the two-parent consent requirement exist if one parent is mentally disabled, imprisoned, or has deserted the family. Based on a peculiarity in the amended statute, a sole parent's consent suffices to justify a child's detention but not to justify the child's discharge (for which both parents must consent). Because the mother fled without leaving contact information, Doyle cannot obtain her consent for the state to discharge the children even after his financial situation improves. First, Doyle unsuccessfully petitions the Minister of Education to discharge the children. He then challenges the statute's constitutionality.

Set in the 1950s, the struggle reflects the tension evident in Stanley v. Illinois. While the legal establishment's position reflects gendered assumptions about the inability of a father to rear children without a mother or mother figure, Doyle (played by Pierce Brosnan) and his legal team (which includes Stephen Rea, Aidan Quinn, and Alan Bates) contend that Section 10 of the Children Act of 1941 violates the Irish Constitution's protections for family matters. Specifically, Doyle's challenge invokes constitutional provisions guaranteeing "inalienable and imprescriptible rights, antecedent and superior to all positive law"; "[the] inalienable right and duty of parents to provide, according to their means, for the . . . education of their children"; and a provision stating that "The State shall not oblige parents . . . to send their children to schools established by the State." Michael Asimow, Evelyn — The Best Legal Movie of 2002?, Picturing Justice, The On-Line Journal of Law & Popular

Culture, Jan. 21, 2003, available at http://www.usfca.edu/pj/evelyn_
asimow.htm (quoting Articles 41.1, 42.1, and 42.3.1 of the Irish
Constitution of 1937). The courtroom scenes include one of Evelyn
on the witness stand.

Despite the odds, including warnings that a father's removal of his
children from protective custody would undermine the fundamental
principles of Irish family law, Doyle persists and ultimately prevails in
a case that the film portrays as the first in which the Irish Supreme
Court set aside a statute as unconstitutional. As the film ends, Bernadette (Julianna Margulies), to whom Doyle develops a romantic attachment, moves in to help him care for the children upon their return.
Thus, do the gendered assumptions underlying the controversy
prevail as well?

For Evelyn's autobiographical account, see Evelyn Doyle, Tea
and Green Ribbons: Evelyn's Story (2004). For additional comparisons between the film and the historical events it represents, see
Asimow, supra. Asimow points out that, with divorce unavailable
in Ireland, Doyle and the Bernadette character cannot marry. Id. But
does the unavailability of divorce perhaps explain the mother's
desertion — her only opportunity for exit?

8. *Presumption of legitimacy.* The presumption of legitimacy has a long
history in British common law, which included Lord Mansfield's rule, barring
spousal testimony that might show another man's paternity. Professor
Michael Grossberg traces American adherence to such principles to the strong
reluctance to stigmatize illegitimate children in the post-Revolutionary period.
He adds that this reluctance ultimately found expression in the creation of
common law marriage, the exclusion of evidence that would bastardize the
child of a married woman, the recognition of the offspring of annulled marriages as legitimate, and the adoption of the doctrine of putative marriage. As
Grossberg elaborates:

> In the agonizing conflict between a man's right to limit his paternity
> only to his actual offspring and the right of a child born to a married
> woman to claim family membership, the common law, first in England
> and then in America, generally made paternal rights defer to the larger
> goal of preserving family integrity.

Michael Grossberg, Governing the Hearth: Law and the Family in Nineteenth-
Century America 201-202 (1985).

9. *Other paternity presumptions.* While children born to married women
acquired legal fathers by presumption, judicial proceedings to establish paternity provided the traditional way to identify the father of nonmarital children
and to impose support duties upon them, if the law made them financially
responsible at all. Such proceedings took the form of criminal "bastardy" pro-
secutions or civil suits often brought by the child's mother. Compare, e.g.,
State v. Camp, 209 S.E.2d 754 (N.C. 1974), and Miller v. State, 20 So. 392

(Ala. 1896), with, e.g., Berry v. Chaplin, 169 P.2d 442 (Cal. Dist. Ct. App. 1946). Today, under directives attached to conditional federal funding, paternity is often established via administrative proceedings (with the state seeking reimbursement for support it provided for a needy child) or through voluntary paternity establishment by affidavit. See, e.g., Jeffrey A. Parness, New Federal Paternity Laws: Securing More Fathers at Birth for the Children of Unwed Mothers, 45 Brandeis L.J. 59 (2006). Should nonmarital children also have access to paternity presumptions?

a. *The original UPA.* The movement toward equal rights for nonmarital children, initiated by a series of Supreme Court decisions, including Weber v. Aetna Casualty & Surety Co., 406 U.S. 164 (1972), had scholarly roots. In particular, the original Uniform Parentage Act (UPA), promulgated in 1973, was influenced by Professor Harry Krause's classic book, Illegitimacy: Law and Social Policy (1971), which called for an end to discrimination against nonmarital children. (Krause became the Reporter for the UPA, drafted by the National Conference of Commissioners on Uniform State Laws (NCCUSL), now renamed the Uniform Law Commission (ULC).) The original UPA recognized that according treatment to nonmarital children equal to that enjoyed by their marital counterparts first requires identifying the fathers of the former. The presumption of legitimacy identified the legal father of a marital child; to help achieve equal treatment for children born to unmarried women, the original UPA developed a network of presumptions for identifying fathers. These presumptions rested on marriage (including attempted marriage and invalid marriage); a man's receiving a child into his home and holding the child out as his own before the child's majority; and the filing of a written acknowledgment of paternity. Unif. Parentage Act §4 (1973), 9B U.L.A. 393-394 (2001).

Suppose more than one presumption applies, as in *Michael H.*? The statute says: "If two or more presumptions arise which conflict with each other, the presumption which on the facts is founded on the weightier considerations of policy and logic controls." Unif. Parentage Act §4(a)(5) (1973), 9B U.L.A. 394 (2001). Further, a presumption can be rebutted by clear and convincing evidence. Unif. Parentage Act §4(b) (1973), 9B U.L.A. 394 (2001). Eighteen states adopted the original UPA. 9B U.L.A. at 377. (Eight have now repealed their statutes and enacted the 2000 UPA, infra. See http://www.nccusl.org/Update/uniformact_factsheets/uniformacts-fs-upa.asp (last visited Oct. 11, 2008).)

b. *Revised UPA.* In 2000, NCCUSL promulgated a new UPA, which it revised in 2002. Although the drafters determined that technological advances (including ARTs and increasingly accurate genetic testing) called for an updated statute, the new UPA reaffirms the original policy of equal treatment of children regardless of their parents' marital status. Unif. Parentage Act §202 (2000), 9B U.L.A. 309 (2001). This statutory scheme provides for the establishment of both the mother-child relationship and the father-child relationship. Unif. Parentage Act §201 (2000, revised 2002), 9B U.L.A. 15 (Supp. 2008). Like its predecessor, it rests paternity presumptions on marriage (including attempted and invalid marriage) and on "holding out." Specifically, a presumption of paternity applies to a man if "for the first two years of the child's life, he resided in the same household with the child and openly held out the child as his own." Unif. Parentage Act §204(a)(5) (2000, revised 2002), 9B U.L.A. 16-17 (Supp. 2008). A presumption of paternity can be rebutted only by an adjudication in a paternity proceeding, covered in Article 6. Unif. Parentage Act §204(b) (2000, revised 2002), 9B U.L.A. 16-17 (Supp. 2008). Article 6, in turn, authorizes paternity proceedings, including genetic testing. For children with no presumed father, a paternity proceeding can be brought at any time. Unif. Parentage Act §606 (2000, revised 2002); 9B U.L.A. 36 (Supp. 2008). The following limitations apply to a child with a presumed father:

> (a) Except as otherwise provided in subsection (b), a proceeding brought by a presumed father, the mother, or another individual to adjudicate the parentage of a child having a presumed father must be commenced not later than two years after the birth of the child.
> (b) A proceeding seeking to disprove the father-child relationship between a child and the child's presumed father may be maintained at any time if the court determines that:
> (1) the presumed father and the mother of the child neither cohabited nor engaged in sexual intercourse with each other during the probable time of conception; and
> (2) the presumed father never openly held out the child as his own.

Unif. Parentage Act §607 (2000, revised 2002), 9B U.L.A. 38 (Supp. 2008).

When initially drafted in 2000, the new UPA omitted a presumption based on "holding out" a child as one's own, on the theory that accurate genetic evidence made conduct-based rules unnecessary. 9B U.L.A. 17 (Supp. 2008) (cmt. to §204). In 2002, however, the drafters inserted §204(a)(5), quoted supra. Why? What is the reason for the two-year requirement in the presumption based on "holding out" and the two-year limitation period for adjudicating parentage for a child with a presumed father? How would a court following the new UPA, as amended, decide the controversy in the *Michael H.* case?

10. *Purpose of presumptions.* What is the purpose of the presumption of legitimacy and the other paternity presumptions? Some commentators contend that such presumptions offered a crude way of determining biological paternity before proof of such relationships became scientifically possible. See, e.g., Marjorie Maguire Shultz, Reproductive Technology and Intent-Based Parenthood: An Opportunity for Gender Neutrality, 1990 Wis. L. Rev. 297, 317. *Michael H.* suggests that the presumption was designed to preserve marital harmony and establish the marital family as the norm. See also Theresa Glennon, Somebody's Child: Evaluating the Erosion of the Marital Presumption of Paternity, 102 W. Va. L. Rev. 547, 590-591 (2000) (suggesting that the presumption reflects a legal consensus that "parenthood within marriage best protects children"). Others emphasize the presumption's facilitation of private, rather than public, support for children. Katharine K. Baker, Bargaining or Biology? The History and Future of Paternity Law and Parental Status, 14 Cornell J.L. & Pub. Pol'y 1 (2004); June Carbone & Naomi Cahn, Which Ties Bind? Redefining the Parent-Child Relationship in an Age of Genetic Certainty, 11 Wm. & Mary Bill Rts. J. 1011 (2003).

11. *Weight of genetic evidence.* At one time, the presumption of legitimacy was conclusive when the spouses were cohabiting at the time of conception and the husband was not sterile, impotent, or racially different from the child. See, e.g., Kusior v. Silver, 354 P.2d 657, 668 (Cal. 1960); In re Estate of Jones, 8 A.2d 631, 635-636 (Vt. 1939). What explains the race-based exception? Today, federal child support legislation gives the states the option of making the presumption rebuttable or conclusive, depending on genetic test results indicating a threshold probability that the alleged father is the father of the child. 42 U.S.C. §666 (a)(5)(G) (2008). Most states now have a rebuttable presumption of legitimacy. Paula Roberts, Truth and Consequences: Part I. Disestablishing the Paternity of Non-Marital Children, 37 Fam. L.Q. 35 n.5 (2003).

Given that parenthood currently can be scientifically determined for any child, what role *should* genetic evidence play? See Katharine K. Baker, Bionormativity and the Construction of Parenthood, 42 Ga. L. Rev. 649 (2007). Should genetic evidence always trump presumptions resting on social factors, such as marriage or "holding out" the child as one's own? See, e.g., In re T.K.Y., 205 S.W.3d 343 (Tenn. 2006). Should legal paternity rest exclusively on biological paternity? To what extent would a regime of fatherhood resting exclusively on genetics best achieve equal treatment of all children, regardless of the marital status or living arrangements of their mothers? Alternatively, when genetic evidence conflicts with the presumption of legitimacy or one of the other paternity presumptions, should courts consider a child's best interests in resolving the conflict? What factors do "best interests" include in this context? See, e.g., In re Nicholas H., 46 P.3d 932 (Cal. 2002); Department of Soc. Servs. ex rel. Byer v. Wright, 678 N.W.2d 586 (S.D. 2004). But see B.E.B. v. R.L.B., 979 P.2d 514 (Alaska 1999) (application of paternity by estoppel rests only on risk of financial harm, not emotional harm to child). Cf. Bay County Prosecutor v. Nugent, 740 N.W.2d 678 (Mich. Ct. App. 2007) (requiring consideration of equities to decide whether to permit revocation of paternity affidavit filed by a man who had believed he was child's father and now sought to retain that legal status, even after learning that the mother conceived the child with his 14-year-old son). With the advent of advanced genetic testing, should the law eliminate presumptions altogether? See Veronica Sue Gunderson, Personal Responsibility in Parentage: An Argument Against the Marital Presumption, 11 U.C. Davis J. Juv. L. & Pol'y 335 (2007).

12. *Paternity disestablishment.* Increasingly, some jurisdictions are permitting, by case law or statute, the disestablishment of paternity, generally on the basis of paternity fraud. Typically, a former husband or nonmarital father will attempt to invalidate a support obligation after genetic evidence shows that his children are not biologically his offspring. Some states require that the man act within a prescribed time. A few jurisdictions impose criminal penalties for mothers who intentionally establish paternity for a man who is not the biological father. See generally Paula Roberts, Truth and Consequences: Part III. Who Pays When Paternity Is Disestablished?, 37 Fam. L.Q. 69 (2003). Does disestablishment constitute sound policy? See Melanie B. Jacobs, When Daddy Doesn't Want to Be Daddy Anymore: An Argument Against Paternity Fraud Claims, 16 Yale J.L. & Feminism 193 (2004). Should all children undergo genetic testing at birth to avoid such situations? Why?

Should a man be permitted to disestablish paternity once he has already assumed the role of the child's father? Courts sometimes deny disestablishment claims based on principles of equitable estoppel. See, e.g., Hubbard v. Hubbard, 44 P.3d 153 (Alaska 2002); In re Shondel J. v. Mark D., 853 N.E.2d 610 (N.Y. 2006). See also Department of Hum. Resources ex rel. Duckworth v. Kamp, 949 A.2d 43 (Md. Ct. Spec. App. 2008) (laches), *cert. granted*, 956 A.2d 201 (Md. 2008). Other courts bar paternity disestablishment based on res judicata principles, treating as a final judgment the divorce decree or child support order establishing paternity. See, e.g., State v. R.L.C., 47 P.3d 327 (Colo. 2002); In re Marriage/Children of Betty L.W. v. William E.W., 569 S.E.2d 77, 88 (W.Va. 2002). See also DNW v. Department of Fam. Servs., 154 P.3d 990 (Wyo. 2007) (holding paternity affidavit binding, despite later genetic evidence). But see In re Briggs, 746 N.W.2d 279 (Iowa Ct. App. 2008). See generally Diane S. Kaplan, Immaculate Deception: The Evolving Right of Paternal Renunciation, 27 Women's Rts. L. Rep. 139 (2006); Jeffrey A. Parness, No Genetic Ties, No More Fathers: Voluntary Acknowledgment Rescissions and Other Paternity Disestablishments Under Illinois Law, 39 J. Marshall L. Rev. 1295 (2006).

If a would-be father is permitted to disestablish paternity, who becomes responsible for child support? The biological father? Suppose he cannot be found? The state? See *B.E.B.*, supra; Jana Singer, Marriage, Biology, and Paternity: The Case for Revitalizing the Marital Presumption, 65 Md. L. Rev. 246 (2006) (arguing for support from mother's husband, regardless of biology). But see Ronald K. Henry, The Innocent Third Party: Victims of Paternity Fraud, 40 Fam. L.Q. 51 (2006) (calling for reforms, including DNA tests, to stop paternity fraud). May a "disestablished father" recover reimbursement from the genetic father? See R.A.C. v. P.J.S., 927 A.2d 97 (N.J. 2007).

13. *How many fathers? Michael H.* rests on the assumption that a child may have only one father. What is the basis for this assumption? Given modern sexual mores and the high divorce rate, does such an assumption continue to make sense? If the dissenters would afford constitutional protection to Michael's interests because he, Carole, and Victoria lived together as a family for a time, would they afford similar protection to any interests asserted by Scott, another man with whom Carole and Victoria lived? Why or why not?

According to Professor Theresa Glennon, one state (Louisiana) has adopted the concept of dual paternity:

> An alleged biological father may assert his paternity, if done in a timely manner and proven by genetic testing. However, the establishment of the alleged biological father's paternity does not disrupt the rights and responsibilities of the legally presumed father, and the alleged biological father is only permitted visitation with the child if he demonstrates his worthiness to participate in the child's life. If his participation in the child's life does not meet the best interests of the child, the legally recognized biological father retains a support obligation but cannot claim the privilege of parental rights.

Glennon, supra, at 577. Reportedly, Louisiana predicted that the Supreme Court would eventually require recognition of biological fathers, even for children born to married women. Dual paternity was designed to afford parental status to the mother's husband in the face of such constitutional interpretation. Cf. Katherine Shaw Spaht, Who's Your Momma?, Who Are Your Daddies?, 67 La. L. Rev. 307, 321-324 (2007). For other advocates of dual paternity, see Nancy E. Dowd, Multiple Parents/Multiple Fathers, 9 J.L. & Fam. Stud. 231 (2007); Mary Louise Fellows, A Feminist Determination of the Law and Legitimacy, 7 Tex. J. Women & L. 195, 207 (1998); Jacobs, supra. Is the concept of dual paternity a workable solution to *Michael H.*? For case law recognizing three legal parents for a given child, see Chapter 6, section B2.

14. *Response to* Michael H. Discomfort with the plurality's decision is evident in legislative and judicial responses to the case. Dissatisfaction with the case led the state legislature in California (the site of *Michael H.*) to amend the conclusive presumption of legitimacy to allow a putative father to move for blood tests within two years of birth in some cases (i.e., if the man who is not the husband has received the child into his home and openly held out the child as his). Cal. Fam. Code §7541(b) (2008), enacted by Stats. 1992, c. 162 (A.B. 2650), §10, amending former Cal. Evid. Code §621.

Eight states (Alabama, Delaware, North Dakota, Oklahoma, Texas, Utah, Washington, and Wyoming) have adopted the new UPA. Uniform Parentage Act: Legislative Fact Sheet, available at http://www.nccusl.org/Update/uniformact_factsheets/uniformacts-fs-upa.asp (last visited Oct. 26, 2008). The new UPA incorporates California's two-year limitation on the putative father's ability to request blood tests, subject to estoppel principles (regarding the conduct of the parties, the equities of disproving the father-child relationship between the child and the presumed or acknowledged father, or the best interests of the child). Unif. Parentage Act §§607-608, 9B U.L.A. 38-41 (Supp. 2008).

As explained above, most states now hold that the common law presumption of legitimacy is rebuttable. Moreover, many states have enacted statutes that permit men like Michael H. to bring actions to establish their paternity to a child born to a married woman. Glennon, supra, at 573. Nonetheless, the policies underlying the presumption persist, with several states making rebuttal difficult. E.g., J.N.R. v. O'Reilly, 264 S.W.3d 587 (Ky. 2008); Barnes v. Jeudevine, 718 N.W.2d 311 (Mich. 2006); Pearson v. Pearson, 182 P.3d 353 (Utah 2008).

## PROBLEM

DeAndre, born out of wedlock, is killed in an auto accident at age 20. Although a judicial proceeding established his biological father's paternity years before, his father never openly acknowledged his son. After DeAndre's death, the young man's mother sues to sever any inheritance rights that his father might claim. State law precludes the father of a nonmarital child from inheriting from the child if the father either failed or refused to provide support or openly acknowledge the child as his own. The father challenges the statute as an unconstitutional gender-based classification because unmarried mothers need not meet any requirements before inheriting from their children. DeAndre's mother and the state argue that the statute differentiates not on the basis of gender but rather distinguishes fathers who openly acknowledge their nonmarital children and those who do not. They also argue that the statute advances the state interest in encouraging fathers to take responsibility for their nonmarital children by precluding an uninvolved father from profiting from the child's death. What result and why? See Rainey v. Chever, 510 S.E.2d 823 (Ga. 1999), *cert. denied*, 527 U.S. 1044 (1999); Linda Kelly Hill, Equal Protection Misapplied: The Politics of Gender and Illegitimacy and the Denial of Inheritance, 13 Wm. & Mary J. Women & L. 129 (2006); Eleanor Mixon, Note, Deadbeat Dads: Undeserving of the Right to Inherit from the Illegitimate Children and Undeserving of Equal Protection, 34 Ga. L. Rev. 1773, 1775-1776 (2000). See also In re Rogiers, 933 A.2d 971 (N.J. Super. Ct. App. Div. 2007).

### b. Extending Paternity Laws to Same-Sex Couples

The preceding materials focus on constitutional and statutory frameworks for identifying a child's father. As shown, in some situations social factors and legal relationships trump genetic paternity in establishing parentage. Because these parentage rules were developed with traditional understandings of "mother" and "father" in mind, the legal recognition of same-sex couples in some states challenges such limited conceptualizations.

The following materials focus on these questions: Should paternity laws apply in a gender-neutral manner to women as well as men? Put another way, what role should paternity laws play in the establishment of the rights of children of lesbian couples and corresponding parental obligations? How should such laws apply to gay male couples and their children? How might the development of parentage rules for same-sex couples inform the way that parentage is understood in more traditional contexts?

ELISA B. v. SUPERIOR COURT

117 P.3d 660 (Cal. 2005)

MORENO, J. . . .

On June 7, 2001, the El Dorado County District Attorney filed a complaint in superior court to establish that Elisa B. is a parent of two-year-old twins Kaia B. and Ry B., who were born to Emily B., and to order Elisa to pay child support. [Elisa denied being the twins' parent.] Elisa testified that she entered into a lesbian relationship with Emily in 1993. They began living together six months later. Elisa obtained a tattoo that read "Emily, por vida," which in Spanish means Emily, for life. They introduced each other to friends as their "partner," exchanged rings, opened a joint bank account, and believed they were in a committed relationship.

Elisa and Emily discussed having children and decided that they both wished to give birth. Because Elisa earned more than twice as much money as Emily, they decided that Emily "would be the stay-at-home mother" and Elisa "would be the primary breadwinner for the family." At a sperm bank, they chose a donor they both would use so the children would "be biological brothers and sisters." [Each attended the other's insemination procedures, prenatal medical appointments, labor, and delivery.] Elisa gave birth to Chance in November, 1997, and Emily gave birth to Ry and Kaia prematurely in March, 1998. Ry had medical problems; he suffered from Down's Syndrome, and required heart surgery.

They jointly selected the children's names, joining their surnames with a hyphen to form the children's surname. They each breast fed all of the children. Elisa claimed all three children as her dependents on her tax returns and obtained a life insurance policy on herself naming Emily as the beneficiary so that if "anything happened" to her, all three children would be "cared for." Elisa believed the children would be considered both of their children.

Elisa's parents referred to the twins as their grandchildren and her sister referred to the twins as part of their family and referred to Elisa as their mother. Elisa treated all of the children as hers and told a prospective employer that she had triplets. Elisa and Emily identified themselves as coparents of Ry at an organization arranging care for his Down's Syndrome.

Elisa supported the household financially. Emily was not working. Emily testified that she would not have become pregnant if Elisa had not promised to support her financially, but Elisa denied that any financial arrangements were discussed before the birth of the children. Elisa later acknowledged in her testimony, however, that Emily "was going to be an at-home mom for maybe a couple of years and then the kids were going to go into day care and she was going to return to work."

They consulted an attorney regarding adopting "each other's child," but never did so. Nor did they register as domestic partners or execute a written agreement concerning the children. Elisa stated she later reconsidered adoption because she had misgivings about Emily adopting Chance.

Elisa and Emily separated in November, 1999. Elisa promised to support Emily and the twins "as much as I possibly could" and initially paid the mortgage payments [and later the rent for Emily and the twins. Then she stopped providing such support.] At the time of trial, Elisa was earning $95,000 a year.

[The superior court found that Elisa and Emily had rejected the option of using a private sperm donor because "[t]hey wanted the child to be raised *exclusively* by them as a couple"; that they intended to create a child and "acted in all respects as a family"; that Elisa was obligated to support the twins under the doctrine of equitable estoppel. The superior court concluded:] "The need for the application of [equitable estoppel] is underscored by the fact that the decision of Respondent to create a family and desert them has caused the remaining family members to seek county assistance. One child that was created has special needs that will require the remaining parent or the County to be financially responsible of those needs. The child was deprived of the right to have a traditional father to take care of the financial needs of this child. Respondent chose to step in those shoes and assume the role and responsibility of the 'other' parent. This should be her responsibility and not the responsibility of the taxpayer." Elisa was subsequently ordered to pay child support in the amount of $907.50 per child for a total of $1815 per month. . . .

We must determine whether the Court of Appeal erred [in reversing, ruling under California's version of the original Uniform Parentage Act (UPA), Cal. Fam. Code §7600 et seq.] that Elisa could not be a parent of the twins born to her lesbian partner, and thus had no obligation to support them. . . . The UPA defines the " '[p]arent and child relationship' " as "the legal relationship existing between a child and the child's natural or adoptive parents. . . . The term includes the mother and child relationship and the father and child relationship." (§7601). One purpose of the UPA was to eliminate distinctions based upon whether a child was born into a marriage, and thus was "legitimate," or was born to unmarried parents, and thus was "illegitimate." Thus, the UPA provides that . . . : "The parent and child relationship extends equally to every child and to every parent, regardless of the marital status of the parents." (§7602.). . . .

Section 7611 provides several circumstances in which "[a] man is presumed to be the natural father of a child," including: if he is the husband of the child's mother, is not impotent or sterile, and was cohabiting with her (§7540); if he signs a voluntary declaration of paternity stating he is the "biological father of the child" (§7574, subd. (b)(6)); and if "[h]e receives the child into his home and openly holds out the child as his natural child" (§7611, subd. (d)). [Although] the UPA contains separate provisions defining who is a mother and who is a father, it expressly provides that in determining the existence of a mother and child relationship, "[i]nsofar as practicable, the provisions of this part applicable to the father and child relationship apply." (§7650.)

The Court of Appeal correctly recognized that, under the UPA, Emily has a parent and child relationship with each of the twins because she gave birth to them. (§7610, subd. (a)). . . . Relying upon our statement in Johnson v. Calvert, [851 P.2d 776 (Cal. 1993)], that "for any child California law recognizes only one natural mother," the Court of Appeal reasoned that Elisa, therefore, could not also be the natural mother of the twins and thus "has no legal maternal relationship with the children under the UPA."

The Attorney General, appearing pursuant to section 17406 to "represent the public interest in establishing, modifying, and enforcing support obligations," argues that the Court of Appeal erred, stating: "*Johnson's* one-natural-mother comment cannot be thoughtlessly interpreted to deprive the child of same-sex couples the same opportunity as other children to two parents and to two sources of child support when only two parties are eligible for parentage." As we shall explain, the Attorney General is correct that our statement in *Johnson* that a child can have "only one natural mother" does not mean that both Elisa and Emily cannot be parents of the twins [because this case is distinguishable.]

In *Johnson*, [a dispute arising from a gestational surrogacy arrangement], we addressed the situation in which three people claimed to be the child's parents: the husband, who undoubtedly was the child's father, and two women [the biological mother versus surrogate mother], who presented conflicting claims to being the child's mother. We rejected the suggestion of amicus curiae that both the wife and the surrogate could be the child's mother, stating that a child can have only one mother, but what we considered and rejected in *Johnson* was the argument that a child could have three parents: a father and two mothers.[4] . . . The Court of Appeal in the present case erred, therefore, in

---

4. We have not yet decided "(whether there exists an overriding legislative policy limiting a child to two parents." [Sharon S. v. Superior Court, 73 P.3d 554, 561 (Cal. 2003)].

concluding that our statement in *Johnson* that a child can have only one mother under California law resolved the issue presented in this case. . . .

We perceive no reason why both parents of a child cannot be women. That result now is possible under the current version of the domestic partnership statutes [providing that: "The rights and obligations of registered domestic partners with respect to a child of either of them shall be the same as those of spouses." Cal. Fam. Code §297.5(d).] Prior to the effective date of the current domestic partnership statutes, we recognized in an adoption case that a child can have two parents, both of whom are women. [Sharon S. v. Superior Court, 73 P.3d 554 (Cal. 2003).] If both parents of an adopted child can be women, we see no reason why the twins in the present case cannot have two parents, both of whom are women.

[W]e proceed to examine the UPA to determine whether Elisa is a parent to the twins in addition to Emily. . . . Subdivision (d) of section 7611 states that a man is presumed to be the natural father of a child if "([h]e receives the child into his home and openly holds out the child as his natural child." The Court of Appeal in [In re Karen C., 124 Cal. Rptr. 2d 677 (Ct. App. 2002)], held that subdivision (d) of section 7611 "should apply equally to women." [W]e must determine whether Elisa received the twins into her home and openly held them out as her natural children [pursuant to Cal. Fam. Code §7611]. There is no doubt that Elisa satisfied the first part of this test. . . . Our inquiry focuses, therefore, on whether she openly held out the twins as her natural children.

The circumstance that Elisa has no genetic connection to the twins does not necessarily mean that she did not hold out the twins as her "natural" children under section 7611. We held in [In re Nicholas H., 46 P.3d 932 (Cal. 2002)] that the presumption under section 7611, subdivision (d), that a man who receives a child into his home and openly holds the child out as his natural child is not necessarily rebutted when he admits he is not the child's biological father. The presumed father [Thomas, who was *not* the biological father] in *Nicholas H.*, [was] named as the child's father on his birth certificate and provided a home for the child and his mother for several years [and subsequently sought custody when the court removed the child from the mother's care].

We held in *Nicholas H.* that Thomas was presumed to be Nicholas's father despite his admission that he was not Nicholas's biological father. . . . We noted, however, that the UPA does not state that the presumption under section 7611, subdivision (d), *is* rebutted by evidence that the presumed father is not the child's biological father, but rather that it *may* be rebutted in an appropriate action by such evidence. We held that *Nicholas H.* was not an appropriate action in which to rebut the presumption because no one had raised a conflicting claim to being the child's father. Applying the presumption, therefore, would produce the "harsh result" of leaving the child fatherless. . . .

The Court of Appeal in In re Karen C., [124 Cal. Rptr. 2d 677 (Ct. App. 2002)], applied the principles discussed in *Nicholas H.* regarding presumed fathers and concluded that a woman with no biological connection to a child [but who had raised a child from birth] could be a presumed mother under section 7611, subdivision (d). . . .

We conclude that the present case, like *Nicholas H.* . . . , is not "an appropriate action" in which to rebut the presumption of presumed parenthood with proof that Elisa is not the twins' biological parent. . . . It is undisputed that Elisa actively consented to, and participated in, the artificial insemination of her partner with the understanding that the resulting child or children would be raised by Emily and her as coparents, and they did act as coparents for a substantial period of time. Elisa received the twins into her home and held them out to the world as her natural children. . . .

Declaring that Elisa cannot be the twins' parent and, thus, has no obligation to support them because she is not biologically related to them would produce a result similar to the situation we sought to avoid in *Nicholas H.* of leaving the child fatherless. . . . Rebutting the presumption that Elisa is the twin's parent would leave them with only one parent and would deprive them of the support of their second parent. Because Emily is financially unable to support the twins, the financial burden of supporting the twins would be borne by the county, rather than Elisa.

In establishing a system for a voluntary declaration of paternity in section 7570, the Legislature declared: "There is a compelling state interest in establishing paternity for all children. Establishing paternity is the first step toward a child support award, which, in turn, provides children with equal rights and access to benefits, including, but not limited to, social security, health insurance, survivors' benefits, military benefits, and inheritance rights. . . ." By recognizing the value of determining paternity, the Legislature implicitly recognized the value of having two parents, rather than one, as a source of both emotional and financial support, especially when the obligation to support the child would otherwise fall to the public. . . .

We observed in dicta in *Nicholas H.* that it would be appropriate to rebut the section 7611 presumption of parentage if "a court decides that the legal rights and obligations of parenthood should devolve upon an unwilling candidate." But we decline to apply our dicta in *Nicholas H.* here, because we did not consider in *Nicholas H.* a situation like that in the present case.

Although Elisa presently is unwilling to accept the obligations of parenthood, this was not always so. . . . We conclude, therefore, that Elisa is a presumed mother of the twins under section 7611, subdivision (d). . . .

## NOTES AND QUESTIONS

1. *Rationale.* On what basis does the court determine that Elisa B. is obligated to pay child support? To what extent is the court's recognition of Elisa as a parent of the children born to Emily a prerequisite of her duty of support? In other words, could the court have obligated Elisa to support the twins without recognizing her as their parent? Even if the court's ruling, recognizing two mothers, appears groundbreaking, can you think of a reason why Elisa should *not* be held responsible for child support on these facts?

What theory makes parents financially responsible for their children? To the extent that children constitute community assets, the next generation of citizens, why shouldn't taxpayers assume responsibility — as they do for public education, for example? See, e.g., Scott Altman, A Theory of Child Support, 17 Int'l J. L. Pol'y & Fam. 173 (2003). Note that the litigation in *Elisa B.* began when the state sought to collect private child support so that the twins would not be dependent on public assistance.

2. *Benefit.* Who benefits from the court's ruling in *Elisa B.*? Lesbian partners like Elisa B.? Birth mothers like Emily? The children? The state? If Elisa must pay support, does it follow that she can seek visitation rights, too?

3. *UPA.* What reasons support extending paternity statutes, such as the Uniform Parentage Act (see supra section B1a), to women like Elisa B.? What counterarguments might apply? Which particular provision(s) of the UPA does the court apply? Why? Is the court's reasoning persuasive that the UPA's paternity provisions should apply to women? Prior to *Elisa B.*, several commentators proposed that states adopt a statutory scheme that permits adjudications of maternity in order to treat same-sex partners as legal parents. See, e.g., Melanie B. Jacobs, Micah Has One Mommy and One Legal Stranger: Adjudicating Maternity for Nonbiological Lesbian Co-Parents, 50 Buff. L. Rev. 341 (2002); Margaret S. Osborne, Note, Legalizing Families: Solutions to Adjudicate Parentage for Lesbian Co-Parents, 49 Vill. L. Rev. 363 (2004).

4. *Domestic partnership provisions.* What is the relevance to the ruling in *Elisa B.* of California's enactment of domestic partnership legislation? As the California Supreme Court notes, state domestic partnership legislation would have made both women parents, if they had registered, through a provision that operates in parallel fashion to the presumption of legitimacy. Cal. Fam. Code §297.5(d) (2008).[1] See Charisma R. v. Kristina S., 44 Cal. Rptr. 3d 332 (Ct. App. 2006). See also Vt. Stat. Ann. tit. 15, §1204(f) (2007). To what extent does a system that turns on the formal actions of adults, such as registering as domestic partners, replicate the inequality problems that the traditional preference for marital children created? See Grace Ganz Blumberg, Legal Recognition of Same-Sex Conjugal Relationships: The 2003 California Domestic Partner Rights and Responsibilities Act in Comparative Civil Rights and Family Law Perspective, 51 UCLA L. Rev. 1555 (2004). On the conflict of laws issues that different state approaches to parentage for same-sex couples make inevitable, see Chapter 8, section A.

5. *Estoppel.* What role, if any, does the doctrine of estoppel play in the court's analysis? What facts give rise to estoppel? In a companion case, Kristine H. v. Lisa R., 117 P.3d 690 (Cal. 2005), the California Supreme Court invoked estoppel more explicitly. Having participated in a prebirth judicial proceeding that stipulated that Kristine and Lisa were both parents of the child whom Kristine, seven months pregnant, was expecting, Kristine was estopped from questioning the stipulation later, after the women's relationship dissolved. The court limited its decision, however, declining to decide the validity of the stipulated judgment for other purposes. Id. at 695. See also, e.g., In re

---

[1] After *Elisa B.*, the state supreme court struck down the exclusion of same-sex couples from marriage, ruling that the domestic partnership laws fail to accord equal dignity to gays, lesbians, and their families. In re Marriage Cases, 183 P.3d 384, 401 (Cal. 2008). The domestic partnership law went back into effect, however, when a majority of voters supported a ballot initiative, which the court will review, amending the state constitution to reinstate same-sex couples' exclusion from marriage. Jesse McKinley, With Same-Sex Marriage, a Court Takes on the People's Voice, N.Y. Times, Nov. 21, 2008, at A18.

H.H., 879 N.E.2d 1175 (Ind. Ct. App. 2008) (estopping mother from denying ex-boyfriend's paternity).

The American Law Institute's Principles of the Law of Family Dissolution (ALI Principles) recognize "parents by estoppel." "Parents by estoppel" have the same rights and responsibilities as legal parents, but parental status by estoppel arises only in the context of dissolution of the family relationship. American Law Institute, Principles of the Law of Family Dissolution: Analysis and Recommendations §2.03 (2002). The status arises when a man has lived with the child for two years (or since birth) and believed that he was the biological father and continued assuming parental responsibilities even after the belief no longer existed; alternatively, the status arises when an adult has lived with the child since birth or for two years, accepting full and permanent responsibilities and holding the child out as his or her own, pursuant to a co-parenting agreement with the parent or parents, and recognition as a parent would serve the child's best interests. Id. at §2.03(b)(ii)-(iv). On what basis would the ALI Principles recognize Elisa B. as a parent by estoppel? See also, e.g., H.M. v. E.T., 851 N.Y.S.2d 58 (Fam. Ct. 2007). Should a man who truly but erroneously believed that he was the biological father be estopped from denying paternity when he later learns the truth? Compare San Diego County v. Arzaga, 62 Cal. Rptr. 3d 329 (Ct. App. 2007), with In re Shondel J. v. Mark D., 853 N.E.2d 610 (N.Y. 2006). In addition, parentage by estoppel can arise when one is ordered to pay child support. ALI Principles §203(b)(i). Why should parental status follow from support duties? See In re J.B., 953 A.2d 1186 (N.H. 2008); Jane Muller-Peterson, Expanding the Definition of Parenthood: Why Equitable Estoppel as Used to Impose a Child Support Obligation on a Lesbian Domestic Partner Isn't Equitable: A Case Study, 4 Geo. J. Gender & L. 781 (2003). But see A.H. v. M.P., 857 N.E.2d 1061 (Mass. 2006) (financial contribution to family, although a parenting function, does not make one a parent by estoppel); Heatzig v. MacLean, 664 S.E.2d 347 (N.C. Ct. App. 2008) (rejecting theory of "parent by estoppel"). See generally Katharine K. Baker, Asymmetric Parenthood, in Reconceiving the Family: Critique on the American Law Institute's Principles of the Law of Family Dissolution 121 (Robin Fretwell Wilson ed., 2006) (contrasting *Principles'* expansive approach to child custody rights with narrow approach to child-support obligations). Besides recognizing parents by estoppel, the ALI Principles recognize as de facto parents some adults who have provided care for children. See infra section B2b.

6. *Parentage by contract.* If parentage may rest on estoppel, should courts also recognize parentage by contract — and the accompanying parental rights and obligations? Compare In re Parentage of A.B., 818 N.E.2d 126 (Ind. Ct. App. 2004) (holding that agreement makes both women parents), *vacated by* King v. S.B., 837 N.E.2d 965 (Ind. 2005) (remanding to trial court for determination of child's best interests), with Wakeman v. Dixon, 921 So. 2d 669 (Fla. Dist. Ct. App. 2006) (holding partners' co-parenting agreement unenforceable); T.F. v. B.L., 813 N.E.2d 1244 (Mass. 2004) (rejecting parentage by contract between former lesbian partners). See generally Katharine K. Baker, Bargaining or Biology? The History and Future of Paternity Law and Parental Status, 14 Cornell J.L. & Pub. Pol'y 1 (2004); Caroline P. Blair, Note, It's More Than a One-Night Stand: Why a Promise to Parent Should Obligate a Former

Lesbian Partner to Pay Child Support in the Absence of a Statutory Requirement, 39 Suffolk U. L. Rev. 465 (2006).

7. *Rebuttal.* If genetic evidence is increasingly permitted to rebut parentage presumptions, what will this development signify for same-sex couples? What limitations on rebuttal does the *Elisa B.* court's reasoning suggest? Is the case governed by the reasoning in *Nicholas H.*, as the court asserts? Would the analysis of the rebuttal of presumed parentage differ if Elisa and Emily had registered as domestic partners? If genetic evidence controls, what good are parentage presumptions for same-sex couples, who must always use some donated genetic material? What do these questions suggest about rebuttal in more traditional contexts?

8. *Numerical limits.* Does *Elisa B.* suggest that two parents are always better than one? To what extent does *Elisa B.*'s preference for two parents rest on economic issues alone? Might more than two parents be better still? Contrast *Michael H.*, supra, which declined to recognize dual paternity, with footnote 4 in *Elisa B.*, where the court cautions that it has not decided "whether there exists an overriding legislative policy limiting a child to two parents" (citing a case permitting a woman's second-parent adoption of the biological child of her partner). Should the law fix a specific number of parents as the maximum for all children? See Chapter 6, section B2.

9. *Gender neutrality versus gender exceptionalism?* Does the court's holding make Elisa the twins' father? Their second mother? Their parent — without any more precise designation? Does it matter? Cf. Michael Levenson, Birth Certificate Policy Draws Fire: Change Affects Same-Sex Couples, Boston Globe, July 22, 2005, at B1 (noting that the Governor ordered Massachusetts hospitals to cross out "father" on birth certificates of children born to women in same-sex marriages and replace term with "parent," over the opposition of couples who fear that such altered documents could prove legally invalid). Does the holding in *Elisa B.* follow from the recent move toward eliminating gender-specific role assignments in family law?

Writing before *Elisa B.*, Professor Susan Dalton criticized the law for its asymmetrical treatment of parentage for males and females and the underlying incapacity for "imagining a gender-free subject" in this context. Susan E. Dalton, From Presumed Fathers to Lesbian Mothers: Sex Discrimination and the Legal Construction of Parenthood, 9 Mich. J. Gender & L. 261, 266 (2003). While the law has accorded a man parental status based on social factors such as marriage to the child's mother or holding out a child as his own, biological ties remained essential for a woman to achieve such status. See id. at 289. To what extent has the California Supreme Court addressed Dalton's critique? If traditional parentage rules should apply in a gender-neutral way, then should the law recognize as a child's legal mother the biological father's wife, when she is not the biological mother? See In re Amy G. v. M.W., 47 Cal. Rptr. 3d 297 (Ct. App. 2006), *cert. denied*, 550 U.S. 934 (2007).

Should mothers and fathers have identical support duties? In contrast to the norm of equal responsibility now imposed on mothers and fathers to provide child support, Professor Martha Fineman articulates a different vision: The state should provide financial support for mothers so that they can care for their children, because childcare is work that ought to be valued. See generally

Martha Albertson Fineman, The Autonomy Myth: A Theory of Dependency (2004). See also Anne L. Alstott, No Exit: What Parents Owe Children and What Society Owes Parents (2004). This approach rejects current "welfare reform" measures, included in the federal Personal Responsibility and Work Opportunity Reconciliation Act of 1996, requiring custodial mothers of young children to work outside the home (with states permitted to have some exemptions). See 42 U.S.C. §607(b)(5) (2008). Evaluate Fineman's proposal. See generally, e.g., Lee Anne Fennell, Relative Burdens: Family Ties and the Safety Net, 45 Wm. & Mary L. Rev. 1453 (2004); Symposium, The Structures of Care Work, 76 Chi.-Kent L. Rev. 1389-1786 (2001).

10. *Gay male couples.* How do the doctrines and statutes examined in *Elisa B.* apply to gay male couples? What would Dalton's call for gender neutrality, supra, mean here? In dissenting from the Massachusetts Supreme Judicial Court's conclusion that anything less than marriage would fail to remedy the constitutional violation found in Goodridge v. Department of Pub. Health, 798 N.E.2d 941 (Mass. 2003), Justice Cordy wrote:

> [T]he presumption of paternity . . . reflects reality with respect to an overwhelming majority of those children born of a woman who is married to a man. As to same-sex couples, however, who cannot conceive and bear children without the aid of a third party, the presumption is, in every case, a physical and biological impossibility. It is also expressly gender based: if a married man impregnates a woman who is not his wife, the law contains no presumption that overrides the biological mother's status and presumes the child to be that of the biological father's wife. By comparison, if a married woman becomes impregnated by a man who is not her husband, the presumption makes her husband the legal father of the child, depriving the biological father of what would otherwise be his parental rights [citing, inter alia, *Michael H.*] Applying these concepts to same-sex couples results in some troubling anomalies: applied literally, the presumption would mean very different things based on whether the same-sex couple was comprised of two women as opposed to two men. For the women, despite the necessary involvement of a third party, the law would recognize the rights of the "mother" who bore the child and presume that the mother's female spouse was the child's "father" or legal "parent." For the men, the necessary involvement of a third party would produce the exact opposite result — the biological mother of the child would retain all her rights, while one (but not both) of the male spouses could claim parental rights as the child's father. . . .

Opinions of the Justices to the Senate, 802 N.E.2d 565, 577 n.3 (Mass. 2004) (Cordy, J., dissenting). Is Justice Cordy correct? Does the involvement of a "surrogate mother" for gay male couples require them to adopt the child, preventing them from achieving parentage through a default rule like the presumption of legitimacy? See In re Roberto d. B., 923 A.2d 115 (Md. 2007), reprinted Chapter 7, section C2.

Assuming that parity with married couples is the goal of those jurisdictions giving same-sex couples access to marriage (or to a similar status with equal rights and benefits), what parentage rules best achieve parity for all couples?

See Susan Frelich Appleton, Presuming Women: Revisiting the Presumption of Legitimacy in the Same-Sex Couples Era, 86 B.U. L. Rev. 227 (2006); Jessica Hawkins, My Two Dads: Challenging Gender Stereotypes in Applying California's Recent Supreme Court Cases to Gay Couples, 41 Fam. L.Q. 623 (2007). To what extent would the imposition of greater legal hurdles (such as adoption proceedings) for gay male couples to secure parental status, as compared to their lesbian counterparts, reinforce negative stereotypes about such men? See E. Gary Spitko, From Queer to Paternity: How Primary Gay Fathers Are Changing Fatherhood and Gay Identity, 24 St. Louis U. Pub. L. Rev. 195 (2005). For the law applicable to adoption and surrogacy arrangements, see Chapter 6, section A2; Chapter 7, section C2.

## 2. PARENTAL AUTONOMY

*Elisa B.* emphasizes the duties and responsibilities ensuing from parental status. As the following materials show, recognition as a parent invests adults with important rights and authority as well.

### a. The Power to Control a Child's Upbringing

TROXEL v. GRANVILLE

530 U.S. 57 (2000)

Justice O'CONNOR announced the judgment of the Court and delivered an opinion, in which the CHIEF JUSTICE, Justice GINSBURG, and Justice BREYER join. . . .

Tommie Granville and Brad Troxel shared a relationship that ended in June 1991. The two never married, but they had two daughters, Isabelle and Natalie. Jenifer and Gary Troxel are Brad's parents, and thus the paternal grandparents of Isabelle and Natalie. After Tommie and Brad separated in 1991, Brad lived with his parents and regularly brought his daughters to his parents' home for weekend visitation. Brad committed suicide in May 1993. Although the Troxels at first continued to see Isabelle and Natalie on a regular basis after their son's death, Tommie Granville informed the Troxels in October 1993 that she wished to limit their visitation with her daughters to one short visit per month.

[Two months later, the Troxels filed this petition for visitation.] At trial, the Troxels requested two weekends of overnight visitation per month and two weeks of visitation each summer. Granville did not oppose visitation altogether, but instead asked the court to order one day of visitation per month with no overnight stay. [T]he Superior Court [ordered] visitation one weekend per month, one week during the summer, and four hours on both of the petitioning grandparents' birthdays.

[The Court of Appeals reversed the visitation order based on their statutory interpretation that nonparents lack standing unless a custody action is pending. The state supreme court held that the state statute granting visitation rights to "any parent" at "any time" (Wash. Rev. Code §26.10.160 (3) (1994)) infringed on parents' fundamental right to rear their children. While the appeal was pending, the mother remarried, and her husband adopted the children.]

The demographic changes of the past century make it difficult to speak of an average American family. The composition of families varies greatly from household to household. While many children may have two married parents and grandparents who visit regularly, many other children are raised in single-parent households. In 1996, children living with only one parent accounted for 28 percent of all children under age 18 in the United States. Understandably, in these single-parent households, persons outside the nuclear family are called upon with increasing frequency to assist in the everyday tasks of child rearing. In many cases, grandparents play an important role. For example, in 1998, approximately 4 million children — or 5.6 percent of all children under age 18 — lived in the household of their grandparents.

The nationwide enactment of nonparental visitation statutes is assuredly due, in some part, to the States' recognition of these changing realities of the American family. Because grandparents and other relatives undertake duties of a parental nature in many households, States have sought to ensure the welfare of the children therein by protecting the relationships those children form with such third parties. The States' nonparental visitation statutes are further supported by a recognition, which varies from State to State, that children should have the opportunity to benefit from relationships with statutorily specified persons — for example, their grandparents. The extension of statutory rights in this area to persons other than a child's parents, however, comes with an obvious cost. For example, the State's recognition of an independent third-party interest in a child can place a substantial burden on the traditional parent-child relationship. . . .

The liberty interest at issue in this case — the interest of parents in the care, custody, and control of their children — is perhaps the oldest of the fundamental liberty interests recognized by this Court. More than 75 years ago, in Meyer v. Nebraska, 262 U.S. 390, 399, 401 (1923), we held that the "liberty" protected by the Due Process Clause includes the right of parents to "establish a home and bring up children" and "to control the education of their own." Two years later, in Pierce v. Society of Sisters, 268 U.S. 510, 534-535 (1925), we again held that the "liberty of parents and guardians" includes the right "to direct the upbringing and education of children under their control." We explained in *Pierce* that "the child is not the mere creature of the State; those who nurture him and direct his destiny have the right, coupled with the high duty, to recognize and prepare him for additional obligations." 268 U.S. at 535. We returned to the subject in Prince v. Massachusetts, 321 U.S. 158 (1944), and again confirmed that there is a constitutional dimension to the right of parents to direct the upbringing of their children. "It is cardinal with us that the custody, care and nurture of the child reside first in the parents, whose primary function and freedom include preparation for obligations the state can neither supply nor hinder." 321 U.S. at 166. . . . In light of this extensive precedent, it cannot now be doubted that the Due Process Clause of the Fourteenth Amendment protects the fundamental right of parents to make decisions concerning the care, custody, and control of their children.

Section 26.10.160(3), as applied to Granville and her family in this case, unconstitutionally infringes on that fundamental parental right. The Washington nonparental visitation statute is breathtakingly broad. According to the statute's text, *[a]ny person* may petition the court for visitation rights *at any time*, and the court may grant such visitation rights whenever "visitation may serve *the best interest of the child.*" §§26.10.160(3) (emphases added). That language effectively permits any third party seeking visitation to subject any decision by a parent concerning visitation of the parent's children to state-court review. Once the visitation petition has been filed in court and the matter is placed before a judge, a parent's decision that visitation would not be in the child's best interest is accorded no deference. Section 26.10.160(3) contains no requirement that a court accord the parent's decision any presumption of validity or any weight whatsoever. Instead, the Washington statute places the best-interest determination solely in the hands of the judge. Should the judge disagree with the parent's estimation of the child's best interests, the judge's view necessarily prevails. Thus, in practical effect, in the State of Washington a court can disregard and overturn any decision by a fit custodial parent concerning visitation whenever a third party affected by the decision files a visitation petition, based solely on the judge's determination of the child's best interests. . . .

Turning to the facts of this case, the record reveals that the Superior Court's order was based on precisely the type of mere disagreement we have just described and nothing more. The Superior Court's order was not founded on any special factors that might justify the State's interference with Granville's fundamental right to make decisions concerning the rearing of her two daughters. [T]he combination of several factors here compels our conclusion that §26.10.160(3), as applied, exceeded the bounds of the Due Process Clause.

First, the Troxels did not allege, and no court has found, that Granville was an unfit parent. That aspect of the case is important, for there is a presumption that fit parents act in the best interests of their children. [S]o long as a parent adequately cares for his or her children (i.e., is fit), there will normally be no reason for the State to inject itself into the private realm of the family to further question the ability of that parent to make the best decisions concerning the rearing of that parent's children.

The problem here is not that the Washington Superior Court intervened, but that when it did so, it gave no special weight at all to Granville's determination of her daughters' best interests. More importantly, it appears that the Superior Court [adopted "a commonsensical approach [that] it is normally in the best interest of the children to spend quality time with the grandparent" and placed] on Granville, the fit custodial parent, the burden of *disproving* that visitation would be in the best interest of her daughters. . . .

The decisional framework employed by the Superior Court directly contravened the traditional presumption that a fit parent will act in the best interest of his or her child. In that respect, the court's presumption failed to provide any protection for Granville's fundamental constitutional right to make decisions concerning the rearing of her own daughters. In an ideal world, parents might always seek to cultivate the bonds between grandparents and their grandchildren. Needless to say, however, our world is far from perfect, and in it the decision whether such an intergenerational relationship would be beneficial in any specific case is for the parent to make in the first instance. And, if a fit parent's decision of the kind at issue here becomes subject to judicial review, the court must accord at least some special weight to the parent's own determination.

Finally, we note that there is no allegation that Granville ever sought to cut off visitation entirely. Rather, the present dispute originated when Granville informed the Troxels that she would prefer to restrict their visitation with Isabelle and Natalie to one short visit per month and special holidays. . . . The Superior Court gave no weight to Granville's having assented to visitation even before the filing of any visitation petition or subsequent court intervention. . . . Significantly, many other States expressly provide by statute that courts may not award visitation unless a parent has denied (or unreasonably denied) visitation to the concerned third party.

Considered together with the Superior Court's reasons for awarding visitation to the Troxels, the combination of these factors demonstrates that the visitation order in this case was an unconstitutional infringement on Granville's fundamental right to make decisions concerning the care, custody, and control of her two daughters. The Washington Superior Court failed to accord the determination of Granville, a fit custodial parent, any material weight. In fact, the Superior Court made only two formal findings in support of its visitation order. First, the Troxels "are part of a large, central, loving family, all located in this area, and the [Troxels] can provide opportunities for the children in the areas of cousins and music." Second, "[t]he children would be benefitted from spending quality time with the [Troxels], provided that that time is balanced with time with the childrens' [sic] nuclear family." These slender findings, in combination with the court's announced presumption in favor of grandparent visitation and its failure to accord significant weight to Granville's already having offered meaningful visitation to the Troxels, show that this case involves nothing more than a simple disagreement between the Washington Superior Court and Granville concerning her children's best interests. The Superior Court's announced reason for ordering one week of visitation in the summer demonstrates our conclusion well: "I look back on some personal experiences. . . . We always spen[t] as kids a week with one set of grandparents and another set of grandparents, [and] it happened to work out in our family that [it] turned out to be an enjoyable experience. Maybe that can, in this family, if that is how it works out." [T]he Due Process Clause does not permit a State to infringe on the fundamental right of parents to make childrearing decisions simply because a state judge believes a "better" decision could be made. [W]e hold that §26.10.160(3), as applied in this case, is unconstitutional. . . .

Because we rest our decision on the sweeping breadth of §26.10.160(3) and the application of that broad, unlimited power in this case, we do not consider the primary constitutional question passed on by the Washington Supreme Court—whether the Due Process Clause requires all nonparental visitation statutes to include a showing of harm or potential harm to the child as a condition precedent to granting visitation. We do not, and need not, define today the precise scope of the parental due process right in the visitation context. [T]he constitutionality of any standard for awarding visitation turns on the specific manner in which that standard is applied. . . . Because much state-court adjudication in this context occurs on a case-by-case basis, we would be hesitant to hold that specific nonparental visitation statutes violate the Due Process Clause as a *per se* matter. . . .

[In separate omitted concurring opinions, Justice Souter would uphold the state court's determination of the statute's facial unconstitutionality, and Justice Thomas asserted that strict scrutiny ought to apply.]

Justice STEVENS, dissenting.

. . . While, as the Court recognizes, the Federal Constitution certainly protects the parent-child relationship from arbitrary impairment by the State, we have never held that the parent's liberty interest in this relationship is so inflexible as to establish a rigid constitutional shield, protecting every arbitrary parental decision from any challenge absent a threshold finding of harm. The presumption that parental decisions generally serve the best interests of their children is sound, and clearly in the normal case the parent's interest is paramount. But even a fit parent is capable of treating a child like a mere possession.

Cases like this do not present a bipolar struggle between the parents and the State over who has final authority to determine what is in a child's best interests. There is at a minimum a third individual, whose interests are implicated in every case to which the statute applies—the child. . . . A parent's rights with respect to her child have thus never been regarded as absolute, but rather are limited by the existence of an actual, developed relationship with a child, and are tied to the presence or absence of some embodiment of family. These limitations have arisen, not simply out of the definition of parenthood itself, but because of this Court's assumption that a parent's interests in a child must be balanced against the State's long-recognized interests as parens patriae, and, critically, the child's own complementary interest in preserving relationships that serve her welfare and protection.

While this Court has not yet had occasion to elucidate the nature of a child's liberty interests in preserving established familial or family-like bonds, it seems to me extremely likely that, to the extent parents and families have fundamental liberty interests in preserving such intimate relationships, so, too, do children have these interests, and so, too, must their interests be balanced in the equation. At a minimum, our prior cases recognizing that children are, generally speaking, constitutionally protected actors require that this Court reject any suggestion that when it comes to parental rights, children are so much chattel. The constitutional protection against arbitrary state interference with parental rights should not be extended to prevent the States from protecting children against the arbitrary exercise of parental authority that is not in fact motivated by an interest in the welfare of the child.

This is not, of course, to suggest that a child's liberty interest in maintaining contact with a particular individual is to be treated invariably as on a par with that child's parents' contrary interests. Because our substantive due process case law includes a strong presumption that a parent will act in the best interest of her child, it would be necessary, were the state appellate courts actually to confront a challenge to the statute as applied, to consider whether the trial court's assessment of the "best interest of the child" incorporated that presumption. . . . But presumptions notwithstanding, we should recognize that there may be circumstances in which a child has a stronger interest at stake than mere protection from serious harm caused by the termination of visitation by a "person" other than a parent. The almost infinite variety of family relationships that pervade our ever-changing society strongly counsel against the creation by this Court of a constitutional rule that treats a biological parent's liberty interest in the care and supervision of her child as an isolated right that may be exercised arbitrarily. It is indisputably the business of the States, rather than a federal court employing a national standard, to assess in the first instance the relative importance of the conflicting interests that give rise to disputes such as this. . . .

[In separate omitted dissenting opinions, Justice Scalia declined to recognize unenumerated constitutional rights, and Justice Kennedy reasoned that the best interest doctrine is not always an unconstitutional standard in visitation cases.]

## NOTES AND QUESTIONS

1. *Constitutional liberty.* As *Troxel* explains, the Court has long recognized that parents have the authority to direct the upbringing of their children, as a substantive "liberty" protected by the Fourteenth Amendment's Due Process Clause. Thus, in Meyer v. Nebraska, 262 U.S. 390 (1923), the Court struck down a law barring the teaching of German to children, on the ground that parents, not the state, should decide what their children may learn. Similarly, in Pierce v. Society of Sisters, 268 U.S. 510 (1925), the Court invalidated a law requiring all children to attend public school and disallowing private schooling. The particular parental prerogative at stake in *Troxel* concerns choosing those with whom the child will spend time.

Thus, legal recognition as a child's "parent" has significant consequences. What reasons justify investing parents with such authority? Does such control provide a quid pro quo in exchange for child support, which the state obligates parents to pay and seeks to maintain as a private, rather than a public, responsibility? See, e.g., Katharine T. Bartlett, Re-Expressing Parenthood, 98 Yale L.J. 293, 298 (1988) (theorizing "exchange view" of parenthood). Does the law presume that parents act in their children's best interests? See, e.g., Parham v. J.R., 442 U.S. 584 (1979) (denying right to a hearing for minors committed to state mental health institutions by their parents). Cf. Bellotti v. Baird, 443 U.S. 622 (1979) (recognizing exceptions to parental control for minors seeking abortions). Or does a principle of utility underlie the protection of parental liberty? See Laurence D. Houlgate, Children's Rights, State Intervention, Custody and Divorce, Contradictions in Ethics and Family Law 163 (2005).

2. *Children as property.* Although revered as "liberal icons" that protect privacy and promote pluralism, *Meyer* and *Pierce* express a conservative attachment to the patriarchal family and a view of children as property owned by their parents, according to Professor Barbara Bennett Woodhouse in "Who

Owns the Child?": *Meyer* and *Pierce* and the Child as Property, 33 Wm. & Mary L. Rev. 995, 996 (1992). After examining the historical context of the cases, she concludes:

> By constitutionalizing a patriarchal notion of parental rights, *Meyer* and *Pierce* interrupted the trend of family law moving toward children's rights and revitalized the notion of rights of possession. . . . Patriarchal notions of ownership do not lend themselves to a child-centered theory of custody or parenthood. . . .
>
> [O]ur legal system fails to respect children. Children are often used as instruments, as in *Meyer* and *Pierce*. The child is denied her own voice and identity and becomes a conduit for the parents' religious expression, cultural identity, and class aspirations. The parents' authority to speak for and through the child is explicit in *Meyer*'s "right of control" and *Pierce*'s "high duty" of the parent to direct his child's destiny. . . .

Id. at 1113-1114. If property ownership provides the wrong legal model for the parent-child relationship, what alternatives might prove more helpful? See, e.g., Merry Jean Chan, Note, The Authorial Parent: An Intellectual Property Model of Parental Rights, 78 N.Y.U. L. Rev. 1186 (2003) (positing parenting as a form of creative expression, protected by the First Amendment); Anne C. Dailey, Developing Citizens, 91 Iowa L. Rev. 431 (2006) (examining developmental approach, with focus on caregiving as a precondition for preparing children for democratic citizenship); Elizabeth S. Scott & Robert E. Scott, Parents as Fiduciaries, 81 Va. L. Rev. 2401 (1995). More recently, Woodhouse writes that the conventional focus on parental rights versus state intervention overlooks realities, such as modern mass-market culture, which require an examination of the larger context of childhood today. Barbara Bennett Woodhouse, Reframing the Debate about the Socialization of Children: An Environmental Paradigm, 2004 U. Chi. Legal F. 85. For an examination of how investing authority in each child's parents necessarily means unequal life chances for children, see Anne L. Alstott, Is the Family at Odds with Equality? The Legal Implications of Equality for Children, 82 S. Cal. L. Rev. 1 (2008). If the law made children's interests paramount, how would it treat parentage and parental autonomy? See generally James G. Dwyer, The Relationship Rights of Children (2006).

3. *Limits of parental autonomy.* Despite constitutional protection, parental rights are not unlimited, as the *Troxel* opinions note. When the family is no longer intact, as when married parents divorce, courts make orders of custody, visitation, and child support. See, e.g., Schmehl v. Wegelin, 927 A.2d 183 (Pa. 2007) (upholding grandparent visitation statute applicable when parents divorce or separate). Further, when parental conduct or decisionmaking subjects the child to harm or the risk of harm, the state may intervene, according to Prince v. Massachusetts, 321 U.S. 158 (1944), which upheld under child labor laws the conviction of a guardian, whose ward had accompanied her to distribute copies of "Watchtower" and "Consolation," as required for the Jehovah's Witnesses, according to the tenets of the religion. Under this harm principle, the state has authority to assert jurisdiction over children suffering abuse and neglect or otherwise in need of help. In such cases, the state may order a variety of dispositions, including home visits by child welfare authorities to monitor

the family and parent educational sessions. How significant must a risk of harm be in order to justify intrusions on parental autonomy? Cf. Smith v. Organization of Foster Families for Equality and Reform, 431 U.S. 816 (1977), reprinted infra section B2b; Santosky v. Kramer, 455 U.S. 745 (1982), reprinted Chapter 2, section A.

Critics note how cultural biases shape the doctrine of parental autonomy. For example, a federal statute criminalizes genital surgeries on female minors (usually called "female genital mutilation," a traditional practice in some cultures) "while the law ignores mainstream practices where parents invade the bodily integrity of their children for nonmedical reasons. . . ." Elaine M. Chiu, The Cultural Differential in Parental Autonomy, 41 U.C. Davis L. Rev. 1773, 1780 (2008). What other examples might support this argument?

4. *Limits of* Troxel. In *Troxel*, the plurality held that the Washington statute, as applied, violated the Due Process Clause. In what way(s) was the application defective? How much deference to parental decisions does *Troxel* require? Compare Koshko v. Haining, 921 A.2d 171 (Md. 2007), with In re Madison C., 2007 WL 3317477 (Ohio Ct. App. 2007).

By holding the statute unconstitutional as applied, the Court avoided a ruling that the statute was facially unconstitutional. The Court also evaded identifying the appropriate standard of review. What standard of review should courts apply to third-party visitation statutes? Should courts be especially protective of parental interests and apply strict scrutiny (as Justice Thomas reasons in an omitted concurrence)? Rational relationship? The undue burden standard (i.e., whether visitation unduly burdens the parents' constitutional rights)? See, e.g., In re Howard, 661 N.W.2d 183 (Iowa 2003); In re R.A., 891 A.2d 564 (N.H. 2005); Harrold v. Collier, 836 N.E.2d 1165 (Ohio 2005) (all applying strict scrutiny to grandparent visitation disputes). See also Blakely v. Blakely, 83 S.W.3d 537 (Mo. 2002) (finding no undue burden imposed by visitation order under statute).

Accordingly, the Justices also disagreed on what the state must show to justify interference with a parent's decision about third-party visitation. What should the test be? The best interests of the child (as Justice Stevens and, in an omitted concurrence, Justice Kennedy assert)? Potential harm to the child if visitation is not granted, as suggested by *Prince*, supra? What are the advantages and disadvantages of applying each test? Compare Doe v. Doe, 172 P.3d 1067 (Haw. 2007) (requiring harm standard), with Hiller v. Fausey, 904 A.2d 875 (Pa. 2006) (finding unnecessary a showing of harm). If the court requires the third party to prove that the child would be harmed by denial of visitation, what should be the standard of proof? Compare Roth v. Weston, 789 A.2d 431 (Conn. 2002) (requiring clear and convincing evidence in applying broad visitation statute), with Moriarty v. Bradt, 827 A.2d 203 (N.J. 2003), and Vibbert v. Vibbert, 144 S.W.3d 292 (Ky. Ct. App. 2004) (both adopting preponderance standard). How substantial must the harm be? See Blixt v. Blixt, 774 N.E.2d 1052, 1060 (Mass. 2002) (requiring significant harm that adversely affects health, safety, or welfare plus a significant preexisting relationship).

Do the opinions suggest different standards for intact families versus families altered by divorce or death? See *Schmehl*, supra. For grandparents denied visitation altogether, versus those for whom parents allow some access?

See *Blakely*, supra. In *Troxel*, the mother decided to reduce (but not eliminate) the grandparents' visitation after she married a man with children and found that unpredictable visits undercut her effort to "nurture her new blended family." Brief for Respondents at 10, Troxel v. Granville, 530 U.S. 57 (2000), available at 1999 WL 1146868. Of what relevance are such reasons?

5. *"Extraordinary" families?* Professor Ariela Dubler notes the contrasting judicial portrayals of the families in *Michael H.*, supra, on the one hand, and *Troxel*, on the other. Of the former, Justice Scalia says "[t]he facts of this case are, we must hope, extraordinary." Some might regard the family in the latter as unusual, too—with a couple who never married, their two children, the woman's three children from her first marriage, her two stepchildren from her new marriage, one child from the new marriage, her new husband's adoption of the two children from the nonmarital relationship, assorted grandparents, and a suicide. How do you explain the "narrative normalization of family fissure and reconstitution" that Professor Dubler discerns in *Troxel*? See Ariela R. Dubler, Constructing the Modern American Family: The Stories of Troxel v. Granville, in Family Law Stories 95, 109 (Carol Sanger ed., 2008). How do the opinions accomplish this normalization? Justice O'Connor's plurality opinion cites demographic data to challenge the notion of "an average American family." Similarly, Justice Stevens's dissent invokes the "almost infinite variety of family relationships that pervade our ever-changing society." Why are these observations relevant to the constitutionality of the Washington statute?

6. *A functional approach?* Arguably, in citing such demographic data these Justices are also acknowledging a functional approach through which family law purports to reflect "the reality of family life," even if individuals do not comply with formal criteria for recognition, such as marriage. See Braschi v. Stahl Associates Co., 543 N.E.2d 49, 54 (N.Y. 1989) (applying functional approach to anti-eviction provisions of New York's rent control law). What are the advantages of a functional approach? The disadvantages?

7. *Parents versus third parties.* Note that *Troxel* assumes a classification that makes an adult either a child's parent or a third party. Parents, in turn, presumptively have authority to decide what relationship, if any, their children have with such third parties or "legal strangers." See generally Family Boundaries: Symposium on Third-Party Rights and Obligations with Respect to Children, 40 Fam. L. Q. 1-147 (2006). In place of the parent/third party binary, should the law recognize a continuum of relationships for children? For example, recall that in *Michael H.*, supra, Justice Stevens would have recognized Michael as someone entitled to an opportunity for a hearing on visitation, not as a "parent" but instead as "any other person having an interest in the welfare of the child." To what extent does *Troxel* and its binary reflect "a dominant White, middle-class, nuclear family model in which parents alone raise their children"? Solangel Maldonado, When Father (or Mother) Doesn't Know Best: Quasi-Parents and Parental Deference after Troxel v. Granville, 88 Iowa L. Rev. 865, 897 (2003).

In fact, every state has departed from the common law to enact grandparent-visitation statutes, perhaps reflecting an appreciation that children have important relationships beyond those with their parents. (These statutes might also reflect the power of grandparents in state legislatures.) At the same time, adults deemed "legal strangers" in some states include a stepparent and a biological parent's long-term partner after the dissolution of the partners' relationship. See e.g., Alison D. v. Virginia M., 572 N.E.2d 27 (N.Y. 1991); Melanie B. Jacobs, Micah Has One Mommy and One Legal Stranger: Adjudicating Maternity for Nonbiological Lesbian Co-Parents, 50 Buff. L. Rev. 341 (2002). Today, several jurisdictions use a functional approach, developing doctrines to accord parental status to some such adults. See, e.g., Kristine H. v. Lisa R., 117 P.3d 690 (Cal. 2005) (estoppel); T.B. v. L.R.M., 786 A.2d 913 (Pa. 2001) (in loco parentis); Marquez v. Caudill, 656 S.E.2d 737 (S.C. 2008) (psychological parent); In re Parentage of L.B., 122 P.3d 161 (Wash. 2005) (common law status of de facto parent). Thus, these doctrines create opportunities for "third parties" to become "parents." But see, e.g., In re Senturi N.S.V., 652 S.E.2d 490 (W. Va. 2007). Still, despite visitation statutes, grandparents ordinarily remain distinct from parents. See Philbrook v. Theriault, 957 A.2d 4 (Me. 2008) (holding that intermittent care by grandparents does not make them de facto parents). For consideration of the American Law Institute's recognition of parents by estoppel, see supra section B1b; for consideration of the American Law Institute's recognition of de facto parents, see infra section B2b.

Should a functional approach to adult-child relationships look beyond ways to extend parental status and instead reflect the reality that many adults who do *not* act as parents nonetheless provide childcare and perform child-rearing? What would such legal recognition of nonparents entail? What consequences would it have? See, e.g., Melissa Murray, The Networked Family: Reframing the Legal Understanding of Caregiving and Caregivers, 94 Va. L. Rev. 385 (2008); Laura A. Rosenbury, Between Home and School, 155 U. Pa. L. Rev. 833 (2007).

8. *Deconstructing parenthood?* Traditionally, the law has treated parenthood as comprehensive, indivisible, and exclusive. See Katharine T. Bartlett, Rethinking Parenthood as an Exclusive Status: The Need for Legal Alternatives When the Premise of the Nuclear Family Has Failed, 70 Va. L. Rev. 879 (1984). Under a functional approach, can parenthood instead be conceptualized as a bundle of rights and responsibilities that might be fragmented and exercised by multiple individuals? See Melanie B. Jacobs, Why Just Two? Disaggregating Traditional Parental Rights and Responsibilities to Recognize Multiple Parents, 9 J.L. & Fam. Stud. 309 (2007). Consider, for example, the "parenting plan" that many statutes now require each divorcing parent to submit—a blueprint that informs, but does not bind, the court in adjudicating child custody. Such plans cover specific allocations of time with a child over every day of the year; details of decisionmaking authority in different areas of the child's life, from education to health care; and responsibility for particular expenses. See, e.g., Mo. Rev. Stat. §452.310(7) (2008). How does such disaggregation of parental functions inform the understanding of what parentage and parenthood mean?

### b. Less than Autonomous Parents: The Case of Foster Care

In exercising its authority to infringe parental autonomy in response to harm or the risk of harm, the state often invokes the jurisdiction of the juvenile or family court over abused, neglected, and dependent children. If this court decides that the problem requires removal of the child from the home, the court's disposition often entails placement in a foster family. As the following case shows, foster parents exercise some but not all of the usual parental prerogatives, thus challenging the traditional understanding of an indivisible and comprehensive set of parental rights and responsibilities. Who benefits from the state's reliance on foster care? This hybrid arrangement, which gives roles to parents, the state, and foster parents, is often justified by its ability to offer the advantages of a family-like setting for children in need while maintaining state supervision and promoting reunification with the family of origin. Yet, sometimes foster care constitutes a transitional arrangement, if termination of the original parents' rights and adoption ultimately follow. Consider whether foster care's simulation of the parent-child relationship and its occasional connection to adoption also might create disadvantages and ambiguities — for children and adults alike.

## SMITH V. ORGANIZATION OF FOSTER FAMILIES FOR EQUALITY AND REFORM (OFFER)

431 U.S. 816 (1977)

Mr. Justice BRENNAN delivered the opinion of the Court.

Appellees, individual foster parents[1] and an organization of foster parents, brought this civil rights class action pursuant to 42 U.S.C. §1983 . . . on their own behalf and on behalf of children for whom they have provided homes for a year or more. They sought declaratory and injunctive relief [alleging] that the procedures governing the removal of foster children from foster homes [N.Y. Soc. Serv. Law §§383(2), 400, and 18 N.Y.C.R.R. §450.14] violated the Due Process and Equal Protection Clauses. . . . A group of natural mothers of children in foster care[5] were granted leave to intervene on behalf of themselves and others similarly situated. [The district court determined that the preremoval

---

1. Appellee Madeleine Smith is the foster parent with whom Eric and Danielle Gandy have been placed since 1970. The Gandy children, who are now 12 and 9 years old respectively, were voluntarily placed in foster care by their natural mother in 1968, and have had no contact with her at least since being placed with Mrs. Smith. The foster-care agency has sought to remove the children from Mrs. Smith's care because her arthritis, in the agency's judgment, makes it difficult for her to continue to provide adequate care. . . .

Appellees Ralph and Christiane Goldberg were the foster parents of Rafael Serrano, now 14. His parents placed him in foster care voluntarily in 1969 after an abuse complaint was filed against them. [The Goldbergs eventually separated, placing Rafael in residential care].

Appellees Walter and Dorothy Lhoton were foster parents of the Wallace sisters, who were voluntarily placed in foster care by their mother in 1970. The two older girls were placed with the Lhotons in that year, their two younger sisters in 1972. In June 1974, the Lhotons were informed that the agency had decided to return the two younger girls to their mother and transfer the two older girls to another foster home. The agency apparently felt that the Lhotons were too emotionally involved with the girls and were damaging the agency's efforts to prepare them to return to their mother. [The children eventually were returned to their mother.]

5. Intervenor Naomi Rodriguez, who is blind, placed her newborn son Edwin in foster care in 1973 because of marital difficulties. When Mrs. Rodriguez separated from her husband three months later, she sought return of her child. Her efforts over the next nine months to obtain return of the child were resisted by the agency, apparently because it felt her handicap prevented her from providing adequate care. [She] finally prevailed, three years after she first sought return of the child. . . .

procedures worked an unconstitutional deprivation of due process by denying the foster child a hearing before transfer to another foster home or return to the natural parents. 418 F. Supp. 277, 282 (S.D.N.Y. 1976).]

The expressed central policy of the New York system is that "it is generally desirable for the child to remain with or be returned to the natural parent because the child's need for a normal family life will usually best be met in the natural home, and . . . parents are entitled to bring up their own children unless the best interests of the child would be thereby endangered," Soc. Serv. Law §384-b(1)(a)(ii). But the State has opted for foster care as one response to those situations where the natural parents are unable to provide the "positive, nurturing family relationships" and "normal family life in a permanent home" that offer "the best opportunity for children to develop and thrive." §§384-b(1)(b), (1)(a)(i). [T]he distinctive features of foster care are, first, "that it is care in a *family*, it is noninstitutional substitute care," and, second, that it is for a *planned* period — either temporary or extended. This is unlike adoptive placement, which implies a *permanent* substitution of one home for another.

Under the New York scheme children may be placed in foster care either by voluntary placement or by court order. Most foster care placements are voluntary. They occur when physical or mental illness, economic problems, or other family crises make it impossible for natural parents, particularly single parents, to provide a stable home life for their children for some limited period. [Under voluntary placements, a written agreement between the parent and agency may provide for the child's return at a specified date, but if not, the child must be returned within 20 days of notice from the parent.]

The agency . . . commonly acts under its authority to "place out and board out" children in foster homes. Foster parents, who are licensed by the State or an authorized foster-care agency, provide care under a contractual arrangement with the agency, and are compensated for their services. The typical contract expressly reserves the right of the agency to remove the child on request. . . .

The New York system divides parental functions among agency, foster parents, and natural parents, and the definitions of the respective roles are often complex and often unclear. The law transfers "care and custody" to the agency, but day-to-day supervision of the child and his activities, and most of the functions ordinarily associated with legal custody, are the responsibility of the foster parent. Nevertheless, agency supervision of the performance of the foster parents takes forms indicating that the foster parent does not have the full authority of a legal custodian. Moreover, the natural parent's placement of the child with the agency does not surrender legal guardianship; the parent retains authority to act with respect to the child in certain circumstances [e.g. consent to surgery, etc.]. The natural parent has not only the right but the obligation to visit the foster child and plan for his future; failure of a parent with capacity to fulfill the obligation for more than a year can result in a court order terminating the parent's rights on the ground of neglect.

Children may also enter foster care by court order. . . . The consequences of foster-care placement by court order do not differ substantially from those for children voluntarily placed, except that the parent is not entitled to return of the child on demand . . . ; termination of foster care must then be consented to by the court.

The provisions of the scheme specifically at issue in this litigation come into play when the agency having legal custody determines to remove the foster child from the foster home, either because it has determined that it would be in the child's best interests to transfer him to some other foster home, or to return the child to his natural parents in accordance with the statute or placement agreement. Most children are removed in order to be transferred to another foster home. The procedures by which foster parents may challenge a removal made for that purpose differ somewhat from those where the removal is made to return the child to his natural parent.

Section 383(2), n.3, supra, provides that the "authorized agency placing out or boarding (a foster) child . . . may in its discretion remove such child from the home where placed or boarded." Administrative regulations implement this provision. The agency is required, except in emergencies, to notify the foster parents in writing 10 days in advance of any removal. The notice advises the foster parents that if they object to the child's removal, they may request a "conference" with the Social Services Department. The department schedules requested conferences within 10 days of the receipt of the request. The foster parent may appear with counsel at the conference, where he will "be advised of the reasons (for the removal of the child), and be afforded an opportunity to submit reasons why the child should not be removed." §450.10(a). The official must render a decision in writing within five days after the close of the conference, and send notice of his decision to the foster parents and the agency. The proposed removal is stayed pending the outcome of the conference.

If the child is removed after the conference, the foster parent may appeal to the Department of Social Services for a [full adversary administrative hearing which is subject to judicial review]; however, the removal is not automatically stayed pending the hearing and judicial review.

This statutory and regulatory scheme applies statewide.[28] In addition, regulations [applicable to New York City] provide even greater procedural safeguards [in the form of a *preremoval* trial, upon request of the foster parents, if a child is being transferred to another foster home]. One further preremoval procedural safeguard is available. [Soc. Serv. Law §392] provides a mechanism whereby a foster parent may obtain preremoval judicial review of an agency's decision to remove a child who has been in foster care for 18 months or more.

Foster care of children is a sensitive and emotion-laden subject, and foster-care programs consequently stir strong controversy. [F]oster care has been condemned as a class-based intrusion into the family life of the poor. See, e.g., Jenkins, Child Welfare as a Class System, in Children and Decent People

---

28. There is some dispute whether the procedures set out in 18 N.Y.C.R.R. §450.10 and Soc. Serv. Law §400 apply in the case of a foster child being removed from his foster home to be returned to his natural parents. [N]othing in either the statute or the regulations limits the availability of these procedures to transfers within the foster-care system. Each refers to the decision to remove a child from the foster family home, and thus on its face each would seem to cover removal for the purpose of returning the child to its parents. . . .

3 (A. Schorr ed. 1974). It is certainly true that the poor resort to foster care more often than other citizens. . . .

The extent to which supposedly "voluntary" placements are in fact voluntary has been questioned on other grounds as well. For example, it has been said that many "voluntary" placements are in fact coerced by threat of neglect proceedings and are not in fact voluntary in the sense of the product of an informed consent. Mnookin, [Foster Care In Whose Best Interests?, 43 Harv. Educ. Rev. 599, 601 (1973)]. Studies also suggest that social workers of middle-class backgrounds, perhaps unconsciously, incline to favor continued placement in foster care with a generally higher-status family rather than return the child to his natural family, thus reflecting a bias that treats the natural parents' poverty and lifestyle as prejudicial to the best interests of the child. This accounts, it has been said, for the hostility of agencies to the efforts of natural parents to obtain the return of their children.

Appellee foster parents as well as natural parents [note] that children often stay in "temporary" foster care for much longer than contemplated by the theory of the system. The District Court found as a fact that the median time spent in foster care in New York was over four years. Indeed, many children apparently remain in this "limbo" indefinitely. Mnookin, [Child-Custody Adjudication: Judicial Functions in the Face of Indeterminacy, 39 Law & Contemp. Probs., Summer 1975, at 226, 273]. The District Court also found that the longer a child remains in foster care, the more likely it is that he will never leave. . . . It is not surprising then that many children, particularly those that enter foster care at a very early age and have little or no contact with their natural parents during extended stays in foster care, often develop deep emotional ties with their foster parents.[40]

Yet such ties do not seem to be regarded as obstacles to transfer of the child from one foster placement to another. The record in this case indicates that nearly 60% of the children in foster care in New York City have experienced more than one placement, and about 28% have experienced three or more. [E]ven when it is clear that a foster child will not be returned to his natural parents, it is rare that he achieves a stable home life through final termination of parental ties and adoption into a new permanent family.

[W]e present this summary in the view that some understanding of those criticisms is necessary for a full appreciation of the complex and controversial system with which this lawsuit is concerned. [But, our] task is only to determine whether the District Court correctly held that the present procedures preceding the removal from a foster home of children resident there a year or more are constitutionally inadequate. . . .

---

40. The development of such ties points up an intrinsic ambiguity of foster care that is central to this case. The warmer and more homelike environment of foster care is intended to be its main advantage over institutional child care, yet because in theory foster care is intended to be only temporary, foster parents are urged not to become too attached to the children in their care. Mnookin, [43 Harv. Educ. Rev.,] at 613. Indeed, the New York courts have upheld removal from a foster home for the very reason that the foster parents had become too emotionally involved with the child. In re Jewish Child Care Assn. (Sanders), 5 N.Y.2d 222, 183 N.Y.S.2d 65, 156 N.E.2d 700 (1959). See also the case of the Lhotans, named appellees in this case. . . .

Our first inquiry is whether appellees have asserted interests within the Fourteenth Amendment's protection of "liberty." . . . The appellees' basic contention is that when a child has lived in a foster home for a year or more, a psychological tie is created between the child and the foster parents which constitutes the foster family the true "psychological family" of the child. That family, they argue, has a "liberty interest" in its survival as a family protected by the Fourteenth Amendment. Upon this premise they conclude that the foster child cannot be removed without a prior hearing satisfying due process. Appointed counsel for the children, . . . however, disagrees, and has consistently argued that the foster parents have no such liberty interest independent of the interests of the foster children, and that the best interests of the children would not be served by procedural protections beyond those already provided by New York law. The intervening natural parents of children in foster care . . . also oppose the foster parents, arguing that recognition of the procedural right claimed would undercut both the substantive family law of New York, which favors the return of children to their natural parents as expeditiously as possible, and their constitutionally protected right of family privacy, by forcing them to submit to a hearing and defend their rights to their children before the children could be returned to them.

[We] turn to appellees' assertion that they have a constitutionally protected liberty interest . . . in the integrity of their family unit. This assertion clearly presents difficulties. . . . There does exist a "private realm of family life which the state cannot enter," Prince v. Massachusetts, 321 U.S. 158, 166 (1944), that has been afforded both substantive and procedural protection. But is the relation of foster parent to foster child sufficiently akin to the concept of "family" recognized in our precedents to merit similar protection? [W]e are not without guides to some of the elements that define the concept of "family" and contribute to its place in our society.

First, the usual understanding of "family" implies biological relationships, and most decisions treating the relation between parent and child have stressed this element. Stanley v. Illinois, 405 U.S. 645, 651 (1972), for example, spoke of "(t)he rights to conceive and to raise one's children" as essential rights. . . . A biological relationship is not present in the case of the usual foster family. But biological relationships are not exclusive determination of the existence of a family. . . . No one would seriously dispute that a deeply loving and interdependent relationship between an adult and a child in his or her care may exist even in the absence of blood relationship. At least where a child has been placed in foster care as an infant, has never known his natural parents, and has remained continuously for several years in the care of the same foster parents, it is natural that the foster family should hold the same place in the emotional life of the foster child, and fulfill the same socializing functions, as a natural family. For this reason, we cannot dismiss the foster family as a mere collection of unrelated individuals.

But there are also important distinctions between the foster family and the natural family. First, unlike the earlier cases recognizing a right to family privacy, the State here seeks to interfere, not with a relationship having its origins entirely apart from the power of the State, but rather with a foster family which has its source in state law and contractual arrangements. . . . Here, however, whatever emotional ties may develop between foster parent and foster child have their origins in an arrangement in which the State has been a partner from the outset. . . .

A second consideration related to this is that ordinarily procedural protection may be afforded to a liberty interest of one person without derogating from the substantive liberty of another. Here, however, such a tension is virtually unavoidable. Under New York law, the natural parent of a foster child in voluntary placement has an absolute right to the return of his child in the absence of a court order obtainable only upon compliance with rigorous substantive and procedural standards, which reflect the constitutional protection accorded the natural family. Moreover, the natural parent initially gave up his child to the State only on the express understanding that the child would be returned in those circumstances. These rights are difficult to reconcile with the liberty interest in the foster family relationship claimed by appellees. It is one thing to say that individuals may acquire a liberty interest against arbitrary governmental interference in the family-like associations into which they have freely entered, even in the absence of biological connection or state-law recognition of the relationship. It is quite another to say that one may acquire such an interest in the face of another's constitutionally recognized liberty interest that derives from blood relationship, state-law sanction, and basic human right — an interest the foster parent has recognized by contract from the outset. Whatever liberty interest might otherwise exist in the foster family as an institution, that interest must be substantially attenuated where the proposed removal from the foster family is to return the child to his natural parents.

As this discussion suggests, appellees' claim to a constitutionally protected liberty interest raises complex and novel questions. It is unnecessary for us to resolve those questions definitively in this case, however, for like the District Court, we conclude that "narrower grounds exist to support" our reversal. We are persuaded that, even on the assumption that appellees have a protected "liberty interest," the District Court erred in holding that the preremoval procedures presently employed by the State are constitutionally defective.

Where procedural due process must be afforded because a "liberty" or "property" interest is within the Fourteenth Amendment's protection, there must be determined "what process is due" in the particular context. . . . Consideration of the procedures employed by the City and State of New York [in light of the factors in Mathews v. Eldridge, 414 U.S. 319 (1976), i.e., the private interest affected; the risk of an erroneous deprivation of such interest by the procedures; and, the government's interest, including avoiding fiscal or administrative burdens that additional or substitute procedural requirements would entail] requires the conclusion that those procedures satisfy constitutional standards.

Turning first to the procedure applicable in New York City, [SSC Procedure No. 5] provides that before a child is removed from a foster home for transfer to another foster home, the foster parents may request an "independent review." . . . Such a procedure would appear to give a more elaborate trial-type hearing to foster families than this Court has found required in other contexts of administrative determinations. The District Court found the procedure inadequate on four grounds, none of which we find sufficient to justify the holding that the procedure violates due process.

First, the court held that the "independent review" administrative proceeding was insufficient because it was only available on the request of the foster parents. [That is,] the proceeding should be provided as a matter of course, because the interests of the foster parents and those of the child would not necessarily be coextensive, and it could not be assumed that the foster parents would invoke the hearing procedure in every case in which it was in the child's interest to have a hearing. . . . We disagree. As previously noted, the constitutional liberty, if any, sought to be protected by the New York procedures is a right of *family* privacy or autonomy, and the basis for recognition of any such interest in the foster family must be that close emotional ties analogous to those between parent and child are established when a child resides for a lengthy period with a foster family. If this is so, necessarily we should expect that the foster parents will seek to continue the relationship to preserve the stability of the family; if they do not request a hearing, it is difficult to see what right or interest of the foster child is protected by holding a hearing. . . .

Second, the District Court faulted the city procedure on the ground that participation is limited to the foster parents and the agency and the natural parent and the child are not made parties to the hearing. This is not fatal in light of the nature of the alleged constitutional interests at stake. When the child's transfer from one foster home to another is pending, the interest arguably requiring protection is that of the foster family, not that of the natural parents. Moreover, . . . nothing in the New York City procedure prevents consultation of the child's wishes. . . . Such consultation, however, does not require that the child or an appointed representative must be a party with full adversary powers in all preremoval hearings.

The other two defects in the city procedure found by the District Court must also be rejected. One is that the procedure does not extend to the removal of a child from foster care to be returned to his natural parent. But as we have already held, whatever liberty interest may be argued to exist in the foster family is significantly weaker in the case of removals preceding return to the natural parent, and the balance of due process interests must accordingly be different. . . . Similarly, the District Court pointed out that the New York City procedure coincided with the informal "conference" and postremoval hearings provided as a matter of state law. This overlap in procedures may be unnecessary or even to some degree unwise, but a State does not violate the Due Process Clause by providing alternative or additional procedures beyond what the Constitution requires.

Outside New York City, where only the statewide procedures apply, foster parents are provided not only with the procedures of a preremoval conference and postremoval hearing provided by 18 N.Y.C.R.R. §450.10 and Soc. Serv. Law §400, but also with the preremoval *judicial* hearing available on request to foster parents who have in their care children who have been in foster care for 18 months or more, Soc. Serv. Law §392. [A] foster parent in such case may obtain an order that the child remain in his care.

The District Court found . . . defects in this full judicial process. First, a §392 proceeding is available only to those foster children who have been in foster care for 18 months or more. . . . We do not think that the 18-month limitation [renders] the New York scheme constitutionally inadequate. The assumed liberty interest to be protected in this case is one rooted in the emotional attachments that develop over time between a child and the adults who care for him. But there is no reason to assume that those attachments ripen at less than 18 months or indeed at any precise point. . . . Finally, the §392 hearing is available to foster parents, both in and outside New York City, even where the removal sought is for the purpose of returning the child to his natural parents. Since this remedy provides a sufficient constitutional pre-removal hearing to protect whatever liberty interest might exist in the continued existence of the foster family when the State seeks to transfer the child to another foster home, a fortiori the procedure is adequate to protect the lesser interest of the foster family in remaining together at the expense of the disruption of the natural family.

. . . Since we hold that the procedures provided by New York State in §392 and by New York City's SSC Procedure No. 5 are adequate to protect whatever liberty interest appellees may have, the judgment of the District Court is reversed.

Mr. Justice Stewart, with whom the Chief Justice and Mr. Justice Rehnquist join, concurring in the judgment.

. . . I cannot understand why the Court thinks itself obliged to decide these cases on the assumption that either foster parents or foster children in New York have some sort of "liberty" interest in the continuation of their relationship. Rather than tiptoeing around this central issue, I would squarely hold that the interests asserted by the appellees are not of a kind that the Due Process Clause of the Fourteenth Amendment protects.

[T]he predicate for invoking the Due Process Clause — the existence of state-created liberty or property — [is] missing here. New York confers no right on foster families to remain intact, defeasible only upon proof of specific acts or circumstances. Similarly, New York law provides no basis for a justifiable expectation on the part of foster families that their relationship will continue indefinitely. . . .

What remains of the appellees' argument is the theory that the relation of the foster parent to the foster child may generate emotional attachments similar to those found in natural families. The Court surmises that foster families who share these attachments might enjoy the same constitutional interest in "family privacy" as natural families. . . .

But under New York's foster-care laws, any case where the foster parents had assumed the emotional role of the child's natural parents would represent not a triumph of the system, to be constitutionally safeguarded from state intrusion, but a failure. The goal of foster care, at least in New York, is not to provide a permanent substitute for the natural or adoptive home, but to prepare the child for his return to his real parents or placement in a permanent adoptive home by giving him temporary shelter in a family setting. . . . Perhaps it is to be expected that children who spend unduly long stays in what should have been temporary foster care will develop strong emotional ties with their foster parents. But this does not mean, and I cannot believe, that such breakdowns of the New York system must be protected or forever frozen in their existence by the Due Process Clause of the Fourteenth Amendment.

One of the liberties protected by the Due Process Clause, the Court has held, is the freedom to "establish a home and bring up children." Meyer v. Nebraska, supra, 262 U.S., at 399. . . . But this constitutional concept is simply not in point when we deal with foster families as New York law has defined them. The family life upon which the State "intrudes" is simply a temporary status which the State itself has created. It is a "family life" defined and con-trolled by the law of New York, for which New York pays, and the goals of which New York is entitled to and does set for itself.

## NOTES AND QUESTIONS

1. *A protected liberty interest?* *OFFER* holds that the preremoval hearing regulations afforded by New York City and the state accorded sufficient due process protection to foster parents. Must such a hearing be provided before removal, or can a social services agency rely on less formal interviews? In other words, how should the Court decide the issue that Justice Stewart accuses the majority of "tiptoeing around"? Several other courts have answered this question after *OFFER*, refusing to recognize the liberty interests of foster families, even after long-term care and the initiation of adoption proceedings. See Rodriguez v. McLoughlin, 214 F.3d 328 (2d Cir. 2000), *cert denied*, 532 U.S. 1051 (2001); Terese B. v. Commissioner of Children & Families, 789 A.2d 1114 (Conn. App. Ct. 2001); In re C.M., 86 P.3d 1025 (Kan. Ct. App. 2004); In re McDaniel, 2004 WL 1144390 (Ohio Ct. App. 2004).

2. OFFER *and parentage.* What does *OFFER* contribute to the understanding of legal parentage and the autonomy that the Constitution protects for par-ents? On the one hand, *OFFER* rejects the approach of *Stanley* and *Elisa B.*, refusing to recognize as parents adults whom the law traditionally excluded. To that extent, *OFFER* is compatible with the plurality opinion of *Michael H.* On the other hand, *OFFER* complicates the traditional understanding of paren-tal prerogatives, as depicted in *Troxel*, because the "natural parents" retain their status but with significant limitations on their authority to direct the child's upbringing. The role recognized for foster parents in *OFFER* thus challenges both the conventional parent/third party binary and the usual exclusion of the state from the day-to-day upbringing of children.

3. *Kinship care.* Should courts treat foster parents who are relatives differ-ently from those who are nonrelatives in terms of family recognition? See Gabrielle A. Paupeck, Note, When Grandma Becomes Mom: The Liberty Inter-ests of Kinship Foster Parents, 70 Fordham L. Rev. 527 (2001) (arguing that kinship foster parents and their foster children should enjoy a due process right of family association). Like the children in *OFFER*, most children in foster care are placed in unrelated family homes. An increasing number, however, are placed with close relatives (a practice known as "kinship care").

Federal law now provides financial incentives to encourage the develop-ment of kinship foster care programs. See 42 U.S.C. §5106 (a)(4) (2008); see also id. §5113 (b)(6). See also Fostering Connections to Success and Increasing

Adoptions Act of 2008, Pub. L. 110-351 (2008) (promoting kinship placements in Title I). Why? The benefits of kinship care include family continuity, reduced trauma from separation from biological parents, and — according to evolutionary biology — better treatment than that from unrelated caregivers. See David J. Herring, Kinship Foster Care: Implications of Behavioral Biology Research, 56 Buffalo L. Rev. 495 (2008). Yet, data show that children in kinship care are more likely to live in poverty and also to have caregivers who are older, less financially stable, less well educated, and burdened with more health problems than nonkin caregivers. In addition, the child's parents are more likely to have access to a child in kinship care — a particularly problematic situation when placement results from parental abuse. See Cynthia G. Hawkins-Leon & Carla Bradley, Race and Transracial Adoption: The Answer is Neither Simply Black or White Nor Right or Wrong, 51 Cath. U. L. Rev. 1227, 1278 (2002). See generally Margaret F. Brinig & Steven L. Nock, How Much Does Legal Status Matter? Adoptions by Kin Caregivers, 36 Fam. L.Q. 449 (2002). To the extent that foster care is designed to serve as a transitional step to permanent outcomes, either family reunification or adoption, how does the rise of kinship care challenge the goal of permanence? See Sacha Coupet, Swimming Upstream Against the Great Adoption Tide: Making the Case for "Impermanence," 34 Cap. U. L. Rev. 405 (2005).

According to Census Bureau figures, over 6 million adults are living with their own minor grandchildren. Roughly 60 percent are white, 20 percent African-American, and 23 percent are of Hispanic or Latino origin (of any race). Fourteen percent are reported to live below the poverty level, and in 15 percent of the households the grandchild's own parent is not present. U.S. Census Bureau, United States, S1002, Grandparents (2007 American Community Survey 1-Year Estimates), available at http://factfinder.census.gov/servlet/STTable?_bm=y&-geo_id=01000US&-qr_name=ACS_2007_1YR_G00_S1002&ds_name=ACS_2007_1YR_G00_&-_lang=en&-redoLog=false&-format=&-CONTEXT=st. What changes in the principles and assumptions of *Troxel*, supra, might follow from the co-residence of grandparents and grandchildren? See, e.g., Solangel Maldonado, When Father (or Mother) Doesn't Know Best: Quasi-Parents and Parental Deference after Troxel v. Granville, 88 Iowa L. Rev. 865 (2003); Sonia Gipson Rankin, Note, Why They Won't Take the Money: Black Grandparents and the Success of Informal Kinship Care, 10 Elder L.J. 153 (2002).

4. *Historical background.* Foster care's history traces back to practices such as placing out and apprenticeship, which were adoption's antecedents, as well as the Progressive Era's childsaving efforts, including the use of "orphan trains." See supra section A.

5. *Voluntary surrender.* As *OFFER* explains, a parent often initiates foster placement. Given *OFFER*'s depiction of the foster care system, what factors complicate the distinction between such "voluntary" surrenders and those imposed by the state? See Dorothy Roberts, Shattered Bonds: The Color of Child Welfare 82-89 (2002) (citing various pressures and power imbalances faced by poor parents).

6. *Psychological parent doctrine.* Appellees' argument that legally cognizable emotional bonds develop within foster families relies on the concept of

"psychological parent" formulated by Joseph Goldstein, Anna Freud, and Alfred Solnit in Beyond the Best Interests of the Child (1973). Their theory asserts that children often may begin to regard a caregiving adult as a parent and may suffer traumatic loss from the disruption of such relationships, even if they were meant to be temporary. This theory proved influential with courts in their efforts to apply the indeterminate standard of "best interests of the child." See, e.g., Painter v. Bannister, 140 N.W.2d 152 (Iowa 1966); John Batt, Child Custody Disputes and the Beyond the Best Interests Paradigm: A Contemporary Assessment of the Goldstein/Freud/Solnit Position and the Group's Painter v. Bannister Jurisprudence, 16 Nova L. Rev. 621 (1992); Peggy C. Davis, "There Is a Book Out . . .": An Analysis of Judicial Absorption of Legislative Facts, 100 Harv. L. Rev. 1539 (1987) (analyzing judicial decisions influenced by Goldstein et al.'s psychological parent theory); Carol Weisbrod, Painter v. Bannister: Still, 2006 Utah L. Rev. 135. Although some states have responded by enacting a preference for biological parents over "third parties" in custody disputes, e.g., Mo. Rev. Stat. §452.375.5 (2008), the psychological parent theory still operates to allow recognition of nonbiological parents in nontraditional families. See, e.g., V.C. v. M.J.B., 748 A.2d 539 (N.J. 2000) (recognizing biological mother's former partner as psychological parent).

Does *OFFER* adequately protect the "psychological parent-child" relationship? To the extent that the theory focuses on the child's interests, can the foster parents assert these interests? Note that the foster parents suing in *OFFER* did so on their own behalf and on behalf of the children. In an omitted footnote 44, the Court addressed the argument that the foster parents lacked standing to raise the children's interests:

> Ordinarily, it is true, a party would not have standing to assert the rights of another, himself a party in the litigation; the third party himself can decide how best to protect his interests. But children usually lack the capacity to make that sort of decision, and thus their interest is ordinarily represented in litigation by parents or guardians. In this case, however, the State, the natural parents, and the foster parents, all of whom share some portion of the responsibility for guardianship of the child, are parties, and all contend that the position they advocate is most in accord with the rights and interests of the children. In this situation, the District Court properly appointed independent counsel to represent the children, so that the court could have the benefit of an independent advocate for the welfare of the children, unprejudiced by the possibly conflicting interests and desires of the other parties. It does not follow, however, that that independent counsel, who is not a guardian *ad litem* of the children, is solely authorized to determine the children's best interest.
>
> [The foster parents'] standing to raise the rights of the children in their attack on those procedures is a prudential question. We believe it would be most imprudent to leave entirely to court-appointed counsel the choices that neither the named foster children nor the class they represent are capable of making for themselves, especially in litigation in which all parties have sufficient attributes of guardianship that their views on the rights of the children should at least be heard.

431 U.S. at 842 n.44. Does that solve the problem? Cf. Annette Ruth Appell, Representing Children Representing What? Critical Reflections on Lawyering for Children, 39 Colum. Hum. Rts. L. Rev. 573 (2008).

Evaluate dissenting Justice Stewart's assertion that the child's emotional ties to the foster parents constitute "breakdowns" of the system that the Due Process Clause should not protect. Does it follow that a child should be moved to a new foster home once such ties begin to develop? See In re Jewish Child Care Assn. (Sanders), 156 N.E.2d 700 (N.Y. 1959). For the significance of emotional attachment in the context of adoptive placements that fail because of defects in the birth parents' consent, see Chapter 2, sections B1 & B2.

Does a foster child have an independent, constitutionally protected liberty interest in maintaining contact with a foster-psychological parent, after the foster placement ends? See Harriet II v. Alex LL, 740 N.Y.S.2d 162 (App. Div. 2002). See also Stephanie Moes, Note, Being Seen and Heard: Webster v. Ryan's Constitutional Protection for Children's Right to Maintain Contact with Foster Parents, 71 U. Cin. L. Rev. 331 (2002).

7. *De Facto parents.* Building on the notion of psychological parents, the ALI Principles recognize de facto parents, in addition to parents by estoppel (discussed supra section B1b). To be a de facto parent, the adult must have lived with the child and

> for reasons primarily other than financial compensation, and with the agreement of a legal parent to form a parent-child relationship, or as a result of a complete failure or inability of any legal parent to perform caretaking functions, (A) regularly performed the majority of the caretaking functions for the child, or (B) regularly performed a share of caretaking functions at least as great as that of the parent with whom the child primarily lived.

American Law Institute, Principles of the Law of Family Dissolution: Analysis and Recommendations §2.03(1)(c) (2002). If the child's emotional attachments justify recognition of de facto parents, how do you explain the requirement that the adult act "for reasons primarily other than financial compensation"? The comments state that the law cannot assume that adults acting for financial compensation "are motivated by love and loyalty," which in turn protect the child's best interests. Id. at §2.03 cmt. c.ii. Might there be other reasons? See Jensen v. Bevard, 168 P.3d 1209, 1214 (Or. Ct. App. 2007) (expressing concern that "parents who, for some employment or other reason, need to be away from their children for regular extended periods [would be] at risk of losing custody of their offspring to child care providers to whom the offspring have formed strong attachments"). Further, those recognized as de facto parents may obtain some allocation of custody, but legal parents and parents by estoppel receive priority in determinations of primary custody and decisionmaking authority. ALI Principles §2.03 cmt. b; §2.09(2).

Does the ALI Principles' approach make sense? Why do the Principles devalue a child's bonds with foster parents and nannies? See Susan Frelich Appleton, Parents by the Numbers, 37 Hofstra L. Rev. 11 (2008); Pamela Laufer-Ukeles, Money Caregiving, and Kinship: Should Paid Caregivers Be Allowed to Obtain De Facto Parental Status?, 74 Mo. L. Rev. ____ (forthcoming

2009). Why must the parent agree to the relationship or completely fail to provide caretaking? Why should parents by estoppel (who may gain their status by having been ordered to pay child support) take priority over those who perform caretaking functions? Why distinguish those who receive money from those who pay it?

8. *Foster Care Population.*

a. *Entry into foster care.* When *OFFER* was decided, the typical parent who placed a child in foster care was a divorced spouse with financial problems, an unwed mother, or a mother on welfare who was unable temporarily to care for a child because of illness or financial problems. A leading authority identified family disruption, financial difficulties, and medical reasons as the primary factors. Alfred Kadushin, Child Welfare Services 366 (1976). Neglect, abuse, and abandonment also accounted for many children's entry into foster care. Beginning in the mid 1980s, significant changes occurred in the numbers of children in foster care, their characteristics, and the reasons for their entrance into care. In 1980 approximately 300,000 children were in foster care. That number practically doubled by 1998. Sandra Bass et al., Children, Families, and Foster Care: Analysis and Recommendations, in 14 The Future of Children 5, 8 (2004). More African-American, Hispanic, and Native American children entered foster care, and more sibling groups needed to be placed together. A considerable number of children entered foster care because their families lacked adequate housing. Substance abuse was another contributing factor — the increasing use of crack cocaine led to the placement of more infants in foster care, based on drug toxicity at birth, substance-related abandonment, or inadequate parenting. Children with HIV or whose parents died of AIDS further enlarged the foster care population. As a result of these factors, many children entered foster care with special needs.

b. *Current characteristics.* According to a 2008 report reflecting data from 2006, an estimated 510,000 children were in foster care. Of these children, 46 percent were in nonrelative foster family homes, 24 percent were in relative foster homes, 17 percent were in group homes or institutions, 3 percent were in pre-adoptive homes, 6 percent were in other types of placements, and 2 percent were runaways. The median age of children in foster care was 10.2 years. In terms of racial characteristics, 40 percent of children in foster care were white/non-Hispanic, 32 percent were Black/non-Hispanic, 19 percent were Hispanic, and 9 percent were children of other racial/ethnic origins. Slightly more than half of the children in foster care were male. The mean time spent in foster care was 28.3 months; however, over one quarter who left foster care had been in care for more than 2 years, and 7 percent had been in care for 5 or more years. Of 289,000 children who exited foster care in 2006, 53 percent were reunited with parent(s) or primary caretakers(s), 17 percent were adopted, 16 percent went to live with a relative or guardian, and 9 percent were emancipated. U.S. Dept. of Health & Human Servs., Administration for Children & Families, The AFCARS Report #14: Preliminary FY2006 Estimates as of January 2008, available at http://www.acf.hhs.gov/programs/cb/stats_research/afcars/tar/report14.pdf.

9. *Epilogue.* Although the Supreme Court reversed the district court's finding of unconstitutionality in *OFFER*, the case had an impact. First, the Gandy

children (see footnote 1) were permitted to remain with their foster mother Mrs. Smith. Eventually, she adopted them. Second, the litigation put on notice those states without any preremoval conferences that their procedures might have constitutional flaws. Third, the litigation resulted in new procedural protections in New York City (although not statewide) regarding the formal hearings prior to intrafoster care transfers. Foster parents (who must request these hearings) may appear with counsel; witnesses are sworn and subject to cross-examination; and expert testimony is often taken. Although only a small number of such hearings are held, the reversal rate for these contested decisions is quite high. David L. Chambers & Michael S. Wald, Smith v. OFFER, in In the Interest of Children: Advocacy, Law Reform, and Public Policy 114-116 (Robert H. Mnookin ed. 1985).

10. *Foster care reform.*

a. *Adoption Assistance and Child Welfare Act.*  Foster care was envisioned as a temporary solution to family dysfunction or disruption. However, in the 1970s, public attention began focusing on the problem of "foster care drift" or "foster care limbo." The terms signify the experience of foster care children who undergo multiple foster care placements, moving continuously from foster home to foster home without any hope of family reunification or adoption. Many commentators criticized the practice and highlighted its psychological harm to children. See, e.g., Goldstein et al., supra; Robert H. Mnookin, Foster Care — In Whose Best Interest?, 43 Harv. Educ. Rev. 599 (1973); Michael S. Wald, State Intervention on Behalf of "Neglected" Children, 28 Stan. L. Rev. 623 (1976). The United States Supreme Court added fuel to the debate with its critique in *OFFER.*

Such concerns motivated legislative reform on the federal and state levels. In 1980 Congress enacted the Adoption Assistance and Child Welfare Act (AACWA), Pub. L. No. 96-272, 94 Stat. 500 (1980). The primary objective of the AACWA was to facilitate finding permanent homes for children (by preventing the need for removal, returning children to their families, or placing them for adoption). The AACWA provides federal matching funds to states for administering foster care and adoption services (emphasizing preventive and rehabilitative services) subject to certain requirements.

To qualify for federal funding, AACWA requires that (1) states must formulate case plans ("permanency planning") that are designed to achieve placement in the least restrictive setting possible and that focus on family reunification; (2) states must conduct periodic case reviews (case files must be reviewed by agencies and courts every 6 months with dispositional hearings held after 18 months); and (3) states must make "reasonable efforts" to prevent the need to remove a child from the home and to facilitate the child's return as soon as possible. See 42 U.S.C. §671 (2008). Even before Congress passed the AACWA, individual states were acting independently to adopt legislation that pointed in the same direction. After 1980, states adopted legislation to conform to the minimum requirements for federal funding set out by the AACWA.

b. *Adoption and Safe Families Act.*  AACWA's emphasis on family preservation and reunification ultimately evoked criticism. According to critics, these policies exposed children to unnecessary risks (by leaving children in or returning them to dangerous homes) and perpetuated foster care drift and foster care limbo (by delaying adoption). In 1997, Congress enacted the Adoption and Safe Families Act (ASFA), 42 U.S.C. §675(5) (2008). ASFA recognizes that reunification is not possible or advisable in all cases and provides for speedier termination of parental rights with a goal of promoting adoption, as discussed in more detail Chapter 2, section A; Chapter 3, section A1a.

c. *Fostering Connections to Success and Increasing Adoptions Act of 2008.* This statute, Pub.L. 110-351, became law in October, 2008. In providing funds to the states, it gives them the option of subsidizing kinship care and otherwise promoting kinship connections; the law also permits states to receive funding while continuing to provide foster care for those up to 21 years of age, in contrast to the traditional and often criticized approach under which youths "age out" of foster care upon turning 18. See, e.g., Pew Charitable Trusts, Time for Reform: Aging Out and on Their Own—More Teens Leaving Foster Care without a Permanent Family (2007), available at http://www.pewtrusts.org/uploadedFiles/wwwpewtrustsorg/Reports/Foster_care_reform/Kids_are_Waiting_TimeforReform0307.pdf; Jennifer Sapp, Note, Aging Out of Foster Care: Enforcing the Independent Living Program Through Contract Liability, 29 Cardozo L. Rev. 2861 (2008).

## PROBLEM

Ernest and Regina Twigg sought discovery to determine the paternity of Kimberly Mays. They allege that Kimberly, who was reared by Robert Mays and his wife (now deceased), was actually the Twiggs' daughter, who had been switched at birth at the hospital. (The daughter reared by the Twiggs, born on the same date at the same hospital, had died of a heart ailment; during the course of her medical treatment, the Twiggs first learned that she was not their biological daughter.) Can a court order the blood tests over Mays's objection? Must it do so? Why?

Suppose blood tests take place and corroborate the Twiggs' claim. They sue for custody of Kimberly (now age 15), who wants to remain with Mays. What result and why? See Twigg v. Mays, 1993 WL 330624 (Fla. Cir. Ct. 1993). Alternatively, suppose Kimberly prefers to live with the Twiggs. See Kim Mays Happy with Family, St. Petersburg Times, Nov. 15, 1994, at 5B. See generally Cynthia R. Mabry, The Tragic and Chaotic Aftermath of a Baby Switch: Should Policy and Common Law, Blood Ties, or Psychological Bonds Prevail?, 6 Wm. & Mary J. Women & L. 1 (1999).

How, if at all, would your analysis of the custody dispute change if Kimberly were age seven and had come to live with Mays three years earlier, after her biological parents, the Twiggs, had temporarily entrusted her to his care during a particularly difficult time? Suppose that, thereafter, Kimberly began to regard Mays as her father and expert testimony established that she was thriving in his care. Then, when the Twiggs sought her return, Mays refuses to send her back. Now, what result and why? See Painter v. Bannister, 140 N.W.2d 152 (Iowa 1966).

Suppose Kimberly were age seven when her biological parents, the Twiggs, discover that the daughter they thought had been killed as an infant in a fire had, in fact, been kidnapped by Mays and reared as his own. Would Kimberly's desire to remain with Mays, even if expert testimony showed her to be thriving, carry any weight at all? Why? See Jacqueline Soteropoulos, Woman Sentenced for Kidnapping Infant in 1997, Phil. Inquirer, Sept. 24, 2005, at domestic news.

# CHAPTER 2

# *ENDING THE ORIGINAL PARENT-CHILD RELATIONSHIP*

Adoption creates a new legal relationship of parent and child. With traditional rules limiting a child to no more than two parents and making parentage a comprehensive, exclusive, and indivisible status, the ordinary prerequisites for adoption include bringing to an end any existing parent-child relationship. Two primary tracks lead to this result: the state's termination of parental rights (TPR), even over the objection of the parents, and parental decisions to relinquish or surrender a child for adoption.

## A. INVOLUNTARY TERMINATION OF PARENTAL RIGHTS

SANTOSKY V. KRAMER

455 U.S. 745 (1982)

Justice BLACKMUN delivered the opinion of the Court. . . .

Under New York law, the State may terminate, over parental objection, the rights of parents in their natural child upon a finding that the child is "permanently neglected." The New York Family Court Act §622 requires that only a "fair preponderance of the evidence" support that finding. Thus, in New York, the factual certainty required to extinguish the parent-child relationship is no greater than that necessary to award money damages in an ordinary civil action. . . . The question here is whether New York's "fair preponderance of the evidence" standard is constitutionally sufficient.

Petitioners John Santosky II and Annie Santosky are the natural parents of Tina and John III. In November 1973, after incidents reflecting parental neglect, respondent Kramer, Commissioner of the Ulster County Department of Social Services, initiated a neglect proceeding under Fam. Ct. Act §1022 and removed Tina from her natural home. About 10 months later, he removed John III and placed him with foster parents. On the day John was taken, Annie Santosky gave birth to a third child, Jed. When Jed was only three days old, respondent transferred him to a foster home on the ground that immediate removal was necessary to avoid imminent danger to his life or health.

In October 1978, respondent petitioned the Ulster County Family Court to terminate petitioners' parental rights in the three children. [When petitioners challenged the "preponderance" standard,] [t]he Family Court Judge rejected this constitutional challenge, and weighed the evidence under the statutory standard. While acknowledging that the Santoskys had maintained contact with their children, the judge found those visits "at best superficial and devoid of any real emotional content." After deciding that the agency had made " 'diligent efforts' to encourage and strengthen the parental relationship," he concluded that the Santoskys were incapable, even with public assistance, of planning for the future of their children. The judge later held a dispositional hearing and ruled that the best interests of the three children required permanent termination of the Santoskys' custody. [Petitioners unsuccessfully appealed.]

Last Term in Lassiter v. Department of Social Services, 452 U.S. 18 (1981), this Court [held] that the Fourteenth Amendment's Due Process Clause does not require the appointment of counsel for indigent parents in every parental status termination proceeding. The case casts light, however, on the two central questions here — whether process is constitutionally due a natural parent at a State's parental rights termination proceeding, and, if so, what process is due. . . .

The fundamental liberty interest of natural parents in the care, custody, and management of their child does not evaporate simply because they have not been model parents or have lost temporary custody of their child to the State. Even when blood relationships are strained, parents retain a vital interest in preventing the irretrievable destruction of their family life. If anything, persons faced with forced dissolution of their parental rights have a more critical need for procedural protections than do those resisting state intervention into ongoing family affairs. When the State moves to destroy weakened familial bonds, it must provide the parents with fundamentally fair procedures.

In Lassiter, the Court and three dissenters agreed that the nature of the process due in parental rights termination proceedings turns on a balancing of the "three distinct factors" specified in Mathews v. Eldridge, 424 U.S. 319, 335 (1976): the private interests affected by the proceeding; the risk of error created by the State's chosen procedure; and the countervailing governmental interest supporting use of the challenged procedure. . . . Evaluation of the three Eldridge factors compels the conclusion that use of a "fair preponderance of the evidence" standard in [termination] proceedings is inconsistent with due process.

"The extent to which procedural due process must be afforded the recipient is influenced by the extent to which he may be 'condemned to suffer grievous loss.' " Whether the loss threatened by a particular type of proceeding is sufficiently grave to warrant more than average certainty on the part of the factfinder turns on both the nature of the private interest threatened and the permanency of the threatened loss.

Lassiter declared it "plain beyond the need for multiple citation" that a natural parent's "desire for and right to 'the companionship, care, custody, and management of his or her children' " is an interest far more precious than any property right. 452 U.S., at 27 quoting Stanley v. Illinois, 405 U.S., at 651. When the State initiates a parental rights termination proceeding, it seeks not merely to infringe that fundamental liberty interest, but to end it. . . . Thus, the first *Eldridge* factor — the private interest affected — weighs heavily against use of the preponderance standard at a state-initiated permanent neglect proceeding. . . .

[T]he factfinding hearing pits the State directly against the parents. The State alleges that the natural parents are at fault. The questions disputed and decided are what the State did — "made diligent efforts," — and what the natural parents did not do — "maintain contact with or plan for the future of the child." The State marshals an array of public resources to prove its case and disprove the parents' case. Victory by the State not only makes termination of parental rights possible; it entails a judicial determination that the parents are unfit to raise their own children.[10]

[U]ntil the State proves parental unfitness, the child and his parents share a vital interest in preventing erroneous termination of their natural relationship. Thus, at the factfinding, the interests of the child and his natural parents coincide to favor use of error-reducing procedures. . . .

Under Mathews v. Eldridge, we next must consider both the risk of erroneous deprivation of private interests resulting from use of a "fair preponderance" standard and the likelihood that a higher evidentiary standard would reduce that risk. . . . In New York, the factfinding stage of a state-initiated permanent neglect proceeding bears many of the indicia of a criminal trial. . . . The State, the parents, and the child are all represented by counsel. The State seeks to establish a series of historical facts about the intensity of its agency's efforts to reunite the family, the infrequency and insubstantiality of the parents' contacts with their child, and the parents' inability or unwillingness to formulate a plan for the child's future. The attorneys submit documentary evidence, and call witnesses who are subject to cross-examination. [T]he judge then determines whether the State has proved the statutory elements of permanent neglect by a fair preponderance of the evidence.

At such a proceeding, numerous factors combine to magnify the risk of erroneous factfinding. Permanent neglect proceedings employ imprecise substantive standards that leave determinations unusually open to the subjective values of the judge. [T]he court possesses unusual discretion to underweigh probative facts that might favor the parent. Because parents subject to termination proceedings are often poor, uneducated, or members of minority groups, such proceedings are often vulnerable to judgments based on cultural or class bias.

---

10. The Family Court judge in the present case expressly refused to terminate petitioners' parental rights on a "non-statutory, no-fault basis." Nor is it clear that the State constitutionally could terminate a parent's rights without showing parental unfitness. See Quilloin v. Walcott, 434 U.S. 246, 255 (1978) ("We have little doubt that the Due Process Clause would be offended '[i]f a State were to attempt to force the breakup of a natural family, over the objections of the parents and their children, without some showing of unfitness and for the sole reason that to do so was thought to be in the children's best interest,'" quoting Smith v. Organization of Foster Families, 431 U.S. 816, 862-863 (1977) (Stewart, J., concurring in judgment)).

The State's ability to assemble its case almost inevitably dwarfs the parents' ability to mount a defense. No predetermined limits restrict the sums an agency may spend in prosecuting a given termination proceeding. The State's attorney usually will be expert on the issues contested and the procedures employed at the factfinding hearing, and enjoys full access to all public records concerning the family. The State may call on experts in family relations, psychology, and medicine to bolster its case. Furthermore, the primary witnesses at the hearing will be the agency's own professional caseworkers whom the State has empowered both to investigate the family situation and to testify against the parents. Indeed, because the child is already in agency custody, the State even has the power to shape the historical events that form the basis for termination.[13]

The disparity between the adversaries' litigation resources is matched by a striking asymmetry in their litigation options. Unlike criminal defendants, natural parents have no "double jeopardy" defense against repeated state termination efforts. If the State initially fails to win termination, as New York did here, it always can try once again to cut off the parents' rights after gathering more or better evidence. Yet even when the parents have attained the level of fitness required by the State, they have no similar means by which they can forestall future termination efforts.

Coupled with a "fair preponderance of the evidence" standard, these factors create a significant prospect of erroneous termination. A standard of proof that by its very terms demands consideration of the quantity, rather than the quality, of the evidence may misdirect the factfinder in the marginal case. . . .

Raising the standard of proof would have both practical and symbolic consequences. . . . An elevated standard of proof in a parental rights termination proceeding would alleviate "the possible risk that a factfinder might decide to [deprive] an individual based solely on a few isolated instances of unusual conduct [or] . . . idiosyncratic behavior." Addington v. Texas, 441 U.S., at 427. "Increasing the burden of proof is one way to impress the factfinder with the importance of the decision and thereby perhaps to reduce the chances that inappropriate" terminations will be ordered. Ibid.

The Appellate Division approved New York's preponderance standard on the ground that it properly "balanced rights possessed by the child . . . with those of the natural parents. . . ." 427 N.Y.S.2d, at 320. By so saying, the court suggested that a preponderance standard properly allocates the risk of error *between* the parents and the child. That view is fundamentally mistaken.

The court's theory assumes that termination of the natural parents' rights invariably will benefit the child.[15] Yet we have noted above that the parents and the child share an interest in avoiding erroneous termination. Even

---

13. In this case, for example, the parents claim that the State sought court orders denying them the right to visit their children, which would have prevented them from maintaining the contact required by Fam. Ct. Act §614.1.(d). The parents further claim that the State cited their rejection of social services they found offensive or superfluous as proof of the agency's "diligent efforts" and their own "failure to plan" for the children's future. . . .

15. This is a hazardous assumption at best. Even when a child's natural home is imperfect, permanent removal from that home will not necessarily improve his welfare. See, e.g., Wald, State Intervention on Behalf of "Neglected" Children: A Search for Realistic Standards, 27 Stan. L. Rev.

accepting the court's assumption, we cannot agree with its conclusion that a preponderance standard fairly distributes the risk of error between parent and child. Use of that standard reflects the judgment that society is nearly neutral between erroneous termination of parental rights and erroneous failure to terminate those rights. For the child, the likely consequence of an erroneous failure to terminate is preservation of an uneasy status quo. For the natural parents, however, the consequence of an erroneous termination is the unnecessary destruction of their natural family. A standard that allocates the risk of error nearly equally between those two outcomes does not reflect properly their relative severity.

Two state interests are at stake in parental rights termination proceedings — a parens patriae interest in preserving and promoting the welfare of the child and a fiscal and administrative interest in reducing the cost and burden of such proceedings. A standard of proof more strict than preponderance of the evidence is consistent with both interests.

. . . As parens patriae, the State's goal is to provide the child with a permanent home. Yet while there is still reason to believe that positive, nurturing parent-child relationships exist, the parens patriae interest favors preservation, not severance, of natural familial bonds. . . . We cannot believe that it would burden the State unduly to require that its factfinders have the same factual certainty when terminating the parent-child relationship as they must have to suspend a driver's license. [Without deciding the outcome under a constitutionally proper standard], we vacate the judgment of the Appellate Division and remand the case for further proceedings not inconsistent with this opinion. . . .

Justice REHNQUIST, with whom the CHIEF JUSTICE, Justice WHITE, and Justice O'CONNOR join, dissenting.

. . . New York has created an exhaustive program to assist parents in regaining the custody of their children and to protect parents from the unfair deprivation of their parental rights. And yet the majority's myopic scrutiny of the standard of proof blinds it to the very considerations and procedures which make the New York scheme "fundamentally fair." . . .

The three children to which this case relates were removed from petitioners' custody [pursuant to New York's procedures] and in response to what can only be described as shockingly abusive treatment.[10]

---

985, 993 (1975) ("In fact, under current practice, coercive intervention frequently results in placing a child in a more detrimental situation than he would be in without intervention").

Nor does termination of parental rights necessarily ensure adoption. Even when a child eventually finds an adoptive family, he may spend years moving between state institutions and "temporary" foster placements after his ties to his natural parents have been severed.

10. Tina Apel, the oldest of petitioners' five children, was removed from their custody by court order in November 1973 when she was two years old. Removal proceedings were commenced in response to complaints by neighbors and reports from a local hospital that Tina had suffered injuries in petitioners' home including a fractured left femur, treated with a home-made splint; bruises on the upper arms, forehead, flank, and spine; and abrasions of the upper leg. The following summer, John Santosky III, petitioners' second oldest child, was also removed from petitioner's custody. John, who was less than one year old at the time, was admitted to the hospital suffering malnutrition, bruises on the eye and forehead, cuts on the foot, blisters on the hand, and multiple pin pricks on the back. Jed Santosky, the third oldest of petitioners' children, was removed from his parents' custody when only three days old as a result of the abusive treatment of the two older children.

[P]etitioners received training by a mother's aide, a nutritional aide, and a public health nurse, and counseling at a family planning clinic. In addition, the plan provided psychiatric treatment and vocational training for the father, and counseling at a family service center for the mother. Between early 1976 and the final termination decision in April 1979, the State spent more than $15,000 in these efforts to rehabilitate petitioners as parents.

Petitioners' response to the State's effort was marginal at best. They wholly disregarded some of the available services and participated only sporadically in the others. As a result, and out of growing concern over the length of the children's stay in foster care, the Department petitioned in September 1976 for permanent termination of petitioners' parental rights so that the children could be adopted by other families. Although the Family Court recognized that petitioners' reaction to the State's efforts was generally "non-responsive, even hostile," the fact that they were "at least superficially cooperative" led it to conclude that there was yet hope of further improvement and an eventual reuniting of the family. Accordingly, the petition for permanent termination was dismissed. [In October 1978, the agency again filed a termination proceeding because petitioners had made few efforts to take advantage of social services or to visit their children.]

[T]he State's extraordinary 4-year effort to reunite petitioners' family was not just unsuccessful, it was altogether rebuffed by parents unwilling to improve their circumstances sufficiently to permit a return of their children. At every step of this protracted process petitioners were accorded those procedures and protections which traditionally have been required by due process of law. . . . It is inconceivable to me that these procedures were "fundamentally unfair" to petitioners. . . . The interests at stake in this case demonstrate that New York has selected a constitutionally permissible standard of proof.

On one side is the interest of parents in a continuation of the family unit and the raising of their own children. The importance of this interest cannot easily be overstated. Few consequences of judicial action are so grave as the severance of natural family ties. . . . On the other side of the termination proceeding are the often countervailing interests of the child. A stable, loving homelife is essential to a child's physical, emotional, and spiritual well-being. . . .

In addition to the child's interest in a normal homelife, "the State has an urgent interest in the welfare of the child." Lassiter v. Department of Social Services, 452 U.S., at 27. Few could doubt that the most valuable resource of a self-governing society is its population of children who will one day become adults and themselves assume the responsibility of self-governance. . . .

When, in the context of a permanent neglect termination proceeding, the interests of the child and the State in a stable, nurturing homelife are balanced against the interests of the parents in the rearing of their child, it cannot be said that either set of interests is so clearly paramount as to require that the risk of error be allocated to one side or the other. Accordingly, a State constitutionally may conclude that the risk of error should be borne in roughly equal fashion by use of the preponderance-of-the-evidence standard of proof. . . .

## NOTES AND QUESTIONS

1. *Standard.* What do the various participants in TPR proceedings have at stake in the distribution of the risk of error? Why does the majority reject neutrality as the appropriate stance toward erroneous terminations of parental rights and erroneous failures to terminate those rights? What are the consequences of each type of erroneous decision? Does the clear-and-convincing standard, required in *Santosky*, adequately protect family autonomy? Adequately protect the interests of children? Ensure that children spend lengthy periods in foster care? See Sharon B. Hershkowitz, Due Process and the Termination of Parental Rights, 19 Fam. L.Q. 245, 292-295 (1985). States may require a higher standard still. See generally Linda Lee Reimer Stevenson, Comment, Fair Play or a Stacked Deck?: In Search of a Proper Standard of Proof in Juvenile Dependency Hearings, 26 Pepp. L. Rev. 613 (1999). Should they do so?

2. *Establishing parentage compared.* Should the same standard govern termination of parental rights and the establishment of parentage? How does the risk of error cut in this context? In Rivera v. Minnich, 483 U.S. 574 (1987), Jean Marie Minnich, an unmarried woman, sought child support for her three-week-old son, alleging that Gregory Rivera was the father. Rivera argued that due process required "clear and convincing" evidence, relying on *Santosky*. Rejecting the higher standard, the Court held that due process requires only the "preponderance of the evidence" standard of proof in paternity proceedings. The Court distinguished the state's imposition of parent-child obligations from the termination of those obligations because of the latter's severe consequences (that is, the elimination of preexisting rights). Justice Brennan, dissenting, argued that paternity proceedings result in "the imposition of a lifelong relationship with significant financial, legal, and moral dimensions." Id. at 583. Is neutrality with respect to erroneous decisions more appropriate for establishing paternity than for terminating parental rights? Is it more problematic for the "wrong" father to be recognized or for no father at all to meet the test?

3. *Scope.* How far does the *Santosky* standard extend? To restrictions on parental rights that fall short of complete termination? See In re R.W., 10 P.3d 1271 (Colo. 2000) (requiring only preponderance standard when parental rights were limited by guardianship). To a termination hearing following a parent's voluntary relinquishment of a child? See Coleman v. Smallwood, 800 S.W.2d 353, 356 (Tex. App. 1990) (requiring clear and convincing evidence).

4. *Stages of intervention.* TPR proceedings generally evolve over several stages of state intervention. Initially, state child welfare workers ask a family or juvenile court to assert jurisdiction over the child. (In an emergency, the state might use summary seizure to remove the child from home, followed by a jurisdictional proceeding.) For the state to be able to exercise its authority, the court must find that the child meets statutory criteria, which typically provide for jurisdiction over abused, neglected, and dependent children. Because of the constitutional status of family integrity as a fundamental right, some authorities require the application of strict scrutiny to such initial intervention. See, e.g., In re Juvenile Appeal (83-CD), 455 A.2d 1313 (Conn. 1983). Assuming satisfaction of this jurisdictional threshold, the court then selects a disposition.

Dispositional alternatives include, inter alia, educational sessions for parents, ongoing home visits, or placement of the child in foster care, with efforts to address the problem and reunify the family. The dissenting opinion in *Santosky* discusses several of these options.

As *Santosky* explains, if the problem requiring removal of the child from home persists, the state may seek TPR. Such proceedings, in turn, entail an initial stage at which the court makes a determination of unfitness (the "unfitness stage") and a subsequent stage at which the court determines whether TPR would serve the child's best interests (sometimes called "the best interests stage"). (*Santosky* refers somewhat differently to the stages of a child neglect proceeding, pursuant to New York statute, as "the fact-finding hearing" at which the state is required to prove permanent neglect and "the dispositional hearing" at which the court determines which placement serves the child's best interests.) These stages may occur in a single hearing.

Although *Santosky* requires the clear and convincing standard before TPR, many states reason that *Santosky* applies only to the determination of unfitness and therefore adopt different standards of proof for the best interests stage. Brian C. Hill, Comment, The State's Burden of Proof at the Best Interests Stage of a Termination of Parental Rights, 2004 U. Chi. Legal F. 557, 559. Is a heightened standard also appropriate at this subsequent stage? See, e.g., In re D.T., 818 N.E.2d 1214 (Ill. 2004) (adopting preponderance of the evidence standard for best interests stage). What light does *Santosky* shed on this question?

5. *Substantive implications.* Although *Santosky* resolves an issue of procedural due process, what implications does it have for constitutionally required substantive standards? Would a law that based TPR exclusively on a showing of the child's best interest survive constitutional review? Why? What inferences do you draw from the majority's footnote 10? In an omitted passage, the dissent responds:

> By holding that due process requires proof by clear and convincing evidence the majority surely cannot mean that any state scheme passes constitutional muster so long as it applies that standard of proof. A state law permitting termination of parental rights upon a showing of neglect by clear and convincing evidence certainly would not be acceptable to the majority if it provided no procedures other than one 30-minute hearing. Similarly, the majority probably would balk at a state scheme that permitted termination of parental rights on a clear and convincing showing merely that such action would be in the best interests of the child.

455 U.S. at 772-773 (Rehnquist, J., dissenting).

6. *ASFA.* In response to criticisms that children were too often languishing in foster care because of an overemphasis on parents' rights, Congress in 1997 enacted the Adoption and Safe Families Act (ASFA), Pub. L. No. 105-89, 111 Stat. 2115 (codified as amended in scattered sections of 42 U.S.C.). ASFA eliminates the requirement that the state undertake reasonable efforts to reunify the family in certain severe cases (i.e., torture, sexual abuse, parental murder of another child, or loss of parental rights to a sibling) (42 U.S.C. §671(a)(15)(D) (2008)). In addition, ASFA aims to facilitate adoption by reducing the amount

of time that children spend in foster care. ASFA shortens the period triggering permanency hearings to no later than 12 months after the child's entry into foster care and also requires states to seek termination of parental rights for children who have been in foster care for 15 of the last 22 months (Id. at §675(5)(E)). States need not file such petitions if (a) a relative cares for the child, (b) a state agency believes that termination would not be in the best interests of the child, or (c) a state agency has failed to provide the family with reunification services.

7. *Parent's right to counsel.* The Supreme Court examined the parent's right to counsel in TPR proceedings in Lassiter v. Department of Soc. Servs., 452 U.S. 18 (1981), discussed in *Santosky.* The Court rejected the argument that procedural due process requires the appointment of counsel for indigent parents. Applying a case-by-case balancing test, the Court weighed (a) the state's and parent's shared interest in the accuracy of the decision; (b) the cost of providing indigent parents with counsel; (c) the state's interest in informal procedures; (d) the complexity of the issues; (e) the incapacity of the indigent parent; and (f) the risk of error. The Court held that, although petitioner had not made a sufficient showing of these factors, in a case in which the parent's interests were especially high and the state's interests were particularly low, due process might require the appointment of counsel. Is *Santosky* consistent with *Lassiter*? Which procedural protection, a right to counsel or a heightened standard of proof, is more valuable to parents fighting terminations? Which offers better protection of children's interests? Which imposes greater costs on the state?

Despite the Supreme Court's holding in *Lassiter*, many states guarantee indigent parents the right to counsel in TPR proceedings. Trisha M. Anklam, The Price of Justice: In Light of *LaVallee*, What Should Massachusetts Courts Do When Attorneys Are Not Available to Represent Indigent Parents Involved in Care and Protection Matters?, 32 N. Eng. J. on Crim. & Civ. Confinement 111, 112 (2006).

8. *Alternatives to termination.* Even if the state decides that parents are unfit to rear their children, must TPR follow? What are the advantages of the traditional view of parenthood as an "all or nothing" status? The disadvantages? See Katharine T. Bartlett, Rethinking Parenthood as an Exclusive Status: The Need for Legal Alternatives When the Premise of the Nuclear Family Has Failed, 70 Va. L. Rev. 879 (1984). Long-term foster care or guardianship without TPR provides one alternative that would allow the retention of ties with biological families.

Professor Marsha Garrison takes a different approach, invoking as her point of departure the divorce context, in which "the child's relationship with a noncustodial parent is almost invariably described as a positive factor in her development that should be encouraged and facilitated [through visitation]." Marsha Garrison, Parents' Rights v. Children's Interests: The Case of the Foster Child, 22 N.Y.U. Rev. L. & Soc. Change 371, 373 (1996). By contrast, in the context of foster care, "the noncustodial parent is typically seen as a threat to the child's relationship with her foster parent or her opportunity to obtain adoptive parents[, and] termination of parental rights is urged whenever the child's return home cannot be accomplished quickly." Id. at

374. Garrison proposes preservation of visitation with biological parents after the foster child's adoption:

> Adoption's powerful symbolism not only obscures the very real benefits that this solution confers on the taxpayer, but it imposes direct costs on the children we intend to help. The positive future symbolized by an adoption order inexorably darkens the past and stigmatizes both the child's former parents and identity. Her acceptance of a new family implies abandonment of her biological family and the death of her old self. . . . Many older foster children cannot face such a loss, and even those who are willing to do so pay a heavy price. . . .
>
> Divorce law today potentially affects all children while child welfare law is reserved for those who are poor. . . . We have expected poor children, and only poor children, to gratefully sacrifice their past lives in order to obtain the benefits it suits us to provide. In the process, we have further stigmatized the lives of the children for whom foster placement will be inevitable, and subjected many of them to the further impermanence of "revolving door" care.
>
> But the emotional lives of poor children are not different from those of the more fortunate. Their parents are equally significant. Their need for evidence of parental love and for opportunities for reconciliation are just as great. For most, loving foster or adoptive parents will not, any more than stepparents, erase the ties that bind parent and child. . . .

Id. at 394-395. Do you find Garrison's proposal sound? Her reasoning persuasive?

## PROBLEMS

1. Bobby B. is placed in foster care at age two because of his single mother's repeated drug use and her chronic liver disease. She will need a transplant for long-term survival, and her substance abuse has placed her near the bottom of those awaiting organs. Bobby's mother wants him to return home so that she can spend her remaining time with him. To achieve this goal, she completes parenting classes and a drug rehabilitation program, as ordered by the Juvenile Court. She has not yet found employment, as directed by the court, but is participating in a job-training program to achieve that goal. All of these efforts require more time than usual because of frequent interruptions caused by her health difficulties.

The governing statute requires "reasonable efforts" to reunite biological families. You are Bobby's court-appointed guardian ad litem. You have learned that, although Bobby had regular supervised visits with his mother, he has bonded with his foster mother and father whom he regards as his psychological parents. The foster parents seek to adopt Bobby, and the state Department of Family Welfare supports this outcome because of Bobby's mother's poor prognosis. In deciding how to handle Bobby's case, you must address the following questions posed by the judge: Should a child in a loving foster home be put through a wrenching separation when the parent seeking return is likely to die or become seriously ill? Alternatively, is time with a parent so important to a child's identity that it should override other considerations? What result? See Felicia R. Lee, Difficult Custody Decisions Being Complicated by AIDS, N.Y. Times, Mar. 4, 1995, at 1, 16.

2. The Commissioner of Children and Families sought to terminate Anthony M.'s and Jessica C.'s parental rights to their three minor children. The commissioner alleges that the parents, who had neglected the children, could not benefit from the reunification efforts of the Department of Children and Families. The trial court appointed separate counsel for the respondent mother and father and their children, as required by state statute. During the three-day evidentiary hearing, the attorney representing the children supported the commissioner's position that TPR would serve the best interests of the children. At the end of the trial, the court acknowledged the mutual love between the parents and their children, but it found that the commissioner had proven the allegations and, accordingly, terminated the parents' rights.

In their appeal, the parents fault the trial court for having failed to appoint not only an attorney to represent the children's legal rights, but also a guardian ad litem to advocate for their best interests. In particular, they contend that children subject to a TPR petition have a constitutional right to effective assistance of counsel. They also argue that the trial court had an obligation, sua sponte, to ensure that there was no conflict between the children's legal interests and their best interests, given evidence in the record that the children's attorney was not advocating for the expressed wishes of the children. In response, the commissioner contends that the parents in TPR proceedings lack standing to assert the constitutional rights of their children. The commissioner also contends that children have no constitutional right to representation by counsel in TPR proceedings. Assuming an adequate record, how should the court decide the parents' appeal? Why? See In re Christina M., 908 A.2d 1073 (Conn. 2006). See also Annette Ruth Appell, Representing Children Representing What?: Critical Reflections on Lawyering for Children, 39 Colum. Hum. Rts. L. Rev. 573 (2008); Linda D. Elrod, Client-Directed Lawyers for Children: It Is the "Right" Thing to Do, 27 Pace L. Rev. 869 (2007); Jacob Ethan Smiles, A Child's Due Process Right to Legal Counsel in Abuse and Neglect Dependency Proceedings, 37 Fam. L.Q. 485 (2003).

# B. PARENTAL RELINQUISHMENT

## 1. VALIDITY AND REVOCABILITY

### Scarpetta v. Spence-Chapin Adoption Service

269 N.E.2d 787 (N.Y. 1971)

Jasen, J.

This appeal involves the return of an out-of-wedlock infant to its natural mother after she had executed a purported surrender of the child to an authorized adoption agency. . . .

The infant child was born on May 18, 1970, to Olga Scarpetta, who was unmarried and 32 years old. She had become pregnant in her native Colombia by a married Colombian in the summer of 1969. Seeking to minimize the shame of an out-of-wedlock child to herself and her family, Miss Scarpetta came to New York for the purpose of having her child. She was well acquainted with this country and its language. She had had her early schooling in New Jersey and her college education in California. Indeed, she had been trained in the social sciences.

Four days after the birth of the child, she placed the infant for boarding care with Spence-Chapin Adoption Service, an agency authorized by statute to receive children for adoption. Ten days later, a surrender document was executed by Miss Scarpetta to the agency, and on June 18, 1970, the baby was placed with a family for adoption. Five days later, on June 23, 1970, the mother repented her actions and requested that the child be returned to her.

After several unsuccessful attempts to regain her child from the agency, the mother commenced this habeas corpus proceeding. Before the surrender, the mother had had a number of interviews with representatives of the adoption agency. On the other hand, shortly before or after the birth of the child, her family in Colombia, well-to-do, and devout in their religion, were shocked that she should put out her child for adoption by strangers. They assured her of their support and backing and urged her to raise her own child. [The courts below ruled in favor of Scarpetta. This court affirms.]

The resolution of the issue of whether or not a mother, who has surrendered her child to an authorized adoption agency, may regain the child's custody, has received various treatment by the legislatures and courts in the United States. At one extreme, several jurisdictions adhere to the rule that the parent has an absolute right to regain custody of her child prior to the final adoption decree. On the other hand, some jurisdictions adhere to the rule that the parent's surrender is final, absent fraud or duress. The majority of the jurisdictions, however, place the parent's right to regain custody within the discretion of the court — the position which, of course, our Legislature has taken. The discretionary rule allows the court leeway to approve a revocation of the surrender when the facts of the individual case warrant it and avoids the obvious dangers posed by the rigidity of the extreme positions.

In New York, a surrender executed by a mother, in which she voluntarily consents to a change of guardianship and custody to an authorized agency for the purpose of adoption, is expressly sanctioned by law. (Social Services Law, §384.) The statute nowhere endows a surrender with irrevocability foreclosing a mother from applying to the court to restore custody of the child to her. In fact, the legislation is clear that, until there has been an actual adoption, or the agency has met the requirements of the Social Services Law [requiring agency or court approval of surrender following notice], the surrender remains under, and subject to, judicial supervision.

Inherent to judicial supervision of surrenders is the recognition that documents of surrender are unilateral, not contracts or deeds, and are almost always executed under circumstances which may cast doubt upon their voluntariness or on understanding of the consequences of their execution. . . . Of necessity, therefore, there is always an issue about the fact of surrender, document or no document. On the other hand, the courts have the strongest obligation not to permit surrenders to be undone except for the weightiest reasons. . . .

Having the power to direct a change of custody from the agency back to the natural parent, notwithstanding the document of surrender, the court should exercise it only when it determines "that the interest of such child will be promoted thereby and that such parent is fit, competent and able to duly maintain, support and educate such child." (Social Services Law, §383, subd. 1.) . . . It has repeatedly been determined, insofar as the best interests of the child are concerned, that "[the] mother or father has a right to the care and custody of a child, superior to that of all others, unless he or she has abandoned that right or is proved unfit to assume the duties and privileges of parenthood." [Citations omitted.]

The primacy of status thus accorded the natural parent is not materially altered or diminished by the mere fact of surrender under the statute, although it is a factor to be considered by the court. To hold, as the agency suggests — that a surrender to an authorized adoption agency constitutes, as a matter of law, an abandonment — would frustrate the policy underlying our legislation, which allows a mother to regain custody of her child, notwithstanding the surrender to the agency, provided, of course, that there is some showing of improvidence in the making of the surrender, that the interest of such child will be promoted and "that such parent is fit, competent and able to duly maintain, support and educate such child." . . .

In no case, however, may a contest between a parent and nonparent resolve itself into a simple factual issue as to which affords the better surroundings, or as to which party is better equipped to raise the child. It may well be that the prospective adoptive parents would afford a child some material advantages over and beyond what the natural mother may be able to furnish, but these advantages, passing and transient as they are, cannot outweigh a mother's tender care and love unless it is clearly established that she is unfit to assume the duties and privileges of parenthood.

We conclude that the record before us supports the finding by the courts below that the surrender was improvident and that the child's best interests — moral and temporal — will be best served by its return to the natural mother.

Within 23 days after the child had been given over to the agency, and only 5 days after the prospective adoptive parents had gained provisional custody of the child, the mother sought its return. If the matter had been resolved at that time, much heartache and distress would have been avoided. . . .

[The court rejects the prospective adoptive parents' petition to intervene on the ground that intervention would necessarily lead to disclosure of the names of the natural parents and prospective adoptive parents to each other in violation of the policy of secrecy, which relies on the adoption agency to serve as intermediary.] Similarly, we find no merit to the contention that the failure to allow the prospective adoptive parents to intervene in the instant proceeding deprived them of due process of law so as to render the court's determination awarding custody of the child to the mother, constitutionally invalid. The prospective adoptive parents do not have legal custody of the baby. Spence-Chapin, the adoption agency, by virtue of the mother's surrender, was vested with legal custody. The agency, in turn, had placed the baby with the prospective adoptive parents pursuant to an arrangement reached between them, for the purpose of prospective adoption of the child. This arrangement is, of course, subject to our adoption statutes, and in no way conveys any vested rights in the child to the prospective adoptive parents. . . .

---

Although American adoption statutes long have reflected a child-centered policy (see supra at Chapter 1, section A), historians have observed that, following World War II, adoption practice shifted its focus to the needs of infertile couples, who faced stigma in an era of "compulsory parenthood." See Elaine Tyler May, Barren in the Promised Land: Childless Americans and the Pursuit of Happiness 127-149 (1997). Nevertheless, adoption's traditional child-welfare rhetoric remained strong because white unmarried mothers were regarded as deviant and unfit to parent—so children needed to be "saved" from such dysfunctional families. Rickie Solinger, Beggars and Choosers: How the Politics of Choice Shapes Adoption, Abortion, and Welfare in the United States 69-70 (2001). Thus, such birth mothers faced enormous pressure to relinquish, both because of the perceived dangers that their deviance posed to their children and because of the valuable resources (babies) they could provide for married infertile couples. See id. Further, according to the conventional wisdom, adoption also "saved" these birth mothers, who could forget about their sexual transgressions and reconstitute their lives as if nothing had happened—all under a shroud of secrecy that would protect their own reputations and their families'. The narratives of birth mothers who experienced these policies now cast doubt on the premises and effectiveness of this approach, as the following excerpt shows:

### Ann Fessler, the Girls Who Went Away: The Hidden History of Women who Surrendered Children for Adoption in Days Before Roe v. Wade (2006)

207-210 (footnotes omitted)

I guess once I got married I felt more normal but still, it's kind of like being in a black hole somewhere. It's as if part of you went away when that happened. A really big part of you went away and you pretend that it didn't. You don't know who you are anymore. It's like suddenly you got cut in half. So what you really end up being is half a person who pretends she's whole. Even though I got married twice, I had two kids, and I have a very successful business, nothing takes away that black hole. Because you're always lying, you're always pretending. You're not true to who you really are.

*—Ann*

Surrendering a child for adoption has been described by many of the women I interviewed as the event that defined their identity and therefore influenced every major decision they made thereafter. Since most of these women surrendered when they were between the ages of sixteen and twenty-three, the event shaped their entire adult lives. It affected the timing of, or ability to pursue, their educational goals, their choice of a career, their decision about having subsequent children, their parenting style, and their relationships with parents, friends, and partners.

Women who said they never entertained the idea of parenting at the time of their surrender often described the same lifelong grief as those who fought to bring their baby home. Their grief has been exacerbated, and in some cases become chronic, because they were not permitted to talk about or properly grieve their loss. Not only was the surrender of their child not recognized as a loss; the implication was they should be grateful that others had taken care of their problem.

> It was never to be mentioned, it was never to be grieved, it was just to be denied. Then little by little, I started picking up with life, but I think I was filled with rage. I have to say, it was the most altering event of my whole life — a defining moment, a defining time. I believe that the way that I led my life, let's say the first ten years after, was reckless, was without regard for myself, my health, well-being, anything, because I had no value. And it was probably without regard for other people as well, because it was difficult for me to respect other people, it was difficult for me to trust.
>
> I'm sure people looked at my life and thought I had everything all together. I have a lot of aunts and uncles and I can remember being called nice little Kathi and thinking, "If you only knew." I felt like I was a demon. It wasn't until I went into therapy that I ever reached the point of feeling I deserved to be valued; it was all about deserving. People do not have a clue what people's lives are like from appearances. Appearances are just the greatest illusion. I think if somebody feels they're all alone, that's one of the worst feelings.
>
> *–Kathi*

Studies that have examined the grief of relinquishing mothers have identified a sense of loss that is unique and often prolonged. In one such study, the grief was likened to the separation loss experienced by a parent whose child is missing, or by a person who is told their loved one is missing in action. Unlike the grief over the death of a child, which is permanent and for which there is an established grieving process, the loss of a child through adoption has no clear end and no social affirmation that grief is even an appropriate response.

> Afterward I was very introverted. I could not have a close friend because I felt like such a fraud. How could I consider myself a close friend without them knowing about this? And, of course, I wasn't supposed to tell anyone. I was a good girl and was going to do what I was told. It just makes you feel like a lesser person, because you've done this horrible thing, this unspeakable thing. I just kind of withdrew. It's like the person that you are was put on hold and you're somebody else, you're flawed.
>
> *–Connie III*

Anger, guilt, and depression are normal grief responses to a major loss. And though grief may never go away, it generally subsides with time. For relinquishing mothers, however, the grief may actually intensify over time. One study has shown that high levels of unresolved grief in women were found to correlate with the "lack of opportunity to express feelings about the loss, the lack of finality of the loss (the child continues to exist), the perception of coercion, and the resulting guilt and shame over the surrender."

Before I went into that place I was always very happy, liked everybody, would talk to everybody, was a class officer in high school, a cheerleader. I was *that* kind of a person. I came out of there a different person. It changed me. It really changed my personality. I got very sad. I was very withdrawn.

I went back to school after that happened and everybody would say to me, "What's your problem? What's the matter with you? Did someone die in your family?" Well, having a child, giving it up for adoption is like having a death in the family. The only difference is you can't publicly be sad; you gotta be sad by yourself. I think it hardened me. I was really nasty to people. I was mad at the world. I was mad at my parents, I was mad at everybody, even if they had nothing to do with it.

*–Cathy II*

The National Mental Health Association has issued a list of the best ways to cope with a major loss, like the death of a loved one. The list suggests that the grieving person should "seek out people who understand your feelings of loss; tell others how you feel; take care of your physical health and be aware of the danger of developing a dependence on medication or alcohol; make an effort to live in the present and not dwell on the past; try to take time to adjust to your loss by waiting to make major changes such as moving, remarrying, changing jobs or having another child; seek outside help when grief seems like it is too much to bear; and be patient because it can take months or years to absorb a major loss." Without proper guidance or counseling, most of the women I interviewed took action that was precisely the opposite of these recommendations, some of it on the advice of professionals.

I got married. I thought, "I better get myself off the streets. This is not going well." I was just living this lie, this lie, this lie. "Do you have children?" "No." It's like being Judas every time. You're denouncing who you are, who they are. You just feel terrible. I married this man under false pretenses. Did he ever know I had children? Absolutely not. I didn't tell him.

I had a wedding, the wedding that my sister wanted. Everything was a lie. I didn't want a wedding, but he was Italian and Catholic, and you had to have a wedding. Oh, God. Then he says, "We can have children." I looked at him, like, "Are you insane?" The last thing I ever wanted to be was pregnant. I said, "I'm too young to get pregnant." That's what I told him. I was twenty, twenty-one at the time. He was an airline pilot, I was a stewardess. I said, "Well, maybe in five years, I don't know." But the whole idea was so repellent to me. It was all mixed up with this grief and this guilt. No, I just couldn't.

So I'm married and everything is so perfect. We go on a Hawaiian honeymoon — everything is just so, so, nice. We lived on forty acres of land, we built this beautiful house, we had so much money. Every weekend we were going over to my parents' house and having steak dinners and barbecues. I remember one of these Sundays as we pulled into my parents' suburban neighborhood I just started hitting my head against the seat of the car. I was just going a little crazy. It was all the things I couldn't say. It was July. The birth month. So July was always horrible, horrible, horrible. Even if my mind didn't remember, my body remembered. This really lives in your body.

*–Diane IV*

## NOTES AND QUESTIONS

1. *Epilogue.* After the court's decision in *Scarpetta*, the adoptive family (the DiMartinos) fled with "Baby Lenore" to Florida. Scarpetta filed a habeas corpus action there, claiming full faith and credit for the New York decision. The DiMartinos successfully argued that they should not be bound by litigation in which they were not permitted to participate. At the ensuing trial, the court focused on the child's best interests. Experts testified about her development with the DiMartinos and the trauma separation would cause. The Florida court ruled the DiMartinos should retain custody. Henry H. Foster, Jr., Adoption and Child Custody: Best Interests of the Child?, 22 Buff. L. Rev. 1, 8 (1972). The U.S. Supreme Court denied certiorari, DiMartino v. Scarpetta, 404 U.S. 805 (1971). For exploration of the problems that can arise when adoption cases involve more than one jurisdiction, see Chapter 5.

In response to the case, New York amended the statute. It now provides that in contested revocation cases parents who consented "have no right to the custody of the child superior to that of the adoptive parents" and custody "shall be awarded solely on the basis of the best interests of the child," with no presumption favoring any particular disposition. N.Y. Dom. Rel. Law §115-b(6)(d)(v) (2008). Evaluate this approach.

2. *Agency placement.* The adoption process often begins, as *Scarpetta* illustrates, when the birth parent voluntarily relinquishes (or "surrenders") the child to a state-licensed or state-operated agency. The agency takes legal custody and selects an adoptive family. After a residential period under the agency's supervision, a court issues an adoption decree. Traditionally, neither the birth parents nor the adopters learn the others' identities. Moreover, if the placement fails during the trial period, the child returns to the agency's care, not to the birth parent whose rights are terminated by the relinquishment. Advocates claim that only agency adoptions serve the birth parents' needs for counseling and support, the child's needs for placement with capable and prepared adopters, and the adopters' needs for a full range of services. See L. Jean Emery, Agency Versus Independent Adoption: The Case for Agency Adoption, The Future of Children, Spring 1993, at 139, 140-142; Susan A. Munson, Comment, Independent Adoption: In Whose Best Interest?, 26 Seton Hall L. Rev. 803, 804-809 (1996). Today, most agency placements involve older children who spent time in foster care. Ruth-Arlene W. Howe, Adoption Laws and Practices in 2000: Serving Whose Interests?, 33 Fam. L.Q. 677, 681-683 (1999).

3. *The relinquishment experience.* According to *Scarpetta*, why did the birth mother relinquish her child? Why did she change her mind? What does the excerpt from Ann Fessler's book add to your understanding of Scarpetta's experience? To your evaluation of the *Scarpetta* case? Consider the thesis of historian Rickie Solinger, developed from communications with birth mothers:

> Based on what I've learned about the experiences of birthmothers in the United States, I want to suggest that the conventional understanding of adoption should be turned on its head. Almost everybody believes that on some level, birthmothers *make a choice to give their babies away.* . . . I argue that adoption is

rarely about mothers' choices; it is, instead, about the abject choicelessness of some resourceless women.

Solinger, supra, at 67. How have these social constraints evolved over time?

In balancing the competing interests in a case like *Scarpetta*, what weight should be accorded to the emotional experiences of birth parents in relinquishment? See Holli Ann Askren & Kathaleen C. Bloom, Postadoptive Reactions of the Relinquishing Mother: A Review, JOGNN, July/Aug. 1999, at 395 ("at risk for long-term physical, psychologic, and social repercussions"). Validating the narratives collected by Fessler, advocates of reform have questioned the traditional postrelinquishment goal of encouraging the birth mother to "reconstitute her life quickly by bolstering the defenses of denial and repression at the cost of other emotional needs." Eva Y. Deykin et al., The Postadoption Experience of Surrendering Parents, 54 Am. J. Orthopsychiatry 271, 272 (1984).

4. *Revocation of consent. Scarpetta* surveys different approaches to revocation. Which is most sound? What can states do to improve the consent process and minimize attempted revocations? See Elizabeth J. Samuels, Time to Decide? The Laws Governing Mothers' Consents to the Adoption of Their Newborn Infants, 72 Tenn. L. Rev. 509 (2005); Karen D. Laverdiere, Note and Comment, Content Over Form: The Shifting of Adoption Consent Laws, 25 Whittier L. Rev. 599 (2004). Jurisdictions recognize several bases for revoking consent to adoption:

a. *Time period.* One approach makes determinative the timing of consent or revocation. To be valid, consent must take place after birth. In re N.J.G., 891 N.E.2d 60 (Ind. Ct. App. 2008). Under the Uniform Adoption Act (UAA), a parent can revoke relinquishment of consent within 192 hours (8 days) of the child's birth. Unif. Adoption Act §§2-408, 2-409, 9 U.L.A. (pt. IA) 60-63 (1999). See also, e.g., In re Adoption of Baby Girls Mandell, 572 N.E.2d 359 (Ill. App. Ct. 1991) (12-month limit). An alternative approach makes voidable consents executed less than a certain number of days after birth. See In re Baby Girl T., 21 P.3d 581 (Kan. Ct. App. 2001) (upholding statute's 12-hour period). Finally, some jurisdictions allow withdrawal of consent anytime before the final decree of termination of parental rights or adoption. E.g., 25 U.S.C. §1913(c) (2008) (Indian Child Welfare Act). How much time for revocation ought to be allowed?

b. *Fraud or duress.* Many states invalidate consent procured by fraud or coercion. E.g., Ariz. Rev. Stat. §8-106(D) (2008); Va. Code Ann. §63.2-1234(2) (2008); Gruett v. Nesbit, 17 P.3d 1090, *reconsideration denied*, 21 P.3d 168 (Or. Ct. App. 2001) (setting aside adoption because of agency's misrepresentation of birth father's lack of interest); Gunderman v. Helms, 68 P.3d 1021 (Utah Ct. App. 2003) (remanding to determine birth mother's claim of duress). The South Carolina supreme court permitted the revocation of a 39-year-old mother's consent because of "emotional stressors" she was experiencing at the time. McCann v. Doe, 660 S.E.2d 500 (S.C. 2008). How do "emotional stressors" differ from "duress"? Might all consents be vulnerable on this ground?

5. *Law reform.* Given the problems revealed in the examination of attempted revocations, should the law tighten adoption consent

requirements? Precisely how? See Samuels, supra. What do you think of a new law in South Dakota permitting birth parents to consent to adoption by telephone? S.D. Codified Laws §25-5A-14 (2008). Does your answer change if this procedure is available only to incarcerated birth parents?

6. *Consent substitutes.* Can a state constitutionally grant an adoption *without* valid parental consent? Involuntary termination of parental rights comporting with all procedural and substantive requirements dispenses with the need for parental consent. See Santosky v. Kramer, supra. Can a state replace consent or the usual grounds for termination of parental rights with a showing that adoption serves the child's best interests? See, e.g., Mass. Gen. Laws Ann. ch. 210, §3(a)(ii) & (c) (2008) (so permitting); In re D.H., 917 A.2d 112 (D.C. 2007); Gray v. Bourne, 614 S.E.2d 661 (Va. Ct. App. 2005). But see In re Adoption of D.D.H., 184 P.3d 967 (Kan. Ct. App. 2008) (rejecting best interests as basis for termination). What considerations should a best interests analysis include? See, e.g., In re Davonta V., 940 A.2d 733 (Conn. 2008) (holding that termination will serve child's interests in permanence and stability, although an adoptive family has not yet been found); M.B. v. D.W., 236 S.W.3d 31 (Ky. Ct. App. 2007) (relying on daughter's reaction to father's sex reassignment surgery); In re Adoption/Guardianship of Harold H., 911 A.2d 464 (Md. Ct. Spec. App. 2006) (holding sufficient mother's stroke-induced neurological deficits); In re D.A., 862 N.E.2d 829 (Ohio 2007) (holding insufficient parents' limited cognitive abilities). Will a statutory time period in foster care meet the constitutional test? Compare In re H.G., 757 N.E.2d 864 (Ill. 2001), with Doe v. Roe, 578 S.E.2d 733 (S.C. Ct. App. 2003).

If the state can dispense with parental consent, can it do so in a way that treats birth fathers and mothers differently? The next section explores this question.

## 2. UNMARRIED BIRTH FATHERS' RIGHTS IN NEWBORN ADOPTIONS

The Supreme Court has recognized constitutional protections for the interests of some unmarried fathers who have developed a relationship with their children. Compare Stanley v. Illinois with Michael H. v. Gerald D., Chapter 1, section B1. What does this doctrine mean for the interests of an unmarried father when a newborn's mother decides to relinquish the child for adoption?

ADOPTION OF KELSEY S.

823 P.2d 1216 (Cal. 1992)

BAXTER, J.

The primary question in this case is whether the father of a child born out of wedlock may properly be denied the right to withhold his consent to his child's adoption by third parties despite his diligent and legal attempts to obtain custody of his child and to rear it himself, and absent any showing of the father's unfitness as a parent. . . .

Kari S. gave birth to Kelsey, a boy, on May 18, 1988. The child's undisputed natural father is petitioner Rickie M. He and Kari S. were not married to one another. At that time, he was married to another woman but was separated from her and apparently was in divorce proceedings. He was aware that Kari planned to place their child for adoption, and he objected to her decision because he wanted to rear the child.

Two days after the child's birth, petitioner filed an action in superior court under Civil Code section 7006 to establish his parental relationship with the child and to obtain custody of the child. [The court awarded petitioner temporary custody, stayed all adoption proceedings, and prohibited contact with the prospective adopters.] On May 24, 1988, Steven and Suzanne A., the prospective adoptive parents, filed an adoption petition under Civil Code section 226[, alleging] that only the mother's consent to the adoption was required because there was no presumed father under section 7004, subdivision (a). [The court modified its order and awarded the birth mother temporary custody.] The court ordered the mother to live with the child in a shelter for unwed mothers. [T]he trial court prohibited visitation by either the prospective adoptive parents or petitioner. [The prospective adopters then petitioned under §7017 to terminate petitioner's parental rights.] The superior court consolidated that proceeding with the adoption proceeding. The court allowed petitioner to have supervised visitation with the child at the women's shelter where the child was living with his mother. The court also allowed the prospective adoptive parents to have unsupervised visitation at the shelter.

[Despite a stipulation of petitioner's biological paternity, the court below held that he was not a "presumed father" under the controlling statute. After four days of hearings, including arguments by the child's attorney that petitioner should retain parental rights, the court held that the child's best interests required termination of his parental rights, by a bare preponderance of the evidence.] Petitioner appealed. He contended the superior court erred by: (1) concluding that he was not the child's presumed father; (2) not granting him a parental placement preference; and (3) applying a preponderance-of-the-evidence standard of proof. The Court of Appeal rejected each of his contentions. . . .

Section 7004 states, "A man is presumed to be the natural father of a child . . ." if the man meets any of several conditions set forth in the statute. Whether a biological father is a "presumed father" under section 7004 is critical to his parental rights. If the mother of a child . . . consents to the child's adoption, [t]he child's best interest is the sole criterion where there is no presumed father. As in the present case, the trial court's determination is frequently that the child's interests are better served by a third party adoption than by granting custody to the unwed natural father. [The relevant statutes are now Cal. Fam. Code §§7611, 7611.5, & 7612 (2008).]

Mothers and presumed fathers have far greater rights. [A] mother or a presumed father must consent to an adoption absent a showing by clear and convincing evidence of that parent's unfitness. . . .

A man becomes a "presumed father" under section 7004, subdivision (a)(4) if *"[h]e receives the child into his home* and openly holds out the child as his natural child." (Italics added.) It is undisputed in this case that petitioner openly held out the child as being his own. Petitioner, however, did not physically receive the child into his home. He was prevented from doing so by the mother, by court order, and allegedly also by the prospective adoptive parents. . . .

There remains . . . the question of whether a natural father's federal constitutional rights are violated if his child's mother is allowed to unilaterally preclude him from obtaining the same legal right as a presumed father to withhold his consent to his child's adoption by third parties. [This question] has not been addressed by the United States Supreme Court. We are guided, however, by a series of high court decisions dealing with the rights of unwed fathers. [The court then analyzed three Supreme Court precedents: Stanley v. Illinois, 405 U.S. 645 (1972); Quilloin v. Walcott, 434 U.S. 246 (1978); and Caban v. Mohammed, 441 U.S. 380 (1979). These cases are noted Chapter 1, section B1a.]

The high court again considered the rights of biological fathers only four years later in Lehr v. Robertson (1983) 463 U.S. 248. The father and mother lived together before the child's birth, and he visited the child in the hospital when the child was born. He did not, however, live with either the mother or child after its birth, and he did not provide them with any financial support. Nor did he offer to marry the mother. Eight months after the child's birth, the mother married another man. When the child was two years old, the mother and her new husband began adoption proceedings. One month later, the biological father filed an action seeking a determination of his paternity, an order of support, and visitation with the child. Shortly thereafter, the biological father learned of the pending adoption proceeding, and almost immediately he sought to have it stayed pending the determination of his paternity petition. The state court informed him that it had already signed the adoption order earlier that day, and then dismissed his paternity action. . . . The *Lehr* court, held that, "because appellant, like the father in *Quilloin*, has never established a substantial relationship with his daughter . . . the New York statutes at issue in this case did not operate to deny appellant equal protection [in treating him differently from other fathers]."

[*Lehr*] did not purport to decide the legal question in the present case, that is, whether the mother may constitutionally prevent the father from establishing the relationship that gives rise to his right to equal protection. The *Lehr* court, however, recognized the uniqueness of the biological connection between parent and child. "The significance of the biological connection is that it offers the natural father an opportunity that no other male possesses to develop a relationship with his offspring. If he grasps that opportunity and accepts some measure of responsibility for the child's future, he may enjoy the blessings of the parent-child relationship and make uniquely valuable contributions to the child's development." (Id., at p.262.) *Lehr* can fairly be read to mean that a father need only make a reasonable and meaningful attempt to establish a relationship, not that he must be successful against all obstacles.

[The court then considered Michael H. v. Gerald D., 491 U.S. 110 (1989), reprinted Chapter 1, section B1a.]

[O]ne unifying and transcendent theme emerges. The biological connection between father and child is unique and worthy of constitutional protection if the father grasps the opportunity to develop that biological connection into a full and enduring relationship. . . .

Petitioner asserts a violation of equal protection and due process under the federal Constitution; more specifically, that he should not be treated differently from his child's mother. . . . Respondents do not adequately explain how an unwed mother's control over a biological father's rights [substantially furthers the state's important] interest in the well-being of the child. The linchpin of their position, however, is clear although largely implicit: Allowing the biological father to have the same rights as the mother would make adoptions more difficult because the consent of both parents is more difficult to obtain than the consent of the mother alone. This reasoning is flawed in several respects.

A. Respondents' view too narrowly assumes that the proper governmental objective is adoption. [T]he constitutionally valid objective is the protection of the child's well-being. . . . If the possible benefit of adoption were by itself sufficient to justify terminating a parent's rights, the state could terminate an unwed mother's parental rights based on nothing more than a showing that her child's best interest would be served by adoption. . . .

B. Nor is there evidence before us that the statutory provisions allowing the mother to determine the father's rights are, in general, substantially related to protecting the child's best interest. [Respondent] assumes an unwed mother's decision to permit an immediate adoption of her newborn is always preferable to custody by the natural father, even when he is a demonstrably fit parent. . . .

C. The lack of any substantial relationship between the state's interest in protecting a child and allowing the mother sole control over its destiny is best demonstrated by the results that can arise when a mother prevents the father from obtaining presumed status under section 7004, subdivision (a). . . . Under the statute, the father has basically two ways in which to achieve that status: he can either marry the mother, or he can receive the child into his home and hold it out as his natural child. Of course, the first alternative is entirely within the mother's control. . . . The system also leads to irrational distinctions between fathers. Based solely on the mother's wishes, a model father can be denied presumed father status, whereas a father of dubious ability and intent can achieve such status by the fortuitous circumstance of the mother allowing him to come into her home, even if only briefly — perhaps a single day. . . .

D. We must not lose sight of the way in which the present case and others like it come before the courts. A mother's decision to place her newborn child for adoption may be excruciating and altogether altruistic. Doing so may reflect the extreme of selflessness and maternal love. As a legal matter, however, the mother seeks to sever all ties with her child. [Yet even if] the mother somehow has a greater connection than the father with their child and thus should have greater rights in the child, the same result need not obtain when she seeks to relinquish custody and to sever her legal ties with the child and the father seeks to assume his legal burdens. . . .

E. In summary, we hold that section 7004, subdivision (a) and the related statutory scheme [are unconstitutional]. If an unwed father promptly comes forward and demonstrates a full commitment to his parental responsibilities — emotional, financial, and otherwise — his federal constitutional right to due process prohibits the termination of his parental relationship absent a showing of his unfitness as a parent. Absent such a showing, the child's well-being is presumptively best served by continuation of the father's parental relationship. Similarly, when the father has come forward to grasp his parental responsibilities, his parental rights are entitled to equal protection as those of the mother.

A court should consider all factors relevant to that determination. The father's conduct both before and after the child's birth must be considered. Once he knows or reasonably should know of the pregnancy, he must promptly attempt to assume his parental responsibilities as fully as the mother will allow and his circumstances permit. In particular, the father must demonstrate "a willingness himself to assume full custody of the child — not merely to block adoption by others." [In Matter of Raquel Marie, 559 N.E.2d 418, 428 (N.Y. 1990).] A court should also consider the father's public acknowledgement of paternity, payment of pregnancy and birth expenses commensurate with his ability to do so, and prompt legal action to seek custody of the child. . . .

[I]f (but only if) the trial court finds petitioner demonstrated the necessary commitment to his parental responsibilities, there will arise the further question of whether he can be deprived of the right to withhold his consent to the adoption. . . . For purposes of remand, . . . any finding of petitioner's unfitness must be supported by clear and convincing evidence. Absent such evidence, he shall be permitted to withhold his consent to the adoption.

[If] the trial court concludes that petitioner has a right to withhold consent, that decision will bear only on the question of whether the adoption will proceed. Even if petitioner has a right to withhold his consent (and chooses to prevent the adoption), there will remain the question of the child's custody. That question is not before us, and we express no view on it. . . .

## NOTES AND QUESTIONS

1. *Independent placement.* The independent adoption in *Kelsey S.* contrasts with the agency placement in *Scarpetta*. Generally, in independent adoptions the birth parents select the adopters themselves, often with the assistance of an intermediary such as an attorney, and place the child directly with the adopters, pending the issuance of a final adoption decree. The UAA has several distinct provisions for "direct" and agency placements (for example, §§2-102, 2-103, Unif. Adoption Act, 9 U.L.A. (pt. IA) 30-33 (1999)). A few states prohibit or strictly limit independent placements. See Elizabeth J. Samuels, Time to Decide? The Laws Governing Mothers' Consents to the Adoption of Their Newborn Infants, 72 Tenn. L. Rev. 509, 519 n.68 (2005).

Critics claim independent adoptions primarily help adults seeking a child to adopt, at the expense of child welfare. L. Jean Emery, Agency Versus

Independent Adoption: The Case for Agency Adoption, The Future of Children, Spring 1993, at 139, 143. Supporters assert: (a) birth parents prefer independent adoption because it allows them to select the adopters; (b) adopters avoid long waiting lists and play an active role in the process; and (c) children avoid the necessity of spending a transitional period in foster care. Mark T. McDermott, Agency Versus Independent Adoption: The Case for Independent Adoption, The Future of Children, Spring 1993, at 146, 147. Because adoptive parents often pay birth parents' expenses in independent placements, some call these "gray market" adoptions. See generally Madelyn Freundlich, The Market Forces in Adoption (2000).

2. *Thwarted fathers.* *Kelsey S.* considers the rights of a "thwarted father" to veto an infant's adoption planned by the birth mother. In deciding in favor of the father, the *Kelsey S.* court considers a series of Supreme Court precedents: Stanley v. Illinois, 405 U.S. 645 (1972); Quilloin v. Walcott, 434 U.S. 246 (1978); Caban v. Mohammed, 441 U.S. 380 (1979); Lehr v. Robertson, 463 U.S. 248 (1983); and Michael H. v. Gerald D., 491 U.S. 110 (1989) (all examined or noted Chapter 1, section B1.). Compare in particular the *Kelsey S.* court's portrayal of the facts in *Lehr* with the version presented by Justice White's dissent in *Lehr*. See Lehr v. Robertson, 463 U.S. 248, 268-269 (1983) (White, J., dissenting). Justice White describes how Lehr and the mother had cohabited, how he had visited her and the infant in the hospital upon birth, and how later he "never ceased his efforts to locate" them (even hiring a detective), despite the mother's efforts to conceal their whereabouts. Lehr also offered financial support. What implications follow? If Justice White's recitation of the facts in *Lehr* is accurate, then the Supreme Court had already rejected the equal protection claims of a father who tried to maintain a relationship with his child but was thwarted by the mother's unilateral actions. Do the two cases warrant different approaches because *Lehr*, unlike *Kelsey S.*, concerned a stepparent adoption in which the birth mother would continue to rear the child?

Are there constitutionally acceptable reasons for giving biological mothers greater authority than fathers to determine placement of a nonmarital child? See generally Mary L. Shanley, Unwed Fathers' Rights, Adoption, and Sex Equality: Gender-Neutrality and the Preservation of Patriarchy, 95 Colum. L. Rev. 60 (1995).

3. *Competing interpretations.* Professor David Meyer identifies two different ways to interpret the Supreme Court precedents. Under the "child centered" view, only an actual parent-child relationship matters, not the efforts of a father whom the mother successfully thwarts. David D. Meyer, Family Ties: Solving the Constitutional Dilemma of the Faultless Father, 41 Ariz. L. Rev. 753, 764 (1999). Under a second reading, "the Supreme Court is concerned not simply with the existence or non-existence of a meaningful father-child relationship, but ultimately also with the strength of the father's moral claim [, that is,] whether the claimant has acted in a way deserving of protection." Id. Which view do you discern in the Supreme Court cases, including the opinions in *Michael H.*, in Chapter 1, section B1a? In *Kelsey S.*?

Under the second reading, how does a father show he is deserving? Should sending one holiday card prevent a finding of abandonment? See In re Peshek, 759 N.E.2d 411 (Ohio Ct. App. 2001). Does an *offer* to provide support for the mother suffice? See In re Adoption of Anderson, 624 S.E.2d 626 (N.C. 2006). See also Escobedo v. Nickita, 231 S.W.3d 601 (Ark. 2006). Does marriage to the mother alone suffice? Cf. Powell v. Lane, 2008 WL 5191061 (Ark. 2008). Can the father's prebirth conduct toward the mother be determinative? Compare In re Adoption of Baby E.A.W., 658 So. 2d 961 (Fla. 1995) (father's prebirth "abandonment" of mother suffices to free child for adoption), with Ex parte F.P., 857 So. 2d 125 (Ala. 2003) (limiting application of prebirth abandonment statute). If there are several possible fathers, must they all take affirmative steps before birth to preserve their rights? See In re Adoption of D.M.M., 955 P.2d 618 (Kan. Ct. App. 1997) (yes). Does the father's criminal conduct prevent a finding that he is deserving, for purposes of halting an adoption? Compare In re C.D.M., 39 P.3d 802 (Okla. 2001) (stalker-father could not invoke protective order, which prohibited contact with child, as excuse for abandonment), and In re Adoption of J.K.W., 2007 WL 161048 (Tenn. Ct. App. 2007) (rejecting constitutional challenge to statute authorizing termination of parental rights after incarceration for ten years, when the child is under eight years of age), with In re Adoption of TLC, 46 P.3d 863 (Wyo. 2002) (rejecting reliance on father's incarceration to show willful failure to support). If the child is conceived as the result of a sexual assault, is the biological father's consent required? An omitted footnote in *Kelsey S.* states that the constitutional protections do not apply in such circumstances. 823 P.2d at 1237 n.14. Cf. In re Kyle F., 5 Cal. Rptr. 3d 190 (Ct. App. 2003) (distinguishing statutory rape from forcible rape to allow father to demonstrate right to withhold consent to adoption). But see LeClair v. Reed, 939 A.2d 466 (Vt. 2007) (holding that conception by sexual assault does not deprive man of standing to establish parentage).

A review of the recent case law, including state court interpretations of the Supreme Court's opinions about unmarried fathers and their parental rights, appears in Laura Oren, Thwarted Fathers or Pop-Up Pops: How to Determine When Putative Fathers Can Block the Adoption of Their Newborn Children, 40 Fam. L.Q. 153 (2006). See also Jennifer Hendricks, Essentially a Mother, 13 Wm. & Mary J. Women & L. 429 (2007) (contending that the Supreme Court modeled the test for unmarried fathers on essential attributes of motherhood).

4. *Maternal deception.* Suppose the mother purposely misidentifies the father when relinquishing the child. Later, she marries the biological father and joins with him to halt adoption proceedings. Should the pair regain custody? See In the Interest of B.G.C., 496 N.W.2d 239 (Iowa 1992) ("Baby Jessica" case, reprinted Chapter 5, section A). Will recognition of the biological father's rights raise the "specter of newly named genetic fathers, upsetting adoptions, perhaps years later"? Id. at 247 (Snell, J., dissenting). Should (could) a state require a woman to identify the father correctly or to notify him of her pregnancy as a precondition to adoption? Cf. In re Termination of Parental Rights of Biological Parents of Baby Boy W., 988 N.W.2d 1270 (Okla. 1999).

Consider the highly publicized "Baby Richard" case, in which the mother falsely told the father the newborn had died. Later they married and sought the child's return. The court held the father had shown sufficient interest in the child to preclude termination of his rights based solely on the child's best interests. It invalidated the adoption, removing the child from his family of four years. In re Petition of John Doe, 638 N.E.2d 181 (Ill.), *cert. denied*, 513 U.S. 994 (1994). The birth father then successfully sought a writ of habeas corpus, requiring the child's transfer to his custody. In re Petition of Kirchner, 649 N.E.2d 324 (Ill.), *stay denied sub nom.* O'Connell v. Kirchner, 513 U.S. 1138 (1995). Later the birth parents separated, leaving the child in the birth mother's custody. Dirk Johnson, Father Who Won Custody Case Over Adopted Boy Moves Out, N.Y. Times, Jan. 22, 1997, at A10.

What time limits should govern the right to challenge an adoption for defective parental consent? When a birth father claims that the birth mother practiced deception but the state imposes time limits on challenging adoptions, should the limitations period begin to run only once he has discovered the fraud? See McCallum v. Salazar, 636 S.E.2d 486 (Va. Ct. App. 2006). See also In re Marquette S., 734 N.W.2d 81 (Wis. 2007) (holding that court must consider unmarried father's efforts after he discovers child's existence and before termination of his rights).

5. *The child's rights.* How should a court balance the rights of biological parents against the child's asserted liberty interest in remaining with a "psychological family"? In Baby Richard's case and similar controversies, courts have declined to allow a child's best interests to trump a thwarted father's rights. See *John Doe*, 638 N.E.2d 181; *B.G.C.*, 496 N.W.2d 239. Do you agree with this approach? For another account of a child returned to his birth mother after his birth father challenged his adoption, see Caught in Tangle of Adoption Laws, Children Suffer, USA Today, Jan. 24, 2005, at 10A (Evan Scott case).

If a court makes the child's best interests determinative, should it focus on short-term or long-term interests? What weight should a court accord to potential trauma from separation from the psychological family? According to psychological theory, disrupted early attachment jeopardizes the formation of later intimate relationships. See Marcus T. Boccaccini & Eleanor Willemsen, Contested Adoption and the Liberty Interest of the Child, 10 St. Thomas L. Rev. 211, 291 (1998). Media reports, however, claim that Baby Jessica and Baby Richard have fared well despite their traumatic removal from long-term adoptive placements and the subsequent dissolutions of their birth parents' relationships. See Leonard Greene, Heartbreak Kids Enjoy Normal Childhoods, N.Y. Post, Mar. 9, 2001, at 19; Gregory A. Kelson, In the Best Interest of the Child: What Have We Learned from Baby Jessica and Baby Richard?, 33 J. Marshall L. Rev. 353, 362, 370-371 (2000).

6. *Statutory reforms.*

a. *Expanded definitions.* In the wake of high-profile challenges to adoptive placements by the thwarted fathers of Baby Jessica and Baby Richard, several states expanded the grounds for terminating parental rights, broadening definitions of "abandonment" and "unfitness." Most of these laws, however, have not been interpreted to allow "no-fault" terminations. See Meyer, supra, at 770-792.

b. *Registries.* Several states use "putative father registries," which eliminate the need for adoption notification or consent for a man who failed to take the initiative by registering. See id. at 756-757. The Supreme Court approved reliance on a registry system in *Lehr*, supra. The Uniform Parentage Act (UPA), revised in 2000 and amended in 2002, follows this approach to facilitate and expedite infant adoptions, where "time is of the essence," while requiring notification to fathers of older children and exempting fathers of infants who initiate timely proceedings to establish paternity. 9B U.L.A. 27 (Supp. 2008) (cmt. on Art. 4). See also Unif. Parentage Act §402 (2000), 9B U.L.A 322 (2001) (requiring registration no later than 30 days after birth or commencement of paternity proceedings before termination of his parental rights). What information must the risk-averse man provide if he registers before he knows of a pregnancy? What problems do you see in this approach? See Tamar Lewin, Unwed Fathers Fight for Babies Placed for Adoption by Mothers, N.Y. Times, March 19, 2006, §1, at 1. See generally Laurence C. Nolan, Preventing Fatherlessness Through Adoption While Protecting the Parental Rights of Unwed Fathers: How Effective Are Paternity Registries?, 4 Whittier J. Child & Fam. Advoc. 289 (2005).

Can biological fathers who have not registered still file actions for paternity? The Illinois Supreme Court has construed the state's registry law, which applies to provide notice of adoption, to be inapplicable to proceedings under the state's Parentage Act, which allows a man to establish paternity. J.S.A. v. M.H., 863 N.E.2d 236 (Ill. 2007). Thus, a biological father who has not registered can file an action for paternity when no adoption proceeding is pending or contemplated. Cf. In re N.L.B., 212 S.W.3d 123 (Mo. 2007) (fathers who do not fall within statutory categories may still contest adoptions). See also Michelle Kaminsky, Note, Excessive Rights for Putative Fathers: *Heart of Adoptions* Jeopardizes Rights of Mother and Child, 57 Cath. U.L. Rev. 917 (2008) (criticizing Florida case protecting rights of biological father who failed to register).

c. *Publication.* Another approach requires notifying unidentified fathers by posting or publication. See, e.g., §3 Unif. Putative and Unknown Fathers Act, 9C U.L.A. 63, 67-68 (2001) (allowing court to order publication or posting of notice if likely to lead to actual notice of father). How well will these methods achieve actual notification if they exclude the mother's name to protect her privacy? See Jones v. South Carolina Dept. of Soc. Servs., 534 S.E.2d 713 (S.C. Ct. App. 2000); Adoption Place, Inc. v. Doe, 2007 WL 4322014 (Tenn. Ct. App. 2007).

Florida enacted a controversial approach designed to enhance actual notification of an unknown father, requiring preadoption publication to include the minor's birth name, each city in which conception might have occurred, and the name of the mother and any man she reasonably believes might be the father. Does the measure violate the right to privacy by interfering with both a woman's autonomy in choosing adoption and her interest in protecting intimate personal information from disclosure, without satisfying strict scrutiny? G.P. v. State, 842 So. 2d 1059 (Fla. Dist. Ct. App. 2003) (holding statutory requirements violate state constitutional right to privacy). See Alison S. Pally, Father by Newspaper Ad: The Impact of In re the Adoption of a Minor Child on the Definition of Fatherhood, 13 Colum. J. Gender & L. 169 (2004) (critiquing Florida's "biology only" test for fathers); Claire L. McKenna, Note, To Unknown Male: Notice of Plan for Adoption in the Florida 2001 Adoption Act, 79 Notre Dame L. Rev. 789 (2004) (analyzing Florida requirements under compelled speech doctrine).

d. *Presumed paternity.* In revising the original UPA in 2000, the drafters initially eliminated the presumption at issue in *Kelsey S.*, reasoning that increasingly accurate genetic tests make conduct-based presumptions obsolete. Two years later, however, the drafters reconsidered and included a limited "holding out" rule: In order for such conduct to create a presumption of paternity, "for the first two years of the child's life, [the man must have] resided in the same household with the child and openly held out the child as his own." What explains the reconsideration? Is it relevant that the drafters had retained the traditional marital presumption (discussed Chapter 1, section B1a)? See Unif. Parentage Act §204(a)(5) (2000, revised 2002) & cmts. to 2002 version, 9B U.L.A. 16-18 (Supp. 2008). Does the new UPA's approach address the problem of the "thwarted father" in adoption cases? Why must the necessary conduct occur during the first two years of the child's life?

e. *Uniform Adoption Act.* The UAA allows termination of the rights of a birth father who has not demonstrated an interest in parenting his child unless he can show a "compelling reason" for his failure to do so. Unif. Adoption Act, §3-504(c)-(d), 9 U.L.A. (pt. IA) 86-87 (1999). Even so, the court can nevertheless terminate his rights if it finds evidence that failure to terminate will be "detrimental" to the child or granting custody to him would pose a risk of "substantial harm" to the child's well-being. Id. Although the act protects a birth mother's right to remain silent about the birth father, it requires advising her that her choice may delay the adoption or subject it to challenge, that the lack of information about the father's medical and genetic history may be detrimental to the adoptee, and that she faces a civil penalty for knowingly misidentifying the father. Unif. Adoption Act §3-404, id. at 79-80.

7. *Adoption versus custody. Kelsey S.* explicitly distinguishes adoption from custody, stating that even if the biological father can block the adoption, custody remains a separate issue. Does the court suggest that the prospective adoptive parents might retain custody even without an adoption decree? See also In re Adoption of Daniele G., 105 Cal. Rptr. 2d 341 (Ct. App. 2001) (applying *Kelsey S.* to award guardianship to would-be adopters because removal would be detrimental); People ex rel. A.J.C., 88 P.3d 599 (Colo. 2004) (ruling child's best interests determine custody after failed adoption). Cf. In re Baby Girl L., 51 P.3d 544 (Okla. 2002) (interpreting "best interests" to require showing of severe psychological harm to justify continued custody with would-be adopters). Yet if custody might remain with the adopters, why does the court say that to prevail in blocking an adoption a birth father must demonstrate a willingness to assume *full custody*? The UAA follows the court's approach, allowing a court that denies an adoption petition to determine the child's legal custody. Unif. Adoption Act §3-506, 9 U.L.A. (pt. IA) 90 (1999). See Meyer, supra, at 792-812 (critiquing Illinois and other laws allowing custody without adoption, in response to Baby Richard's case). Professor Meyer proposes instead adoption with visitation rights for biological parents, in other words, "non-consensual open adoption." Id. at 833-845. Evaluate this proposal. Recall the similar proposal by Professor Garrison, noted supra section A. See Marsha Garrison, Parents' Rights v. Children's Interests: The Case of the Foster Child, 22 N.Y.U. Rev. L. & Soc. Change 371 (1996).

By contrast, the Utah supreme court has rejected the separate consideration of long-term custody in failed adoptions. In re P.N., 148 P.3d 927 (Utah 2006). In this case, the mother had contractually agreed to be inseminated, to bear a child for the biological father, and to relinquish the child to his care. When the biological father landed in prison, the mother relinquished the child to a prospective adoptive couple but later changed her mind. The trial court decided that, despite the failed adoption, the prospective adopters should get custody based on a best-interests analysis. The supreme court reversed, holding that the statute on contested adoptions

> cannot be used to permanently cut off custody and visitation to parents who have not been found unfit and who have not consented to such placement. It cannot be used to give permanent custody of a child to legal strangers, which is what the [prospective adopters] became once the court dismissed their petition for adoption.

Id. at 930. This result follows, said the court, even "where a custody battle between two biological parents looms once the adoption fails." Id. See also Barnes v. Solomon, 158 P.3d 1097 (Utah 2007).

8. *Estoppel.* In a concurring and dissenting opinion in *Kelsey S.*, Justice Mosk would have reached the same result based on equitable estoppel: The conduct of the biological mother and adoptive parents, thwarting the father's efforts, should equitably estop them from challenging his status as a presumed father. Mosk claims this approach would avoid an unnecessary declaration of unconstitutionality and "needless uncertainty in the application of statutory categories that have been consistently employed for almost 20 years," to the detriment of all parties, "especially the child." 823 P.2d at 1239. Is this approach preferable?

Can a putative father be estopped from *preventing* an adoption? See In re Adoption of S.A.J., 838 A.2d 616 (Pa. 2003) (father's denial of paternity estops him from subsequently claiming paternity to prevent stepparent adoption). Can estoppel *create* parental rights requiring termination before others can adopt the child? Suppose a birth mother and her partner obtain a prebirth decree recognizing both as parents. See Kristine H. v. Lisa R., 117 P.3d 690 (Cal. 2005); American Law Institute, Principles of the Law of Family Dissolution §§2.03, 3.03 (2002).

9. *Empirical evidence.* An early classic study reveals that surrender of a child for adoption long remains an emotional issue for birth fathers. Eva Y. Deykin et al., Fathers of Adopted Children: A Study of the Impact of Child Surrender on Birthfathers, 58 Am. J. Orthopsychiatry 240, 246-247 (1988). This survey of self-identified birth fathers reports that most had negative views of the surrender and some felt obsessed with finding the child. Id. at 244, 246. Despite such data, other studies reveal that many birth mothers, adoptive parents, and adoptees hold negative attitudes about birth fathers, associating them with desertion and failure to take responsibility. Most respondents did not support the release of identifying information on adoptees to birth fathers even when supporting the same for birth mothers. Paul Sachdev, The Birth Father: A Neglected Element in the Adoption Equation, 72 Fam. Soc'y: J. Contemp. Hum. Servs. 131 (1991). Compare Elizabeth S. Cole & Kathryn S. Donley,

History, Values, and Placement Policy Issues in Adoption, in The Psychology of Adoption 273, 285 (David M. Brodzinsky & Marshall D. Schecter eds., 1990) (research fails to justify negative views of birth fathers), with Anne B. Brodzinsky, Surrendering an Infant for Adoption: The Birthmother Experience, in The Psychology of Adoption, supra, at 295, 315 ("interested, committed birthfathers remain in the minority").

## 3. WHEN THE BIRTH PARENT IS A MINOR

What difference does the birth parent's age make for the validity of the relinquishment? For any attempt to revoke consent for adoption? May the actions of a minor birth parent's own parent control? Should special procedural protections apply in such cases? Consider the following controversy:

ADOPTION OF **D.N.T.**

843 So. 2d 690 (Miss. 2003) (en banc)

CARLSON, Justice, for the Court . . . .

D.N.T. (Diane), born September 8, 1999, is the daughter of C.M.T. (Camille), born August 26, 1983. In January 1999, Camille, who was hardly unaccustomed to living in various places for short periods of time,[3] became pregnant while living with D.W.P. (Dan) in Lufkin, Texas.[4] After Camille became pregnant, she moved back to Yuma, Arizona, to live with her mother, S.T. (Sally); however, Camille soon returned to Texas in an effort to make amends with Dan and to stay with her father, C.R.T. (Curt). Within a few days after her sixteenth birthday, Camille gave birth to Diane in Llano, Texas, where she had been living with her father for about five months prior to Diane's birth. When Diane was born, her father (Dan) was living in Llano. Camille and Diane remained in Texas with Camille's father, for about two and a half months after Diane's birth, at which time Camille and Diane returned to Yuma, Arizona, on approximately November 17, 1999, to resume living with Sally.

Camille had received prenatal care in both Arizona and Texas, and she had relied on her mother for support during the pregnancy and after the birth of the child. Diane's father (Dan) never supported Diane and rarely called to check on the child. Dan and Camille never married, and Dan never took legal action to be recognized as Diane's father.

By going to a store in Yuma, Arizona, and purchasing a packet, Sally, Diane's maternal grandmother, established a "do-it-yourself" guardianship in Arizona, whereby Sally became the "guardian" of Diane. This guardianship, was established so that Diane could benefit from Sally's insurance coverage. These "do-it-yourself papers" were filed by Sally and Camille with the Yuma County Clerk's Office in October 2000. This guardianship was established

---

3. The record reveals that Camille had a history of living for awhile with her mother in Arizona, then living with her father in whatever city or state he happened to be living at the time, as well as living with different men for short periods of time.

4. This was Camille's second pregnancy. Camille's mother (Sally) testified that Camille became sexually active at age 12, became pregnant at age 13, and had an abortion in Arizona.

without consultation with an attorney. Camille testified that she took this action because "I wanted a responsible adult to have guardianship of Diane and my mother could put her (Diane) on her insurance if she was listed as a dependent." [W]e are able to conclude that a judge entered an order appointing Sally as Diane's guardian though no documentation appears in the record regarding the guardianship papers. This "guardianship" was still in effect when Camille and Diane came to Mississippi.

Camille and Diane left Arizona for Mississippi approximately one week before Christmas 2000, for the purpose of visiting Camille's father (Curt), who had by that time moved from Texas to Wesson, Mississippi. Camille stated that she wanted her father to "get to know his granddaughter." Camille testified that at the time she left Arizona, she planned to return Diane to Sally's home in Yuma, Arizona, in mid-January 2001, and that although she came to visit in Mississippi, she felt like she would "end up back in Arizona."

Camille stayed with her father for one week, but then she met C.A.H. and R.D.H. (Carol and Rick), on Christmas Day 2000, and Camille and Diane promptly moved in with Rick and Carol in Stonewall, Clarke County, Mississippi. Camille lived with Rick and Carol from Christmas 2000, through the time the adoption petition was filed in March 2001, and Camille relied on Carol for support. In addition, Carol's mother and Camille's father (Curt) lived together.[6] . . . Camille testified that she did not always stay with Rick and Carol at night, but that she was there during the day.[7] While Camille was away at night, Carol would keep Diane. At the time of the chancery court hearing, Diane had lived continuously with Rick and Carol for several months, and Rick and Carol had fully supported her.

Around January 10, 2001, Carol helped Camille write a letter to a judge in Arizona to terminate the guardianship Sally and Camille had established. Camille testified she took efforts to terminate the guardianship "so Carol could adopt Diane." On the other hand, Sally testified she never intended to relinquish any rights over Diane when Camille went to Mississippi. The Arizona guardianship over Diane was judicially terminated on or about February 14, 2001.

On March 8, 2001, Rick and Carol filed in the Chancery Court of Clarke County, Mississippi, a sworn Complaint for Adoption, also signed under oath by Camille; however, on March 23, 2001, Camille [decided she did not wish to relinquish Diane, so she] filed an Objection to Proceedings, requesting the chancery court to "set aside, cancel and hold for naught any documents [she] signed or executed in anticipation of the [adoption] matter." Notwithstanding the objection filed by Camille, the chancellor entered a temporary judgment of custody in favor of Rick and Carol on April 2, 2001. On April 6, 2001, Camille and Sally, through counsel, filed a Complaint to

---

6. Additionally, Camille's father (Curt) and mother (Sally), though having lived separately for some nine years, were still married.

7. Camille admitted under oath that for the first two weeks after moving in with Rick and Carol, she was there "day and night," but then she began to only stay with Carol and Diane during the day, spending her nights with C.M. (Calvin), having sex and smoking marihuana, and returning to Rick and Carol's home each morning around 7:00 a.m., about the time that Diane was waking up.

Revoke Consent and For Custody of Minor Child [challenging, inter alia, the court's jurisdiction and Camille's capacity to consent].

[The chancellor held that the case was a contested adoption and that a guardian ad litem must be appointed. After a hearing, the chancellor concluded, inter alia, that Camille was not the victim of undue influence or fraud and ruled in favor of Carol and Rick. Camille and Sally appealed.] [W]henever reviewing adoption proceedings, we must always remember that the best interests of the child are paramount. . . .

Miss. Code Ann. §93-15-103(2) (Supp. 2002) states:

> (2) The rights of a parent with reference to a child, including parental rights to control or withhold consent to an adoption, and the right to receive notice of a hearing on a petition for adoption, *may be relinquished and the relationship of the parent and child terminated by the execution of a written voluntary release, signed by the parent, regardless of the age of the parent.*

(Emphasis added).

Camille originally joined in the adoption complaint, as evidenced by her signature on the document. [Invoking Mississippi authority for the principle that abandonment may result from a single decision of a parent at a particular point in time, the] chancellor found this act on the part of Camille constituted an abandonment by her of Diane and found that the appropriate Mississippi court had jurisdiction. . . .

Miss. Code Ann. §93-17-7 states in pertinent part:

> No infant shall be adopted to any person if either parent, after having been summoned, shall appear and object thereto before the making of a decree for adoption, unless it shall be made to appear to the court from evidence touching such matters that the parent so objecting had abandoned or deserted such infant or is mentally, or morally, or otherwise unfit to rear and train it. . . .

[W]e must next determine whether the consent was voluntary and abandonment was both physical and legal. C.C.I. v. Natural Parents, 398 So. 2d 220 (Miss. 1981). "Absent a showing by the parent(s) establishing either fraud, duress, or undue influence by clear and convincing evidence, surrenders executed in strict compliance with the safeguard provision of §93-17-9, supra [applicable to relinquishments to adoption agencies], are irrevocable." Id. at 226. . . . In C.C.I., we also stated:

> Undue influence is one of several grounds demonstrating a lack of voluntary consent on the part of the parents. Several of the means which may constitute undue influence include over-persuasion, threat of economic detriment or promise of economic benefit, the invoking of extreme family hostility both to the child and mother, and undue moral persuasion. Because undue influence is such a broad concept, cases must be resolved upon their particular facts. [The party asserting undue influence has the burden of establishing it by clear and convincing evidence.]

C.C.I., 398 So. 2d at 222-23.

Turning to the facts of this case, Carol testified that she helped Camille word a letter to have Sally's guardianship in Arizona terminated, and the guardianship was in fact terminated by an Arizona judge in February 2001. Sally testified that she was not able to afford a lawyer to contest the termination of the guardianship. Carol also testified that the "ideas" in the letter to the Arizona judge were both hers and Camille's. On the other hand, Camille testified that she had no intention of putting Diane up for adoption until Carol brought it up "jokingly"; that she never initiated any conversations about adoption; that Carol also confided in her that she had considered "cheating on Rick to get pregnant"; that the idea of writing the letter to terminate the guardianship was Carol's idea; that Carol actually wrote the letter; that Rick and Carol were providing food and shelter and spending money for her and that she was not working at all; that when she told her mother (Sally) of her second thoughts about the adoption on March 18 or 19, Sally immediately left Arizona to come for Camille in Mississippi; that she was afraid to tell Rick and Carol of her change of heart until her mother was close by; that as soon as she told Carol she wanted to withdraw her consent to the adoption, Carol began crying; and, that when Rick found out, he told Camille to get the "f — out of his house" and that "no one was going to take this baby from them — that he would hurt anyone that tried."

At the close of the case-in-chief as presented by Sally and Camille, Rick and Carol, through counsel, made an ore tenus motion to dismiss pursuant to Miss. R. Civ. P. 41(b), which was granted by the chancellor, but only after a detailed finding of fact which consumed approximately seven pages of the trial record. The chancellor found:

> [Camille] knew for a substantial amount of time prior to the time that the adoption papers were drawn up that the adoption was in the works. She knew when Rick and Carol went to the attorney's office; she knew that the adoption papers were being drawn up, and she went without Rick and Carol to the lawyer's office.
>
> She could have called her father or her mother at any time during the time that she remained with Rick and Carol. She was not under Rick and Carol's direct control at all times. She spent substantial periods of time with her boyfriend, Calvin, and could have called either parent at any time.
>
> She had a contemporary with her when she went to the lawyer's office to sign the papers and that contemporary told her she wouldn't sign adoption papers, she wouldn't give up her child, and yet Camille made the decision to go in to the lawyer's office and complete the process of signing the consent forms.
>
> At the time that she signed the consent forms she was in a relationship with her boyfriend who had asked her to marry [him] and even offered to raise the minor child as his own.

The chancellor's findings of fact are amply supported by the record. . . . The record clearly reveals that Camille signed the original complaint for adoption, though she later changed her mind and attempted to withdraw her consent. Under Miss. Code Ann. §93-15-103(2) . . . , the chancellor was eminently correct in finding that upon joining in the sworn complaint for adoption and requesting, inter alia, that Diane be permanently adopted to Rick and Carol, Camille had in effect relinquished her parental rights to Diane. The record likewise clearly supports the chancellor's finding that Camille (and Sally) failed to prove by clear and convincing evidence that Camille's consent to the adoption was procured by Rick and Carol's exercise of "undue influence or fraud." *C.C.I.,* 398 So. 2d at 222-23.

The record is replete with bad decisions Camille has made her entire life. She has proven herself immature beyond understanding, as evidenced adequately by her own testimony of leaving Diane with almost strangers (Rick and Carol) while she spent the nights at her new boyfriend's house having sex and smoking marihuana with him.

The brief of Camille and Sally lists a litany of things minors may not do including voting, entering into binding contracts, etc. Likewise, Camille and Sally discuss in their brief the Mississippi statutory requirement for consent by the parents or legal guardian of an unemancipated minor before that minor may have an abortion, as opposed to no such requirement of parental or guardian consent before an unmarried minor gives her child up for adoption. After all, argue Camille and Sally, both a consent to an abortion and a consent to an adoption result in the minor mother being forever deprived of her child. With this, the Court cannot argue. On the other hand, perhaps the learned chancellor in this case said it best when responding to the abortion vs. adoption argument propounded by Camille and Sally:

> [The attorney for Camille and Sally] asks the Court to compare allowing a minor to consent to an adoption with not allowing a minor to consent to an abortion. A minor who is contemplating an abortion has not yet become a parent and there is a clear distinction in the law between the way a minor child contemplating an abortion is treated and the way that a minor child contemplating an adoption is considered and it's the fact of that child's parenthood that makes that decision different.
>
> There comes a point when a child must become responsible for his or her decisions and our Legislature has set out that a child who has given birth has the capacity to consent to an adoption.

Our adoption statutes state specifically that age does not matter when it comes to voluntarily releasing the child for adoption. . . . Camille was competent to waive process and has, under our case law and statutes, effectively done so. Additionally her actions, under Mississippi law, constituted an abandonment of Diane, and the chancellor was eminently correct in so ruling.

[The court then decides that failure to join Sally as a party was not fatal to the adoption.] The statute makes no mention of a requirement that the guardian of a minor parent be joined. Camille and Sally assert that "No minor in Mississippi may sue or be sued in his or her own right." That is the case in nearly all civil settings, but we have express exceptions to this rule through our adoption statutes. . . .

Though the testimony of Camille and Sally suggests at least an inference of undue influence, the chancellor was there on the scene and not only heard the testimony of the witnesses, but also had the opportunity to observe their manner and demeanor and ultimately make findings of fact based on the record before the court. Accordingly, the chancellor did not manifestly err by finding

Camille had failed to meet her burden of proof. As such, the chancellor did not err in granting the dismissal. . . .

Cobb, Justice, Concurring:

I agree with the majority's application of existing law to all issues presented in this case, and I strongly support the very important and valid public policy of encouraging, facilitating, and promptly finalizing adoptions. However, I believe that this Court has moved too far away from protecting vulnerable minor parents in the adoption process. Thus I write separately to express this concern, with the hope that either by case law or by statute, some protection might be made available in certain circumstances.

Here, an unmarried 17-year-old mother was taken in by a childless couple who had expressed an interest in her 15 month old daughter from the moment the couple met her. By taking the mother and child into their home and effectively supporting them, the couple applies strong emotional pressure on the mother to let them adopt her daughter, promising, inter alia, that the mother will be allowed ample contact with the child afterwards. Without independent legal counsel, the young mother goes to the couple's lawyer and signs away her full legal rights to the child. Only three weeks later, the mother realizes the gravity of what she has done, regrets her decision, and asks for her child back. But she is virtually thrown out of the couple's house and denied any future contact with her child. Going to court, she finds that she has no recourse, and learns, too late, that the moment she signed the document consenting to the adoption was her last moment as her baby's legal parent, as established by prior decisions of this state.

In addition to the interests of the infant child D.N.T., there are also the interests of the other minor in this case, C.M.T., which should not be forgotten. I question the analysis of the trial court and the majority which concludes that the physical act of giving birth automatically bestows upon a minor mother, however young and vulnerable, the capacity to consent to an adoption without any advice or counsel from lawyer or layman, regarding the law and the consequences of signing a consent form. I am not at all convinced that the Legislature, when it enacted Miss. Code Ann. §93-15-103(2), contemplated this Court's pronouncement that the single act of signing a consent to adoption could forever remove the child from its parent without counsel, especially with regard to a minor mother.

I am mindful of the fact that it is not the place of this Court to rewrite the statutes. That should not end the issue, however, because this Court [under its equity powers] does have a constitutional *duty* to protect children — be they 15 months old or 17 years old — insofar as that is consistent with the law. . . .

Where the minor parent's own parent or guardian is not involved with the adoption, the minimum safeguard for protecting the minor parent's rights is independent legal counsel. A guardian ad litem should be appointed by the court where the minor is unable to secure such counsel. The relatively insignificant delay and expense involved in appointing a guardian ad litem should not outweigh the importance of ensuring that the minor parent understands the irrevocable nature of the proceedings. . . .

[T]here is no conflict between a minor parent's having the power to consent to an adoption and her being provided adequate legal advice as to the nature and consequences of her act. . . . It is time for this Court to seriously consider adopting the practice of our neighboring states. Alabama and Arkansas specifically provide for independent legal counsel for minor parents in adoption proceedings. . . . Many other states also have some requirement that the minor parent be provided counsel before entering into a momentous and irreversible surrender of her precious parental rights.

Further, in all equity, providing a guardian ad litem to a minor parent presents no impediment to legitimate adoptions (and even should make them all the more secure from challenge), whereas it offers literally the only chance under our rigorous statutory and case law to protect a minor parent from unjust and unfair pressures and misrepresentations.

Our case law has evolved, almost heartlessly, and it now says that once the paper is signed, the child is considered "abandoned," and any hope of reversing the proceeding is effectively lost, unless the minor can meet an extraordinarily high burden of proof to show undue influence.[17] This is true no matter whether the change of heart occurs within a day or two, a week or two, or a year or two. How can this be considered equitable? It is crucial, in my opinion, that the court of equity should be completely satisfied that the minor parent has been advised as to what signing the document to consent to the adoption of her child really means. Adoptive parents and their legal counsel cannot be relied upon to protect the minor parent's interest. Only independent legal counsel, if necessary a guardian ad litem, can fulfill the court's duty to the minor parent.

In any event, these arguments come too late for C.M.T. Her daughter has been living with the adoptive parents for three years, thinking of them as her parents, and it is unlikely that her best interests would be served by disrupting her life further. However, this Court has the opportunity, from this day forward, to implement a simple and adequate safeguard to uphold the most sacred and fundamental of rights in the field of family law, a parent's right regarding her child. . . .

McRae, Presiding Justice (joined by Diaz, J.,), Dissenting:

I dissent . . . The facts show that the adoptive parents all but held the mother's hand while she signed the papers. They used every manipulative tactic available to convince the mother, a seventeen-year-old child herself, that she should allow them to adopt her child. Their coercion and underhandedness are obvious; therefore the majority's abandonment argument is without merit since the totality of the circumstances does not evidence voluntary abandonment.

---

17. It is disconcerting to contrast our case law on wills, where a confidential relationship creates the presumption of undue influence, with our case law on adoption. Had it been a question of C.M.T. bequeathing them something of monetary value, the adoptive parents surely would have been found to be in a confidential relationship with C.M.T., and she would have been entitled to the presumption. But since she was only giving them her child, the law says otherwise. This is contrary to logic, reason, and common sense.

Second, the adopted child's father was not given adequate notice of the adoption proceeding. . . . I believe that under the circumstances of this case, the natural father was entitled to notice. Had the parties to the adoption been unaware of the natural father's name and location, the failure to serve him with notice of the proceedings may have been justified. . . . The record shows that the father has had very little contact with the adoptive child since her birth, but some contact is more than none. . . .

Third, the minor mother did not have capacity to execute the papers to relinquish her rights. It is well-established law in Mississippi that minors have limited contract rights and are not able to waive constitutionally protected rights even in civil litigation. In civil and criminal litigation, a minor's right to waive the protection of certain liberties and constitutional rights are so too limited. . . . Yet, here this Court allows a seventeen-year-old girl to consent to an adoption without the advice of counsel or her guardian; i.e. her mother. Furthermore, when the minor mother went to sign the adoption papers she was told she could not leave the lawyer's office with the papers to look them over and the attorney who prepared the papers was not available for questions regarding their content. Could it be any clearer that this girl was being taken advantage of and did not have had the mental capacity and knowledge to consent to the adoption? . . .

. . . After reviewing the facts of this action, it is apparent that the adoptive parents exerted undue influence over the mother. The majority omits many facts regarding this action. In December 2000, the mother brought the child with her to Mississippi to visit her father and his live-in girlfriend who is the mother of the adopting mother. During their visit, the adopting parents began showing a great deal of affection toward both the mother and child. They suggested that the girls move in with them for a while until they returned to Arizona. During the first week of her living with them, the adoptive parents began making comments about how they were unable to have children and were trying desperately to adopt. The adoptive mother often came to the mother crying about her inability to have a child or adopt. They treated the mother and child like daughters and often encouraged the mother to go out with friends. In fact they began giving the mother spending money for that very purpose. Less than one month after meeting them, the adoptive parents encouraged the mother to end the guardianship of the child by her maternal grandmother. They drafted the paperwork and paid for the proceedings to end guardianship. Then the adoptive parents took their final step only after three (3) months of knowing the mother and child. Through coercion and manipulation, they convinced the mother that she should sign papers allowing the child to be adopted by them. They even promised her that she had six months to change her mind and that if the adoption went through she would be able to spend as much time with the child as she liked. Their attorney drew up the paperwork and had the mother sign the documents without even explaining their significance or advising her to get counsel. Less than a week after the papers were signed the mother realized their significance. She went to the adoptive mother and told her that she did not want to give her child up for adoption. There could not be a more clear cut case of undue influence and coercion. The adoptive parents preyed on an innocent and uneducated teenager. They even had an inside track. The mother of the adoptive mother was the live-in girl-friend of the child's mother's father who undoubtedly played a role in convincing the child's mother that adoption was the right thing to do. . . .

Fourth, the majority fails to give appropriate consideration for the best interest of the child. Mississippi has consistently and repeatedly held that "the best interest of the child is a polestar consideration in the granting of any adoption." . . . Here, the child was one year and four months (16 months) old when she and her mother came to Mississippi to visit her grandfather. Children at this age are very attached to their parents. Their only security in life are those who have cared for them since birth. The child only knew the adoptive parents for three months before they filed their complaint for adoption. Only ten months after the child met the adoptive parents, the Chancery Court of Clarke County, Mississippi entered an order granting the adoption. There is no way the child could have known the adoptive parents well enough to be emotionally stable with her adoption and placement with them. The child had only two persons close to her: her mother and her maternal grand-mother. It can not be in the best interest of this child to allow this adoption. Furthermore, the majority seems to emphasize on the mother's personal life as a reason why it would be in the best interest of the child to be adopted, but her personal decisions do not justify its findings. After all, this Court has always ruled that a parent's personal choices which are not in view of their child and that have no negative impact on their child rearing are not sufficient for a finding that it would not be in the child's best interest to be placed on remain with the parent. . . .

## NOTES AND QUESTIONS

1. *Minors' relinquishments.* In most settings, parents have the responsibility to support minors, minors remain subject to parental control, and the contracts that minors enter are voidable. Emancipation, however, confers adult status on children for many legal purposes. See, e.g., State v. C.R., 797 P.2d 459 (Utah Ct. App. 1990); Cal. Fam. Code §7050 (2008). The criteria for emancipation vary from jurisdiction to jurisdiction. For example, in some states pregnancy and parenthood trigger emancipation; in others, they do not, if the minor has not become self-supporting. Compare Purdy v. Purdy, 578 S.E.2d 30 (S.C. Ct. App. 2003) (pregnancy, cohabitation, and employment are insufficient if minor not self-supporting), with Caldwell v. Caldwell, 823 So. 2d 1216, 1221 (Miss. Ct. App. 2002) (child's "adult decisions," such as becoming pregnant, help show emancipation).

Against this background, how should the law approach the relinquishment for adoption of a minor's child? Evaluate the Mississippi statute, applied in *D.N.T.*, which makes the birth parent's age irrelevant. See also T.R. v. Adoption Servs., Inc., 724 So. 2d 1235 (Fla. Dist. Ct. App. 1999) (youth and poverty do not constitute duress). Should courts be required to appoint a guardian ad litem for minor birth parents for the relinquishment to be valid? Or should court-appointed counsel be required? See In re Adoption of A.L.O., 132 P.3d

543 (Mont. 2006). Some jurisdictions address this problem by requiring the consent of the minor birth parent's parents. See, e.g., Minn. Stat. §259.24(2) (2007) (also requiring an opportunity for the minor to consult an attorney, member of the clergy, or physician). But see Mo. Rev. Stat. §453.050 (2008) (waiver of consent valid even if parent is under age 18). Can a minor birth parent who subsequently seeks to revoke consent be bound by her own parents' consent?

Should the same rules govern minor females' and minor males' consent to adoption? Evaluate the dissenting judge's assertion that the rights of Diane's father were not properly terminated.

2. *Minors' abortions.* D.N.T. contrasts the law governing minors' abortions. According to the U.S. Supreme Court's abortion jurisprudence, the Constitution permits greater state regulation of minors' abortion rights compared to those of adults. Why? In Bellotti v. Baird, 443 U.S. 622, 634 (1979), a plurality of the Supreme Court invoked the vulnerability of youth; their inability to make mature, informed decisions; and the need to foster the parental role in child-rearing. While these reasons support parental-involvement requirements for minors' abortions, *Bellotti* went on to say that states with such laws must also provide an alternative to allow some minors to proceed without their parents, specifically when they are sufficiently mature to make their own abortion decisions or when terminating the pregnancy will serve their best interests. A number of states with abortion restrictions responded, creating procedures for a minor to appear before a judge to "bypass" the parental consent or notification otherwise required; the judge, in turn evaluates the minor's maturity and best interests. See, e.g., Hodgson v. Minnesota, 497 U.S. 417 (1990); Lambert v. Wiklund, 520 U.S. 292 (1997).

Should the law require a similar assessment of maturity and best interests before a minor carries her pregnancy to term and gives birth? See Planned Parenthood of Cent. N.J. v. Farmer, 762 A.2d 620 (N.J. 2000); see also Nanette Dembitz, The Supreme Court and a Minor's Abortion Decision, 80 Colum. L. Rev. 1251, 1255-1256 (1980). Before a minor relinquishes a baby for adoption, as in *D.N.T.*? Critics of parental involvement laws and bypass proceedings for abortions cite studies that have examined the decisionmaking processes of adolescents and adults and that find few, if any, differences in cognitive abilities, at least for those adolescents who are age 14 and older. See J. Shoshanna Ehrlich, Grounded in the Reality of Their Lives: Listening to Teens Who Make the Abortion Decision Without Involving Their Parents, 18 Berkeley Women's L.J. 61, 150 (2003); Preston A. Britner et al., Psychology and the Law: Evaluating Juveniles' Competence to Make Abortion Decisions: How Social Science Can Inform the Law, 5 U. Chi. L. Sch. Roundtable 35 (1998). To what extent do these analyses of abortion laws have implications for the issue of minors' consent to adoption, as in D.N.T.?

3. *Teen sexuality.* What value judgments and attitudes about Camille's sexuality appear in the majority opinion? What bearing do (should) Camille's sexuality have on the issue presented?

a. *Information and education.* What role should the state play in educating young persons (or even their parents) about sexuality and ways to communicate about it? See, e.g., Susan Frelich Appleton, Toward a "Culturally Cliterate" Family Law?, 24 Berkeley J. Gender L. Just. 267 (2008).

Many of those depicted in Fessler's book, supra, gave birth as teenagers. They had little understanding of heterosexual activity and its consequences. One of those depicted in the book, "Nancy I," reminisces about the conversation she had with her mother just before "going away" to continue her pregnancy in secret, give birth, and relinquish the child:

> The night before I was scheduled to leave, . . . I had the very first, possibly the only, honest conversation I'd ever had with [my mother]. I felt safe enough . . . to ask her this question: "How do they get rid of the mark when they take the baby out?" I'd seen people in bathing suits and I could never tell if they'd had children. She stood there, three feet from me, with a look of horror on her face and said, "My God, Nancy, that baby comes out the same way it went in." I said, "You have got to be kidding me." She said, "No."
>
> I mean, it's borderline child abuse not to share this kind of information. How can anyone think that we will just absorb it naturally, or that it's our responsibility as children to figure it out? It just mystifies me. I had no idea. I mean, we never had pets. I didn't live on a farm. We had a very puritanical, Beaver Cleaver lifestyle, and it just wasn't anything that was ever discussed. I mean, as amazing as it sounds, I was sixteen and pregnant and I did not know how babies were born. It's pathetic, but it's true.

Fessler, supra, at 49. Should we presume that Camille, in the principal case, had more knowledge because she had been pregnant before (see footnote 4)?

The federal government currently provides funds exclusively for abstinence-only programs. 42 U.S.C. §710 (2008). On the continuing debates about sex education, see, e.g., Judith Levine, Harmful to Minors: The Perils of Protecting Children from Sex (2002); Kristin Luker, When Sex Goes to School (2006); Linda C. McClain, Children and Education: Some ABCs of Feminist Sex Education (in Light of the Sexuality Critique of Legal Feminism), 15 Colum. J. Gender & L. 63 (2006); Danielle LeClair, Comment, Let's Talk About Sex Honestly: Why Federal Abstinence-Only-Until-Marriage Education Programs Discriminate Against Girls, Are Bad Public Policy, and Should be Overturned, 21 Wis. Women's L.J. 291 (2006). In contrast to the official emphasis on abstinence, contemporary American culture sexualizes girls, even very young girls, according to a critical report of the American Psychological Association. See American Psychological Association, Report of the APA Task Force on the Sexualization of Girls (2007).

b. *Sexual activity.* Nearly half of all 15- to 19-year-olds in the United States have had sex at least once; by age 15 only 13 percent have had sex, but by age 19, 7 of 10 have had sexual intercourse. Guttmacher Institute, In Brief, Facts on American Teens' Sexual and Reproductive Health, Sept. 2006, available at http://www.guttmacher.org/pubs/fb_ATSRH.pdf. Overall, 1 in 4 American teenage females has a sexually transmitted infection, but rates vary by race, with half of African-American teenage girls having such infections compared to 20 percent for whites. Lawrence K. Altman, Sex Infections Reported in Quarter of Teenage Girls, N.Y. Times, Mar. 12, 2008, at A1 (reporting announcement at health conference). For an examination of the gender differences characterizing the practice of "hooking up," see Paula England et al., Hooking Up and Forming Romantic Relationships on Today's College Campuses, in The Gendered Society Reader 531 (Michael S. Kimmel & Amy Aronson eds., 2008).

c. *Pregnancy and birth rates.* The rates of teen pregnancy and birth in the United States are the highest among developed countries, with about 75 pregnancies per 1000 females aged 15 to 19 each year. Guttmacher Institute, supra. Again, the data (and analyses) vary by race. Between 1990 and 2000, the nationwide teen pregnancy rate for African-Americans declined 32 percent; for whites 28 percent; and for Hispanics 15 percent. Alan Guttmacher Institute, U.S. Teenage Pregnancy Statistics: Overall Trends, Trends by Race and Ethnicity and State-by-State Information 2 (Feb. 19, 2004) (summary), available at http://www.guttmacher.org/pubs/state_pregnancy_trends.pdf. Despite such declines, in 2006 the teen birthrate in the United States rose for the first time in 14 years. Centers for Disease Control & Prevention, Teen Birth Rate Rises for First Time in 14 Years, Dec. 5, 2007 (press release), available at http://www.cdc.gov/media/pressrel/2007/r071205.htm. What might explain the high rates of teen pregnancy and births in the United States and the other data cited?

In contrast to the mainstream view of teen motherhood's devastating consequences (educational, economic, and psychological), some challenge this conventional wisdom for African-American teens, asserting that considerations of health, kinship support, and insurance networks make youthful childbearing rational, as a collective or cultural matter. Arline T. Geronimus, Teenage Childbearing and Social and Reproductive Disadvantage: The Evolution of Complex Questions and the Demise of Simple Answers, 40 Fam. Relations 463 (1991).

d. *Abortion.* The abortion rate for teenagers in 2000 was 24.0 per 1,000 young women aged 15-19. Guttmacher Institute, U.S. Teenage Pregnancy, supra. Broken down by race, the rate was 54.9 for African-Americans, 17.9 for whites, and 30.3 for Hispanics.

4. *Independent placement redux.* While *Scarpetta* (supra section B1) depicts an agency placement and *Kelsey S.* (supra section B2) illustrates one form of independent placement, consider the variation of this process illustrated in *D.N.T.* In particular, consider the arrangement by which Diane and Camille resided with Carol and Rick for a period proceeding the relinquishment. What are the advantages of this increasingly common practice? The risks? See also, e.g., In re Adoption of E.H., 103 P.3d 177 (Utah Ct. App. 2004), *remanded,* 137 P.3d 809 (Utah 2006).

5. *Abandonment.* Note how the *D.N.T.* court's treatment of Camille's initial consent as abandonment blurs the distinction between children who have become available for adoption as the result of involuntary termination of parental rights, as in *Santosky* (supra section A), versus those available by parental relinquishment. This analysis also makes initial consent to adoption irrevocable.

Similar issues surfaced in a highly publicized case in which adult birth parents from China, the Hes, successfully contested the termination of their parental rights even after their eight-year-old daughter, Anna Mae, had spent more than seven years with a Tennessee couple, the Bakers, who wished to adopt her. In re Adoption of A.M.H., 215 S.W.3d 793 (Tenn. 2007). In the United States, the birth parents had signed a consent order transferring custody (temporarily, they asserted), but they had refused to agree to adoption. The birth mother spoke little English; the father, a student, faced deportation for charges of alleged rape, on which he was acquitted by a jury; and they could not obtain medical insurance for their child. After the Hes' efforts to visit Anna Mae and later to obtain her return were thwarted, a trial court terminated their parental rights based on abandonment, on the ground that they willfully failed to visit their daughter for four months.

On appeal, the state supreme court rejected the argument that the Hes had abandoned Anna Mae, given their active pursuit of legal remedies, the animosity between them and the Bakers, and a judicial order of no contact with Anna Mae. Further, applying the test that only a showing of substantial harm can overcome parents' superior right to care and custody, the court found no such showing here, despite the length of time the child had spent with the couple wishing to adopt her.

Media coverage of the case highlighted the close friendship that Anna Mae developed with the Bakers' daughter, Aimee — a relationship that ultimately reconciled the two families after the Hes won on appeal and Anna Mae rejoined her biological family. As a result, overcoming years of fierce legal contests (including the Bakers' efforts to have the Hes deported), both families together celebrated Anna Mae's ninth birthday. Soon thereafter, however, the Hes — facing deportation now that the stay granted in connection with the custody proceedings had ended — returned to China. See For the Love of Anna Mae: Two Families Come Together After Custody Battle, Only to be Torn Apart, ABC News, 20/20, Feb. 7, 2008, available at http://abcnews.go.com/TheLaw/Story?-id=4250114&page=1. Earlier, the court had considered the possibility that the Hes would move with Anna Mae to China, but concluded that this possibility would not support a finding of that Anna Mae's return to her parents would pose a threat of substantial harm. 215 S.W.3d at 813.

6. *"Safe haven" laws.* In response to highly publicized cases of abandonment and infanticide by teen parents, several states have enacted statutes that provide anonymity and immunity from prosecution for parents who leave their babies at designated safe sites. See generally Michael S. Raum & Jeffrey L. Skaare, Encouraging Abandonment: The Trend Towards Allowing Parents to Drop Off Unwanted Newborns, 76 N.D. L. Rev. 511 (2000). Although 47 states have enacted such laws, their effectiveness remains uncertain. See, e.g., Cara Buckley, Safe-Haven Laws Fail to End Discarding of Babies, N.Y. Times, Jan. 13, 2007, at B1. Some critics say the laws have received insufficient publicity among the populations needing them most, specifically young, unmarried girls still living with their parents and in denial about the pregnancy and birth. Other critics note that such laws target mothers and ignore the rights and roles of fathers. See Jeffrey A. Parness, Lost Paternity in the Culture of Motherhood: A Different View of Safe Haven Laws, 42 Val. U. L. Rev. 81 (2007). Still others contend that such laws, properly understood, constitute efforts to promote a "culture of life" and to eliminate legal abortion. See Carol

Sanger, Infant Safe Haven Laws: Legislating in the Culture of Life, 106 Colum. L. Rev. 753 (2006).

Nebraska's safe haven law received extensive publicity when its failure to limit application to infants prompted parents from several different states to leave older children, often teens, at hospitals and other designated sites; the legislature changed the law just after the total of such children reached 36. Associated Press, Boy Left in Nebraska as a Law Is Changed, N.Y. Times, Nov. 23, 2008, at A30. Observers discerned in the response to the original version of the law evidence of the inadequate services available for families with troubled children. Erik Eckholm, Nebraska Limits Safe Haven Law to Infants, N.Y. Times, Nov. 22, 2008, at A10.

---

### Depictions in Popular Culture:
### Juno (2007)

This film, reviewed as a comedy, presents a lighthearted look at a teen's unplanned pregnancy. Wisecracking Juno tries out sexual intercourse once with her nerdy friend, Paulie; rejects abortion; confesses her pregnancy to her blue-collar and supportive father and stepmother; opts "to kick it out old school," choosing a "yuppie" childless couple to adopt her baby—while remaining in high school throughout these developments. Although the adoptive couple's own story turns out to be less ideal than Juno first imagines, she follows through on the planned relinquishment, remains close to Paulie, and never looks back.

Some observers detect in Juno and contemporaneous films (e.g., *Knocked Up* (2007) and *Waitress* (2007)) a positive attitude toward unplanned pregnancy, perhaps reflected in data showing a recent increase in the teen birth rate. See Meghan Daum, Knocked Up but Not Out: Why Has the Teenage Birthrate Increased After Years of Decline?, L.A. Times, Dec. 15, 2007 (opinion column) (wondering whether the increased birth rate results not from a lack of education but "a lack of mortification"). Others see a "fairy tale" that ignores the lifelong effects of surrendering a child and minimizes the very different consequences of sexual activity for girls and boys. See Caitlin Flanagan, Sex and the Teenage Girl, N.Y. Times, Jan. 13, 2008, at WK13 (op-ed). Still others disagree whether *Juno* assumes a conservative stance in the "culture wars" or challenges the views of both warring factions. Compare Melissa Fletcher Stoeltje, Hollywood's New Family Values?, San Antonio Express-News, Jan. 28, 2008, S.A. Life, at 1D, with Ann Hulbert, Juno and the Culture Wars: How the Movie Disarms the Family Values Debate, Slate, Dec. 18, 2007, available at http://www.slate.com/id/2180275/. How do you interpret the film's portrayal of teen pregnancy and the decision to relinquish a baby?

---

## PROBLEMS

1. Mark (then 20) asks Stephanie (then 15) to marry after a short relationship. She declines. A few months later they learn Stephanie is pregnant. They decide on adoption. Stephanie then leaves Arizona to visit California. After meeting John and Margaret there, she chooses them to adopt the baby.

On her return to Arizona, Stephanie's relationship with Mark deteriorates. Stephanie excludes him from birthing classes. Following two violent outbursts, Mark attempts suicide and enters drug rehabilitation therapy. He then informs Stephanie he no longer favors adoption.

Stephanie returns to California, gives birth, places the child with John and Margaret, and consents to their adoption. Mark, when he learns of the birth a week later, immediately consults an attorney, sends out birth announcements, and purchases baby supplies. Thereafter, he consistently expresses his desire to take full parental responsibilities.

John and Margaret seek to terminate Mark's parental rights in California. They claim that *Kelsey S.* gives Mark no veto over the adoption because he failed to demonstrate full commitment to parental responsibilities throughout the pregnancy. Mark also invokes *Kelsey S.*, counterarguing that he attempted to maintain a relationship with Stephanie during the pregnancy and that since birth he has done everything possible to assume full parental responsibility. He also claims that John and Margaret's interpretation of *Kelsey S.* discriminates by allowing mothers to decide after birth to withhold consent for adoption while requiring fathers to decide early in the pregnancy.

What result and why? What policy issues does each reading of *Kelsey S.* raise? See Adoption of Michael H., 898 P.2d 891 (Cal. 1995); Carol A. Gorenberg, Fathers' Rights vs. Children's Best Interests: Establishing a Predictable Standard for California Adoption Disputes, 31 Fam. L.Q. 169 (1997).

2. T.W. gives birth to twin daughters in Missouri. While the premature twins are hospitalized, T.W. brings them breast milk. Because T.W. is rearing three other children, she explores the possibility of placing the twins for adoption. Seeking an open adoption (which Missouri does not permit), she chooses a California couple whom she finds with help from an adoption professional and the Internet. Later, she reclaims the twins, within the permissible time period for revocation, because she concludes that the couple would not respect her preference for continuing contact. Next, she chooses a British couple, and an Arkansas court issues the adoption decrees. After British social service workers find this couple unfit and the Arkansas adoption is set aside for lack of jurisdiction, the twins are placed in foster care in Missouri. T.W., who by then changes her mind about adoption, seeks the twins' return to her custody.

The family court terminates T.W.'s parental rights on the ground that she abandoned the twins and emotionally abused them by relinquishing them twice for adoption. T.W. appeals, contending that she neither abandoned nor abused the twins and asserting that no other permissible basis for termination exists. What result and why? See In re K.A.W., 133 S.W.3d 1 (Mo. 2004); Robert Patrick, Mom Set to See 'Net Twins,' Now 5, St. Louis Post-Dispatch,

March 21, 2006, at A1. Of what relevance is T.W.'s use of the Internet to find a placement? If the foster parents now wish to adopt the children, *should* the court resolve the dispute by deciding whether adoption or their return to T.W. will serve their best interests? See Moore v. Asente, 110 S.W.3d 336 (Ky. 2003). *Can* the court decide on the basis of the twins' best interests? Cf. In re R.C., 745 N.E.2d 1233 (Ill. 2001).

# CHAPTER 3

# CHOOSING AN ADOPTIVE FAMILY

## A. THE REGULATION AND PROFESSIONALIZATION OF CHILD PLACEMENT

Imagine a child available for adoption and many families applying to have the child placed with them. How does the selection take place? What characteristics of the prospective adopters and the child are important? Which ones should be important? Who should decide the relevance of such characteristics? Legislators? Judges? Social workers at adoption agencies? Lawyers or other intermediaries? The birth parents themselves? What standard should be used?

Historian Julie Berebitsky, in the excerpt below, shows how adoption began to enjoy popular acceptance in the United States, how adoption assumed an important role in defining the normative family, and how adoptive placement came within the special jurisdiction of social workers. As you read the materials that follow the excerpt, consider the extent to which Berebitsky's observations about the past remain apt today.

JULIE BEREBITSKY, LIKE OUR VERY OWN: ADOPTION AND THE
CHANGING CULTURE OF MOTHERHOOD, 1851-1950

---

52-56, 62, 103-104, 113-117, 121-127, 129-138 (2000)

In October 1907, the *Delineator* [a popular women's magazine] published "The Child without a Home," which told of the 25,000 poor, primarily immigrant children who lived without a mother's love in institutions throughout New York. [In the months thereafter, the magazine's "Child Rescue Campaign"] would feature the photos and life stories of dependent children who were available to any interested reader who wanted to take them out of an institution and into her home. [The campaign, which emphasized how adoption would save homeless children, save marriages, and save the nation from the social threat of those reared without a mother's love,] generated a tremendous amount of reader response. . . . The first letters the *Delineator* published expressed the intense longing for children felt by childless women and women whose children had died; they all hoped to adopt the children to "fill the vacancy in [their] home[s] and still the ache in [their] heart[s]." The *Delineator* had urged women to adopt the children by appealing to their sense of patriotic and civic duty, in addition to their motherly instinct. Yet these letters suggest that women responded on a personal level; they needed the children as much as the children needed them. Nonetheless, adoption at the turn of the century was uncommon enough, and fears about bad heredity prevalent enough[, as reflected in the eugenics movement], that many women needed assurance, encouragement, and a place to voice their fears before they could comfortably adopt a child. . . .

The series also articulated a definition of motherhood based on a woman's capacity to love and nurture a child, not on blood ties. . . . If motherhood was a spiritual state, an attitude, and not the result of a physical experience, then a woman's marital status also bore no relation to her maternal instincts. Consequently, the *Delineator* sometimes advocated that single women adopt. Motherhood was woman's highest calling, . . . so shouldn't single women also have the opportunity to experience it, especially since countless children suffered for lack of mothering? . . . Physicians and others doing private adoption placement who were interviewed for these stories agreed that it was natural for unmarried women to find an outlet for their maternal longings through adoption. . . . As long as the culture understood single adoptive mothers as "mother-women," they were acceptable, because they posed no challenge to traditional gender roles; in fact, they seemed to celebrate them. . . .

In the 1920s, [however,] an array of voices, which included social workers, sociologists, psychologists, members of the legal profession, and married adoptive parents, began to inveigh against allowing single women to adopt. . . . By the 1920s, children had become a "priceless commodity," fathers had become vital to a child's healthy psychological development, and women had become sexual beings. An assortment of social scientists and other professionals defined the best "family" as one in which husband and wife enjoyed emotional intimacy and sexual pleasure and nurtured a few children, to the personal fulfillment of all involved. . . .

It appears that by the 1920s, adoption was becoming more popular among married childless couples and that virtually all healthy, adoptable young children could find homes in such families. Given that demand far exceeded supply, many felt that it was only natural that childless couples should be given first choice. Yet a close examination of the reservations expressed by those set against allowing single women to adopt shows more than just concern for the well-being of the child. These critiques of single adoptive mothers are as much about cultural fears surrounding lesbianism, the maintenance of distinct male-female gender roles, and the stability of the traditional family as they are about the best interests of children. They also reflect the growing influence of psychology, not only in adoption but also in the definition of appropriate adult emotional adjustment and the determination of child-development practices. . . . As this study argues throughout, adoption serves as a site on which the culture plays out its fears about the stability of the family and, more broadly, its anxieties about the ever-changing, unknowable future. . . .

The first two decades of the twentieth century [also] witnessed efforts by social workers to establish their occupation as a profession distinct from the sentimental philanthropy of volunteers. The principle underlying social work held that those dispensing aid should be guided not by social class, the rich helping the poor, but by science, the expert assisting the uninformed. A six-week summer training course for charity workers held in New York in 1898 marked the beginning of social work education; by 1920, seventeen schools of social work existed. . . .

Social workers, however, came to adoption slowly. The idea of adoption conflicted with their efforts toward family preservation and their belief in the primacy of the blood tie. Social workers thought that unwed mothers should keep their infants, a philosophy that continued unchallenged within the profession through the 1930s. In addition, beginning in the 1910s, social workers, influenced by the findings of the new intelligence tests, felt that a definite link existed between illegitimacy and inherited feeblemindedness — a link that they believed made most illegitimate children unadoptable. Consequently, social workers focused their efforts on issues other than adoption.

Meanwhile, in the 1910s, individuals, generally well-to-do women, began to establish private adoption agencies. Imbued with a philanthropic spirit, they strongly disagreed with social workers, especially regarding the disposition of illegitimate infants. They believed that these children were adoptable and that an unwed mother and her child did not make a real family. . . . In Chicago, Florence Walrath found herself in the adoption business after locating an infant for her sister, whose firstborn child had died shortly after birth. Soon word of Walrath's success spread, and friends and acquaintances began to approach her to find infants for them. Walrath officially opened the Cradle, Chicago's first formal adoption agency, in 1923. The Cradle quickly achieved a national reputation as such Hollywood stars as George Burns and Gracie Allen flew to Chicago to claim their own bundles of joy. . . .

As a result, social workers had an uphill battle in the 1920s when they began to look at child placing and tried to bring adoption under their professional jurisdiction. They had to both assert their unique qualifications to be in charge and convince the public that the current practices were dangerous to the child, the adoptive parent, the biological parent, *and* society at large. . . . Changing popular opinion and behavior was a daunting task. Legislative efforts focused on establishing laws that required an investigation into the circumstances surrounding the placement by a child welfare professional or the state welfare department and a six-month trial period of residence in the prospective home before any adoption could be finalized. In 1917, Minnesota passed the first such law, and by the end of 1941, thirty-four states required an investigation before the court issued an adoption decree. [I]n placements made by public agencies, social workers had almost complete authority; the court was in no way involved with an agency's initial decision to reject or approve an applicant and virtually always granted an adoption that a public agency recommended. Still, despite social workers' increased involvement, even in states that required an investigation, judges had the ultimate power to deny or approve a petition. . . .

. . . Social workers argued that child placing was a "most exacting" science that required "careful preparation and study." . . . As social workers developed adoption policy and refined the practice in the 1920s, 1930s, and 1940s, they claimed expertise in three areas of special concern to prospective adopters. First, social workers spoke to adopters' fear of a child's heredity. Social workers promised to evaluate a child's heritage thoroughly by extensive interviewing and testing. Second, and directly related to the first, social workers maintained that through the extensive evaluation of a child and his or her biological parents, they could "match" a child to the adoptive parents. Social workers asserted that they could find a child "who might have been born to you." Children would "fit" their adoptive homes in physical characteristics, intellectual capacities, temperament, and religious and ethnic affiliation. The policy of matching assumed that this affinity would lead to easier assimilation. And finally, responding to the adoptive parents' fear of biological parents changing their minds, social workers maintained that their procedures ensured that the child was really free to be adopted and that the biological parents would stick to their decision. . . .

## 1. PLACEMENT CRITERIA

### a. Matching

CRUMP v. MONTGOMERY

154 A.2d 802 (Md. 1959)

PRESCOTT, J.

This is an appeal by the petitioners below, Lloyd R. and Dorothy V. Crump, (the Crumps) from a decree entered by the Circuit Court for Wicomico County, dismissing the petition of the Crumps for the adoption of a minor child and decreeing the adoption of said child by Arthur P. and Blanche P. Montgomery, (the Montgomerys), who had also petitioned the court for the adoption of the child.

The child, Johnnie, was born in May of 1957 to an unwed mother. When he was seven days old, he was placed by the Montgomery County Welfare Board (Montgomery Board), which later received from his mother a written right to consent to his adoption, in the home of the Crumps, in Montgomery County, for foster care and pre-adoptive study. The Crumps had received five other foster children from the Montgomery Board and cared for them satisfactorily—not more than two being in their home at any one time. When first placed with the Crumps, it was thought Johnnie would be placed for adoption within three to six months. However, they were notified in a few months by a welfare worker that he was not adoptable, because of his showing in his early psychological tests. In later psychological tests, the child showed such improvement (his rating was then slightly below average) that he was rated as eligible for adoption and the Crumps were informed of this fact in

September of 1958. During the intervening months (about 15) that Johnnie had been in their home, the Crumps had become very much attached to him and strongly desired him to be their adopted son. Oral requests concerning the adoption of Johnnie were frequently made by the Crumps to the Montgomery Board worker, but they were told, as they had been before, that they were not eligible as adoptive parents, due to the fact that they were foster parents, and also because the Montgomery Board had "closed its adoption list."

Following the determination that Johnnie was adoptable, his name was placed on the roll of children in that category with the State Welfare Department in Baltimore, which roll is designated as a child "Pool." The testimony does not make the method of operation of this "Pool" certain, but it seems that the children's names (probably minus their surnames), together with their backgrounds, are sent to Baltimore, where they are, in turn, sent to the various Welfare Boards throughout the state to be considered for adoption by prospective adoptive parents who have made application to them. Johnnie's name came to the attention of the Wicomico County Welfare Board (Wicomico Board), which had such an application from the Montgomerys, who had already adopted one child through that Board. The Wicomico Board notified the Montgomerys, who, after consultation with the Board, consideration of Johnnie's background and an interview with him in Montgomery County, decided they would like to have him as their adopted son. . . .

The Montgomery Board, over the protests of the Crumps, placed the custody of the child in the Wicomico Board for adoption, and thereafter, without any independent investigation of their own of the Montgomerys and without investigating the Crumps as possible *adoptive* parents, joined the Wicomico Board in consenting to the adoption of Johnnie by the Montgomerys. . . .

[At trial, the] testimony disclosed that Mr. and Mrs. Crump were 34 and 32 years of age, respectively, and had been married 12 years; they had one natural daughter, aged eleven, who was living with them; Mr. Crump had been an orphan himself and stated he desired to give some of the things that he had missed as a child to Johnnie; for the last six years they had lived in a modern brick bungalow in a desirable residential neighborhood in Silver Spring, Maryland; that Mr. Crump had been employed by the United States Government for nine years and was a scientist and engineer, receiving a salary of $7,200 per year, which was supplemented by approximately $5,000 per year, from his publications, inventions and private enterprises; one witness said that he was a "brilliant scientist"; that he was a steady, reliable and industrious worker; that Mrs. Crump was unemployed and spent her time in the care of the home, her child and the foster children; that neither Mr. nor Mrs. Crump indulged in alcoholic beverages and they were a compatible and congenial couple; and that the children in their home were receiving proper religious instructions.

In summary, the learned Chancellors below found that the testimony of "all of the witnesses who were familiar with the situation shows the Crump home to be an excellent one, the care given to little Johnnie was all that could be desired, and no one, certainly not this Court, offers the slightest criticism of their conduct while the little boy was in their custody," but "[o]n the contrary, we wholeheartedly commend their conduct and what they have done for this little boy."

The testimony also disclosed that the Montgomerys are splendid people and maintain a nice home. Mr. Montgomery was 41 years of age — his wife 31 — and they had been married about 15 years. They were living in a "comfortable, modest and attractive" home in a wholesome residential community on the outskirts of Salisbury, with one daughter — 4 years of age — whom they had previously adopted. His home and automobile were fully paid for and he had money in the bank. The wife was a high school graduate, while the husband had stopped his formal education when through the eleventh grade, but had taken several vocational courses when in the armed services during the war. Mr. Montgomery had been employed by the Eastern Shore Public Service Company since 1948, starting as a member of a line crew and his "job," at the time of the hearing below, was "maintenance and utility." He received $2.18, per hour, from which he derived about $5,000 yearly. He and Mrs. Montgomery were, also, a compatible couple, who were attentive to, and mindful of, their children's welfare. She was unemployed and spent her time in the care of her home where she saw that the children were receiving proper religious training. The Chancellors expressed their "complete approval and satisfaction with Mr. and Mrs. Montgomery as well as with the home they maintain."

The Montgomery Board objected to the Crumps as adoptive parents for Johnnie on two grounds: first, that in their opinion the child would be "over-placed"; and, second, it had not investigated their home for adoptive purposes *in accordance with their policies*. The Montgomery Board, while it advocated the wisdom of its established policy (not consistently applied) of not considering foster-care parents as eligible to become adoptive parents, concedes that this policy is not binding upon a court, which has the final authority to approve or disapprove a proposed adoption.

The "over-placed" objection was based upon the fact that Mr. Crump was a well-educated, highly intelligent young man, who might, because Johnnie was slightly "below average" in his psychological tests, become dissatisfied with the boy and exert "pressure" upon him if the child were unable to exhibit a very high degree of intellectual ability.[3] The Chancellors expressed serious doubt upon this point, stating: "We are not altogether in agreement with the position that an intelligent man should be penalized by being prohibited from adopting a child whose home and background is not apparently up to his standard, and especially is this so when the child is only 18 or 20 months old, and any determination of the capacity of the child to grow in intelligence must be speculative at this stage of his life. . . . *We would be inclined to say that such a home would be more beneficial to him.*" (Emphasis supplied.) . . .

Had the matter of alleged over-placing been fully explored, it may have satisfied the Chancellors that their opinion, quoted above, was sound. . . . The results of Johnnie's early psychological tests would possibly be a matter of real concern as to his "over-placement" if they disclosed some serious impediment in his mentality, or if they could be correlated to his mental potential at any

---

3. This objection is based on one of the elements that comes under a general heading usually termed "matching." Rule 517.1 of the Board of Public Welfare calls for "likeness in temperament, intelligence and racial heritage." 1 Schapiro, A Study of Adoption Practice, p. 84, lists ten factors considered as important in "matching."

time in the future. . . . In considering further the relative intellectual powers of the prospective adoptive father, Mr. Crump, and the boy, it was noted above that it was suggested that because Mr. Crump is a well-educated, intelligent man he might, if permitted to adopt Johnnie, become dissatisfied with the union and exert undue pressure upon the boy if he failed to attain a high level of mental development. In order to give this its proper relative importance, it should be noted that the intellectual feature of matching is only one of many factors, such as race, religion, physical likeness, etc., that should be considered under the general heading of "matching adoptive parents with adoptive children." . . .

Schapiro, op. cit., Vol. 1, p. 84, recognizes that matching is an important part of agency practice in adoptions, but points out there is "no one rule for appraising the qualitative contributions that any single factor can make to the general atmosphere of a home, as [t]here is no unanimity of opinion on what constitutes sound matching," and "matching has become more flexible because agencies have begun to recognize that some adoptive parents are frequently able to accept differences." See also, Child Welfare League of America Standards for Adoption Service, p. 23, par. 4.3, "Matching."

Thus, we have two families that have been passed as eligible for adoptive purposes — both desiring to adopt the same child. The Child Welfare League of America Standards for Adoption Service, p. 23, says the selection of a family for an adoptive child should be made on the basis of an appraisal of their suitability for each other, and suitability "should be appraised in terms of the capacity of adoptive parents to meet the individual needs of the particular child, and of the child to benefit by placement with them and to bring them the satisfaction of parenthood." It will be noticed the emphasis here is on the benefit to the child. . . .

In making short qualitative analyses of the two families involved herein, we make no reference to the qualifications where they seem to be equal, but only to those that differ. The Crumps have the better educational-occupational status (unless it is ultimately determined that the mental attainments of Mr. Crump will probably interfere with his accepting the child, or that he is likely to exert undue pressure upon the child to attain a level of mental development of which the child is incapable); they have a larger income, $12,200, per year, as compared to $5,000; they have a slightly better residence; and Mr. Montgomery demonstrated in his testimony that he does not speak grammatically in simple, ordinary statements of speech. On the other hand, the daughter of the Montgomerys was nearer the age of Johnnie than the daughter of the Crumps (4 years as compared to 11), and Mr. Montgomery's mental development is not such as to raise any question about his accepting the child. Another matter that the Chancellors should have thoroughly considered and weighed is that the adoption of Johnnie by the Montgomerys involved a change from the home, locality and environment in which he had been, practically, since birth. . . .

[I]t is plainly seen that the Chancellors adopted the decision and judgment of the Montgomery Board as to which family would better subserve the welfare and best interests of Johnnie by his adoption, and made no actual finding of their own upon the subject, although clearly intimating that their conclusion was contrary to the Board's. [The statute] places the responsibility for the granting of adoptions in the counties of this State upon the Circuit Courts, and, in granting adoptions, it is the duty of said courts to determine what will best promote the welfare and interests of the child. . . . In view of the fact that the Chancellors failed to make a definite finding of their own with reference to the welfare and best interests of the child, and the testimony in regards to certain aspects of the case is not so complete as it might be, as previously indicated in this opinion, we have decided . . . to remand the case without affirmance or reversal so that the court below may take such additional testimony as it desires, have an independent investigation made of the prospective adoptive parents and the infant if it deems the same necessary or desirable, and render a final and definitive finding, insofar as that court is concerned, as to what will best serve the welfare and best interests of Johnnie. . . .

## NOTES AND QUESTIONS

1. *Epilogue.* After remand, the attorneys for the two families and the Welfare Board of Montgomery County met with the judges and appointed a committee charged with making a "complete study of, and report to the court on, the 'home situations' of the potential adoptive couples." 168 A.2d 355, 356 (Del. 1961). Psychiatrists and psychologists examined the individuals, most of whom recommended that Johnnie stay with the Montgomerys, where he had lived since being removed from the Crumps' home. Finding sufficient support for this conclusion, the court affirmed while observing that the transfer from the Crumps' home was handled poorly and opining that tact and diplomacy in dealing with the Crumps might have avoided the litigation. Id. Does the outcome mean that the court believes the Montgomerys' home was always a better placement for Johnnie, or only that it became so with the passage of time?

2. *Adoption process.* In this classic case illustrating matching practices in adoption, what is the division of authority between the agency, on the one hand, and the court, on the other? Note that the adoption process usually includes a close evaluation of the prospective adopters, often called a "home study" or a "preplacement investigation." See, e.g., Iowa Code §600.8 (2008); 23 Pa. Cons. Stat. §2530 (2008). Under the Uniform Adoption Act (UAA), most adopters must have a favorable preplacement evaluation. Unif. Adoption Act §§2-102, 2-104, 7-101, 9 U.L.A. (pt. IA) 30-31, 33-34, 124 (1999). All placements require an evaluation before the adoption becomes final. Unif. Adoption Act §§3-601 through 3-603, 9 U.L.A. (pt. IA) at 91-92. What explains such regulation of adoptive placements, compared to the absence of regulation (or "privacy") for those who become parents biologically? Do you agree with the criticism that such regulation of adoption reflects a preference for biological relationships and signals distrust of those who would raise a "child born to another" or who seek to parent "someone else's child." Elizabeth Bartholet, Family Bonds: Adoption, Infertility, and the New World of Child Production 69 (1999). See id. at 34, 93.

3. *Placement preferences.* The UAA lists in order of preference priority an agency should consider in determining a child's best interests in the selection

of adoptive parents: the previous adoption of a sibling, characteristics requested by the minor's birth parent or guardian, custody of the minor for 6 months within the preceding 24 months or half the child's life, and status as relative with whom the child has established a positive emotional relationship by one who makes a written adoption request. After considering these possibilities, the agency can consider other individuals. Unif. Adoption Act §2-104, 9 U.L.A. (pt. IA) at 33-34. Alternatively, the child's parent or guardian can select an adoptive family and place the child directly. Unif. Adoption Act §2-102, 9 U.L.A. (pt. IA) at 12. Case law raises numerous questions about the factors that agencies and the state can (and cannot) consider in choosing an adoptive placement. See, e.g., Adoption of Richardson, 59 Cal. Rptr. 323 (Ct. App. 1967) (adopters' deafness); Brett M. ex rel. Children's Home Soc'y v. Vesely, 757 N.W.2d 360 (Neb. 2008) (prospective adopter's undisclosed pregnancy); McClement v. Beaudoin, 700 N.Y.S.2d 570 (App. Div. 1999) (adopters' age); Depew v. Depew, 42 P.3d 873 (Okla. Civ. App. 2001) (couple's divorce). See also James Hohmann, After Receiving Gastric Bypass in Dallas, He Loses Custody Appeal, Dallas Morning News, Sept. 7, 2007, at 8B (obesity).

4. *Foster parents as adopters.* If the Crumps were deemed qualified to serve as Johnnie's foster parents, why were they not considered suitable adoptive parents for him? Do adoptive parents need different skills and characteristics? In contrast to the strict distinction between foster parents and adoptive parents illustrated by Smith v. OFFER, Chapter 2, section B, and *Crump*, modern practice under ASFA (see Chapter 2, section A & infra at 133-134) reflects a more fluid approach in which many foster placements are expressly designed to serve as pre-adoptive placements (even though termination of parental rights might not occur) and permanency planning concurrently pursues both reunification and adoption.

5. *Who benefits?* Whom does matching benefit? The concern about "over-placement" in *Crump* suggests that matching serves the child's interests. Might matching also have helped adoptive families "pass" as biological families in a day when infertility had even more stigmatizing effects than it does now? Will matching always achieve equilibrium between supply and demand?

Today, critics challenge attempts to create "the 'as if' family" through adoption, emphasizing the importance of how a family functions, rather than whether it "imitates nature." E.g., Mary Lyndon Shanley, Making Babies, Making Families: What Matters Most in an Age of Reproductive Technologies, Surrogacy, Adoption, and Same-Sex and Unwed Parents 15-20 (2001). Some of the most vigorous contemporary debates about matching explore the role of race and cultural heritage in adoption, as the following materials show.

ELIZABETH BARTHOLET, WHERE DO BLACK CHILDREN BELONG? THE POLITICS OF RACE MATCHING IN ADOPTION

139 U. Pa. L. Rev. 1163, 1164-1188, 1237 (1991)

When I first walked into the world of adoption, I was stunned at the dominant role race played. . . . Early in the process of exploring how I might adopt, I discovered that the first order of business for the agencies responsible for matching children waiting for homes with prospective parents is to sort and allocate by race. The public and most of the traditional private adoption agencies would not consider assigning a waiting minority child to me, a white person, except as a last resort, and perhaps not even then. The organizations and individual entrepreneurs that arrange independent adoptions, while more willing to place across racial lines, also sorted children by race. In this part of the adoption world, minority children might actually be easier for the white prospective parent to find than a white child, and they were often available for a lesser fee. . . .

The familiar refrain that there are no children available for adoption is a reflection of the racial policies of many adoption agencies and the racial preferences of many adoptive parents. The reality is that there are very few *white* children by comparison to the large pool of would-be white adopters. But there are many *non-white* children available to this pool, both through independent adoption in this country and through international adoption. And there are many non-white children waiting in foster care who are unavailable solely because of adoption agency insistence that they not be placed transracially.

Racial thinking dominates the world of international adoption as well. [Bartholet, a single mother of one child from an early marriage, adopted two children from Peru.] I discovered during my two adoption trips to Peru something about how children may be rated in racial terms in their own country as well as here. Most of the children available for adoption in Peru are of mixed indian and spanish heritage. But there is tremendous variety in ethnic features and skin color. For my second adoption I was offered by the government adoption agency an unusually white, one-month-old baby. My initial reaction upon meeting him was disappointment that he did not look like my first child from Peru. Christopher's brown-skinned face with its indian features had become the quintessence of what a child — my child — should look like. But I decided that it was foolish to look for another baby-Christopher, as I had decided years earlier that it would be foolish to look in adoption for a clone of my biological son. I took this baby home and named him Michael. Within twenty-four hours I found myself tearing through the streets in a taxi, mopping his feverish body with a wet cloth, and terrified, as I saw his eyes lose contact with mine and begin to stare off into the middle distance, that he would die in my arms before we got to the hospital emergency room. . . . Sometime during that taxi ride, or in the hospital room, I became hopelessly attached.

Several weeks later I sat with a blanketed Michael in my arms in the office of one of Lima's fanciest pediatricians. Michael had recovered from the fever but had been suffering from nausea and diarrhea almost ever since. . . . I had been to three different doctors. . . . I told this new doctor the story of Michael's troubles, trying with my words and tone to convey my sense of desperation — to make him understand that if he didn't help us Michael might die. The doctor sat impassively, interrupting me only when my three-year old Christopher wandered over to the bookshelves. Pointing with apparent disgust, as if some small and dirty animal had invaded his office, the doctor asked, "What is he?" I thought the question truly peculiar and the answer rather obvious, but explained that this was my son (perhaps he thought it was the child of the Peruvian nanny who was with me?). At the end of my story the doctor, who had still made no move to look at Michael, assured himself that the nanny spoke no English, and he then proceeded to tell me that he could get me another child, in a way that would avoid all the troublesome procedures of a Peruvian adoption. Women were giving birth in his hospital all the time who would not keep their babies. He could have the birth certificate for one of these babies made out showing me as the mother and the baby would be mine.

When I finally realized that this hospital baby was being suggested as a substitute for the one on my lap, I said in what I hoped was a polite but firm tone that I planned to keep this child and that I was here because I was afraid the child was seriously ill. I asked if the doctor could please now examine the child. . . . I put Michael on the table and started to undress him, and for the first time the doctor looked at him. . . . It was overwhelmingly clear that Michael's value had been transformed in the doctor's eyes by his whiteness. Whiteness made it comprehensible that someone would want to cure and keep this child rather than discard him. . . .

I learned more about my own feelings about race as I puzzled through the process of creating my adoptive family. Adoption compels this kind of learning. You don't just get at the end of one general child line when you're doing adoption. There are a lot of lines, each identified by the race, disabilities, and age of the children available, together with the length of wait and the difficulty and cost of adoption. In choosing which line to join, I had to think about race, and to think on a level that was new to me. I had to try to confront without distortion the reality of parenting someone of another race — since the child and I would have to live that reality. . . . I had to think about whether it would be racist to look for a same-race child or racist to look for a child of another race. . . .

[O]ne day, when he is three and one-half, Christopher says to me across the kitchen table at dinner, "I wish you looked like me." . . . I am left to puzzle at the meaning of this pain. . . . Is it, as the opponents of transracial adoption would have us believe, a piece of a permanent anguish at the sense that he does not truly belong in the place where he should most surely belong — his family? Or should I simply take it as a signal that living as a part of a multi-racial, multi-ethnic, multi-cultural family will force us to confront the meaning of racial and other differences on a regular basis?

This child is as inside my skin as any child could be. It feels entirely right that he should be there. Yet the powers that be in today's adoption world proclaim with near unanimity that race-mixing in the context of adoption should be avoided if at all possible, at least where black or brown-skinned American children are involved. . . .

[C]urrent racial matching policies represent a coming together of powerful and related ideologies — old fashioned white racism, modern-day black nationalism, and what I will call "biologism" — the idea that what is "natural" in the context of the biological family is what is normal and desirable in the context of adoption. Biological families have same-race parents and children. The laws and policies surrounding adoption in this country have generally structured adoption in imitation of biology, giving the adopted child a new birth certificate as if the child had been born to the adoptive parents, sealing off the birth parents as if they had never existed, and attempting to match adoptive parents and children with respect to looks, intellect and religion. The implicit goal has been to create an adoptive family which will resemble as much as possible "the real thing" — the "natural" or biological family that is not. . . .

But the question is . . . whether today's powerful racial matching policies make sense from the viewpoint of either the minority children involved or the larger society. . . . Minority children are pouring, in increasing numbers, into the already overburdened foster care system, and current policies stand in the way of placing these children with available adoptive families. . . .

The controversy over transracial adoption that has arisen in recent decades has primarily involved the placement of children generally identified as black with white families. . . . Through the middle of this century there were near-absolute barriers to transracial adoption posed by adoption agency practice, by social attitudes, and by the law. As adoption agencies gained increasing power in the late nineteenth and early twentieth centuries to screen prospective parents and to assign waiting children to particular homes, they helped to institutionalize the racial barriers. Agencies adopted a powerful "matching" philosophy. Prospective parents were ideally to be matched with children who were physically and mentally as close a match as possible to the biological children they might have produced. This kind of matching was thought to maximize the chances for a successful bonding and nurturing relationship between parent and child. . . .

The 1960s represented a period of relative openness to transracial adoption. Foreign adoptions helped pave the way. In the aftermath of the Korean War, South Korea made many of its abandoned and orphaned children available for adoption. Large numbers of these were mixed race children who had been fathered by black American soldiers stationed in Korea. . . . The civil rights movement in this country brought increasing attention to the plight of the minority children who had languished in the foster care systems over the years. This movement's integrationist ideology made transracial adoption a sympathetic idea to many adoption workers and prospective parents. Transracial adoption also served the needs of the waiting white parents, for whom there were not enough color-matched children available, as well as the interests of the agencies in putting together adoptive families and reducing the foster care population. And so agencies began to place waiting black children with white parents when there were no black parents apparently available. The reported number of transracial placements rose gradually to 733 in 1968, and it more than tripled in the next three years to reach a peak of 2574 in 1971. . . .

In 1972 this brief era of relative openness to transracial adoption came to an abrupt end. That year an organization called the National Association of Black Social Workers (NABSW) issued a position statement against transracial adoption [calling it a form of "genocide"]. It stated:

> Black children should be placed only with Black families whether in foster care or for adoption. Black children belong, physically, psychologically and cultur-ally in Black families in order that they receive the total sense of themselves

and develop a sound projection of their future. Human beings are products of their environment and develop their sense of values, attitudes and self concept within their family structures. Black children in white homes are cut off from the healthy development of themselves as Black people. . . .

Others joined in the attack on transracial adoption, arguing with the NABSW that transracial adoption constituted an attack upon the black community and that it harmed black children by denying them their black heritage and the survival skills needed for life in a racist society.

The attack on transracial adoption appeared to have an immediate and significant impact. The numbers fell from a peak of 2574 in 1971 [to 831 in 1975]. [The Child Welfare League and adoption] agency bureaucrats moved swiftly to accommodate the position taken by the NABSW. . . . A parallel development occurred with respect to the adoptive placement of Native American children. [My own] investigation has made clear to me that race is used as the basis for official decision-making in adoption in a way that is unparalleled in a society that has generally endorsed an anti-discrimination and pro-integration ideology. . . .

This matching scheme confronts a major problem in the fact that the numbers of children falling into the black and the white pools do not "fit," proportionately, with the number of prospective parents falling into their own black and white pools. In 1987, 37.1% of the children in out-of-home placement were black as compared with 46.1% white. Although no good statistics are available, the general understanding is that a very high percentage of the waiting adoptive parent pool is white. . . .

The matching process surfaces, to a degree, in written rules and documented cases. But it is the unwritten and generally invisible rules that are central to understanding the nature of current policies. . . . The rules generally make race not simply "a factor," but an overwhelmingly important factor in the placement process. . . .

[A]doption is not supposed to be about parent or community rights and interests, but rather about serving the best interests of children. Adoption laws throughout this country provide that agencies are to make children's interests paramount in placement decisions. Arguments can be made that black children in general will benefit from efforts to strengthen the black community, and that racial matching policies represent one such effort. The problem is that . . . racial matching policies seem contrary to the immediate and long-term interests of the specific black children waiting for homes. . . .

---

DOROTHY ROBERTS, SHATTERED BONDS: THE COLOR OF CHILD WELFARE

---

165-172 (2002)

The shift in federal policy from family preservation toward adoption [exemplified by the Adoption and Safe Families Act of 1997 (ASFA)] corresponded with the change in the federal position on transracial adoption. The relationship between these two trends was more than a coincidence of timing. The new adoption law was tied to the growing movement to remove barriers to adoption of Black children by white middle-class couples. White adoptive families are seen as a major source for reducing the large numbers of Black children in foster care. At the same time, family preservation policies are seen as a hindrance to white families' ability to adopt them. Although the federal adoption law is racially neutral on its face, its connection to transracial adoption reveals the racial politics that undergirds its popularity. Most of the biological families whose bonds the law disparages are Black, whereas most of the adoptive families whom the law favors are white.

For decades, the federal government permitted public adoption agencies to enforce race-matching policies that sought to place Black children exclusively with Black adoptive families. But in the 1990s, after aggressive lobbying by supporters of transracial adoption, Congress took steps to remove barriers to whites willing to adopt children of other races. Transracial adoption was championed as a critical step in increasing the numbers of adoptions of Black children, the population with the lowest rate of exit from foster care. Advocates argued that race-matching policies forced Black children to languish in foster care awaiting scarce Black adoptive parents when they could have been adopted. . . .

Adoption policy has historically tracked the market for children, serving the interests of adults seeking to adopt more than the interests of children needing stable homes. Foster care and adoption have a supply and demand relationship. While the foster care system provides a source of children for adopters, adoption provides a source of homes for children in foster care. For example, in the early 1900s, child welfare officials softened the child rescue philosophy of the nineteenth century and refrained from terminating parental rights when the supply of newborns available for adoption exceeded demand. In more recent decades, however, the growing demand for adoptable older children as babies became scarce helped to generate policies that free children for adoption by terminating parental rights quickly. . . . Roe v. Wade's protection of women's right to abortion and the diminished social stigma attached to single motherhood have drastically cut the numbers of white women who give up their babies for adoption, creating what has been called the "White Baby Famine." Until recently, the number of adoptions in the United States steadily declined since reaching a peak of 175,000 in 1970.

All of the literature advocating the elimination of racial considerations in child placements focuses on making it easier for white people to adopt Black children. . . . Transracial adoption advocates don't mention the possibility of Blacks adopting white children. Nor do they acknowledge that most race-matching in adoption involves matching white adoptive parents with white children. Child welfare agencies routinely allow whites to choose the white foster children they prefer . . .

[Congressional and media] rhetoric supporting ASFA praised reforms in federal child welfare policy for removing the twin barriers to adoption—race-matching restrictions and prolonged family preservation efforts. Terminating parents' rights faster and abolishing race-matching policies were linked as a strategy for increasing adoptions of Black children by white families. Connecting these two issues—family preservation and transracial adoption—allowed commentators to claim that the foster care problems could be solved by moving more Black children from their families into white adoptive homes. . . .

Transracial adoption becomes especially explosive in the context of terminating parental rights to free children for adoption. . . . These contests bring to the surface a theme that runs more subtly through some of the discourse supporting transracial adoption — the belief that black children fare better if raised by white adoptive families than if returned home. Advocates of transracial adoption frequently assert the benefits of racial assimilation that Black children and white parents experience by living together. . . . As in the rhetoric promoting ASFA, the rhetoric promoting transracial adoption supports the dissolution of poor Black families by depicting adoptive homes as superior to children's existing family relationships.

The picture painted by the media and advocates of transracial adoption as a panacea for the foster care crisis bears little connection to the real world adoption market. The transracial adoption issue is a red herring. It diverts attention from the main harms the child welfare system inflicts on Black families. The white couples the public envisions as adoptive parents are typically not interested in the poor Black children who make up the bulk of the foster care population. The vast majority of white adoptive parents are only willing to take a white child. . . .

Even when they adopt outside their race, whites generally prefer non-Black children of Asian or Latin American heritage. . . . The notion that state agencies are turning away thousands of white parents anxious to adopt Black foster children is ludicrous. Yet this mirage is held out as a reason for opposing policies that preserve Black families. . . .

## IN RE BABY BOY C.

805 N.Y.S.2d 313 (App. Div. 2005)

GONZALEZ, J. . . .

[Baby Boy C. was born in California on March 22, 2004, to Rita C. and her boyfriend Justin W. Rita is one-half Native American Indian and is a registered member of the Tohono O'odham Nation tribe.] Justin is Caucasian and Jewish. On April 13, 2004, Rita and Justin executed extrajudicial consents in Arizona to the termination of their parental rights and the adoption of the child by petitioners Jeffrey A. and Joshua A., who have been certified as qualified adoptive parents in New York. Included in Rita's executed consent were representations that she was a member of the Tribe, that the child may be an "Indian child" under [the Indian Child Welfare Act (ICWA), 25 U.S.C. §1901 et. seq.,] and that she was aware of the placement preferences in ICWA but desired that they be waived, and that a finding of good cause [be] entered to permit the child's adoption by petitioners. [An Arizona court accepted the consents and terminated the birth parents' rights. The Tribe received notice but did not appear. Meanwhile, petitioners took custody of the child, returned to New York, and commenced this adoption proceeding in April 2004. Over petitioners' opposition, the Tribe moved to intervene in the adoption proceeding.]

[After a hearing], Family Court found that ICWA did not apply since the Tribe failed to meet its burden of proving that the subject child was part of an "existing Indian family." The court found that Rita's ties to the Tribe were mainly in her childhood and adolescence, but that as an adult she had "divorced herself from the community affairs, politics and social and religious life of the Tribe," thereby demonstrating a "rejection of her Indian heritage." [Rita had also testified that neither of her other children was being reared in an Indian setting and she had no interest in having this child reared in the tribal culture.] Rita's rejection of her own Indian heritage, in turn, "has acted to break the link between the Tribe and Rita's nuclear family." [After a subsequent best-interests hearing, the court decided the proposed adoption should go forward. The Tribe appeals.]

ICWA was enacted by Congress in 1978 as a product of the rising concern in the mid-1970s over the effect on Indian children, families and tribes of abusive welfare practices that separated large numbers of Indian children from their families and tribes through adoption or foster care placement in non-Indian homes (Mississippi Choctaw Indians Band v Holyfield, 490 U.S. 30, 32 [1989]). ICWA's stated purpose is "to protect the best interests of Indian children and to promote the stability and security of Indian tribes and families by the establishment of minimum Federal standards for the removal of Indian children from their families and the placement of such children in foster or adoptive homes which will reflect the unique values of Indian culture" (25 USC §1902). . . . ICWA seeks to achieve this goal by establishing "a Federal policy that, where possible, an Indian child should remain in the Indian community" and ensuring that Indian child welfare determinations are not based on "a white, middle-class standard which, in many cases, forecloses placement with [an] Indian family" [citing legislative history].

[T]he plain language of ICWA makes the act applicable to this adoption proceeding. As noted, ICWA applies to any "child custody proceeding" involving an "Indian child" (25 USC §1903[1], [4]. [P]etitioners' argument that ICWA is inapplicable rests entirely on its claim that the ["existing Indian family" (EIF)] exception removes this proceeding from the Act. . . . The EIF exception was first articulated by the Supreme Court of Kansas in Matter of Adoption of Baby Boy L. (643 P.2d 168 [1982]). [In finding the ICWA inapplicable, the court said:]

> "[T]he overriding concern of Congress and the proponents of the Act was the maintenance of the family and tribal relationships existing in Indian homes and to set minimum standards for the removal of Indian children from their existing Indian environment. It was not to dictate that an illegitimate infant who has never been a member of an Indian home or culture, and probably never would be, should be removed from its primary cultural heritage and placed in an Indian environment over the express objections of its non-Indian mother." (Id. at 205-206.). . . .

. . . The common rationale behind [*Baby Boy L.* and similar decisions from other states] was that because Congress's primary goal in passing ICWA was to prevent the removal of Indian children from Indian families, that purpose would not be served by applying the Act to children who had never been a part of an existing Indian family.

The legal landscape surrounding the EIF exception changed in 1989, when the United States Supreme Court decided [*Holyfield*]. *Holyfield* involved twin babies born out of wedlock to parents who were both enrolled members of the petitioner tribe. Although both parents lived on the reservation, they traveled 200 miles away from the reservation for the birth [and consented to adoption by a specific non-Indian couple whom they had selected. The Court held that] under federal domicile law, the children were domiciled on the reservation within the meaning of ICWA's exclusive tribal court jurisdiction provision, even though the children had never been physically present on the reserva-tion. . . . In rejecting the notion that ICWA could be avoided by the fact that the parents had "voluntarily surrendered" the child, the *Holyfield* court stated that tribal jurisdiction was not meant to be defeated by the actions of individual tribe members or parents, "for Congress was concerned not solely about the interests of Indian children and families, *but also about the impact on the tribes themselves of the large number of Indian children adopted by non-Indians*" ([490 U.S.] at 49 [emphasis added], citing 25 USC §1901[3] ["there is no resource that is more vital to the continued existence and integrity of Indian tribes than their children"]).

The *Holyfield* Court also emphasized that a major concern of Congress was the "detrimental impact" on the Indian children themselves of being placed outside their culture in non-Indian homes. To this end, Congress made ICWA's jurisdictional and placement provisions applicable not only to involuntary removals of Indian children, but also to voluntary adoptions involving place-ment with non-Indian families "because of concerns going beyond the wishes of individual parents."

In the wake of *Holyfield*, many state courts rejected the EIF exception. . . . Notwithstanding *Holyfield*, two districts of the California Court of Appeals not only adopted the EIF exception to ICWA, but also held that ICWA was uncon-stitutional absent the EIF exception. [In In re Bridget R., 49 Cal. Rptr. 2d 507 (Ct. App. 1996),] the court held that ICWA does not apply to a voluntary termination of parental rights proceeding respecting an Indian child who is not domiciled on an Indian reservation unless the parents are of American Indian descent and "maintain a significant social, cultural or political relation-ship with their tribe." Otherwise, the *Bridget R.* court held, ICWA would violate the child's constitutional rights. . . .

[*Bridget R.*] found that a child had a fundamental right to placement in a stable and permanent home, thereby triggering strict scrutiny, which requires that the legislation serve a compelling governmental interest and be actually necessary and effective in accomplishing that purpose. Although the court found that the compelling interest prong had been met, it held that ICWA's purpose of preserving American Indian culture would not be served by apply-ing it to children whose biological parents did not have a significant relation-ship with an Indian community. Applying ICWA to remove such a child from a home in which he or she had formed familial bonds, the *Bridget R.* court deter-mined, would violate the child's substantive due process rights.

[*Bridget R.*] also found that ICWA violated the child's equal protection rights because it required different treatment of Indian and non-Indian children who were similarly situated. It reasoned that although disparate treat-ment was not constitutionally offensive when it was based on the social, cul-tural and political relationships between Indian children and their tribes, where such "relationships do not exist or are very attenuated, the only remaining basis for applying ICWA rather than state law in proceedings affecting an Indian child's custody is the child's genetic heritage in other words, race." . . .

Having considered the various arguments and authorities for and against the acceptance of the EIF exception, we reject it as fundamentally inconsistent with both the plain language of ICWA and one of its core purpose of preserving and protecting the interests of Indian tribes in their children. We also conclude that, contrary to Family Court's holding, ICWA is constitutional because it is rationally related to fulfilling this expressed purpose.

[As a matter of statutory interpretation, because] Congress has clearly delineated the nature of the relationship between an Indian child and tribe necessary to trigger application of the Act, judicial insertion of an additional [criterion] for applicability is plainly beyond the intent of Congress and must be rejected. Another problem with the EIF exception is that its acceptance would undermine the significant tribal interests recognized by the Supreme Court in *Holyfield*. . . . If the EIF exception were applied in this instance, Rita would have succeeded in nullifying ICWA's purpose at the expense of the interests of the Tribe. . . . Where, as here, Rita has rejected Indian life and culture and, then, voluntarily relinquished her newborn Indian child to be adopted by a non-Indian couple, the detriment to the Tribe is quite significant — the loss of two generations of Indian children instead of just one.

The EIF exception also conflicts with the Congressional policy underlying ICWA that certain child custody determinations be made in accordance with Indian cultural or community standards. The EIF exception is clearly at odds with this policy because it requires state courts to make the inherently subjective factual determination as to the "Indianness" of a particular Indian child or parent, a determination that state courts "are ill-equipped to make." . . .

We also find that ICWA is not constitutionally infirm absent the EIF exception. . . . The decisions finding ICWA unconstitutional without the EIF exception, such as *Bridget R.*, are premised on the existence of a fundamental right or suspect classification. [A child has no fundamental right to adoption, which is strictly a creature of statute.] [With regard to the equal protection claim, courts] have consistently held that federal laws that treat Indians differently from non-Indians do not derive from race, but rather from the political status of the parents or children and the quasi-sovereign nature of the tribe [citations omitted]. [With neither a fundamental right nor a suspect classification implicated, the court applies the rational basis test, finding ICWA reasonably related to the protection of Indian tribes and families and to the fulfillment of Congress's unique guardianship obligation toward Indians.]

Perhaps the most fundamental flaw in the reasoning of the courts that have accepted the EIF exception is the failure to give adequate consideration to the statutory "good cause" exception in 25 USC §1915, which permits state courts to depart from the placement preferences upon a showing of good cause. . . . Although ICWA does not define "good cause," regulations promulgated by the Bureau of Indian Affairs provide that good cause must be based on one or more of the following considerations: (1) the request of the biological parents or the child when of sufficient age; (2) the extraordinary physical or emotional needs of the child as established by testimony of a qualified expert witness; and (3) the unavailability of suitable Indian families for placement (see 44 Fed. Reg. 67,584; 67,594 f.3 [1979]).

The EIF exception loses much of its force when viewed in light of the "good cause" exception, since that provision already provides state courts with the flexibility to deviate from the placement preferences in circumstances where the interests of the parent or child outweigh the tribe's interest in the strict application of those preferences. Here, had Family Court found ICWA applicable and held a placement preference/good cause hearing, it may well have reached the same result of permitting the adoption to proceed without having to rely on a judicially created exception to ICWA that is inconsistent with its language and purpose. [The court also decides that ICWA does not grant the Tribe intervention as a matter of right in adoption proceedings but that New York's civil practice rules permit tribal intervention on remand here.]

## NOTES AND QUESTIONS

1. *The debate.* What role should race play in choosing an adoptive family? Ethnic and cultural background? Why does the law prefer the placement of Native American children with Native American families, according to *Baby Boy C.*? Do similar reasons justify race matching in adoption? To what extent can or should the law specify such placement preferences for minority children without doing the same for white children? Whose analysis do you find more persuasive, Professor Bartholet's or Professor Roberts's? See also Hawley Fogg-Davis, The Ethics of Transracial Adoption (2002); Randall Kennedy, Interracial Intimacies: Sex, Marriage, Identity, and Adoption 402-446; 480-518 (2003) (opposing race matching and ICWA's preferences); Rachel F. Moran, Interracial Intimacy: The Regulation of Race and Romance 127-153 (2001) (emphasizing complexities of determining proper role of race and background); Twila L. Perry, The Transracial Adoption Controversy: An Analysis of Discourse and Subordination, 21 N.Y.U. Rev. L. & Soc. Change 33 (1993-1994) (critiquing political agenda underlying transracial adoption and the emotional strains placed on adoptees). What does the debate about transracial adoption say about mothering, hierarchy, and other themes emphasized in feminist analysis? See Twila L. Perry, Transracial and International Adoption: Mothers, Hierarchy, Race, and Feminist Legal Theory, 10 Yale J.L. & Feminism 101 (1998) (excerpted in Chapter 5, section C); Black Children and Their Families in the 21st Century: Surviving the American Nightmare or Living the American Dream?, 26 B.C. Third World L.J. 1-129 (2006) (symposium including articles on transracial adoption by Professors Twila L. Perry, Michele Goodwin, and Angela Mae Kupenda).

2. *Constitutional limits.* In challenges to some of the restrictive policies described by Bartholet, usually by white adults seeking to adopt African-American children, courts early on held unconstitutional absolute prohibitions on transracial adoptions. Compos v. McKeithen, 341 F. Supp. 264 (E.D. La. 1972); In re Adoption of Gomez, 424 S.W.2d 656 (Tex. Civ. App. 1967). Can race constitute *one* factor in state placement decisions? See In re Petition of R.M.G., 454 A.2d 776 (D.C. 1982).

In Palmore v. Sidoti, 466 U.S. 429 (1984), the Supreme Court overturned the modification of a child custody arrangement because the modification improperly rested on race, in violation of the Equal Protection Clause of the Fourteenth Amendment. The case arose after a Caucasian couple divorced in Florida, the court awarded the mother custody of their three-year-old daughter, and the father successfully got the earlier decree changed (so that custody was awarded to him) once the mother began cohabiting with an African-American man, whom she married two months later.

The court that granted the father's request for modification justified its outcome on the best interests of the child. It stated (in language later quoted by the United States Supreme Court):

> The father's evident resentment of the mother's choice of a black partner is not sufficient to wrest custody from the mother. It is of some significance, however, that the mother did see fit to bring a man into her home and carry on a sexual relationship with him without being married to him. Such action tended to place gratification of her own desires ahead of her concern for the child's future welfare. *This Court feels that despite the strides that have been made in bettering relations between the races in this country, it is inevitable that Melanie will, if allowed to remain in her present situation and attains school age and thus more vulnerable to peer pressures, suffer from the social stigmatization that is sure to come.*

Id. at 431 (emphasis in Supreme Court opinion).

In the Supreme Court's view, the lower "court correctly stated that the child's welfare was the controlling factor, [but] made no effort to place its holding on any ground other than race." Id. at 432. Is that a correct reading of the quoted paragraph?

Turning to the Fourteenth Amendment, the Supreme Court identified as a "core purpose" the elimination of "all governmentally imposed discrimination based on race." Id. Yet, the Court acknowledged both that racial prejudice exists and that the "goal of granting custody based on the best interests of the child is indisputably a substantial governmental interest for purposes of the Equal Protection Clause." Id. at 433. The Supreme Court concluded with the following effort to balance these competing considerations:

> The question, however, is whether the reality of private biases and the possible injury they might inflict are permissible considerations for removal of an infant child from the custody of its natural mother. We have little difficulty concluding that they are not. The Constitution cannot control such prejudices but neither can it tolerate them. Private biases may be outside the reach of the law, but the law cannot, directly or indirectly, give them effect. . . . The effects of racial prejudice, however real, cannot justify a racial classification removing an infant child from the custody of its natural mother found to be an appropriate person to have such custody.

Id.

Following the U.S. Supreme Court's decision, the mother filed a petition in Texas (where the father and child had moved) for a writ of habeas corpus to recover the child and, in Florida, a motion to compel the return of the child (that was opposed there by the father). The Florida court declined jurisdiction in favor of the Texas court. When the mother appealed that decision, the Florida Court of Appeals affirmed, stating:

> The Supreme Court's decision [in *Palmore*] was that the modification of custody could not be predicated upon the mother's association with a black man. Its opinion did not direct a reinstatement of the original custody decree and the immediate return of the child. The Supreme Court did not say that a Florida court could not defer to a Texas court.

472 So. 2d 843, 846 (Fla. Dist. Ct. App. 1985). The court then determined that it would serve the child's best interests to remain in her father's custody given the passage of time and the already "substantial upheavals" in the child's life. Id. at 847.

How far does *Palmore* extend? Does it bar all considerations of race in child custody decisions? Only in modifications? Only when race provides the sole basis for the custody decision? See, e.g., Gamble v. Woodson, 853 N.E.2d 847 (Ill. App. Ct. 2006). What implications does it have for considerations of race in adoptive placements?

Some cases limiting the use of race in adoption rely on *Palmore*. See, e.g., In re D.L., 479 N.W.2d 408 (Minn. Ct. App. 1991). Does *Palmore* apply to adoptions? What factors differentiate postdissolution custody adjudications from adoption? If *Palmore* applies, does it foreclose the possibility that race matching might satisfy strict scrutiny? See *R.M.G.*, supra. See also David D. Meyer, *Palmore* Comes of Age: The Place of Race in the Placement of Children, 18 U. Fla. J.L. & Pub. Pol'y 183 (2007) (advocating strict scrutiny and case-by-case analysis).

3. *Relative preferences.* To what extent can states promote race matching, while avoiding constitutional problems, by promulgating preferences for adoptive placements with relatives? See, e.g., *D.L.*, supra; Moran, supra, at 131. What considerations support such preferences? Recall the observation in the Berebitsky excerpt, supra, that social workers initially resisted adoption because they valued family preservation and blood ties. Would adoptive placements with relatives offer a middle ground? What difficulties do relative preferences pose? State statutes and practices vary. Compare In re Adoption of B.C.S., 793 N.E.2d 1054 (Ind. Ct. App. 2003) (statute contains no preference for relatives), and In re Adoption of D.M., 710 N.W.2d 441 (S.D. 2006) (no statutory right of relatives to intervene), with Baker v. Webb, 127 S.W.3d 622 (Ky. 2004) (setting aside adoption to allow second cousins to intervene), and State ex rel. D.B. v. M.O., 870 So. 2d 1143 (La. Ct. App. 2004) (applying statutory preference for adoption by relatives). See also Debbie G. v. State, 132 P.3d 1168 (Alaska 2006) (rejecting parental right to choose relative to adopt the child); G.S. v. T.B., 985 So. 2d 978 (Fla. 2008) (holding that a trial court abuses its discretion in denying adoption petition of fit maternal grandparents in order to ensure involvement of paternal grandparents in child's life). Does the Constitution give relatives a right to adopt over strangers? Do their biological connections to the child require the same analysis applicable to unmarried fathers? Why? See Mullins v. Oregon, 57 F.3d 789 (9th Cir. 1995). As noted below, the ICWA contains a relative preference for Native American children. Does equal protection require extending this preference to all children?

4. *Empirical data.* According to data from 2000, 15 percent of all adoptions from foster care are transracial (defined as one in which the child's race differs from at least one adoptive parent). Madelyn Freundlich, Transracial & Transcultural Adoptions, 27 Fam. Advoc. 40, 40 (2004). Empirical studies support transracial adoption as a "basically positive" alternative to long-term foster care. Rita J. Simon et al., The Case for Transracial Adoption 74, 155 (1994) (20-year study of 83 families). In 1991, approximately 108 transracial adoptees, then young adults, were asked whether they wished they had had a same-race placement. Seven percent answered affirmatively, 67 percent answered negatively, 4 percent were not sure, and 22 percent did not reply. Rita J. Simon & Rhonda M. Roorda, In Their Own Voices: Transracial Adoptees Tell Their Stories 21, 25 (2000). Can you think of reasons why such data might not accurately address the concerns raised by opponents of transracial adoption? Recent studies have looked beyond general data showing no significant differences overall between transracial and same-race adoptees to identify specific challenges confronting transracial adoptees: "coping with 'being different'"; struggling "to identify a positive racial/ethnic identity"; and acquiring "the ability to cope with discrimination." Evan B. Donaldson Adoption Institute, Finding Families for African American Children: The Role of Race & Law in Adoption from Foster Care — Policy & Practice Perspective 5-6 (2008), available at http://www.adoptioninstitute.org/publications/MEPApaper20080527.pdf. At the same time, the foster care system includes a disproportionate number of African-American children (32 percent, although African-American children constitute 15 percent of the U.S. child population), and such children take longer to achieve permanency than other foster children. Id. at 11-12.

Increasingly, the literature includes memoirs reflecting personal experiences with transracial adoption. E.g., Barbara Katz Rothman, Weaving a Family: Untangling Race and Adoption (2005) (adoptive parent's perspective); Susan R. Harris, Race, Search, and My Baby-Self: Reflections of a Transracial Adoptee, 9 Yale J.L. & Feminism 5 (1997); Andrew Morrison, Transracial Adoption: The Pros and Cons and the Parents' Perspective, 20 Harv. BlackLetter L.J. 167 (2004) (adoptive sibling's view). See Kennedy, supra, at 447-479 (summarizing such literature).

5. *Federal statutes.* Federal legislation now shapes the way states approach several different aspects of adoptive placements. As you consider the following laws, evaluate both the benefits and disadvantages of federal intervention in this area traditionally relegated to the states. See, e.g., Vivek S. Sankaran, Innovation Held Hostage: Has Federal Intervention Stifled Efforts to Reform the Child Welfare System?, 41 U. Mich. J.L. Reform 281 (2007).

a. *"Barriers to interethnic adoption."* As Roberts indicates in the excerpt above, Congress has legislated the "removal of barriers to interethnic adoption" by providing that no state nor other entity in a state receiving federal funds can "deny to any individual the opportunity to become an adoptive or a foster parent, on the basis of the race, color, or national origin of the individual, or of the child, involved." 42 U.S.C. §1996b (2008) (amending the earlier, and less restrictive, federal Multi-Ethnic Placement Act). Does this statute limit only the practices of adoption agencies, or does it bind judges as well? See In re Adoption of Vito, 712 N.E.2d 1188, 1196 (Mass. App. Ct. 1999) (federal law does not constrain judge in "crafting an order she determines to be in the child's best interests"), *vacated and remanded*, 728 N.E.2d 292, 305 n.27 (Mass. 2000) (avoiding this issue). Some states have enacted laws that complement the federal statute's goal of facilitating transracial adoption. For example, a Texas law provides as follows:

> Unless an independent psychological evaluation specific to a child indicates that placement with a family of a particular race or ethnicity would be detrimental to the child, the department, county child-care or welfare unit, or licensed child-placing agency may not deny, delay, or prohibit the adoption of a child because the department, county, or agency is attempting to locate a family of a particular race or ethnicity.

Tex. Fam. Code Ann. §162.308(b) (2007). Further, the Texas legislature has established an advisory committee to promote the adoption of minority children. Id. at §162.309. See also generally, Lynette Clemetson & Ron Nixon, Breaking Through Adoption's Racial Barriers, N.Y. Times, Aug. 17, 2006, at A1.

The debate continues in response to the federal statute. In 2008, the Evan B. Donaldson Adoption Institute published a report calling for amendments to the federal statute that would permit consideration of race and ethnicity in permanency planning and in the preparation of adoptive parents. According to the report, "[s]ound, ethical adoption practice requires attention to racial and ethnic issues, so that the original [standard from the Multi-Ethnic Placement Act] — which provided that race is *one factor, but not the sole factor*, to be considered in selecting a foster or adoptive parent for a child in foster care — should be reinstated." Evan B. Donaldson Adoption Institute, supra, at 44. The report cautions that the child's best interests should provide the paramount standard, that race should not delay placement, and that "all foster and adoptive families [should] receive some level of training in parenting children of culturally diverse backgrounds [with] families who adopt transracially or transculturally [receiving] additional training and other supportive services to help them meet their children's racial, ethnic, cultural, and linguistic needs." Id. For another critique of the current federal law, see David J. Herring, The Multiethnic Placement Act: Threat to Foster Child Safety and Well-Being?, 41 U. Mich. J.L. Reform 89 (2007). By contrast, Bartholet commends recent efforts to enforce the federal statute, as written. Elizabeth Bartholet, Commentary: Cultural Stereotypes Can and Do Die: It's Time to Move on with Transracial Adoption, 34 J. Am. Acad. Psychiatry & L. 315 (2006).

b. *ASFA*. Congress enacted the Adoption and Safe Families Act 1997 to promote adoption by, inter alia, requiring states to seek terminations of parental rights after a limited period of foster care (42 U.S.C. §675(5) (2008)) and providing financial incentives for states to increase adoptions of children in foster care (id. at §673b). To what extent do these measures encourage transfer of African-American children to white families — serving the needs of adopters rather than children, as Roberts contends? What reforms would address these problems? Cf., e.g., Nell Clement, Note, Do "Reasonable Efforts" Require Cultural Competence? The Importance of Culturally Competent

Reunification Services in the California Child Welfare System, 5 Hastings Race & Poverty L. J. 397 (2008) (noting high number of child welfare cases involving families outside the dominant culture and urging recognition of culture in family reunification efforts). ASFA's time limits pose special problems for incarcerated parents. See Arlene F. Lee et al., The Impact of the Adoption and Safe Families Act on Children of Incarcerated Parents: Critical Issues (2005) (published by the Child Welfare League of America).

Given ASFA's emphasis on permanency, is a showing of an approved placement required before parental rights can be terminated? Compare In re Thomas R., 51 Cal. Rptr. 3d 864 (Ct. App. 2006) (parents have due process right to test sufficiency of evidence of children's adoptability), with In re A.J.G., 148 P.3d 759 (Nev. 2007) (no showing of adoptive placement required), and In re K.C.F., 928 A.2d 1046 (Pa. Super. Ct. 2007) (termination statute does not require preadoptive placement). See also In re Adoption of Victor A., 872 A.2d 662 (Md. 2005) (holding that same best interests standard applies to TPR for all children, regardless of special needs).

c. *ICWA.* As *Baby Boy C.* illustrates, the Indian Child Welfare Act gives Native American background a prominent, if not decisive, role, with preference accorded (absent good cause) to placement with: (1) a member of the child's extended family, (2) other members of the Indian child's tribe, or (3) other Indian families. 25 U.S.C. §1915(a) (2008). In removing "barriers to interethnic adoption," Congress explicitly left intact the ICWA's placement preferences. 42 U.S.C. §1996b(3) (2008). Why? Do the frequent analyses of the ICWA's preferences as race-matching measures expose a fundamental misunderstanding about Indian identity? See Barbara Ann Atwood, Flashpoints Under the Indian Child Welfare Act: Toward a New Understanding of State Court Resistance, 51 Emory L.J. 587 (2002); Carole Goldberg, Critical Race Studies: Descent into Race, 49 UCLA L. Rev. 1373 (2002). See also Solangel Maldonado, Race, Culture, and Adoption: Lessons from Mississippi Band of Choctaw Indians v. Holyfield, 17 Colum. J. Gender & L. 1 (2008).

Given the interpretation of the ICWA in *Baby Boy C.*, what constitutes good cause to depart from the act's preferences? Do "the prevailing social or cultural standards of the [parent's or extended family's] community," which apply to meeting the ICWA's preference requirements (25 U.S.C. §1915 (2008)), also govern the determination of good cause? See In re Adoption of Sara J., 123 P.3d 1017 (Alaska 2005). Did the *Baby Boy C.* correctly reject the EIF exception? Most courts have done so. See *Baby Boy C.*, 805 N.Y.S. 2d at 322 n.4 (listing states). Why do some courts reason that, without the exception, the ICWA would be unconstitutional? Compare In re Santos Y., 112 Cal. Rptr. 2d 692 (Ct. App. 2001), with Hoots v. K.B., 663 N.W.2d 625 (N.D. 2003). See also In re A.W., 741 N.W.2d 793 (Iowa 2007). For critiques of the judge-made EIF exception, see, e.g., Atwood, supra; Goldberg, supra, at 1380-1388. Although *Baby Boy C.* rejects the argument that the tribe may intervene as a matter of right, other courts have held that the ICWA gives tribes independent standing to challenge adoptions of Native American children voluntarily relinquished by their parents. See In re Phillip A.C., 149 P.3d 51 (Nev. 2006). The Alaska supreme court has ruled that Native American villages can sue state officials for damages under 42 U.S.C. §1983 for violations of the ICWA and the Adoption

Assistance and Child Welfare Act. State Dept. of Health v. Native Village of Curyung, 151 P.3d 388 (Alaska 2007).

6. *Classifying: criticisms.* The controversy over the EIF reveals a larger problem about classifications in adoptive placement. The ICWA defines "Indian child" as "any unmarried person who is under age eighteen and is either (a) a member of an Indian tribe or (b) is eligible for membership in an Indian tribe and is the biological child of a member of an Indian tribe." 25 U.S.C. §1903(4) (2000). Does this definition promote the ICWA's goals? Optimize child placements?

To the extent that race plays a role in adoptive placements, what families provide a good "match" for children of mixed race? See Moran, supra, at 139-140; Jane Maslow Cohen, Race-Based Adoption in a Post-*Loving* Frame, 6 B.U. Pub. Int. L.J. 653 (1997); Jennifer L. Rosato, "A Color of Their Own": Multiracial Children and the Family, 36 Brandeis J. Fam. L. 41 (1997-1998). Professor Ruth-Arlene W. Howe predicts that eliminating consideration of race will actually increase discrimination:

> Elimination of race from all placement decisionmaking sets the stage for reinforcing old prejudices and discriminatory practices toward African Americans and for anachronistic recommodification of *young* African American children, without providing any strong assurance that the needs of such children will be met appropriately. Instead, white adults seeking healthy infants now have an opportunity to "garner the market" on the only expanding "crop" of healthy newborns—voluntarily relinquished biracial nonmarital infants (many with one black and one white parent). Prior to Interethnic Adoption Provisions, these babies would be considered black under the customary "one-drop" rule for determining race.

Ruth-Arlene W. Howe, Adoption Laws and Practices in 2000: Serving Whose Interests?, 33 Fam. L.Q. 677, 684-685 (1999).

7. *Religious matching.* How should the law classify children for purposes of religious matching? What problems does this practice pose? New York law includes a preference for placing children with caregivers of the same religion. N.Y. Soc. Serv. Law §373 (2008). In *Baby Boy C.*, the lower court noted the Tribe's argument that Jewish law would not recognize the child as Jewish, despite his Jewish birth father, given the mother's identity. 784 N.Y.S.2d 334, 337 (Fam. Ct. 2004).

8. *Parental autonomy.* What weight should the law give to birth parents' preferences in adoptive placements? For example, in *Baby Boy C.*, the birth mother consented to the child's adoption by Joshua and Jeffrey, stating "I . . . approve and agree that the child be brought up in the Jewish faith." 784 N.Y.S.2d at 336. See also Ark. Code Ann. §9-9-102 (2008) (directing courts to honor genetic parents' religious preferences for placement, if possible); Mass. Gen. Laws Ann. ch. 210, §5B (2008) (directing courts to honor parents' religious designation of child, unless inconsistent with best interests). What constitutional issues do these laws raise?

Should the policies of the ICWA give way to birth parents' autonomy? How does Mississippi Band of Choctaw Indians v. Holyfield, 490 U.S. 30 (1989), summarized in *Baby Boy C.*, resolve this issue? For the story behind *Holyfield* and information about the aftermath, see Maldonado, supra. See also see Cherokee Nation v. Nomura, 160 P.3d 967 (Okla. 2007) (applying Oklahoma's Indian Child Welfare Act to hold that protection of tribal interests trumps birth parents' autonomy in choosing an out-of-state non-Indian placement); Perry, Transracial and International Adoption, supra, at 150-151 (feminists must address conflict between parental autonomy and argument for deference to ethnic groups' desires for intra-ethnic placement).

Professor Richard Banks argues that, even without state race-matching policies, accommodating adoptive parents' race-based preferences makes the state complicit in discrimination. R. Richard Banks, The Color of Desire: Fulfilling Adoptive Parents' Racial Preferences through Discriminatory State Action, 107 Yale L.J. 875 (1998). Cf. Fogg-Davis, supra, at 74-92. Should (must?) the state ignore such preferences when placing children?

As an alternative to Professor Banks's proposal, consider Professor Solangel Maldonado's approach to discouraging race-based preferences in adoption. She recommends a statute along the following lines:

> . . . To deter United States citizens from adopting internationally for race-based reasons and to encourage United States citizens to adopt U.S.-born children, agencies are required to wait one year before processing United States citizens' applications to adopt internationally unless the applicants show that (1) they have sought to adopt a U.S.-born child of similar age, health status, sex, etc., without regard to race, but have been unsuccessful, or (2) they rebut the presumption that their reasons for seeking to adopt internationally are race-based.

> Foreign adoptees' entry into the United States would be contingent on their parents' compliance with the statute. . . .

Solangel Maldonado, Discouraging Racial Preferences in Adoptions, 39 U.C. Davis L. Rev. 1415, 1472-1473 (2006). Evaluate this proposal.

## Depictions in Popular Culture: Losing Isaiah (1985)

After unmarried and drug-addicted African-American Khalia Richards (Halle Berry) abandons her infant during winter in a garbage dump, hospital-based social worker Margaret Lewin (Jessica Lange) bonds with the child, who had been rescued by garbage collectors after they heard a cry. The child, Isaiah, experiences withdrawal from his own drug addiction acquired during Khalia's pregnancy and comes to live with Margaret, her husband, and teenage daughter, Hannah — all Caucasians. In the meantime, Khalia, haunted by fears that she must have caused Isaiah's death, is arrested, and she begins a long struggle to rehabilitate herself, through work as a nanny, reading instruction, and counseling. Her counselor, an African-American woman who has overcome her own past substance abuse, investigates Khalia's reluctantly recounted story of Isaiah's abandonment and presumed death only to discover his completed adoption by the Lewin family.

Khalia finds an attorney who will sue to overturn the adoption, based on inadequate notice of the TPR, because the case is "socially relevant." He later explains to Khalia, "This goes way beyond you. Black babies belong with Black mothers." Even the Lewins' African-American attorney remarks on the complexity of transracial adoption: "You might raise a Black child with the best intentions in the world, color-blind, but in the end the world is still out there. He needs to know who he is." To bring the point home, in the next scene the hands of Hannah and Isaiah meet while the two are playing; Hannah asks what is different about their hands; and Isaiah responds: "My hand's smaller."

Having left behind her old life and living arrangement with another addicted mother, a very well-groomed and determined Khalia goes to court, and—after several witnesses take the stand—the judge rules in Khalia's favor, overturning the adoption. Devastated, the Lewins must hand over a screaming Isaiah to a social worker who brings him to Khalia. Isaiah's transition to his new life proves excruciatingly difficult. Finally, Khalia, distraught by his pain and unmistakable longing for Margaret, asks her to help. Because Khalia loves Isaiah, she wants him to live with the Lewins "till he can understand all this." She explains to Margaret, "You might not like me but you're going to have to deal with me."

What stereotypes does this film bring to life? Promotional materials feature the question: "Who Decides What Makes a Mother?" How does the film answer this question? Note that the denouement, entailing a cooperative effort by Khalia and Margaret, resembles the suggestions for postadoption visitation by birth parents proposed by Professor Garrison and Professor Meyer (see Chapter 2, sections A & B2). What message does the denouement send? Is this resolution a "happy ending"? Why?

Note that another tale of a disputed adoption in popular culture ends in a similar fashion. In Barbara Kingsolver's pair of novels, *The Bean Trees* (1988) and *Pigs in Heaven* (1993), a non-Indian woman, Taylor Greer, traveling across the country finds a child foisted into her care. She rears the child, who becomes attached to her, but subsequent publicity reveals the child's Cherokee identity. Pursuant to the ICWA, the child's Cherokee grandfather is appointed her legal guardian, but he must share custody with Taylor. Is such shared parenting a fairy tale? Or a realistic solution to an otherwise intractable problem? What does the allure of this ending suggest?

## PROBLEM

Most states require that older children, typically those age 14 and above, consent to adoption. See, e.g., Hefner v. Hefner, 859 N.E.2d 388 (Ind. Ct. App. 2006); James G. Dwyer, The Relationship Rights of Children 36 (2006).

Suppose Max, an African-American who is ten years old and has a history of "acting out" in several foster placements with Caucasian families, insists that he wants to be adopted only by a married African-American couple. What weight *may* the state social services agency give to Max's preference? See Elizabeth Bartholet, Commentary, supra, at 319. What weight *should* such expressed preferences receive? See generally American Bar Association Child Custody and Adoption Pro Bono Project, Hearing Children's Voices and Interests in Adoption and Guardianship Proceedings, 41 Fam. L.Q. 385 (2007).

### b. Sexual Orientation

LOFTON V. SECRETARY OF THE DEPARTMENT OF
CHILDREN AND FAMILY SERVICES

358 F.3d 804 (11th Cir. 2004), cert. denied, 543 U.S. 1081 (2005)

BIRCH, Circuit Judge

In this appeal, we decide the states' rights issue of whether Florida Statute §63.042(3), which prevents adoption by practicing homosexuals, is constitutional. . . . For purposes of this statute, Florida courts have defined the term "homosexual" as being "limited to applicants who are known to engage in current, voluntary homosexual activity," thus drawing "a distinction between homosexual orientation and homosexual activity." During the past twelve years, several legislative bills [and court challenges have failed to overturn the provision, which was enacted in 1977.]

Six plaintiffs-appellants bring this case. The first, Steven Lofton, is a registered pediatric nurse who has raised from infancy three Florida foster children, each of whom tested positive for HIV at birth. By all accounts, Lofton's efforts in caring for these children have been exemplary, and his story has been chronicled in dozens of news stories and editorials as well as on national television. . . .

John Doe, also named as a plaintiff-appellant in this litigation, was born on 29 April 1991. Testing positive at birth for HIV and cocaine, Doe immediately entered the Florida foster care system. Shortly thereafter, Children's Home Society, a private agency, placed Doe in foster care with Lofton, who has extensive experience treating HIV patients. At eighteen months, Doe seroreverted and has since tested HIV negative. In September of 1994, Lofton filed an application to adopt Doe but refused to answer the application's inquiry about his sexual preference and also failed to disclose Roger Croteau, his cohabitating partner, as a member of his household. After Lofton refused requests from the Department of Children and Families ("DCF") to supply the missing information, his application was rejected pursuant to the homosexual adoption provision. [In 1997,] in light of the length of Doe's stay in Lofton's household, DCF offered Lofton the compromise of becoming Doe's legal guardian. This arrangement would have allowed Doe to leave the foster care system and DCF supervision. However, because it would have cost Lofton over $300 a month in lost foster care subsidies and would have jeopardized Doe's Medicaid coverage, Lofton declined the guardianship option unless it was an interim stage toward adoption. Under Florida law, DCF could not accommodate this condition, and the present [constitutional challenge] ensued. . . .

### B.   Florida's Adoption Scheme

. . . Under Florida law, "adoption is not a right; it is a statutory privilege." Unlike biological parentage, which precedes and transcends formal recognition by the state, adoption is wholly a creature of the state.

In formulating its adoption policies and procedures, the State of Florida acts in the protective and provisional role of *in loco parentis* for those children who, because of various circumstances, have become wards of the state. Thus, adoption law is unlike criminal law, for example, where the paramount substantive concern is not intruding on individuals' liberty interests, see, e.g., [Lawrence v. Texas, 539 U.S. 558 (2003)]; Roe v. Wade, 410 U.S. 113 (1973), and the paramount procedural imperative is ensuring due process and fairness. . . . Because of the primacy of the welfare of the child, the state can make classifications for adoption purposes that would be constitutionally suspect in many other arenas. For example, [in] screening adoption applicants, Florida considers such factors as physical and mental health, income and financial status, duration of marriage, housing, and neighborhood, among others. . . .

The decision to adopt a child is not a private one, but a public act. [A] person who seeks to adopt is asking the state to conduct an examination into his or her background and to make a determination as to the best interests of a child in need of adoption. In doing so, the state's overriding interest is not providing individuals the opportunity to become parents, but rather identifying those individuals whom it deems most capable of parenting adoptive children and providing them with a secure family environment. . . .

### C.   Appellants' Due Process Challenges

#### 1.   Fundamental Right to "Family Integrity"

Neither party disputes that there is no fundamental right to adopt, nor any fundamental right to be adopted. . . . Nevertheless, appellants argue that, by prohibiting homosexual adoption, the state is refusing to recognize and protect constitutionally protected parent-child relationships between Lofton and Doe. . . . Only by being given the opportunity to adopt, appellants assert, will they be able to protect their alleged right to "family integrity."

[Appellants] seize on a few lines of dicta from [Smith v. Organization of Foster Families for Equality and Reform, 431 U.S. 816 (1977),] in which the Court acknowledged that "biological relationships are not [the] exclusive determination of the existence of a family," [id. at 842,] and noted that "adoption, for instance, is recognized as the legal equivalent of biological parenthood," id. at 844 n.51. Extrapolating from *Smith*, appellants argue that parental and familial rights should be extended to individuals such as foster parents and legal guardians and that the touchstone of this liberty interest is not biological ties or official legal recognition, but the emotional bond that develops between and among individuals as a result of shared daily life.

We do not read *Smith* so broadly. . . . The emotional connections between Lofton and his foster child . . . originate in arrangements that have been subject to state oversight from the outset. We conclude that Lofton [and the other appellants] could have no justifiable expectation of permanency in their relationships. Nor could [they] have developed expectations that they would be allowed to adopt, in light of the adoption provision itself. . . .

### 2.   Fundamental Right to "Private Sexual Intimacy"

. . . Appellants argue that the Supreme Court's recent decision in Lawrence v. Texas, 539 U.S. 558 (2003), which struck down Texas's sodomy statute, identified a hitherto unarticulated fundamental right to private sexual intimacy. They contend that the Florida statute, by disallowing adoption to any individual who chooses to engage in homosexual conduct, impermissibly burdens the exercise of this right.

. . . *Lawrence*'s holding was that substantive due process does not permit a state to impose a criminal prohibition on private consensual homosexual conduct. The effect of this holding was to establish a greater respect than previously existed in the law for the right of consenting adults to engage in private sexual conduct. Nowhere, however, did the Court characterize this right as "fundamental" [or apply strict scrutiny.] We are particularly hesitant to infer a new fundamental liberty interest from an opinion whose language and reasoning are inconsistent with standard fundamental-rights analysis. [The court also distinguishes *Lawrence* because adoption involves minors and entails official recognition, not private, consensual, adult conduct.]

### D.   Appellants' Equal Protection Challenge

[Finding neither a fundamental right nor a suspect class,] we review the Florida statute under the rational-basis standard. . . . Florida contends that the statute is only one aspect of its broader adoption policy, which is designed to create adoptive homes that resemble the nuclear family as closely as possible. Florida argues that the statute is rationally related to Florida's interest in furthering the best interests of adopted children by placing them in families with married mothers and fathers. Such homes, Florida asserts, provide the stability that marriage affords and the presence of both male and female authority figures, which it considers critical to optimal childhood development and socialization. In particular, Florida emphasizes a vital role that dual-gender parenting plays in shaping sexual and gender identity and in providing heterosexual role modeling. . . .

. . . Florida argues that its preference for adoptive marital families is based on the premise that the marital family structure is more stable than other household arrangements and that children benefit from the presence of both a father and mother in the home. Given that appellants have offered no competent evidence to the contrary, we find this premise to be one of those "unprovable assumptions" that nevertheless can provide a legitimate basis for legislative action. Paris Adult Theatre I v. Slaton, 413 U.S. 49, 62-63

(1973). Although social theorists from Plato to Simone de Beauvoir have pro-posed alternative child-rearing arrangements, none has proven as enduring as the marital family structure, nor has the accumulated wisdom of several mil-lennia of human experience discovered a superior model. See, e.g., Plato, The Republic, Bk. V, 459d-461e; Simone de Beauvoir, The Second Sex (H. M. Parshley trans., Vintage Books 1989) (1949). . . .

. . . Arguing that the statute is both overinclusive and underinclusive, appellants contend that the real motivation behind the statute cannot be the best interest of adoptive children. . . . Appellants note that Florida law permits adoption by unmarried individuals and that, among children coming out [of] the Florida foster care system, 25% of adoptions are to parents who are currently single. . . .

. . . The Florida legislature could rationally conclude that homosexuals and heterosexual singles are not "similarly situated in relevant respects." It is not irrational to think that heterosexual singles have a markedly greater probabil-ity of eventually establishing a married household and, thus, providing their adopted children with a stable, dual-gender parenting environment. More-over, as the state noted, the legislature could rationally act on the theory that heterosexual singles, even if they never marry, are better positioned than homosexual individuals to provide adopted children with education and guidance relative to their sexual development throughout pubescence and adolescence. . . ."

Appellants make much of the fact that Florida has over three thousand children who are currently in foster care and, consequently, have not been placed with permanent adoptive families. According to appellants, because excluding homosexuals from the pool of prospective adoptive parents will not create more eligible married couples to reduce the backlog, it is impossible for the legislature to believe that the statute advances the state's interest in placing children with married couples.

. . . Appellants misconstrue Florida's interest, which is not simply to place children in a permanent home as quickly as possible, but, when placing them, to do so in an optimal home, i.e., one in which there is a heterosexual couple or the potential for one. According to appellants' logic, every restriction on adoptive-parent candidates, such as income, instate residency, and criminal record — none of which creates more available married couples — are likewise constitutionally suspect as long as Florida has a backlog of unadopted foster children. The best interests of children, however, are not automatically served by adoption into *any* available home merely because it is permanent. . . .

Noting that Florida law permits homosexuals to become foster parents and permanent guardians, appellants contend that this fact demonstrates that Florida must not truly believe that placement in a homosexual household is not in a child's best interests. . . . Foster care and legal guardianship are designed to address a different situation than permanent adoption, and "the legislature must be allowed leeway to approach a perceived problem incrementally." . . .

Appellants cite recent social science research and the opinion of mental health professionals and child welfare organizations as evidence that there is no child welfare basis for excluding homosexuals from adopting.[23] . . . In considering appellants' argument, we must ask not whether the latest in social science research and professional opinion *support* the decision of the Florida legislature, but whether that evidence is so well established and so far beyond dispute that it would be irrational for the Florida legislature to believe that the interests of its children are best served by not permitting homosexual adoption. Also, we must credit any conceivable rational reason that the legislature might have for choosing not to alter its statutory scheme in response to this recent social science research. We must assume, for example, that the legislature might be aware of the critiques of the studies cited by appellants — critiques that have highlighted significant flaws in the studies' methodologies and conclusions, such as the use of small, self-selected samples; reliance on self-report instruments; politically driven hypotheses; and the use of unrepresentative study populations consisting of disproportionately affluent, educated parents.[24] Alternatively, the legislature might consider and credit other studies that have found that children raised in homosexual households fare differently on a number of measures, doing worse on some of them, than children raised in similarly situated heterosexual households.[25] Or the legislature might consider, and even credit, the research cited by appellants, but find it premature to rely on a very recent and still developing body of research, particularly in light of the absence of longitudinal studies following child subjects into adulthood and of studies of adopted, rather than natural, children of homosexual parents.[26]

We do not find any of these possible legislative responses to be irrational. Openly homosexual households represent a very recent phenomenon, and sufficient time has not yet passed to permit any scientific study of how children raised in those households fare as adults. [I]t is hardly surprising that the question of the effects of homosexual parenting on childhood development is

---

23. For the sake of simplicity, our discussion here will attribute to appellants not only their own arguments but also the arguments made in the amicus brief filed jointly on their behalf by the Child Welfare League of America, Children's Rights, Inc., the Evan B. Donaldson Adoption Institute, and the National Center for Youth Law.

24. See e.g., D. Baumrind, Commentary on Sexual Orientation: Research and Social Policy Implications, 31 Developmental Psychol. 130 (No. 1, 1995) (reviewing various studies and questioning them on "theoretical and empirical grounds" because of flaws such as small sample sizes, reliance on self-report instruments, and self-selected, unrepresentative study populations); R. Lerner & A. K. Nagai, No Basis: What the Studies Don't Tell Us About Same-Sex Parenting, Marriage Law Project (Jan. 2001) (reviewing forty-nine studies on same-sex parenting and finding recurring methodological flaws, including failure to use testable hypotheses, lack of control methods, unrepresentative study populations, self-selected sample groups, and use of negative hypotheses); J. Stacey & T. Biblarz, (How) Does the Sexual Orientation of Parents Matter, 66 Am. Soc. Rev. 159, 166 (2001) (reviewing 21 studies and finding various methodological flaws, leading authors to conclude that "there are no studies of child development based on random, representative samples" of same-sex households).

25. See, e.g., K. Cameron & P. Cameron, Homosexual Parents, 31 Adolescence 757, 770-774 (1996) (reporting study findings that children raised by homosexual parents suffer from disproportionately high incidence of emotional disturbance and sexual victimization); Stacey & Biblarz, supra, at 170 (concluding, based on study results, that "parental sexual orientation is positively associated with the possibility that children will attain a similar orientation, and theory and common sense also support such a view").

26. We also note Justice Cordy's extensive, and persuasive, discussion of the currently available body of research on the question of homosexual parenting in his dissenting opinion in Goodridge v. Dep't of Health, 798 N.E.2d 941 (Mass. Nov. 18. 2003). . . .

one on which even experts of good faith reasonably disagree. Given this state of affairs, it is not irrational for the Florida legislature to credit one side of the debate over the other. Nor is it irrational for the legislature to proceed with deliberate caution. . . .

### III.  Conclusion

. . . The State of Florida has made the determination that it is not in the best interests of its displaced children to be adopted by individuals who "engage in current, voluntary homosexual activity," [Department of Health & Rehab. Servs. v. Cox, 627 So. 2d 1210, 1215 (Fla. Dist. Ct. App. 1993)], and we have found nothing in the Constitution that forbids this policy judgment. Thus, any argument that the Florida legislature was misguided in its decision is one of legislative policy, not constitutional law. The legislature is the proper forum for this debate, and we do not sit as a superlegislature "to award by judicial decree what was not achievable by political consensus." . . .

## NOTES AND QUESTIONS

1. *Background and epilogue.* Lofton, Croteau, and their five foster children moved to Portland, Oregon. All five tested HIV-positive at the time of placement, as did another child who died of AIDS complications. The three eldest children remained under the supervision of Florida, which made the initial foster placements and which requested Lofton quit his job to stay home with the children. (He did so.) The dispute in the principal case arose when Bert ("John Doe") seroconverted to HIV-negative, in turn becoming "adoptable." Florida continued to look for an adoptive home for Bert, who had lived with Lofton and Croteau since placement as an infant in 1991. See Fred A. Bernstein, Married or Not, It's a Full House, N.Y. Times, Nov. 20, 2003, §F, at 1.

Despite *Lofton,* some Florida state courts have declared unconstitutional the statute barring adoption by gays and lesbians. See In re Adoption of Doe, 34 Fam. L. Rep. 1531 (BNA) (Sept. 30, 2008) (summarizing case, which struck down the law as an unconstitutional bill of attainder and special law and a violation of separation of powers); In re Adoption of Doe, 2008 WL 5006172 (Fla. Cir. Ct. 2008) (invoking expert testimony and goals of Florida's child welfare policy to hold the law violates equal protection without serving any rational basis).

2. *State restrictions.* Adoption by gays and lesbians has emerged as "a second front in the culture wars." Andrea Stone, Drives to Ban Gay Adoption Heat Up; In 16 States Laws or Ballot Votes Proposed, USA Today, Feb. 21, 2006, at 1A. Although several states explicitly permit adoptions without regard to sexual orientation (as shown by the authorization of second-parent adoptions, examined Chapter 4, section B), by early 2006, 16 states had taken steps to impose restrictions on adoptions by gays and lesbians through legislation or ballot initiatives. Stone, supra. In 2008, citizens of Arkansas voted by ballot initiative to prevent cohabiting but unmarried couples from adopting children or providing foster care, in turn prompting a challenge by the American Civil Liberties Union. See Associated Press, Arkansas: Adoption Law Is Challenged, N.Y. Times, Dec. 31, 2008, at A16. Utah has long had a similar law, which

prohibits adoption by a person cohabiting with another but not in a valid marriage and expresses a preference for placement with married couples, subject to certain exceptions. Utah Code Ann. §78B-6-117(3) & (4) (2008). See also Chapter 5, section B (exploring Oklahoma's statutory ban on recognition of other states' adoption decrees to same-sex couples).

To what extent do restrictions such as those upheld in *Lofton* provide a modern illustration of the thesis advanced by Berebitsky, supra, that adoption provides a template for the normative family? Cf. id. at 172-176 (adoption's radical potential to challenge conventional family realized by "the creation of families across the boundaries of race and sexuality"). For a critique of these restrictive laws, see Carlos A. Ball, The Immorality of Statutory Restrictions on Adoption by Lesbians and Gay Men, 38 Loy. U. Chi. L.J. 379 (2007). A symposium, *Lofton* and the Future of Gay and Lesbian Adoption, appears in 18 St. Thomas L. Rev. 207-691 (2005).

In contrast to Florida's approach, at least twelve jurisdictions reportedly have laws explicitly prohibiting reliance on sexual orientation to prevent adoptions. These states are California, Connecticut, the District of Columbia, Illinois, Indiana, Maryland, Massachusetts, Nevada, New Jersey, New York, Pennsylvania, and Vermont. Angeline Acain, Equal Rights: Anti-Gay Laws Hurt Adoption Advances, Myrtle Beach Sun News, June 3, 2007, at D5. But see Conn. Gen. Stat. §45a-726a (2008) (permitting consideration of sexual orientation in adoption, notwithstanding antidiscrimination provisions). According to the attorney general of Tennessee, state law does not prohibit adoption by a same-sex couple. Opinion No. 07-140, Tenn. Atty. Gen., Oct. 10, 2007, 2007 Tenn. AG LEXIS 140. The same result obtains in Maine, by judicial decision. See Adoption of M.A., 930 A.2d 1088 (Me. 2007). State Senate bill 200, which would have permitted gays and lesbians to adopt in Florida under some circumstances, died in committee on May 2, 2008. Florida Legislature—Regular Session—2008: History of Senate Bills 10 (2008), available at http://www.flsenate.gov/data/session/2008/citator/Daily/senhist.pdf.

3. *Lofton's precedents.* In Bowers v. Hardwick, 478 U.S. 186 (1986), the United States Supreme Court rejected a constitutional challenge to Georgia's criminal sodomy statute. Michael Hardwick, asserting that he was "a practicing homosexual," had sued after being arrested in his bedroom while engaged in consensual sex with another male. He argued that the law and its enforcement violated his constitutional right to privacy, which the Court had previously recognized in a number of cases concerning contraception, abortion, and family decisionmaking, usually under the Fourteenth Amendment's Due Process Clause. A majority of the Court rejected his arguments, stating:

> [W]e think it evident that none of the rights announced in those [earlier] cases bears any resemblance to the claimed constitutional right of homosexuals to engage in acts of sodomy that is asserted in this case. No connection between family, marriage, or procreation on the one hand and homosexual activity on the other has been demonstrated. . . .

Id. at 190-191. The majority went on to apply rational basis review to the statute, deciding that deference to the moral values of Georgia's citizens (as reflected in the actions of their elected representatives) satisfied the test.

In Lawrence v. Texas, 539 U.S. 558 (2003), a majority of the Justices overruled *Bowers*, announcing that "*Bowers* was not correct when it was decided, and it is not correct today." Id. at 577. The Court did not rely on the right to privacy in this challenge to a Texas statute criminalizing same-sex sodomy and enforced in this case after officers, responding to a weapons disturbance, reportedly found two men engaged in the prohibited conduct in a bedroom. Rather, the Court invoked the Fourteenth Amendment Due Process Clause's protection for liberty and autonomy, while also emphasizing the discrimination and stigma of the challenged statute, which singles out same-sex activity for punishment. See generally, e.g., Pamela Karlen, Foreword: Loving *Lawrence*, 102 Mich. L. Rev. 1447, 1449 (2004); Laurence H. Tribe, essay, Lawrence v. Texas: The "Fundamental Right" That Dare Not Speak Its Name, 117 Harv. L. Rev. 1893, 1911 (2004). Without identifying the applicable standard of review, the majority stated that the statute "furthers no legitimate state interest, which can justify its intrusion into the personal and private life of the individual." 539 U.S. at 578.

The majority also suggested, however, limits to its ruling:

> The present case does not involve minors. It does not involve persons who might be injured or coerced or who are situated in relationships where consent might not easily be refused. It does not involve public conduct or prostitution. It does not involve whether the government must give formal recognition to any relationship that homosexual persons seek to enter. The case does involve two adults who, with full and mutual consent from each other, engaged in sexual practices common to a homosexual lifestyle. The petitioners are entitled to respect for their private lives. The State cannot demean their existence or control their destiny by making their private sexual conduct a crime. Their right to liberty under the Due Process Clause gives them the full right to engage in their conduct without intervention of the government.

Id.

Justice O'Connor wrote a separate concurring opinion, which would find the law unconstitutional as a violation of the Fourteenth Amendment's Equal Protection Clause (because the law punished sodomy only when the participants were of the same sex). In a dissent joined by Chief Justice Rehnquist and Justice Thomas, Justice Scalia asserted that the majority's overruling of *Bowers* "effectively decrees the end of all morals legislation," including "criminal laws against fornication, bigamy, adultery, adult incest, bestiality, and obscenity." Id. at 599 (Scalia, J., dissenting). Further, according to Justice Scalia, the equal protection challenge, if successful, would doom laws denying access to marriage by same-sex couples. Id. at 599-600.

Just months after *Lawrence*, the Supreme Judicial Court of Massachusetts invoked the state constitution's protection of liberty and equality to invalidate state laws denying to same-sex couples marriage's many benefits. Goodridge v. Department of Pub. Health, 798 N.E.2d 941 (Mass. 2003). Among the reasons given, the court noted that the law unfairly penalized the children being raised by same-sex couples who could not marry. In a subsequent ruling, the court decided that only access to marriage (not a "second-class" alternative, such as civil unions) would remedy the constitutional violation. Opinion of the Justices to the Senate, 802 N.E.2d 565 (Mass. 2004).

California's supreme court followed with a similar ruling, finding inadequate the state's domestic partnership law. In re Marriage Cases, 183 P.3d 384 (Cal. 2008). Similarly, same-sex marriage became available in Connecticut, after the supreme court ruled in October 2008 that the state had failed to justify its two-track system, marriage for male-female couples and civil unions for same-sex couples. Kerrigan v. Commissioner of Pub. Health, 957 A.2d 407 (Conn. 2008).

The volatile and divisive character of the issue persists, however. Even before *Lawrence, Goodridge,* and the later cases, Congress enacted the federal Defense of Marriage Act, limiting the federal definition of marriage to male-female couples and stating that one state need not recognize a same-sex marriage celebrated in another state. 1 U.S.C. §7, 28 U.S.C. §1738C (2008). In addition, many states have enacted statutes or amended their constitutions to ban same-sex marriage, while a few have provided for marriage-like regimes through laws governing domestic partnerships or civil unions. Christine Vestal, Gay Marriage Ripe for Decision in 3 States, available at http://www.stateline.org/live/ViewPage.action?siteNodeId=136&languageId=1&contentId=20695 (updated June 15, 2007). Several courts rejected challenges to marriage restrictions. E.g., Conaway v. Deane, 932 A.2d 571 (Md. 2007); Lewis v. Harris, 908 A.2d 196 (N.J. 2006); Hernandez v. Robles, 855 N.E.2d 1 (N.Y. 2006); Andersen v. King County, 138 P.3d 963 (Wash. 2006). And on the heels of the California ruling, a majority of voters supported a ballot initiative, which the court will review, amending the state constitution to reinstate same-sex couples' exclusion from marriage. Jesse McKinley, With Same-Sex Marriage, a Court Takes on the People's Voice, N.Y. Times, Nov. 21, 2008, at A18.

In upholding Florida's ban on adoptions by gay men and lesbians, *Lofton* dismisses arguments based on the Supreme Court ruling in *Lawrence.* On what bases is *Lawrence* distinguishable? Indistinguishable? According to *Lofton,* the Florida adoption statute, as interpreted by the state courts, "draw[s] a distinction between homosexual orientation and homosexual conduct." In fact, throughout, the *Lawrence* majority opinion refers variously to "homosexual conduct," "homosexual persons," and "a homosexual lifestyle." What is the connection among these? Of what relevance to *Lofton* is the *Lawrence* majority's observation that laws targeting the sexual conduct of gay men and lesbians create a stigma and invite status-based discrimination? Does the Florida adoption statute, as interpreted by state courts, avoid this problematic effect? What does *Lawrence's* reasoning mean for the Florida adoption statute's distinction between "practicing" and celibate homosexuals? Does *Lofton's* critique of *Lawrence's* standard of review mean that *Lawrence* has no precedential value at all?

See generally, e.g., Christopher D. Jozwiak, Lofton v. Secretary of the Department of Children & Family Services: Florida's Gay Adoption Ban Under Irrational Equal Protection Analysis, 23 Law & Ineq. 407 (2005); Benjamin C. Morgan, Comment, Adopting *Lawrence*: Lawrence v. Texas and Discriminatory Adoption Laws, 53 Emory L.J. 1491 (2004); *Lofton* and the Future of Gay and Lesbian Adoption, 18 St. Thomas L. Rev. 207-691 (2005) (symposium); Note, Unfixing *Lawrence*, 118 Harv. L. Rev. 2858, 2868-2869

(2005). For a defense of *Lofton*, see Lynn D. Wardle, Preference for Marital Couple Adoption—Constitutional and Policy Reflections, 5 J.L. Fam. Stud. 345 (2003).

4. *Constitutional protections in adoption.* A number of authorities, like *Lofton*, disclaim the existence of a right to adopt. See, e.g., Griffith v. Johnston, 899 F.2d 1427, 1437 (5th Cir. 1990); Ruth-Arlene W. Howe, Adoption Laws and Practices in 2000: Serving Whose Interests?, 33 Fam. L.Q. 677, 678-679 (1999). What consequences follow from this principle? Can state actors reject adoption applications for *any* reason? Do applicants have a right to a statement of reasons for rejection or fair procedures? Would the Crumps in Crump v. Montgomery, supra, have a procedural due process argument? Does the reasoning in *Lofton* leave room for race-based matching and other placement criteria designed to find the "best" adoptive home for a child? How would the analysis change if the law recognized a child's fundamental right to adoption? See Barbara Bennett Woodhouse, Waiting for *Loving*: The Child's Fundamental Right to Adoption, 34 Cap. U. L. Rev. 297 (2005). See also Mark Strasser, Deliberate Indifference, Professional Judgment, and the Constitution: On Liberty Interests in the Child Placement Context, 15 Duke J. Gender L. & Pol'y 223 (2008).

5. *Adoption versus foster care.* Reminiscent of one of the issues in *Crump*, supra, Florida law permits gays and lesbians to serve as foster parents, even on a long-term basis, while refusing to permit them to adopt. Why? How does the court address the apparent inconsistencies in the Florida system? See John A. Robertson, Gay and Lesbian Access to Assisted Reproductive Technology, 55 Case W. Res. L. Rev. 323, 338-339 (2004). Does the Florida restriction contravene the "best interests" standard? See Lauren Schwartzreich, Restructuring the Framework for Legal Analyses of Gay Parenting, 21 Harv. BlackLetter J. 109 (2005). On the other hand, given the ongoing de facto relationship of Lofton and his children, what would be the advantages of adoption versus foster care? Recall that Florida continued to search for adoptive parents for Bert. See also Margaret F. Brinig & Steven L. Nock, How Much Does Legal Status Matter? Adoptions by Kin Caregivers, 36 Fam. L.Q. 449, 462 (2002) (finding "foster care does not compare favorably with adoption for any children").

Data show that adoptions by gay men and lesbians will significantly increase the number of homes for parentless children. See Evan B. Donaldson Adoption Institute, Expanding Resources for Waiting Children II: Eliminating Legal and Practice Barriers to Gay and Lesbian Adoption from Foster Care (2008), available at http://www.adoptioninstitute.org/publications/2008_09_Expanding_Resources_Legal.pdf (last visited Nov. 30, 2008). Without such adoptions, some of these children will have no parents at all. Allen P. Fisher, Still "Not Quite as Good as Having Your Own"? Toward a Sociology of Adoption, 29 Ann. Rev. Soc. 335, 349 (2003). One reason might be that adoption remains socially devalued among all prospective parents except gays, lesbians, and single persons. Id. at 356. See also Tanya M. Washington, Throwing Black Babies Out With the Bathwater: A Child-Centered Challenge to Same-Sex Adoption Bans, 6 Hastings Race & Poverty L.J. 1 (2009) (examining impact of such adoption restrictions on Black orphans, who are overrepresented in the child welfare system).

6. *Religious objections.* The advent of same-sex marriage in Massachusetts, the state's antidiscrimination laws, the license requirement for all adoption agencies, and the Catholic Church's opposition to adoptions by gays and lesbians (labeled "a form of violence against children") combined to spark a crisis there. Mary Szaniszlo, Holy Wars: State, Agency Mum on Church Gay-Adopt Stance, The Boston Herald, Dec. 8, 2005, news section, at 5. Ultimately, Catholic Charities stopped providing adoption services. See Dana Wilkie, Reactions to Unions Are Mixed in Mass.; In 2004, State Became First to Let Gays Wed, San Diego Union-Trib., June 30, 2008, at A-1. Should the legislature create a special exemption from the antidiscrimination laws for such religious adoption agencies? See Scott Helman, Romney Shifts Tone on Gay Adoption, Boston Globe, March 14, 2006, at A1 (Governor's proposal).

7. *Social science evidence.* Evaluate *Lofton*'s consideration of empirical studies under the rational basis test. Should the court have noted that the studies were not undertaken in the context of adoption? Even if all the existing studies find no difference in the outcomes of children reared by gay and lesbian parents and those raised by heterosexual parents, would the court have reached the same result? What does the court's analysis of the evidence say about the court's (and legislature's) understanding of the "cause" of one's sexual orientation? Does the court's analysis of the evidence assume that all children themselves are heterosexual? For reviews of the social science literature, see Carlos A. Ball, Lesbian and Gay Families: Gender Nonconformity and the Implications of Difference, 31 Cap. U. L. Rev. 691 (2003) (analyzing report of American Academy of Pediatrics finding no meaningful difference for children based on parents' orientation and essay of sociologists Stacey and Biblarz finding evidence of some differences); Fisher, supra, at 348-349 (concluding that evidence does not show harm to children of gay and lesbian parents); Charlotte Patterson, Children of Lesbian and Gay Parents: Summary of Research Findings, in Same-Sex Marriage: Pro and Con: A Reader 240 (Andrew Sullivan ed., rev. ed. 2004) (finding no appreciable difference in terms of children's gender identity, gender-role behavior, and sexual identity).

Does the application of the rational basis test necessarily mean that social science evidence cannot displace the legislature's decision? Consider the reasoning of a Florida circuit court judge in a more recent challenge to the statutory ban:

> The quality and breadth of research available, as well as the results of the studies performed about gay parenting and children of gay parents, is robust and has provided the basis for a consensus in the field. [R]eports and studies find that there are no differences in the parenting of homosexuals or the adjustment of their children. These conclusions have been accepted, adopted and ratified by the American Psychological Association, the American Psychiatry Association, the American Pediatric Association, the American Academy of Pediatrics, the Child Welfare League of America and the National Association of Social Workers. [T]his Court is satisfied that the issue is so far beyond dispute that it would be irrational to hold otherwise; the best interests of children are not preserved by prohibiting homosexual adoption.

Adoption of Doe, 2008 WL 5006172 at *20.

Can social science investigations that suggest harm successfully disentangle the impact of parental gender from the effects of stigma from a disapproving legal and social environment? See In re Marriage Cases, 183 P.3d 384, 401 (Cal. 2008). How might the analysis be informed by the Supreme Court's treatment of public disapproval and its effect on a child in the context of race discrimination (see Palmore v. Sidoti, 466 U.S. 429, 433 (1984), discussed supra section A1a)? To what extent does the *Lofton* court's concept of "harm" to children living in nontraditional family settings rest on assumptions about gender performance and role modeling? Do these assumptions, in turn, presume distinct behavior and roles for males and females? Some data assert that daughters reared by lesbian mothers are more "masculine" than those raised by heterosexual parents. See Philip A. Belcastro et al., A Review of Data Based Studies Addressing the Effects of Homosexual Parenting on Children's Sexual and Social Functioning, in Same-Sex Marriage, supra, at 250, 253. See also David K. Flaks et al., Lesbians Choosing Motherhood: A Comparative Study of Lesbian and Heterosexual Parents and Their Children, in Same-Sex Marriage, supra, at 246, 248 (noting more effective parenting skills in lesbian couples, compared to other families, probably because of gender differences, rather then sexual orientation). Can this basis for prohibiting adoptions by gays and lesbians survive challenge under the Supreme Court precedents that find equal protection violations in official role assignments resting on gender stereotypes? See Chapter 1, section B1a. See also Kari E. Hong, Parens Patri[archy]: Adoption, Eugenics, and Same-Sex Couples, 40 Cal. W. L. Rev. 1 (2003). Consider a gay adoptive father's account of how he addressed some "role model" questions raised by his young son, as recounted in the excerpt below:

DAN SAVAGE, THE COMMITMENT: LOVE, SEX,
MARRIAGE, AND MY FAMILY (2005)

---

236-238

. . . D.J. [age 6] woke up in the middle of the night with an earache. . . . I got some Children's Tylenol into D.J., and we curled up together on the couch in the living room waiting for the medicine to do its job. It was three in the morning on a Sunday. . . .

"I want to be gay with Joshua [the child's best friend] when I grow up," D.J. suddenly said. It was a radical change of topic, but it wasn't a bolt from the blue. . . .

It was one of those through-the-looking-glass moments unique to gay parents, like the moment we saw our names on our adopted child's birth certificate on the lines marked "mother" and "father." I didn't want to tell D.J. he *couldn't* be gay when he grew up, but I didn't believe he was going to be gay when he grew up. It would be misleading to present gayness and straightness to him as an "either/or" proposition. Telling him he would be one or the other, gay or straight, would give the false impression that sexual orientation was a coin toss.

But the odds weren't fifty/fifty; the odds were so clearly stacked in favor of D.J. being straight that I almost told him he wouldn't be gay. . . . But on the off chance that he wasn't going to be straight, I starting naming all the couples we knew, gay and straight, and D.J. joined in. . . .

"Most of the men we know are with. . . . ?" I asked.

"Girls," D.J. said.

"That's because most men wind up falling in love with women when they grow up, and most women wind up falling in love with men. Those kind of men are called 'straight.' Men who fall in love with men, like me and Daddy, are called 'gay.' "

"Am I going to be gay?"

"I don't know, but probably not," I said. "Most men aren't gay. You could be gay when you grow up, but it's much more likely that you're going to be straight like Uncle Bill or Uncle Eddie or Tim or Brad or Barak."

"But I want to be gay like you and Daddy."

Ah, I thought, somewhere a fundamentalist Christian's heart is breaking. This is precisely what they worry about, they insist, when they condemn gay parents. Our kids will want to be gay, they will emulate their parents, and adopt their sexuality. If you believe — against all the evidence — that sexuality is a matter of choice, it may be a rational fear. But sexuality isn't a matter of choice, it's an inborn trait, and D.J. could no more choose to be gay, like his parents, than I could choose to be straight, like mine.

"It's not a decision you get to make," I said. "It's not a decision I got to make. It's a decision your heart makes."

"When?"

"When you're older," I said. "One day your heart will let you know whether you're going to be the kind of man who falls in love with a woman or a man." . . .

## PROBLEMS

1. Megan relinquishes her son for adoption. Subsequently, she marries and then two years after the relinquishment and a series of foster home placements for her son, she learns (through media publicity) about the state agency's placement of her son with a gay male couple for prospective adoption. Megan describes this placement as her "worst nightmare." Should the court allow Megan to revoke her consent, now that the gay couple is petitioning to adopt? If not, should it allow her and her husband also to petition to adopt the child, enabling the court to consider the two available adoptive placements? See In re Dependency of G.C.B., 870 P.2d 1037 (Wash. Ct. App.), *review denied*, 881 P.2d 254 (Wash. 1994); Shannon E. Phillips, Note, Preventing Bidding Wars in Washington Adoptions: The Need for Statutory Reform After In re Dependency of G.C.B., 70 Wash. L. Rev. 277 (1995). Cf. Avery v. Department of Soc. & Health Servs., 78 P.3d 634 (Wash. 2003).

2. Christine knowingly relinquished her baby for adoption by a same-sex couple. Under state statutes, the biological parent can select the adoptive parents so long as a court determines the placement serves the child's best interests. During the adoption proceedings, Christine's parents (with whom she

and the baby lived for four months after the birth) submit a competing petition to adopt the child. They argue that, despite a favorable home study for the placement Christine chose, adoption by homosexuals is not in the child's best interests. They also attack the constitutionality of the adoption statutes, arguing that (a) the Constitution requires a preference for placement with relatives, particularly those who have established a relationship with the child; (b) the absence of a statutory preference for placement with relatives in the adoption statute violates equal protection, given the relative preference in the foster care statute; and (c) the adoption statutes are unconstitutional because they permit the biological parent to select a placement to the exclusion of other biological relatives, to the detriment of the child. Are these arguments persuasive? See In re Adoption of M.J.S., 44 S.W.3d 41 (Tenn. Ct. App. 2000). See also In re Petition to Adopt T.L.A., 677 N.W.2d 428 (Minn. Ct. App. 2004).

3. Some scholars propose that states screen and license *all* parents, not only those who take children into their homes through adoption and foster care. They claim that parenting entails responsibilities at least as significant as operating a motor vehicle, which requires a driver's license. See, e.g., Hugh LaFollette, Licensing Parents, 9 Phil. & Pub. Aff. 182 (1980). See also James G. Dwyer, The Relationship Rights of Children 36 (2006). With the development of long-term contraceptives for women, the means of implementing a parental licensing program exist. The program might include the same sort of home study, investigation, and evaluation required for adoptive parents. Would this program be desirable? Constitutional? If neither, what justifies parental screening and state approval for adoption? For literature supporting the idea, see Roger W. McIntire, Parenthood Training or Mandatory Birth Control: Take Your Choice, Psychology Today, Oct. 1973, at 34; Claudia Pap Mangel, Licensing Parents: How Feasible?, 22 Fam. L.Q. 17 (1988). For a counterargument, see Lawrence E. Frisch, On Licentious Licensing: A Reply to Hugh LaFollette, 11 Phil. & Pub. Aff. 173 (1982).

## 2. THE ATTORNEY'S ROLE

### Stark County Bar Association v. Hare

791 N.E.2d 966 (Ohio 2003)

Per Curiam. . . .

In April 2000, respondent [David B. Hare, an attorney since 1989,] attempted to arrange an adoption for the first time. The birth mother, whom respondent had represented in a divorce and who still owed him $2,300 in legal fees, was pregnant with twins. Respondent learned of the pregnancy at a debtor's exam in March 2000, at which time he also learned that the birth mother was unemployed and unmarried and did not intend to marry the biological father. They discussed adoption, and he advised that he would be willing to help with the arrangements.

. . . Although respondent had never done an adoption before, [the birth mother] testified that he said he had handled "a lot" of adoptions. She also testified that respondent offered to pay her for her time off work during pregnancy and for six to eight weeks after the twins' delivery, her medical bills and other expenses, and "anything" else she needed. . . .

The birth mother, who was scheduled to deliver in June 2000, agreed to have respondent arrange the adoption of her unborn children. Between April and June of that year, respondent issued eight checks totaling $2,889 for the birth mother's use [which she applied] to rental payments, a motor vehicle inspection, a daughter's trip to Washington, D.C., and [other] expenses. . . . Respondent disputed the birth mother's testimony, insisting that as far as he knew all of these checks had been issued to the birth mother to pay for medical expenses. . . .

On April 28, 2000, respondent interviewed a couple who wanted to adopt the twins. He demanded a $1,500 nonrefundable retainer to pay for their interview and advised that the twins' adoptions would cost $50,000. Respondent decided to charge this amount because he knew parents who had adopted one child from a foreign country, and they had paid $25,000 in legal fees. The couple agreed to proceed, and respondent interviewed them about their background. Three days later, respondent selected the couple as the prospective adoptive parents.

Respondent told the prospective adoptive parents that in addition to the $50,000 legal fee, they would also have to pay $10,000 for the birth mother's medical expenses before the births. In total, the couple paid respondent $61,500: $1,500 for the interview, $20,000 on May 12, 2000, and $40,000 on June 19, 2000. Respondent picked up the $40,000 check himself at the couple's home, explaining that he needed the money to finish paying the bills for the adoptions.

Between April and June 2000, the birth mother, biological father, and prospective adoptive parents completed preliminary adoption requirements. During those proceedings, respondent assured the adoptive mother that although the court had concerns about her previous divorces, they would be able to complete the adoption because he was a friend of the probate judge. At some point, respondent also told the birth mother that he could no longer represent her in the adoption because of a conflict of interest [and] arranged for her representation by another attorney, telling the other attorney first that his fee would be either $134 or $143 and later that his representation would have to be on a pro bono basis . . . because the birth mother did not have any money.

The birth mother delivered the twins on June 22, 2000. On June 27, 2000, respondent filed preliminary estimated accountings in probate court that were required to disclose any disbursements of value in connection with the adoptions. Respondent, who had paid living expenses to the birth mother and had received over $60,000 from the prospective adoptive parents, represented in those filings that no such disbursements had been made. . . .

Also on June 27, 2000, respondent appeared on the adoptive parents' behalf in probate court, along with the birth mother and her counsel and the birth father, for the initial consent hearing. The court awarded temporary custody of the twins to the adoptive parents subject to a final consent hearing six months later.

Prior to the June 2000 hearing, respondent had permitted the birth mother to use a 1993 Oldsmobile that he said was worth $6,000. In July 2000, after the birth mother gave her initial consent to the adoptions, respondent transferred title of the vehicle to her. Respondent also filed a notice of satisfaction of the $2,300 judgment he had against the birth mother. The birth mother testified that respondent told her, "I let you go" on the judgment amount, which he quoted as $2,700. Respondent denied this and testified that he declared the judgment satisfied because he knew the birth mother had no assets. Thereafter, respondent stopped assisting the birth mother financially [including refusing to pay the medical bills that she submitted].

In anticipation of the final consent hearing, respondent forwarded for the birth parents' signature the final accountings for the twins' adoptions. Again, these documents did not list any disbursements for medical expenses or attorney fees. The adoptive mother asked respondent why he had omitted the $50,000 in legal fees and $10,000 in medical expenses they had paid. Respondent explained that "in a private adoption, the monies involved do not need to be disclosed." . . . The adoptive parents signed the accounts, and respondent filed them with the probate court on November 20, 2000. . . .

On December 28, 2000, at what was to be the final adoption hearing, the birth mother withdrew her consent to the adoption, citing her unpaid medical bills. She testified that she no longer trusted respondent's representations about the twins' placement. At the same hearing, the birth mother's attorney asserted a conflict of interest and withdrew.

Thereafter, the birth mother retained a third attorney, who also eventually represented the birth father. The new attorney arranged for the birth mother to become more familiar with the adoptive parents. At the birth mother's request and with the adoptive parents' consent, respondent subsequently withdrew from representing the adoptive parents. Notwithstanding this withdrawal, respondent advised the adoptive parents prior to a meeting with the birth mother and her new attorney "not to discuss money whatsoever because money in a private adoption is private."

[With a new attorney, the birth parents consented again; the adoptive parents disclosed to the court their payment to Hare; and the twins, who had been removed from the adoptive parents and placed in foster care, were returned to them. They recouped some of their money and completed the adoption requirements again.] The probate court approved the twins' adoptions in July 2002.

The panel found that by charging the adoptive parents a $50,000 legal fee in these adoptions, respondent clearly violated DR 2-106(A) (charging or collecting a clearly excessive fee). The panel cited evidence indicating that local adoption lawyers charged hourly rates of $125 to $150 for customary total fees of $2,000 to $3,000 and the fact that respondent had formally accounted for only a few hours of work.

The panel also found respondent in violation of DR 5-101(A)(1) (accepting employment in a conflict of interest without a client's consent after full disclosure) because he had acquired an interest in these adoptions through improper payments to the birth mother and also had not disclosed these payments to the adoptive parents. The panel further found violations of DR

5-103(A) (acquiring an improper proprietary interest in a client's case) and (B) (providing improper financial assistance to a client) because respondent had paid the birth mother's personal expenses and given her a car, neither of which was a permissible advance of court costs or other litigation expenses.

The panel additionally found respondent in violation of DR 7-102(A)(3) (knowingly failing to disclose that which an attorney is required by law to reveal [i.e., the fees and payments]), (4) (knowingly using perjured or false evidence), (5) (making a false statement of law or fact), (6) (creating or preserving evidence the attorney knows or should know is false), and (7) (counseling a client in conduct the attorney knows is illegal or fraudulent). . . . Finally, the panel found that respondent violated DR 9-102(A) (failing to keep client's funds in a separate and identifiable trust account) by depositing into his personal accounts all the money paid to him by the adoptive parents, which included unearned and unapproved attorney fees as well as funds intended to be used for the birth mother's medical expenses. . . .

. . . The panel concluded that respondent had dishonestly and selfishly attempted to conceal the exorbitant fee he charged for these adoptions. [R]espondent has attempted to evade responsibility for and conceal evidence of his shameful betrayal of his clients' interests and professional oath. Disbarment is the only appropriate sanction. . . .

## NOTES AND QUESTIONS

1. *Attorneys in private placements.* Private adoptions present a host of challenges for the attorney. Beyond the ethical violations cited in the principal case, consider the following: On what basis did Hare select the adoptive parents? What obligation, if any, does he have to ensure their suitability as parents? What difficulties does his representation of both the birth mother and the adopters, even temporarily, pose?

2. *"Baby broker" laws.* Statutes in many states impose tight restrictions on child placement. For example, New York prohibits all placements except those by "an authorized agency" or "a parent, legal guardian or relative with the second degree." N.Y. Soc. Serv. Law §374(2) (2008). The statute defines the prohibited conduct, "plac[ing] out," as arranging for the child's free care in a family other than that of a relative, "for the purpose of adoption or for the purpose of providing care." N.Y. Soc. Serv. Law §371(12) (2008). See also, e.g., Ala. Code §26-10A-33 (2008); Del. Code Ann. tit. 13, §904 (2008); Mass. Gen. Laws ch. 210, §11A (2008).

Such "baby broker" laws were enacted both to prevent commercial trafficking in babies ("baby selling") and to prevent placement by the untrained. See In re Preadoption Certificate Concerning Carballo, 521 N.Y.S.2d 375 (Fam. Ct. 1987). Given the latter goal, what activities do such statutes prohibit? Why do such laws exempt parents and some relatives? To what extent can attorneys or other third parties serve as intermediaries under the New York statute? For what can attorneys receive fees? See also Galison v. District of Columbia, 402 A.2d 1263 (D.C. 1979); People v. Schwartz, 356 N.E.2d 8 (Ill. 1976).

3. *Fees and expenses.* Despite the usual exemption for parents in placement restrictions, of course, even parents cannot "sell" their children.

See Maryland v. Runkles, 605 A.2d 111 (Md. 1992). On the other hand, payment of the birth mother's medical expenses by the adoptive parents has long been permissible. See, e.g., Okla. Stat. Ann., tit. 10, §7505-3.2 (2008) (2007); In re Baby Boy P., 700 N.Y.S.2d 792 (Fam. Ct. 1999). What other costs can be reimbursed? See N.Y. Soc. Serv. Law §374(6) (2008) (listing reimbursable expenses); In re D.S.D., 19 P.3d 204 (Kan. Ct. App. 2001) (adopters may pay indigent biological father's attorneys fees); In re Adoption No. 9979, 591 A.2d 468 (Md. 1991) (not maternity clothes); In re Baby Girl D., 517 A.2d 925 (Pa. 1986) (no reimbursement for counseling, housing, medical expenses not directly beneficial to the child, including Lamaze classes and sonograms).

The UAA prohibits payments for placement, parental consent, or relinquishment, subject to a civil penalty. Unif. Adoption Act, §7-102, 9 U.L.A. (pt. IA) 125 (1999). The UAA permits, however, payment for the services of an agency, advertising, medical and travel expenses, counseling, living expenses for the birth mother for a reasonable period, disclosure of the child's medical and psychological history, legal services and court costs, evaluations of the adopters, and any other service the court finds reasonably necessary. Such payments cannot be made contingent on placement, relinquishment, or consent to adoption. Unif. Adoption Act, §7-103, 9 U.L.A. (pt. IA) at 126.

4. *Ethical challenges.* May an attorney ethically keep a file of adults interested in adopting and then select one over the others when a birth parent seeks help in placement? See In re Petrie, 742 P.2d 796 (Ariz. 1987). Does the birth mother's attorney, who facilitates her plan to relinquish her newborn for adoption, have any obligation to the birth father and his parents, who want to rear the child? Does the duty to the birth mother require the attorney to assist in thwarting the father's effort to establish a relationship with the child? Does the father have any remedies against the attorney? See Sprouse v. Eisenman, 2005 WL 289460 (Ohio Ct. App. 2005). In a malpractice action against an attorney who negligently advised birth parents that they could revoke their consent, what damages should they recover for loss of exclusive care of the child? See Collins v. Missouri Bar Plan, 157 S.W.3d 726 (Mo. Ct. App. 2005).

5. *Multiple clients.* Under what circumstances can one attorney represent both the adoptive parents, whom the attorney has selected, and the birth mother or father? Do such parties always have adverse interests? According to *Petrie,* supra, having such multiple clients is permissible only if it is obvious that the attorney can adequately represent the interests of each and if each consents after full disclosure of the possible effects. The Model Rules of Professional Conduct, addressing attorneys as intermediaries, requires full disclosure of the implications of common representation, client consent thereto, full explanations of each decision to be made, and withdrawal from the matter upon request or dissatisfaction. Further, the attorney must reasonably believe that the matter can be resolved impartially and consistent with the clients' best interests. Model Rules Prof'l Conduct R. 2.2 (LEXIS 2008). Does this *general* rule provide appropriate regulation of adoption intermediaries *in particular*?

Although the American Bar Association has stated expressly that "a lawyer may not ethically represent both the adoptive and biological parents in a private adoption proceeding," it recognizes that "some authorities have held otherwise." ABA Comm. on Ethics and Prof'l Responsibility, Informal Op. 1523

(1987). See also, e.g., In re Adoption of Gustavo G., 776 N.Y.S.2d 15 (App. Div. 2004) (rejecting per se disqualification of adopter's attorney, which previously represented placing foster care agency); Restatement (Third) of the Law Governing Lawyers §130 (2000) (requiring consent for multiple representation in nonlitigated matter if there is a substantial risk of material and adverse effect on one client's interests). For example, California treats as unethical joint representation in independent adoptions absent both parties' written consent. The consent must include, inter alia, notice to the birth parents of the right to independent counsel with reasonable attorneys' fees assumed by the adoptive parents, waiver by the birth parents of independent representation, and an agreement that the attorney for the adoptive parents will represent the birth parents. Cal. Fam. Code §8800 (2007). See also Debra Lyn Bassett, Three's A Crowd: A Proposal to Abolish Joint Representation, 32 Rutgers L.J. 387 (2001).

6. *Adoption facilitators.*  When only parents and licensed agencies can place children, what services can nonagency intermediaries provide to assist a parent in selecting a placement? According to the Nevada Attorney General, a lawyer who merely sends video or audio tapes, letters, resumes, or other information describing prospective adoptive parents to the birth mother violates a statute prohibiting adoptive placement by a person not licensed to place children. A statute makes it a misdemeanor for any unlicensed person or organization to place, arrange the placement of, or assist in placing or arranging the placement of any child for adoption. Nev. Rev. Stat. Ann. §127.310 (2008). This statute defines "[a]rrange the placement of a child" as "to make preparations for or bring about any agreement or understanding concerning the adoption of a child." Id. at §127.220. Would this statute also cover new avenues now available thanks to modern technology, for example, the creation of websites on which birth parents can read profiles of hopeful adoptive parents? See, e.g., http://www.parentprofiles.com/(website established by Adoption Profiles, LLC) (last visited Nov. 28, 2008). See also Butler v. Adoption Media, LLC, 486 F. Supp. 2d 1022 (N.D. Cal. 2007), discussed Chapter 5, section B.

How would the sending of tapes, letters, and resumes or the establishment of a website fare under the following statute?

> The selection of a prospective adoptive parent or parents shall be personally made by the child's birth parent or parents and may not be delegated to an agent. The act of selection by the birth parent or parents shall be based upon his, her, or their personal knowledge of the prospective adoptive parent or parents.

Cal. Fam. Code §8801(a) (2008). The statute then lists specific information required to satisfy "personal knowledge." Id. at §8801(b). But see also id. at §8637 (attorneys as adoption facilitators).

7. *The commodification controversy.*  Despite the prohibition on buying and selling children, most authorities agree that today's practice of independent adoption often entails the payment of money, particularly for white infants. See Madelyn Freundlich, The Market Forces in Adoption 11-13 (2000); Adam Pertman, Adoption Nation: How the Adoption Revolution Is Transforming America 185-203 (2000). But see Martha M. Ertman, What's Wrong With a

Parenthood Market? A New and Improved Theory of Commodification, 82 N.C. L. Rev. 1 (2003); Amanda C. Pustilnik, Note, Private Ordering, Legal Ordering, and the Getting of Children: A Counterhistory of Adoption Law, 20 Yale L. & Pol'y Rev. 263 (2002).

Birth parents often have the opportunity to choose from several competing prospective adopters, as dramatized on a prime-time televised broadcast that tracked a young woman's interviews with five couples seeking to adopt her baby and her ultimate selection of one. ABC News, 20/20, Be My Baby, Apr. 30, 2004 (available on LEXIS). Sometimes, the birth mother lives temporarily with the prospective adopters to assess personally their parenting styles and inter- actions with the child. See, e.g., In re Adoption of E.H., 103 P.3d 177 (Utah Ct. App. 2004), *remanded*, 137 P.3d 809 (Utah 2006). What are the advantages and disadvantages of this selection process? Recall *D.N.T.*, Chapter 2, section B3.

Why not legitimize baby selling, given the existence of a market and con- troversy about matching and other longstanding placement practices? A provocative article contends that an adopter's willingness to pay ensures the child will be well cared for. Elisabeth M. Landes & Richard A. Posner, The Economics of the Baby Shortage, 7 J. Legal Stud. 323 (1978). The authors attrib- ute discomfort with the idea to concerns about overreaching, racial ranking, and the specter of baby breeding. Nonetheless, citing the current availability of abor- tion and the decreased stigma of rearing nonmarital children, they ask: "[W]hat social purposes are served by encouraging these alternatives to the baby sale?" Id. at 346. Is this analysis persuasive? Judge Posner advocates removing the "price ceiling" for independent adoptions, given the decreasing supply of available children. Richard A. Posner, Sex and Reason 409-416 (1992).

## Note: Adoption of Children with Special Needs

Despite market analyses that suggest a "baby shortage," many children with disabilities, children of color, older children, and children in foster care with histories of abuse and neglect await placement. These children are often called "children with special needs" or "hard to place children" — terms that also include sibling groups and children with HIV infection.[1] What infer- ences about adoption's objectives arise from the coexistence of an alleged "baby shortage" and the number of children awaiting placement? See, e.g., Susan Frelich Appleton, Adoption in the Age of Reproductive Technology, 2004 U. Chi. Legal F. 393, 402-405.

To encourage adoptions of "hard to place" children, state and federal pro- grams provide financial assistance. See generally Seth A. Grob, Adoption Sub- sidies: Advocating for Children with Special Needs, 7 U.C. Davis J. Juv. L. & Pol'y 83 (2003). Tax law offers incentives, including some credits and

---

[1] See Judith K. McKenzie, Adoption of Children with Special Needs, The Future of Children, Spring 1993, at 62, 63. On September 30, 2003, 523,085 children were in foster care, with 118,761 awaiting adoption. The largest fraction of the waiting children, 40 percent, were classified as "Black Non-Hispanic." During 2003, 282,000 children exited foster care, but only 18 percent left for adoption. U.S. Dept. of Health and Human Servs., Administration for Children and Families, Administration on Children, Youth and Families, Children's Bureau, The AFCARS Report, Interim FY 2003 Estimates as of June 2006 (10) (available athttp://www.acf.hhs.gov/programs/cb/stats_ research/afcars/tar/report10.htm) (last visited Nov. 28, 2008).

exclusions. See I.R.C. §§23, 137 (2008). The UAA requires agencies receiving federal funds to make diligent efforts to recruit adopters for these children. Unif. Adoption Act §2-105, 9 U.L.A. (pt. IA) 35-36 (1999).

Adoptions of children with special needs have risen to constitute over half of all domestic adoptions by nonrelatives.[2] Although most adopters of children with special needs report satisfaction with these placements, some such placements end before the final decree is issued. Most of these disrupted adoptions involve older children, while placements of younger children with disabilities and serious medical problems produce higher success rates. Like age, emotional and behavioral problems (including a past history of physical and sexual abuse) are predictors of disruption. Adopters' unrealistic expectations and their rigidity in family interactions also tend to correlate with poor outcomes.[3] (For stories of the problems ensuing from such placements and disruptions and the legal responses thereto, see Chapter 4, section D.)

According to some critics, existing governmental support is inadequate. Adoptive families complain about the state's failure to disclose the full extent of the problems experienced by some children in subsidized adoption programs, preventing appropriate treatment; they also contend that more services are necessary to make such placements work. See Griffith v. Johnston, 899 F.2d 1427 (5th Cir. 1990). Child welfare advocates recommend improved efforts to recruit adopters, the removal of barriers to nontraditional families, acceleration of the process by which children removed from parental custody become available for adoption, and provision of postadoption services.[4] Because children of color are usually included in the definition of children with special needs, the debate about transracial adoption inevitably surfaces in these calls for reform. See, e.g., Sarah Ramsey, Fixing Foster Care or Reducing Child Poverty: The Pew Commission Recommendations and the Transracial Adoption Debate, 66 Mont. L. Rev. 21 (2005). See also Tanya M. Washington, Throwing Black Babies Out With the Bathwater: A Child-Centered Challenge to Same-Sex Adoption Bans, 6 Hastings Race & Poverty L.J. 1 (2009) (noting impact of sexuality restrictions on orphans with special needs, including Black orphans).

Other critics, like Professor Roberts, supra section A1A, condemn legislation like the Adoption and Safe Families Act (ASFA) for favoring adoptive homes over birth families and for failing to encourage systemic reform. See also, e.g., Amy Wilkinson-Hagen, Note, The Adoption and Safe Families Act of 1997: A Collision of Parens Patriae and Parents' Constitutional Rights, 11 Geo. J. on Poverty L. & Pol'y 137, 138 (2004) (critiquing goal of "permanency at any cost—even the cost of unnecessary state termination proceedings"). But see Elizabeth Bartholet, Nobody's Children: Abuse and Neglect, Foster Drift, and the Adoption Alternative 188-189 (1999). Preliminary empirical evidence associates ASFA with an increase in adoptions of young children, a possible shift to adoption from reunification with birth parents, and an

---

[2] National Council for Adoption, Adoption Factbook IV 8 (2007) (60 percent in 2002, up from 48.5 percent in 1996). See id. at 28-29.

[3] These conclusions are reported in James A. Rosenthal, Outcomes of Adoption of Children with Special Needs, The Future of Children, Spring 1993, at 77, 79-81.

[4] See McKenzie, supra note [1], at 73-75; Rosenthal, supra note [3], at 84-86.

increase in older children with no legal parents because adoption often does not follow the termination of parental rights. Richard P. Barth et. al., From Anticipation to Evidence: Research on the Adoption and Safe Families Act, 12 Va. J. Soc. Pol'y & L. 371, 381-383, 392-395 (2005).

# B. BEYOND CHILD PLACEMENT: OTHER PATHS TO ADOPTION

Not all adoptions reflect the stereotypical child placement scenario depicted in the foregoing cases and materials. This next section examines two important departures from the usual scenario, equitable adoption and adult adoption. Two other significant departures, stepparent adoptions and second-parent adoptions, are covered in Chapter IV because of the questions that they also raise about the legal consequences of adoption.

## 1. EQUITABLE ADOPTION

ESTATE OF FORD

82 P.3d 747 (Cal. 2004)

WERDEGAR, J.

Terrold Bean claims the right to inherit the intestate estate of Arthur Patrick Ford as Ford's equitably adopted son. . . . Born in 1953, Bean was declared a ward of the court and placed in the home of Ford and his wife, Kathleen Ford, as a foster child in 1955. Bean never knew his natural father, whose identity is uncertain, and he was declared free of his mother's control in 1958, at the age of four. Bean lived continuously with Mr. and Mrs. Ford and their natural daughter, Mary Catherine, for about 18 years, until Mrs. Ford's death in 1973, then with Ford and Mary Catherine for another two years, until 1975.

During part of the time Bean lived with the Fords, they cared for other foster children and received a county stipend for doing so. Although the Fords stopped taking in foster children after Mrs. Ford became ill with cancer, they retained custody of Bean. The last two other foster children left the home around the time of Mrs. Ford's death, but Bean, who at 18 years of age could have left, stayed with Ford and Mary Catherine.

Bean knew the Fords were not his natural parents, but as a child he called them "Mommy" and "Daddy," and later "Mom" and "Dad." Joan Malpassi, Mary Catherine's friend since childhood and later administrator of Ford's estate, testified that Bean's relationship with Mary Catherine was "as two siblings" and that the Fords treated Bean "more like Mary rather than a foster son, like a real son was my observation." Mary Catherine later listed Bean as her brother on a life insurance application.

Bean remained involved with Ford and Mary Catherine even after leaving the Ford home and marrying. Ford loaned Bean money to help furnish his new household and later forgave the unpaid part of the debt when Bean's marriage was dissolved. Bean visited Ford and Mary Catherine several times per year both during his marriage and after his divorce. When Ford suffered a disabling stroke in 1989, Mary Catherine conferred with Bean and Malpassi over Ford's care; Ford was placed in a board and care facility, where Bean continued to visit him regularly until his death in 2000.

Mary Catherine died in 1999. Bean and Malpassi arranged her funeral. Bean petitioned for Malpassi to be appointed Ford's conservator, and with Malpassi's agreement Bean obtained a power of attorney to take care of Ford's affairs pending establishment of the conservatorship. Bean also administered Mary Catherine's estate, which was distributed to the Ford conservatorship. When a decision was needed as to whether Ford should receive medical life support, Malpassi consulted with Bean in deciding he should. When Ford died, Bean and Malpassi arranged the funeral.

The Fords never petitioned to adopt Bean. Mrs. Ford told Barbara Carter, a family friend, that "they wanted to adopt Terry," but she was "under the impression that she could not put in for adoption while he was in the home." She worried that if Bean was removed during the adoption process he might be put in "a foster home that wasn't safe."

Ford's nearest relatives at the time of his death were the two children of his predeceased brother, nephew John J. Ford III and niece Veronica Newbeck. Neither had any contact with Ford for about 15 years before his death, and neither attended his funeral. John J. Ford III filed a petition to determine entitlement to distribution (Prob. Code, §11700), listing both himself and Newbeck as heirs. Bean filed a statement of interest claiming entitlement to Ford's entire estate under [Probate Code §6455 (equitable adoption). After trial, the court ruled against Bean because it found no clear and convincing evidence of "an intent to adopt." Bean appealed.]

### I. Criteria for Equitable Adoption

[The judicial doctrine] of equitable adoption allows a person who was accepted and treated as a natural or adopted child, and as to whom adoption typically was promised or contemplated but never performed, to share in inheritance of the foster parents' property. . . .[2] California decisions have explained equitable adoption as the specific enforcement of a contract to adopt. Yet it has long been clear that the doctrine, even in California, rested less on ordinary rules of contract law than on considerations of fairness and intent for, as Justice Schauer put it [in his dissenting opinion in Estate of Radovich, 308 P.2d 14, 24 (Cal. 1957)], the child "should have been" adopted and would have been but for the decedent's "inadvertence or fault." [M]oreover, the contracts purportedly being enforced were made between foster parents and their minor charges, yet neither court addressed the children's capacity to contract, suggesting, again, that the contract served mainly as evidence of the parties' intent, rather than as an enforceable legal basis for transmission of property.

---

2. In California, at least, adoption itself is "purely statutory in origin and nature." (Estate of Radovich[, 308 P.2d 14 (Cal. 1957)] (dis. opn. of Schauer, J.).) The effect of an equitable adoption finding, therefore, is limited to the child's inheritance rights and does not in other respects equate the child's rights with those of a statutorily adopted child.

Bean urges that equitable adoption be viewed not as specific enforcement of a contract to adopt, but as application of an equitable restitutionary remedy he has identified as quasi-contract or, as his counsel emphasized at oral argument, as an application of equitable estoppel principles. While we have found no decisions articulating a quasi-contract theory, courts in several states have, instead of or in addition to the contract rationale, analyzed equitable adoption as arising from "a broader and vaguer equitable principle of estoppel." (Clark, The Law of Domestic Relations in the United States, [926 (2d ed. 1988)]). Bean argues Mr. Ford's conduct toward him during their long and close relationship estops Ford's estate or heirs at law from denying his status as an equitably adopted child.

For several reasons, we conclude the California law of equitable adoption, which has rested on contract principles, does not recognize an estoppel arising merely from the existence of a familial relationship between the decedent and the claimant. The law of intestate succession is intended to carry out [the decedent's likely intent]. The existence of a mutually affectionate relationship, without any direct expression by the decedent of an intent to adopt the child or to have him or her treated as a legally adopted child, sheds little light on the decedent's likely intent regarding distribution of property. [E]quitable adoption in California is neither a means of compensating the child for services rendered to the parent nor a device to avoid the unjust enrichment of other, more distant relatives who will succeed to the estate under the intestacy statutes. Absent proof of an intent to adopt, we must follow the statutory law of intestate succession.

In addition, a rule looking to the parties' overall relationship in order to do equity in a given case, rather than to particular expressions of intent to adopt, would necessarily be a vague and subjective one, inconsistently applied, in an area of law where "consistent, bright-line rules" are greatly needed. Such a broad scope for equitable adoption would leave open to competing claims the estate of *any* foster parent or stepparent who treats a foster child or stepchild lovingly and on an equal basis with his or her natural or legally adopted children. . . .

While a California equitable adoption claimant need not prove all the elements of an enforceable contract to adopt, therefore, we conclude the claimant must demonstrate the existence of some direct expression, on the decedent's part, of an intent to adopt the claimant. [I]n addition to a contract or other direct evidence of the intent to adopt, the evidence must show "objective conduct indicating mutual recognition of an adoptive parent and child relationship to such an extent that in equity and good conscience an adoption should be deemed to have taken place."

## II.  Standard of Proof of Equitable Adoption

. . . Several good reasons support the rule [requiring clear and convincing evidence, the standard used by the court below.] First, the claimant in an equitable adoption case is seeking inheritance outside the ordinary statutory course of intestate succession and without the formalities required by the adoption statutes. . . . Second, the claim involves a relationship with persons who have died and who can, therefore, no longer testify to their intent. Finally, too relaxed a standard could create the danger that "a person could not help out a needy child without having a de facto adoption foisted upon him after death." [Jan Ellen Rein, Relatives by Blood, Adoption, and Association: Who Should Get What and Why, 37 Vand. L. Rev. 711, 782 (1984).]

Although the evidence showed the Fords and Bean enjoyed a close and enduring familial relationship, evidence was totally lacking that the Fords ever made an attempt to adopt Bean or promised or stated their intent to do so; they neither held Bean out to the world as their natural or adopted child (Bean, for example, did not take the Ford name) nor represented to Bean that he was their child. Mrs. Ford's single statement to Barbara Carter was not clear and convincing evidence that Mr. Ford intended Bean to be, or be treated as, his adopted son. [Affirmed.]

## NOTES AND QUESTIONS

1. *Background.* Equitable adoption is a judicially created doctrine. The majority of courts (among those that have considered the issue) recognize the doctrine. See R. Brent Drake, Note, Status or Contract? A Comparative Analysis of Inheritance Rights Under Equitable Adoption and Domestic Partnership Doctrines, 39 Ga. L. Rev. 675, 681 (2005) (27 jurisdictions recognize the doctrine by case law). The practice traces back to the era when "orphan trains" brought indigent children from urban centers to families in the west. See Johnson v. Johnson, 617 N.W.2d 97, 101-102 (N.D. 2000). See also Hendrik Hartog, Someday All This Will Be Yours: Inheritance, Adoption, and Obligation in Capitalist America, 79 Ind. L.J. 345 (2004).

2. *Theories.* Jurisdictions rely on one of two theories to establish equitable adoption: implied contract or equitable estoppel. Under the former, a court enforces a foster parent's *implied promise* to adopt a child. Under the latter, a court considers the child's performance of filial services to protect the child from the adoptive parents' *neglect to finalize* the adoption. Drake, supra, at 684. In contrast, many jurisdictions refuse to recognize the doctrine because adoption is purely legislative in origin, so a court may not grant an adoption absent compliance with the statutory formalities. See generally Tracy Bateman Farrell, Annot., Modern Status of Law as to Equitable Adoption or Adoption by Estoppel, 122 A.L.R.5th 205 (2004) (citing authority).

3. *Criticisms.* Each of the theoretical bases has shortcomings. The implied contract approach suffers because of conceptual difficulties in applying specific performance (e.g., enforcement after the death of a party, a reluctance to enforce personal service contracts, the lack of a meeting of the minds). Estoppel raises questions about the child's detrimental reliance on the contract, especially a child who is too young to understand the contract and who lacks meaningful alternatives. See Jan Ellen Rein, Relatives by Blood, Adoption, and Association: Who Should Get What and Why?, 37 Vand. L. Rev. 711, 774-777 (1984) (discussing these and other criticisms).

Under either theory, courts usually condition relief on a showing of some agreement between the foster parents and the biological parent(s). E.g., Hulsey v. Carter, 588 S.E.2d 717 (Ga. 2003). Did any such agreement exist in Terry Bean's case? Why or why not? Can the requisite agreement ever arise when foster parents take custody of a child through a court's assertion of its dependency jurisdiction?

4. *Intent to adopt.* Although *Ford* adheres strictly to the requirement of an intent to adopt, other courts adopt a more liberal approach. For example, the court in Smalley v. Parks, 108 S.W.3d 138, 141 (Mo. Ct. App. 2003), reasons that the requisite agreement may be shown by "acts, conduct, and admissions of the adopting parent." Would Terry Bean have been more successful under this approach? What possible reasons might explain Mrs. Ford's reluctance to formally adopt Terry? Might agency policy have played a role (i.e., the discouragement of the formation of ties between foster parents and foster children, in turn leading to Mrs. Ford's fear that Terry might be removed from their home)?

5. *Status-based approach.* Many commentators criticize reliance on the contract theory and advocate instead a status-based approach. See Drake, supra, at 684, 712. To date, West Virginia alone follows this approach:

> While the existence of an express contract of adoption is very convincing evidence, an implied contract of adoption is an unnecessary fiction created by courts as a protection from fraudulent claims. We find that if a claimant can, by clear, cogent and convincing evidence, prove sufficient facts to convince the trier of fact that his status is identical to that of a formally adopted child, except only for the absence of a formal order of adoption, a finding of an equitable adoption is proper without proof of an adoption contract.

Wheeling Dollar Savings & Trust Co. v. Singer, 250 S.E.2d 369, 374 (W. Va. 1978). Under the status-based approach, what criteria should be used to determine whether a child has been equitably adopted? Does the so-called "functional approach" to establishing parentage, Chapter 1, section B2a, provide any guidance? According to *Wheeling*, supra, the claimant must prove by clear and convincing evidence that she or he was treated the same, from a young age, as a formally adopted child. Relevant circumstances include love and affection, filial obedience, reliance, representation that the child is a natural or adopted child, an invalid or ineffectual adoption proceeding, and the birth parent's surrender of ties. 250 S.E.2d at 373-374. How would Terry Bean fare under this approach?

Should application of the equitable adoption doctrine depend on the adoptee's good faith belief that he or she was a legally adopted child or a biological child? Did Terry Bean have such a belief? Should application of the doctrine require severance of the child's ties to the biological parents? For example, *Hulsey*, supra, held that a stepchild failed to establish equitable adoption because, in part, she continued to have contact with her biological father and his extended family. Does this rationale hark back to the traditional notion that a child can have only one set of parents?

6. *Legal obstacle.* In a common scenario in equitable adoption cases, an impediment prevents the foster parents from finalizing the adoption. For example, in the classic case of Estate of Wilson, 168 Cal. Rptr. 533 (Ct. App. 1980), a child's adoption failed when the birth mother could not be found to provide consent. As an adult, the petitioner discovered only after the foster parents' deaths that he had not been adopted. When he sought recognition as their heir, the court applied equitable adoption, citing the requisite agreement

to adopt and continuation of the parent-child relationship during their joint lifetimes.

The legislature codified the *Wilson* holding, permitting the establishment of a parent-child relationship in the context of both foster parenthood and stepparenthood. Cal. Prob. Code §6454 (2008). Specifically, the statute requires a personal relationship between the claimant and the decedent that began during the child's minority and continued for their joint lifetimes and also a legal barrier but for which the foster parent would have adopted the child. Terry Bean originally brought claims under this statutory provision as well as the equitable adoption doctrine. Why was this former statute inapplicable in *Ford*?

Under this test and several others, the relationship and/or agreement to adopt must occur during the child's minority. See, e.g., Samek v. Sanders, 788 So. 2d 872 (Ala. 2000). Why? See also In re Bovey, 132 P.3d 510 (Mont. 2006) (noting how some states require the individual to live during his or her minority as a "regular member" of the deceased's household in order to inherit by intestate succession through the adopter). In *Bovey*, a woman lived in the home of her mother's lover for two years as a teenager, and he adopted her as an adult to prevent other heirs from receiving at his death the residue of a trust created by his mother. The court held that the adopted woman could not inherit by intestate succession through the adopter because she had not been a "regular member" of his household during her minority. What is the purpose of this requirement? Does it have the same purpose as the rule for equitable adoption that the relationship and/or agreement to adopt must occur during the child's minority? What light does *Bovey* shed on the purposes of this limitation of equitable adoption?

7. *Scope.* Should the doctrine of equitable adoption apply only to inheritance questions? Traditionally, the doctrine has had this narrow scope. Recall footnote 2 in *Ford*. Indeed, most states restrict the doctrine to intestacy cases. E.g., In re Estate of Musil, 965 So. 2d 1157 (Fla. Dist. Ct. App. 2007) (listing elements of virtual adoption). See also Poncho v. Bowdoin, 126 P.3d 1221 (N.M. Ct. App. 2005) (disallowing equitable adoption by mother's husband as a means for biological father to avoid support duties); In re M.L.P.J., 16 S.W.3d 45 (Tex. App. 2000) (doctrine inapplicable to claims for child support and health insurance). Even with such restrictions, some courts recognize the equitably adopted child's right to inherit only *from* the would-be adopter. E.g., Estate of Furia, 126 Cal. Rptr. 2d 384 (Ct. App. 2002); see also Sanderson v. Bathrick, 76 P.3d 1236 (Wyo. 2003) (doctrine inapplicable to anti-lapse statute, when would-be adopter dies testate). What explains this narrow scope? Should the doctrine apply in other contexts? Which ones?

May a contract impose child support obligations in a jurisdiction that does not recognize equitable adoption for support purposes? See In re Marriage of Eilers, 205 S.W.3d 637 (Tex. App. 2006) (holding enforceable "power of attorney delegating parental responsibility" and upholding order of child support based thereon). But see Dial v. Dial, 621 S.E.2d 461 (Ga. 2005). For a critique of the limited definition of "family" reflected in many such cases, see Michael J. Higdon, When Informal Adoption Meets Intestate Succession: The Cultural Myopia of the Equitable Adoption Doctrine, 43 Wake Forest L. Rev. 223 (2008).

8. *Equitable parent doctrine.* Despite the traditionally narrow scope, courts increasingly are recognizing a broader modern variation of equitable adoption, often called the "equitable parent doctrine." In one prevalent fact pattern, some states recognize as an equitable parent a man who first learns upon divorce that his wife's child (whom he had treated as his own) is not his biological offspring. In these cases, the doctrine allows the man parental custodial or visitation rights, or it may result in support duties. See, e.g., In re Marriage of Gallagher, 539 N.W.2d 479 (Iowa 1995) (recognizing husband as equitable parent based on estoppel against mother, with remand to determine child's best interests); Hinshaw v. Hinshaw, 237 S.W.3d 170 (Ky. 2007) (applying equitable estoppel to postdissolution custody, following mother's deception); Atkinson v. Atkinson, 408 N.W.2d 516, 519 (Mich. Ct. App. 1987) (requiring mutual acknowledgment as father and child or cooperation of the mother in the development of the relationship, husband's desire to have parental rights, and his willingness to pay child support); *Johnson*, supra (holding equitable adoption applicable to postdissolution child support). Nonetheless, some courts limit or reject the equitable parent approach in such cases. See, e.g., Van v. Zahorik, 597 N.W.2d 15 (Mich. 1999) (refusing to extend doctrine to man who met functional criteria but had not married the mother). Compare D.G. v. D.M.K., 557 N.W.2d 235 (S.D. 1996) (rejecting doctrine for a man who knew all along that he was not the child's father), with In re Paternity of H.H., 879 N.E.2d 1175 (Ind. Ct. App. 2008) (estopping mother from asserting former paramour was not the child's father after they filed paternity affidavit, although both knew he was not the biological father).

In a second increasingly common fact pattern, a lesbian couple who agreed to rear children together become involved in a custody, visitation, or child-support dispute after their relationship dissolves. Initially, courts recognized only the biological or adoptive mother as a parent in such disputes, giving her exclusive authority to control access to the child (and the exclusive responsibility for support), regardless of her former partner's participation in childrearing or the child's attachment. E.g., Alison D. v. Virginia M., 572 N.E.2d 27 (N.Y. 1991). More recently, courts have accorded parental prerogatives based on estoppel or other equitable principles. See Kristine H. v. Lisa R., 117 P.3d 690 (Cal. 2005) (estoppel based on prebirth stipulation of parentage); In re L.B., 122 P.3d 161 (Wash. 2005) (recognizing common law de facto parentage under court's equitable authority), *cert. denied*, 547 U.S. 1143 (2006). See also American Law Institute, Principles of the Law of Family Dissolution: Analysis and Recommendations §§2.03, 3.03 (2002) (recognizing parents by estoppel and de facto parents). But see, e.g., Janice M. v. Margaret K., 948 A.2d 73 (Md. 2008). Some courts bypass an estoppel-based analysis, instead expansively construing "parent" in the state's parentage statutes. E.g., Elisa B. v. Superior Ct. (reprinted Chapter 1, section B1b). Cf. In re A.B., 837 N.E.2d 965 (Ind. 2005), *vacating and remanding* 818 N.E.2d 126 (Ind. Ct. App. 2004). Should supporting the child financially (i.e., playing the stereotypical breadwinner's role in the family) suffice to create parental status on equitable grounds? See A.H. v. M.P., 857 N.E.2d 1061, 1071 (Mass. 2006) (distinguishing caretaking functions from other parenting functions); B.F. v. T.D., 194 S.W.3d 310 (Ky. 2006).

Given these decisions extending parental prerogatives in situations in which everyone knows that the mother's former female partner is not the child's biological parent, why do some courts declare that a man can achieve recognition as an equitable parent only if he mistakenly believed that he was the child's biological father, as in *D.G.*, supra? Should the method of conception, donor insemination versus sexual intercourse, matter? See Chapter 6. Should it matter whether the would-be equitable parent is seeking recognition (as in a custody and visitation dispute) or disclaiming recognition (as in a child-support dispute)? Compare, e.g., *A.B.*, supra, with *Elisa B.*, supra.

## 2. ADULT ADOPTION

IN RE P.B. AND S.B.

---

920 A.2d 155 (N.J. Super. Ct. Ch. Div. 2006)

JULIO L. MENDEZ, P.J.F.P.

A married couple, P.B. and S.B., ages fifty and fifty-three, respectively, seek to adopt an unmarried fifty-two-year-old female, L.C. L.C. has resided with the couple for over ten years and wishes to formalize her familial relationship with P.B. and S.B. through adoption and changing her last name to theirs. At the adoption hearing on July 14, 2006, the parties testified as to how they operate as a "team" and desire the adoption in order to make their relationship permanent. L.C. testified that she had been married twice previously, had a troubled relationship with her birth parents and siblings, is currently disabled, and has no valuable personal property. P.B. and S.B. currently rent a two-bedroom mobile home, and testified that they are childless, do not seek to adopt L.C. for inheritance, tax, or other such purposes, but instead seek to make their "family unit" official in the eyes of the law. The parties are assumed to have a platonic relationship, although it should be noted that there was testimony indicating S.B. and L.C. share a bedroom. P.B., S.B., and L.C. presented themselves as a team of three equals.

The issue before the court is whether an adult adoption should be granted when the statutorily-required minimum age difference of ten years between the adopter and adoptee is not satisfied. No case law in this State addresses this issue.

Adoption is solely a creature of statute; it did not exist at common law. In researching adult adoption, this Court has found that there are several common reasons for why one adult would choose to adopt another. The first such reason concerns inheritance. See In re the Adoption of Swanson, 623 A.2d 1095 (Del. 1993). Creating a parent-child relationship through adult adoption allows the adoptee to have legally recognizable inheritance rights. A second main reason for adult adoption is to formalize an existing parent-child relationship. For instance, a step-child who has developed a strong relationship with a step-parent may be adopted as an adult by the step-parent. Similarly, a former foster child who had grown close to the foster family, but was not legally available for adoption as a child, could choose to be adopted as an adult. Another common reason for adult adoption is to provide for perpetual care of the adoptee. This allows an adoptee of diminished capacity or abilities some assurance of lifetime care under family insurance and inheritance rights. Finally, in some states adult adoption is used to create a legally binding relationship where marriage is not available.[1]

In New Jersey, there are three statutory sections concerning adult adoption, N.J.S.A. 2A:22-1, -2 and -3. The first section, N.J.S.A. 2A:22-1, provides the standards for adult adoptions, allowing an unmarried adult or a jointly consenting married couple to adopt an adult person if

> [t]he adopting parent or parents are of good moral character and of reputable standing in their community, and . . . the adoption will be to the advantage and benefit of the person to be adopted.

The second section addressing adult adoption, N.J.S.A. 2A:22-2, further stipulates that an adult adoption will not be granted unless: (1) there is an age difference of at least 10 years between adopting parents and the adoptee; and (2) the adoptee has requested the adoption (and change of name, if desired) in writing. The court may waive these requirements if the best interests of adoptee would be promoted by the adoption. Ibid. The third and last section, N.J.S.A. 2A:22-3, deals with inheritance rights of an adopted adult.

Here, the parties arguably do meet many of the above-listed statutory requirements. . . . The statutory terms of N.J.S.A. 2A:22-2 do allow the court to waive the age difference requirement, if the court is "satisfied that the best interests of the person to be adopted would be promoted by granting the adoption." Therefore, this court must next consider whether L.C.'s best interests would be promoted by granting this adoption.

But before [doing so], the court will examine why the New Jersey Legislature chose to enact the age difference requirement. On March 13, 1925, the Legislature first approved "An Act Relating To And Providing For The Adoption Of Adults," whose terms in large part remain unchanged today. *N.J.S.A. 2:39-2, 3.* However, one major difference was the initial requirement that "the person or persons petitioning aforesaid shall be at least fifteen years older than the person sought to be adopted." Ibid. Notably, the 1925 statute did not provide for judicial waiver of this age difference requirement. In 1977, the Legislature reduced the fifteen year age difference requirement to ten years solely to "conform the age differential" of adult adoption with that of minor adoption.[2]

---

1. Gay and lesbian couples routinely use adult adoption as such a vehicle in California and various other states. This is a moot issue in New Jersey because of the newly enacted domestic partnership act, N.J.S.A. 26:8A-1 to -13.

2. The full text of the Assembly Statement No. 541, dated June 20, 1977, reads as follows:

> . . . This bill amends the law concerning adoption of adults. Under present law persons who are adopting a minor must be at least 10 years older than the minor, but persons who are adopting an adult must be at least 15 years older than the adult. This can result in situations whereby a 27-year-old may adopt a 17-year-old, while a 28-year-old may not adopt an 18-year old.
>
> This bill would require a 10 year age differential between the adopter and the adoptee regardless of whether the person to be adopted was a minor or an adult.
>
> Furthermore, the court would be allowed discretion in waiving this 10 year differential if it determined that such waiver would be in the best interest of the person being adopted.
>
> [Assembly Institutions, Health and Welfare Committee Statement to A. 541 (June 20, 1977).]

This court believes that the age difference requirement was intended by the New Jersey Legislature as a method of ensuring that at least a semblance of a parent-child relationship existed between the adult parties. In fact, this court cannot conceive of any other reason why the Legislature would mandate such a requirement but to ensure such a parent-child relationship. Indeed, it is widely accepted that adult adoption law in most states derives from the ancient Roman principle of *adoptio naturam imitatur*, i.e., adoption imitates nature. Walter J. Wadlington, Minimum Age Difference as a Requisite for Adoption, 1966 Duke L.J. 392 (1966). This principle has formed the basis of legislative safeguards such as the age difference requirement which disallow adoptions between those persons not old enough to be the adoptee's natural parent. It seems reasonable to surmise then that the New Jersey Legislature enacted this requirement to safeguard against illogical adult adoptions, where there is no semblance of a parent-child relationship. . . .

The limited case law in New Jersey concerning adult adoption has not confronted the age difference requirement, or its waiver. . . . In [In the Matter of the Estate of Maria Fenton, 901 A.2d 455 (N.J. Super. Ct. App. Div. 2006),] the validity of the adoption was challenged by appellants, *inter alia*, on the basis that the adoption had been spitefully and improperly undertaken by Maria Fenton for the purpose of diverting the trust fund proceeds. [T]he Appellate Division found no evidence of the alleged spiteful motivation and determined that Ms. Fenton's statement that she desired a "nice, close family" was a sufficient motivation for the adoption. In any event, the Appellate Division found that Ms. Fenton's motivation for the adoption was moot, and emphasized that "New Jersey does not require adoptive parents to indicate their reasons for the adoption," id. at 416, 901 A.2d 455, although it cautioned that courts should always be "mindful of the possibility of fraud."

The Appellate Division in *Fenton* continued to echo the prevailing sentiment of existing New Jersey case law in describing adult adoption as "ordinarily quite simple and almost in the nature of a civil contract." The Appellate Division further found that the adult adoption statute "reflects the State's public policy of allowing 'adoption[s] between consenting persons . . . when there is a strong benefit to be gained,'" and a "'mutually beneficial adoptive relationship will result.'"

Due to the Appellate Division's characterization of adult adoption as practically a civil contract requiring little inquiry into the parties' purpose, it might appear that inquiry into the presence of a parent-child relationship would not be proper. This court agrees that existing case law, including *Fenton*, supports limited inquiry into the parties' purpose, and thus, by extension, inquiry into the existence of a parent-child relationship, *as long as the initial statutory requirements are met*. Here, unlike *Fenton* and all other previously-published cases concerning adult adoption, the court is confronted with a case in which the parties cannot satisfy the statutorily required age difference, and is asked to waive this requirement. Because this court believes that the age difference requirement was enacted by the New Jersey Legislature as a means of ensuring a semblance of a parent-child relationship, it logically follows that, if this age difference cannot be met, the court must examine whether the parties' purpose is to legally solidify their already existing parent-child relationship. If the parties do not have a parent-child relationship and are not separated in age by ten years, the adoption petition must necessarily be denied, as it is contrary to the Legislature's intent. Otherwise, courts would be providing a legal stamp of approval to illogical and on some occasions bizarre relationships without any consideration or weight given to the statutory age difference requirement.

[T]he court turns for further guidance to the case law of other jurisdictions. . . . In New York, the Court of Appeals has held that where the relationship between the adult parties is utterly incompatible with the creation of a parent-child relationship, an adoption should not be granted by the court. In the Matter of the Adoption of Robert Paul P., 471 N.E.2d 424 (N.Y. 1984). In this case, a fifty-seven-year-old male sought to adopt his fifty-year-old male homosexual partner. The Court of Appeals decided that adoption is "plainly not a quasi-matrimonial vehicle to provide non-married partners with a legal imprimatur for their sexual relationship, be it heterosexual or homosexual." The Court found that since adoption was unknown at common law, legislative purposes and mandates must be strictly observed. The Court of Appeals further found that, under New York's statute, an adult adoption must still be in the adoptee's "best interests," and the relevant "familial, social, religious, emotional, and financial circumstances" of the adoptive parents still must be investigated. The Court held that permitting adults to feign a parent and child union through the adoption process could not have been the Legislature's intent.

In sharp contrast, the Supreme Court of Delaware held that evidence of a parent-child relationship between the parties is not a condition to adult adoption. In re the Adoption of James A. Swanson, an adult, 623 A.2d 1095 (Del. 1993). In *Swanson*, a sixty-six-year-old male sought to adopt his fifty-one-year-old male homosexual companion in order to formalize their emotional relationship and to facilitate their estate planning. The Delaware Court explained that most jurisdictions limit judicial inquiry into the motives behind adult adoption, but that adult adoption for the purpose of creating inheritance rights has been expressly approved. . . .

Like New York's statute requiring inquiry into the adoptee's best interests, New Jersey's adoption statute similarly requires the trial court to inquire into the adoptee's best interests if the statutory requirements are not met and the parties seek waiver of these requirements. . . . This court concludes that N.J.S.A. 2A:22-2 supports a similar finding. The New Jersey State Legislature can likewise be presumed to have intended adult adoption to require a pre-existing parent-child relationship, especially when the age difference requirement is not met, due to the best interests analysis required before waiver can be granted.

In the instant case, not only is the age difference requirement not met, the adoptee, L.C., is older than one of her potential adoptive parents. Therefore, this court finds that inquiry into L.C.'s best interests—which entails inquiry to the existence of a parent-child relationship—is necessary to determine if this statutory mandate should be waived. The court can discern no reason why the parties desire the adoption other than to obtain legal recognition for their emotional bond. Each party testified that the three operate as a "team" of equals. The court saw no evidence of a parent-child relationship between the parties, and the parties never characterized their relationship as such. Further, the court finds no other compelling evidence as to why it would be in L.C.'s best interests to grant the adoption and waive the age difference requirement. The parties testified that they did not seek the adoption to establish inheritance rights or to address issues of perpetual care, but to solidify their emotional connection as a family.

The court understands that this adoption factored as an important emotional milestone in the parties' relationship, and that the parties appear to want nothing more than to have their relationship made "official" in the eyes of the law. This court's denial of the adoption does not lessen the significance of the parties' relationship. Indeed, "[t]he law does not require or prohibit love or kindness. It deals only with legal rights and duties." In re Adoption of A., 286 A.2d 751 (Cty. Ct. 1972). P.B. and S.B. have the right to treat L.C. as a family member of equal standing without adopting her. They may also provide her with love and affection or provide for her in their wills. If L.C. wants to change her last name to theirs, she may do so without an adoption decree. . . .

## NOTES AND QUESTIONS

1. *Reasons for adult adoption.* Why did the parties in the principal case seek an adoption decree? Adult adoption provides one vehicle that unmarried adults, including same-sex partners, have used to create a legally recognized relationship for inheritance purposes. Persons may resort to adult adoption not only to create inheritance rights, but also to obtain decisionmaking authority for a partner in cases of emergency or incapacity, to secure hospital visitation rights, and to obtain benefits under insurance policies or employee benefit packages. To what extent does the advent of same-sex marriage and laws permitting domestic partnerships and civil unions address these purposes? Would such reforms have obviated the interest in adoption in the principal case?

2. *General rule and exceptions.* Almost all states permit adult adoption. Angie Smolka, Note, That's the Ticket: A New Way of Defining Family, 10 Cornell J.L. & Pub. Pol'y 629, 638-639 (2001) (pointing out that Alabama and Nebraska are exceptions). Adult adoption generally requires only the consent of the parties (unlike the adoption of a child, which is predicated on the best interests of the child). However, a few states have particular requirements (i.e., co-residence, consanguinity, or age restrictions) that preclude gays or lesbians from adopting their partners. For example, some statutes include requirements that the adoptee be a stepchild, birth child, or close relative. E.g., Va. Code Ann §63.2-1243 (2008). Why? Other states require that the adoptee's relationship be commenced during the latter's minority. E.g., Idaho Code §16-1501 (2008). Why? Finally, as the principal case illustrates, some states require that the adoptee be some statutorily specified age younger than the adopter. See Joanna Grossman, Adopting Adults: An Estate Planning Device for Gay Partners, available at http://writ.news.findlaw.com/grossman/20010116.html (last visited Jan. 24, 2009) (pointing out that two thirds of the states allow

adult adoption, and one third permit it with restrictions). Why? Case law on adult adoption as a vehicle for estate-planning purposes remains divided, as the precedents surveyed in principal case show. In one legendary case involving a childless couple, Kentucky upheld the husband's adoption of his wife, undertaken to make her his lawful heir and thereby defeat the claims of cousins and charities to the remainder of an earlier testamentary trust established by the husband's mother. Bedinger v. Graybill's Executor & Trustee, 302 S.W.2d 594 (Ky. 1957). See generally Jan Ellen Rein, Relatives by Blood, Adoption, and Association: Who Should Get What and Why, 37 Vand. L. Rev. 711, 752-753 (1984).

3. *Challenges to adult adoptions.* Although adoption may be used as an estate-planning tool, it does not ensure inheritance rights because an adoption may still be contested (for example, on grounds of fraud or undue influence) even after the adopter's death. Professor Sherman suggests methods by which a same-sex partner may attempt to insulate an adoption from subsequent attack.

> It might still be advantageous for the homosexual testator to adopt his lover, however, if he promptly informs his prospective heirs of the adoption. A number of states have statutes of limitations requiring that actions to vacate adoption decrees be brought within a certain period of time. [I]f the homosexual [adopter] informs his prospective heirs of the adoption as soon as it occurs, it is likely that they will be compelled either to object to the adoption then and there or to acquiesce in it permanently, and they may be most unwilling to challenge the adoptor face to face.

Jeffrey G. Sherman, Undue Influence and the Homosexual Testator, 42 U. Pitt. L. Rev. 225, 260-261 (1981).

In a much publicized recent case, Olive Watson, a granddaughter of the founder of IBM, adopted her same-sex partner of 14 years, Patricia Spado, in 1991. They broke up a year later. At that time, Watson paid Spado $500,000 and wrote her a letter affirming that "I shall not at any time initiate any action to revoke or annul my adoption of you." The validity of the adoption became an issue upon the 2005 death of Watson's mother, who left millions of dollars in trusts established by her late husband to be divided among 18 grandchildren; Spado claimed that the adoption made her a grandchild too, eligible for a share of the trusts. Watson family lawyers presently are attempting to abrogate the adoption, arguing that the adoption violated the statutory requirement that either the adoptive parent reside in Maine or the child live in the state. At the time of the adoption, Watson lived in New York City, and Spado gave her address as Watson's summer house in Maine. Pam Belluck & Alison Leigh Cowan, Partner Adopted by an Heiress Stakes Her Claim, N.Y. Times, Mar. 19, 2007, at A1; Gregory D. Kesich, Ex-Lover's Adoption Hinges on Key Point, Portland Press Herald, Apr. 19, 2007, at B1. The Supreme Court of Maine set aside a default judgment vacating the adoption and remanded the case for further proceedings. Adoption of Spado, 912 A.2d 578 (Me. 2007).

4. *Other disadvantages of adoption as an estate-planning tool.* Other disadvantages also exist if same-sex partners resort to adoption as an estate-planning tool. One primary disadvantage is that the adoption relationship cannot be rescinded if the partners later choose to dissolve their relationship. Another

disadvantage is that the rights of the adoptee's biological parents terminate upon adoption, thereby severing the adoptee's right to inherit from his or her biological parents or relatives. Maureen B. Cohon, Where the Rainbow Ends: Trying to Find a Pot of Gold for Same-Sex Couples in Pennsylvania, 41 Duq. L. Rev. 495, 499 (2003); Grossman, supra. How will the same-sex marriage movement and the rise of domestic partnership laws affect the use of adult adoption as a planning vehicle for gays and lesbians? See generally Joan M. Burda, Estate Planning for Same-Sex Couples (2004).

5. *Friends as family?* Why did the petitioners in this case seek adoption? Why does their notion of family, for which they sought recognition, defy what the law permits? Is adoption an appropriate vehicle? What would be the implications of extending the legal recognition of family law to groups of close friends or others who choose to live their lives as a "team" of equals rather than as a conjugal couple or parent(s) with children? Compare Laura A. Rosenbury, Friends with Benefits?, 106 Mich. L. Rev. 189 (2007), with Katherine M. Franke, Longing for *Loving*, 76 Fordham L. Rev. 2685 (2008).

## PROBLEM

In Florida, Donald, age 88 and childless, adopted his life partner, Gordon, age 72. Donald was the beneficiary of a trust, and his niece, Silvia, would get the trust remainder if Donald died childless. Several years later, upon Donald's death, Silvia petitions a Florida court to set aside Donald's adoption of Gordon. She contends that the Florida statute upheld in *Lofton*, supra, invalidates the adoption. What result and why? On what theory might she argue that this adoption constitutes a fraud on the court? See Rickard v. McKesson, 774 So. 2d 838 (Fla. Dist. Ct. App. 2000).

# LEGAL CONSEQUENCES OF ADOPTION

If adoption creates a legal fiction, what consequences does this fiction entail? This chapter explores this question, from doctrinal, policy-based, and emotional perspectives.

## A. THE "CUTOFF" RULE

MATTER OF PIEL

884 N.E.2d 1040 (N.Y. 2008)

KAYE, Chief Judge:

In *Matter of Best* [485 N.E.2d 1010 (1985)], this Court relied on strong policy considerations to conclude that a child adopted out of the family by strangers does not presumptively share in a class gift to the biological parent's issue established in the biological grandmother's 1973 testamentary trust. This appeal presents the same scenario, but with class gifts created by 1926 and 1963 irrevocable trusts. Despite the time difference, we conclude that the policy considerations that were determinative in *Best* equally determine the case before us, and that the adopted-out child does not share in the trust proceeds.

### Background

Florence Woodward created two irrevocable trusts, one in 1926 and a second in 1963, for the lifetime benefit of her daughter, Barbara W. Piel, and upon her death the trusts directed the trustee (successor-in-interest Fleet Bank) to distribute the principal to Barbara's descendants. Specifically, the 1926 trust net income was to be paid "to her descendants, if any, in equal shares, per stirpes. . . ." The 1963 trust principal was to be divided equally for "each then living child of hers. . . ." Barbara Piel died in July 2003, and in October 2004 Fleet Bank instituted two proceedings for judicial settlement of the final account for each trust. This appeal concerns the distribution of approximately $9.7 million in trust principal.

Barbara Piel gave birth to three daughters. Her first daughter, intervenor-respondent Elizabeth McNabb, was born out of wedlock on August 15, 1955 in Portland, Oregon. Within days, Barbara signed a Consent to Adoption, relinquishing her parental rights and agreeing to Elizabeth's adoption by strangers. An Oregon court finalized the adoption in November 1955 and Elizabeth lived her life in Oregon as a member of the Jones family. There is no indication that Florence Woodward knew of Elizabeth's birth or adoption. Barbara's other two daughters, Stobie Piel, born in 1959, and Lila Piel-Ollman, born in 1961, are the children of her marriage to Michael Piel.

Fleet Bank cited Stobie and Lila in the October 2004 proceedings, but failed to include Elizabeth or her children as interested persons. In November 2004 Elizabeth moved for permission to intervene and file objections to the accounts, later joined by her two children. Elizabeth objected to each account because it failed to provide her with a one-third distribution of the principal and income of each trust. [On cross-motions for summary judgment, the Surrogate's Court dismissed Elizabeth's objections, but the intermediate appellate court reversed. Here, the court reverses and reinstates the decision of the Surrogate's Court.]

### Analysis

We begin with the fundamental premise that a court must first look within the four corners of a trust instrument to determine the grantor's intent. . . . The question in *Best*, as here, was whether the adopted-out child was an intended beneficiary of the class gift. . . . Before addressing the policy considerations relied upon in *Best*, we outline the significant change in the Domestic Relations Law that distinguishes the present facts, but not the result.

From 1896 through 1963, an adopted child's right "to inheritance and succession" from the biological family "remain[ed] unaffected" by the order of adoption (Domestic Relations Law §64, as codified by L 1896, ch 272). . . . Unclear, however, is whether an adopted-out child was presumptively included in a class gift to a biological parent's issue, descendants or children. In 1963 the Legislature amended Domestic Relations Law §117 by terminating—for the first time since 1896—an adopted child's rights to inheritance and succession from the biological family. Effective March 1, 1964, the amendments included a savings clause for wills and irrevocable instruments executed prior to that date.

In 1985, when *Best* was decided, Domestic Relations Law §117 provided that the "rights of an adoptive child to inheritance and succession from and through his natural parents shall terminate upon the making of the order of adoption. . . ." Subsection 2 clarified that the termination of rights applied "only to the intestate descent and distribution of real and personal property and *shall not affect the right of any child to distribution of property under the will . . . or under any inter vivos instrument* . . . executed by such natural parent or his or her kindred." Significantly, the Court determined that this statutory provision "does not mandate that [an adopted-out] child receive a gift by implication[,]" but only protects an adopted-out child's right to inherit when specifically identified in the instrument. Thus, section 117(2) merely preserved rights of inheritance expressly intended by the grantor; it did not create additional rights.

As in *Best*, the Domestic Relations Law in effect at the time Florence Woodward executed the trusts does not create rights for an adopted-out child to share in a class gift by implication. *Best* determined that question, concluding that similar statutory language did not create such a right. Nothing in the pre-1964 legislative history or case law, moreover, indicates that an adopted-out child would share in a class gift to a biological parent's issue, descendants or children.

Having determined that the statutory law effective prior to March 1, 1964 does not require a different result, we turn to the strong policy considerations supporting adherence to *Best*. In excluding adopted-out children from class gifts to the biological parent's issue, the Court highlighted the legislative objective of fully assimilating the adopted child into the adoptive family and, relatedly, the importance of keeping adoption records confidential. From the very inception of the adoption law [in 1896] the Legislature has sought to promote assimilation of the adopted child by providing the new family with the "legal relation of parent and child." Additionally, by 1924 the Legislature had explicitly recognized the importance of confidentiality in adoption records, and in 1938 it mandated the sealing of those records. These policy considerations pre-date the execution of both Woodward trusts.

The facts of this case also compellingly demonstrate the importance of the third policy concern identified in *Best*. As the Court noted, the finality of judicial decrees would be compromised if adopted-out children were included in such class gifts "because there would always lurk the possibility, no matter how remote, that a secret out-of-wedlock child had been adopted out of the family by a biological parent or ancestor of a class of beneficiaries." That lurking possibility materialized here. In this case the adopted-out child intervened and relieved the trustee of the duty to identify and cite her. In other cases, neither the family nor the child may be aware of a birth or adoption, thereby placing on a trustee seeking closure the onerous burden of searching out unknown potential beneficiaries.

This case raises additional policy concerns: here we address classes of beneficiaries created in irrevocable instruments prior to 1964. The chances of unearthing adoption decrees potentially dating back to the late 1800s, or of identifying witnesses to recall the details of an adoption, dwindle as time passes. Permitting adopted-out children to participate in a class created by a pre-1964 instrument would pose greater practical problems to the procedural administration of a gift, and—without any legal basis for doing so—would create two classes of beneficiaries, those receiving a gift in an instrument executed before 1964 and those after. The policy interests of finality in court decrees and stability in property titles weigh heavily in favor of consistency with *Best*.

Therefore, we conclude that the *Best* rule of construction also applies to irrevocable trusts executed prior to March 1, 1964. Where, as here, the grantor's intent is indiscernible and the statutory intent at best ambiguous, we conclude that the policy considerations disfavoring inclusion of adopted-out children in such a class determine this case. . . .

## NOTES AND QUESTIONS

1. *Adoption and inheritance.* An adoption decree terminates or "cuts off" the legal relationship between the adoptee and all biological relatives and replaces it with ties to the adoptive family. This principle treats the adoptee as if she were a legitimate blood descendant of the adopter for all purposes. It follows, as *Piel* indicates in its discussion of New York's statutes, that adopted children inherit by intestate succession from their adoptive, but not from their biological, parents. What reasons support this rule? According to a comment in the 1969 version of the Uniform Adoption Act (UAA):

> The termination of relationship of parent and child between the adopted person and his natural parents and the family of the natural parents follows the trend of modern statutes and is desirable for many reasons. It eases the transition from old family to new family by providing for a clean final "cutoff" of legal relationships with the old family. It also preserves the secrecy of adoption proceedings . . . by reducing the selfish reasons an individual might have to discover his antecedents.

Unif. Adoption Act §14, 9 U.L.A. (pt. IA) 199 (1999). Nonetheless, some statutes provide for inheritance by adopted children from their biological parents. See, e.g., Tex. Fam. Code Ann. §161.206 (2007).

At one time, the "stranger-to-the-adoption" doctrine prevailed in construing wills and trusts. Under this doctrine, class-gift language — such as "children," "issue," or "heirs" — does not include an adoptee when the testator or settlor was not the adoptive parent. Wills and trusts written today, however, carry a presumption that inclusion is intended, unless the document expressly excludes adoptees. See Unif. Probate Code §2-611, 8 U.L.A. (pt. I) 434 (1998) (Prior Art. II); In re Estate of Jenkins, 904 P.2d 1316 (Colo. 1995). Cf. Watson v. Baker, 829 N.E.2d 648 (Mass. 2005) (applying prior statute).

2. *Other consequences.* The general rule that adoption creates new relationships in place of biological ties raises questions other than inheritance. For example, does the preference for placing siblings together still apply once one sibling has been adopted? See In re Shanee Carol B., 550 S.E.2d 636 (W. Va. 2001). See also In re Miguel A., 67 Cal. Rptr. 3d 307 (Ct. App. 2007); In re Adoption of J.E.F., 902 A.2d 402 (Pa. 2006).

Should laws barring marriages between close relatives (incest restrictions) apply to relationships by adoption? Compare Israel v. Allen, 577 P.2d 762 (Colo. 1978), with In re MEW, 4 Pa. D. & C.3d 51 (C.P. Allegheny 1977). See also State v. Hall, 48 P.3d 350 (Wash. 2002) (biological father guilty of incest despite daughter's adoption).

3. *Policy considerations.* To what extent do the policy considerations cited in *Piel* and noted in the UAA comment, supra, remain compelling today? Do the diminution of secrecy in adoptive placements, the rise of open adoption, and the recognition of psychological reasons prompting adoptees to seek out their birth parents (all explored infra) require rethinking the "cutoff" rule? Are there situations in which "cutoff" of the original parent-child relationship works to the child's detriment?

In fact, contemporary authorities show increasing flexibility about whether the consequences of adoption must be "all or nothing." For example, the new UAA, while adhering to the general rule severing legal ties with the biological family, provides that adoption does not terminate a former parent's duty to pay arrearages for child support. Unif. Adoption Act §§1-104, 1-105, 9 U.L.A. (pt. IA) 23-24 (1999).

# B. STEPPARENT AND SECOND-PARENT ADOPTIONS

In the typical stepparent adoption, one birth parent terminates his parental rights (or fails to assert them or dies) while the spouse of the second birth parent steps in, assuming parental rights by adoption. How do stepparent adoptions resemble so-called "stranger adoptions"? How do they differ? What underlying assumptions do the two practices share — about the optimal number of parents for each child, the gender of those parents, and the relationship between those parents? The following pair of cases challenges such assumptions in the legal construction of "family."

ADOPTION OF TAMMY

619 N.E.2d 315 (Mass. 1993)

GREANEY, J.

In this case, two unmarried women, Susan and Helen, filed a joint petition in the Probate and Family Court Department under G.L. c. 210, §1 (1992 ed.) to adopt as their child Tammy, a minor, who is Susan's biological daughter. . . . Based on [a] finding that Helen and Susan "are each functioning, separately and together, as the custodial and psychological parents of [Tammy]," and that "it is the best interest of said [Tammy] that she be adopted by both," the judge entered a decree allowing the adoption. Simultaneously, the [Probate and Family Court] judge reserved and reported to the Appeals Court the evidence and all questions of law, in an effort to "secure [the] decree from any attack in the future on jurisdictional grounds." We transferred the case to this court on our own motion. We conclude that the adoption was properly allowed under G.L. c. 210.

. . . Helen and Susan have lived together in a committed relationship, which they consider to be permanent, for more than ten years. In June, 1983, they jointly purchased a house in Cambridge. Both women are physicians specializing in surgery. At the time the petition was filed, Helen maintained a private practice in general surgery at Mount Auburn Hospital and Susan, a nationally recognized expert in the field of breast cancer, was director of the Faulkner Breast Center and a surgical oncologist at the Dana Farber Cancer Institute. Both women also held positions on the faculty of Harvard Medical School.

For several years prior to the birth of Tammy, Helen and Susan planned to have a child, biologically related to both of them, whom they would jointly parent. Helen first attempted to conceive a child through artificial insemination by Susan's brother. When those efforts failed, Susan successfully conceived a child through artificial insemination by Helen's biological cousin,

Francis. The women attended childbirth classes together and Helen was present when Susan gave birth to Tammy on April 30, 1988. Although Tammy's birth certificate reflects Francis as her biological father, she was given a hyphenated surname using Susan and Helen's last names.

Since her birth, Tammy has lived with, and been raised and supported by, Helen and Susan. Tammy views both women as her parents, calling Helen "mama" and Susan "mommy." Tammy has strong emotional and psychological bonds with both Helen and Susan. Together, Helen and Susan have provided Tammy with a comfortable home, and have created a warm and stable environment which is supportive of Tammy's growth and over-all well being. Both women jointly and equally participate in parenting Tammy, and both have a strong financial commitment to her. . . . Francis does not participate in parenting Tammy and does not support her. His intention was to assist Helen and Susan in having a child, and he does not intend to be involved with Tammy, except as a distant relative. Francis signed an adoption surrender and supports the joint adoption by both women.

Helen and Susan, recognizing that the laws of the Commonwealth do not permit them to enter into a legally cognizable marriage, believe that the best interests of Tammy require legal recognition of her identical emotional relationship to both women. Susan expressed her understanding that it may not be in her own long-term interest to permit Helen to adopt Tammy because, in the event that Helen and Susan separate, Helen would have equal rights to primary custody. Susan indicated, however, that she has no reservation about allowing Helen to adopt. Apart from the emotional security and current practical ramifications which legal recognition of the reality of her parental relationships will provide Tammy, Susan indicated that the adoption is important for Tammy in terms of potential inheritance from Helen. Helen and her living issue are the beneficiaries of three irrevocable family trusts. Unless Tammy is adopted, Helen's share of the trusts may pass to others. . . .

Over a dozen witnesses, including mental health professionals, teachers, colleagues, neighbors, blood relatives and a priest and nun, testified to the fact that Helen and Susan participate equally in raising Tammy, that Tammy relates to both women as her parents, and that the three form a healthy, happy, and stable family unit. . . . [Both extended families unreservedly endorsed the adoption. The home study conducted by the Department of Social Services, the psychiatrist appointed as Tammy's guardian ad litem, and the attorney appointed to represent her interests all supported the adoption for her best interests.]

1. The initial question is whether the Probate Court judge had jurisdiction under G.L. c. 210 to enter a judgment on a joint petition for adoption brought by two unmarried cohabitants in the petitioners' circumstances. We answer this question in the affirmative.

There is nothing on the face of the statute which precludes the joint adoption of a child by two unmarried cohabitants such as the petitioners. Chapter 210, §1, provides that "[a] person of full age may petition the probate court in the county where he resides for leave to adopt as his child another person younger than himself, unless such other person is his or her wife or husband, or brother, sister, uncle or aunt, of the whole or half blood." Other than requiring that a spouse join in the petition, if the petitioner is married and the spouse is competent to join therein, the statute does not expressly prohibit or require joinder by any person. [I]t is apparent from the first sentence of G.L. c. 210, §1, that the Legislature considered and defined those combinations of persons which would lead to adoptions in violation of public policy. Clearly absent is any prohibition of adoption by two unmarried individuals like the petitioners. . . .

In this case all requirements in [the statute] are met, and there is no question that the judge's findings demonstrate that the directives [in the statute,] and in case law, have been satisfied. Adoption will not result in any tangible change in Tammy's daily life; it will, however, serve to provide her with a significant legal relationship which may be important in her future. At the most practical level, adoption will entitle Tammy to inherit from Helen's family trusts and from Helen and her family under the law of intestate succession, to receive support from Helen, who will be legally obligated to provide such support, to be eligible for coverage under Helen's health insurance policies, and to be eligible for social security benefits in the event of Helen's disability or death. Of equal, if not greater significance, adoption will enable Tammy to preserve her unique filial ties to Helen in the event that Helen and Susan separate, or Susan predeceases Helen. . . . The conclusion that the adoption is in the best interests of Tammy is also well warranted.

2. The judge also posed the question whether, pursuant to G.L. c. 210, §6 (1992 ed.), Susan's legal relationship to Tammy must be terminated if Tammy is adopted. Section 6 provides that, on entry of an adoption decree, "all rights, duties and other legal consequences of the natural relation of child and parent shall . . . except as regards marriage, incest or cohabitation, terminate between the child so adopted and his natural parents and kindred." Although G.L. c. 210, §2, clearly permits a child's natural parent to be an adoptive parent, §6 does not contain any express exceptions to its termination provision. The Legislature obviously did not intend that a natural parent's legal relationship to its child be terminated when the natural parent is a party to the adoption petition.

Section 6 clearly is directed to the more usual circumstances of adoption, where the child is adopted by persons who are not the child's natural parents (either because the natural parents have elected to relinquish the child for adoption or their parental rights have been involuntarily terminated). The purpose of the termination provision is to protect the security of the child's newly-created family unit by eliminating involvement with the child's natural parents. . . . Reading the adoption statute as a whole, we conclude that the termination provision contained in §6 was intended to apply only when the natural parents (or parent) are not parties to the adoption petition. . . .

ADOPTION OF GARRETT

841 N.Y.S.2d 731 (Sur. Ct. 2007)

RANDAL B. CALDWELL, J.

Before this Court is a petition for adoption filed by the natural mother of the child, Pamela V., and the proposed adoptive father, Michael J. The proposed adoptive father is the biological brother of the natural mother and they have resided at the same address only since December 2006.

The background to this adoption proceeding is found in the recent divorce decree of the biological parents of the child, present Petitioner Pamela and her ex-husband, Chad, dated June 13, 2007. The decree incorporates an opting-out agreement between the parties which provides that the father execute an irrevocable consent to the adoption of the child by his ex-wife and an unnamed "another male." In return, the mother agreed that the payment of $4,000 would satisfy the obligation to pay the outstanding child support arrears of $7,628.00 and that his child support obligation would cease. In essence, the father of the child agreed to relinquish all parental rights in exchange for the ending of his future support obligation and a favorable settlement of the past due amount.

It is undeniable that the area of adoption law has undergone a significant transformation in recent years whereby same-sex couples were deemed eligible to adopt (see, Matter of Jacob, [660 N.E.2d 397 (N.Y. 1995)]), and unmarried heterosexual couples were also permitted to adopt (see, Matter of Carl, [709 N.Y.S.2d 905 (Fam. Ct. 2000)]). Indeed this Court was the venue of one of the leading cases in this area, decided by former Surrogate John G. Ringrose, namely Matter of Joseph, [684 N.Y.S.2d 760 (Sur. Ct. 1998)], which held that an unmarried couple, residing together, would be permitted to adopt their foster child even though neither adoptive parent was the child's biological parent. Notably, however, all of these decisions have been predicated on the rationale that the relationship between the proposed adoptive parents is the functional equivalent of the traditional husband-wife relationship, albeit between same-sex couples or unmarried partners. The first case in Matter of Jacob, supra, involved the biological mother of the child and her unmarried heterosexual partner who had been living together for three years, and the second case involved the natural mother of the child and her lesbian partner who had lived together in a relationship for nineteen years. In analyzing the terms of the statute, the Court stated:

> The statute uses the word "together" only to describe married persons and thus does not preclude an unmarried person *in a relationship* with another unmarried person from adopting.

(86 N.Y.2d at p. 660, emphasis added).

The Court also discussed the nature of the changing American family where "at least 1.2 of the 3.5 million American households which consist of an unmarried adult couple have children under 15 years old". Similarly, in Matter of Carl, supra, the Court expressly considered the length of the relationship between the unmarried petitioners in that case and in Matter of Joseph, . . . in contrast to the high rate of divorce for married persons.

As recently noted by the Appellate Division of the Fourth Department, the adoption statute must be strictly construed as adoption is solely the creature of statute (Matter of Zoe D.K., [804 N.Y.S.2d 197 (App. Div. 2005)]). In that case, the Fourth Department would not permit the adoption of a child born out of wedlock by her unmarried biological parent where the effect would be to terminate the rights of the natural father while leaving unchanged the rights and responsibilities of the mother. The Court noted that the adoption did not foster the goals of providing the best possible home for the child or giving legal recognition to an existing family unit.

We are now asked to further expand the prior holdings to virtually unlimited boundaries, namely to authorize the adoption of a child by a natural parent and another member of that parent's family, namely the brother of the natural mother. This Court finds that the reasoning employed in the prior decisions expanding the right to adopt is simply inapplicable to the present case. In absence of direction by a higher Court that the right to adopt should be extended in this fashion, this Court will dismiss the pending petition. . . .

## NOTES AND QUESTIONS ON *TAMMY* AND *GARRETT*

1. *Stepparents and stepchild generally.*
a. *Prevalence.* Census data reveal that 5 percent of all children of householders are stepchildren. Bureau of the Census, U.S. Dept. of Commerce, Adopted Children and Stepchildren: 2000, 3, 6 (Oct. 2003). Stepparent adoptions comprise approximately half of all adoptions. Typically, the adopter is the spouse of one biological parent, who retains parental rights. See Unif. Adoption Act, 9 U.L.A. (pt. IA) 103-104 (1999) (cmt. on Art. 4).
b. *Support.* In the absence of adoption, the common law imposed no duty on stepparents to support their stepchildren either during a marriage or following its dissolution; courts and legislatures are changing these rules, however. See generally Margaret M. Mahoney, Stepfamilies and the Law (1994). Several states have statutes imposing financial responsibility on a stepparent who receives a child into the family, so long as the parent's and the stepparent's marriage continues. E.g., Wash. Rev. Code §26.16.205 (2008). Others simply codify the doctrine of in loco parentis, presuming a stepparent who accepts and supports a child does so as a parent but allowing unilateral termination of that status at any time, e.g., Okla. Stat. Ann. tit. 10, §15 (2008) (phrased in terms of husband's support of wife's children by former husband), or look to stepparents only when a child would otherwise become destitute, e.g., Vt. Stat. Ann. tit. 15, §296 (2007). The obligation does not continue, however, upon dissolution of that marriage. See, e.g., Weinand v. Wienand, 616 N.W.2d 1 (Neb. 2000) (ex-stepparent granted visitation not required to pay child support).

The ALI Principles do not recognize a general duty of support by stepparents. One who agrees or undertakes to assume a parental support obligation to a child, however, might later be estopped from denying a parental support obligation. American Law Institute, Principles of the Law of Family Dissolution: Analysis and Recommendations §3.03(1)(a) (2002). Under such circumstances, a court could impose a child support obligation on the stepparent after the dissolution of the relationship with the child's parent. See id. at cmt. b. An adult obligated to pay child support is a parent by estoppel for purposes of determining custodial and decisionmaking responsibility. Id. at §2.03. See Chapter 1, section B1b. See also Mary Ann Mason & Nicole Zayac, Rethinking Stepparent Rights: Has the ALI Found a Better Definition?, 36 Fam. L.Q. 227 (2002).

c. *Custody and visitation.* Traditionally, if a former stepparent sought post-dissolution custody in the face of parental objection, that stepparent had to overcome the legal preference for the biological parent. See David R. Fine & Mark A. Fine, Learning from Social Sciences: A Model for Reformation of the Laws Affecting Stepfamilies, 97 Dick. L. Rev. 49, 56 (1992) (citing survey finding that 38 states have such presumptions). Even if stepparents had a legally cognizable relationship with the child during the marriage, such recognition ended when the marriage terminated. See June Carbone, The Legal Definition of Parenthood: Uncertainty at the Core of Family Identity, 65 Louisiana L. Rev. 1295, 1312 (2005). Courts have become increasingly willing to grant visitation rights to former stepparents, especially given a long-term relationship with the child. Fine & Fine, supra, at 56. Some states accomplish this result by application of equitable doctrines such as in loco parentis. Carbone, supra, at 1328. Others have statutes that spell out the conditions under which a "third party" can win custody or visitation. E.g., Mo. Rev. Stat. §452.375.5(5)(a) (2008).

Does an award of stepparent visitation infringe a biological parent's constitutional rights as articulated in Troxel v. Granville, reprinted Chapter 1, section B2a? Compare Robinson v. Ford-Robinson, 208 S.W.3d 140 (Ark. 2005) (holding that court may award visitation to a stepparent standing in loco parentis over the biological parent's objection, distinguishing *Troxel* because petitioner was similar to a noncustodial parent), with In re Marriage of Engelkens, 821 N.E.2d 799 (Ill. App. Ct. 2004) (holding facially unconstitutional a statute allowing reasonable visitation to a stepparent if the court determines that it is in child's best interests). See also In re C.T.G. ex rel. P.G., 179 P.3d 213 (Colo. App. 2007) (reviewing limited standing of stepparents to seek visitation); McFall v. Watson, 2008 WL 4456957 (Ohio Ct. App. 2008) (reviewing statute allowing "any relative" of an unmarried mother, including child's stepparent, to seek visitation).

d. *Policy.* Professor David Chambers has observed that empirical studies find stepparents play an important family role:

> Some empirical evidence suggests that when residential stepparents enter children's lives, the children generally see their absent parents less often than they did before. [D]espite the ambiguities of the stepparent relationship, many individual stepparents do form strong emotional bonds with their stepchildren. They are seen by the child as "parent." And, of course, there is ample corresponding evidence that biologic fathers who do not live with their children will not pay child support unless compelled to do so and that they visit their children less and less as time passes, whether or not the mother remarries. In the future, we may come to view residential stepparents as replacing absent parents and assuming some or all of their responsibilities.

David L. Chambers, Stepparents, Biologic Parents, and the Law's Perceptions of "Family" after Divorce, in Divorce Reform at the Crossroads 102, 117 (Stephen D. Sugarman & Herma Hill Kay eds., 1990).

e. *Surnames.* Should stepchildren use the same surname as the members of the stepfamily? Or should they retain their original surnames? Compare In re Name Change of L.M.G., 738 N.W.2d 71 (S.D. 2007), with Hunter v. Haunert, 270 S.W.3d 339 (Ark. Ct. App. 2007). See generally Merle H. Weiner, "We Are

Family": Valuing Associationalism in Disputes Over Children's Surnames, 75 N.C. L. Rev. 1625 (1997).

2. *Stepparent adoptions: applicable standard.* What standard should a court use to decide whether to decree a stepparent adoption? Even if the child's best interests support formal recognition of the new family unit created when a custodial parent remarries, does that test suffice for terminating the non-custodial parent's rights, the traditional prerequisite of adoption? Does Santosky v. Kramer (reprinted Chapter 2, section A) apply in this context? Should a more permissive substantive standard govern TPR before stepparent adoption than for other adoptions? Or, should the law permit formal recognition for stepparents without necessarily terminating an original parent's rights? What weight, if any, does the custodial parent's autonomy carry in such cases? The Illinois supreme court has held that indigent biological parents, facing loss of their rights via a stepparent adoption, have a constitutional right to appointed counsel. In re Adoption of L.T.M., 824 N.E.2d 221 (Ill. 2005). See also M.E.K. v. R.L.K., 921 So. 2d 787 (Fla. Dist. Ct. App. 2006) (recognizing indigent parent's right to counsel in involuntary private adoption proceeding brought by a relative, because even private adoptions constitute state action).

3. *Legal consequences of stepparent adoptions.* Should the "cutoff" rule, supra, apply to stepparent adoptions? Why? Under the UAA, stepparent adoptions do not affect:

> (1) the relationship between the adoptee and the adoptee's parent who is the adoptive stepparent's spouse or deceased spouse;
> (2) an existing order for visitation or communication with a minor adoptee by an individual related to the adoptee through the parent who is the adoptive stepparent's spouse or deceased spouse;
> (3) the right of the adoptee or a descendant of the adoptee to inheritance or intestate succession through or from the adoptee's former parent; or
> (4) a court order or agreement for visitation or communication with a minor adoptee which is approved by the court. . . .

Unif. Adoption Act §4-103, 9 U.L.A. (pt. IA) 106 (1999).

Such statutory protections raise the possibility of dual inheritance, affording adoptees an advantage denied to biological children. The Uniform Probate Code's general rule against dual inheritance does not explicitly prevent an adoptee from inheriting from biological and adoptive relatives. Unif. Probate Code §2-113, 8 U.L.A. (pt. I) 91 (1998) (Rev. Art. II). Indeed, this Code creates an exception to the general rule in stepparent adoptions, providing that the adoptee and his or her descendants continue to inherit from and through the biological noncustodial parent in cases of intestate succession. Unif. Probate Code §2-114(b), 8 U.L.A. (pt. I) 91 (1998) (Rev. Art. II).

Why permit dual inheritance in these cases? See e.g., Raley v. Spikes, 614 So. 2d 1017 (Ala. 1993). Note that, without such provisions, courts might deny stepparent adoptions because the loss of intestate inheritance from the biological parent would prevent the adoption from serving the child's best interest. See Matter of Gerald G.G., 403 N.Y.S.2d 57 (App. Div. 1978).

4. *Second-parent adoption. Tammy* permits a practice called second-parent adoption. See, e.g., Jane S. Schacter, Constructing Families in a

Democracy: Courts, Legislatures, and Second-Parent Adoption, 75 Chi.-Kent L. Rev. 933 (2000). How does the practice resemble stepparent adoption? How does it differ? See Peter Wendel, Inheritance Rights and the Step-Partner Adoption Paradigm: Shades of Discrimination Against Illegitimate Children, 34 Hofstra L. Rev. 351 (2005).

Before Vermont permitted same-sex couples to enter civil unions, its supreme court allowed second-parent adoptions to come within the statutory exception for stepparents. In re Adoptions of B.L.V.B. & E.L.V.B., 628 A.2d 1271 (Vt. 1993). The legislature later codified this holding. Vt. Stat. Ann., tit. 15A, §1-102(b) (2007). The UAA follows this approach, indicating in comments that the provisions on stepparent adoptions should apply. Unif. Adoption Act §4-102 (cmts.), 9 U.L.A. (pt. IA) 105 (1999). Will courts necessarily construe "stepparent" to cover someone like Helen in *Tammy*? Why? Why not? See S.J.L.S. v. T.L.S., 265 S.W.3d 804, 822-828 (Ky. Ct. App. 2008) (rejecting concept of " 'stepparent-like' adoption" as inconsistent with state adoption laws).

5. *Statutory construction.* On what basis does the majority decide that the Massachusetts adoption statute permits Susan and Helen to adopt Tammy jointly? An omitted dissent rejects this conclusion, despite deciding that Helen can adopt Tammy while Susan retains her parental rights (the majority's second approach). Which presents the more persuasive statutory interpretation regarding joint adoption, the majority or the dissent? If Susan and Helen can jointly adopt Susan's biological child, would they be able to adopt jointly a child not related to either of them? See In re Infant Girl W., 845 N.E.2d 229 (Ind. Ct. App. 2006); In re Adoption of Carolyn B., 774 N.Y.S.2d 227 (App. Div. 2004) (permitting the joint adoption).

Alternatively, consider the second approach, reading the statute to permit Helen to adopt while Susan retains parental rights, despite the usual "cutoff" rule. Courts divide on this issue. Compare In re Adoption of Luke, 640 N.W.2d 374 (Neb. 2002) (finding child ineligible for adoption under statute without relinquishment by birth mother), with In re Adoption by R.B.F., 803 A.2d 1195 (Pa. 2002) (construing statutory amendment to permit adoption without termination of parental rights for good cause shown). See also Sharon S. v. Superior Ct., 73 P.3d 554 (Cal. 2003) (permitting second-parent adoption before effective date of California's domestic partnership legislation or recognition of same-sex marriage).

Some states now have statutes explicitly permitting the practice under some circumstances. E.g., Cal. Fam. Code §9000(b) (2008) (for domestic partners); Conn. Gen. Stat. Ann. §45a-724(a)(3) (2008) (for one who shares parental responsibility). On the question of interstate recognition of second-parent adoptions, see Finstuen v. Crutcher, reprinted Chapter 5, section B.

6. *Revocation.* Do the statutory difficulties in states without explicit legislation authorizing second-parent adoption make such adoptions vulnerable to revocation? Mothers, who earlier had consented to a second-parent adoption, have sometimes invoked both problems of statutory construction and public policy in later seeking to bar the child's contact with the second parent, after the adult relationship dissolves. See, e.g., *Sharon S.*, supra; Wheeler v. Wheeler,

642 S.E.2d 103 (Ga. 2007); In re Adoption Petition of Rebecca M., 178 P.3d 839 (N.M. Ct. App. 2008); Goodson v. Castellanos, 214 S.W.3d 741 (Tex. App. 2007) (all siding with second parent). See also Schott v. Schott, 744 N.W.2d 85 (Iowa 2008) (reversing trial court's attack sua sponte on the validity of previous second-parent adoptions).

7. *Policy considerations.* The division of authority on second-parent adoption highlights the tension between two oft-stated principles: that adoption law is purely statutory and that adoption law should serve a child's best interests. See, e.g., Mark Strasser, Courts, Legislatures, and Second-Parent Adoptions: On Judicial Deference, Specious Reasoning, and the Best Interests of the Child, 66 Tenn. L. Rev. 1019 (1999); Amanda C. Pustilnik, Note, Private Ordering, Legal Ordering, and the Getting of Children: A Counterhistory of Adoption Law, 20 Yale L. & Pol'y Rev. 263, 291-295 (2002).

Considering the child's best interests, what are the advantages to Tammy of the second-parent adoption? First, second-parent adoptions ensure that Tammy will be able to maintain her ties with Helen even if the relationship between Helen and Susan dissolves. Without such official recognition, some courts have denied standing to co-parents and permitted the biological mother to foreclose visitation. E.g., Alison D. v. Virginia M., 572 N.E.2d 27 (N.Y. 1991). Such adoptions can also ensure postdissolution support for the child and resolve disputes about the child between a co-parent and a deceased biological mother's relatives. E.g., Mariga v. Flint, 822 N.E.2d 620 (Ind. Ct. App. 2005) (allowing biological mother to sue adoptive mother for child support after relationship ended); Clifford K. v. Paul S. ex rel. Z.B.S., 619 S.E.2d 138 (W. Va. 2005) (granting custody to co-parent in litigation with deceased mother's father). Second, such adoptions provide benefits while the couple's relationship remains intact, for example, permitting the co-parent to consent to medical treatment for the child, to have access to school records, or to obtain insurance coverage for the child through an employer. See In re Adoption of Jacob, 660 N.E.2d 397, 399 (N.Y. 1995); American Bar Association, House of Delegates, Report 112A (Aug. 11-12, 2003) (report supporting resolution in favor of joint adoptions and second-parent adoptions) (available at http://www.abanet.org/leadership/2003/journal/112.pdf). Do these benefits also support "third-parent adoptions," for example, in cases in which a lesbian couple uses a known semen donor and all three adults plan to have a role in the child's upbringing? See A.A. v. B.B., 83 O.R. (3d) 561 (2007); Pamela Gatos, Note, Third-Parent Adoption in Lesbian and Gay Families, 26 Vt. L. Rev. 195 (2001). See also Chapter 6, section B2.

Emphasizing the benefits to children, the American Academy of Pediatrics supports second-parent adoption. See Erica Goode, Group Wants Gays to Have Right to Adopt a Partner's Child, N.Y. Times, Feb. 4, 2002, at A17. Are there child welfare reasons to disallow such adoptions? See, e.g., William C. Duncan, In Whose Best Interests: Sexual Orientation and Adoption Law, 31 Cap. U. L. Rev. 787, 798-802 (2003). Cf. *Clifford K.*, 619 S.E.2d at 161 (Maynard, J., dissenting in part).

8. *Same-sex marriage.* If Susan and Helen could have married (which Massachusetts would now permit), would the second-parent adoption become

unnecessary?[1] Beyond making statutory provisions on stepparent adoptions expressly applicable, would the automatic rules of parentage for a mother's spouse obviate the need for Helen to go to court to formalize her relationship with Tammy? See Chapter 1, section B1. To what extent should the availability of same-sex marriage and second-parent adoption diminish the availability of equitable remedies designed to fill gaps in the law that nontraditional families have faced? See, e.g., Titchenal v. Dexter, 693 A.2d 682 (Vt. 1997). See also Julie Shapiro, A Lesbian-Centered Critique of Second-Parent Adoptions, 14 Berkeley Women's L.J. 17, 32-25 (1999) (using *Titchenal*, supra, to illustrate problems posed for lesbians by second-parent adoptions).

Does the ruling in *Tammy* compel recognition of same-sex marriage? Once a state permits second-parent adoptions, what reason supports restricting marriage to heterosexual couples? Are children who are the subject of such second-parent adoptions disadvantaged compared to children of married parents? In holding that the Massachusetts constitution prohibits denying same-sex couples access to the benefits of marriage, the court relied on *Tammy* to reject the state's arguments identifying procreation as the essential element of marriage and supporting marriage restrictions as a means to ensure an optimal setting for childrearing. Goodridge v. Department of Pub. Health, 798 N.E.2d 941, 962 n.24, 963, 966 n.30 (Mass. 2003). But see id. at 1000 (Cordy, J., dissenting).

9. *Only conjugal couples?* Given the well-established place of stepparent adoptions that follow a parent's remarriage and new variations such as second-parent adoptions within same-sex couples, why does *Garrett* reject the proposed adoption? Why did the various approaches to statutory construction in *Tammy* not apply in *Garrett*? Why does *Garrett* require a conjugal relationship in order for two persons to share legal parenthood of a child? Children are not expected to witness their parents' sexual activities, so why would a sexual relationship constitute a prerequisite for the proposed adoption? Given the number of marriages and nonmarital conjugal relationships that dissolve, wouldn't the mother and her brother, as in the principal case, provide an even more stable family for the child than a traditional stepparent adoption? Given the two-parent norm and the recognition of the superior ability of two parents, over one, to support a child (see Elisa B. v. Superior Ct., reprinted Chapter 1, section B1b), why shouldn't two individuals such as the mother and her brother here be eligible to adopt? What of one parent and a close friend? If such adoptions should be permitted, must the two adults live together? Why? To what extent do the answers to the questions depend on the alternative in the absence of the proposed adoption—whether the maintenance of the second biological parent's rights, continuation of single parenthood, or a continued wait for an adoptive placement? See

---

[1] In fact, the couple (who had moved to Los Angeles) married in San Francisco when same-sex weddings were being performed there and before the judicial invalidation of such marriages. Helen Cooksey, Susan Love, N.Y. Times, Feb. 22, 2004, §9, at 12 (weddings and celebrations). Same-sex marriages resumed in California in 2008 after the state supreme court held a ban unconstitutional, In re Marriage Cases, 183 P.3d 384 (Cal. 2008), but became unavailable again after the passage of Proposition 8. See supra Chapter 1, section B1b.

Jessica R. Feinberg, Friends as Co-Parents, 43 U.S.F. L. Rev. _____ (forthcoming 2009); Angela Mae Kupenda, Two Parents Are Better Than None: Whether Two Single African American Adults — Who Are Not in a Traditional Marriage or a Romantic or Sexual Relationship with Each Other — Should Be Allowed to Jointly Adopt and Co-Parent African American Children, 35 U. Louisville J. Fam. L. 703 (1996-1997).

## C. SECRECY VERSUS DISCLOSURE

### 1. SEALED-RECORD LAWS

Secrecy has long shrouded the adoption process in most states. To maintain this secrecy, statutes provide for the issuance of a new birth certificate upon adoption, changing the name of the adoptee to that of the adoptive parents. (The original birth certificate is then sealed.) Professor Elizabeth Samuels, offers the following historical summary:

> [I]n the 1940s and 1950s, a variety of expert voices advised states to seal court and birth records but to recognize in adult adoptees an unrestricted right of access to the birth records. The reason given for the closing of court and birth records to the parties as well as the public was to protect adoptive families from possible interference by birth parents. In contrast, no reason was generally offered in specific support of the closings of birth records to adult adoptees that did occur from the 1930s through the 1960s. It appears that the early closings of birth records to adult adoptees were not the result of articulated reasons, nor merely the result of confusion or happenstance. The early closings may have been, in no small part, the consequence of a contemporary social attitude or understanding, that is, of the social context in which they occurred. Adoption was beginning to be perceived as a means of creating a perfect and complete substitute for a family created by natural childbirth. Over time, as legal rules established a nearly universal regime of secrecy with respect to all persons' access to court records and all persons' except adult adoptees' access to birth records, the regime of secrecy itself inevitably influenced social attitudes and understandings. Actions once thought natural, such as attempts by adoptees to learn information about their birth families, came to be socially disfavored and considered abnormal. Such attempts acquired negative social meanings: they were the psychologically unhealthful product of unsuccessful adoptions that had failed to create perfect substitutes for natural families created by childbirth, and they indicated adoptees' rejection of and ingratitude toward adoptive parents. Eventually, lifelong secrecy would be viewed as an essential feature of adoptions in which birth and adoptive parents did not know one another.

Elizabeth J. Samuels, The Idea of Adoption: An Inquiry into the History of Adult Adoptee Access to Birth Records, 53 Rutgers L. Rev. 367, 370-371 (2001). Another account attributes the practice of secrecy to the corrupt efforts of Georgia Tann, who arranged thousands of adoptions in Tennessee between 1924 and 1950 and sought to cover up the kidnapping and baby selling that were frequently part of her placement service. Barbara Bisantz Raymond,

The Baby Thief: The Untold Story of Georgia Tann, the Baby Seller Who Corrupted Adoption 188-189, 209 (2007).

In the early 1970s, support and advocacy groups such as the Adoptees' Liberation Movement Association (the ALMA Society) began to press for the opening of sealed records. Courts rejected adult adoptees' constitutional challenges to sealed-record laws, concluding that the right to privacy does not include a fundamental "right to know" one's biological parents and that adoptees do not constitute a suspect class for equal protection purposes. The laws survived rational basis review as protection for the interests of all parties. See, e.g., In re Roger B., 418 N.E.2d 751 (Ill.), *appeal dismissed sub nom.* Barth v. Finley, 454 U.S. 806 (1981). Commentators suggest that, today, courts would reach different results for adult adoptees, given the recognized importance of identity interests and other developments in family law, including challenges to the traditional unitary family. Naomi Cahn & Jana Singer, Adoption, Identity, and the Constitution: The Case for Opening Closed Records, 2 U. Pa. J. Const. L. 150 (1999); Jennifer R. Racine, Comment, A Fundamental Rights Debate: Should Wisconsin Allow Adult Adoptees Unconditional Access to Adoption Records and Original Birth Certificates?, 2002 Wis. L. Rev. 1435. But see In re Adoption S.J.D., 641 N.W.2d 794 (Iowa 2002) (rejecting adoptee's First Amendment challenge to sealed birth records).

Most sealed-record statutes permit disclosure on a showing of good cause. E.g., Ga. Code Ann. §19-8-23(a) (2008). Courts have been more willing to find good cause for medical (such as for diagnosis of genetic disease) than psychological reasons. Compare, e.g., Doe v. Ward Law Firm, P.A., 579 S.E.2d 303 (S.C. 2003) (child's health problems constitute good cause), with In re Philip S., 881 A.2d 931 (R.I. 2005) (rejecting asserted religious basis for good cause). See also In re Adoption of Sherman, 2007 WL 703498 (V.I. 2007) (rejecting birth mother's petition to open records and finding that her wish to see her son and include him in her will do not constitute good cause). Although courts have declined to treat a psychological "need to know" as good cause, in a concurring opinion in In Application of Maples, 563 S.W.2d 760 (Mo. 1978), Judge Seiler explained the need adoptees have for finding their origins: "All of us need to know our past, not only for a sense of lineage and heritage, but for a fundamental and crucial sense of our very selves: our identity is incomplete and our sense of self retarded without a real personal historical connection. . . ." Id. at 767. Experts in other fields view adoptees' searches as a helpful response to the psychological problems caused by secrecy. See, e.g., Robert S. Andersen, Why Adoptees Search: Motives and More, 67 Child Welfare 15, 18 (1988). See also Annette Baran & Reuben Pannor, Open Adoption, in The Psychology of Adoption 316, 318 (David M. Brodzinsky & Marshall D. Schechter eds., 1990).

Sealed records can create special problems for adoptive parents of "special needs" children whose medical histories might yield important information about their current problems. Some states now routinely authorize release of the child's medical history (and that of the parents and grandparents) to adoptive parents. See Okla. Stat. Ann. tit. 10, §7504-1.1 (2008). Further, without health information about their birth families, adult adoptees have trouble providing for their children's medical care. See Carol Barbieri, Your Mother Would Know, N.Y. Times, Nov. 29, 2005, at A1 (op-ed).

## Depictions in Popular Culture: A.M. Homes, The Mistress's Daughter: A Memoir (2007)

In this memoir, novelist and writer for popular television shows, A.M. Homes recounts, with painstaking self-reflection, her feelings and experiences after her birth parents, who relinquished her for adoption as an infant, initiated contact 31 years later, through her adoptive parents. Homes learns that she was conceived during an extramarital affair of her biological father, Norman, with a much younger unmarried woman, Ellen. Ellen dies during the course of the events covered in the book.

At one point, Norman insists that he and Homes have DNA tests. They go to a lab. Homes poignantly describes a moment of recognition:

> As Norman walks up to the counter, I notice that his butt looks familiar; I am watching him and I'm thinking: There goes my ass. That's my ass walking away. His blue sport coat covers it halfway, but I can see it broken into sections, departments of ass, high and low just like mine. I notice his thighs — chubby, thick, not a pretty thing. This is the first time I have seen anyone else in my body.
>
> I stare as he turns and comes back to me. I look down at his shoes, white loafers, country-club shoes, stretched out, fading. Inside the shoe, his feet are wide and short. I look up; his hands are the same as mine, square like paws. He is an exact replica, the male version of me. . . .

Id. at 51. Later, after Ellen's death, Homes has a similar experience when she finds in Ellen's pants pockets a wad of money, just as she keeps in her own pockets: "It creeps me out, this indescribable subtlety of biology. In her pockets I find the same things I find in mine. . . ." Id. at 102. Homes reflects on the resulting "hum of identification, a sense of wholeness and well-being," while later realizing how hard she must work to find information that her birth relatives "have lived with all along — information that is theirs for the asking. . . ." Id. at 149-151.

In bringing to life the emotions of one adopted individual, what implications, if any, does this memoir have for adoption law and policy?

## 2. LAW REFORM

Two states, Alaska and Kansas, have long allowed adult adoptees to view their birth records. Alaska Stat. §18.50.500 (2008); Kan. Stat. Ann. §65-2423 (2006). The modern wave of legislative reform elsewhere includes different approaches. (1) Some states have created voluntary registries that will provide information when both parties, e.g., birth family member and adoptee, have registered. E.g., Ark. Code Ann. §9-9-503 (2008). Voluntary matching over the Internet, without state assistance, has made such laws obsolete, however. Adam Pertman, Adoption Nation: How the Adoption Revolution Is Transforming America 32 (2000). (2) Some states have statutes under which an intermediary will contact one party to obtain consent to release information once the other party has registered. E.g., Ind. Code Ann. §31-19-24-2 (2008). (3) Some states have enacted laws honoring a party's request for information in the absence of a veto registered by the other party. E.g., Mich. Comp. Laws Ann. §710.68(7) (2008). See generally Caroline B. Fleming, Note, The Open-Records Debate: Balancing the Interests of Birth Parents and Adult Adoptees, 11 Wm. & Mary J. Women & L. 461, 474-475 (2005) (examining reforms).

More recently, some states have gone further. For example, Tennessee enacted both a disclosure provision opening adoption records and a "contact veto" to be exercised if one party does not want communication from the other. Tenn. Code Ann. §§36-1-127; 36-1-128 (2008). A 1998 ballot initiative in Oregon, Measure 58, gave adult adoptees access to their birth records. See Or. Rev. Stat. Ann. §432.240 (2007). These laws were unsuccessfully challenged by birth mothers who relinquished children under promises of confidentiality along with opponents who claimed the reforms will encourage abortion and discourage adoption. Both state and federal courts have rejected arguments that these reforms unconstitutionally impair vested rights and the obligation of contracts and violate the rights of reproductive privacy and nondisclosure. See Doe v. Sundquist, 106 F.3d 702 (6th Cir.), *cert. denied,* 522 U.S. 810 (1997); Doe 1 v. State, 993 P.2d 822 (Or. Ct. App. 1999), *rev. denied,* 6 P.3d 1098 (Or.), *stay denied,* 530 U.S. 1228 (2000); Doe v. Sundquist, 2 S.W.3d 919 (Tenn. 1999). See generally Pertman, supra; Cahn & Singer, supra; Fleming, supra; Samuels, supra. For a review of recent reforms here and abroad, see D. Marianne Brower Blair, The Impact of Family Paradigms, Domestic Constitutions, and International Conventions on Disclosure of an Adopted Person's Identities and Heritage: A Comparative Examination, 22 Mich. J. Int'l L. 587 (2001).

## Depictions in Popular Culture: Secrets and Lies (1996)

In this classic and well-received film by famed British director Mike Leigh, Cynthia's depressing, anxiety-ridden, and economically stressed existence with her sullen daughter Roxanne, a street sweeper, is abruptly interrupted when an older daughter she relinquished as an infant finds her. Hortense, a sophisticated young London optometrist whose adoptive parents recently died, locates Cynthia because of "the 1975 Act" opening birth records to adult adoptees. Just as Hortense, who is Black, is shocked to learn that her mother is Caucasian, so too does Cynthia believe there must be an error in the identity of the daughter whom she refused to see after birth for fear that she would become too emotionally attached to let go. Hortense's arrival adds a new dimension to her own life as well as to the lives of Cynthia and Roxanne. Further, Cynthia's revelations of her own "secrets and lies" spark other family revelations, including the infertility and resulting deep shame of Cynthia's financially successful brother and his wife.

In beginning her search, Hortense is warned that she should not get her hopes up, that her birth mother legitimately never expected to see her again, but that the law had changed. Indeed, although Hortense initiates the search and contact and Cynthia initially resists (hanging up the telephone when Hortense first summons the courage to call), it is Cynthia and those around her who are "reborn" as the result of the reunion. Rita Kempley, "Secrets & Lies": Human Right Down to the Heart, Wash. Post, Oct. 11, 1996, at D1. By contrast, Hortense's "life was fine before the action starts and will continue on an even keel afterward." Roger Ebert, Sharing "Secrets"; Leigh Has Us Rooting for Family, Chi. Sun Times, Oct. 25, 1996, Weekend Plus section, at 40. What implications, if any, does this story have for law reform?

Despite the uniqueness of each story of an adoption search and reunion, what do the different races of Cynthia and Hortense add to this particular story? According to one reviewer, "this story has more to do with classism — that perennial British obsession — than racism." Kempley, supra. See also Ebert, supra ("[R]ace is not really on anyone's mind in this film."). In turn, what does the relative insignificance of race in this story reveal — given the historical emphasis on race in adoption in the United States?

### 3. "OPEN ADOPTION"

The movement to open adoption records has focused on adoptees who have reached adulthood. In addition, the asserted "need to know" and the belief that secrecy can result in psychological difficulties for all parties have prompted a new approach, "open adoption," that focuses on young adoptees.[2]

GROVES V. CLARK

982 P.2d 446 (Mont. 1999)

Justice WILLIAM E. HUNT, SR. delivered the Opinion of the Court. . . .

This is the second appeal filed in this case concerning post-adoption visitation between Groves and L.C. A more detailed account of the facts of this

[2] Open adoption was introduced in the literature in 1976 in an article noting the absence of secrecy in adoption in traditional Hawaiian culture. Annette Baran et al., Open Adoption, 21 Soc. Work 97 (1976). See Reuben Pannor & Annette Baran, Open Adoption as Standard Practice, 63 Child Welfare 245 (1984).

case can be found in Groves v. Clark, 920 P.2d 981 [(Mont. 1996)]. To summarize, in January 1994, when L.C. was three years old, Groves signed a document terminating her parental rights to L.C., relinquishing custody of L.C. to Lutheran Social Services (LSS), and consenting to adoption. Groves and the Clarks signed a written visitation agreement which provided the following: Groves would have unrestricted visitation with L.C. so long as she gave the Clarks two days notice; Groves would have unrestricted telephone contact with L.C.; and Groves would have the right to take L.C. out of school in the event she had to "go to Butte for some emergency." This agreement was drafted by the LSS and neither party consulted an attorney before signing it. In February 1994, the District Court entered an order terminating Groves' parental rights to L.C. and awarding custody of L.C. to LSS. In September 1994, the Clarks legally adopted L.C.

Groves and the Clarks abided by the terms of the visitation agreement until June 5, 1995, when Groves notified the Clarks that she wanted to take L.C. to Butte for the weekend and the Clarks refused. The Clarks told Groves that she was welcome to visit L.C. in their home, but could not take L.C. on extended out-of-town trips. [Groves then sought specific performance of the visitation agreement, and the Clarks objected, moving for summary judgment. The District Court denied Groves' petition for specific performance on the ground that the post-adoption visitation agreement was void and unenforceable. Groves appealed to this Court, which reversed, holding:]

> [B]irth parents and prospective adoptive parents are free to contract for post-adoption visitation and . . . trial courts must give effect to such contracts when continued visitation is in the best interest of the child.

We remanded the case to the District Court for a hearing on whether enforcement of the parties' visitation agreement would be in the best interest of L.C.

Based on the evidence produced at trial, the [District Court] found that a bond existed between Groves and L.C. and that it was highly likely L.C. would suffer from issues of abandonment, identity, and grieving unless appropriate visitation with Groves was granted. Ultimately, the court found that continued visitation between Groves and L.C. was in L.C.'s best interest. . . . Specifically, the court granted Groves unsupervised monthly weekend visitation with L.C. and required the parties to share equally in the transportation costs. Additionally, the court granted Groves telephone contact with L.C. at least once per week. The court recommended that the parties seek adoption counseling and attempt to agree upon future visitation modifications that may be appropriate as L.C. matures.

[On appeal,] the Clarks assert that the adoptive parents' wishes are paramount in deciding whether a post-adoption visitation agreement should be enforced. The Clarks cite several cases from other jurisdictions purportedly holding that adoptive parents have the right to determine whether it is in the best interest of the adopted child to maintain contact with the birth mother. [Citations omitted.] The Clarks also cite cases from other jurisdictions purportedly holding that the mere fact that the adoptive parents oppose visitation provides a sufficient basis for finding that visitation is not in the best interest of the child. [Citations omitted.]

We reject the Clarks' assertions. . . . The law in Montana, which also happens to be the law of this case, is clear: whether a post-adoption visitation agreement is enforceable shall be decided by the District Court pursuant to a "best interests" analysis. The adoptive parents' wishes is but one factor among many to be considered by the District Court.

Next, the Clarks argue that the court did not adequately consider and evaluate the evidence when applying the "best interests" standard. [The Clarks] testified that visitation adversely affected L.C. in that afterward she would evidence insecurity about her adoption status, would be moody and difficult to discipline. On the other hand, the court heard the testimony of the [Groves'] experts including Kathy Gerhke [an adoptive parenting instructor] and Debbie O'Brien [a family counselor] which explained this as a normal occurrence. Based on their testimony, this court finds that it is highly likely L.C. will suffer from issues of abandonment, identity, and grieving unless appropriate visitation is granted. L.C. lived with her mother for over three years. The evidence, including from a visitation facilitator, was that visitation was a happy experience for L.C. . . .

[T]he Clarks assert that visitation with Groves is not in L.C.'s best interests because the Clarks do not know the details of the visitation such as where L.C. will be, what L.C. will be doing, and with whom L.C. will be associating. The Clarks have expressed concern over L.C.'s sleeping arrangements at Groves' residence. The Clarks disapprove of L.C. snowmobiling and riding in a car without wearing a seatbelt. . . . These concerns were not presented to the District Court at trial. . . .

[W]e determine that the court's finding that visitation between Groves and L.C. was in the best interest of L.C. was not clearly erroneous. The finding was supported by substantial evidence, the court did not misapprehend the effect of the evidence, and we do not believe a mistake was committed. . . . We [also] agree with the District Court that modification of the parties' original visitation agreement was within its discretion in accordance with determining the best interests of L.C. The policy of this state is that "in matters relating to children, the best interests of the children are paramount." [F]ailure to apply this rule to disputes involving post-adoption visitation agreements could potentially lead to absurd results. It would be incongruous for a court to hold that visitation is in the best interest of a child and then enforce a visitation agreement that was not in the best interest of the child. For these reasons, we determine that the District Court did not abuse its discretion in modifying the parties' post-adoption visitation agreement. . . .

## NOTES AND QUESTIONS

1. *Background.* The rise of open or cooperative adoption emerged from several developments: First, an increasing number of older children, with established bonds to their birth families, have been freed for adoption. Second, because of the decreased availability of the most sought-after infants for adoption following the legalization of abortion, birth parents can demand

enhanced conditions in placement, including open-adoption arrangements. Finally, experts claim that an open system avoids the damaging psychological effects of anonymity for adoptees, birth parents, and adopters. See, e.g., Annette Ruth Appell, The Move Toward Legally Sanctioned Cooperative Adoption: Can It Survive the Uniform Adoption Act?, 30 Fam. L.Q. 483, 483 (1996). See also Adam Pertman, Adoption Nation: How the Adoption Revolution Is Transforming America 47 (2000).

With the prevalence of both adoptions by stepparents and relatives and also adoptions of foster children, most adoptions today are not anonymous.

2. *Enforcement.* Several states allow voluntary open adoption but permit the adoptive parents to determine whether to abide by such agreements. *Groves* cites cases from Arizona, Colorado, Maryland, and Pennsylvania taking this position. Alternatively, some states authorize judicial approval of such agreements upon a finding of best interests and then enforcement of agreements so approved. See, e.g., Minn. Stat. Ann. §259.58 (2007); Birth Mother v. Adoptive Parents, 59 P.3d 1233, 1236 (Nev. 2002) (rejecting enforcement "if the agreement is not incorporated in the adoption decree"); Fast v. Moore, 135 P.3d 387 (Or. Ct. App. 2006) (enforcement of agreement requires prior court approval).

The UAA expressly provides for judicial enforcement of visitation agreements in stepparent adoptions. Unif. Adoption Act §4-113, 9 U.L.A. (pt. IA) 110-112 (1999). Otherwise, however, it permits "mutually agreed-upon communication between birth and adoptive families" without making such agreements enforceable. See id. at 15 (Prefatory Note ¶9). The UAA's failure to dictate enforceability has evoked criticism from proponents of open adoption. See, e.g., Appell, supra.

3. *Open adoption in practice.* For a review of the applicable statutes and preliminary empirical data about their use, see Annette R. Appell, Survey of State Utilization of Adoption with Contact, 6 Adoption Q. 75 (2003). Professor Appell found that states with such statutes generally lack "formal mechanisms to inform relatives and prospective adoptive parents about the adoption with contact option." Id. at 80. Further, "only Oregon and California have formal programs to assist parties to reach, and draft, postadoption contact agreements." Id. Appell also found that concerns about informal contact agreements often motivated the enactment of such statutes and that child welfare agencies play an important role in the use of postadoption contact mechanisms. Id. at 83. See also Kirsten Widner, Comment, Continuing the Evolution: Why California Should Amend Family Code 8616.55 to Allow Visitation in All Postadoption Contact Agreements, 44 San Diego L. Rev. 355, 382-384 (2007) (arguing for required notification of birth parents about the option of postadoption contact).

4. *Parental rights.* Why does *Groves* go beyond all of these approaches, allowing courts to fashion arrangements that the parties have not chosen? Does *Groves* make adoptive parents "second-class" parents? Should adoptive parents have the same rights as other parents to determine the extent of their children's visitation, if any, with legal strangers? See Troxel v. Granville, Chapter 1, section B2a. In *Groves,* who should resolve the asserted disputes about snowmobiling and seatbelts? Does open adoption conflict with

the very concept of adoption, as some older cases have held? E.g., Hill v. Moorman, 525 So. 2d 681 (La. Ct. App. 1988); Cage v. Harrisonburg Dept. of Soc. Servs., 410 S.E.2d 405 (Va. Ct. App. 1991). Recall and evaluate Professor Meyer's proposal for nonconsensual open adoptions to solve the legal problem posed by birth parents' flawed consent in cases such as those of Baby Jessica and Baby Richard, noted Chapter 2, section B2. See David D. Meyer, Family Ties: Solving the Constitutional Dilemma of the Faultless Father, 41 Ariz. L. Rev. 753, 833-846 (1999).

5. *Status.* What is the legal status of biological parents after an open adoption? Do they remain parents? Are they legal strangers to the child? Do they occupy some intermediate status?

An Alabama appellate court has ruled that a biological father has standing to file a dependency petition for a child, who had been adopted but with whom he maintained a relationship, based on his belief that the adoptive parents were not properly supervising the child. W.C.R. v. D.A.L., 963 So. 2d 99 (Ala. Civ. App. 2007). Although the biological father (who also sought custody or visitation) no longer had parental rights because of the adoption, he had standing to bring the dependency action because of his knowledge of the facts underlying his dependency allegations. See also Morgan v. Weiser, 923 A.2d 1183 (Pa. Super. Ct. 2007) (recognizing that biological father, whose rights were terminated, might seek custody or visitation as a third party, but rejecting his claim to in loco parentis status because he never lived with the child and because he could not achieve such status in defiance of legal (adoptive) parents' wishes).

---

## Depictions in Popular Culture: Immediate Family (1989)

After struggling with the stress and disappointment of infertility, Linda (Glenn Close) and Michael (James Woods), an upper-middle-class couple living in a beautiful home with a breathtaking view in Seattle, consult an attorney who recommends the "relatively new procedure" of open adoption. Lucy (Mary Stuart Masterson) and Sam (Kevin Dillon), blue-collar teenagers from Ohio, choose Linda and Michael as adoptive parents for their expected baby. Lucy travels to Seattle to give birth, and Sam joins her there. Lucy, who has lived with a stepfather ever since her mother died when Lucy was only seven, finds in Linda and Michael the parental figures missing from her life; Michael and Linda find themselves negotiating an awkward and unfamiliar role in their developing relationship with Lucy and Sam and their anticipation of adding a baby to their lives. Lucy experiences a period of uncertainty but ultimately completes the relinquishment—explaining that the child should know that she based her decision on love. Closing scenes depict the next year, when the child celebrates his first birthday, Lucy and Sam seem to have achieved some economic stability, and the presence of a photograph in Lucy's possession shows that communication between the birth parents and the adoptive parents has continued.

> Despite the trite plot and the predictable denouement, the film provides a glimpse of the collaborative familial relationships that open adoption creates and that might flourish even without legal supervision. Should Linda and Michael treat Lucy and Sam as their teenage kids? But then what would that mean for their relationship with the baby? Will the connections among these people, from different states and different backgrounds, go beyond the mailing of occasional photographs? What will the open adoption — however it plays out in the coming years — mean for the child? Will he have the best of both worlds or feel longing and distress? What stance should the law take with respect to open adoption? Why?

6. *Grandparent visitation.* Some states have special rules authorizing post-adoption visitation by grandparents. E.g., Tex. Fam. Code §161.206(c) (2007). Why not rely on the general best interests test for such cases? To what extent does *Troxel* make these laws constitutionally vulnerable? Compare Ex Parte D.W., 835 So. 2d 186 (Ala. 2002) (distinguishing *Troxel* to uphold authorization of visitation by "natural grandparents" after intrafamily adoption), with Visitation of Cathy L.(R.) M. v. Mark Brent R., 617 S.E.2d 866 (W. Va. 2005) (*Troxel* requires giving adoptive parents special weight in deciding whether biological grandparents can visit, even in intrafamily adoptions). How should courts analyze such cases in the absence of special grandparent visitation statutes? See In re Adoption of R.S., 231 S.W.3d 826 (Mo. Ct. App. 2007).

7. *Sibling visitation.* Are special rules warranted for postadoption visitation by biological siblings? Why? Compare In re Adoption of Anthony, 448 N.Y.S.2d 377 (Fam. Ct. 1982) (ordering visitation in child's best interests), and Cocose v. Diane B., 803 N.Y.S.2d 17 (Fam. Ct. 2005) (refusing to dismiss petition for sibling visitation, despite adoptive parents' argument based on *Troxel*), with In re Adoption of T.J.F., 798 N.E.2d 867 (Ind. Ct. App. 2003) (using adopted child's best interests to halt visitation with biological sibling), and Adoption of Pierce, 790 N.E.2d 680 (Mass. App. Ct. 2003) (upholding dismissal of sister's claim for visitation with her adopted brother). Should preservation of a child's relationship with a biological sibling operate as a reason to reject adoption as the best permanency plan for the child? Should the court consider the impact on both siblings or only the child to be adopted? See In re Celine R., 71 P.3d 787 (Cal. 2003). See generally William Wesley Patton, The Status of Siblings' Rights: A View Into the New Millennium, 51 DePaul L. Rev. 1 (2001); Angela Ferraris, Comment, Sibling Visitation as a Fundamental Right in Herbst v. Swan, 39 New Eng. L. Rev. 715 (2005); Meghann M. Seifert, Note, Sibling Visitation after Adoption: The Implications of the Massachusetts Sibling Visitation Statute, 84 B.U. L. Rev. 1467 (2004).

For the findings of an empirical study on sibling contact, see Jerica M. Berge et al., Adolescent Sibling Narratives Regarding Contact in Adoption, 9 Adoption Q. 81 (2006) (using interviews to examine experiences of 58 nonbiologically adopted siblings with varying levels of contact with their birth families).

## Note: Guardianship

Open adoption forms part of a larger debate about whether the parent-child relationship must be complete and exclusive or whether the law ought to recognize a child's connections with multiple parental figures. See, e.g., Katharine T. Bartlett, Rethinking Parenthood as an Exclusive Status: The Need for Legal Alternatives When the Premise of the Nuclear Family Has Failed, 70 Va. L. Rev. 879 (1984). Professor Brigitte Bodenheimer pioneered a new approach, suggesting as a "compromise" in contested adoption cases naming a guardian without terminating biological parents' rights. Brigitte M. Bodenheimer, New Trends and Requirements in Adoption Law and Proposals for Legislative Change, 49 S. Cal. L. Rev. 10, 41 (1975).

Traditionally, parents serve as a child's "natural guardians," but courts appoint a guardian for a minor (or incompetent) when parental care is unavailable or inadequate to serve a particular need of the child. See, e.g., Cotton v. Wise, 977 S.W.2d 263 (Mo. 1998). Cf. Freeman v. Rushton, 202 S.W.3d 485 (Ark. 2005) (statutory preference for fit parent as guardian does not require his selection as guardian). Most courts defer to parental autonomy in the appointment of a minor's guardian even after the parent's death. See, e.g., Bristol v. Brundage, 589 A.2d 1 (Conn. App. Ct. 1991). But see Wild v. Adrian, 155 P.3d 1036 (Wyo. 2007) (disallowing intervention to modify custody by the couple whom the father, now deceased, had designated as his children's guardian when their mother survives). Generally, guardianship of a minor ends upon the age of majority. E.g., In re Hollins, 872 N.E.2d 1214 (Ohio 2007).

States often distinguish guardianship generally or guardianship of the person, which entails rights and duties of custody and decisionmaking, from guardianship of the estate, which entails responsibility for the ward's property and financial interests. Compare, e.g., Conn. Gen. Stat. Ann. §17a-93(d) (2008), with Conn. Gen. Stat. Ann. §45a-629 (2008). Guardians ad litem advocate for or represent the minor's or incompetent individual's interests in connection with legal proceedings. See, e.g., People v. Delores W., 888 N.E.2d 15 (Ill. 2008) (upholding appointment of guardian ad litem for a mentally disabled mother who already had a guardian of the person). Some courts hold that a guardian ad litem is appropriate for children only when they are parties to a proceeding, not when they are the subjects of a proceeding, as in an adoption case. E.g., In re Doe, 848 N.Y.S.2d 820, 821-822 (Sur. Ct. 2007).

Different standards typically prevail for an adult to be named a child's guardian rather than an adoptive parent. For example, recall that in *Lofton*, reprinted Chapter 3, section A1b, the state allowed the petitioner to become the child's guardian but not his adoptive parent. Similarly, courts have expressed skepticism of the use of guardianship to interfere with parental rights without meeting otherwise applicable standards. See, e.g., Devine v. Martens, 263 S.W.3d 515, 526 (Ark. 2007) (overturning permanent guardianship for grandparents, while noting that "courts should not be in the business of permanently removing children from their parents' custody simply because the parents have exercised poor judgment in caring for their children"); Guardianship of Estelle, 875 N.E.2d 515 (Mass. Ct. App. 2007) (rejecting guardianship unless surviving parent is found unfit); Fischer v. Fischer, 157 P.3d 682 (Mont. 2007) (reversing temporary guardianship granted to a custodial father's friends during his military deployment because of respect required for the rights of a noncustodial fit mother). But see Smith v. Thomas, 2008 WL 2055207 (Ark. 2008).

The HIV/AIDS epidemic prompted the development of a new type of guardianship, standby guardianship, enabling parents suffering from a terminal illness to plan for the future of their children before death or incapacitation. This approach responds to the particular needs of ill single mothers by allowing for a "backup" guardian without requiring the mother to relinquish parental rights. See, e.g., Va. Code Ann. §§16.1-349 to -355 (2008). Likewise, absence for military service might prompt a parent to name a guardian. E.g., Lebo v. Lebo, 886 So. 2d 491 (La. Ct. App. 2004).

Finally, reforms aimed at meeting the needs of the numerous children in foster care include proposals for subsidized guardianships. See Sarah Ramsey, Fixing Foster Care or Reducing Child Poverty: The Pew Commission Recommendations and the Transracial Adoption Debate, 66 Mont. L. Rev. 21, 46-48 (2005); Mark F. Testa, The Quality of Permanence — Lasting or Binding? Subsidized Guardianship and Kinship Foster Care as Alternatives to Adoption, 12 Va. J. Soc. Pol'y & L. 499 (2005).

In particular, kinship foster parents often prefer to be named guardians rather than to pursue adoption for several reasons, "which may include a strong personal desire not to terminate the parental rights of their own daughter or son, a desire to maintain existing familial relationships, a desire to one day see the biological parent be able to parent successfully again, and a desire to utilize culturally based caregiving practices. . . ." Sacha Coupet, Swimming Upstream Against the Great Adoption Tide: Making the Case for "Impermanence," 34 Cap. U. L. Rev. 405, 433 (2005). Although the preference for "permanence" under ASFA (Chapter 2, section A; Chapter 3, section A1a) and related state laws often made ineligible for subsidies these kinship foster parents, who want neither to adopt nor to allow nonfamily members to adopt the child, such support became available under reforms enacted in 2008. See 42 U.S.C. §5106 (a)(4) (2008); id. at §5113 (b)(6); Fostering Connections to Success and Increasing Adoptions Act of 2008, Pub. L. 110-351 (2008). See also, e.g., In re Fernando M., 41 Cal. Rptr. 3d 511 (Ct. App. 2006) (preserving relationship with siblings can constitute exceptional circumstance warranting guardianship instead of adoption).

# D. ADOPTION FAILURE

IN RE LISA DIANE G.

537 A.2d 131 (R.I. 1988)

KELLEHER, J.

The single but significant issue presented by this controversy is whether a Family Court justice can grant relief to the plaintiffs, the adoptive parents of a daughter who was eight years old in 1983 when the decree of adoption was entered in the Family Court. The gist of the parents' complaint is that the adoption decree was procured by the fraudulent conduct or misrepresentations of certain representatives of the Department of Children and Their Families (DCF). The parents contend that DCF never informed them that the staff at Bradley Hospital, an institution noted for its treatment of the emotionally disturbed, had informed DCF that the eight-year-old, because of her behavioral problems, should not be placed for adoption. In the Family Court the parents sought nullification of the adoption decree and compensation for the expenses they incurred in caring for the child. . . .

[W]e have ruled that a natural mother who has consented to have her child placed for adoption but subsequently seeks to vacate the adoption decree must prove her claim to relief by clear and convincing evidence. We believe that the same standard should be satisfied in situations in which, as here, the adopting parents are the ones seeking to invalidate the adoption decree. . . .

The Legislature has seen fit to vest exclusive jurisdiction in the area of adoptions in the Family Court. If the adoptive parents are to prevail on their claim of fraud or misrepresentation that has been perpetrated on them, the fraud or the misrepresentation has also been perpetrated on the Family Court. In these circumstances [of asserted fraud] we are of the belief that the Family Court, because of its exclusive jurisdiction in the subject matter of adoption, has the inherent power to adjudicate the claim now put forth by the adoptive parents.

. . . Any determination of the plaintiff's claim in the Family Court will necessarily involve a consideration of the child's best interest. However, this consideration must be balanced against the harm suffered by the adoptive parents as a result of the alleged conduct of DCF.

Accordingly the adoptive parents' appeal is sustained, and the dismissal order is vacated. The case is remanded to the Family Court for a trial and adjudication of the plaintiffs' claim.

### DANIEL GOLDEN, WHEN ADOPTION DOESN'T WORK . . .

Boston Globe, June 11, 1989, Magazine Section, at 16

[This excerpt amplifies the facts of In re Lisa Diane G.]

For years after Sheila was born in 1968, Bob and Joan Gordon wanted another child, but the timing never seemed right. Even with two incomes — he was a mechanic, she a lab technician — they barely scraped by. They couldn't afford for Joan to take a maternity leave, never mind paying for day care.

[In 1981,] Joan heard that Rhode Island, like other states, was offering older children for adoption. Here, she thought, was a practical alternative. She would not have to quit her job, and Sheila's longing for a younger sister might be fulfilled at last.

The Gordons, whose names have been changed in this story to protect their privacy, were very specific when social workers from the Rhode Island Department of Children and Their Families visited their suburban home. They wanted a girl between the ages of 6 and 10 who would be in school while they worked. She could have a physical disability, they said, but not an emotional one. The Gordons knew their limits: A troubled girl would need more care than they felt ready to give. . . .

When Joan saw blond, blue-eyed Lisa, the hard-headed attitude she had maintained throughout the adoption process yielded to her heart. "Something instinctively told me to go with this child," she says. "Her background was so traumatic. You wanted to just reach out and love this little girl."

Only 6 years old, Lisa had suffered a lifetime's worth of pain and separation. She never knew her father, and her mother abused her. Covered with bites and bruises, she was placed in a foster home. She was adored there, but her stay ended abruptly when her foster father died of a heart attack. She was removed from her next foster home after the family accused her of killing its cat and trying to smother a baby. She was then sent to a state-supervised group home. Along the way, she lost contact with her older brother and sister, who had been adopted.

Lisa's social worker assured the Gordons that Lisa had emerged from these upheavals emotionally intact. . . ." We were led to believe that once she was part of a good, secure home, she would be fine, and her problems would disappear," Joan says. Assuming they had been told all, the Gordons never asked to read Lisa's file. . . .

Adoption is supposed to last a lifetime. Like marriage, it is meant to be an unswerving commitment, for better or for worse. Yet, while adoption has a far higher success rate than marriage, it too is plagued by divorce. Today, an increasing number of adoptive parents are relinquishing their children to the state, or even going to court to nullify the adoption. Most of these "disruptions," as they are termed, involve adoptions of older children with physical or emotional problems stemming from abuse by their natural parents. Infant adoptions are less prone to break up. . . .

Beset by lawsuits from disenchanted parents, adoption agencies are reassessing their credo that all children can be adopted. . . . The main reason for the surge in disruptions is a shift in the type of children being adopted. Until the 1970s, only infants were considered adoptable. Then an increase in abortions, coupled with greater social acceptance of single mothers, reduced the pool of available infants. At the same time, the number of abused and neglected older children was on the rise. Advocacy groups argued that these children, who were often warehoused in institutions or shunted from one foster home to another, needed adoptive homes. In 1980, a federal law enshrined "permanency planning" as a goal for children in state care; the law also expanded subsidies for adoptive parents. Like the deinstitutionalization of mental patients in the same era, this policy was both humanely intended and inexpensive, but it had the consequence of dumping some difficult people into a society that was not equipped to handle them. . . .

Once Lisa Gordon's adoption was finalized in 1983, the Department of Children and Their Families closed her case. Soon afterward, Joan Gordon decided that her daughter needed psychotherapy, and she asked the department to pay for it. . . . Late in 1984, Joan finally obtained medical insurance that covered therapy, and the family began seeing a psychologist. Instead of helping, Joan says, "the therapy was a catalyst for her to get worse." [For example, Lisa, who disliked the chore of fetching wood from the backyard, set fire to the wood pile.]

By 1985, the Gordons' house simmered with antagonism. Sensing the tension, Sheila's friends stopped coming over. . . . Bob's relationship with Lisa was, by turns, more antagonistic and more affectionate than Joan's. Lisa could goad her father into angry outbursts one minute and cuddle up to him the next. So Joan was not surprised one morning in April 1986 when Lisa . . . volunteered to fix the soup that Bob, as was his custom, would take to work. When Lisa gave him the thermos on his way out the door, he opened the lid and smelled something unusual. It was the disinfectant Lysol. . . .

It took one more incident for Joan to make up her mind. [Lisa told the school nurse her father had hit her with a board.] Obeying the law, the nurse reported the allegation to the state. After an investigation, the charges were dropped, and Joan went to the office of the state Department of Children and Their Families, saying she wouldn't leave until Lisa was removed from her house. State officials gave in and arranged for Lisa to be evaluated at Bradley Hospital, a psychiatric facility for children in Rhode Island.

Three members of the hospital's staff listened to Lisa describe the Lysol episode in a passionless monotone. One of them asked, "Did you want to kill him?" She said, simply, "Yes." She was admitted to the hospital immediately. . . .

## NOTES AND QUESTIONS

1. *Epilogue.* On remand, the court revoked the adoption. Lisa was institutionalized. The adoptive parents, who had also sought damages, withdrew that request. Subsequently, they dissolved their marriage, in part because of the stress Lisa had created. Telephone interview with Stephen E. Cicilline, attorney for plaintiffs (July 23, 1997).

2. *Failures.* Adoption failure occurs either when the child is removed before the adoption is final (disruption) or when a final adoption is abrogated or annulled (dissolution). See Jennifer F. Coakley & Jill D. Berrick, Research Review: In a Rush to Permanency: Preventing Adoption Disruption, 13 Child & Fam. Soc. Work 101, 102 (2007). Most studies place the current rate of disruption between 6 and 11 percent. Id. The adoption failure rate increased with the growing number of placements of special needs children (including older children) and children with previous foster care. Id. at 102, 107. See generally Lita Linzer Schwartz, When Adoption Goes Wrong: Psychological and Legal Issues of Adoption Disruption (2006).

3. *Standards.* Must the agency that placed the child consent to abrogation? Must the adopters have a reasonable basis for seeking to relinquish parental rights? See In re J.F., 862 A.2d 1258 (Pa. Super. Ct. 2004). When, if ever, should a court set aside an adoption? Suppose an adoptive father alleges that he relied on fraudulent assurances that the child, born to a married woman, was his biological son? See McAdams v. McAdams, 109 S.W.3d 649 (Ark. 2003) (holding suit time-barred). Does abrogation ever serve the child's best

interests? See In re Adoption of B.J.H., 564 N.W.2d 387, 392-393 (Iowa 1997); In re Adoption of Hemmer, 619 N.W.2d 848 (Neb. 2000).

Should cases be decided by courts based on equitable discretion or legislative criteria? See, e.g., Cal. Fam. Code §9100 (2008) (developmental disability or mental illness arising from conditions prior to adoption); Ky. Rev. Stat. Ann. §199.540(1) (2008) (different racial heritage). Who may petition for abrogation? What time limits, if any, should control? See, e.g., Mich. Comp. Laws Ann. §710.64(1) (2008) (21 days); Neb. Rev. Stat. §43-116 (2008) (2 years). Does abrogation infringe the adoptee's constitutional rights? See In re Adoption of Kay C., 278 Cal. Rptr. 907 (Ct. App. 1991) (no).

4. *Consequences.* When adopters surrender their parental rights after a failed adoption, who is responsible for supporting the child? See Greene County Dept. of Soc. Servs. ex rel. Ward v. Ward, 870 N.E.2d 1132 (N.Y. 2007) (imposing support duty on adoptive mother who permanently surrendered rights to a child with special needs and behavioral problems); State ex rel. C.V. v. Visser, 2007 WL 1462235 (Tenn. Ct. App. 2007) (holding that voluntary surrender of a child because of his behavioral problems does not relieve adoptive parents of support duties until the child is adopted (again)). What implications do such outcomes have for the policy of encouraging adoptions of children with special needs?

5. *Wrongful adoption.* As an alternative to abrogation, some parents have successfully sued adoption agencies for fraud or the tort of "wrongful adoption," based on the defendant's concealment of the child's medical condition. See, e.g., Jackson v. State, 956 P.2d 35 (Mont. 1998); Mallette v. Children's Friend & Serv., 661 A.2d 67 (R.I. 1995). What public policy issues do such negligence suits raise? Compare Richard P. v. Vista Del Mar Child Care Serv., 165 Cal. Rptr. 370, 374 (Ct. App. 1980), with M.H. v. Caritas Fam. Servs., 488 N.W.2d 282, 288 (Minn. 1992).

Must plaintiffs prove they would not have adopted but for the misrepresentation? See McKinney v. State, 950 P.2d 461 (Wash. 1998) (jury must find proximate cause). Can plaintiffs recover punitive damages? See Ross v. Louise Wise Servs., Inc., 868 N.E.2d 189 (N.Y. 2007) (no). Can they recover for emotional distress? Compare Price v. State, 57 P.3d 639 (Wash. 2002) (permitting recovery), with Rowey v. Children's Friend & Servs., 2003 WL 23196347 (R.I. Super. 2003) (only when supported by medical evidence). Can agencies obtain valid waivers of disclosure? See Ferenc v. World Child, Inc., 977 F. Supp. 56 (D.D.C. 1997), *aff'd,* 172 F.3d 919 (D.C. Cir. 1998) (yes). Does the adopted child have a claim? See Dresser v. Cradle of Hope Adoption Ctr., Inc., 358 F. Supp. 2d 620, 640-642 (E.D. Mich. 2005) (agency owes a duty to the child to provide medical information so adopters can obtain proper treatment). But see *Rowey,* supra. Should governmental immunity protect state placement agencies from such claims? Compare Young v. Van Duyne, 92 P.3d 1269 (N.M. Ct. App. 2004), with Eischen v. Stark County Bd. of Comm'rs., 2002 WL 31831395 (Ohio Ct. App. 2002). Apart from a negligence claim, does the placement agency have a fiduciary responsibility to provide information about family health history to adoptive parents? See Dahlin v. Evangelical Child & Fam. Agency, 252 F. Supp. 2d 666 (N.D. Ill. 2002) (plaintiffs must prove at trial).

In the adoptive parents' suit for damages, can a court compel an adult adoptee to release his or her medical treatment records? See Sirca v. Medina County Dep't of Human Servs., 762 N.E.2d 407 (Ohio Ct. App. 2001).

6. *Disclosure laws.* Several modern statutes require full disclosure to prospective adoptive parents of the child's medical history, e.g., Ariz. Rev. Stat. Ann. §8-129(A) (2008); Cal. Fam. Code §8706 (2008).

The UAA contains a detailed list of background information that must be disclosed to prospective adopters before they accept physical custody of the child. The list includes current medical and psychological history (including prenatal care), genetic diseases or drug addictions of the genetic parent, performance in school, and allegations of parental abuse or neglect. Unif. Adoption Act §2-106, 9 U.L.A. (pt. IA) 36-37 (1999). How readily can such information be obtained? For exploration of this question, see Marianne Brower Blair, The Uniform Adoption Act's Health Disclosure Provisions: A Model That Should Not Be Overlooked, 30 Fam. L.Q. 427 (1996). Should preadoptive genetic testing become a part of the placement process? Would such tests violate privacy rights? See Jessica Ann Schlee, Notes & Comments, Genetic Testing: Technology That Is Changing the Adoption Process, 18 N.Y.L. Sch. J. Hum. Rts. 133 (2001).

Should required disclosure include only individualized medical and familial histories or also data gathered from adoptions more generally? Asserting that "[d]isproportionate percentages of adopted children have learning disabilities and/or mental illness," one commentator (an adoptive parent) contends that the disclosure necessary for adopters' informed consent must include not only specific information about a particular child's history but also "general adoption information — such as the general rates of disability and mental illness in adopted populations." Ellen Wertheimer, Of Apples and Trees: Adoption and Informed Consent, 25 Quinnipiac L. Rev. 601, 601-602 (2007). See also Donovan M. Steltzner, Note, Intercountry Adoption: Toward a Regime That Recognizes the "Best Interests" of Adoptive Parents, 35 Case W. Res. J. Int'l L. 113 (2003) (calling for "consumer protection" laws for adopters who obtain children abroad, many of whom have spent time in institutional settings).

7. *Policy.* To what extent do sealed-record laws, supra section C, facilitate fraud by adoption agencies? Do biological parents have a duty of full disclosure in relinquishing their children? To the extent that such laws impose disclosure duties on birth parents upon relinquishment, should these duties include updating the information in the event of subsequent familial health problems? See R. Scott Smith, Disclosure of Post-Adoption Family Medical Information: A Continuing Birth Parent Duty, 35 Fam. L.Q. 553 (2001). Will subsidized adoption of children with special needs reduce the incidence of fraud?

## PROBLEMS

1. Barbara gives birth to a child and relinquishes him to the Children's Home Society (CHS), a state-licensed private adoption agency, which places the baby in an adoptive family. As part of the relinquishment process, CHS

provides counseling for Barbara. It also obtains detailed health and background information from her. Ten years later Barbara marries and has two children, a daughter and a son. When this son dies in infancy, Barbara learns she carries a genetic defect that afflicts male offspring. Barbara contacts CHS to determine the health of her first son and learns from CHS that he, too, suffers from the genetic disease.

Barbara sues CHS for wrongful death, negligent and intentional infliction of emotional distress, and fraud. In essence, she claims CHS had a duty to inform her of the genetic disease of the son she relinquished, to enable her to make informed choices about future childbearing. What result? See Olson v. Children's Home Soc'y, 252 Cal. Rptr. 11 (Ct. App. 1988). But cf. Molloy v. Meier, 679 N.W.2d 711 (Minn. 2004).

2. John and Mary Roe sue the Jewish Children's Bureau of Chicago with a complaint sounding in fraud, negligence, and breach of contract. Their complaint also includes a count sounding in negligence on behalf of their daughter, Jane. Assume the following underlying facts: In applying to adopt a child from defendants, the plaintiffs stated they would accept only a child whose parents were normal mentally, intellectually, and emotionally and who had no history of psychiatric problems. In 1974, defendants placed Larry (born in 1973) with plaintiffs, asserting that Larry's mother "wears glasses for far-sightedness, has no known allergies, is in good physical health." In 1975, plaintiffs adopted Larry, and in 1976, plaintiffs adopted a second child, Jane, placed by defendants. Soon thereafter, Larry's physicians diagnosed him with a psychiatric disorder with features of autism and schizophrenia. In 1991, Larry's biological father contacted the Roes, informing them that Larry's biological mother had a history of physical complaints seemingly often hysterical in origin and a history of self-induced epileptic seizures, with a diagnosis of "hysterical character disorder" and amphetamine addiction. At the time of Larry's placement, it was not believed that mental illness was inheritable.

Do these facts suffice to assert a cause of action by the Roes? What of their claim on behalf of Jane? As a matter of policy, would recognition of a cause of action "place an unbearable burden upon adoption agencies" by requiring them to guarantee the future health and happiness of the children whom they place? Alternatively, what benefit to adopted children generally might flow from recognition of a cause of action here? If defendants seek to show that plaintiffs' claims are time-barred, does the statute of limitations begin to run once Larry's physicians diagnosed his mental problems (around 1976) or only after the Roes obtained the additional information from Larry's biological father (in 1991)? See Roe v. Jewish Children's Bureau of Chicago, 790 N.E.2d 882 (Ill. App. Ct. 2003). See also Lubin v. Jewish Children's Bureau of Chicago, 765 N.E.2d 1138 (Ill. App. Ct. 2002).

3. Henry and Wilma, a married couple, adopted Denise when she was 15. Sometime thereafter, the marriage of Henry and Wilma failed, and a court ultimately granted Wilma's divorce petition. At age 22, Denise gave birth to a son, Sam. No one contests that Henry is Sam's father and that Sam must have been conceived before the court dissolved Henry's and Wilma's marriage. Denise and Henry now wish to marry to legitimize Sam. State incest laws,

however, bar marriages between fathers and daughters, including those whose relationship rests on adoption. As a result, Denise sues to abrogate Henry's adoption of her, while leaving her adoption by Wilma undisturbed; Henry and Wilma both support Denise's petition. What result and why? See In re Adoption of M., 722 A.2d 615 (N.J. Super. Ct. Ch. Div. 1998).

# CHAPTER 5

# *ADOPTION ACROSS STATE AND NATIONAL BOUNDARIES*

Mobility characterizes contemporary society, and birth parents, adopters, and children often travel among jurisdictions with different legal regimes. This chapter "maps" adoption, exploring the issues posed by cases with connections to more than one state or country.

## A. ADOPTION JURISDICTION

### IN RE BABY GIRL CLAUSEN

502 N.W.2d 649 (Mich. 1993)

PER CURIAM. . . .

[O]n February 8, 1991, Cara Clausen gave birth to a baby girl in Iowa. . . . On February 10, 1991, Clausen signed a release of custody form, relinquishing her parental rights to the child. Clausen, who was unmarried at the time of the birth, had named Scott Seefeldt as the father. On February 14, 1991, he executed a release of custody form.

[On February 25, 1991, petitioners Roberta and Jan DeBoer, Michigan residents, petitioned a juvenile court in Iowa to adopt the child. At a hearing held the same day,] the parental rights of Cara Clausen and Seefeldt were terminated, and petitioners were granted custody of the child during the pendency of the proceeding. The DeBoers returned to Michigan with the child, and she has lived with them in Michigan continuously since then.

However, the prospective adoption never took place. On March 6, 1991, nine days after the filing of the adoption petition, Cara Clausen filed a motion in the Iowa Juvenile Court to revoke her release of custody. In an affidavit accompanying the request, Clausen stated that she had lied when she named Seefeldt as the father of the child, and that the child's father actually was Daniel Schmidt. Schmidt filed an affidavit of paternity on March 12, 1991, and on March 27, 1991, he filed a petition in the Iowa district court, seeking to intervene in the adoption proceeding initiated by the DeBoers. [He and Clausen married in April, 1992.]

[The Iowa district court found that Schmidt was the biological father and that the DeBoers failed to establish either that Schmidt had abandoned the child or that his rights should be terminated. It determined that a best interests of the child analysis becomes appropriate only after a showing of abandonment.] On the basis of these findings, the court concluded that the termination proceeding was void with respect to Schmidt, and that the DeBoers' petition to adopt the child must be denied. Those decisions have been affirmed by the Iowa appellate courts. [In re BGC, 496 N.W.2d 239 (Iowa, 1992). On remand, the Iowa district terminated the DeBoers' rights as temporary guardians and custodians.]

On the same day their rights were terminated in Iowa, the DeBoers filed a petition in Washtenaw Circuit Court [in Michigan], asking the court to assume jurisdiction under the UCCJA. The petition requested that the court enjoin enforcement of the Iowa custody order and find that it was not enforceable, or, in the alternative, to modify it to give custody to the DeBoers. [The Michigan court] entered an ex parte temporary restraining order, which directed that the child remain in the custody of the DeBoers, and ordered Schmidt not to remove the child from Washtenaw County.

[The Michigan court] found that it had jurisdiction to determine the best interests of the child. It denied Schmidt's motion for summary judgment [to dissolve the preliminary injunction and enforce the Iowa judgment], and directed that the child remain with the DeBoers until further order of the court.[9] [The court of appeals reversed, concluding Michigan lacked jurisdiction under the UCCJA and the DeBoers lacked standing. Following a petition for declaratory and injunctive relief by the child's guardian ad litem, the circuit court entered an order temporarily continuing the status quo. This court granted the DeBoers' application to appeal, limited to issues of jurisdiction and standing, and the Schmidts' application to appeal, limited to the question whether the complaint should be dismissed for failure to state a claim.]

Interstate enforcement of child custody orders has long presented vexing problems. This arose principally from uncertainties about the applicability of the Full Faith and Credit Clause of the United States Constitution. Because custody decrees were generally regarded as subject to modification, states had traditionally felt free to modify another state's prior order.

The initial attempt to deal with these jurisdictional problems was the drafting of the Uniform Child Custody Jurisdiction Act, promulgated by the National Conference of Commissioners on Uniform State Laws in 1968. That uniform act has now been enacted, in some form, in all fifty states, the District of Columbia, and the U.S. Virgin Islands. . . . In 1980, Congress

---

9. [P]roceedings have continued in Iowa. On January 27, 1993, the Iowa district court held the DeBoers in contempt of court, and issued bench warrants for their arrest. The Iowa juvenile court entered an order on February 17, 1993, restoring Cara (Clausen) Schmidt's parental rights.

A best interests of the child determination hearing began in Washtenaw Circuit Court on January 29, 1993, and continued for eight days. In a decision rendered from the bench on February 12, 1993, the Washtenaw Circuit Court found that it was in the best interests of the child for her to remain with the DeBoers. That decision is not at issue in the instant appeal.

[enacted] the Parental Kidnapping Prevention Act, 28 U.S.C. §1738A. The PKPA "imposes a duty on the States to enforce a child custody determination entered by a court of a sister State if the determination is consistent with the provisions of the Act." Thompson v. Thompson, 484 U.S. 174, 175-176 (1988). The PKPA includes provisions similar to the UCCJA, and emphatically imposes the requirement that sister-state custody orders be given effect. . . .

In its March 29, 1993, opinion, the Court of Appeals agreed with Daniel Schmidt that the Washtenaw Circuit Court lacked jurisdiction to modify the Iowa custody orders and was instead required to enforce them. [It explained that adoption proceedings are custody proceedings under the UCCJA; that the custody matter was still pending in Iowa, where further proceedings had been scheduled; and that Iowa did not fail to conform to the UCCJA when it did not determine the best interests of the child.]

The congressionally declared purpose of the PKPA is to deal with inconsistent and conflicting laws and practices by which courts determine their jurisdiction to decide disputes between persons claiming rights of custody. Inconsistency in the determination by courts of their jurisdiction to decide custody disputes contributes to "the disregard of court orders, excessive relitigation of cases, [and] obtaining of conflicting orders by the courts of various jurisdictions. . . ." For these reasons, among others, Congress declared that the best interests of the child required the establishment of a uniform system for the assumption of jurisdiction. . . .

The [DeBoers' argument] that in this context the best interests purpose of the PKPA mandates a best interests analysis in Iowa, failing which the Iowa decision is not entitled to full faith and credit, would permit the forum state's view of the merits of the case to govern the assumption of jurisdiction to modify the foreign decree. . . .

It has been aptly noted that the vulnerability of a custody decree to an out-of-state modification presented the greatest need of all for the reform effort of the PKPA. . . . Certainty and stability are given priority under the PKPA, which gives the home state exclusive continuing jurisdiction. Thus, the PKPA expressly provides that if a custody determination is made consistently with its provisions, the appropriate authorities of every State *shall* enforce [it] according to its terms, and *shall not* modify that custody decision. 28 U.S.C. §1738A(a) (emphasis added). . . . At the time of commencement of both the termination and adoption proceedings, Iowa unquestionably had jurisdiction under its own laws and Iowa was unquestionably the home state of the child. . . .

Where the custody determination is made consistently with the provisions of the PKPA, the jurisdiction of the court that made the decision is exclusive and continuing as long as that state "remains the residence of the child or of any contestant," and it still has jurisdiction under its own laws. 28 U.S.C. §1738A(d). Unquestionably, Daniel Schmidt continues to reside in Iowa. Furthermore, Iowa law provides for continuing jurisdiction in custody matters. . . . The courts of this state may only modify Iowa's order if Iowa has declined to exercise its jurisdiction to modify it. 28 U.S.C. §1738A(f). Iowa has not declined to exercise its jurisdiction to modify its custody order; it has simply declined to order the relief sought by the DeBoers. . . .

The DeBoers advance a variety of arguments in support of their claim that they have standing to litigate regarding the custody of the child. [Yet] when the temporary custody order was rescinded, they became third parties to the child and no longer had a basis on which to claim a substantive right of custody. . . .

[T]he next friend for the child argues that we should recognize the right of a minor child to bring a Child Custody Act action and obtain a best interests of the child hearing regarding her custody. . . . We do not believe that the Child Custody Act can be read as authorizing such an action. The act's consistent distinction between the "parties" and the "child" makes clear that the act is intended to resolve disputes among adults seeking custody of the child.

It is true that children, as well as their parents, have a due process liberty interest in their family life. However, in our view those interests are not independent of the child's parents. [T]he natural parent's right to custody is not to be disturbed [absent a showing of unfitness], sometimes despite the preferences of the child. [The court rejected the due process and equal protection arguments raised on the child's behalf.] In the Iowa proceedings, a challenge to Daniel Schmidt's fitness was vigorously prosecuted by the DeBoers, and they failed to prove that he was unfit . . .[48] . . .

We direct the Washtenaw Circuit Court to enter an order enforcing the custody orders entered by the Iowa courts. In consultation with counsel for the Schmidts and the DeBoers, the circuit court shall promptly establish a plan for the transfer of custody [within 31 days]. It is now time for the adults to move beyond saying that their only concern is the welfare of the child and to put those words into action by assuring that the transfer of custody is accomplished promptly with minimum disruption of the life of the child.

Levin, J. (dissenting).

I would agree with the majority's analysis if the DeBoers had gone to Iowa, purchased a carload of hay from Cara Clausen, and then found themselves in litigation in Iowa with Daniel Schmidt, who also claimed an interest in the hay. It could then properly be said that the DeBoers "must be taken to have known" that, rightly or wrongly, the Iowa courts might rule against them, and they should, as gracefully as possible, accept an adverse decision of the Iowa courts. Michigan would then have had no interest in the outcome, and would routinely enforce a decree of the Iowa courts against the DeBoers. But this is not a lawsuit concerning the ownership, the legal title, to a bale of hay. . . .

The PKPA was enacted to protect the child. . . . Congress enacted the PKPA, not because of an abstract concern about "interstate controversies over child custody," but rather "in the interest of greater stability of home environment and of secure *family relationships* for the child." . . . Congress identified the "home state" of the child as the "state which can best decide the case in the interest of the child." "Home state" is defined as the "State in which, immediately preceding the time involved, the child lived with his parents, a parent, *or a person acting as a parent, for at least six consecutive months*, and in the

---

48. Even if we were to conclude that the child has [constitutional] interests that were not adequately represented in the previous Iowa proceedings, the PKPA would require that any new action on her behalf be brought in Iowa, which has continuing exclusive jurisdiction. . . .

case of a child less than six months old, the State in which the child lived from birth with any of such persons." (Emphasis added.) . . .

Michigan is the child's home state because she has lived in Michigan with the DeBoers, persons "acting as a parent," for at least six consecutive months — actually for over two years. Michigan, the home state, would also qualify as the state having jurisdiction under the PKPA pursuant to the alternative "significant connection" test for a case where no state is the home state. . . . There is more substantial evidence concerning the child's present or future care, protection, training and personal relationships in Michigan than in Iowa. . . . There was no contact between Daniel Schmidt and the child in Iowa, minimum contact between Cara Schmidt and the child in Iowa, and maximum contact between the child and the DeBoers in Michigan. . . . Assuming that the PKPA applies to adoption proceedings, and that is the assumption on which the majority opinion is predicated, the underlying themes of the act must be observed. . . .

Professor Clark wrote that subject matter jurisdiction in adoption should be given to the home state of the child. . . . As Professor Clark explains, the only issues in an adoption proceeding with respect to the natural parents, are "whether the consent is genuine, or whether the alleged abandonment or neglect did occur. These resemble *the issues in the ordinary transitory lawsuit*, and there is thus no need for any requirements of domicile or residence on the part of the natural parents."[53]

But, suggests Professor Clark, "since adoption consists of matching a child with a new parent or set of parents," there is a need for a "thorough opportunity to study the child and his background. To give the court this opportunity, the child must be present and available in the jurisdiction."[54] He concludes . . . that that subject matter jurisdiction in adoption should be where the adoptive parents reside and the child is physically present. . . .

A decree rendered by a state other than the home state is not a determination made "consistent with the provisions" of the PKPA. A decree rendered without consideration of the child's best interests is not a decree that the Congress intended that all other states must enforce. [Michigan law would require a best interests hearing.]

The sympathetic portrayal of the Schmidts in the majority opinion ignores that it was Cara Schmidt's fraud on the Iowa court and on Daniel Schmidt that is at the root of this controversy. . . . To fault the DeBoers is unwarranted. [They left Iowa with the child in good faith.] Why should they have believed that Cara Schmidt was telling the truth when she said she had fraudulently named the other man as the father? The DeBoers discovered that Schmidt had a dismal record as a father. . . . The Iowa courts thought there was sufficient merit in the DeBoers' claims that they maintained custody of the child with the DeBoers until after the Iowa Supreme Court ruled. One [dissenting] justice agreed with the DeBoers. . . .

If the danger confronting this child were physical injury, no one would question her right to invoke judicial process to protect herself against such

---

53. [2 Clark, Domestic Relations, 2d ed., §21.3,] p. 595. (Emphasis added.)
54. Id., §21.3, p. 596.

injury. There is little difference, when viewed from the child's frame of reference, between a physical assault and a psychological assault. . . . It is only because this child cannot speak for herself that adults can avert their eyes from the pain that she will suffer.

## NOTES AND QUESTIONS

1. *Epilogue.* The litigation in the principal case, often called "the Baby Jessica case," gripped the nation. The United States Supreme Court refused to stay the order entered pursuant to the Michigan Supreme Court's opinion. 509 U.S. 1301 (1993). After the transfer, Baby Jessica became Anna Schmidt. Although Anna's home life has been marked by parental unemployment and divorce, she has fared well by all accounts, despite the emotional trauma predicted when she left the DeBoers' custody. See Brian Dickerson, A Child's Life Shows Folly of Adults, Media, Detroit Free Press, Feb. 24, 2003, at 1B. The DeBoers adopted again, then divorced, but later reconciled and remarried. Pair Who Fought for Baby Jessica Plan to Remarry, Atlanta J. & Atlanta Const., Feb. 4, 2001, at A6; Milestones, Time Magazine, June 20, 1994, at 23.

2. *Background material on child custody jurisdiction.* The statutes examined in *Baby Girl Clausen* originated as responses to particular problems in child custody litigation. By way of background, consider the following:

Issues of child custody often arise in cases of divorce or other family dissolutions. Traditionally, one parent would receive custody (including the prerogative of deciding how the child should be reared) and the other visitation. More recently, joint custody awards have become widely used, with the law distinguishing "joint legal custody" (or shared decisionmaking authority) from "joint physical custody" (or shared residential time).

In choosing a particular custodial arrangement over available alternatives, most states use "the best interests of the child" as the ultimate standard, despite criticisms of this standard's indeterminacy, which in turn invites judges to resort to their own subjective views. See, e.g., American Law Institute, Principles of the Law of Family Dissolution: Analysis and Recommendations 95-106 (2002) (§2.02, comments thereto, and reporter's notes); Robert H. Mnookin, Child-Custody Adjudication: Judicial Functions in the Face of Indeterminacy, 39 Law & Contemp. Probs., Summer 1975, at 226 (1975). Further, custody determinations are modifiable because the wide range of facts that prove influential under the best interests standard might change, in turn prompting an order that alters the previous custody arrangement.

Based on an influential California case, courts long regarded jurisdiction to decide child custody matters to exist concurrently in the state of the child's domicile, a state of the child's physical presence (even in the absence of domicile), and a state with personal jurisdiction over both parents. See Sampsell v. Superior Court, 197 P.2d 739 (Cal. 1948). The perceived importance of protecting the child's best interests purported to justify the flexibility reflected by this concurrent jurisdiction approach. Similar reasoning supported the view that the routine obligation for one state to accord full faith and credit to the judicial judgments and decrees of sister states should give way in matters as delicate and important as child custody. See, e.g., Kovacs v. Brewer, 356 U.S.

604, 611-613 (1958) (Frankfurter, J., dissenting). See also May v. Anderson, 345 U.S. 528, 535-536 (1953) (Frankfurter, J., concurring). Indeed, courts have left unclear whether the constitutional duty of full faith and credit applies to modifiable decrees; even if it does, however, modification in a second state of the first state's *modifiable* custody determination does not conflict with that obligation. See, e.g., New York ex rel. Halvey v. Halvey, 330 U.S. 610, 615 (1947); *Kovacs*, 356 U.S. at 607. As a result, a child custody award in one state was traditionally modifiable elsewhere. See generally Leonard Ratner, Child Custody Jurisdiction in a Federal System, 62 Mich. L. Rev. 795 (1964).

The indeterminacy of the best interests test, the availability of modification, and concurrent jurisdiction all combined to create unstable custody decrees. A parent, dissatisfied with a court's custody decision, often took the child to another state (or refused to return a child following visitation in another state) and sought modification, in the hope that this second court would take a different view of the child's best interests than the first court had. One Supreme Court Justice condemned the regime that fostered this practice as "a rule of seize-and-run." *May*, 345 U.S. at 542 (Jackson, J., dissenting).

The Uniform Child Custody Jurisdiction Act (UCCJA) was drafted in 1968 to reduce jurisdictional competition and confusion, as well as to deter parents from forum shopping to religitate custody. Unif. Child Custody Jurisdiction Act, 9 U.L.A. (pt. IA) 261 (1999). A version of the UCCJA, which applied to initial custody decisions as well as modifications, was adopted in every state by 1981. In that year, Congress spoke up with the Parental Kidnapping Prevention Act (PKPA), 28 U.S.C. §1738A (2008), which built on the basic principles of the UCCJA to mandate full faith and credit for custody determinations made in compliance with the PKPA's jurisdictional requirements. Finally, in 1997, the National Conference of Commissioners on Uniform State Laws revisited the UCCJA and promulgated a refined version, the Uniform Child Jurisdiction and Enforcement Act (UCCJEA), which more closely tracks the PKPA. Unif. Child Custody Jurisdiction and Enforcement Act, 9 U.L.A. (pt. IA) at 655. Forty-eight states or territories have enacted the UCCJEA, and it is pending in three others. See http://www.nccusl.org/Update/uniformact_factsheets/uniformacts-fs-uccjea.asp (last visited Sept. 23, 2008).

All three reform measures—the UCCJA, the PKPA, and the UCCJEA— share several important features, which lawmakers became more adept at articulating with each successive legislative effort and which respond to particular problems surfacing in custody adjudications:

First, these measures seek to limit jurisdiction. Responding to the difficulties posed by concurrent jurisdiction, the PKPA and UCCJEA clearly indicate that only one state at a time has the authority to decide a given child custody matter.

Second, these reforms reflect an understanding of child custody adjudications as intensely fact-specific assessments in which evidence about the child's day-to-day interactions and the availability of witnesses with knowledge of the child and his or her environment loom large. Hence, the drafters expressly incorporated a preference for a forum with "maximum rather than minimum contact" with the child, specifically the child's "home state." See Unif. Child Custody Jurisdiction Act §3 (comment), 9 U.L.A. (pt. IA) at 309. As the PKPA and UCCJEA make clear, only when there is no home state (defined usually as a state where the child lived for at least six consecutive months) may one of the states meeting alternative requirements, listed in order of priority, assert jurisdiction. Further, in personam jurisdiction over a parent provides neither a necessary nor a sufficient condition for jurisdiction. In other words, based on the rationale that child custody adjudications resolve issues of status, like ex parte divorce (which does not require in personam jurisdiction), a parent need not have minimum contacts with the forum. But see Barbara Ann Atwood, Child Custody Jurisdiction and Territoriality, 52 Ohio St. L.J. 369 (1991) (critiquing this approach).

Third, the court initially deciding custody retains exclusive, continuing jurisdiction, so that modification proceedings must take place there — unless all the parties and the child have left this state. Finally, under these statutes, other states must respect and enforce custody adjudications made consistent with the legislation's jurisdictional rules; thus, these measures include a statutory requirement of full faith and credit.

The PKPA, invoked in *Baby Girl Clausen*, illustrates these features. In full, this statute provides:

§1738A. Full faith and credit given to child custody determinations

(a) The appropriate authorities of every State shall enforce according to its terms, and shall not modify except as provided in subsections (f), (g), and (h) of this section, any custody determination or visitation determination made consistently with the provisions of this section by a court of another State.

(b) As used in this section, the term —

(1) "child" means a person under the age of eighteen;

(2) "contestant" means a person, including a parent or grandparent, who claims a right to custody or visitation of a child;

(3) "custody determination" means a judgment, decree, or other order of a court providing for the custody of a child, and includes permanent and temporary orders, and initial orders and modifications;

(4) "home State" means the State in which, immediately preceding the time involved, the child lived with his parents, a parent, or a person acting as parent, for at least six consecutive months, and in the case of a child less than six months old, the State in which the child lived from birth with any of such persons. Periods of temporary absence of any of such persons are counted as part of the six-month or other period;

(5) "modification" and "modify" refer to a custody or visitation determination which modifies, replaces, supersedes, or otherwise is made subsequent to, a prior custody or visitation determination concerning the same child, whether made by the same court or not;

(6) "person acting as a parent" means a person, other than a parent, who has physical custody of a child and who has either been awarded custody by a court or claims a right to custody;

(7) "physical custody" means actual possession and control of a child;

(8) "State" means a State of the United States, the District of Columbia, the Commonwealth of Puerto Rico, or a territory or possession of the United States; and

(9) "visitation determination" means a judgment, decree, or other order of a court providing for the visitation of a child and includes permanent and temporary orders and initial orders and modifications.

(c) A child custody or visitation determination made by a court of a State is consistent with the provisions of this section only if—

(1) such court has jurisdiction under the law of such State; and

(2) one of the following conditions is met:

(A) such State (i) is the home State of the child on the date of the commencement of the proceeding, or (ii) had been the child's home State within six months before the date of the commencement of the proceeding and the child is absent from such State because of his removal or retention by a contestant or for other reasons, and a contestant continues to live in such State;

(B) (i) it appears that no other State would have jurisdiction under subparagraph (A), and (ii) it is in the best interest of the child that a court of such State assume jurisdiction because (I) the child and his parents, or the child and at least one contestant, have a significant connection with such State other than mere physical presence in such State, and (II) there is available in such State substantial evidence concerning the child's present or future care, protection, training, and personal relationships;

(C) the child is physically present in such State and (i) the child has been abandoned, or (ii) it is necessary in an emergency to protect the child because the child, a sibling, or parent of the child has been subjected to or threatened with mistreatment or abuse;

(D) (i) it appears that no other State would have jurisdiction under subparagraph (A), (B), (C), or (E), or another State has declined to exercise jurisdiction on the ground that the State whose jurisdiction is in issue is the more appropriate forum to determine the custody or visitation of the child, and (ii) it is in the best interest of the child that such court assume jurisdiction; or

(E) the court has continuing jurisdiction pursuant to subsection (d) of this section.

(d) The jurisdiction of a court of a State which has made a child custody or visitation determination consistently with the provisions of this section continues as long as the requirement of subsection (c)(1) of this section continues to be met and such State remains the residence of the child or of any contestant.

(e) Before a child custody or visitation determination is made, reasonable notice and opportunity to be heard shall be given to the contestants, any parent whose parental rights have not been previously terminated and any person who has physical custody of a child.

(f) A court of a State may modify a determination of the custody of the same child made by a court of another State, if—

(1) it has jurisdiction to make such a child custody determination; and

(2) the court of the other State no longer has jurisdiction, or it has declined to exercise such jurisdiction to modify such determination.

(g) A court of a State shall not exercise jurisdiction in any proceeding for a custody or visitation determination commenced during the pendency of a proceeding in a court of another State where such court of that other State is exercising jurisdiction consistently with the provisions of this section to make a custody determination.

(h) A court of a State may not modify a visitation determination made by a court of another State unless the court of the other State no longer has jurisdiction to modify such determination or has declined to exercise jurisdiction to modify such determination.

3. *Applying the statutes.* In *Baby Girl Clausen*, how sound is the majority's premise that the UCCJA and the PKPA control in termination and adoption proceedings? Several courts have applied these statutes to such cases. See, e.g., In re Adoption of Asente, 734 N.E.2d 1224, 1231 (Ohio 2000) (majority of jurisdictions apply UCCJA and PKPA to adoptions). See also People ex rel. A.J.C., 88 P.3d 599 (Colo. 2004) (applying UCCJA and PKPA to custody battle after failed adoption); In re H.L.A.D., 646 S.E.2d 425 (N.C. Ct. App. 2007) (applying UCCJEA's requirement of continuing exclusive jurisdiction to termination proceedings); In re Adoption of H.L.C., 706 N.W.2d 90 (S.D. 2005) (UCCJA applies to termination proceedings to free child for adoption and yields same result dictated by PKPA).

Do custody and adoption proceedings differ in ways that call for different jurisdictional rules? See generally Bernadette W. Hartfield, The Uniform Child Custody Jurisdiction Act and the Problem of Interstate Adoption: An Easy Fix?, 43 Okla. L. Rev. 621 (1990); Herma Hill Kay, Adoption in the Conflict of Laws: The UAA, Not the UCCJA, Is the Answer, 84 Cal. L. Rev. 703, 712-728 (1996).

4. *Home state.* Assuming that the UCCJA and the PKPA apply, which analysis in *Baby Girl Clausen* is more convincing, the majority's or the dissent's? Did Iowa satisfy the requirements for "home state" or any other jurisdictional basis? Do the statutes require a best interests inquiry? Will the majority's reasoning invite fraudulent identification of a child's father (as the dissent predicts)? Will the dissent's approach encourage prospective adopters to delay returning a child, despite an impediment to adoption in the state where the child was relinquished, in hopes of obtaining in their domicile a more favorable outcome based on a best interests analysis (as the majority fears)? Might the home state nonetheless constitute an inconvenient forum, so that it should abstain from asserting jurisdiction? See In re Adoption of Baby Boy M., 193 P.3d 520 (Kan. Ct. App. 2008).

5. *Nexus to forum.* If the UCCJA and the PKPA do not apply, what connections with the forum state confer adoption jurisdiction? Considerable authority uses as an alternative domicile, traditionally that of the child, or according to some modern courts, that of the adoptive parent. Eugene F. Scoles et al., Conflict of Laws §16.5 (4th ed. 2004); see Homer H. Clark, The Law of Domestic Relations in the United States 870-872 (2d ed. 1988); Restatement (Second) of Conflict of Laws §78 (1971). Is domicile preferable to the bases used under the UCCJA, PKPA, and UCCJEA? Where is an infant domiciled? See Mississippi Band of Choctaw Indians v. Holyfield, 490 U.S. 30, 47-48 (1989) (common law assigns nonmarital children their mother's domicile; hence, a child's domicile of origin may be a place where child has never been).

Must a court at the child's or adopter's domicile have personal jurisdiction over the child's birth parents, absent a previous termination of parental rights? Cf. Armstrong v. Manzo, 380 U.S. 545 (1965). Would this requirement remain controlling if the custody jurisdiction statutes govern adoptions?

In Division of Youth & Family Services v. M.Y.J.P., 823 A.2d 817 (N.J. Super. Ct. App. Div. 2003), a mother who remained in Haiti after the father took their son to live in New Jersey challenged that state's jurisdiction to terminate her parental rights. In New Jersey, the child had been removed from the father and placed with foster parents, who wished to adopt him. The lower court decided it had jurisdiction, based on its parens patriae authority to serve the child's best interests. On appeal, the court affirmed, invoking both the "status exception" to the minimum-contacts requirement and the mother's purposeful availment of New Jersey's benefits when she acceded to the care of her son by state child welfare authorities. Do you agree with the outcome? Which rationale works best — parens patriae, the status exception, or purposeful availment? Why?

6. *Interstate compact.* The widely enacted Interstate Compact on the Placement of Children (ICPC) also governs multistate adoptions. See, e.g., Mo. Ann. Stat. §210.620 (2008) (with note listing complementary laws in 50 other jurisdictions). The statute specifies procedural requirements for transferring the custody of a child to adoptive parents from another state but does not establish jurisdiction. *Asente*, 734 N.E.2d at 1230-1231. See also Alternative Options & Servs. for Children v. Chapman, 106 P.3d 744 (Utah Ct. App. 2004) (holding statute inapplicable when out-of-state pregnant women travel to Utah to give birth and relinquish children there). Courts have cited failure to comply with the ICPC as a reason to allow revocation of parental consent to adoption. See, e.g., In re Adoption of A.M.M., 949 P.2d 1155 (Kan. Ct. App. 1997).

Recent criticism of the ICPC points out that the law's procedural requirements often result in long waits for approval of placements with relatives, including noncustodial parents, who live in other states. According to one report: "In the 2007 fiscal year, for example, Michigan sent requests to other states to place 563 children. [As of June, 2008,] 359 cases have been resolved, with the receiving states taking more than 60 days to complete a home study in 195 of them. In half of the resolved cases, the relatives have been declared unsuitable by the other states." Eric Eckholm, Waits Plague Transfers of Children to Relatives' Care, N.Y. Times, June 27, 2008, at A11. See Vivek S. Sankaran, Out of State and Out of Luck: The Treatment of Noncustodial Parents Under the Interstate Compact on the Placement of Children, 25 Yale L. & Pol'y Rev. 63 (2006). But see In re Alexis O., 959 A.2d 176 (N.H. 2008) (holding that ICPC's plain language makes it inapplicable to placement with parents). A revised version of the ICPC attempts to address some of these problems by, inter alia, narrowing the ICPC's applicability and imposing time limits. See http://www.aphsa.org/Policy/ICPC-REWRITE/Resource%20Materials/HIGHLIGHTS%20OF%20PROPOSED%20COMPACT%20PROVISIONS.pdf (last visited Jan. 24, 2009). Seven states have enacted the new version. See http://www.aphsa.org/Policy/icpc2006rewrite.htm (last visited Sept. 23, 2008). Critics contend that these reforms fail to go far enough. See Vivek Sankaran, Perpetuating the Impermanence of Foster Children: A Critical Analysis of Efforts to Reform the Interstate Compact on the Placement of Children, 40 Fam. L.Q. 435 (2006); Robert G. Spector & Cara N. Rodriguez, Jurisdiction Over Children in Interstate Placement: the UCCJEA, Not the ICPC, Is the Answer, 41 Fam. L.Q. 145 (2007).

7. *Jurisdictional reform.* Drafted in the wake of Baby Jessica's case, the Uniform Adoption Act (UAA) modifies the UCCJA to account for the distinctive features of adoption proceedings, in which there is often no "home state." According to the UAA:

> (a) Except as otherwise provided . . . , a court of this State has jurisdiction over a proceeding for the adoption of a minor commenced under this [Act] if:
>
> (1) immediately before commencement of the proceeding, the minor lived in this State with a parent, a guardian, a prospective adoptive parent, or another person acting as parent, for at least six consecutive months, excluding periods of temporary absence, or, in the case of a minor under six months of age, lived in this State from soon after birth with any of those individuals and there is available in this State substantial evidence concerning the minor's present or future care;
>
> (2) immediately before commencement of the proceeding, the prospective adoptive parent lived in this State for at least six consecutive months, excluding periods of temporary absence, and there is available in this State substantial evidence concerning the minor's present or future care;
>
> (3) the agency that placed the minor for adoption is located in this State and it is in the best interest of the minor that a court of this State assume jurisdiction because:
>
> (i) the minor and the minor's parents, or the minor and the prospective adoptive parent, have a significant connection with this State; and
>
> (ii) there is available in this State substantial evidence concerning the minor's present or future care;
>
> (4) the minor and the prospective adoptive parent are physically present in this State and the minor has been abandoned or it is necessary in an emergency to protect the minor because the minor has been subjected to or threatened with mistreatment or abuse or is otherwise neglected; or
>
> (5) it appears that no other State would have jurisdiction under prerequisites substantially in accordance with paragraphs (1) through (4), or another State has declined to exercise jurisdiction on the ground that this State is the more appropriate forum to hear a petition for adoption of the minor, and it is in the best interest of the minor that a court of this State assume jurisdiction. . . .

Unif. Adoption Act §3-101, 9 U.L.A. (Pt. IA) at 67-68. The section goes on to disallow a state from exercising jurisdiction if a proceeding is pending in another state (with jurisdiction under the Act) or another state has issued a decree, unless that state no longer has jurisdiction. This legislation would not displace the ICPC, supra; rather, once a court assumes jurisdiction under the UAA, it considers whether the parties complied with the ICPC. See Joan Heifetz

Hollinger, The Uniform Adoption Act: Reporter's Ruminations, 30 Fam. L.Q. 345, 368 (1996).

How would the UAA apply in Baby Jessica's case? See Joan Heifetz Hollinger, Adoption and Aspiration: The Uniform Adoption Act, the DeBoer-Schmidt Cases, and the American Quest for the Ideal Family, 2 Duke J. Gender L. & Pol'y 15 (1995); Kay, supra. Only Vermont has enacted the UAA. See http://www.nccusl.org/Update/uniformact_factsheets/uniformacts-fs-aa94.asp (last visited Sept. 23, 2008).

To eliminate any confusion, the UCCJEA, which revises the UCCJA to make it more consistent with the PKPA, explicitly states that it does not apply to adoption proceedings, with a comment explaining that the UAA governs adoption jurisdiction. Unif. Child Custody Jurisdiction and Enforcement Act §103, 9 U.L.A. (pt. IA) at 660-661. See, e.g., White v. Adoption of Baby Boy D., 10 P.3d 212 (Okla. 2000). How likely is this approach to eliminate jurisdictional conflicts and achieve uniformity, given that only one state (Vermont) has enacted the UAA? By contrast, 48 jurisdictions have enacted the UCCJEA, with a few states, including Vermont, yet to do so. See http://www.nccusl.org/Update/uniformact_factsheets/uniformacts-fs-uccjea.asp (last visited Jan. 24, 2009). What jurisdictional principles govern adoption in these states?

Specifically, does the UCCJEA preclude a state's jurisdiction despite proceedings pending elsewhere, given the statute's disclaimer of its application to adoption? In *A.J.C.*, supra, the Colorado Supreme Court concluded that Colorado could assert jurisdiction to decide whether a couple there could retain custody of a child following a failed adoption in Missouri — the state where the child was born and initially relinquished, where the Colorado couple had filed their adoption petition, where the birth mother withdrew her consent, and where the court then halted the adoption proceedings. With the UCCJEA (enacted in Colorado) inapplicable to adoptions, the supreme court concluded that the failure to consider the child's best interests in Missouri (where the earlier UCCJA remained in force) amounts to a declination of jurisdiction, leaving room for Colorado courts to decide custody. See 88 P.3d at 611. Even if the UCCJEA does not apply to adoptions, might the PKPA remain applicable? Why? See In re Baby Girl F., 2008 WL 5195638 (Ill. App. Ct. 2008).

Other courts in failed or disputed adoptions have also looked to custody jurisdiction statutes on the theory that the "case involve[s] more than adoption, it involve[s] the custody of the child as well." D.B. v. M.A., 975 So. 2d 927, 936 (Ala. Civ. App. 2006), *aff'd*, Ex Parte D.B., 975 So. 2d 940 (Ala. 2007). Cf. Doe v. Baby Girl, 657 S.E.2d 455 (S.C. 2008) (using custody jurisdiction statutes to disregard Illinois order and to reinstate South Carolina adoption petition, although child has no "home state"); In re E.H., 137 P.3d 809 (Utah 2006) (invoking policy favoring settlements to respect parties' stipulations to determine custody in contested adoption).

Have these courts all forgotten the history of the UCCJA, PKPA, and the UCCJEA? Assess the concerns of the dissenting judge in *A.J.C.*, supra, about "the jurisdictional free-for-all that will surely result from the majority's approach and the harm done to children who will be forced to suffer under conflicting custody orders and perpetual jurisdictional disputes." 88 P.3d at 614 (Coats, J., dissenting).

## PROBLEMS

1. Reconsider the facts of Adoption of D.N.T., Chapter 2, section B3. In their effort to regain Diane, Camille and her mother Sally contend that Mississippi lacks jurisdiction over the adoption that Carol and Rick are pursuing there. Who should prevail and why? Should the same jurisdictional rules govern consensual adoptions and contested adoptions, like this one? Why? See *D.N.T.*, 843 So. 2d at 697-706.

2. Thomaszine moves from Texas to Washington state four months before giving birth to a son. A few weeks after the birth, Carl and Yvonne, a married couple living in Oregon, meet Thomaszine in Washington to discuss adopting the child. Because Thomaszine is not ready to relinquish him permanently, no agreement results. For the next several months, Thomaszine and her son live in a crisis shelter. When forced to move, she places the child in foster care, and the state (Washington) initiates dependency proceedings.

When her son is seven months old, Thomaszine finally decides to place him for adoption. Her physician contacts Carl and Yvonne, who travel to Washington to pick up the child. Thomaszine signs a consent, stating that Carl and Yvonne "will car[e] for the child during the adoptive process, after which they will become his legal parents." Carl and Yvonne return to Oregon with the child. A week later, the dependency proceedings are dismissed. Two months thereafter, Thomaszine informs Carl and Yvonne she wants her child back and no longer consents to adoption. In Oregon, Carl and Yvonne have just completed a home study and have prepared a petition for adoption.

As attorney for Carl and Yvonne, what would you advise? Should they return the child to Thomaszine? What "compromises" might you explore? Alternatively, if they insist on filing their adoption petition, what problems should they anticipate? Which state has jurisdiction under the UCCJA and PKPA? The UCCJEA and UAA? Suppose, instead, the biological father (whom Thomaszine refused to identify) contacts you just before the adoption petition is filed to convey his refusal to consent? See Stubbs v. Weathersby, 892 P.2d 991 (Or. 1995). But see In re Hayes, 979 P.2d 779 (Or. Ct. App. 1999).

3. Iva Sue became pregnant while living in Illinois, where six of her other children had become wards of the state. As the date of delivery approached, Iva Sue asked her caseworker what would happen to her new baby if she gave birth in Illinois. She learned that the Department of Family and Children's Services would investigate and determine whether to take custody of the baby. Fearing the loss of her baby, Iva Sue decided to move to Tennessee, where two of her other children lived with their father. En route, Iva Sue gives birth in Indiana. Where is the baby's home state under the UCCJEA? Why? See In re D.S., 840 N.E.2d 1216 (Ill. 2005). Even if Indiana is not otherwise the baby's home state, would it become the home state if Iva Sue relinquishes the baby to an adoption agency there? Why? See Adoption House, Inc. v. A.R. 820 A.2d 402 (Del. Fam. Ct. 2003). If Illinois has legal custody of Iva Sue's children because they had been adjudicated dependent and neglected there, does Illinois retain jurisdiction even after the children and their parents all have left the state? See In re Z.T.S., 2008 WL 371184 (Tenn. Ct. App. 2008).

# B. RECOGNITION IN OTHER STATES

Finstuen v. Crutcher

---

496 F.3d 1139 (10th Cir. 2007)

Ebel, Circuit Judge. . . .

Three same-sex couples and their adopted children have challenged the following amendment to Oklahoma's statute governing the recognition of parent-child relationships that are created by out-of-state adoptions.

> §7502-1.4. Foreign adoptions
> A. The courts of this state shall recognize a decree, judgment, or final order creating the relationship of parent and child by adoption, issued by a court or other governmental authority with appropriate jurisdiction in a foreign country or in another state or territory of the United States. The rights and obligations of the parties as to matters within the jurisdiction of this state shall be determined as though the decree, judgment, or final order were issued by a court of this state. Except that, this state, any of its agencies, or any court of this state shall not recognize an adoption by more than one individual of the same sex from any other state or foreign jurisdiction.

Okla. Stat. tit. 10, §7502-1.4(A) (the "adoption amendment").

Each of the three families has a different set of circumstances. Mr. Greg Hampel and Mr. Ed Swaya are residents of Washington, where they jointly adopted child V in 2002. V was born in Oklahoma, and pursuant to an "open" adoption agreement with V's biological mother, the men agreed to bring V to Oklahoma to visit her mother "from time to time." However, they do not state any plans to move to Oklahoma or have any ongoing interactions with the state of Oklahoma. After V's adoption, Mr. Hampel and Mr. Swaya requested that OSDH issue a new birth certificate for V. OSDH did so on July 7, 2003, but named only Mr. Hampel as V's parent. Mr. Hampel and Mr. Swaya contested that action, prompting OSDH to seek an opinion from the Oklahoma attorney general as to whether it must fulfill the request to list both fathers on the birth certificate. The attorney general opined that the U.S. Constitution's Full Faith and Credit Clause required Oklahoma to recognize any validly issued out-of-state adoption decree. OSDH subsequently issued V a new birth certificate naming both men as parents. The state legislature responded one month later by enacting the adoption amendment.

Lucy Doel and Jennifer Doel live with their adopted child E in Oklahoma. E was born in Oklahoma. Lucy Doel adopted E in California in January 2002. Jennifer Doel adopted E in California six months later in a second-parent adoption, a process used by step-parents to adopt the biological child of a spouse without terminating the parental rights of that spouse. OSDH issued E a supplemental birth certificate naming only Lucy Doel as her mother. The Doels have requested a revised birth certificate from OSDH that would acknowledge Jennifer Doel as E's parent, but OSDH denied the request.

Anne Magro and Heather Finstuen reside in Oklahoma with their two children. Ms. Magro gave birth to S and K in New Jersey in 1998. In 2000, Ms. Finstuen adopted S and K in New Jersey as a second parent, and New Jersey subsequently issued new birth certificates for S and K naming both women as their parents.

These three families brought suit against the state of Oklahoma seeking to enjoin enforcement of the adoption amendment. . . . OSDH appeals from the district court's conclusion that the Doels and the Finstuen-Magro family have standing and its ruling that the adoption amendment is unconstitutional. The Oklahoma governor and attorney general did not appeal. In addition, Mr. Hampel, Mr. Swaya and their child V timely appeal from the denial of standing, and reassert their claim that the Oklahoma amendment violates their constitutional right to travel. . . . [On appeal, the court decides that only the Doels have standing to challenge the Oklahoma amendment and that their case is not moot although OSDH asserts that the amendment applies only to adoptions by same-sex couples that take place in a single proceeding, not sequential adoptions.]

. . . The district court concluded that the adoption amendment was unconstitutional because the Full Faith and Credit Clause requires Oklahoma to recognize adoptions—including same-sex couples' adoptions—that are validly decreed in other states. . . . We affirm, because there is "no roving 'public policy exception' to the full faith and credit due judgments," Baker ex rel. Thomas v. Gen. Motors Corp. 522 U.S. 222, 233 (1998), and OSDH presents no relevant legal argument as to why the Doels' out-of-state adoption judgments should not be recognized under the Full Faith and Credit Clause.

The Constitution states that "Full Faith and Credit shall be given in each State to the public Acts, Records, and judicial Proceedings of every other State." U.S. Const. art. 4, §1. The Supreme Court has often explained the purpose and policies behind the Full Faith and Credit Clause.

> The very purpose of the full faith and credit clause was to alter the status of the several states as independent foreign sovereignties, each free to ignore obligations created under the laws or by the judicial proceedings of the others, and to make them integral parts of a single nation throughout which a remedy upon a just obligation might be demanded as of right, irrespective of the state of its origin.

Milwaukee County v. M. E. White Co., 296 U.S. 268, 276-77 (1935). . . . In applying the Full Faith and Credit Clause, the Supreme Court has drawn a distinction between statutes and judgments. *Baker*, 522 U.S. at 232-33. Specifically, the Court has been clear that although the Full Faith and Credit Clause applies unequivocally to the judgments [including judicial decrees and orders] of sister states, it applies with less force to their statutory laws. [W]ith respect to final judgments entered in a sister state, it is clear there is no "public policy" exception to the Full Faith and Credit Clause:

> Regarding judgments . . . the full faith and credit obligation is exacting. A final judgment in one State, if rendered by a court with adjudicatory authority over the subject matter and persons governed by the judgment, qualifies for recognition throughout the land. For claim and issue preclusion (res judicata) purposes, in other words, the judgment of the rendering State gains nationwide force. . . .

> A court may be guided by the forum State's 'public policy' in determining the law applicable to a controversy. But our decisions support no roving 'public policy exception' to the full faith and credit due judgments.

*Baker*, 522 U.S. at 232-33 (citations, footnotes omitted). . . .

OSDH stops short of arguing that the Full Faith and Credit Clause permits states to invoke a "policy exception," but contends that requiring Oklahoma to recognize an out-of-state adoption judgment would be tantamount to giving the sister state control over the effect of its judgment in Oklahoma. Specifically, OSDH argues that the recognition of adoptive status in Oklahoma would extend the gamut of rights and responsibilities to the parents and child of the adoption order, including the right of a child to inherit from his parents, and therefore would constitute an impermissible, extra-territorial application of California law in Oklahoma. OSDH argues that inheritance is an Oklahoma property right which California courts lack the power to confer.

OSDH's argument improperly conflates Oklahoma's obligation to give full faith and credit to a sister state's judgment with its authority to apply its own state laws in deciding what state-specific rights and responsibilities flow from that judgment. . . . A California court made the decision, in its own state and under its own laws, as to whether Jennifer Doel could adopt child E. That decision is final. If Oklahoma had no statute providing for the issuance of supplementary birth certificates for adopted children, the Doels could not invoke the Full Faith and Credit Clause in asking Oklahoma for a new birth certificate. However, Oklahoma has such a statute—i.e., it already has the necessary "mechanism[] for enforcing [adoption] judgments." See id. The Doels merely ask Oklahoma to apply its own law to "enforce" their adoption order in an "even-handed" manner. See id.

Oklahoma continues to exercise authority over the manner in which adoptive relationships should be enforced in Oklahoma and the rights and obligations in Oklahoma flowing from an adoptive relationship. . . . By way of illustration, the right of a parent in Oklahoma to authorize medical treatment for her minor child, id., §170.1, extends by virtue of §7505-6.5 to adoptive parents as well. Whatever rights may be afforded to the Doels based on their status as parent and child, those rights flow from an application of Oklahoma law, not California law.

OSDH argues that Oklahoma is not bound by the Full Faith and Credit Clause to recognize out-of-state adoptions to which the Commissioner of Health was not a party. . . . OSDH's theory misconstrues the Doels' lawsuit and the role of the state being asked to give full faith and credit to a sister state's prior judgment. The Doels do not seek to enforce their adoption order against Dr. Crutcher in his official capacity for the state of Oklahoma as a matter of claim or issue preclusion. Instead, the Doels assert in their Oklahoma suit that Dr. Crutcher and OSDH are obligated under Oklahoma law to issue a supplemental birth certificate and that they have failed to fulfill the constitutionally-imposed duty on states to recognize another state's judgment. . . . The rights that the Doels seek to enforce in Oklahoma are Oklahoma rights and the Doels have clearly established jurisdiction over Dr. Crutcher and OSDH in Oklahoma. . . .

We hold today that final adoption orders and decrees are judgments that are entitled to recognition by all other states under the Full Faith and Credit Clause. Therefore, Oklahoma's adoption amendment is unconstitutional in its refusal to recognize final adoption orders of other states that permit adoption by same-sex couples. Because we affirm the district court on this basis, we do not reach the issues of whether the adoption amendment infringes on the Due Process or Equal Protection Clauses. . . .

## NOTES AND QUESTIONS

1. *Full faith and credit. Finstuen* relies on the same principle that compels recognition of, for example, an out-of-state divorce decree issued by a forum, even in other states that have stricter grounds for divorce based on public policy. See, e.g., Williams v. North Carolina, 317 U.S. 287 (1942). The policies of finality and national uniformity reflected also can be found in several statutes enacted by Congress pursuant to its authority to implement the Constitution's Full Faith and Credit Clause. For example, one such enactment codifies the obligation of interstate respect by providing, in pertinent part, that "Acts, records and judicial proceedings or copies thereof . . . shall have the same full faith and credit in every court within the United States and its Territories and Possessions as they have by law or usage in the courts of such State, Territory or Possession from which they are taken." 28 U.S.C. §1738 (2008). Another, the Parental Kidnapping Prevention Act, 28 U.S.C. §1738A (2008), played a central role in the jurisdictional analysis in *Baby Girl Clausen*, supra. Both of these statutes seek to ensure consistency and uniformity among the states.

The principle applied in *Finstuen* assumes that the court issuing the adoption decree has jurisdiction to do so, in turn making particularly salient the available bases for adoption jurisdiction, including the PKPA or the UAA, examined after *Baby Girl Clausen*, supra. See, e.g., Russell v. Bridgens, 647 N.W.2d 56 (Neb. 2002). Cf. also Schott v. Schott, 744 N.W.2d 85 (Iowa 2008) (rejecting collateral attack when rendering court had jurisdiction).

Consistently with *Finstuen*, several scholars argue that full faith and credit requires interstate recognition of adoptions involving same-sex couples. E.g., Barbara J. Cox, Adoptions by Lesbian and Gay Parents Must Be Recognized by Sister States Under the Full Faith and Credit Clause Despite Anti-Marriage Statutes that Discriminate against Same-Sex Couples, 31 Cap. U. L. Rev. 751 (2003); Robert G. Spector, The Unconstitutionality of Oklahoma's Statute Denying Recognition to Adoptions by Same-Sex Couples from Other States, 40 Tulsa L. Rev. 467 (2005); Ralph U. Whitten, Choice of Law, Jurisdiction, and Judgment Issues in Interstate Adoption Cases, 31 Cap. U. L. Rev. 803 (2003). What reasons might exempt such adoptions from recognition in other states? See Lynn D. Wardle, A Critical Analysis of Interstate Recognition of Lesbigay Adoptions, 3 Ave Maria L. Rev. 561 (2005) (examining six reasons not to recognize such adoptions from other states).

2. *Same-sex adoptions versus same-sex marriages.* Why should adoptions involving same-sex couples, for example, receive different treatment from, say, same-sex marriages? See Rhonda Wasserman, Are You Still My Mother? Interstate Recognition of Adoptions by Gays and Lesbians, 58 Am. U. L. Rev. 1 (2008).

3. *Effect of DOMAs.* Despite federal statutes promoting consistency and uniformity under the Full Faith and Credit Clause, Congress departed from this policy in enacting the "Defense of Marriage Act" (DOMA), which provides in part:

> No State, territory, or possession of the United States, or Indian tribe, shall be required to give effect to any public act, record, or judicial proceeding of any other State, territory, possession, or tribe respecting a relationship between persons of the same sex that is treated as a marriage under the laws of such other State, territory, possession, or tribe, or a right or claim arising from such relationship.

28 U.S.C. §1738C (2008). To what extent does this provision address the question presented in *Finstuen*? Does it relieve a state like Oklahoma from the obligation to recognize adoptions by same-sex parents? Against the background of DOMA, evaluate the court's response to the argument that required recognition of an adoption granted to a same-sex couple by another state constitutes "an impermissible, extra-territorial application" of the initial forum's law and policy.

Even without reaching the question of full faith and credit, a majority of the Virginia Supreme Court ruled that statutes require changing birth certificates to show both parents following the second-parent adoptions of Virginia children decreed in other states. Davenport v. Little-Bowser, 611 S.E.2d 366 (Va. 2005). Should the court have considered the public policy expressed in Virginia's own failure to authorize second-parent adoption and its "mini DOMA," which makes void in Virginia a same-sex marriage celebrated elsewhere and "any contractual rights created by such marriage" (Va. Code Ann. §20-45.2 (2008))? See *Davenport*, 611 S.E.2d at 374-375 (Hassell, C.J., dissenting). See also Va. Code Ann. §20-45.3 (2008). See also Adar v. Smith, 2008 WL 5378130 (E.D. La. 2008).

4. *Discrimination?* May Oklahoma treat adoption decrees issued out of state differently from the way it treats adoption decrees issued in Oklahoma? May it treat adoption decrees issued to same-sex couples out of state differently from the way it treats adoption decrees issued to heterosexual couples out of state? Cf. Estin v. Estin, 334 U.S. 541 (1948) (addressing discrimination issues in the context of divorce and support awards). Does *Finstuen* answer these questions? See Spencer B. Ross, Survey, Finstuen v. Crutcher: The Tenth Circuit Delivers a Significant Victory for Same-Sex Couples, 85 Denv. U.L. Rev. 685, 694-699 (2008).

5. *Law reform strategies.* What does *Finstuen* teach about methods of effectuating law reforms designed to achieve equality for same-sex couples and their families? What does recognition of same-sex adoptions portend for recognition of same-sex marriage? See June Carbone, The Role of Adoption in Winning Public Recognition for Adult Partnerships, 35 Cap. U. L. Rev. 341 (2006); Vanessa A. Lavely, The Path to Recognition of Same-Sex Marriage: Reconciling the Inconsistencies Between Marriage and Adoption Cases, 55 UCLA L. Rev. 247 (2007); Jason N.W. Plowman, Note, When Second-Parent Adoption Is the Second-Best Option: The Case for Legislative Reform as the Next Best Option for Same-Sex Couples in the Face of Marriage Inequality, 11 Scholar 57 (2008).

## PROBLEMS

1. Michael and Richard registered as domestic partners in California. Hoping to start a family, they received approval as prospective adoptive parents in California and then sought to post their profiles on a website operated by an Arizona-based Adoption Media, LLC, which operates the largest, most active, and most well-known Internet adoption-related business in the United States. Adoption Media, LLC rejected their request, based on a policy restricting eligibility to opposite-sex married couples. California has civil rights statutes prohibiting discrimination based on sexual orientation and marital status. Arizona prohibits neither sexual-orientation discrimination nor marital-status discrimination; it does not have a law on domestic partnerships; and its citizens recently rejected a proposed constitutional amendment that would have prohibited recognizing same-sex relationships akin to marriage. Michael and Richard sue Adoption Media, LLC in California, seeking damages under California's civil rights statutes. Adoption Media argues that California lacks jurisdiction and, even if it has jurisdiction, its statutes do not apply. What result and why? See Butler v. Adoption Media, LLC, 486 F. Supp. 2d 1022 (N.D. Cal. 2007).

2. K.M., from Utah, became pregnant during a one-week visit to Oklahoma. Back in Utah, she informed T.C. of Oklahoma of her pregnancy and her plan to relinquish the baby for adoption. Although K.M. communicated with T.C. several times and told him how to reach her, she did not name him as the father on the birth certificate when she delivered the baby, K.J.C., in Utah. After K.M. relinquished the baby to a social services agency in Utah, the agency and the state conducted paternity searches; finding no registration of paternity rights, the agency placed K.J.C. for adoption with C.J. and A.J. Three days later, in Oklahoma, T.C. filed a petition to determine the baby's paternity. Should (must) the Utah court now decline to finalize the petition for adoption filed by C.J. and A.J.? Specifically, what effect does T.C.'s paternity proceeding in Oklahoma have in the Utah adoption case? Why? See In re K.C.J., 184 P.3d 1239 (Utah Ct. App. 2008).

## C. INTERCOUNTRY ADOPTION

ELIZABETH BARTHOLET, WHERE DO BLACK CHILDREN BELONG?<br>THE POLITICS OF RACE MATCHING IN ADOPTION

---

139 U. Pa. L. Rev. 1163, 1164-1188, 1237 (1991)

Review the excerpt, reprinted Chapter 3, p. 119.

TWILA L. PERRY, TRANSRACIAL AND INTERNATIONAL ADOPTION:<br>MOTHERS, HIERARCHY, RACE, AND FEMINIST LEGAL THEORY

---

10 Yale J.L. & Feminism 101, 130-131, 134-137 (1998)

International adoptions began primarily as a humanitarian response by North Americans to the problem of European children orphaned by World

War II. After the war, when Europe was rebuilt and its economic condition stabilized, the problem of orphaned children was resolved. Since that time, birthrates have fallen in the West, abortion and reliable methods of contraception have become available, and the stigma against women bearing children outside of marriage has declined, resulting in fewer white women surrendering babies for adoption. These factors have led to a decline in the number of children available for adoption in the West. At the same time, birthrates in the Third World have increased. The result has been a rise in the adoption of children from Third World countries by Westerners. . . .

To some extent, transracial adoption and the international adoption of children from Latin America and Asia raise different issues. Some of the countries involved in international adoptions, at least in the past, actively supported or promoted such activity. Many of the children adopted are infants whose mothers presumably gave them up knowing that they were to be adopted by Westerners. Indeed, some of these mothers may be pleased that their children will have a chance to have a more economically comfortable life in America than they would have been able to offer in their often impoverished circumstances. Finally, in the United States, the adoption of children from Asia and Latin America may pose fewer social difficulties than the adoption of Black American children. . . . If Asian or Hispanic children are more accepted by white society than are Black children, the "best interests" and/or "survival skills" issues that are so controversial in the transracial adoption of Black children may not seem as controversial with respect to children from these groups.

Still, international adoptions have also been subject to controversy and criticism. . . . A number of countries from which children of color come have a history of colonialism—military and economic domination by Western nations at some point in their histories. Obviously, colonial relationships exist to serve the needs of the colonizing countries; the result is generally exploitation of the people and resources of the country that is dominated. However, colonialism is not simply military and economic—it also has a cultural component. This cultural component often finds expression in the belief that the country that is being militarily and economically subjugated is comprised of an inferior people, and in the eyes of the conqueror, this inferiority justifies the conquest and continued domination. A phenomenon occurs wherein over time, as Edward Said [author of *Orientalism* (1978)] has noted, the dominant group substitutes its own view or representation of the other culture for positive knowledge about it, and the relationship becomes one of "power, of domination, of varying degrees of a complex hegemony. . . ." While the era of actual colonialism may be over in much of the world, the racist and ethnocentric rationales for it linger.

The United States has never formally held colonies in Latin America. Nevertheless, our government has had strong military ties to numerous governments in that area of the world. It has often financed military endeavors favorable to United States' interests, and it has developed economic interests and relationships that favor American businesses. The United States has also been a dominant military force in a number of the Asian countries, such as Korea and Vietnam where many internationally adopted children have been born. The kind of economic and military relationships that the United States has had with some third-world countries can engender the same kind of cultural imperialism that results from more formal colonial relationships.

As troubling as it may be for many to admit, a conception of poor, third-world countries as subordinate nations fits very comfortably with the practice of international adoption. This kind of view translates easily into the idea that Western adoptive parents are simply saving unfortunate third-world children by bringing them out of primitive, impoverished and disease-ridden countries into the more affluent life that the West can offer. It permits a discourse that allows Westerners to take the high ground and portray their international adoptions as simple acts of humanitarianism and altruism.

Admittedly, there is a humanitarian aspect to many international adoptions. Obviously, there are children adopted from poor countries who would face a very bleak life or even death in their homelands. However, a feminist analysis of international adoption should go farther than a simple altruism narrative. Indeed, an appropriate question might not be what Westerners are giving to the children of impoverished countries, but what they are taking from those countries or from the poor women who live in them. "Taking" might appear to be a harsh word in the context of a situation in which women have voluntarily surrendered their children. However, the "voluntariness" of these surrenders must be examined in light of the economic, social, and political circumstances under which the mothers often live. . . .

Patriarchy and racism can also be important factors in the availability of children for international adoption, although these phenomena take different forms in different countries. In some countries, patriarchy may be the dominant factor. In Asian countries such as Korea, adoption historically has only been considered as a means to perpetuate family lines in families without a male heir. Because adoption has been unpopular as a general practice, it has been difficult to place children for adoption within the country.

In China, the availability of many baby girls for adoption is also largely a function of patriarchy. The Chinese tradition of favoring male children, combined with the policy limiting families to one child, results in many families choosing to keep a male child and putting female infants in orphanages, or sometimes even putting them to death. Adoption by foreigners has sometimes been a fortunate alternative to these fates. In Vietnam, children fathered by foreigners, often by American soldiers, have not been easily accepted by the society. Where the children have obviously been fathered by Blacks, racial prejudice can compound the factors of foreign blood and birth outside of marriage, placing on these children a triple burden. . . .

## NOTES AND QUESTIONS

1. *Numbers.* Adoptions of children born outside the United States have increased in this country, with annual rates climbing from 7,700 in the 1980s to 18,000 by 2000 and more than 22,000 in 2005. Rose Kreider, Foreign Born Adopted Children in the U.S., 2000, in Adoption Factbook IV at 133 (National Council for Adoption 2007). In 2000, about 13 percent of adopted children in the United States were foreign-born. Id. at 138-139. What accounts for these numbers? Authorities state that U.S. citizens seek children from abroad in part because of the shortage of "highly desirable" adoptees, as well

as agency restrictions on adopters. Further, the highly publicized cases of Baby Richard, noted Chapter 2, section B2, and Baby Jessica, supra, which returned children to biological parents after lengthy periods with adoptive families, reportedly sparked increased interest in intercountry adoptions, believed by many to be less vulnerable to such disruptions. See, e.g., Alison Fleisher, Note, The Decline of Domestic Adoption: Intercountry Adoption as a Response to Local Adoption Laws and Proposals to Foster Domestic Adoption, 13 S. Cal. Rev. L. & Women's Stud. 171 (2003).

2. *Applicable laws.* Several bodies of law might ordinarily apply to international adoptions: federal immigration laws, state adoption standards, and the foreign country's relinquishment requirements. Two adoptions were routinely required, the first in the country of origin to enable the child to travel to the United States and the second in the adoptive parents' state, given the absence of full faith and credit for decrees from foreign countries. Cf. In re Doe, 868 N.Y.S.2d 40 (App. Div. 2008) (holding act of state doctrine inapplicable in domestic "readoption" to shield foreign adoption from reexamination).

Significant changes have occurred in recent years. For example, federal law, which limits entry to foreign adoptees who are "orphans," expanded the definition of the term to include not only children whose parents both have died but also those whose parents both have disappeared, abandoned or deserted them, or become separated or lost from them, as well as children for whom the sole surviving parent cannot provide care and has irrevocably released the child for adoption and emigration. 8 U.S.C. §1101(b)(1)(F) (2008). In addition, some jurisdictions stopped requiring a full state proceeding if a foreign adoption has been completed. See, e.g., In re Adoption of W.J., 942 P.2d 37 (Kan. 1997). Moreover, federal legislation now provides that, when certain statutory conditions are met, children adopted from abroad by U.S. citizens automatically become U.S. citizens. 8 U.S.C. §1431(b) (2008). This Child Citizenship Act thus treats children adopted abroad by U.S. citizens the same as those born abroad to U.S. citizens. See also 8 U.S.C. §1101(b)(1)(F) (2008) (immediate relative classification for such children).

Now, the Hague Convention on Protection of Children and Cooperation in Respect for Intercountry Adoption has ushered in even more notable reforms. This Convention, which applies only when both countries involved are Convention parties, is designed to regularize international adoptions by requiring a finding that the child is adoptable and a determination that the adoption would serve the child's best interests. For example, the Convention lists the following requirements for intercountry adoptions:

**Article 4**
An adoption within the scope of the Convention shall take place only if the competent authorities of the State of origin—

*a)* have established that the child is adoptable;
*b)* have determined, after possibilities for placement of the child within the State of origin have been given due consideration, that an intercountry adoption is in the child's best interests;
*c)* have ensured that
(1) the persons, institutions and authorities whose consent is necessary for adoption, have been counselled as may be necessary and duly informed of the effects of their consent, in particular

whether or not an adoption will result in the termination of the legal relationship between the child and his or her family of origin,

(2) such persons, institutions and authorities have given their consent freely, in the required legal form, and expressed or evidenced in writing,

(3) the consents have not been induced by payment or compensation of any kind and have not been withdrawn, and

(4) the consent of the mother, where required, has been given only after the birth of the child; and

*d)* have ensured, having regard to the age and degree of maturity of the child, that

(1) he or she has been counselled and duly informed of the effects of the adoption and of his or her consent to the adoption, where such consent is required,

(2) consideration has been given to the child's wishes and opinions,

(3) the child's consent to the adoption, where such consent is required, has been given freely, in the required legal form, and expressed or evidenced in writing, and

(4) such consent has not been induced by payment or compensation of any kind.

**Article 5**

An adoption within the scope of the Convention shall take place only if the competent authorities of the receiving
State —

*a)* have determined that the prospective adoptive parents are eligible and suited to adopt;

*b)* have ensured that the prospective adoptive parents have been counselled as may be necessary; and

*c)* have determined that the child is or will be authorized to enter and reside permanently in that State.

Hague Conference on Private International Law, 33: Convention of 29 May 1993 on Protection of Children and Co-operation in respect of Intercountry Adoption, available at http://www.hcch.net/index_en.php?act=conventions. pdf&cid=69. The Convention also establishes supervisory Central Authorities to impose minimum norms and procedures and mandates recognition of such adoptions in other signatory countries.

In 2000, the United States enacted implementing legislation for this convention, 42 U.S.C. §§14901-14954 (2008), but ratification here did not occur until 2007, with the convention entering into force in this country on April 1, 2008. For additional details, including a list of other countries that have ratified the Convention, see 34 Fam. L. Rep. 1239 (BNA Apr. 1, 2008).

The Convention has met with both praise and criticism. Observers predict that this regime will facilitate U.S. citizens' intercountry adoptions by removing procedural hurdles, such as the need for readoption in the parents' domicile, while also creating new barriers and increasing expenses. Elizabeth Bartholet, International Adoption: Thoughts on the Human Rights Issues, 13 Buff. Hum. Rts. L. Rev. 151, 174-177 (2007). For example, the requirements are difficult for small adoption agencies to satisfy. See Amy Grillo Kales, Note, The Intercountry Adoption Act of 2000: Are Its Laudable Goals Worth Its Potential

Impact on Small Adoption Agencies, Independent Intercounty Adoptions, and Ethical Independent Adoption Professionals?, 36 Geo. Wash. Int'l L. Rev. 477 (2004). Further, concern persists that the U.S. regulations issued pursuant to the Convention fail to address payments to birth parents and might increase child trafficking. See Trish Maskew, The Failure of Promise: The U.S. Regulations on Intercountry Adoption Under the Hague Convention, 60 Admin. L. Rev. 487 (2008).

3. *A controversial practice.* Like transracial adoption, intercountry adoption provokes controversy. Supporters insist that intercountry adoptions provide opportunities for growth, love, and well-being that would otherwise elude certain children, while also demonstrating the importance of our shared humanity. Thus, intercountry adoption has passionate supporters like Professor Elizabeth Bartholet, whose own story appears in the excerpt in Chapter 3, section A1a. She contends that child-focused advocacy necessarily favors international adoption, based on imagining with empathy what children living in institutions or on the streets in other countries would want, if they could think rationally and make informed choices. Elizabeth Bartholet, International Adoption: The Child's Story, 24 Ga. St. L. Rev. 333 (2007). On the other hand, critics point out the similarity to baby selling, given the predominance of market behavior. Jacqueline Bhabha, Moving Babies: Globalization, Markets, and Transnational Adoption, 28-Sum. Fletcher F. World Aff. 181 (2004); David M. Smolin, Intercountry Adoption as Child Trafficking, 39 Val. U. L. Rev. 281 (2004). See also Sara Corbett, Where Do Babies Come From?, N.Y. Times, June 16, 2002, §6 (Magazine), at 42 (cover story examining "baby laundering" and the "mysterious origins of Cambodian 'orphans' — and the complex ethics for Americans adopting them").

What insights does Professor Twila Perry's excerpt add to the controversy? See also, e.g., Shani King, Challenging MonoHumanism: An Argument for Changing the Way We Think About Intercountry Adoption, 30 Mich. J. Int'l L. ___ (forthcoming 2009), available at http://ssrn.com/abstract=1298464 (last visited Jan. 24, 2009). Consider the following observation of historian Rickie Solinger: "[T]he incidence of adoption, that is, the transfer of babies from women of one social classification to women in a higher social classification or group (within the same country or transnationally), may be a very accurate index of the vulnerable status of women in the country of the birth mother." Rickie Solinger, Beggars and Choosers: How the Politics of Choice Shapes Adoption, Abortion, and Welfare in the United States 67 (2001). See also id. at 28.

Who benefits from intercountry adoption? Whom does it harm? What impact does it have on the adoption of U.S.-born children? What law reforms would you suggest? See, e.g., Patricia Meier, Note, Small Commodities: How Child Traffickers Exploit Children and Families in Intercountry Adoption and What the United States Must Do to Stop Them, 12 J. Gender Race & Just. 185 (2008).

For a range of other perspectives on intercountry adoption, see generally, e.g., Kathleen Ja Sook Bergquist et al., International Korean Adoption: A Fifty-Year History of Policy and Practice (2007); Veronica S. Root, Development, Angelina and Madonna: Why All the Fuss? An Exploration of the Rights of the Child and Intercountry Adoption Within African Nations, 8 Chi. J. Int'l L. 323 (2007); Elisabeth J. Ryan, Note, For the Best Interests of the Children: Why the Hague Convention on Intercountry Adoption Needs to Go Farther, as Evidenced by Implementation in Romania and the United States, 29 B.C. Int'l & Comp. L. Rev. 353 (2006); David M. Smolin, Child Laundering as Exploitation: Applying Anti-Trafficking Norms to Intercountry Adoption Under the Coming Hague Regime, 32 Vt. L. Rev. 1 (2007); Barbara Stark, Baby Girls from China in New York: A Thrice-Told Tale, 2003 Utah L. Rev. 1231.

4. *A changing landscape.* Some countries that previously permitted adoptions by Americans have tightened restrictions, revoking the accreditation of U.S. adoption agencies and imposing new rules for adopters. See, e.g., Vanessa Hua, Russian Adoptions Held Up by Red Tape; Agencies Lose Accreditation Under Tighter Controls, S.F. Chron., Feb. 23, 2006, at B4. In the meantime, new sites have gained prominence. See, e.g., Jane Gross & Will Connors, Surge in Adoptions Raises Concerns in Ethiopia, N.Y. Times, June 4, 2007, at A1.

Recent publicity has focused on Guatemala, once the second most popular source of intercountry adoptions by Americans (after China). At one time, nearly 1 percent of all Guatemalan children were adopted by Americans, with many birth mothers receiving payments and the country itself benefiting from adoption tourism. See Marc Lacey, Guatemala System Is Scrutinized as Americans Rush in to Adopt, N.Y. Times, Nov. 6, 2006, §1, at 1. When the Hague Convention, supra, entered into force in the United States, however, Guatemala's procedures had not yet become Hague compliant. See 24 Fam. L. Rep. 1239 (BNA Apr. 1, 2008). Indeed, reports of babies stolen from birth parents and then sold for adoption surfaced. See, e.g., Tests Link Stolen Baby to Adoption, Chi. Trib., July 24, 2008, News section, at 14. Subsequently, the U.S. Department of State's website, which posts country-by-country information relevant to intercountry adoption, stated that adoptions from Guatemala had ceased. http://adoption.state.gov/country/guatemala.html (updated Oct. 2008) (last visited Dec. 20, 2008).

## Depictions in Popular Culture: Anne Tyler, Digging to America (2006)

This novel, a *New York Times* bestseller, tells the story of two families, one Iranian American, the Yazdans, and one with less obvious and less recent immigrant roots, the Donaldsons, who meet at the airport while awaiting the arrival of daughters whom they are adopting from Korea. Although the Donaldsons name their daughter Jin-Ho and affirmatively seek to emphasize her ties to her native country, the assimilated Yazdans rear their daughter, Susan, without explicitly formulating such a cultural agenda. Ordinary family life, with its joys and misfortunes, unfolds as the two families celebrate together, year after year, the date of arrival of Jin-Ho and Susan. All the while, Maryam, Susan's adoptive and widowed grandmother, discovers through her new connections with Susan and the Donaldsons that, even after 35 years in the United States, she still has not fully addressed the meaning of her own "foreignness."

The two families exemplify sharply contrasting approaches to childrearing. Such different choices are protected by parental autonomy and family privacy, Chapter 1, section B2. Nonetheless, what are the merits and disadvantages of each approach, given the background of Jin-Ho and Susan? How do the situations of children who come to the United States as intercountry adoptees both differ from and also resemble the situation of others who immigrate to the United States, such as Maryam? To what extent can one achieve "belonging" without some loss of cultural distinctiveness and identity?

## Depictions in Popular Culture: Casa de los Babys (2003)

As this film presenting many perspectives on intercountry adoption by acclaimed director John Sayles opens, one sees a large room with dozens of cribs, each containing a brown-skinned baby, while an attendant softly sings to one baby she holds in her arms. Meanwhile, six women from the United States meet and spend weeks together in an upscale South American hotel, nicknamed "Casa de los Babys," while awaiting the babies they have traveled to adopt. Although each woman has her own story, all of them are white. Juxtaposed with depictions of the women's habits, disappointments, concerns, and dreams — from fitness regimens to tragic losses of biological children to opportunistic behavior to idealized visions of motherhood — are scenes of the abject poverty of many homeless children who live on the streets in the community. In a particularly poignant exchange, one of the women, Eileen, candidly describes her fantasy of spending a snowy day with the young daughter she hopes to rear at her home in Boston; in response, the hotel maid, Asuncion, tells of her own biological daughter, Esmeralda, whose "other mother up there in the North" Asuncion hopes is just like Eileen. Because Eileen speaks only English and Asuncion only Spanish, however, the two women do not understand one another's stories. Yet, perhaps by coincidence, when Eileen is about to meet her baby daughter, she mentions to another prospective adopter that she will name her Esmeralda.

The film raises but does not answer numerous questions. Who benefits from the practices examined here? Do the impoverished lives of the street children justify the corruption of local adoption officials and the "cultural imperialism" that one character perceives in the adopters' quest for children? Or, should we blame the stark class differences within the local community — between the hotel operator and her brother, the adoption attorney, on the one hand,

and the hotel workers and the homeless, on the other? Why are the U.S. women adopting internationally? Why are they all Caucasian? Could the money spent on their travel, hotel stays, legal expenses, and payoffs address the plight of the poorest members of the community, perhaps making many of the relinquishments unnecessary? Are some of these women not fit to be mothers? On what basis? Will the adoptive mothers feel like "real mothers"? And, why have the adoptive fathers all remained in the United States?

## PROBLEM

At a family gathering, your cousin and your cousin's spouse approach you for a private conversation after hearing you mention that you have been taking a course on adoption. They want to adopt a child, but they are having difficulty making sense of the conflicting stories and opinions from well-meaning friends and web-based support groups about both the advantages and disadvantages of domestic adoption, on the one hand, and intercountry adoption, on the other. They ask you what considerations you would find important as they try to choose which option to pursue. What would you say? How, if at all, would your statement change if you were an attorney counseling clients who had asked for similar advice?

# ASSISTED REPRODUCTION

Although the law and discourse of adoption long have emphasized child welfare, the preceding materials reveal how adoption also serves the needs of adults—needs often shaped by powerful social, cultural, and legal norms. To the extent that adoption provides a way for childless adults to construct a family, however, medicine and science now offer alternatives: assisted reproductive technologies or ARTs. Further, the market for such advances has flourished in response to the insufficient supply of the most sought-after adoptees—white infants.

This part considers two primary ARTs: alternative insemination (once called "artificial insemination") and in vitro fertilization (IVF), with a chapter devoted to each. As these materials demonstrate, however, the legal and social meanings of these techniques vary based on context, including gender, race, class, and the participants' intentions. The final chapter in this part explores the consequences of the differences among jurisdictions in their approaches to ARTs, including the attraction of travel for those seeking a hospitable regime.

Throughout these materials, three salient points warrant emphasis. First, even if adults regard adoption and ARTs as two options for constructing a family, significant differences mark the legal treatment of these would-be alternatives. Second, as a general matter, this divergence in legal treatment reflects an absence of law governing many ARTs, in contrast to the close regulation of adoption. Indeed, such legal silence about many forms of assisted reproduction has helped cultivate a thriving practice and consumer industry—so that the rare disputes about ARTs that make their way into court and then into these materials constitute the exception, not the rule. Thus, recurring questions concern what regulation might be desirable and why. Finally, these materials suggest that the contrasting legal regimes governing adoption and ARTs have the power to shape not only the preferences of adults considering these two options but also the understanding of family itself.

# CHAPTER 6

# *ALTERNATIVE INSEMINATION*

The earliest and simplest technique permitting procreation without sex was once called "artificial insemination." Today, authorities prefer the term "alternative insemination."[1] Why? Who benefits from this technique?

## A. CREATING TRADITIONAL FAMILIES

### 1. DONOR INSEMINATION

IN RE ADOPTION OF ANONYMOUS

345 N.Y.S.2d 430 (Sur. Ct. 1973)

SOBEL, Surrogate. . . .

As a preliminary, there are two types of artificial insemination. Homologous insemination is the process by which the wife is artificially impregnated with the semen of her husband [(AIH).] Heterologous insemination is the artificial insemination of the wife by the semen of a third-party donor [(AID).] The utilization of AID procedures is bound to increase because of the unavailability — no doubt due to the "pill" and liberalized abortion laws — of adoptive children. Relatively recent too is the practice of AID where the husband's family has a history of hereditary disease or where RH incompatibility has led to repeated stillbirths. . . .

The facts in this proceeding are briefly stated. During the marriage the child was born of consensual AID. The husband was listed as the father on the birth certificate. Later the couple separated and the separation was followed by a divorce. Both the separation agreement and the divorce decree declare the child to be the "daughter" and "child" of the couple. The wife was granted support and the husband visitation rights. He has faithfully visited

---

[1] Mary Lyndon Shanley, Making Babies, Making Families: What Matters Most in an Age of Reproductive Technologies, Surrogacy, Adoption, and Same-Sex and Unwed Parents 80 (2001).

and performed all the support conditions of the decree. The wife later remarried and her new husband is petitioning to adopt the child. The first husband has refused his consent. Confronted with that legal impediment, the petitioner has suggested that the first husband's consent is not required since he is not the "parent" of the child. . . . If the husband is the "parent" of a child born of consensual AID, in the absence of his consent to the adoption, the petition must be dismissed. . . .

The leading case . . . is People v. Sorensen[, 437 P.2d 495 (Cal. 1968)]. *Sorensen* was a criminal prosecution on complaint of the welfare authorities against the husband for failure to support a minor child born during the marriage of consensual AID. The California Supreme Court without dissent held: the defendant is the lawful father of a dependent child born of consensual AID; that the term "father" as used in the penal statute is not limited to a biologic or natural father; the determinative factor is whether the legal relationship of father and child exists. The court reasoned that a child conceived through AID does not have a "natural" father; that the anonymous donor is not the "natural" father; that he does have a "lawful" father and the intent of the Legislature was to include a lawful father in the penal sanctions; further, that "In light of these principles of statutory construction, a reasonable man who, because of his inability to procreate, actively participates and consents to his wife's artificial insemination in the hope that a child will be produced whom they will treat as their own, knows that such behavior carries with it the legal responsibilities of fatherhood and criminal liability for nonsupport. . . ." This is the principle of equitable estoppel found in several other cases. . . .

[Gursky v. Gursky, 242 N.Y.S.2d 406 (Sup. Ct. 1963), the leading New York case,] is not persuasive. It is the only published decision which flatly holds that AID children are illegitimate. It has been criticized. (Note, 1968 U. of Ill. L. Forum 203, 208.) The "historical concept" and the statutory definition of "a child born out of wedlock" upon which it relies were developed and enacted long before the advent of the practice of artificial insemination. The birth of AID children was not then contemplated. An AID child is not "begotten" by a father who is not the husband; the donor is anonymous; the wife does not have sexual intercourse or commit adultery with him; if there is any "begetting" it is by the doctor who in this specialty is often a woman. The suggestion that the husband might not regard the child as his own has been dispelled by our gratifying experience with adoptive parents. Since there is consent by the husband, there is no marital infidelity. The child is not born "out of wedlock" but in and during wedlock. And finally legislative inaction is an unsound basis for any inferences favorable or unfavorable. . . .

Basically the problem of the status of AID children vis-à-vis the "father" is one of policy. . . . New York has a strong policy in favor of legitimacy [so] it would seem absurd to hold illegitimate a child born during a valid marriage, of parents desiring but unable to conceive a child, and both consenting and agreeing to the impregnation of the mother by a carefully and medically selected anonymous donor. [O]ur liberal policy is for the protection of the child, not the parents. It serves no purpose whatsoever to stigmatize the AID child; or to compel the parents formally to adopt in order to confer upon the AID child the status and rights of a naturally conceived child.

[A] child born of consensual AID during a valid marriage is a legitimate child entitled to the rights and privileges of a naturally conceived child of the same marriage. The father of such child is therefore the "parent" (Domestic Relations Law, §111) whose consent is required to the adoption of such child by another. . . .

## NOTES AND QUESTIONS

1. *History and background.* Use of AIH as a medical response to male infertility reportedly began in the 1790s and AID in 1884. See Lee M. Silver, Remaking Eden: How Genetic Engineering and Cloning Will Transform the American Family 178-179 (1998). The popularity of AID (or donor insemination) grew over the years, especially during the "baby boom" following World War II. See Elaine Tyler May, Barren in the Promised Land: Childless Americans and the Pursuit of Happiness 75-78, 147-149 (1997). On alternative insemination's history, its diffusion into society, and the role of the medical profession and law, see Gaia Bernstein, The Socio-Legal Acceptance of New Technologies: A Close Look at Artificial Insemination, 77 Wash. L. Rev. 1035 (2002).

Statistics show that 6.1 million women and approximately 2.1 million married couples in the United States suffer impaired ability to have children, and 9.3 women use fertility services. Centers for Disease Control, National Center for Health Statistics, Fast Stats, Infertility (available at http://www.cdc.gov/nchs/fastats/fertile.htm) (last visited Dec. 29, 2008). See also Naomi R. Cahn, Test Tube Families: Why the Fertility Market Needs Legal Regulation 32 (2009). Past data show that over 100,000 women undergo alternative insemination in the United States each year. In 1987, the number was 172,000. Congress of the United States, Office of Technology Assessment, Artificial Insemination in the United States: Summary of a 1987 Survey—Background Paper 3 (1988).

Insemination does not require medical intervention. Self-insemination can be performed with semen obtained from a relative, friend, or acquaintance or from a sperm bank, such as the Sperm Bank of California, which often offers the possibility of donor anonymity. See http://thespermbankofca.org/pages/page.php?pageid=1&cat=1 (last visited Dec. 29, 2008).

2. *Statutory responses.* Many jurisdictions now address by statute the issue presented in *Anonymous*. Eighteen have followed the 1973 Uniform Parentage Act, which recognizes as the father the husband who consents in writing to AID performed by a licensed physician and states that the "donor of semen provided to a licensed physician for artificial insemination of a woman other than the donor's wife is treated in law as if he were not the natural father. . . ." Unif. Parentage Act §5 (1973), 9B U.L.A. 377, 407-408 (2001). The new Uniform Parentage Act (new UPA), first promulgated in 2000 and revised in 2002, reaches the same result, providing that the husband's failure to consent to assisted reproduction does not preclude his recognition as father, if the man and woman during the first two years of the child's life reside in the same household with the child and openly hold the child as their own. Unif. Parentage Act §§702, 704 (2000, amended 2002), 9B U.L.A. 355-356 (2001); id. at 53 (Supp. 2008). See also American Law Institute, Principles of the Law of

Family Dissolution: Analysis and Recommendations (ALI Principles) §§2.03, 3.03 (2002) (recognizing parentage by estoppel in such cases).

3. *The adoption analogy. Anonymous* examines Gursky v. Gursky, 242 N.Y.S.2d 406 (Sup. Ct. 1963), in which the husband's duty to support an AID child rested on his implied promise and equitable estoppel. See Chapter 1, section B1b. Does this approach apply the principle of equitable adoption or equitable parenthood (Chapter 3, section B1) to consensual donor insemination? See generally Bridget R. Penick, Note, Give the Child a Legal Father: A Plea for Iowa to Adopt a Statute Regulating Artificial Insemination by Anonymous Donor, 83 Iowa L. Rev. 633 (1998).

What other principles from adoption law should apply to AID cases? Should the husband of a woman who uses AID undertake a stepparent adoption of the child? See Welborn v. Doe, 394 S.E.2d 732 (Va. Ct. App. 1990).

4. *Anonymity versus disclosure.* The 1973 UPA provided for sealed records concerning donor insemination. Unif. Parentage Act §5 (1973), 9B U.L.A. 407-408 (2001). Even while litigation and legislative reform began to give adult adoptees access to information about their birth parents (see Chapter 4, section C2), a norm of secrecy prevailed for donor insemination. Why? What similarities between adoptees and donor-conceived individuals are relevant to an asserted "right to know"? What dissimilarities? See generally Mary Lyndon Shanley, Collaboration and Commodification in Assisted Procreation: Reflections on an Open Market and Anonymous Donation in Human Sperm and Eggs, 36 Law & Soc'y Rev. 257 (2002); Elizabeth Siberry Chestney, Note, The Right to Know One's Genetic Origin: Can, Should, or Must a State That Extends This Right to Adoptees Extend an Analogous Right to Children Conceived with Donor Gametes?, 80 Tex. L. Rev. 365 (2001); Lucy R. Dollens, Note, Artificial Insemination: Right of Privacy and the Difficulty in Maintaining Donor Anonymity, 35 Ind. L. Rev. 213 (2001).

Today, parents often openly discuss their children's origins, sperm banks facilitate donor-child meetings, and children can register on a website designed to introduce them to others conceived by the same donor. See Amy Harmon, Hello, I'm Your Sister. Our Father Is Donor 150, N.Y. Times, Nov. 20, 2005, §1, at 1; Linda Villarosa, Once-Invisible Sperm Donors Get to Meet the Family, N.Y. Times, May 21, 2002, §F, at 5. See also Amy Harmon, Sperm Donor Father Ends His Anonymity, N.Y. Times, Feb. 14, 2007, at A18 (man uses Internet donor sibling registry to reveal his identity to offspring, now teens and young adults).

Some other countries, including the United Kingdom, now make information even more available. Under the 2008 amendments to the Human Fertilisation and Embryology Act (HFEA), individuals conceived by donor gametes may obtain, when they turn 16, nonidentifying information about their genetic parents and their donor-conceived genetic siblings and identifying information, once they turn 18. Human Fertilisation and Embryology Act of 2008, ch. 22, §24 (U.K.) (§31ZA, amending §31 of the 1990 Act). The amendments also provide for the release of information about genetic parentage to those seeking to marry or enter an intimate physical relationship (id. at §31ZB), the release of information about resulting children to gamete donors (id. at §31ZD), and — upon mutual consent — the release of identifying information about donor-conceived genetic siblings (id. at §31ZE). Some of these provisions become effective under a schedule designed to avoid surprise to past donors who expected anonymity. See Human Fertilisation and Embryology Act 2008: Explanatory Notes 24, available at http://www.opsi.gov.uk/acts/acts2008/en/ukpgaen_20080022_en.pdf (explaining that "[d]onor conceived people will be able to request identifying information about their donor from 2023 onwards, in relation to donors who donated identifiably from April 2005" or earlier for donors who reregister as identifiable). In addition, treatment services using donated gametes must be accompanied by counseling, including information about the importance of apprising resulting children of the facts of their conception. Human Fertilisation and Embryology Act of 2008, ch. 22, §14 (6C) (U.K.). See also R. v. Secretary of State for Health, (2002) EWHC 1593 (Q.B. Admin.) Eng. 28 (recognizing right to personal identity in family life, which allows children of donor insemination to seek information and requires balancing against other interests).

Should similar reforms be enacted in the United States? What are the most compelling arguments for such reforms? See, e.g., Katrina Clark, Who's Your Daddy? Mine Was an Anonymous Sperm Donor. That Made Me Mad. So I Decided to Find Him., Wash. Post, Dec. 17, 2006, at B1 ("It's hypocritical of parents and medical professionals to assume that biological roots won't matter to the 'products' of the cryobanks' service, when the longing for a biological relationship is what brings customers to the banks in the first place."). See also Lynne W. Spencer, Sperm Donor Offspring: Identity and Other Experiences (2007); Naomi Cahn, Necessary Subjects: The Need for a Mandatory National Donor Gamete Registry,_____DePaul J. Health Care L. (forthcoming 2008), available at http://papers.ssrn.com/sol3/papers.cfm?abstract_id=1120389 (last visited Jan. 24, 2009); Michelle Dennison, Revealing Your Sources: The Case for Non-Anonymous Gamete Donation, 21 J.L. & Health 1 (2008). What are the countervailing arguments in favor of donor anonymity? See Denise Grady, Shortage of Sperm Donors in Britain Prompts Calls for Change, N.Y. Times, Nov. 12, 2008, at A10; Amy Harmon, Are You My Sperm Donor? Few Clinics Will Say, N.Y. Times, Jan. 20, 2006, at A1.

5. *Policy issues.*

a. *Eugenics.* Assisted reproduction allows recipients to select genetic material, in turn raising criticisms and concerns typically evoked by eugenics. Sperm banks provide elaborate profiles of donors' characteristics, including physical features, educational backgrounds, skills, interests, and talents. See, e.g., The Sperm Bank of California, Donor Catalogue and Profiles, available at http://thespermbankofca.org/pages/page.php?pageid=4&cat=4 (visited Dec. 29, 2008). The Repository of Germinal Choice, established in 1980 by a wealthy Californian, promised to provide the sperm of Nobel Prize winners. For a journalist's investigation and profiles of some of the donors and resulting children, see David Plotz, The Genius Factory: The Curious History of the Nobel Prize Sperm Bank (2005). Despite the perils of eugenics, why shouldn't those using donor insemination be informed and demanding consumers? Instead, should medical personnel make the selection? The state?

b. *Fraud.* The practice of donor insemination resulted in a famous case of fraud. In 1992, Dr. Cecil Jacobson was convicted on 52 counts of fraud and perjury for telling his patients he used semen from anonymous donors for inseminations when in fact he used his own. For federal prosecutors, the case posed unique questions about privacy rights versus law enforcement: On the one hand, the patients had a right to know about their physician's alleged fraud, and genetic testing of the children would be necessary to prove the case. On the other hand, suppose the family members would prefer not to know. How should the prosecutors proceed? See Sabra Chartrand, Parents Recall Ordeal of Prosecuting in Artificial-Insemination Fraud Case, N.Y. Times, Mar. 15, 1992, §1, at 16. The DNA tests ultimately revealed that Jacobson had fathered 15 children in the 7 families participating in the case until conclusion. Id. Jacobson was sentenced to five years in prison and ordered to pay fines and restitution exceeding $116,000. See United States v. Jacobson, 4 F.3d 987, 1993 WL 343172 (4th Cir. 1993) (unpublished opinion upholding convictions on appeal), *cert. denied*, 511 U.S. 1069 (1994). See generally Cyrene Grothaus-Day, Criminal Conception: Behind the White Coat, 39 Fam. L.Q. 707, 712-716 (2005) (calling Jacobson's crime "genetic rape").

6. *Medical regulation.* What role should the state play in screening and checking the medical histories of donors? What records should be kept? What risks follow from inadequate screening and record-keeping? Would you support limits on the use of any one individual's gametes to prevent accidental incest? See Naomi Cahn, Accidental Incest: Drawing the Line—or the Curtain?—for Reproductive Technology, 32 Harv. J.L. & Gender 59 (2009).

In the United States, the practice of donor insemination long remained unregulated, with wide variations in screening performed by physicians providing such treatment. See Congress of the United States, supra. But see N.H. Rev. Stat. Ann. §§168-B:10, 168-B:12 (2008) (medical evaluation of sperm donors and recipients required since 1990). Occasional litigation highlights the risks of improper screening. See Johnson v. Superior Ct., 95 Cal. Rptr. 2d 864 (Ct. App. 2000) (allowing plaintiff family to compel anonymous donor's deposition in negligence action against sperm bank for using semen with family history of kidney disease). By contrast, the United Kingdom uses a licensing regime, conditioning licenses for providing fertility treatment and assisted reproduction on compliance with specific requirements. See generally Human Fertilisation and Embryology Act 2008, ch. 22, Pt. 1 (U.K.).

The Food and Drug Administration (FDA) first took steps to regulate donated reproductive tissue in rules that became effective in May, 2005. See U.S. Department of Health and Human Services, Food and Drug Administration, Center for Biologics and Research, Guidance for Industry: Eligibility Determination for Donors of Human Cells, Tissues, and Cellular and Tissue-Based Products (HCT/Ps) (August 2007) (available at www.fda.gov/cber/gdlns/tissdonor.pdf.). These donor eligibility rules require testing for specific diseases, including HIV and hepatitis. 21 C.F.R. §§1271.45-1271.90 (2008). In accompanying nonbinding recommendations, the FDA now considers at increased risk and thus ineligible any man who has had sex with another man in the preceding five years, effectively precluding gay men from donating semen. See U.S. Department of Health and Human Services, supra. For critiques of this policy, see John G. Culhane, Bad Science, Worse Policy: The Exclusion of Gay Males from Donor Pools, 24 St. Louis U. Pub. L. Rev. 129 (2005); Luke Boso, Note, The Unjust Exclusion of Gay Sperm Donors: Litigation Strategies to End Discrimination in the Gene Pool, 110 W.Va. L. Rev. 843 (2008).

7. *AIH.* *Anonymous* distinguishes AID from AIH, a practice sometimes used when the husband's fertility problems consist of a low sperm count or decreased motility. Families might also use AIH when the husband (or other prospective father) faces a life- or health-threatening situation, such as war or illness. Semen stored in advance can be used even after the man's death. See infra section B1.

In several publicized cases, mix-ups have resulted in use of the wrong man's semen — often a man of a different race. E.g., Sara Lyall, British Judge Rules Sperm Donor Is Legal Father in Mix-Up Case, N.Y. Times, Feb. 27, 2003, at A1 (court recognizes Black donor as father of children born, following clinic error, to white couple, who are permitted to retain custody); Avi Salzman, Looking for Answers After a Mistake at the Start of Life, N.Y. Times, July 25, 2004, §14CN, at 1 (reporting African-American woman's decision not to use emergency contraception after physician discovered using wrong semen (probably of a white man) immediately after insemination). How do you explain the frequency of racial differences in the reported mix-ups? See Dorothy Roberts, Killing the Black Body: Race Reproduction, and the Meaning of Liberty 251-252 (1999). See also Leslie Bender, Genes, Parents, and Assisted Reproductive Technologies: ARTs, Mistakes, Sex, Race & Law, 12 Colum. J. Gender & L. 1 (2003); Raizel Liebler, Are You My Parent? Are You My Child? The Role of Genetics and Race in Defining Relationships After Reproductive Technological Mistakes, 5 DePaul J. Health Care L. 15 (2002). Does similar harm occur from use of semen from the wrong donor, who is the same race but lacks a physical resemblance to the intended father? See Harnicher v. University of Utah Med. Ctr., 962 P.2d 67 (Utah 1998).

---

## Depictions in Popular Culture: Made in America (1993)

This comedy centers on the unexpected relationship between Sarah Matthews (Whoppi Goldberg), a widowed Black woman who runs an Afro-centric bookstore, and Hal Jackson (Ted Danson), a Caucasian "ham" of a car salesman, who meet after Sarah's daughter Zora learns that she was conceived by donor insemination (not by Sarah's deceased husband), and she tracks down Hal as her genetic father. For Sarah and Zora, the idea of a genetic father who is not African-American comes as a disorienting shock. As advertisements for the film describe the problem: "At the sperm-bank, she asked for a tall, intelligent, black man. One out of three ain't bad." To add insult to injury, Hal, well-known for his outlandish television commercials, is not the sort of man whom the thoughtful Sarah or the studious Zora can easily welcome into the family. By the end of the film, however, Sarah and Hal have developed a genuine affection for one another, and Zora has come to see Hal as her father, completely apart from genetics.

Although the film paints with a broad and often unbelievable brush, it raises questions about race matching in donor insemination, about the quest of many offspring for their donor fathers, and about the biological versus functional understandings of parentage. What legal regulation, if any, would you suggest on these matters?

## PROBLEM

Marcia wants to have children but her husband Eric does not. Marcia decides to pursue AID. Although Eric voices his objection, Marcia proceeds. She later gives birth to a son, whom blood tests show cannot be Eric's biological child. In divorce proceedings that begin before the baby's birth, Marcia seeks child support from Eric. She argues the child has a right to support. In claiming that he has no duty to pay, Eric invokes a state statute like the provision of the 1973 Uniform Parentage Act expressly referring to the husband's consent. What result? See In re Marriage of Witbeck-Wildhagen, 667 N.E.2d 122 (Ill. App. Ct. 1996). Cf. K.S. v. G.S., 440 A.2d 64 (N.J. Super. Ct. Ch. Div. 1981); Lane v. Lane, 912 P.2d 290 (N. M. Ct. App. 1996). If the family had remained intact until after the child's birth, would the husband's behavior prove relevant? See Brown v. Wyatt, 202 S.W.3d 555 (Ark. Ct. App. 2005); R.S. v. R.S., 670 P.2d 923 (Kan. Ct. App. 1983); Laura G. v. Peter G., 830 N.Y.S.2d 496 (Sup. Ct. 2007). See also Unif. Parentage Act §705 (2000, amended 2002), 9B U.L.A. 54 (Supp. 2008).

Who has the burden of proof on the consent issue? See Jackson v. Jackson, 739 N.E.2d 1203 (Ohio Ct. App. 2000); In re Marriage of M.C., 65 S.W.3d 188 (Tex. App. 2001). Can Eric recover in tort from the physician? Cf. Shin v. Kong, 95 Cal. Rptr. 2d 304 (Ct. App. 2000). See generally Karen DeHaan, Note, Whose Child Am I? A Look at How Consent Affects a Husband's Obligation to Support a Child Conceived Through Heterologous Artificial Insemination, 37 Brandeis L.J. 809 (1998-1999).

## 2. TRADITIONAL SURROGACY ARRANGEMENTS

### In Re Baby M

537 A.2d 1227 (N.J. 1988)

WILENTZ, C.J. . . .

In February 1985, William Stern and Mary Beth Whitehead entered into a surrogacy contract. It recited that Stern's wife, Elizabeth, was infertile, that they wanted a child, and that Mrs. Whitehead was willing to provide that child as the mother with Mr. Stern as the father.

The contract provided that through artificial insemination using Mr. Stern's sperm, Mrs. Whitehead would become pregnant, carry the child to term, bear it, deliver it to the Sterns, and thereafter do whatever was necessary to terminate her maternal rights so that Mrs. Stern could thereafter adopt the child. Mrs. Whitehead's husband, Richard, was also a party to the contract; Mrs. Stern was not. Mr. Whitehead promised to do all acts necessary to rebut the presumption of paternity under the Parentage Act. N.J.S.A. 9:17-43a(l), -44a. Although Mrs. Stern was not a party to the surrogacy agreement, the contract gave her sole custody of the child in the event of Mr. Stern's death. . . .

Mr. Stern, on his part, agreed to attempt the artificial insemination and to pay Mrs. Whitehead $10,000 after the child's birth, on its delivery to him. In a separate contract, Mr. Stern agreed to pay $7,500 to the Infertility Center of

New York ("ICNY"). The Center's advertising campaigns solicit surrogate mothers and encourage infertile couples to consider surrogacy. ICNY arranged for the surrogacy contract by bringing the parties together, explaining the process to them, furnishing the contractual form, and providing legal counsel.

The history of the parties' involvement in this arrangement suggests their good faith. William and Elizabeth Stern were married in July 1974, having met at the University of Michigan, where both were Ph.D. candidates. Due to financial considerations and Mrs. Stern's pursuit of a medical degree and residency, they decided to defer starting a family until 1981. . . . Based on the perceived risk [of Mrs. Stern's possible multiple sclerosis,] the Sterns decided to forego having their own children. The decision had special significance for Mr. Stern. Most of his family had been destroyed in the Holocaust. As the family's only survivor, he very much wanted to continue his bloodline.

Initially the Sterns considered adoption, but were discouraged by the substantial delay apparently involved and by the potential problem they saw arising from their age and their differing religious backgrounds. . . .

The paths of Mrs. Whitehead and the Sterns to surrogacy were similar. Both responded to advertising by ICNY. . . . Mrs. Whitehead's response apparently resulted from her sympathy with family members and others who could have no children (she stated that she wanted to give another couple the "gift of life"); she also wanted the $10,000 to help her family. . . . On February 6, 1985, Mr. Stern and Mr. and Mrs. Whitehead executed the surrogate parenting agreement. After several artificial inseminations over a period of months, Mrs. Whitehead became pregnant. The pregnancy was uneventful and on March 27, 1986, Baby M was born. . . .

Mrs. Whitehead realized, almost from the moment of birth, that she could not part with this child. . . . Nonetheless, Mrs. Whitehead was, for the moment, true to her word. Despite powerful inclinations to the contrary, she turned her child over to the Sterns on March 30 at the Whiteheads' home.

The Sterns were thrilled with their new child [whom they named Melissa]. They had planned extensively for its arrival. . . . Later in the evening of March 30, Mrs. Whitehead became deeply disturbed, disconsolate, stricken with unbearable sadness. She had to have her child. . . . The Sterns, concerned that Mrs. Whitehead might indeed commit suicide, not wanting under any circumstances to risk that, and in any event believing that Mrs. Whitehead would keep her word [that she would return her in a week], turned the child over to her. . . .

The struggle over Baby M began when it became apparent that Mrs. Whitehead could not return the child to Mr. Stern. Due to Mrs. Whitehead's refusal to relinquish the baby, Mr. Stern filed a complaint seeking enforcement of the surrogacy contract. . . . After the order [in favor of Stern] was entered, ex parte, the process server, aided by the police, in the presence of the Sterns, entered Mrs. Whitehead's home to execute the order. Mr. Whitehead fled with the child, who had been handed to him through a window while those who came to enforce the order were thrown off balance by a dispute over the child's current name.

The Whiteheads immediately fled to Florida with Baby M. . . . Police in Florida enforced [a court order obtained by Mr. Stern], forcibly removing the child from her grandparents' home. She was soon thereafter brought to New Jersey and turned over to the Sterns. [The *ex parte* order awarding custody to the Sterns *pendente lite* was affirmed.] Pending final judgment, Mrs. Whitehead was awarded limited visitation with Baby M. . . .

The trial took thirty-two days over a period of more than two months. [The trial court] held that the surrogacy contract was valid; ordered that Mrs. Whitehead's parental rights be terminated and that sole custody of the child be granted to Mr. Stern; and, after hearing brief testimony from Mrs. Stern, immediately entered an order allowing the adoption of Melissa by Mrs. Stern, all in accordance with the surrogacy contract. Pending the outcome of the appeal, we granted a continuation of visitation to Mrs. Whitehead, although slightly more limited than the visitation allowed during the trial.

Although clearly expressing its view that the surrogacy contract was valid, the trial court devoted the major portion of its opinion to the question of the baby's best interests. . . . Its rationalization . . . was that while the surrogacy contract was valid, specific performance would not be granted unless that remedy was in the best interests of the child. The factual issues confronted and decided by the trial court were the same as if Mr. Stern and Mrs. Whitehead had had the child out of wedlock, intended or unintended, and then disagreed about custody. . . .

On the question of best interests [raised in this appeal by Mrs. Whitehead, we] agree substantially with both [the trial court's] analysis and conclusions on the matter of custody. The court's review and analysis of the surrogacy contract, however, is not at all in accord with ours. . . .

### Invalidity and Unenforceability of Surrogacy Contract . . .

#### A.   Conflict with Statutory Provisions

The surrogacy contract conflicts with: (1) laws prohibiting the use of money in connection with adoptions; (2) laws requiring proof of parental unfitness or abandonment before termination of parental rights is ordered or an adoption is granted; and (3) laws that make surrender of custody and consent to adoption revocable in private placement adoptions. . . .

(1) Considerable care was taken in this case to structure the surrogacy arrangement so as not to violate [the prohibition on payment in connection with adoption]. The arrangement was structured as follows: the adopting parent, Mrs. Stern, was not a party to the surrogacy contract; the money paid to Mrs. Whitehead was stated to be for her services — not for the adoption; the sole purpose of the contract was stated as being that "of giving a child to William Stern, its natural and biological father"; the money was purported to be "compensation for services and expenses and in no way . . . a fee for termination of parental rights or a payment in exchange for consent to surrender a child for adoption"; the fee to the Infertility Center ($7,500) was stated to be for legal representation, advice, administrative work, and other "services." Nevertheless, it seems clear that the money was paid and accepted in connection with an adoption [in violation of criminal law]. As for the contention that the Sterns are paying only for services and not for an adoption, we need note only that they would pay nothing in the event the child died before the fourth

month of pregnancy, and only $1,000 if the child were stillborn, even though the "services" had been fully rendered. . . .

The prohibition of our statute is strong. Violation constitutes a high misdemeanor, N.J.S.A. 9:3-54c, a third-degree crime, N.J.S.A. 2C:43-lb, carrying a penalty of three to five years imprisonment. N.J.S.A. 2C:43-6a(3). The evils inherent in baby-bartering are loathsome for a myriad of reasons. The child is sold without regard for whether the purchasers will be suitable parents. The natural mother does not receive the benefit of counseling and guidance to assist her in making a decision that may affect her for a lifetime. In fact, the monetary incentive to sell her child may, depending on her financial circumstances, make her decision less voluntary. . . . Baby-selling potentially results in the exploitation of all parties involved. . . .

(2) The termination of Mrs. Whitehead's parental rights, called for by the surrogacy contract and actually ordered by the court fails to comply with the stringent requirements of New Jersey law. Our law, recognizing the finality of any termination of parental rights, provides for such termination only where there has been a voluntary surrender of a child to an approved agency or to the Division of Youth and Family Services ("DYFS"), accompanied by a formal document acknowledging termination of parental rights, N.J.S.A. 9:2-16, -17; N.J.S.A. 9:3-41; N.J.S.A. 30:4C-23, or where there has been a showing of parental abandonment or unfitness. A termination may ordinarily take one of three forms: an action by an approved agency, an action by DYFS, or an action in connection with a private placement adoption. . . .

In this case a termination of parental rights was obtained not by proving the statutory prerequisites but by claiming the benefit of contractual provisions. . . . Since the termination was invalid, it follows, as noted above, that adoption of Melissa by Mrs. Stern could not properly be granted.

(3) The provision in the surrogacy contract stating that Mary Beth Whitehead agrees to "surrender custody . . . and terminate all parental rights" contains no clause giving her a right to rescind. It is intended to be an irrevocable consent. . . .

It is clear that the Legislature so carefully circumscribed all aspects of a consent to surrender custody — its form and substance, its manner of execution, and the agency or agencies to which it may be made — in order to provide the basis for irrevocability. . . . There is only one irrevocable consent, and that is the one explicitly provided for by statute: a consent to surrender of custody and a placement with an approved agency or with DYFS. The provision in the surrogacy contract, agreed to before conception, requiring the natural mother to surrender custody of the child without any right of revocation is one more indication of the essential nature of this transaction: the creation of a contractual system of termination and adoption designed to circumvent our statutes.

### B.   Public Policy Considerations . . .

The surrogacy contract guarantees permanent separation of the child from one of its natural parents. Our policy, however, has long been that to the extent possible, children should remain with and be brought up by both of their natural parents. . . .

The surrogacy contract violates the policy of this State that the rights of natural parents are equal concerning their child, the father's right no greater than the mother's. . . . The whole purpose and effect of the surrogacy contract was to give the father the exclusive right to the child by destroying the rights of the mother.

The policies expressed in our comprehensive laws governing consent to the surrender of a child . . . stand in stark contrast to the surrogacy contract and what it implies. Here there is no counseling, independent or otherwise, of the natural mother, no evaluation, no warning. . . .

Worst of all, however, is the contract's total disregard of the best interests of the child. There is not the slightest suggestion that any inquiry will be made at any time to determine the fitness of the Sterns as custodial parents, of Mrs. Stern as an adoptive parent, their superiority to Mrs. Whitehead, or the effect on the child of not living with her natural mother.

This is the sale of a child, or, at the very least, the sale of a mother's right to her child, the only mitigating factor being that one of the purchasers is the father. Almost every evil that prompted the prohibition on the payment of money in connection with adoptions exists here. . . .

The differences between adoption and a surrogacy contract should be noted, since it is asserted that the use of money in connection with surrogacy does not pose the risks found where money buys adoption. First, and perhaps most important, all parties concede that it is unlikely that surrogacy will survive without money. . . . That conclusion contrasts with adoption; for obvious reasons, there remains a steady supply, albeit insufficient, despite the prohibitions against payment. The adoption itself, relieving the natural mother of the financial burden of supporting an infant, is in some sense the equivalent of payment.

Second, the use of money in adoptions does not produce the problem — conception occurs, and usually the birth itself, before illicit funds are offered. With surrogacy, the "problem," if one views it as such, consisting of the purchase of a woman's procreative capacity, at the risk of her life, is caused by and originates with the offer of money.

Third, with the law prohibiting the use of money in connection with adoptions, the built-in financial pressure of the unwanted pregnancy and the consequent support obligation do not lead the mother to the highest paying, ill-suited, adoptive parents. She is just as well-off surrendering the child to an approved agency. In surrogacy, the highest bidders will presumably become the adoptive parents regardless of suitability, so long as payment of money is permitted. . . .

The main difference, that the unwanted pregnancy is unintended while the situation of the surrogate mother is voluntary and intended, is really not significant. [T]he essential evil is the same, taking advantage of a woman's circumstances (the unwanted pregnancy or the need for money) in order to take away her child. . . . Intimated, but disputed, is the assertion that surrogacy will be used for the benefit of the rich at the expense of the poor. . . . The point is made that Mrs. Whitehead agreed to the surrogacy arrangement, supposedly fully understanding the consequences. Putting aside the issue of how compelling her need for money may have been, and how significant her understanding of the consequences, we suggest that her consent is irrelevant. There are, in a civilized society, some things that money cannot buy. . . .

The long-term effects of surrogacy contracts are not known, but feared — the impact on the child who learns her life was bought, that she is the offspring of someone who gave birth to her only to obtain money; the impact on the natural mother as the full weight of her isolation is felt along with the full reality of the sale of her body and her child; the impact on the natural father and adoptive mother once they realize the consequences of their conduct. . . . In New Jersey the surrogate mother's agreement to sell her child is void.

### Termination . . .

Although the question of best interests of the child is dispositive of the custody issue in a dispute between natural parents, it does not govern the question of termination. It has long been decided that the mere fact that a child would be better off with one set of parents than with another is an insufficient basis for terminating the natural parent's rights. . . . There is simply no basis . . . to warrant termination of Mrs. Whitehead's parental rights. . . .

### Constitutional Issues . . .

The right to procreate, as protected by the Constitution, has been ruled on directly only once by the United States Supreme Court. See Skinner v. Oklahoma, 316 U.S. 535 (forced sterilization of habitual criminals violates equal protection clause of fourteenth amendment). Although Griswold v. Connecticut, 381 U.S. 479, is obviously of a similar class, strictly speaking it involves the right not to procreate. The right to procreate very simply is the right to have natural children, whether through sexual intercourse or artificial insemination. It is no more than that. Mr. Stern has not been deprived of that right. Through artificial insemination of Mrs. Whitehead, Baby M is his child. . . . To assert that Mr. Stern's right of procreation gives him the right to the custody of Baby M . . . would be to assert that the constitutional right of procreation includes within it a constitutionally protected contractual right to destroy someone else's right of procreation. . . .

Mr. Stern also contends that he has been denied equal protection of the laws by the State's statute granting full parental rights to a husband in relation to the child produced, with his consent, by the union of his wife with a sperm donor. N.J.S.A. 9:17-44. The claim really is that of Mrs. Stern. It is that she is in precisely the same position as the husband in the statute: she is presumably infertile, as is the husband in the statute; her spouse by agreement with a third party procreates with the understanding that the child will be the couple's child. . . .

. . . The State has more than a sufficient basis to distinguish the two situations — even if the only difference is between the time it takes to provide sperm for artificial insemination and the time invested in a nine-month pregnancy — so as to justify automatically divesting the sperm donor of his parental rights without automatically divesting a surrogate mother. Some basis for an equal protection argument might exist if Mary Beth Whitehead had contributed her egg to be implanted, fertilized or otherwise, in Mrs. Stern, resulting in the latter's pregnancy. That is not the case here, however.

Mrs. Whitehead, on the other hand, . . . claims the right to the companionship of her child. This is a fundamental interest, constitutionally protected. Furthermore, it was taken away from her by the action of the court below. . . . Having held the contract invalid and having found no other grounds for the termination of Mrs. Whitehead's parental rights, we find that nothing remains of her constitutional claim. We express no opinion on whether a prolonged suspension of visitation would constitute a termination of parental rights, or whether, assuming it would, a showing of unfitness would be required.

## Custody

. . . With the surrogacy contract disposed of, the legal framework becomes a dispute between two couples over the custody of a child produced by the artificial insemination of one couple's wife by the other's husband. Under the Parentage Act the claims of the natural father and the natural mother are entitled to equal weight, i.e., one is not preferred over the other solely because he or she is the father or the mother.[3] [T]he child's best interests determine custody. . . .

. . . The Whiteheads claim that even if the child's best interests would be served by our awarding custody to the Sterns, we should not do so, since that will encourage surrogacy contracts. . . . We disagree. Our declaration that this surrogacy contract is unenforceable and illegal is sufficient to deter similar agreements. We need not sacrifice the child's interests in order to make that point sharper. . . .

The Whiteheads also contend that the award of custody to the Sterns *pendente lite* was erroneous and that the error should not be allowed to affect the final custody decision. [They argue that] one of the most important factors, whether mentioned or not, in favor of custody in the Sterns is their continuing custody during the litigation, now having lasted for one-and-a-half years. . . . We disagree with the premise, however, that in determining custody a court should decide what the child's best interests would be if some hypothetical state of facts had existed. Rather, we must look to what those best interests are, today, even if some of the facts may have resulted in part from legal error. . . .

[Eleven experts testified on the child's best interests.] Our reading of the record persuades us that the trial court's decision awarding custody to the Sterns (technically to Mr. Stern) should be affirmed. . . .

Our custody conclusion is based on strongly persuasive testimony contrasting both the family life of the Whiteheads and the Sterns and the personalities and characters of the individuals. The stability of the Whitehead family life was doubtful at the time of trial. Their finances were in serious trouble (foreclosure by Mrs. Whitehead's sister on a second mortgage was in process).

---

3. . . . This does not mean that a mother who has had custody of her child for three, four, or five months does not have a particularly strong claim arising out of the unquestionable bond that exists at that point between the child and its mother; in other words, equality does not mean that all of the considerations underlying the [sex-based] "tender years" doctrine have been abolished.

Mr. Whitehead's employment, though relatively steady, was always at risk because of his alcoholism, a condition that he seems not to have been able to confront effectively. Mrs. Whitehead had not worked for quite some time, her last two employments having been part-time. One of the Whiteheads' positive attributes was their ability to bring up two children, and apparently well, even in so vulnerable a household. Yet substantial question was raised even about that aspect of their home life. The expert testimony contained criticism of Mrs. Whitehead's handling of her son's educational difficulties. Certain of the experts noted that Mrs. Whitehead perceived herself as omnipotent and omniscient concerning her children. . . . Her inconsistent stories about various things engendered grave doubts about her ability to explain honestly and sensitively to Baby M—and at the right time—the nature of her origin. Although faith in professional counseling is not a *sine qua non* of parenting, several experts believed that Mrs. Whitehead's contempt for professional help, especially professional psychological help, coincided with her feelings of omnipotence in a way that could be devastating to a child who most likely will need such help. . . . The prospects for wholesome, independent psychological growth and development would be at serious risk. [Mrs. Whitehead subsequently divorced, became pregnant by another man and remarried, developments that the court said had no effect on its decision.]

The Sterns have no other children, but all indications are that their household and their personalities promise a much more likely foundation for Melissa to grow and thrive. There is a track record of sorts—during the one-and-a-half years of custody Baby M has done very well, and the relationship between both Mr. and Mrs. Stern and the baby has become very strong. The household is stable, and likely to remain so. Their finances are more than adequate, their circle of friends supportive, and their marriage happy. Most important, they are loving, giving, nurturing, and open-minded people. They have demonstrated the wish and ability to nurture and protect Melissa, yet at the same time to encourage her independence. Their lack of experience is more than made up for by a willingness to learn and to listen, a willingness that is enhanced by their professional training, especially Mrs. Stern's experience as a pediatrician. They are honest; they can recognize error, deal with it, and learn from it. They will try to determine rationally the best way to cope with problems in their relationship with Melissa. When the time comes to tell her about her origins, they will probably have found a means of doing so that accords with the best interests of Baby M. All in all, Melissa's future appears solid, happy, and promising with them. Based on all of this we have concluded . . . that Melissa's best interests call for custody in the Sterns [an outcome favored by the expert witnesses].

Some comment is required on the initial *ex parte* order awarding custody *pendente lite* to the Sterns (and the continuation of that order after a plenary hearing). The issue, although irrelevant to our disposition of this case, may recur; and when it does, it can be of crucial importance. When father and mother are separated and disagree, at birth, on custody, only in an extreme, truly rare, case should the child be taken from its mother *pendente lite*. . . . The probable bond between mother and child, and the child's need, not just the mother's, to strengthen that bond, along with the likelihood, in most cases, of a significantly lesser, if any, bond with the father—all counsel against temporary custody in the father [absent the mother's unfitness or danger to the child.]

Even [the mother's] threats to flee should not suffice to warrant any other relief unless her unfitness is clearly shown. At most, it should result in an order enjoining such flight. The erroneous transfer of custody, as we view it, represents a greater risk to the child than removal to a foreign jurisdiction. . . .

## Visitation

. . . Our reversal of the trial court's order . . . requires delineation of Mrs. Whitehead's rights to visitation. [The experts called by Melissa's court-appointed guardian] were concerned that given Mrs. Whitehead's determination to have custody, visitation might be used to undermine the Sterns' parental authority and thereby jeopardize the stability and security so badly needed by this child. Two of the experts recommended suspension of visitation for five years and the other suspension for an undefined period. [The guardian ad litem] now argues that instead of five years, visitation should be suspended until Melissa reaches majority. . . .

We also note the following for the trial court's consideration: First, this is not a divorce case where visitation is almost invariably granted to the non-custodial spouse. To some extent the facts here resemble cases where the non-custodial spouse has had practically no relationship with the child, but it only "resembles" those cases. In the instant case, Mrs. Whitehead spent the first four months of this child's life as her mother and has regularly visited the child since then. Second, she is not only the natural mother, but also the legal mother, and is not to be penalized one iota because of the surrogacy contract. [A touchstone of visitation is] that it is desirable for the child to have contact with both parents. . . .

We have decided that Mrs. Whitehead is entitled to visitation at some point, and that question is not open to the trial court on this remand. [T]he guardian's recommendation of a five-year delay is most unusual—one might argue that it begins to border on termination. Nevertheless, if the circumstances as further developed by appropriate proofs or as reconsidered on remand clearly call for that suspension under applicable legal principles of visitation, it should be so ordered. . . .

## Conclusion

This case affords some insight into a new reproductive arrangement: the artificial insemination of a surrogate mother. The unfortunate events that have unfolded illustrate that its unregulated use can bring suffering to all involved. . . .

We have found that our present laws do not permit the surrogacy contract used in this case. Nowhere, however, do we find any legal prohibition against surrogacy when the surrogate mother volunteers, without any payment, to act as a surrogate and is given the right to change her mind and to assert her parental rights. Moreover, the Legislature remains free to deal with this most sensitive issue as it sees fit, subject only to constitutional constraints. . . .

The judgment is affirmed in part, reversed in part, and remanded for further proceedings consistent with this opinion.

Lori B. Andrews, Between Strangers: Surrogate Mothers,
Expectant Fathers and Brave New Babies (1989)

11-24

. . . Carol Pavek knew exactly why she was different from the people of Amarillo. She was adopted. She came, at least prenatally, from somewhere else. . . . Carol felt no need to seek out her birth parents. She loved the couple who raised her, and felt she could get from them any help and advice she needed. But when she got pregnant with her own child, her link to her biological mother became crucially important. . . .

[After her child's birth, Carol began training as a midwife. She and her husband Rick were disappointed they could not experience the home birth they had planned for their son.] "We felt unfulfilled," says Carol. "We teased each other that we would keep giving birth until we got it right, only we would have to find families to give the children to."

When their son, Chris, was eighteen months old, their joking took a serious turn. That's when they first heard about the possibility of surrogate motherhood on a television show. The guest on the show was Noel Keane, the Dearborn, Michigan, attorney. . . . As Noel Keane and an infertile couple described surrogate motherhood to the television audience, Carol Pavek recognized how she could connect her dream of a home birth with a couple's dream of a baby. . . . "This was a way for Carol to express herself and do something for others," Rick said later. "There was a lot of altruism. . . ." . . .

It took six months' reflection before Carol actually began to fashion a letter to Noel expressing her interest. "It wasn't actually a letter," she says. "It was more like a book." . . . Carol was candid in her portrait of herself, mentioning her receding chin, heavy hips, and nearsightedness. She was equally blunt about what she was looking for in a couple. They would have to agree, of course, to a home birth and the adoptive mother would have to be present. If possible, the father and any other children in the family should be present as well. Carol would breast-feed the baby for three to five days to pass on her immunities.

At the time Carol contacted Noel, in 1980, surrogate mothers were not being paid. It hadn't even occurred to Carol to ask for any money. Her main concern was the quality of the relationship she would have with the couple. . . .

Noel received the letter the same day he received a desperate call from a couple of modest means who lived in a rural section of northern California. Nancy's first husband had died when she was pregnant with their second child. She raised their two daughters alone through childhood, then required a hysterectomy. When she later married Andy, it was clear that she would not be able to bear children. But now, in part because of his attachment to Nancy's two daughters, they were wishing they could have another child [one with Andy's traits].

By sundown, Andy and Nancy had called Carol. Within a week, they had taken the tiresome three-and-a-half-day bus ride to the Texas panhandle to meet Carol and Rick face-to-face. . . . Carol and Rick immediately took to the couple. . . . Their conversations over the next few days were not at all like a business negotiation; they were getting to know each other like new neighbors. Surrogacy is not like a merger of corporations. It is the creation of a relationship — and, as with any intimate relationship, it takes a certain level of compatibility to allow therelationship to flower. . . .

The first insemination [at Carol's house] did not result in a pregnancy, so the following month, May of 1980, Carol flew out to their home in the California mountains. They lived out in the country in a cabin with a dog and horses, about four miles from an old mining town. Carol was immediately enchanted by the area as the perfect place to raise a child. [E]very other day for a week, Carol artificially inseminated herself. [She became pregnant.]

Four days before the scheduled due date, Andy, Nancy, and the two teen-aged daughters drove down to Amarillo in a motor home. The four of them rushed to Carol's house once her labor began. By this time, Carol had helped with thirty-five successful home births; she hoped her own would be the thirty-sixth. But, again, there was a problem with Carol's delivery and by midnight she was giving birth in a local hospital. . . . Andy and Nancy stayed with Carol through the labor, but once delivery began, they had to leave because no advance arrangements had been made for their presence. Rick was left to coach Carol through and oversee the birth of a ten-pound boy. . . .

The baby was gently lowered onto Carol's abdomen. She slowly opened her eyes, and was relieved to find that she didn't have any feeling of possession. Her only thought was "What a gorgeous baby."

Two hours later, Andy and Nancy wanted to give Carol the baby to breast-feed. A nurse took Nancy aside, saying "Oh you must not let her breast-feed the baby, she will bond."

"I've trusted her this far, I'm going to trust her again," Nancy replied.

Carol fed the baby, then spent a peaceful hour watching Nancy hold her son. Carol thought of how, in traditional adoptions, the hospital staff did everything they could to keep the biological mother and the baby apart. It wasn't right to rip a baby away, Carol thought as she drifted off to sleep; the mother must have a chance to say good-bye.

The next day, back at home, Rick turned to Carol before she fell asleep. "You're already thinking of trying again, aren't you?" he asked. [Carol twice subsequently served as a "surrogate."]

MARY BETH WHITEHEAD WITH LORETTA SCHWARTZ-NOBEL,
A MOTHER'S STORY: THE TRUTH ABOUT THE *BABY M* CASE (1989)

---

25-27

Rick [the then husband of Mary Beth Whitehead] tried to comfort me. He tried everything he knew. Nothing worked. . . . You don't comfort somebody who is giving away her child.

Everybody said, "You have two other children." It wasn't as if my baby were dead. My child was alive, and I had given her to two strangers. . . .

The Sterns and the Infertility Center had told me I was doing a beautiful thing, but I wasn't. All the way through my pregnancy, I had tried to believe it.

I had suppressed the reality; I had denied my feelings. I had not allowed myself to deal with it. But now I couldn't pretend anymore. I just didn't want to be a party to it, no matter how much it was going to disappoint them. I couldn't bear to be a woman who gave away her child. . . .

I began to feel angry and defensive. My body, my soul, my heart, my breathing, my everything had gone into making this baby. What had Bill Stern done? Put some sperm in cup. What had Betsy done? Bought some clothes, a box of diapers, and a case of formula. . . .

. . . I just couldn't stop crying. It just kept coming, and the emptiness that I felt was something I never want to feel again.

Eventually I fell asleep. Suddenly I opened my eyes. The room was dark, and I was lying in a pool of milk. The sheets were full of milk. I knew it was time to feed my baby. I knew she was hungry, but I could not hear her crying. The room was quiet as I sat up in the bed, alone in the darkness, with the milk running down my chest and soaking my nightgown. I held out my empty arms and screamed at the top of my lungs, "Oh, God, what have I done — I want my baby!" . . .

## NOTES AND QUESTIONS

1. *"Traditional surrogacy."* *Baby M* illustrates what has come to be known as "traditional surrogacy," an arrangement pioneered by Michigan attorney Noel Keane, who drafted the first such formal agreement in 1976. Traditional surrogacy entails the same process of insemination used in *Anonymous*, supra, but with a mirror-image purpose: A woman is inseminated with the sperm of a man who (with his wife, if he is married) intends to serve as the child's parent. Thus, the so-called "surrogate" provides both gestation and genes — or is the mother, as some would argue. In part because of the litigation and the outcome of *Baby M*, today traditional surrogacy has given way to more technologically sophisticated collaborations, including "gestational surrogacy," made possible by in vitro fertilization (IVF) and explored in Chapter 7.

2. *The context and legacy of* Baby M. *Baby M* garnered extensive publicity during the legal proceedings that culminated in the principal case, introducing the public to surrogacy arrangements and sparking considerable controversy. Despite the impression left by *Baby M*, studies of the practice indicated that, in the vast majority of surrogacy arrangements, the parties perform their agreements without resort to judicial intervention. See John A. Robertson, Children of Choice: Freedom and the New Reproductive Technologies 131 (1994). See also Susan Fischer & Irene Gillman, Surrogate Motherhood: Attachment, Attitudes and Social Support, 54 Psychiatry 13, 19 (1991) (describing Whitehead as an "anomaly").

Nonetheless, *Baby M* raised two primary questions about surrogacy: First, what legal restrictions ought to apply to consensual arrangements in which all parties are willing to perform? For example, *Baby M* holds that surrogacy for pay constitutes an illegal sale of a child, regardless of the parties' wishes. Second, what rules ought to govern "failed" surrogacy arrangements such as *Baby M*? Note that failure also can occur when the intended parents repudiate the agreement, as when they reject the child because of birth defects. Cf., e.g., Stiver v. Parker, 975 F.2d 261 (6th Cir. 1992). Both questions ask about the appropriate limits on private ordering in what *Baby M* calls "a new way of bringing children into a family." See also, e.g., R.R. v. M.H., 689 N.E.2d 790 (Mass. 1998).

3. *Surrogacy and adoption.* How does surrogacy resemble adoption? *Baby M* looks to adoption law to rule the contract void. Yet, how can the court ignore the contract when, without it, this particular child would not exist? Thus, is not surrogacy distinguishable from adoption?

What are the advantages and disadvantages of surrogacy over adoption? For prospective parents? Birth mothers (surrogates)? Children? Society?

Had the arrangement not failed, adoption by Elizabeth Stern would have followed termination of Mary Beth Whitehead's parental rights. Should the adoption be treated as a stepparent adoption, in which there is typically little screening of adopters, or as an adoption of an unrelated child, in which the state usually intervenes more extensively? See also infra Note 7 (preconception adoption).

4. *Surrogacy and donor insemination.* Alternatively, does the law of donor insemination (rather than adoption) provide a more appropriate framework for surrogacy? Are not the two simply the biologically dictated responses to different kinds of infertility that couples experience? Consider the reasoning of Judge Sorkow, the trial judge in *Baby M.* He reasoned that surrogate mothers must be allowed to sell their services and the intended mother must be recognized as a legal parent because these rules apply to AID: "To rule otherwise denies equal protection of the law to the childless couple, the surrogate, whether male or female, and the unborn child." 525 A.2d 1128, 1165 (N.J. Super. Ct. Ch. Div. 1987). See also Carmel Shalev, Birth Power: The Case for Surrogacy 87 (1989) ("surrogacy presents a mirror situation to that of artificial insemination of a married woman with donor sperm").

What is the biological father's legal status with respect to the child if the surrogate conceives while married, as did Whitehead? Isn't he just a sperm donor with no legal status under AID law? See *R.R.,* 689 N.E.2d at 795-796. Then how could the resulting adoption be classified as a stepparent adoption? If it must be treated as an adoption by a nonrelative, why should the state have more opportunities for intervention in, and thus more control over, surrogacy than AID?

5. *"Gender neutrality."* Given his biological limitations, what more could William Stern — or any man — have done to show his interest in his anticipated child? (Recall *Kelsey S.,* Chapter 2, section B2.) Or do gender-specific contributions to reproduction compel different treatment of mothers and fathers? According to Professor Marjorie Shultz, the *Baby M* court missed an opportunity to treat men and women equally:

> To say that the factual issues are "the same" as if Whitehead and William Stern had simply had a child out of wedlock, ignores the centrally important fact that modern reproductive techniques allow the separation of personal and sexual intimacy from procreation. . . . It ignores that the father here differs in important ways from stereotypical unwed fathers. In particular, it ignores that the child in question exists only because of its progenitors' individual intentions,

their reciprocal decisions, and their behavior and expectations in the wake of such decisions. . . .

. . . Unlike biologically-based variables, the capacity to form and express intentions is gender-neutral. [H]aving rejected any role for intention, the court fell back on gender stereotypes to resolve the issues. . . . The court's decision reinforced stereotypes regarding the desirability of segregating women from the market, the unpredictability of women's intentions and decisions, and the givenness of women's biological destiny. Perhaps worst of all, it acted to lock in existing gender-based spheres of influence in our society, refusing to recognize fragile, emergent male efforts to claim a meaningful role in access to and nurture of children. . . .

Marjorie Maguire Shultz, Reproductive Technology and Intent-Based Parenthood: An Opportunity for Gender Neutrality, 1990 Wis. L. Rev. 297, 376-379. But see Pamela Laufer-Ukeles, Essay, Approaching Surrogate Motherhood: Reconsidering Difference, 26 Vt. L. Rev. 407, 436 (2002) (arguing surrogacy reveals the need for "an asymmetrical notion of [gender] equality").

6. *Feminism and surrogacy. Baby M* engendered sharp divisions among feminists. Some submitted briefs supporting Whitehead, others for the Sterns.[2] In the wake of this case, some feminists advocated the prohibition of surrogacy agreements, even those women willingly make.[3] These scholars condemned surrogacy as a practice that commodifies and exploits women and children.[4] From this point of view, surrogacy reduces women to "baby machines,"[5] subjects them to the patriarchal control of the medical profession,[6] and resembles slavery[7] and prostitution.[8] Surrogacy also reflects racist and eugenic motivations, at the expense of existing children who need homes.[9]

---

[2] Lori B. Andrews, Between Strangers: Surrogate Mothers, Expectant Fathers and Brave New Babies 171-182 (1989).

[3] See, e.g., Shari O'Brien, Commercial Conceptions: A Breeding Ground for Surrogacy, 65 N.C. L. Rev. 127 (1986); Margaret Jane Radin, Market-Inalienability, 100 Harv. L. Rev. 1849 (1987); Robin L. West, Taking Preferences Seriously, 64 Tul. L. Rev. 659 (1990).

[4] See, e.g., Anita L. Allen, Privacy, Surrogacy, and the Baby M Case, 76 Geo. L.J. 1759, 1783, 1791 (1988) (rejecting linkage of freedom-of-contract theory and privacy jurisprudence of *Griswold* because of unique harms risked by surrogates); Cass R. Sunstein, Neutrality in Constitutional Law (With Special Reference to Pornography, Abortion, and Surrogacy), 92 Colum. L. Rev. 1, 47 (1992) ("[A] world in which female sexual and reproductive services are freely traded on markets would legitimate and reinforce a pervasive form of inequality—one that sees the social role of women as that of breeders, and that uses that role to create second-class citizenship.").

[5] See, e.g., Gena Corea, Junk Liberty, in Reconstructing Babylon: Essays on Women and Technology 142, 153-156 (H. Patricia Hynes ed., 1991). See also Robyn Rowland, Living Laboratories: Women and Reproductive Technologies 198 (1992) (use of brain-dead "surrogates" as "female incubators").

[6] See, e.g., Gena Corea, The Mother Machine: Reproductive Technologies from Artificial Insemination to Artificial Wombs (1985).

[7] Professor Allen observes that slavery "had the effect of causing black women to become surrogate mothers on behalf of slave owners." Anita L. Allen, Surrogacy, Slavery and the Ownership of Life, 13 Harv. J.L. & Pub. Pol'y 139, 140 (1990).

[8] E.g., Carole Pateman, The Sexual Contract 209-218 (1988); Margaret Jane Radin, Contested Commodities 131-153 (1996).

[9] Elizabeth S. Anderson, Is Women's Labor a Commodity?, 19 Phil. & Pub. Affairs 71, 91 (1990).

Would banning consensual surrogacy, however, suggest that women need protection from their own decisions? Some feminists thus condemned efforts to outlaw surrogacy as an unwarranted intrusion on reproductive autonomy, reflecting gender stereotypes and paternalism.[10] This position supports legality for surrogacy on the ground that it respects freedom of contract and offers women new employment opportunities.[11]

Still other feminists took an intermediate position, recommending that the law permit surrogacy but allow the birth mother to renounce the contract.[12] Which of these positions is most consistent with the notion of reproductive autonomy, which enjoys some constitutional protection? The increasing importance of gender equality in family law? The best interests of children? How do the stories of Carol Pavek and Mary Beth Whitehead influence your answers?

For additional feminist perspectives, see, e.g., Expecting Trouble: Surrogacy, Fetal Abuse, and New Reproductive Technologies 156 (Patricia Boling ed., 1995); Barbara Katz Rothman, Recreating Motherhood (2000); Patricia J. Williams, On Being the Object of Property, 14 Signs 5 (1988). For a review of different feminist legal theorists' views on surrogacy, see generally Applications of Feminist Legal Theory to Women's Lives: Sex, Violence, Work, and Reproduction 1041-1062 (D. Kelly Weisberg ed., 1996).

## Depictions in Popular Culture: Margaret Atwood, The Handmaid's Tale (1985)

This frightening novel portrays a dystopia in which humans have poisoned the earth's environment, threatening the future of the species, and religious fundamentalists have conscripted women of childbearing age, Handmaids, to carry pregnancies for those in positions of power, namely Commanders and their Wives, whose authority receives reinforcement from women performing supportive functions—from the Aunts (who control thought) to the Marthas (who perform housework). See Christmas Books: Editor's Choice: The Best Books of 1986, N.Y. Times, Dec. 7, 1986, §7, at 3. The Handmaids' status is signified by their appellations: In place of their own names, they must go by words that indicate the men whom they serve,

---

[10] See, e.g., Debra Satz, Markets in Women's Reproductive Labor, 21 Phil. & Pub. Affairs 107, 117 (1992) ("dilemma for those who wish to use the mother-fetus bond to condemn [surrogacy] contracts while endorsing [privacy] right to choose abortion"); Carmel Shalev, Birth Power: The Case for Surrogacy 9-10 (1989) ("[A]mid the serious debate on the morality of [all varieties of] medical reproduction, only surrogacy has been addressed in terms of criminal norms. It occurred to me that the reason for this was the untraditional role that women play in these arrangements."); Marjorie Maguire Shultz, Reproductive Technology and Intent-Based Parenthood: An Opportunity for Gender Neutrality, 1990 Wis. L. Rev. 297.

[11] See, e.g., Shalev, supra note [10], at 160-166 (reviewing how public-private dichotomy excluded women from market and concluding that "exclusion of domestic reproductive labor from the public economy is the ultimate manifestation of a patriarchal double standard").

[12] Martha A. Field, Surrogate Motherhood (1988). See also Lawrence O. Gostin, Surrogacy from the Perspectives of Economic and Civil Liberties, 17 J. Contemp. Health L. & Pol'y 429 (2001).

"Offred," "Ofwarren," and "Ofglen," for example. The reader experiences this world through the words of Offred, who endures her circumstances and the forced rituals designed to induce compliance, all the while mourning a life that we would take for granted in the world as it existed beforehand.

A political allegory, Atwood's novel has been hailed as "a cautionary tale of postfeminist future shock." Id. What does it contribute to the debate over surrogacy arrangements? In an interview over twenty years later, Atwood observes, "You will see that no woman ruler has been successful if she has been an advocate for women at large. Not one, ever." Deborah Solomon, Questions for Margaret Atwood: In the Red, N.Y. Times, Sept. 26, 2008, §M (Magazine), at 21. To what extent does this comment pertain to issues raised by the fictional *The Handmaid's Tale* and by real-life surrogacy arrangements?

7. *Failed surrogacy agreements.* When an arrangement fails (because it is illegal or a court refuses enforcement), numerous questions arise. Using *Baby M* as an example, what is the legal status of Elizabeth Stern, who cannot adopt the child? See Nancy D. Polikoff, This Child Does Have Two Mothers: Redefining Parenthood to Meet the Needs of Children in Lesbian-Mother and Other Nontraditional Families, 78 Geo. L.J. 459, 474-477 (1990). Should courts and legislatures formally recognize long-term caregivers, such as Dr. Stern? See Doe v. Doe, 710 A.2d 1297 (Conn. 1998) (declining to recognize an intended mother as an equitable parent despite her rearing of the child, but awarding her custody as a third party after divorce); ALI Principles §2.03 (recognizing de facto parents only in limited circumstances, i.e., agreement with child's parent or parent's failure to provide care).

Should William Stern and Mary Beth Whitehead share parenting of the child, through joint custody or a custody-visitation arrangement?[13] Even if such arrangements routinely follow divorce or the dissolution of an intimate nonmarital relationship, do they make sense when the parents have only a contractual relationship? What do the best interests of the child dictate in *Baby M*? To what extent does the Constitution permit termination of Mary Beth Whitehead's parental rights altogether on grounds of the child's best interests? When "Baby M" turned 18, she reportedly initiated proceedings to terminate Mary Beth Whitehead's parental rights, and Elizabeth Stern then adopted her. See Jennifer Weiss, Now It's Melissa's Time, New Jersey Monthly Magazine, March, 2007, available at http://www.reproductivelawyer.com/news/babym.asp (last visited Dec. 26, 2008). Does a termination initiated by the now-adult child avoid the constitutional problems arguably posed if the court had taken such action soon after birth? Why?

---

[13] On remand, the court granted Mary Beth Whitehead unsupervised visitation for one eight-hour period per week, increasing to two days every other week beginning in September 1988; overnight visits followed after one year as well as a two-week visit in summer, 1989. 14 Fam. L. Rep. (BNA) 1276 (Apr. 12, 1988).

8. *Legislative responses.* Should legislatures regulate surrogacy? If so, how? What policy considerations should they consider? Should participants face criminal penalties? Which participants? Should the law distinguish commercial surrogacy from unpaid arrangements? What rules should govern in the event of breach?

The National Conference of Commissioners on Uniform State Laws, unable to promulgate a single model in 1988, included two alternatives in the Uniform Status of Children of Assisted Conception Act (USCACA): Alternative A, which regulated surrogacy arrangements through a preconception adoption proceeding, and Alternative B, which made surrogacy agreements void. See Unif. Status of Children of Assisted Conception Act, 9C U.L.A. 373-383 (2001). The new Uniform Parentage Act, UPA, drafted in 2000 and revised in 2002, replaces USCACA, see Unif. Parentage Act (2000, amended 2002), 9B U.L.A. 5-6 (Supp. 2008) (Prefatory Note to UPA). Like Alternative A of USCACA, the new UPA authorizes "gestational agreements," including the payment of consideration; requires a home study of the intended parents and judicial validation of the agreement; and provides for a court order of parentage consistent with the judicially validated agreement upon the child's birth. Unif. Parentage Act §§801, 802, 807 (2000, amended 2002), 9B U.L.A. 58-63 (Supp. 2008).

About half the states have statutes addressing surrogacy, with some banning the practice. E.g., N.Y. Dom. Rel. Law §§121-123 (2008). Some states permit but regulate the practice, typically disallowing payment and allowing the "surrogate" to rescind. See, e.g., Fla. Stat. Ann. §63.212(1)(h) (2008) (allowing "preplanned adoption agreement" but not for valuable consideration beyond expenses and with opportunity for mother to rescind consent within seven days of birth). Some states require advance judicial approval, inspired by USCACA. See, e.g., N.H. Rev. Stat. Ann. §168-B:16 (2008) (requiring "judicial preauthorization"); Va. Code Ann. §§20-160 & 20-162 (2008) (prior judicial approval and reformation). Eight states have enacted the new UPA. See http://www.nccusl.org/Update/uniformact_factsheets/uniformacts-fs-upa.asp (last visited Dec. 31, 2008); only five of these address surrogacy at all (North Dakota, Texas, Utah, Washington, and Wyoming).

Other states take a still more permissive stance: Arkansas declares that the legal parents of such children are the intended parents (including the biological father only, if unmarried). Ark. Code Ann. §9-10-201 (2008). And Nevada exempts surrogacy agreements from the ban on payment in adoptive placements. Nev. Rev. Stat. §127.287(5) (2008).

Following some of the recommendations of the famous Warnock Commission in England, Parliament outlawed commercial surrogacy agencies. §2 Surrogacy Arrangements Act of 1985, ch. 49. See also Human Fertilisation and Embryology Act of 2008, ch. 22, §59 (U.K.) (permitting nonprofit bodies to charge for initiating negotiations for a surrogacy arrangement and for compiling information about surrogacy); Human Fertilisation and Embryology Act 2008: Explanatory Notes 40-41, available at http://www.opsi.gov.uk/acts/acts2008/en/ukpgaen_20080022_en.pdf. British law also makes surrogacy arrangements unenforceable against a party unwilling to perform, while permitting judicial recognition of intended parents when certain require-ments are met. §1A Surrogacy Arrangements Act of 1985 (added by Human Fertilisation and Embryology Act of 1990, ch. 37, §36(1) (U.K.)); Human Ferti-lisation and Embryology Act of 1990, ch. 37, §30 (U.K.). Under the 2008 amendments, a court may issue a parental order to applicants when specified conditions obtain, including use of the gametes of one of the applicants, a relationship between the applicants as spouses or partners, and the free consent of the woman who carried the pregnancy. Human Fertilisation and Embryology Act of 2008, ch. 22, §54 (U.K.).

9. *The attorney's role.* What role should attorneys play in surrogacy arrange-ments? What payments are appropriate? See Joan Heifetz Hollinger, Baby M, Lawyers, and Legal Education, 37 Buff. L. Rev. 675 (1988/1989); Carol Sanger, Developing Markets in Baby-Making: In the Matter of Baby M, 30 Harv. J.L. & Gender 67 (2007). Recall the material on the attorney's role in adoptive placements, Chapter 3, section A2. Should similar limitations apply? Cf. Stiver v. Parker, 975 F.2d 261 (6th Cir. 1992) (broker and physicians owed affirmative duty of protection to mother, her husband, and intended father); Huddleston v. Infertility Ctr. of Am., 700 A.2d 453 (Pa. Super. Ct. 1997) (broker can be liable to surrogate for failing to screen father who fatally abused child).

## PROBLEM

Suppose the *Baby M* court awards custody to Mary Beth Whitehead. Should it now order William Stern to pay child support? What precedents would com-pel this result? Alternatively, what risks would such support duties create? What should the legislature say on this subject? See Martha A. Field, Surrogate Motherhood 98-101 (1988). See also J.F. v. D.B., 941 A.2d 718 (Pa. Super. Ct. 2008); J.F. v. D.B., 848 N.E.2d 873, 879-881 (Ohio Ct. App. 2006), *aff'd in part & rev'd in part*, 879 N.E.2d 740 (Ohio 2007).

# B. CREATING NONTRADITIONAL FAMILIES

## 1. "FATHERLESS" CHILDREN?

### ELISA B. V. SUPERIOR COURT

117 P.3d 660 (Cal. 2005)

Review case, reprinted Chapter 1, p. 30

### GILLETT-NETTING V. BARNHART

371 F.3d 593 (9th Cir. 2004)

BETTY FLETCHER, Circuit Judge.

Plaintiff-Appellant Rhonda Gillett-Netting, on her own behalf and on behalf of her minor children Juliet O. Netting and Piers W. Netting, appeals the district court's grant of summary judgment for the Commissioner of Social Security [denying the children's claim for insurance benefits based on the earnings of their deceased father, Robert Netting.][1]

In December 1994, Netting was diagnosed with cancer. At the time, he and his wife, Gillett-Netting, were trying to have a baby together, but Gillett-Netting suffered from fertility problems that had caused her to miscarry twice. Because doctors advised Netting that chemotherapy might render him sterile, he delayed the start of his treatment for several days so that he could deposit his semen at the University of Arizona Health Sciences Center, where it was frozen and stored for later use by his wife. Netting quickly lost his battle with cancer. He died on February 4, 1995, before his wife was able to conceive. Earlier, Netting confirmed that he wanted Gillett-Netting to have their child after his death using his frozen sperm. In-vitro fertilization of Gillett-Netting's eggs with Netting's sperm was undertaken successfully on December 19, 1995. . . . Juliet and Piers Netting were born on August 6, 1996.

On August 19, 1996, Gillett-Netting filed an application on behalf of Juliet and Piers for Social Security child's insurance benefits based on Netting's earnings. [The Social Security Administration (SSA) and later an Administrative Law judge denied the application on the ground the twins were not dependent on Netting at the time he died].

Under the [Social Security] Act, every child is entitled to benefits if the claimant is the child, as defined in 42 U.S.C. §416(e), of an individual who dies fully or currently insured; the child or the child's representative files an application for benefits; the child is unmarried and a minor (or meets disability requirements) at the time of application; and the child was dependent on the insured wage earner at the time of his death. 42 U.S.C. §402(d)(1). It is undisputed that Netting was fully insured under the Act when he died, that Juliet and Piers are his biological children and are unmarried minors, and that Gillett-Netting filed an application for child's insurance benefits on their behalf. . . .

The Act defines "child" broadly to include any "child or legally adopted child of an individual," as well as a stepchild who was the insured person's stepchild for at least nine months before the insured person died, and a grandchild or stepgrandchild of the insured person under certain circumstances. See 42 U.S.C. §416(e). Courts and the SSA have interpreted the word "child" used in the definition of "child" to mean the natural, or biological, child of the insured.

The Commissioner argues and the district court held that "child" is further defined by 42 U.S.C. §§416(h)(2), (3). . . . Under the current version of §416(h), a claimant whose parentage is disputed is deemed to be the child of an insured individual if: (1) the child would be entitled to take an intestate share of the individual's property under the laws of the state in which the individual resided at death; (2) the child's parents went through a marriage ceremony resulting in a purported marriage between them that, but for a legal impediment

---

1. Gillett-Netting also argues that applying the Act to preclude the award of child's insurance benefits to posthumously conceived children violates the children's right to equal protection of the laws. Because we conclude that Juliet and Piers are entitled to benefits under the Act, we do not reach Gillett-Netting's equal protection claim.

unknown to them at the time, would have been a valid marriage; (3) the deceased wage earner acknowledged the claimant as his or her child in writing; (4) the deceased wage earner, before dying, had been decreed by a court to be the parent of the claimant; (5) the deceased wage earner, before dying, had been ordered by a court to contribute to the support of the claimant because the claimant was his or her child; or (6) the insured individual is shown by evidence satisfactory to the Commissioner to have been the parent of the claimant and to have been living with or contributing to the support of the claimant at the time that he died. See U.S.C. §§416 (h)(2), (3).

Although these provisions offer means of "determining whether an applicant is the child . . . of a fully or currently insured individual," id. at §416(h)(2)(A), when parentage is disputed, nothing in the statute suggests that a child must prove parentage under §416(h) if it is not disputed. We conclude that these provisions do not come into play for the purposes of determining whether a claimant is the "child" of a deceased wage earner unless parentage is disputed. In this case, the Commissioner concedes that Juliet and Piers are Netting's biological children. Therefore, we conclude that the district court erred by holding that Juliet and Piers are not Netting's children for the purposes of the Act.

. . . The only remaining issue is whether Juliet and Piers, the undisputed biological children of a deceased, insured individual, are statutorily deemed dependent on Netting without proof of actual dependency. Under the Act, a claimant must show dependency on an insured wage earner in order to be entitled to child's insurance benefits. 42 U.S.C. §402(d)(1). However, the Act statutorily deems broad categories of children to have been dependent on a deceased, insured parent without demonstrating actual dependency. It is well-settled that all legitimate children automatically are considered to have been dependent on the insured individual, absent narrow circumstances not present in this case. Similarly, "illegitimate" children who prove parentage under 42 U.S.C. §§416(h)(2), (3) are "deemed to be the legitimate child of such individual" and, therefore, are deemed to have been dependent on the insured wage earner. 42 U.S.C. §402(d)(3). Thus, the provisions of §416(h) described above typically come into play to prove dependency rather than parentage. . . .

Juliet and Piers are indisputably Netting's legitimate children under the law of the state in which they reside. "Arizona has eliminated the status of illegitimacy[.]" State v. Mejia, 399 P.2d 116 [(Ariz.1965)]. In Arizona, "[e]very child is the legitimate child of its natural parents and is entitled to support and education as if born in lawful wedlock." Ariz. Rev. Stat. §8-601. . . . Under Arizona law, Netting would be treated as the natural parent of Juliet and Piers and would have a legal obligation to support them if he were alive, although they were conceived using in-vitro fertilization, because he is their biological father and was married to the mother of the children. See Ariz. Rev. Stat. §25-501 (providing that children have a right to support from their natural parents; the biological father of a child born using artificial insemination is considered a natural parent if the father is married to the mother). Although Arizona law does not deal specifically with posthumously-conceived children, *every* child in Arizona, which necessarily includes Juliet and Piers, is the legitimate child of her or his natural parents.[5]

The Commissioner nevertheless argues that Juliet and Piers do not satisfy the "legitimate child" requirement, and therefore cannot be deemed dependent under §402(d)(3), unless they also are able to inherit from Netting under state intestacy laws or meet one of the other provisions of §416(h). This is not the case. Legitimacy in §402(d)(3) is determined in accordance with state law. See Jimenez v. Weinberger, 417 U.S. 628, 635-36 (1974) (noting that children who are considered legitimate under state law are entitled to child's insurance benefits without proving dependency). While §416(h) provides alternative avenues for children to be deemed legitimate, nothing in the Act suggests that a child who is legitimate under state law separately must prove legitimacy under the Act. It would make little sense to require a child whose parents were married to demonstrate legitimacy by showing she meets a test set forth in §416(h), for example by showing that her parent acknowledged her in writing or that a court determined her parentage prior to the parent's death.[6]

Because Juliet and Piers are Netting's legitimate children under Arizona law, they are deemed dependent under §402(d)(3), and need not demonstrate actual dependency nor deemed dependency under the provisions of §416(h). As Netting's legitimate children, Juliet and Piers are conclusively deemed dependent on Netting under the Act and are entitled to child's insurance benefits based on his earnings. . . .

## NOTES AND QUESTIONS ON *ELISA B.* AND *GILLETT-NETTING*

1. *Unmarried women and AID.*  When an unmarried woman uses alternative insemination, does the resulting child have no father on the theory that the law does not recognize semen donors as fathers? If the donor is known, should the law recognize him as the child's father? Note that the term "unmarried women" applies to single women, women in a relationship with a significant other who is not a legal spouse (as in *Elisa B.*), and widows (as in *Gillett-Netting*).

a. *Single women.*  Today, a significant number of "single mothers by choice" achieve their goal of having children via donor insemination. See, e.g., Amy Harmon, First Comes the Baby Carriage, N.Y. Times, Oct. 13, 2005, at G1 (reporting support group with 4,000 members); Jennifer Egan, Wanted: A Few Good Sperm, N.Y. Times, Mar. 19, 2006, §6 (Magazine), at 46. Professor Marsha Garrison criticizes as anomalous rules declaring that such children

---

5. This is not to say that every posthumously-conceived child in Arizona would be eligible for survivorship benefits on the basis of the earnings of the deceased sperm donor. If the sperm donor had not been married to the mother, Arizona would not treat him as the child's natural parent, and he likely would have no obligation to support the child if he were alive. In such circumstances, no eligibility for benefits would exist unless the Commissioner made a determination that the claimant was the dependent child of the deceased wage earner for purposes of the Act by virtue of satisfying one of the requirements in §416(h).

6. Because Juliet and Piers are Netting's legitimate children under Arizona state law, we need not consider whether they could be deemed dependent for another reason, such as their ability to inherit property from their deceased father under Arizona intestacy laws. See generally Woodward [v. Commission of Soc. Security, 760 N.E.2d 257 (Mass. 2002)]. As a practical matter, in most cases legitimate children would be able to inherit under state intestacy laws, but they need not demonstrate their ability to do so in order to be entitled to child's insurance benefits.

have no legal father because "outside the AID context, our legal system grants no parent, male or female, the right to be a sole parent." Marsha Garrison, Law Making for Baby Making: An Interpretive Approach to the Determination of Legal Parentage, 113 Harv. L. Rev. 835, 906 (2000). Some cases involving known donors have reached results consistent with Garrison's view, invoking the child's best interests. See, e.g., C.M. v. C.C., 407 A.2d 849 (N.J. Juv. & Dom. Rel. Ct., Cumberland County 1979) (recognizing donor as father); In re Sullivan, 157 S.W.3d 911 (Tex. App. 2005) (recognizing donor's standing to establish parentage under UPA).

Other states, however, have shown greater solicitude for leaving a child with only one legal parent in such cases. For example, under California law, a woman can foreclose a known donor's parental status so long as a licensed physician performs the insemination. Compare Steven S. v. Deborah D., 25 Cal. Rptr. 3d 482 (Ct. App. 2005), with Jhordan C. v. Mary K., 224 Cal. Rptr. 530 (Ct. App. 1986). More recently, a divided Pennsylvania supreme court reversed the court below and held enforceable a contract in which a man promised to provide sperm for the in vitro fertilization of his former lover so long as he would not be responsible for child support. Ferguson v. McKiernan, 940 A.2d 1236 (Pa. 2007). The state supreme court noted that the situation before it falls between two scenarios that evoke contrasting legal responses: fathers who conceive by sexual intercourse (who cannot contract away their support duties) and semen donors for clinical insemination (who, especially when anonymous, have no support duties). The majority reasoned that a rule of unenforceability "would mean that a woman who wishes to have a baby but is unable to conceive through intercourse could not seek sperm from a man she knows and admires, while assuring him that he will never be subject to a support order and being herself assured that he will never be able to seek custody of the child" — leaving her no choice but to resort to anonymously donated semen. Id. at 1247. Why did the court find this rationale compelling? While protecting donors and facilitating choices by prospective mothers, does the majority's approach undermine the interests of children? See id. at 1248 (noting that children here would not have been born, absent agreement). See also Brown v. Gadson, 654 S.E.2d 179 (Ga. Ct. App. 2007) (holding similar agreement does not violate Georgia's public policy); In re H.C.S., 219 S.W.3d 33 (Tex. App. 2006) (holding donor lacks standing to establish paternity).

What should the default position be in the absence of a formal agreement by the parties? In In re K.M.H., 169 P.3d 1025 (Kan. 2007), a divided court upheld against due process and equal protection challenges a state statute treating a sperm provider as "not the birth father," absent a written agreement to the contrary with the woman. In this case, Daryl Hendrix (a gay man reportedly hopeful about the opportunity to become a parent) alleged both an oral understanding with a friend, Samantha Harrington (an attorney,) that he would be involved in the twins' lives and her assurances that they need not put anything in writing. See Man Fights for Parental Rights, KCTV5-Kansas City, Nov. 23, 2007, available at http://www.kctv5.com/news/14673759/detail.html (last visited Sept. 28, 2008). Having lost in the state courts, Hendrix unsuccessfully sought certiorari in the United States Supreme Court. 129 S. Ct. 36 (2008). Should the Court have reviewed the case? Why? What does the case portend for legislative resolution of the nontraditional parentage issues increasingly confronting the courts? See Elizabeth E. McDonald, Sperm Donor or Thwarted Father? How Written Agreement Statutes Are Changing the Way Courts Resolve Legal Parentage Issues in Assisted Reproduction Cases, 47 Fam. Ct. Rev. _____ (forthcoming 2009). Cf. Jason Oller, Comment, Can I Get That in Writing? Established and Emerging Protections of Paternity Rights (In re K.M.H., 169 P.3d 1025 (Kan. 2007)), 48 Washburn L.J. 209 (2008).

b. *Women in nonmarital relationships.* How does the reasoning in *Elisa B.* resemble that in In re Adoption of Anonymous, supra? How does it differ? To what extent does the court in *Elisa B.* rely on the parties' relationship? On specific conduct by Elisa? Does such reasoning obviate the need for second-parent adoption, as in Adoption of Tammy, reprinted in Chapter 4, section B, or even same-sex marriage (or domestic partnerships) to secure parental rights?

Courts have relied on conduct to recognize the mother's partner as the parent of a child conceived by donor insemination in several other cases involving both heterosexual and same-sex relationships. See, e.g., In re M.J., 787 N.E.2d 144 (Ill. 2003) (allowing mother to proceed on promissory estoppel claim against male former paramour, who did not provide semen); C.E.W. v. D.E.W., 845 A.2d 1146 (Me. 2004) (recognizing mother's former partner as de facto parent with standing to seek award of parental rights); T.B. v. L.R.M., 786 A.2d 913 (Pa. 2001) (recognizing standing for mother's former partner, in loco parentis), *after remand*, 874 A.2d 34 (Pa. 2005); In re L.B., 122 P.3d 161 (Wash. 2005) (recognizing mother's former partner as de facto parent); In re Parentage of J.M.K., 119 P.3d 840 (Wash. 2005) (recognizing as father former partner who provided semen used for in vitro fertilization). See also In re Guardianship of I.H., 834 A.2d 922 (Me. 2003) (no notice required for anonymous donor in guardianship proceeding by mother's same-sex partner). But see, e.g., Heatzig v. MacLean, 664 S.E.2d 347 (N.C. Ct. App. 2008) (rejecting theory of "parent by estoppel" for former partner of biological mother of donor-conceived child). Cf. Tripp v. Hinckley, 736 N.Y.S.2d 506 (App. Div. 2002) (allowing known donor expanded visitation after mother's same-sex relationship ended). See generally Deborah L. Forman, Same-Sex Partners: Strangers, Third Parties, or Parents? The Changing Legal Landscape and the Struggle for Parental Equality, 40 Fam. L.Q. 23 (2006); Courtney G. Joslin, The Legal Parentage of Children Born to Same-Sex Couples: Developments in the Law, 39 Fam. L.Q. 683 (2005).

Despite the variations, might one read these cases to suggest that the law prefers *two parents* (as Garrison, supra, argues) but has become increasingly indifferent about not only the second parent's absence of genetic contribution but also his or her gender? In 2008, British legislation expressly authorized recognition of two women as a child's parents in cases of assisted reproduction, changing a previous provision requiring acknowledgment of a child's "need for a father" to refer instead to the "need for supportive parenting." Human Fertilisation and Embryology Act of 2008, ch. 22, §§14 (2)(b), 42-47 (U.K.); Human Fertilisation and Embryology Act 2008: Explanatory Notes 19, 30-31 available at http://www.opsi.gov.uk/acts/acts2008/en/ukpgaen_20080022_en.pdf.

c. *Posthumous conception.* To what extent does the law's preference for two parents explain *Gillett-Netting*? What purpose does the recognition of Robert Netting as the twins' legal father serve, other than financial? Why is the twins' mother not estopped from seeking government benefits for children whom she knew in advance would not have a second parent's support? On what basis did the court find the twins dependent on a father who died before they were conceived? Children born after a parent's death raise several legal issues, as noted below:

2. *Background.* A posthumous child is a child who was conceived before a parent's death but born thereafter. A common law presumption, now codified in many states, legitimates a child born within nine months after the death of the mother's husband. Reproductive technologies, including cryopreservation of genetic material, have made possible the birth of an increasing number of children who are *conceived* posthumously. The frozen semen, for example, can be used for insemination or to fertilize ova in vitro (see Chapter 7). The occurrence of posthumous conception is likely to increase during wartime because soldiers often freeze semen before deployment. Finally, physicians can now extract semen from men after death. See Lori B. Andrews, The Clone Age: Adventures in the New World of Reproductive Technology 222-236 (2000) ("the sperminator"); Robert Salladay, Advancing the Issue: Reproduction and the Law; Controversy Continues to Dog a Procedure That Allows Human Embryos to Be Frozen for Use at a Later Date: "Dead Dads" Create Legal Issues, Daily Press, June 16, 2004, at A3 (describing case of daughter born four years after postmortem sperm extraction). A model statute proposed by the American Bar Association recognizes the decedent as a parent when assisted reproduction is used after death only if the decedent consented in a record to such posthumous use. American Bar Association Model Act Governing Assisted Reproduction §501.3(f) (February 2008), available at http://www.abanet.org/family/committees/artmodelact.pdf. The United Kingdom also follows this approach. Human Fertilisation and Embryology Act of 2008, ch. 22, §39 (U.K.).

a. *Federal benefits.* Social Security survivors' benefits are available to "dependents" of a deceased wage earner. To qualify for such survivors' benefits under the Social Security Act, a child must prove "dependency" on the deceased parent. Legitimate children are presumed dependent, but many states follow the common law approach noted above, which excludes children *conceived after* the parent's death. How does *Gillett-Netting* address this problem?

*Gillett-Netting* is the culmination of a lengthy battle to secure Social Security survivors' benefits for posthumously conceived children. For earlier cases, see, e.g., In re Estate of Kolacy, 753 A.2d 1257 (N.J. Super. Ct. Ch. Div. 2000); Woodward v. Commissioner of Social Sec., 760 N.E.2d 257 (Mass. 2002); Michael K. Elliott, Tales of Parenthood from the Crypt: The Predicament of the Posthumously Conceived Child, 39 Real Prop. Prob. & Tr. J. 47, 60-62 (2004) (discussing 1991 case, Hart v. Chater).

b. *Inheritance rights.* Only a few states address the issue of the inheritance rights of posthumously conceived children. Some statutes grant rights to such children if the deceased parent gave consent during his lifetime. However, the nature of the required consent varies. Compare La. Rev. Stat. Ann. §9:391.1(A) (2008) (requiring the deceased's authorization that his spouse use his gametes), with Tex. Fam. Code Ann. §160.707 (2007) (requiring that the deceased spouse "consented in a record kept by a licensed physician that if assisted reproduction were to occur after death the deceased spouse would be a parent of the child"). See also In re Martin B., 841 N.Y.S.2d 207 (Sur. Ct. 2007) (ruling that the terms "issue" and "descendants" in trust documents include children conceived with cryopreserved semen of the grantor's adult son when the son was alive at execution of the trust).

What should the law require for a posthumously conceived child to inherit from this parent's intestate estate? *Woodward*, supra, requires the surviving parent to establish in a timely manner the deceased's genetic relationship and affirmative consent both to conceive posthumously and to support the child. 760 N.E.2d at 269. How should the parent manifest consent? Should a presumption of a child's entitlement arise merely from the existence of a parent's cryopreserved reproductive material? See Elliott, supra, at 58. Some states refuse to permit a posthumously conceived child to inherit unless the deceased's will provided for the child. See Fla. Stat. Ann. §742.17(4) (2008). See also Finley v. Astrue, 2008 WL 95775 (Ark. 2008); Khabbaz v. Commissioner, 930 A.2d 1180 (N.H. 2007) (both answering certified questions from federal courts deciding claims for federal benefits and holding that the child cannot inherit as a surviving child under the state intestacy statute).

Given that genetic material can be frozen and brought to term years after the deaths of both biological parents, should states require children's claims for inheritance or benefits to commence within a certain time after the parent's death? What period of time would you propose? See Ronald Chester, Posthumously Conceived Heirs under a Revised Uniform Probate Code, 38 Real Prop. Prob. & Tr. J. 727, 736-738 (2004) (proposing a three-year limitation on actions to determine whether posthumous conceived children are "descendants"). See also La. Rev. Stat. Ann. §9:391.1(A) (2008) (requiring that the child be born within three years of the decedent's death). Do short time periods provide adequate time for the surviving parent to grieve the other's death and to prepare to rear a child alone?

See generally Charles P. Kindregan & Maureen McBrien, Posthumous Reproduction, 39 Fam. L.Q. 579 (2005); Julie E. Goodwin, Not All Children Are Created Equal: A Proposal to Address Equal Protection Inheritance Rights of Posthumously Conceived Children, 4 Conn. Pub. Int. L.J. 234 (2005); Kristine S. Knaplund, Postmortem Conception and a Father's Last Will, 46 Ariz. L. Rev. 91 (2004); Kayla VanCannon, Note, Fathering a Child from the Grave: What Are the Inheritance Rights of Children Born Through New Technology After the Death of a Parent?, 52 Drake L. Rev. 331 (2004). On the different understandings of posthumous procreation in Africa, see Uché Ewelukwa, Posthumous Children, Hegemonic Human Rights, and the Dilemma of Reform — Conversations Across Cultures, 19 Hastings Women's L.J. 211 (2008).

3. *Genetic connection?* Although the father in *Gillett-Netting* supplied the genetic material, should a biological relationship be essential to the child's

status and rights? Should a posthumously conceived child qualify as a dependent for the purpose of federal benefits or inheritance rights if the husband, prior to his death, consented to the wife's use of donor insemination? The new UPA provides:

> If an individual who consented in a record to be a parent by assisted reproduction dies before placement of eggs, sperm, or embryos, the deceased individual is not a parent of the resulting child unless the deceased spouse consented in a record that if assisted reproduction were to occur after death, the deceased individual would be a parent of the child.

Unif. Parentage Act §707 (2000, amended 2002), 9B U.L.A. 55 (Supp. 2008). The comment to this section assumes the use of the deceased's genetic material. Does §707's text clearly impose this requirement? How well does this model provision address the questions raised by posthumous conception? See also Human Fertilisation and Embryology Act of 2008, ch. 22, §40 U.K.) (provision for posthumous parentage when deceased did not provide genetic material).

4. *Property rights.* Posthumous insemination and conception also raise questions about the nature and "ownership" of genetic material. Does one have a right to bequeath such material for use in posthumous reproduction?

Hecht v. Superior Court, 20 Cal. Rptr. 2d 275 (Ct. App. 1993), addressed this question in a will contest between Deborah Hecht, the girlfriend of decedent William Kane, and Kane's adult children from a prior marriage. Before committing suicide, Kane deposited semen in a sperm bank and willed the semen to Hecht. Kane's children urged destruction of the semen, to prevent the birth of children outside "a traditional family" and to protect existing family members from financial and emotional distress. Id. at 279.

The court concluded that "at the time of his death, decedent had an interest, in the nature of ownership, to the extent that he had decisionmaking authority as to the use of his sperm for reproduction. Such interest is sufficient to constitute 'property' within the meaning of [the] Probate Code." Id. at 283. According to the court, California case law and statutes fail to support a public policy against insemination of unmarried women, and Kane's children failed to persuade the court initially that it would be better for a posthumously conceived child not to be born, sufficient to overcome the decedent's decision. The court subsequently ordered release of the sperm to Hecht without deciding whether any resulting child could inherit as Kane's heir. 59 Cal. Rptr. 2d 222, 228 (Ct. App. 1996). See also Hall v. Fertility Inst. of New Orleans, 647 So. 2d 1348 (La. Ct. App. 1994). Cf. Kurchner v. State Farm Fire & Cas. Co., 858 So. 2d 1220 (Fla. Dist. Ct. App. 2003) (treating frozen semen as personal property, so that destruction not covered by insurance policy for bodily injury). If the decedent indicated that the semen should be discarded, should a court balance his interest against his widow's interest in using the semen? See Estate of Kievernagel, 83 Cal. Rptr. 3d 311 (Ct. App. 2008).

5. *"Lifestyle" screening versus access rights.* Should states restrict alternative insemination to traditional families? Some statutes provide that practitioners can perform insemination "only at the request and with the written consent of

the husband and wife." See Okla. Stat. Ann. tit. 10 §553 (2008). Should recipients receive the same screening and state approval (through judicial proceedings) as adoptive parents? Would you support a now superseded British law requiring that fertility clinics consider a child's "need for a father"? Human Fertilisation and Embryology Act of 2008, ch. 22, §14 (2)(b) (U.K.). Why? See generally Richard F. Storrow, Rescuing Children from the Marriage Movement: The Case Against Marital Status Discrimination in Adoption and Assisted Reproduction, 39 U.C. Davis L. Rev. 305 (2006).

Do you agree that "lesbians and/or single women are entitled to the full range of reproductive technologies that married couples enjoy access to"? Justyn Lezin, (Mis) Conceptions: Unjust Limitations on Legally Unmarried Women's Access to Reproductive Technology and Their Use of Known Donors, 14 Hastings Women's L.J. 185, 189 (2003). See Michael S. Wald, Adults' Sexual Orientation and State Determinations Regarding Placement of Children, 40 Fam. L.Q. 381 (2006) (arguing, inter alia, that gays and same-sex couples should have same access to ARTs as others). Assuming state action, what particular constitutional rights are at stake? See generally Catherine DeLair, Ethical, Moral, Economic and Legal Barriers to Assisted Reproductive Technologies Employed by Gay Men and Lesbian Women, 4 DePaul J. Health Care L. 147 (2000). To what extent is posthumous conception a protected right of the deceased, assuming he chose to father a child after his death? See John A. Robertson, Posthumous Reproduction, 69 Ind. L.J. 1027 (1994). Do the children-to-be have rights or interests at stake justifying state restrictions on access to assisted reproduction? See Helen M. Alvaré, The Turn Toward the Self in the Law of Marriage & Family: Same-Sex Marriage & Its Predecessors, 16 Stan. L. & Pol'y Rev. 135, 158-162 (2005). But see John A. Robertson, Gay and Lesbian Access to Assisted Reproductive Technology, 55 Case W. Res. L. Rev. 323, 347 (2004) (noting "nonidentity problem" in attempts to justify restrictions to protect children because "the children sought to be protected by banning . . . access to ARTs will not then be born").

6. *Implications and policy questions.*

a. *Self-insemination.* Women have long performed insemination themselves, without medical assistance. See, e.g., Francie Hornstein, Children by Donor Insemination: A New Choice for Lesbians, in Rita Arditti, et al., Test-Tube Women: What Future for Motherhood 373, 375 (1984) (citing turkey basters as "now synonymous with self-help insemination"). What are the consequences for attempts to regulate the practice? Note that California law, however, protects the woman from the assertion of parental rights by a known donor only if a physician has performed the procedure. See *Jhordan C.*, supra. Nonetheless, a woman can perform self-insemination with semen from an anonymous donor obtained from a sperm bank.

b. *Gender.* What are the implications for gender roles and the traditional family? Judge Posner writes:

> Artificial insemination . . . is rich with social implications. [A]s a practical matter, it places lesbian custody of children beyond the reach of governmental regulation. Beyond that, it allows women to escape having to share parental rights with men, since the sperm donor, whether provided through the

woman's physician or through a sperm bank, is anonymous. It therefore accelerates the shift of economic power from men to women. . . .

Richard A. Posner, Sex and Reason 421 (1992). See also Amy Agigian, Baby Steps: How Lesbian Alternative Insemination Is Changing the World (2004).

c. *Commodification.* According to Professor Martha Ertman, sperm banks pay donors about $60 per donation; recipients pay sperm banks between $120 and $275 per vial of semen; once shipping costs and doctor's visits are added, "alternative insemination can cost between $500 and $1,000 for the first insemination and between $300 and $700 for each subsequent insemination"; and most women become pregnant within six attempts. Martha M. Ertman, What's Wrong with a Parenthood Market? A New and Improved Theory of Commodification, 82 N.C. L. Rev. 1, 14-16 (2003). She continues:

> . . . AI is a literal market and a relatively free, open market. . . . Markets, by definition, exist where supply and demand determine prices for the transfer of goods and services. Banks and recipients demand sperm, and donors and banks supply it. Suppliers (donors and sperm banks) transfer sperm on the condition of donor anonymity and indemnity for any injury or illness. Buyers (sperm banks and prospective mothers), in turn, demand medical and social information about the donor, further protections against disease transmission, and anonymity. . . . Moreover, lack of regulation and a relatively low price for the gametes means that it is both an open market in which a large number of people can participate, and a free market that flourishes because of its comparative freedom from regulation. . . .
>
> Alternative insemination generally involves at least two separate transactions. The sperm bank first purchases sperm from a donor and subsequently sells the sperm to a woman who uses it to become a mother. . . . While the transactions differ in important respects, both transactions commodify gametes, and in doing so commodify parental rights and responsibilities. . . .

Id. at 15-16. Ertman highlights the negative implications of such commodification as well as its benefits, including facilitation of new family forms. Id. at 26-42. How should the law respond?

d. *Comparison to adoption.* For those considering adoption and donor insemination (e.g., a heterosexual couple with male factor infertility, a single woman, or a lesbian couple), how might the law's approach influence preferences? How do the two ways to become parents compare in terms of cost, state regulation, and risks? What other factors should enter the comparison? The scant empirical data on the preferences of infertile couples reveal adoption as a last resort. Why? See Susan Frelich Appleton, Adoption in the Age of Reproductive Technology, 2004 U. Chi. Legal F. 393, 426-433. The data also show gender differences, including a preference for assisted reproduction with donors over adoption among females and vice versa among males. Id. at 431. See also Richard F. Storrow, Marginalizing Adoption Through the Regulation of Assisted Reproduction, 35 Cap. U.L. Rev. 479 (2006) (including international comparisons). For a critique of the status quo and recommendations for law reform, see Elizabeth Bartholet, Family Bonds: Adoption, Infertility, and the New World of Child Production (1999).

## PROBLEMS

1. Ellen and Lee, cohabiting in an intimate relationship, agreed in writing that Lee would have parental rights to and parental responsibilities for the child that Ellen planned to conceive using semen from an anonymous donor. After the child was born and the adults' relationship deteriorated, Lee unsuccessfully sued for recognition as a parent. Lee now commences a separate suit, seeking enforcement of the agreement or, alternatively, damages for its breach. What result and why? Would the result vary depending on whether Lee is male or female? On how long the relationship lasted after the birth? Suppose instead that Ellen is the plaintiff, seeking support from Lee for the child? If both Ellen and Lee are women, does the state's law on same-sex relationships affect the result? Why? Compare Dunkin v. Boskey, 98 Cal. Rptr. 2d 44 (Ct. App. 2000), with T.F. v. B.L., 813 N.E.2d 1244 (Mass. 2004), and Wakeman v. Dixon, 921 So. 2d 669 (Fla. Dist. Ct. App. 2006).

2. Guadalupe and Joanne, committed partners who live together in California, decided they wanted Guadalupe to become pregnant so that they would have a child to rear. After intravaginal self-insemination failed, they sought medical assistance from North Coast Woman's Care Medical Group, Inc. The only available physician licensed to perform the procedure that had been recommended for Guadalupe, intrauterine insemination, refused to do so, based on religious objections. California's civil rights statute requires the provision of full and equal services to all persons, regardless of sexual orientation. Guadalupe sues North Coast and the physician for sexual-orientation discrimination, in violation of the civil rights statute, seeking damages and injunctive relief. Defendants raise the First Amendment's protection for free speech and freedom of religion as affirmative defenses. What result and why? How does a claim for sexual-orientation discrimination differ from a claim for marital-status discrimination? See North Coast Women's Care Medical Group, Inc. v. Superior Ct., 189 P.3d 959 (Cal. 2008). How would any decision by California to authorize same-sex marriage affect such cases going forward? See generally Holly J. Harlow, Paternalism Without Paternity: Discrimination Against Single Women Seeking Artificial Insemination by Donor, 6 S. Cal. Rev. L. & Women's Stud. 173 (1996); Robertson, Gay and Lesbian Access, supra, at 353-355; Richard F. Storrow, The Bioethics of Prospective Parenthood: In Pursuit of the Proper Standard for Gatekeeping in Infertility Clinics, 28 Cardozo L. Rev. 2283 (2007).

## 2. BEYOND THE TWO-PARENT NORM

### JACOB v. SHULTZ-JACOB

923 A.2d 473 (Pa. Super. Ct. 2007)

KELLY, J. . . .

Beginning in 1996, the parties [Appellant, Jennifer Shultz-Jacob, and Appellee, Jodilynn Jacob,] lived together in York County for approximately nine years, during which period they underwent a commitment ceremony in Pittsburgh, and entered into a civil union in Vermont. Of the children who are the subjects of these actions, two, A.J. and L.J., are nephews of Appellee's whom she has adopted. The remaining two, Co.J. and Ca.J., are Appellee's biological children by Appellee Carl Frampton, a long-time friend of Appellant's. At her instigation he agreed to act as sperm donor, and has been involved in the children's lives since their birth.

In February of 2006, after several months during which the parties continued to reside together despite separation as a couple, Appellee relocated with the children from York County to Dauphin County. Shortly after Appellee's departure, Appellant, naming both Appellee and Appellee Carl Frampton as defendants, sought full legal and physical custody of all four children in the York County Court. . . . On April 3, Appellee filed a complaint in Dauphin County seeking child support from Appellant for Ca.J. and Co.J., and was awarded approximately $983 per month. Appellant appealed seeking *de novo* review on the basis that Appellee Frampton was essentially a third parent to Co.J. and Ca.J., and as such was obligated to contribute to their financial support. [Appellant's request to join Frampton was denied.]

[Following a trial, the court] awarded shared legal custody of all four children to the parties. Appellant received primary physical custody of L.J. only, with partial physical custody as to him in Appellee, who was awarded primary physical custody of the other three children, with partial custody in Appellant. Appellee Frampton was awarded partial physical custody, one weekend a month, of Co.J. and Ca.J.

Appellant has filed appeals from both the custody and support orders. Although presenting separate issues, the anomalous circumstances of these actions present basic and interrelated questions concerning the parental rights and responsibilities both of Appellant and of Appellee Frampton given the parties' recognition of her in loco parentis status, as well as his standing as a biological parent. . . .

Our courts have long held that "[the] rights and liabilities arising out of that relation [in loco parentis] are, as the words imply, exactly the same as between parent and child." That status confers on third parties, defined for purposes of custody disputes as persons other than biological parents, standing such as would permit them "the opportunity to litigate fully the issue of whether that relationship [with the child] should be maintained even over a natural parent's objections." However, standing established by virtue of in loco parentis status does not elevate a third party to parity with a natural parent in determining the merits of custody dispute. Jones v. Jones, 884 A.2d 915, 917 (Pa. Super. 2005), *appeal denied*, 912 A.2d 838 (Pa. 2006). Rather, even with standing referable to in loco parentis status,

> where the custody dispute is between a biological parent and a third party, the burden of proof is not evenly balanced. In such instances the parents have a prima facie right to custody which will be forfeited only if convincing reasons appear that the child's best interest[s] will be served by an award to the third party. Thus, even before the proceedings start, the evidentiary scale is tipped, and tipped hard, to the [biological] parents' side.

Under any circumstances, the axiom that the paramount interest to be served in custody disputes is that of the child(ren) remains undisturbed.

"What the judge must do, therefore, is first, hear all evidence relevant to the child's best interest, and then, decide whether the evidence on behalf of the third party is weighty enough to bring the scale up to even, and down on the third party's side."

As to all of Appellant's best interests claims, . . . the trial court here determined that the evidence was not sufficient to override the presumption in favor of the biological parent, nevertheless noting in its decision from the bench that "all parties have had a very positive influence on the lives of the children." [After reviewing the trial court's analysis and applicable precedent,] we do not disagree with the trial court's assessment of the children's best interests, nor do we disturb its custody arrangements.

In her appeal from the support order, Appellant has ostensibly raised three claims concerning the court's denial of her joinder motion. Two of these are, in fact, aspects of the same contention, that Appellee Carl Frampton, having, as the biological father of Co.J. and Ca.J. a *prima facie* right to custody, for the same reason also has the obligation to contribute to their support. That being so, the trial court erred in denying the motion to join him as an indispensable party. As a coda to her primary contention, Appellant argues that the biological mother's failure/unwillingness to pursue support claims against the biological father is irrelevant, and since all of the three persons involved in these matters have been awarded formal rights of custody, all three are obligated to provide support. . . .

. . . The basic inquiry in determining indispensability [of a party] concerns whether, in the absence of the person sought to be joined, justice can be done. Analysis of this claim requires reference to both the nature of the claim and the requested remedy.

In finding that because Appellee Frampton is not obligated to provide child support he is thus not indispensable, the trial court relies on two case authorities. The first, [L.S.K. v. H.A.N., 813 A.2d 872 (Pa. Super. 2002),] explores the financial responsibility of a lesbian partner in a long term relationship where a sperm donor, in that case anonymous, fathered a child to the other partner. Support was not sought from the biological father, who had relinquished all parental rights.

The Court found that the biological mother was owed support by her partner, who had exercised custodial rights on the basis of her in loco parentis status. The duty, however, was not to be derived from the Domestic Relations Code, 23 Pa. C.S.A. §4321(2), governing liability for support of minor children. Rather, the obligation stemmed from principles of equitable estoppel, which "applies to prevent a party from assuming a position or asserting a right to another's disadvantage inconsistent with a position previously taken." *L.S.K.*, supra at 877. Reduced to its essence, the doctrine is one of "fundamental fairness, designed to preclude a party from depriving another of a reasonable expectation when the party inducing the expectation albeit gratuitously knew or should have known that the other would rely on that conduct to his detriment." Thus the trial court in this case held that Appellant, having "asserted custodial rights in relation to [the children], is [] obligated under an equitable theory to provide for their support."

In two basic respects, this case differs from *L.S.K.*: first, Appellant does not deny her own responsibility to support the children; rather, her focus is on the omission of any similar obligation assigned to Appellee Frampton, who, if he has not "asserted custodial rights" by petitioning for them, has sought them informally, and has in no way declined the award of custody. However, *L.S.K.* provides a matrix in which the critical question in this case arises: if fundamental fairness prevents Appellant, identified by law as a third party, from avoiding a support obligation arising from her status as a de facto parent, and she does not, in any event, attempt such an avoidance, does not the same principle operate similarly to estop Appellee Frampton, automatically recognized as the possessor of parental rights based on his biological parenthood, from disclaiming financial responsibility? We find that it does. His obligation is, in fact, statutorily imposed as "[p]arents are liable for the support of their children who are unemancipated and 18 years of age or younger." 23 Pa. C.S.A. §4321(2). As the Court in *L.S.K.*, supra at 877, has opined, stepparents who have held a child out as their own are liable for support; biological parents who have exercised the rights appurtenant to that status can be no less bound. Thus the trial court's conclusion that Appellant's obligation is established by *L.S.K.* is not incorrect, only incomplete.

Further, Appellee Frampton has himself anticipated his obligation by providing support to Co.J. and Ca.J. since their births, having contributed "in excess of $13,000" in the last four years, $3,000 of it during the six months preceding the custody trial; and having borrowed money to provide the parties with a vehicle suited to transporting the children. While these contributions have been voluntary, they evidence a settled intention to demonstrate parental involvement far beyond the merely biological. Further, in addition to having been awarded partial custody, [i.e., shared legal custody and visitation] Appellee [Frampton] was present at the birth of Co.J.; has expressed an interest in relocating closer to the children's home to facilitate both his court ordered monthly partial custody and further contact, which, in fact, already occurs; and has encouraged the children to call him "Papa." If Appellee expresses a need for funds or household items, he supplies them, as well as clothing and toys for the children. Such constant and attentive solicitude seems widely at variance with the support court's characterization of Appellee Frampton's having "played a minimal role in raising and supporting" the children. We find that under such circumstances, the principle which serves to confirm Appellant's obligation operates in the same manner as to Appellee Frampton's.

To address the latter, the trial court finds relevant this Court's decision in Ferguson v. McKiernan, 855 A.2d 121 (Pa. Super. 2004). There the biological mother sought child support from the biological father, her co-worker and former lover, despite having assured him on several occasions that he would have no parental status or obligation. Although recognizing the mother's reprehensible conduct toward the biological father, as well as toward her husband, who filed for divorce on the same day artificial insemination was performed, the Court found a duty of support to be owed by the biological father on grounds that the parties could not bargain away the right of support which accrued not to them but to the children.

The trial court here, which seems erroneously to regard Appellant's desire to join Appellee Frampton as an attempt to escape financial liability altogether, found that appearances notwithstanding, *Ferguson* does not support Appellant's position, as she was already liable for support under the ruling in *L.S.K.* The court also attempted to distinguish *Ferguson* on several bases: specifically, the biological mother there was in the process of divorce and had once been romantically attached to the sperm donor, while the children here were born into an intact family to persons who intended to cooperate in rearing them.

The distinctions drawn by the trial court to support its theory of inapplicability seem less persuasive than distinctions which tend in the opposite direction. Contrary to the trial court's assertion that Appellee Frampton, "like the sperm donor in *Ferguson* who *also* did not assert or seek parental rights," (emphasis added), rather than remaining detached from the children, he became, voluntarily, indeed, enthusiastically, an integral part of their lives. Most pertinently, the court found that Appellee Frampton made no agreement as to the children's support as there was no need for him to do so — two parents were already available to provide the support. This last point is in fact the crux of the court's rationale: "to hold [Appellee] Frampton liable for support would create a situation in which three parties/parents would be liable for support." In the trial court's view the interjection of a third person in the traditional support scenario would create an untenable situation, never having been anticipated by Pennsylvania law. We are not convinced that the calculus of support arrangements cannot be reformulated, for instance, applying to the guidelines amount set for Appellant fractional shares to incorporate the contribution of anther obligee. As the Court in *L.S.K.*, has held, in another anomalous situation:

> We recognize this is a matter which is better addressed by the legislature rather than the courts. However, in the absence of legislative mandates, the courts must construct a fair, workable and responsible basis for the protection of children, aside from whatever rights the adults may have *vis a vis* each other.

Accordingly, we affirm the award of custody, vacate the award of support, and remand to the trial court with directions that Appellee Frampton be joined as an indispensable party for a hearing at which the support obligation of each litigant is to be recalculated. . . .

## NOTES AND QUESTIONS

1. *More than two parents.* If donor insemination can be used to create nontraditional families with one parent, with a deceased parent, or with two parents of the same sex, is there any reason why nontraditional families may not include more than two parents per child? Would such departures from the traditional two-parent model benefit children? Parents? Society? Or would this change present risks of harm? See generally Laura T. Kessler, Community Parenting, 24 Wash. U. J.L. & Pol'y 47 (2007). If a child can have three parents, how about four or five? More specifically, what advantages does an increasing number offer? What disadvantages? Compare Melanie B. Jacobs, Why Just

Two?: Disaggregating Parental Rights and Responsibilities to Recognize Multiple Parents, 9 J.L. & Fam. Stud. 309 (2007), with Emily Buss, "Parental" Rights, 88 Va. L. Rev. 635 (2002). What is the allure of a two-parent model? See Katharine K. Baker, Bionormativity and the Construction of Parenthood, 42 Ga. L. Rev. 649 (2008). See also Commission on Parenthood's Future, The Revolution in Parenthood: The Emerging Global Clash Between Adult Rights and Children's Needs (Elizabeth Marquardt, principal investigator, 2006) (arguing that rearing by two biological parents is better for children and opposing increased parental numbers).

Just before *Jacob*, a court in Ontario, Canada, ruled in a suit for a maternity declaration brought during an ongoing family relationship that a biological mother, her partner (who was seeking the declaration), and the genetic father (who was actively involved in the child's life) could all be recognized as the child's parents. A.A. v. B.B. [2007] 278 D.L.R. (4th) 519 (Can.), *leave to appeal denied sub nom.* Alliance for Marriage and Family v. A.A., [2007] 3 S.C.R. 124. See Laura Nicole Althouse, Three's Company? How American Law Can Recognize a Third Social Parent in Same-Sex Headed Families, 19 Hastings Women's L.J. 171 (2008). Also, Elisa B. v. Superior Ct., (Chapter 1, section B1) makes the following observation: "We have not decided 'whether there exists an overriding legislative policy limiting a child to two parents.' (quoting Sharon S. v. Superior Ct., 73 P.3d 554, 561 n.6 (Cal. 2003))." 117 P.3d 660, 666 n.4 (Cal. 2005). See also Thomas S. v. Robin Y., 618 N.Y.S.2d 356 (App. Div. 1994) (authorizing filiation order for semen donor, already involved in life of child being reared by lesbian couple); LaChapelle v. Mitten, 607 N.W.2d 151 (Minn. Ct. App. 2000) (approving joint custody to mother and former partner, while recognizing some parental rights for known donor). But see Human Fertilisation and Embryology Act, ch. 22, §45 (U.K.) (providing that no man can be treated as the father of a child with two women as parents).

The Ontario case, A.A. v. B.B., involved an intact family in which all three adults supported the suit for the maternity declaration, while *Jacob* presents the parentage issues upon the breakdown of the couple's relationship. Should the context matter for the courts' willingness to recognize more than two parents? Whether recognized by law or not, many nontraditional families include more than two adults functioning as parents. See, e.g., Diane Ehrensaft, Mommies, Daddies, Donors, Surrogates: Answering Tough Questions and Building Strong Families (2005); John Bowe, Gay Donor or Gay Dad?, N.Y. Times, Nov. 19, 2006, §6 (Magazine), at 66.

2. *Disaggregation.* In 1984, Professor Katharine Bartlett described parenthood as comprehensive, exclusive, and indivisible. Katharine T. Bartlett, Rethinking Parenthood as an Exclusive Status: The Need for Legal Alternatives When the Premise of the Nuclear Family Has Failed, 70 Va. L. Rev. 879, 883-884 (1984). Does this description remain accurate today? If so, how can three adults share parental rights and prerogatives? How can two?

Recall the division of authority and responsibilities among birth parents, foster parents, and the state explained in Smith v. OFFER (Chapter 1, section B2b). How does this arrangement resemble the result reached in *Jacob*? How does it differ?

Today, many states' divorce statutes separate legal and physical custody and financial responsibility. Some states go further, prescribing parenting plans, which list separately many discrete parental decisions (e.g., medical decisions and educational decisions), responsibility for specific components of child support, and—in effect—every day of each year when one parent or the other will spend time with the child. See, e.g., Mo. Rev. Stat. §452.310 (7) (2008). What implications follow from these developments? From the rise of grandparent visitation rights? To what extent does such "disaggregation" of parental rights and responsibilities facilitate the legal recognition of multiple parents? See Susan Frelich Appleton, Parents by the Numbers, 37 Hofstra L. Rev. 11 (2008).

Does *Jacob* disaggregate parental rights and responsibilities? Do any of the three adults get "the full bundle"? Which? In a regime of multiple parents, do some have more rights (and responsibilities) than others? See Nancy E. Dowd, Multiple Parents/Multiple Fathers, 9 J.L. Fam. Stud. 231 (2007). To what extent do multiple parents and disaggregation anticipate more fundamental changes, such as "dismantling the legal understanding of parenthood entirely"? See Melissa Murray, The Networked Family: Reframing the Legal Understanding of Caregiving and Caregivers, 94 Va. L. Rev. 385, 453 (2008). See also Appleton, supra.

Does the desire of children who are born with the help of donated genetic material for knowledge about their progenitors suggest the need to develop a hierarchy of parents—with some vested with full rights and responsibilities and others having very limited duties, for example, providing information about medical history or identity? Compare Jacobs, supra, at 333, with Baker, supra, at 711-712. Cf. Annette R. Appell, The Endurance of Biological Connection: Heteronormativity, Same-Sex Parenting and the Lessons of Adoption, 22 BYU J. Pub. L. 289 (2008); Caroline Jones, Why Donor Insemination Requires Developments in Family Law: The Need for New Definitions of Parents (2007).

3. *What counts?* What criteria does *Jacob* use to accord parental status? Once the law moves beyond the traditional criteria of biology or marital relationship to embrace functional definitions, it must identify a functional test—that is, identify the elements that make one a parent. In providing authority to recognize parents by estoppel and de facto parents, the ALI Principles require the consent of the legal parent or parents. ALI Principles, §2.03. Why is that important? Should providing support but not direct caregiving suffice to make one a parent? Why? Compare ALI Principles, §§2.03 (1)(b), 2.03(5), 2.03(6), and 2.08(1) (a), with A.H. v. M.P., 857 N.E.2d 1061, 1071 (Mass. 2006), and B.F. v. T.D., 194 S.W.3d 310 (Ky. 2006). Should residing with the child be a prerequisite? If so, for how long? ALI Principles, §2.03(1) (b) & (c). Should paid caregiving—such as that performed by nannies—count? Compare id. at §2.03(c), with Pamela Laufer-Ukeles, Money Caregiving, and Kinship: Should Paid Caregivers Be Allowed to Obtain De Facto Parental Status? 74 Mo. L. Rev. _____ (forthcoming 2009).

4. *Parenting agreements.* Professor Melanie Jacobs argues that advance agreements about the division of parental rights and responsibilities can

facilitate multiparty parenting while avoiding pitfalls, such as future disputes. See Jacobs, supra. Are such agreements enforceable while the adults' relationship remains intact? After the adults' relationship dissolves?

Ferguson v. McKiernan, a case invoked by *Jacob*, involved an agreement in which the man provided semen in exchange for the woman's promise not to hold him responsible for child support. The opinion cited by *Jacob* ruled the agreement unenforceable because parents cannot bargain away the rights of their children. Subsequently, however, the state supreme court reversed *Ferguson*, 940 A.2d 1236 (Pa. 2007), as summarized p. 269, supra. Does the reversal of this precedent require a changed result in *Jacob*? Why?

5. *Challenging gender.* Professor Laura Kessler contends that "community parenting," as she calls the recognition of more than two parents, would advance family law by helping to "deconstruct traditional gender and sexuality norms." Laura T. Kessler, Community Parenting, 24 Wash. U. J.L. & Pol'y 47, 50 (2007). For example, collaborative childrearing practices among some gay men and lesbians demonstrate how "disconnecting family formation and reproduction from heterosexual relations . . . reveal[s] heterosexuality and biology to be mere symbols of a privileged relationship." Id. at 73. See also Laura T. Kessler, Transgressive Caregiving, 33 Fla. St. U.L. Rev. 1 (2005). Do you agree? Do *Jacob* and *A.A.*, supra, challenge traditional gender categories or reinforce them? Note that the third parent recognized in each supplies a "missing gender" in the family. Would a court have been equally willing to recognize an additional woman?

6. *Extensions?* Should the recognition of more than two parents in alternative insemination cases affect the legal analysis in cases of "conventional insemination"? Why? If not, why should the particular method of conception prove determinative for the number of parents a child may have? Against this background, consider the following Problem:

## PROBLEM

Holly, an unmarried woman, gave birth to Noah while involved in a relationship with Martin. They executed an acknowledgment of parentage at the time of birth, and they stipulated to joint custody of Noah when the relationship ended. When Holly tried to relocate with Noah, Martin sought sole custody. In response, Holly produced DNA evidence identifying Gregory, not Martin, as Noah's biological father—evidence she obtained from tests after noticing Noah's physical resemblance to Gregory, with whom she had had an affair. Based on this evidence, Holly seeks to revoke the earlier acknowledgment of Martin's parentage, and Gregory institutes a paternity action. Martin objects. What result and why? Can the court recognize Gregory as Noah's father without rescinding the earlier acknowledgment of Martin's parentage? Why? See Sinicropi v. Mazurek, 2008 WL 2596217 (Mich. Ct. App. 2008). Does Noah have a right to a relationship with both men? See generally James G. Dwyer, The Relationship Rights of Children (2006); Dowd, supra. To what extent does the recognition of a parent by estoppel or an equitable parent (see Chapter 3, section B1) foreclose the recognition of biological parents?

Do these doctrines assume a maximum of two parents for each child, or—given their emphasis on function rather than biology—do they permit more? See generally Appleton, supra; Deborah H. Wald, The Parentage Puzzle: The Interplay Between Genetics, Procreative Intent, and Parental Conduct in Determining Legal Parentage, 15 Am. U. J. Gender Soc. Pol'y & L. 379 (2007).

# CHAPTER 7

# *IN VITRO FERTILIZATION*

## A. THE SCOPE OF REPRODUCTIVE PRIVACY

Advances in medicine offer new responses to infertility that go well beyond alternative insemination and traditional surrogacy. Many of these ARTs use or build on in vitro fertilization (literally, fertilization in glass and called "IVF"), first successfully used to produce a human birth in England in 1978. Such medical progress has flourished in the United States, in the absence of significant regulation. As you study the materials on IVF and the various arrangements that this technique permits, consider the possible reasons for the regulatory void, such as an understanding of procreative activities as "private," a commitment to a free-market economy, legislative failure to keep pace with medical advances, conflicting views of morality, and the power of repronormativity.[1] Are there other explanations? How *should* the law respond?

LIFCHEZ V. HARTIGAN

735 F. Supp. 1361 (N.D. Ill. 1990)

WILLIAMS, Judge.

Dr. Lifchez represents a class of plaintiff physicians who specialize in reproductive endocrinology and fertility counseling. . . . Dr. Lifchez is suing the Illinois Attorney General and the Cook County State's Attorney, seeking a declaratory judgment that [§6(7)] of the Illinois Abortion Law is unconstitutional. . . .

### Vagueness

Section 6(7) of the Illinois Abortion Law provides as follows:

> No person shall sell or experiment upon a fetus produced by the fertilization of a human ovum by a human sperm unless such experimentation is therapeutic to the fetus thereby produced. Intentional violation of this section is a Class A misdemeanor. Nothing in this subsection (7) is intended to prohibit the performance of in vitro fertilization.

---

[1] See Katherine M. Franke, Essay: Theorizing Yes: An Essay on Feminism, Law, and Desire, 101 Colum. L. Rev. 181, 183-197 (2001).

Ill. Rev. Stat., Ch. 38 para. 81-26, §6(7) (1989). Dr. Lifchez claims that the Illinois legislature's failure to define the terms "experimentation" and "therapeutic" renders the statute vague, thus violating his due process rights under the Fourteenth Amendment. . . .

One of the more common procedures performed by reproductive endocrinologists is amniocentesis. Amniocentesis involves withdrawing a portion of the amniotic fluid in order to test it for genetic anomalies. It is performed on women considered to be at risk for bearing children with serious defects. The purpose of the procedure is to provide information about the developing fetus; this information is often used by women in deciding whether or not to have an abortion. Although now routinely performed, amniocentesis could be considered experimental under at least two of Dr. Lifchez' [proposed] definitions: it could be classified as pure research, since there is no benefit to the fetus, the subject being "experimented" on; it could also be experimental . . . if the particular practitioner or clinic were doing it for the first time.

Amniocentesis illustrates well the problem of deciding at what point a procedure graduates from "experimental" to routine. . . . Dr. Lifchez can hardly be expected to know which of his medical activities would be illegal now if he were to look back on the quick evolution of amniocentesis from (very likely) illegal experiment in 1975 to explicitly endorsed "process" in 1985. [B]ecause of the meteoric growth in reproductive endocrinology, any classification of a particular procedure as either "experimental" or "routine" could easily be out-of-date within six months. . . . A statute is unconstitutionally vague if the mere passage of time can transform conduct from being unlawful to lawful. . . .

Many other procedures that Dr. Lifchez performs on his patients could fall within the ambit of §6(7). Among these are in vitro fertilization and the many techniques spawned through research into in vitro fertilization. The difficulty posed by these procedures is not just whether or not they are "experimental," but whether they are "therapeutic to the fetus." . . . In vitro fertilization itself is explicitly permitted by the statute. Related reproductive technologies are less certain. Embryo transfer, for example, involves removal of an embryo from one woman's uterus and placing it in the uterus of a second woman. The variations on this basic technique are considerable. A donated egg could be fertilized in vitro (with a partner's or a donor's sperm), be placed in a second woman's uterus to gestate for five days, and then be flushed out for implantation in the woman trying to get pregnant. That this procedure is experimental is undisputed. Whether it is "therapeutic to the fetus" (actually, embryo . . . ) is more complicated. . . . Removing an embryo from one woman's uterus, where it is gestating, for implantation in another woman, may be therapeutic for the woman trying to get pregnant, but it is not necessarily therapeutic for that embryo. . . .

[The court concluded that the scienter requirement in §6(7) did not save it from being unconstitutionally vague.]

### Reproductive Privacy

Section 6(7) of the Illinois Abortion Law is also unconstitutional because it impermissibly restricts a woman's fundamental right of privacy, in particular, her right to make reproductive choices free of governmental interference with those choices. Various aspects of this reproductive privacy right have been articulated in a number of landmark Supreme Court cases including Griswold v. Connecticut, 381 U.S. 479 (1965) (striking down statute which forbid use of contraceptives on grounds that statute invaded zone of privacy surrounding marriage relationship); Eisenstadt v. Baird, 405 U.S. 438 (1972) (striking down statute forbidding distribution of contraceptives to unmarried persons on equal protection grounds, but observing in dicta that: "If the right of privacy means anything, it is the right of the *individual*, married or single, to be free from unwarranted governmental intrusion into matters so fundamentally affecting a person as the decision whether to bear or beget a child." Id. at 453); Roe v. Wade, 410 U.S. 113 (1973) (establishing unrestricted right to an abortion in first trimester); and Planned Parenthood of Missouri v. Danforth, 428 U.S. 52 (1976) (striking down provisions of abortion statute requiring spousal consent and parental consent). In Carey v. Population Services International, 431 U.S. 678 (1977), the Court [overturned various restrictions on access to contraceptives,] reviewed its prior privacy cases and declared that

> The decision whether or not to beget or bear a child is at the very heart of this cluster of constitutionally protected choices. That decision holds a particularly important place in the history of the right of privacy, a right first explicitly recognized in an opinion holding unconstitutional a statute prohibiting the use of contraceptives . . . and most prominently vindicated in recent years in the contexts of contraception . . . and abortion.

Id. at 685 (citations omitted).

Section 6(7) intrudes upon this "cluster of constitutionally protected choices." Embryo transfer and chorionic villi sampling [a method of prenatal testing for birth defects] are illustrative. Both procedures are "experimental" by most definitions of that term. Both are performed directly, and intentionally, on the fetus. Neither procedure is necessarily therapeutic to the fetus. . . .

Both procedures, however, fall within a woman's zone of privacy as recognized in Roe v. Wade, Carey v. Population Services International, and their progeny. Embryo transfer is a procedure designed to enable an infertile woman to bear her own child. It takes no great leap of logic to see that within the cluster of constitutionally protected choices that includes the right to have access to contraceptives, there must be included within that cluster the right to submit to a medical procedure that may bring about, rather than prevent, pregnancy. Chorionic villi sampling is similarly protected. The cluster of constitutional choices that includes the right to abort a fetus within the first trimester must also include the right to submit to a procedure designed to give information about that fetus which can then lead to a decision to abort. Since there is no compelling state interest sufficient to prevent a woman from terminating her pregnancy during the first trimester, there can be no such interest sufficient to intrude upon these other protected activities during the first trimester. By encroaching upon this protected zone of privacy, §6(7) is unconstitutional. . . .

## NOTES AND QUESTIONS

1. *Procreative liberty.* *Lifchez* relies on a series of cases from the United States Supreme Court supporting a right to reproductive autonomy to conclude that

the right to privacy protects use of and access to reproductive technologies. The leading proponent of this position, Professor John Robertson, has written that "procreative liberty is a deeply held moral and legal value that deserves a strong measure of respect in all reproductive activities [to be] equally honored when reproduction requires technological assistance." John A. Robertson, Children of Choice: Freedom and The New Reproductive Technologies 4 (1994). Robertson's book goes on to advocate reproductive autonomy for seven major reproductive technologies, including IVF and forms of collaborative reproduction, that is, procreation that requires contribution from parties other than the intended parents. Do cases about a right to avoid procreation (via contraception and abortion) necessarily imply a right to use available interventions to have children? Do they necessarily imply a right to have children who do not share a genetic relationship with the intended parents?

2. *Abortion underpinnings.* Given the reliance in *Lifchez* on Roe v. Wade to recognize a right to reproductive privacy, to what extent does the legal status of IVF depend on the continued vitality of *Roe*? The strict judicial scrutiny and resulting "trimester timetable" that *Roe* prescribed in 1973 for abortion restrictions gave way to a less demanding "undue burden standard" in Planned Parenthood of Southeastern Pennsylvania v. Casey, 505 U.S. 833 (1992), then a minority position that a majority subsequently applied in Gonzales v. Carhart, 550 U.S. 124 (2007), to uphold the federal law called the "Partial Birth Abortion Ban Act." Notably, in *Gonzales*, the majority permitted legislative resolution of medical disagreements (about whether the banned procedure would sometimes be necessary to protect the woman's health) and also justified the statute in part on the ground that it protects women from their own ill-advised choices. Justice Ginsburg dissented vigorously on both points. On such "woman-protective abortion restrictions," see Reva B. Siegel, The New Politics of Abortion: An Equality Analysis of Woman-Protective Abortion Restrictions, 2007 U. Ill. L. Rev. 991 (tracing the rise of this rationale for abortion restrictions, which shifts the anti-abortion focus from fetal interests to women's interests).

In the wake of *Gonzales*, some states considered much more sweeping abortion restrictions. For example, in 2008, Colorado voters rejected a measure that would have extended constitutional protection to "any human being from the moment of conception." What are the implications for IVF? See Electa Draper, Amendment 48 "Personhood" Push Rejected, Denver Post, Nov. 5, 2008, at B4.

3. *Moral and ethical objections.* Assuming that a constitutional right to use reproductive technologies like IVF exists, what state interests justify its infringement? Does the goal of bringing as least some IVF-created embryos to term make inapplicable the state interests traditionally asserted to justify limitations on abortion—interests in protecting fetal life? Might one raise "woman-protective" arguments to restrict IVF and similar procedures?

Early on, feminist scholar Gena Corea raised moral and ethical objections to IVF, claiming that it exploits women. See Gena Corea, The Mother Machine: Reproductive Technologies from Artificial Insemination to Artificial Wombs 100-134 (1985). The Catholic Church has found IVF morally illicit because it deprives the child *"of being the result and fruit of a conjugal act* in which spouses can become 'cooperators with God for giving life to a new person.'"

Congregation for the Doctrine of the Faith, Instruction on Respect for Human Life in its Origin and on the Dignity of Procreation: Replies to Certain Questions of the Day 29-31 (1987). See also Congregation for the Doctrine of the Faith, Instruction Dignitas Personae on Certain Bioethical Questions 8-13 (2008) (condemning IVF, destruction of embryos, and cryopreservation of genetic material). On the other hand, a British commission concluded IVF is ethically acceptable. Department of Health & Social Security, Report of the Committee of Inquiry into Human Fertilisation and Embryology 31-34 (Chairman: Dame Mary Warnock DBE) (Presented to Parliament by Command of Her Majesty, July 1984). Can moral and ethical objections to IVF support state prohibitions? Cf. Lawrence v. Texas, 539 U.S. 558 (2003) (rejecting reliance on majoritarian morality to justify criminal bans on same-sex sodomy). But see *Gonzales*, 550 U.S. at 158 (noting moral concerns underlying ban on "partial birth abortion").

4. *Health and safety.* Could IVF be banned or restricted to protect the health of the children-to-be? How does one assess harm to a not-yet-conceived individual who would not exist without the technology? See Philip G. Peters, Jr., How Safe Is Safe Enough?: Obligations to the Children of Reproductive Technology (2004). Hormones used to induce superovulation can produce dangerous multifetal pregnancies requiring "selective abortion" (killing some fetuses to improve the chances for others) or creating significant risks of premature birth and neurological problems, in addition to health dangers for the mother. See, e.g., Lars Noah, Assisted Reproductive Technologies and the Pitfalls of Unregulated Biomedical Innovation, 55 Fla. L. Rev. 603 (2003).

In addition, some data indicate that children of IVF suffer a disproportionate incidence of birth defects. See Robin Fretwell Wilson, Uncovering the Rationale for Requiring Infertility in Surrogacy Arrangements, 29 Am. J.L. & Med. 337, 343-347 (2003). See also Gina Kolata, Picture Emerging on Genetic Risks of IVF, N.Y. Times, Feb. 17, 2009, at D1. Particular concerns have been prompted by intracytoplasmic sperm injection (ICSI), which entails the injection of a single sperm into the center of an ovum and allows, for example, a man with a very low sperm count to become a genetic father. The process may allow fertilization (in vitro) with unsuitable sperm and risks transmission of genetic abnormalities causing the underlying infertility. ICSI has flourished in the absence of any longitudinal studies about its safety, however. The President's Council on Bioethics, Reproduction and Responsibility: The Regulation of New Biotechnologies 39-40 (2004).

What implications does *Gonzales* have for maternal health? See B. Jessie Hill, The Constitutional Right to Make Medical Treatment Decisions: A Tale of Two Doctrines, 86 Tex. L. Rev. 277 (2007). Given the absence of an exception for maternal health in the ban upheld by the majority (despite some medical opinion that the procedure in question might be the safest for some women), does the *Gonzales* majority suggest that preventing possible postabortion regret constitutes a higher value than preventing risks to present physical and emotional health? In turn, what are the legal consequences for any dangers to maternal health posed by IVF?

5. *Prenatal testing. Lifchez* observes that prenatal testing, like other reproductive technologies, does not benefit the embryo or fetus. Do parents

have a right to such tests to enable them to select the characteristics of their children (or to terminate pregnancies when gestating a fetus with undesired problems)? Today, preimplantation genetic diagnosis (PGD) of embryos created in vitro along with new information from the Human Genome Project are increasing such choices. See, e.g., Maxwell J. Mehlman, The Law of Above Averages: Leveling the New Genetic Enhancement Playing Field, 85 Iowa L. Rev. 517 (2000). See also Michael J. Sandel, The Case Against Perfection, The Atlantic, Apr. 2004, at 50. Does the Americans with Disabilities Act restrict physicians' discretion to turn away ARTs patients with disabilities in order to prevent the birth of children with disabilities? See Carl H. Coleman, Conceiving Harm: Disability Discrimination in Assisted Reproductive Technologies, 50 UCLA L. Rev. 17, 60-67 (2002).

British legislation specifying the requirements for licensed fertility services provides that embryos known to have abnormalities likely to produce a serious disability or illness "must not be preferred to those not known to have such an abnormality." Human Fertilisation and Embryology Act of 2008, ch. 22, §14 (4) (U.K.). Further, the statute's definition of "permitted" eggs and embryos includes those treated "to prevent the transmission of a serious mitochondrial disease." Id. at §3 (adding section 3ZA). How would a preference for an embryo with disabilities arise? See Liza Mundy, A World of Their Own: In the Eyes of His Parents, If Gauvin Hughes McCullough Turns Out to Be Deaf, That Will Be Just Perfect, Wash. Post, Mar. 31, 2002, at W22 (reporting efforts of a deaf couple, two woman, to conceive a deaf child by selecting deaf sperm donor). For an analysis that considers the relationship between the now discredited eugenics movement and the use of new technologies to produce "designer babies," see Sonia M. Suter, A Brave New World of Designer Babies?, 22 Berkeley Tech. L.J. 897 (2007).

Prenatal testing, including amniocentesis and chorionic villi sampling, began to flourish after Roe's legalization of abortion. Such testing and the larger practice of genetic counseling became a form of defensive medicine as families successfully sued for "wrongful birth," claiming that professional negligence resulted in the birth of a child with handicaps whom the parents, if properly informed, would have aborted. E.g., Bader v. Johnson, 732 N.E.2d 1212 (Ind. 2000); Berman v. Allan, 404 A.2d 8 (N.J. 1979). Courts have been less hospitable to "wrongful life" claims brought on behalf of the afflicted child. Compare, e.g., Hester v. Dwivedi, 733 N.E.2d 1161 (Ohio 2000), with Procanik v. Cillo, 478 A.2d 755 (N.J. 1984). See generally Elizabeth Weil, A Wrongful Birth?, N.Y. Times, March 12, 2006, §6 (Magazine), at 48. To whom do health professionals performing genetic testing and counseling owe a duty of care? All the members of the patient's family who might carry or pass on the gene or chromosomal abnormality? See Molloy v. Meier, 679 N.W.2d 711 (Minn. 2004).

Lifchez treats these technologies as a positive development, enhancing reproductive autonomy. Are there negative consequences for pregnant women, who are asked "to accept their pregnancies and their babies . . . and yet be willing to abort the genetically damaged fetus"? Barbara Katz Rothman, The Tentative Pregnancy: How Amniocentesis Changes the Experience of Motherhood 6 (1993).

6. *Feminist perspectives.* Some feminists condemn IVF. Professor Dorothy Roberts observes that "new reproductive technologies, such as in vitro fertilization and surrogacy, function primarily to fulfill men's desires for genetically related offspring." Dorothy E. Roberts, The Genetic Tie, 62 U. Chi. L. Rev. 209, 239 (1995). See also, e.g., Elizabeth Bartholet, Family Bonds: Adoption and the Politics of Parenting 187-229 (1999); Corea, supra; Robyn Rowland, Living Laboratories: Women and Reproductive Technologies (1992). Reports from Egypt substantiate this hypothesis. There, infertile husbands, whose wives could have conceived while young but became too old to bear children, are leaving these wives and remarrying women of reproductive age with whom they can use ICSI to father biological children. Marcia C. Inhorn, Global Infertility and the Globalization of New Reproductive Technologies: Illustrations from Egypt, 56 Soc. Sci. & Med. 1837, 1846 (2003).

What legal conclusions for IVF follow from feminist critiques? A ban on these procedures? Government intervention through mandated warnings to ensure "informed" consent, as some states require for abortions? If the state can outlaw surrogacy in part to protect even those women who want to participate (see Chapter 6, section A2), can it not outlaw IVF despite the wishes of otherwise infertile women? Could women bring a successful sex discrimination challenge to such laws? Or do technologies such as IVF, in contrast to abortion, perpetuate a view of women as, first and foremost, mothers? Suppose some women yearn to contribute to this stereotype?

7. *Infertility and gender.* Both women and men react to infertility with strong emotions. But data suggest gender differences:

> Although men considered childlessness as a painful experience, it did not preclude a full and enjoyable life. . . . Wives spoke of enjoying their quality of life, but described something as missing. [For women, infertility] overtook other aspects of life. It was a continuous, biopsychosocial, spiritual struggle; a loss; a feeling of being passed by; and a feeling of incompleteness or emptiness. . . .

Su An Arnn Phipps, A Phenomenological Study of Couples' Infertility: Gender Influence, 7 Holistic Nurse Prac. 44, 46-47 (1993). See also Judith Daniluk & Joss Hurtig-Mitchell, Themes of Hope and Healing: Infertile Couples' Experiences of Adoption, 81 J. Counseling & Dev. 389, 392 (2003); Laurie Tarkan, Fertility Clinics Begin to Address Mental Health, N.Y. Times, Oct. 8, 2002, at F5. For an historical examination, see generally Elaine Tyler May, Barren in the Promised Land: Childless Americans in Pursuit of Happiness (1995).

Are women to blame for their own infertility? Pointing to inadequacies in leave policies, childcare, and shared parenting by men, sociologist Barbara Katz Rothman writes:

> Shall we blame the woman for putting off childbearing while she became a lawyer, art historian, physician, set designer, or engineer? Or shall we blame the system that makes it so very difficult for young lawyers, art historians, physicians, set designers, and engineers to have children without wives to care for them? Men did not have to delay entry into parenthood for nearly as many years in the pursuit of their careers as women do now. It is easier to blame the individual woman than to understand the political and economic context in which she must act, but it does not make for good social policy.

Barbara Katz Rothman, Recreating Motherhood 98 (2000).

8. *The regulatory scheme.*

a. *Laissez-faire approach.* Whatever the concerns prompted by IVF, a laissez-faire approach to assisted reproduction prevails in the United States, with any limits left up to the market — health care providers, fertility clinics, and patients desperate to explore every possible route to procreation. See Susan Frelich Appleton, Adoption in the Age of Reproductive Technology, 2004 U. Chi. Legal F. 393, 421-426. In the one notable exception to this self-regulation, federal legislation (designed in part to develop "informed consumers") requires ARTs programs to report their pregnancy rates to the Department of Health and Human Services for annual publication and distribution to the public. 42 U.S.C. §§263a-1 to 263a-7 (2008). See U.S. Department of Health and Human Services, Centers for Disease Control and Prevention, Assisted Reproductive Technology Success Rates, 2005 National Summary and Fertility Clinic Reports (October 2007), available at http://www.cdc.gov/art/art2005/508PDF/2005ART508.pdf. The required information now includes the number of singleton (as distinguished from multiple) pregnancies and births. Lyria Bennett Moses, Understanding Legal Responses to Technological Change: The Example of In Vitro Fertilization, 6 Minn. J. L. Sci. & Tech. 505, 590 (2005). For a summary of the patchwork of state regulations, including, for example, New Hampshire's time limits on embryo storage and Pennsylvania's reporting requirements, see id. at 537-538. The birth of IVF octuplets to an unemployed single mother in California with six other IVF children focused attention on the absence of regulation. See Alan Zarembo, Fertility: A Very Private Practice, L.A. Times, Feb. 14, 2009, at A1.

b. *Other countries.* Once a country famous for reproductive innovation, Italy now takes a much more restrictive approach, with laws prohibiting the freezing and testing of embryos and limiting the number of harvested eggs to three. Elisabeth Rosenthal & Elisabetta Povoledo, Vote on Fertility Law Fires Passions in Italy, N.Y. Times, June 11, 2005, at A7. A referendum to repeal the law failed because 50 percent of the eligible voters declined to participate after the Vatican urged a boycott. See Ian Fisher, Italian Vote to Ease Fertility Law Fails for Want of Voters, N.Y. Times, June 14, 2005, at A11.

In examining the specific issue of regulation designed to address the problem of multifetal pregnancies, one writer has identified the following approaches among common law countries: "professional guidelines supplemented by government intervention (United States [which requires information disclosure, noted supra]), professional guidelines with strong incentives to comply (New South Wales), professional guidelines with mandated compliance (Victoria), and regulation by a government authority using a clear rule (United Kingdom)." Moses, supra, at 603-604. Several European countries (Austria, Germany, Ireland, and Switzerland) ban PGD while others (Belgium, Greece, Holland, Italy, Norway, and the United Kingdom) restrict it to medical uses. Bratislav Stankovic, "It's a Designer Baby!": Opinions on Regulation of Preimplantation Genetic Diagnosis, 2005 UCLA J.L. & Tech. 3, 50 (2005). See generally David Adamson, Regulation of Assisted Reproductive Technologies in the United States, 39 Fam. L.Q. 727, 739-742 (2005) (international comparisons); Lori P. Knowles, The Governance of Reproductive

Technology: International Models, in Reprogenetics: Law, Policy, and Ethical Issues 127 (Lori P. Knowles & Gregory E. Kaebnick, eds. 2007); Alison Harvison Young, Possible Policy Strategies for the United States: Comparative Lessons, in Reprogenetics, supra, at 236. On the "reproductive tourism" that has emerged in response to the differences worldwide in laws as well as costs, see Chapter 8, section B.

c. *Recommendations.* The President's Council on Bioethics proposes federally funded data collection to assess the effects of IVF and related procedures on women and the resulting children. The President's Council on Bioethics, supra, at 39-44, 195-198, 210-212. Professor Jennifer Rosato recommends a two-tiered approach under which states would adopt restrictions designed to address the greatest hazards (e.g., limiting the number of embryos implanted to no more than three per cycle), complemented by federal oversight. Jennifer Rosato, The Children of ART (Assisted Reproductive Technology): Should the Law Protect Them From Harm?, 2004 Utah L. Rev. 57. See generally Naomi R. Cahn, Test Tube Families: Why the Fertility Market Needs Legal Regulation (2009).

9. *Paying for IVF.* Is infertility an "illness" and IVF a "treatment" therefor? The issue arises in determining whether the procedure is covered by medical insurance that reimburses only treatment of illness. See Egert v. Connecticut General Life Ins. Co., 900 F.2d 1032 (7th Cir. 1990). Some challenges to restrictive insurance coverage under the Americans with Disabilities Act have succeeded. See, e.g., Pacourek v. Inland Steel Co., 858 F. Supp. 1393 (N.D. Ill. 1994); 916 F. Supp. 797 (N.D. Ill. 1996). See also Bragdon v. Abbott, 524 U.S. 624 (1998). But see Krauel v. Iowa Methodist Med. Ctr., 95 F.3d 674 (8th Cir. 1996). See generally Karen L. Goldstein & Caryn H. Okinaga, Assisted Reproductive Technology, 3 Geo. J. Gender & L. 409, 432-437 (2002) (summarizing pertinent statutes and cases). A Connecticut statute, effective in 2005, requires insurance coverage for two cycles of IVF (with no more than two preembryos implanted per cycle) but only for women no older than 40 years of age. Conn. Gen. Stat. §38a-509 (2008). What reasons explain this particular legislative response? What concerns does it raise? See Bartholet, supra, at 213-214 (criticizing move toward mandated insurance coverage for IVF, because it "would simply stack the deck even more in favor of procreation," rather than adoption).

Beyond questions of insurance, can patients deduct the costs of infertility treatment as medical expenses on their tax returns? See Katherine T. Pratt, Inconceivable? Deducting the Costs of Fertility Treatment, 89 Cornell L. Rev. 1121 (2004); Anna L. Benjamin, The Implications of Using the Medical Expense Deduction of I.R.C. §213 to Subsidize Assisted Reproductive Technology, 79 Notre Dame L. Rev. 1117 (2004). Must a divorcing husband reimburse his wife for a portion of the treatment she pursued while the marriage was intact? See Ewing v. Ewing, 2007 WL 4563458 (Ohio Ct. App. 2007).

Should Medicaid provide assistance for poor persons seeking fertility treatments? What consequences follow from the prevailing approach, under which Medicaid benefits do not cover IVF and most private physicians are unwilling to serve Medicaid recipients? See Dorothy Roberts, Killing the Black Body: Race, Reproduction, and the Meaning of Liberty 253 (1999) (noting that most Blacks are excluded from access). See Cahn, supra, at 37.

## PROBLEMS

1. Melinda's employer, a state university, fires her because she used so many of her available sick leave and vacation days, usually in half-day increments, to undergo (so far unsuccessful) fertility treatments. Melinda sues the university, claiming that her termination violates the Pregnancy Discrimination Act, 42 U.S.C. §2000e(k) (2008). This statute provides the following definitions for the employment discrimination prohibited by Title VII:

> The terms "because of sex" or "on the basis of sex" include, but are not limited to, because of or on the basis of pregnancy, childbirth, or related medical conditions; and women affected by pregnancy, childbirth, or related medical conditions shall be treated the same for all employment-related purposes, including receipt of benefits under fringe benefit programs, as other persons not so affected but similar in their ability or inability to work. . . .

The university moves to dismiss, arguing the PDA does not apply. What result? If applicable, would the Family and Medical Leave Act, 29 U.S.C. §§2601-2654 (2008), provide protection for Melinda's job? This statute accords 12 weeks of leave and protects the employee's right to return to work when the employee seeks to care for a child upon birth or adoptive placement; seeks to care for a son, daughter, spouse, or parent who has a serious medical condition; cannot work because of a serious health condition; or is addressing certain exigencies arising out of the military deployment of a spouse, son, daughter, or parent. Id. at §2612. See Erickson v. Board of Governors, 911 F. Supp. 316 (N.D. Ill. 1995), *rev'd on other grounds*, 207 F.3d 945 (7th Cir. 2000), *cert. denied sub nom.* United States v. Board of Governors, 531 U.S. 1190 (2001). But see Saks v. Franklin Covey Co., 316 F.3d 337 (2d Cir. 2003).

2. You work in the general counsel's office of a large university, whose medical school has a successful program offering patients ARTs, including IVF. The program's directors consult your office about whether they may decline to provide services to HIV-positive women. What reasons, if any, would justify the exclusion of HIV-positive women? What legal and ethical considerations would enter your analysis? What advice would you give? See Nanette R. Elster, HIV and ART: Reproductive Choices and Challenges, 19 J. Contemp. Health L. & Pol'y 415 (2003).

# B. DECIDING THE FATE OF FROZEN EMBRYOS

### A.Z. v. B.Z.

725 N.E.2d 1051 (Mass. 2000)

Cowin, J.

We . . . consider for the first time the effect of a consent form between a married couple and an in vitro fertilization (IVF) clinic (clinic) concerning the disposition of frozen preembryos [at the time of the couple's divorce.] The husband [A.Z.] and wife [B.Z.] were married in 1977. For the first two years of their marriage they resided in Virginia, where they both served in the armed forces. [They moved to Maryland and later to Massachusetts. They experienced fertility problems, including failure to achieve pregnancy with medical assistance, ectopic pregnancies, and removal of wife's fallopian tubes, before they turned to IVF, using wife's ova and husband's sperm.] They underwent IVF treatment from 1988 through 1991. As a result of the 1991 treatment, the wife conceived and gave birth to twin daughters in 1992. During the 1991 IVF treatment, more preembryos were formed than were necessary for immediate implantation, and two vials of preembryos were frozen for possible future implantation.

In the spring of 1995, before the couple separated, the wife desired more children and had one of the remaining vials of preembryos thawed and one preembryo was implanted. [No pregnancy resulted. The husband first learned of this attempt] when he received a notice from his insurance company regarding the procedure. During this period relations between the husband and wife deteriorated. The wife sought and received a protective order against the husband. . . . Ultimately, they separated and the husband filed for divorce [while] one vial containing four frozen preembryos remained in storage at the clinic. . . .

In order to participate in fertility treatment, including . . . IVF, the clinic required egg and sperm donors (donors) to sign certain consent forms for the relevant procedures. . . . The only forms that both the husband and the wife were required to sign were those entitled "Consent Form for Freezing (Cyropreservation) of Embryos" (consent form), one of which is the form at issue here.

Each consent form explains the general nature of the IVF procedure and outlines the freezing process, including the financial cost and the potential benefits and risks of that process. The consent form also requires the donors to decide the disposition of the frozen preembryos on certain listed contingencies: "wife or donor" reaching normal menopause or age forty-five years; preembryos no longer being healthy; "one of us dying"; "should we become separated"; "should we both die." Under each contingency the consent form provides the following as options for disposition of the preembryos: "donated or destroyed — choose one or both." A blank line beneath these choices permits the donors to write in additional alternatives not listed as options on the form, and the form notifies the donors that they may do so. The consent form also informs the donors that they may change their minds as to any disposition, provided that both donors convey that fact in writing to the clinic. . . .

. . . Every time before eggs were retrieved from the wife and combined with sperm from the husband, they each signed a consent form. The husband was present when the first form was completed by the wife in October, 1988. They both signed that consent form after it was finished. The form, as filled out by the wife, stated, inter alia, that if they "should become separated, [they] both agree[d] to have the embryo(s) . . . return[ed] to [the] wife for implant." The husband and wife thereafter underwent six additional egg retrievals for freezing and signed six additional consent forms. . . .

Each time after signing the first consent form in October, 1988, the husband always signed a blank consent form. . . . Each time, after the husband signed the form, the wife filled in the disposition and other information, and then signed the form herself. . . . In each instance the wife specified in the option for "should we become separated," that the preembryos were to be returned to the wife for implantation. . . .

. . . The probate judge [below] determined that the "best solution" was to balance the wife's interest in procreation against the husband's interest in avoiding procreation. Based on his findings, the judge determined that the husband's interest in avoiding procreation outweighed the wife's interest in having additional children and granted the permanent injunction in favor of the husband.

. . . While IVF has been available for over two decades and has been the focus of much academic commentary, there is little law on the enforceability of agreements concerning the disposition of frozen preembryos. Only three States have enacted legislation addressing the issue [citing statutes from Florida, New Hampshire, and Louisiana]. Two State courts of last resort, the Supreme Court of Tennessee and the Court of Appeals of New York, have dealt with the enforceability [after divorce] of agreements between donors regarding the disposition of preembryos and have concluded that such agreements should ordinarily be enforced. [I]n Davis v. Davis 842 S.W.2d 588 (Tenn. 1992), *cert. denied sub nom.* Stowe v. Davis, 507 U.S. 911, (1993), [the] wife sought to donate the preembryos at issue to another couple for implantation. The court stated that agreements between donors regarding disposition of the preembryos "should be presumed valid and should be enforced." 842 S.W.2d at 597. In that case, because there was no agreement between the donors regarding disposition of the preembryos, the court balanced the equitable interests of the two parties and concluded that the husband's interest in avoiding parenthood outweighed the wife's interest in donating the preembryos to another couple for implantation. Id. at 603.

The Court of Appeals of New York, in Kass v. Kass, [696 N.E.2d 174 (N.Y. 1998,] agreed with the Tennessee court's view that courts should enforce agreements where potential parents provide for the disposition of frozen preembryos. . . . The wife sought custody of the preembryos for implantation. According to the New York court, agreements "should generally be presumed valid and binding, and enforced in any dispute between [the donors]." . . . Therefore the court enforced the agreement that provided that the frozen preembryos be donated to the IVF clinic.

. . . This is the first reported case involving the disposition of frozen preembryos in which a consent form signed between the donors on the one hand and the clinic on the other provided that, on the donors' separation, the preembryos were to be given to one of the donors for implantation. In view of the purpose of the form (drafted by and to give assistance to the clinic) and the circumstances of execution, we are dubious at best that it represents the intent of the husband and the wife regarding disposition of the preembryos in the case of a dispute between them. In any event, for several independent reasons, we conclude that the form should not be enforced in the circumstances of this case.

First, the consent form's primary purpose is to explain to the donors the benefits and risks of freezing, and to record the donors' desires for disposition of the frozen preembryos at the time the form is executed in order to provide the clinic with guidance if the donors (as a unit) no longer wish to use the frozen preembryos. The form does not state, and the record does not indicate, that the husband and wife intended the consent form to act as a binding agreement between them should they later disagree as to the disposition. . . .

Second, the consent form does not contain a duration provision. . . . Third, the form uses the term "should we become separated" in referring to the disposition of the frozen preembryos without defining "become separated." Because this dispute arose in the context of a divorce, we cannot conclude that the consent form was intended to govern in these circumstances. Separation and divorce have distinct legal meanings. . . .

The donors' conduct in connection with the execution of the consent forms also creates doubt whether the consent form at issue here represents the clear intentions of both donors. . . . A clinic representative told her that "she could cross out any of the language on the form and fill in her own [language] to fit [the wife's] wishes." Further, although the wife used language in each subsequent form similar to the language used in the first form that she and her husband signed together, the consent form at issue here was signed in blank by the husband, before the wife filled in the language indicating that she would use the preembryos for implantation on separation. . . . Finally, the consent form is not a separation agreement that is binding on the couple in a divorce proceeding pursuant to G. L. c. 208, §34. The consent form does not contain provisions for custody, support, and maintenance, in the event that the wife conceives and gives birth to a child.

With this said, we conclude that, even had the husband and the wife entered into an unambiguous agreement between themselves regarding the disposition of the frozen preembryos, we would not enforce an agreement that would compel one donor to become a parent against his or her will.[22] As a matter of public policy, we conclude that forced procreation is not an area amenable to judicial enforcement. It is well-established that courts will not enforce contracts that violate public policy. . . .

The Legislature has already determined by statute that individuals should not be bound by certain agreements binding them to enter or not enter into familial relationships. [T]he Legislature abolished the cause of action for the breach of a promise to marry [and] provided that no mother may agree to surrender her child "sooner than the fourth calendar day after the date of birth of the child to be adopted" regardless of any prior agreement. . . . In our decisions, we have also indicated a reluctance to enforce prior agreements that bind individuals to future family relationships. In R.R. v. M.H., 689 N.E.2d 790 (1998), we held that a surrogacy agreement in which the surrogate mother agreed to give up the child on its birth is unenforceable unless the agreement

---

22. We express no view regarding whether an unambiguous agreement between two donors concerning the disposition of frozen preembryos could be enforced over the contemporaneous objection of one of the donors, when such agreement contemplated destruction or donation of the preembryos either for research or implantation in a surrogate. . . .

contained, inter alia, a "reasonable" waiting period during which the mother could change her mind. . . .

We glean from these statutes and judicial decisions that prior agreements to enter into familial relationships (marriage or parenthood) should not be enforced against individuals who subsequently reconsider their decisions. This enhances the "freedom of personal choice in matters of marriage and family life." Moore v. East Cleveland, 431 U.S. 494, 499 (1977), quoting Cleveland Bd. of Educ. v. LaFleur, 414 U.S. 632, 639-640 (1974). . . .

In this case, we are asked to decide whether the law of the Commonwealth may compel an individual to become a parent over his or her contemporaneous objection. . . . Enforcing the [1991 consent form against the husband] would require him to become a parent over his present objection to such an undertaking. We decline to do so. . . .

## NOTES AND QUESTIONS

1. *Cryopreservation.* Despite the disputes it can produce, cryopreservation of preembryos offers several advantages. It allows a woman to attempt to achieve pregnancy on several successive occasions without repeating surgery to remove ova. This process also allows for the possibility of replacing preembryos during a spontaneous ovulatory cycle and avoids the risk of multiple pregnancy that inheres in the simultaneous use of numerous preembryos. See, e.g., The Ethics Committee of the American Fertility Society, Ethical Considerations of the New Reproductive Technologies, 53 Fertility and Sterility 58S (Supp. 2 1990) (explaining the process). Finally, the process allows for posthumous reproduction by women. See Anne Reichman Schiff, Arising from the Dead: Challenges of Posthumous Procreation, 75 N.C. L. Rev. 901 (1997).

2. *Classifying embryos.* Early disputes sought to classify frozen preembroyos. In Del Zio v. Presbyterian Hospital, 1978 U.S. Dist. LEXIS 14450 (S.D. N.Y. 1978), a couple won $50,000 for the deliberate destruction of a culture containing their eggs and sperm by health care providers who questioned the safety of this then-untried procedure. The jury based its award on plaintiffs' claims for emotional distress, while rejecting their claims for conversion of property. More recently, an Illinois court held inapplicable the state's wrongful death statute to the destruction of an unimplanted embryo, created by IVF. Miller v. American Infertility Group of Ill., 897 N.E.2d 837 (Ill. App. Ct. 2008). Are embryos property? Compare York v. Jones, 717 F. Supp. 421 (E.D. Va. 1989) (property), with Davis v. Davis, 842 S.W.2d 588, 594-597 (Tenn. 1992) (interim category between "persons" and "property"). Should frozen embryos and frozen sperm be classified the same way? See Hecht v. Superior Ct., 20 Cal. Rptr. 2d 275, 283 (Ct. App. 1993) (relying on *Davis* to conclude that decedent had ownership interest in his frozen sperm at the time of his death sufficient to constitute "property" within Probate Code). See generally Jessica Berg, Of Elephants and Embryos: A Proposed Framework for Legal Personhood, 59 Hastings L.J. 369 (2007); Katheleen R. Guzman, Property, Progeny, Body Part: Assisted Reproduction and the Transfer of Wealth, 31 U.C. Davis L. Rev. 193 (1997); Kermit Roosevelt III, The Newest Property: Reproductive Technologies and the Concept of Parenthood, 39 Santa Clara L. Rev. 79 (1998).

Louisiana has a statutory scheme defining the "in vitro fertilized human ovum" as both a "juridical person" until implanted and a "biological human being" and entitling "such ovum to sue or be sued." La. Rev. Stat. Ann. §§9:121-9:124 (2008). The law prohibits intentional destruction of "viable" fertilized ova, explaining that "[a]n in vitro fertilized human ovum that fails to develop further over a thirty-six hour period except when the embryo is in a state of cryopreservation, is considered nonviable and is not a juridical person." Id. at §9:129. The statute makes available for "adoptive implantation" those fertilized ova for which the IVF patients have renounced their own parental rights for in utero implantation. Id. at §9:130. The law precludes inheritance rights for an ovum unless live birth occurs. Id. at §9:133. Louisiana applies the "best interest of the in vitro fertilized ovum" test in any disputes. Id. at §9:131. Does this test mean that the party seeking implantation must prevail? The trial court in *Davis* so ruled. See 842 S.W.2d at 594. See Diane K. Yang, Note, What's Mine Is Mine, but What's Yours Should Also Be Mine: An Analysis of State Statutes That Mandate the Implantation of Frozen Preembryos, 10 J.L. & Pol'y 587 (2002).

3. *Contract doctrine.* Early cases, such as those reviewed in *A.Z.*, turned on the absence of an express agreement between the parties. For example, writing about Davis v. Davis, 842 S.W.2d 588 (Tenn. 1992), the first of these postdivorce disputes to reach a state high court, Professor Margaret Brinig offers the following analysis:

> The Tennessee Supreme Court [treated] procreative intent as rather like the making of an offer. As first year law students know, the offeror is free to revoke until the offer is accepted. In *Davis*, implantation constituted acceptance. If there is no implantation of the embryo, the father (or mother) is free to have a change of heart: neither is bound. Their genetic contributions are equal, even if their emotional ones may not be. . . .
>
> Although the parties had once intended to create a family together, the *Davis* decision turned on the technical question of contractual intent. Once the marriage had dissolved, the Court regarded the end of the marriage as something like the contractual doctrine of frustration of purpose. Their purpose, having children within their marriage using their own frozen embryos, could no longer be accomplished. The question then became, who "owned" these embryos? Though Mary Sue and Junior each made an equal genetic contribution, the tie went to Junior.

Margaret F. Brinig, The Story of Mary Sue and Junior Davis, in Family Law Stories 195, 204-205, 212 (Carol Sanger ed., 2008).

4. *Precommitment strategies versus contemporaneous consent.* Before *A.Z.*, most authorities read *Davis* and similar cases to mean that agreements and consent forms signed by the "progenitors" would determine the disposition of frozen embryos. As a result, many IVF clinics began routinely to obtain agreements designed to prevent future disputes about disposition. Why does *A.Z.* decline to follow the statement on the consent form? More generally, why does *A.Z.* say that courts should not enforce precommitment strategies, that is, advance directives, to determine the disposition of embryos? The approach adopted by *A.Z.*, requiring contemporaneous mutual consent, derives from an analysis by Professor Carl Coleman. Carl H. Coleman, Procreative Liberty

and Contemporaneous Choice: An Inalienable Rights Approach to Frozen Embryo Disputes, 84 Minn. L. Rev. 55 (1999). See also, e.g., In re Marriage of Witten, 672 N.W.2d 768 (Iowa 2003).

Do you agree with *A.Z.*'s statement that contemporaneous mutual consent safeguards reproductive autonomy ("freedom of personal choice in matters of marriage and family life")? Criticizing *A.Z.*, Professor John Robertson asserts that "a main argument for enforcing precommitments for disposition of frozen embryos is the importance of the freedom that it provides individuals at Time A to control or restrain future reproductive choices at Time B." John A. Robertson, Precommitment Strategies for Disposition of Frozen Embryos, 50 Emory L.J. 989, 1038-1039 (2001). In addition, enforcement promotes efficiency, relieving courts of the burden of resolving such disputes. Id. at 1039. Texas follows this approach. Roman v. Roman, 193 S.W.3d 40 (Tex. App. 2006). See also Cahill v. Cahill, 757 So. 2d 465 (Ala. Civ. App. 2000) (upholding form agreement giving physicians control over embryos). For additional support of a contractual approach, see Sara D. Petersen, Comment, Dealing with Cryopreserved Embryos Upon Divorce: A Contractual Approach Aimed at Preserving Party Expectations, 50 UCLA L. Rev. 1065 (2003); Karissa Hostrup Windsor, Note, Disposition of Cryopreserved Embryos After Divorce, 88 Iowa L. Rev. 1001 (2003). Under a contractual approach, should courts recognize implied agreements? Contract defenses? See Windsor, supra, at 1025-1027. See generally Angela K. Upchurch, A Postmodern Deconstruction of Frozen Embryo Disputes, 39 Conn. L. Rev. 2107 (2007).

5. *Alternative approaches.*

a. *Balancing.* Without a controlling agreement, courts have balanced the progenitors' competing interests. When such disagreements arise in the abortion context, the Supreme Court has said the woman's decision prevails. See Planned Parenthood of Southeastern Pa. v. Casey, 505 U.S. 833, 887-898 (1992). On what basis might one argue that a woman's interest in implanting frozen embryos should trump a man's in avoiding parenthood? See, e.g., Kass v. Kass, 1995 WL 110368 (N.Y. Sup. Ct. 1995), *rev'd*, 663 N.Y.S.2d 581 (App. Div. 1997), *aff'd*, 696 N.E.2d 174 (N.Y. 1998); Ruth Colker, Pregnant Men Revisited or Sperm Is Cheap, Eggs Are Not, 47 Hastings L.J. 1063 (1996); Tracey S. Pachman, Disputes Over Frozen Preembryos & the "Right Not to be a Parent," 12 Colum. J. Gender & L. 128 (2003). Professor Brinig discerns in these disputes about the disposition of frozen embryos a battle "in the war between the sexes" in which men have prevailed because the courts have set "a limit on the supremacy of women's privacy rights in reproduction." Brinig, supra, at 216. Do you agree?

b. *Forced parenthood.* Although *A.Z.* does not expressly use a balancing approach, it suggests that one former spouse's interest in avoiding parenthood outweighs the other's interest in implantation. Several other courts facing such disputes articulate a principle against forcing parenthood on an unwilling party. J.B. v. M.B., 783 A.2d 707 (N.J. 2001); Davis v. Davis, 842 S.W.2d 588, 604 (Tenn. 1992). What, precisely, does the notion of "forced parenthood" entail? Would an agreement to relieve the unwilling party of parental duties address the problem? Would such agreements be enforceable? If the unwilling party's interest lies in avoiding genetic reproduction, can you reconcile these cases with those that impose responsibility on fathers who conceived as the result of birth-control fraud? See Chapter 1, section B1a. Don't support obligations in such cases impose "forced parenthood"? See generally Susan B. Apel, Cryopreserved Embryos: A Response to "Forced Parenthood" and the Role of Intent, 39 Fam. L.Q. 663 (2005); Ellen Waldman, The Parent Trap: Uncovering the Myth of "Coerced Parenthood" in Frozen Embryo Disputes, 53 Am. U.L. Rev. 1021 (2004). See also Robertson, supra, at 1032-1038. To what extent do cases recognizing contraception and abortion rights address unwanted genetic parenthood, apart from unwanted pregnancy? See I. Glenn Cohen, The Constitution and the Rights Not to Procreate, 60 Stan. L. Rev. 1135 (2008) (separating such interests and challenging relevance of constitutional law in private embryo disputes).

c. *Last procreative chance.* In balancing the competing interests or requiring mutual contemporaneous consent, some courts have also considered whether the party seeking implantation has or will have other procreative opportunities. See, e.g., *J.B.*, 783 A.2d at 716-717. In a well-known Israeli case, Nachmani v. Nachmani, F.H. 2401/95, several of the justices noted that the preembryos represented the only chance for the estranged wife (who sought to implant them) to become a genetic mother. See Helene S. Shapo, Frozen Pre-Embryos and the Right to Change One's Mind, 12 Duke J. Comp. & Int'l L. 75, 79 (2002).

Professor Robertson points out the gendered significance of this exception because, "[a]lthough there will be few men who will become infertile during the IVF and embryo storage process, many women might," as their age advances. Robertson, supra, at 1014. In addition, a man facing a disease that threatens his reproductive future can freeze semen, without involving another gamete provider. Unfertilized ova do not freeze as well, however. Thus, for example, upon physicians' advice, a woman in a controversial British decision — diagnosed with tumors requiring the removal of her ovaries — asked her partner to provide semen so she could fertilize some ova, to be preserved for future use. When he later withdrew his consent for her to use the embryos, she lost her only chance to become a genetic parent. See Evans v. United Kingdom (App no. 6339/05), [2007] 1 FLR 1990 (Eur. Ct. H.R. Grand Chamber). Under such circumstances, is not a gender-neutral contemporaneous-consent rule unfair to women? See Anne Donchin, Toward a Gender-Sensitive Assisted Reproduction Policy, 23 Bioethics 28 (2009); Katharine Wright, Competing Interests in Reproduction: The Case of Natallie Evans, 19 King's L.J. 135, 148-150 (2008). (See Chapter 8, section B for additional examination of the *Evans* case.)

Another argument favoring the party seeking parenthood emphasizes the teleology of the parties' earlier agreement: their purpose to develop a parent-child relationship, which in turn undermines subsequent autonomy-based claims. Olivia Lin, Note, Rehabilitating Bioethics: Recontextualizing In Vitro Fertilization Outside Contractual Autonomy, 54 Duke L.J. 485 (2004). See also D. Kelly Weisberg, The Birth of Surrogacy in Israel 86 (2005) (noting that justices in *Nachmani*, supra, invoked such reasoning).

d. *Contract and property law.* In an Oregon case, the spouses had signed an agreement with the clinic stating that the wife would have sole and exclusive rights to authorize transfer or disposition of any remaining frozen embryos.

When the marriage ended, the court held that the agreement created an intangible contractual right constituting personal property to be allocated under the property division statute that applies at divorce. Accordingly, the wife, who wanted to destroy the embryos prevailed over the husband, who wished to donate them to others. In re Marriage of Dahl and Angle, 194 P.3d 834 (Or. Ct. App. 2008). The court also observed that it could find no countervailing reason to impose, as a default principle, a genetic parental relationship on an unwilling party. Id. at 841.

e. *Legislative responses.* A few jurisdictions provide statutorily for the disposition of preembryos. For example, Louisiana law, examined supra, limits destruction. Florida, on the other hand, calls for written agreements between the commissioning couple and the treating physician and spells out default rules for particular situations. Fla. Stat. Ann. §742.17 (2008). Legislation in the United Kingdom requires contemporaneous consent for continued storage or use of cryopreserved genetic material. See *Evans*, supra. For suggestions of what the U.S. could learn from the regulatory schemes in effect in other countries, see Christina C. Lawrence, Note, Procreative Liberty and the Preembryo Problem: Developing a Medical and Legal Framework to Settle the Disposition of Frozen Preembryos, 52 Case W. Res. L. Rev. 721, 745-750 (2002).

6. *Destruction.* What legal rules should govern the continuing storage of the growing number of unused cryopreserved preembryos? British law once imposed a five-year limit, amended to allow additional time if both progenitors consent. See Human Fertilisation and Embryology Act of 1990, ch. 37, §14 (UlK.); Human Fertilisation and Embryology Regulations 1996, SI 1996 No 375, reg 2, Schedule. Six to ten thousand preembryos were destroyed August 1, 1996, pursuant to the law. See Youssef M. Ibrahim, Ethical Furor Erupts in Britain: Should Embryos Be Destroyed?, N.Y. Times, Aug. 1, 1996, at A1. Amendments extended the limit to ten years. Human Fertilisation and Embryology Act of 2008, ch. 22, §15 (U.K.). See Human Fertilisation and Embryology Act 2008: Explanatory Notes 21, available at http://www.opsi.gov.uk/acts/acts2008/en/ukpgaen_20080022_en.pdf. What approach should the United States follow? Under a model law proposed by the American Bar Association, absent a contrary agreement, embryos are deemed abandoned after five years and an unsuccessful search to find the interested participants; disposal of abandoned embryos must follow the most recent recorded agreement between the participants and the storage facility, with a court order for disposition required in the absence of such agreement. American Bar Association Model Act Governing Assisted Reproduction §504 (February 2008), available at http://www.abanet.org/family/committees/artmodelact.pdf.

Recent investigations show that decisions about the disposition of unused embryos pose emotional and ethical difficulties for fertility patients, with some paying for ongoing storage. See Denise Grady, Parents Torn Over Extra Frozen Embryos from Fertility Procedures, N.Y. Times, Dec. 4, 2008, at A26. In 2001, President George W. Bush denied federal funding for stem cell research that would have destroyed frozen preembryos donated for research, while allowing support on cell lines already established from such sources. See Doe v. Shalala, 122 Fed. App'x 600 (4th Cir. 2004) (describing policy and affirming dismissal of embryos' challenge to previous policy). The debate over use of such embryos for research continues, with a number of states committing to support such science and a few private ventures moving forward without federal assistance. See, e.g., David Chen, New Jersey Awards $5 Million in Grants for Stem Cell Research, N.Y. Times, Dec. 17, 2005, at B2; Gina Kolata, Embryonic Cells, No Embryo Needed: Hunting for Ways Out of an Impasse, N.Y. Times, Oct. 11, 2005, at F1. The Obama administration is expected to take action supporting such research. See Andrew Pollack, Milestone in Research in Stem Cells, N.Y. Times, Jan. 23, 2009, at B1.

7. *The biological connection?* How important are physical connections, genetic or otherwise, in *A.Z.* and other judicial analyses of disposition disputes? Suppose, for example, the embryos had been created from donated eggs? Would the fact that the former wife did not endure superovulation and ovum retrieval diminish her interest? Does the forced-parenthood rationale apply to a commissioning adult who used another's genetic material? Suppose she does not plan to gestate herself preembryos conceived from donor eggs but intends to parent the resulting child? See Litowitz v. Litowitz, 48 P.3d 261 (Wash. 2002); Lainie M. C. Dillon, Comment, Conundrums with Penumbras: The Right to Privacy Encompasses Non-Gamete Providers Who Create Embryos with the Intent to Become Parents, 78 Wash. L. Rev. 625 (2003).

# C. IVF'S PROGENY: EGG DONATION, GESTATIONAL SURROGACY, AND "EMBRYO ADOPTION"

IVF's capacity to split once unitary concepts of parentage prompts questions not only about control of frozen preembryos but also about the parental rights to and responsibilities for resulting children, as the following materials demonstrate.

## 1. CHILDREN WITH TWO BIOLOGICAL MOTHERS

### K.M. v. E.G.

117 P.3d 673 (Cal. 2005)

MORENO, J. . . .

[W]e must decide whether a woman who provided ova to her lesbian partner so that the partner could bear children by means of in vitro fertilization is a parent of those children. . . . On March 6, 2001, petitioner K.M. filed a petition to establish a parental relationship with twin five-year-old girls born to respondent E.G., her former lesbian partner. [At a subsequent hearing on K.M.'s motion for custody and visitation,] E.G. testified that she first considered raising a child before she met K.M., at a time when she did not have a partner. She met K.M. in October, 1992, and they became romantically involved in June 1993. E.G. told K.M. that she planned to adopt a baby as a single mother. E.G. applied for adoption in November, 1993. K.M. and E.G.

began living together in March, 1994, and registered as domestic partners in San Francisco.

[Later, E.G., usually along with K.M., visited several fertility clinics and attempted artificial insemination.] K.M. testified that she and E.G. planned to raise the child together, while E.G. insisted that, although K.M. was very supportive, E.G. made it clear that her intention was to become "a single parent." [E.G. then unsuccessfully attempted IVF.]

In January, 1995, [Dr. Mary Martin at the fertility practice of the University of California at San Francisco Medical Center (UCSF)] suggested using K.M.'s ova. E.G. then asked K.M. to donate her ova, explaining that she would accept the ova only if K.M. "would really be a donor" and E.G. would "be the mother of any child," adding that she would not even consider permitting K.M. to adopt the child "for at least five years until [she] felt the relationship was stable and would endure." E.G. told K.M. that she "had seen too many lesbian relationships end quickly, and [she] did not want to be in a custody battle." E.G. and K.M. agreed they would not tell anyone that K.M. was the ova donor.

K.M. acknowledged that she agreed not to disclose to anyone that she was the ova donor, but insisted that she only agreed to provide her ova because she and E.G. had agreed to raise the child together. K.M. and E.G. selected the sperm donor together. K.M. denied that E.G. had said she wanted to be a single parent and insisted that she would not have donated her ova had she known E.G. intended to be the sole parent.

On March 8, 1995, K.M. signed a four-page form on UCSF letterhead entitled "Consent Form for Ovum Donor (Known)." The form states that K.M. agrees "to have eggs taken from my ovaries, in order that they may be donated to another woman." [The form included a waiver of any claim to the donated eggs or any parental rights to the resulting child.] E.G. signed a form entitled "Consent Form for Ovum Recipient" that stated, in part: "I acknowledge that the child or children produced by the IVF procedure is and shall be my own legitimate child or children and the heir or heirs of my body with all rights and privileges accompanying such status." [The parties disagree about their expectations in signing these forms.]

Ova were withdrawn from K.M., and embryos were then created in vitro and implanted in E.G. on April 13, 1995. K.M. and E.G. told K.M.'s father about the resulting pregnancy by announcing that he was going to be a grandfather. The twins were born on December 7, 1995. The twins' birth certificates listed E.G. as their mother and did not reflect a father's name. As they had agreed, neither E.G. nor K.M. told anyone K.M. had donated the ova, including their friends, family and the twins' pediatrician. Soon after the twins were born, E.G. asked K.M. to marry her, and on Christmas Day, the couple exchanged rings.

Within a month of their birth, E.G. added the twins to her health insurance policy, named them as her beneficiary for all employment benefits, and increased her life insurance with the twins as the beneficiary. K.M. did not do the same. E.G. referred to her mother, as well as K.M.'s parents, as the twins' grandparents and referred to K.M.'s sister and brother as the twins' aunt and uncle, and K.M.'s nieces as their cousins. Two school forms listed both K.M. and respondent as the twins' parents. The children's nanny testified that both K.M. and E.G. "were the babies' mother."

The relationship between K.M. and E.G. ended in March, 2001 and K.M. filed the present action. In September, 2001, E.G. and the twins moved to Massachusetts to live with E.G.'s mother. [The courts below rejected K.M.'s claims.]

K.M. asserts that she is a parent of the twins because she supplied the ova that were fertilized in vitro and implanted in her lesbian partner, resulting in the birth of the twins. . . . The Court of Appeal in the present case concluded, however, that K.M. was not a parent of the twins, despite her genetic relationship to them, because she had the same status as a sperm donor. . . . In [Johnson v. Calvert, 851 P.2d 776 (Cal. 1993),] we considered the predecessor statute to [Family Code] section 7613(b), former Civil Code section 7005. We did not discuss whether this statute applied to a woman who provides ova used to impregnate another woman, but we observed that "in a true 'egg donation' situation, where a woman gestates and gives birth to a child formed from the egg of another woman with the intent to raise the child as her own, the birth mother is the natural mother under California law." We held that the statute did not apply under the circumstances in *Johnson* [a gestational surrogacy case], because the husband and wife in *Johnson* did not intend to "donate" their sperm and ova to the surrogate mother, but rather "intended to procreate a child genetically related to them by the only available means."

The circumstances of the present case are not identical to those in *Johnson*, but they are similar in a crucial respect; both the couple in *Johnson* and the couple in the present case intended to produce a child that would be raised in their own home. [Thus, this is not a "true 'egg donation'" case.]

Although the predecessor to section 7613 was based upon the Model [Uniform Parentage Act (UPA)], the California Legislature made one significant change; it expanded the reach of the provision to apply to both married and unmarried women. "[T]he California Legislature has afforded unmarried as well as married women a statutory vehicle for obtaining semen for artificial insemination without fear that the donor may claim paternity, and has likewise provided men with a statutory vehicle for donating semen to married and unmarried women alike without fear of liability for child support." (Jhordan C. v. Mary K., [224 Cal. Rptr. 530 (Ct. App. 1986).]. . . . But there is nothing to indicate that California intended to expand the reach of this provision so far that it would apply if a man provided semen to be used to impregnate his unmarried partner in order to produce a child that would be raised in their joint home. It would be surprising, to say the least, to conclude that the Legislature intended such a result. The Colorado Supreme Court considered a related issue and reached a similar conclusion [in In Interest of R.C., 775 P.2d 27, 29 (Colo. 1989), a case about] the parental rights, if any, of a man who provided semen to a physician that was used to impregnate an unmarried friend of the man. . . . [Here,] K.M. and E.G. were more than "friends" when K.M. provided her ova, through a physician, to be used to impregnate E.G.; they lived together and were registered domestic partners. Although the parties dispute whether both women were intended to be parents of the resulting child, it is undisputed that they intended that the resulting child would be raised in their joint home. Neither the Model UPA, nor section 7613(b) was intended to apply under such circumstances. . . . K.M.'s genetic relationship

with the twins constitutes evidence of a mother and child relationship under
the UPA and, as explained above, section 7613(b) does not apply to exclude
K.M. as a parent of the twins. The circumstance that E.G. gave birth to the
twins also constitutes evidence of a mother and child relationship. Thus, both
K.M. and E.G. are mothers of the twins under the UPA.[6]

It is true we said in *Johnson* that "for any child California law recognizes
only one natural mother." But as we explain in the companion case of Elisa B. v.
Superior Court [Chapter 1, section B1b], this statement in *Johnson* must be
understood in light of the issue presented in that case; "our decision in *Johnson*
does not preclude a child from having two parents both of whom are women."

Justice Werdegar's dissent argues that we should determine whether K.M. is
a parent using the "intent test" [which we applied to choose between two
women when each adduced evidence of maternity, giving birth and genetic
relationship]. It would be unwise to expand application of the *Johnson* intent
test as suggested by Justice Werdegar's dissent beyond the circumstances
presented in *Johnson*. Usually, whether there is evidence of a parent and child
relationship under the UPA does not depend upon the intent of the parent. For
example, a man who engages in sexual intercourse with a woman who assures
him, falsely, that she is incapable of conceiving children is the father of a resulting child, despite his lack of intent to become a father. Justice Werdegar's dissent
states that predictability in this area is important, but relying upon a later judicial determination of the intent of the parties, as the dissent suggests, would not
provide such predictability. The present case is a good example.

The superior court in the present case found that K.M. signed a waiver
form, thereby "relinquishing and waiving all rights to claim legal parentage
of any children who might result." But such a waiver does not affect our determination of parentage. Section 7632 provides: "Regardless of its terms, an
agreement between an alleged or presumed father and the mother or child
does not bar an action under this chapter." A woman who supplies ova to
be used to impregnate her lesbian partner, with the understanding that the
resulting child will be raised in their joint home, cannot waive her responsibility to support that child. Nor can such a purported waiver effectively cause
that woman to relinquish her parental rights.

In light of our conclusion that section 7613(b) does not apply and that
K.M. is the twins' parent (together with E.G.), based upon K.M.'s genetic relationship to the twins, we need not, and do not, consider whether K.M. is presumed to be a parent of the twins under section 7611, subdivision (d), which
provides that a man is presumed to be a child's father if "[h]e receives the child
into his home and openly holds out the child as his natural child." [Reversed.]

KENNARD, J., dissenting.

. . . Because K.M. donated her ova for physician-assisted artificial insemination and implantation in another woman, and knowingly and voluntarily
signed a document declaring her intention *not* to become a parent of any
resulting children, she is not a parent of the twins. . . . In the 12 years since
this court's decision in *Johnson,* an unknown number of Californians have

---

6. Contrary to the suggestion in Justice Werdegar's dissent[, we do not use a best-interests
standard]. We simply follow the dictates of the UPA.

made procreative choices in reliance on it. For example, in the companion case of Kristine H. v. Lisa R. [117 P.3d 690 (Cal. 2005),] a lesbian couple obtained a prebirth stipulated judgment declaring them to be "the joint *intended legal parents*" of the child born to one of them (italics added), language they presumably used in order to bring themselves within *Johnson* where the preconception intent to be come a parent is the determinative inquiry. We do know that prebirth judgments of parentage on behalf of the nonbiologically related partner of a child's biological parent have been entered in this state, and that such judgments were touted to same-sex couples as less expensive and time consuming than second parent adoption. How will today's majority holding affect the validity of the various procreative choices made in reliance on *Johnson*? . . .

. . . The majority amends the sperm-donor statute by inserting a new provision making a sperm donor the legal father of a child born to a woman artificially inseminated with his sperm whenever the sperm donor and the birth mother "*intended that the resulting child would be raised in their joint home,*" even though both the donor and birth mother also intended that the donor *not* be the child's father. Finding nothing in the statutory language or history to support this construction, I reject it. . . .

WERDEGAR, J., dissenting . . .

. . . Precisely because predictability in this area is so important, I cannot agree with the majority that the children in this case do in fact have two mothers. Until today, when one woman has provided the ova and another has given birth, the established rule for determining disputed claims to motherhood was clear: we looked to the intent of the parties. Indeed, we have no other test sufficient to the task. Furthermore, to apply *Johnson*'s intent test to the facts of this case necessarily leads to the conclusion that E.G. is a mother and K.M. is not.

. . . The majority criticizes the [intent] test as basing "the determination of parentage upon a later judicial determination of intent made years after the birth of the child." But the task of determining the intent of persons who have undertaken assisted reproduction is not fundamentally different than the task of determining intent in the context of disputes involving contract, tort or criminal law, something courts have done satisfactorily for centuries. . . . [When two women divide] the genetic and gestational components of motherhood, only an examination of their intent permits us to determine whether we are dealing with an ovum donation agreement, a gestational surrogacy agreement, or neither. If courts can perform one of these tasks acceptably, they can also perform the other.

No more persuasive is the majority's suggestion that to respect the formally expressed intent of the parties to an ovum donation agreement is prohibited by the rule that parental obligations may not be waived by contract. . . . Certainly parental obligations may not be waived by contract. But *Johnson*'s intent test does not *enforce* ovum donation and gestational surrogacy agreements; it merely directs courts to consider such documents, along with all other relevant evidence, in determining preconception intent.

As a final reason for rejecting the intent test, the majority suggests that to apply the test outside the context of *Johnson* might shield from the obligations of fatherhood, contrary to existing law, a man who, lacking the intent to become a father, "engages in sexual intercourse with a woman who assures him, falsely, that she is incapable of conceiving children. . . ." But no one, to my knowledge, proposes to apply the intent test to determine the parentage of children conceived through ordinary sexual reproduction. . . .

The new rule the majority substitutes for the intent test entails serious problems. First, the rule inappropriately confers rights and imposes disabilities on persons because of their sexual orientation. In a standard ovum donation agreement, such as the agreement between K.M. and E.G., the donor confirms her intention to assist another woman to become a parent without the donor becoming a parent herself. The majority's rule vitiates such agreements when its conditions are satisfied — conditions that include the fact the parties to the agreement are lesbian. Although the majority denies that its rule depends on sexual orientation, the opinion speaks for itself. The majority has chosen to use the term "lesbian" no less than six times in articulating its holding. Moreover, the majority prevents future courts from applying its holding automatically to persons other than lesbians by stating that it "decide[s] only the case before us, which involves a lesbian couple who registered as domestic partners." . . . Why should a lesbian not have the same right as other women to donate ova without becoming a mother, or to accept a donation of ova without accepting the donor as a coparent, even if the donor and recipient live together and both plan to help raise the child? [This approach, in turn, requires a formal definition of "lesbian."]

Other problems arise from the majority's attempt to limit its holding to cases in which the ovum donor and birth mother intend to raise the children together. Except in the context of the majority's new rule, a person's preconception intent to participate in *raising* a child has no relevance to the determination of natural parentage. The duty to raise children (by personal care or through payment of child support) is imposed by law regardless of the parents' intent or wishes. Many persons who become parents do not intend to raise children (e.g., casual inseminators and parents who abandon their babies) and, conversely, many people intend to raise children without becoming parents (e.g., nannies and some stepparents and grandparents). . . . Perhaps the most serious problem with the majority's new rule is that it threatens to destabilize ovum donation and gestational surrogacy agreements. One important function of *Johnson*'s intent test was to permit persons who made use of reproductive technology to create, before conception, settled and enforceable expectations about who would and would not become parents. *Johnson*, supra, thus gave E.G. a right at the time she conceived to expect that she alone would be the parent of her children — a right the majority now retrospectively abrogates. E.G.'s expectation has a constitutional dimension. (See Troxel v. Granville[, 530 U.S. 57, 65 (2000) (due process clause protects a parent's fundamental right to make decisions concerning the care, custody and control of her children)]. We cannot recognize K.M. as a parent without diminishing E.G.'s existing parental rights. . . .

The following excerpt describes K.M.'s situation before her victory in the California Supreme Court:

PEGGY ORENSTEIN, THE OTHER MOTHER

N.Y. Times, July 25, 2004, §6 (Magazine), at 24

[K.] hadn't seen the twins, who were living [with her former partner, E., in Massachusetts after their break-up] in a month, and then only for eight hours. For her, the issue was simple: she wanted her daughters back. . . .

[Recalling the form she signed before the first administration of hormones to stimulate superovulation,] K. says it seemed obvious that the form was meant for anonymous donors, not for a live-in lover. (The clinic later stopped requiring lesbian couples to sign it.) One section included the phrase "I agree not to attempt to discover the identity of the recipient." Could K. have challenged the language? Could she have crossed sections out? If so, it didn't occur to her at the time. "I believed I had to sign the form to do the procedure," she says now. "It was something for the clinic — it wasn't anything between my partner and me. We were having a family. I look back on that now, and I think, Oh, my God." . . .

[Although California cases have relied on intent to determine parentage, the] trouble is that, as with K. and E., by the time a couple gets to court, acrimony and regret can obscure intent. In that way, K. and E.'s case is like those of hundreds of gay couples who did not or could not pursue second-parent adoption. Typically, however, only one partner is the biological (or adoptive) parent; the other relies on the evolving notion of "psychological parenthood." Some states, like New Jersey, recognize a second mom or dad who wiped runny noses and helped with homework — who had a clear parental role regardless of the actual legal relationships. In those places, K. might have had an easy case. Other states, like New York, side with birth mothers regardless of what a gay couple's intent may have been. . . .

Everything reminds her of the girls. She pulls out another picture, this one shot on a recent getaway, of two Adirondack chairs overlooking a wine-country valley. "This is where my girls would hang out if they had been there," she says. Nor does she find relief at night: in her dreams she searches for her daughters, trying to swim through turbid water or to run to them on legs that won't obey. She wakes up gasping.

A child's voice floats in through an open window. . . . K. winces. "Sometimes I have to turn on some music so I won't hear that baby," she says.

It is, of course, the children's voices that are missing from this debate. What are their wishes, their feelings, their needs? As with heterosexual couples, gay partners in a hostile split will say and do hurtful things. They will use children as weapons. With no legal recognition of their families, however, without the possibility of marriage or, in some states, second-parent adoption, doing so is just that much easier. Ultimately, it is the children who suffer. . . .

## NOTES AND QUESTIONS

1. *Collaborative reproduction.* Although *Lifchez,* supra, discussed the possibility of "removal of an embryo from one woman's uterus and placing it in the uterus of a second woman," IVF permits several forms of "collaborative reproduction." For example, an intended mother can gestate a fetus conceived with a donor's egg and the sperm of her husband/partner. See, e.g., In re C.K.G., 173 S.W.3d 714 (Tenn. 2005). Or, the intended parents can hire a "gestational surrogate" after creating a preembryo with their own genetic material. See, e.g., Johnson v. Calvert, 851 P.2d 776 (Cal. 1993); Culliton v. Beth Israel Deaconess Med. Ctr., 756 N.E.2d 1133 (Mass. 2001). Sometimes, a gestational surrogate carries donated genetic material (a donated embryo or an embryo created with a donor egg or donor sperm or both) so that one or both intended parents has no biological tie to the resulting child. See, e.g., In re Marriage of Buzzanca, 72 Cal. Rptr. 2d 280 (Ct. App. 1998); Litowitz v. Litowitz, 48 P.3d 261 (Wash. 2002). And, as in *K.M.,* lesbian couples can divide genetic and gestational contributions, giving each woman a biological tie to the child. See, e.g., In re J.D.M., 2004 WL 2272063 (Ohio Ct. App. 2004).

2. *Intent-based parentage.* Dissenting in *K.M.,* Justice Werdegar urges reliance on the parties' intent. Under this approach, as originally advocated by Professor Marjorie Shultz in response to the *Baby M* case (Chapter 6, section A2), "[w]ithin the context of artificial reproductive techniques, intentions that are voluntarily chosen, deliberate, express and bargained-for ought presumptively to determine legal parenthood." Marjorie Maguire Shultz, Reproductive Technology and Intent-Based Parenthood: An Opportunity for Gender Neutrality, 1990 Wis. L. Rev. 297, 323. The California Supreme Court first applied the test in *Johnson,* supra, to recognize as parents the commissioning couple who provided the genetic material and intended to rear the child, rather than the gestational surrogate who decided during the pregnancy not to relinquish the child. Given the conflicting indicia of maternity under California parentage statutes (gestation and genetics), the court broke the "tie" based on the parties' intent and causation (but for the agreement, the child would not exist). Thereafter, *Buzzanca,* supra, invoked intent to rule that divorcing spouses were both legal parents of a child who was created from a frozen embryo that they obtained from a fertility clinic and who was born to a gestational surrogate whom they hired; as a result, John Buzzanca could not avoid paying child support. Despite these precedents, California courts have not used intent to resolve disputes in "traditional surrogacy" cases (in which the gestational surrogate bears her genetic child, as in *Baby M*). See In re Marriage of Moschetta, 30 Cal. Rptr. 2d 893 (Ct. App. 1994).

What are the advantages of intent-based parentage? The disadvantages? How should a court determine the parties' intent when they offer conflicting testimony, as in *K.M.*?

3. *Alternatives to intent.*

a. *Uniform Parentage Act of 1973.* The 1973 version of the Uniform Parentage Act (UPA), which California enacted, indicates that genetic parentage establishes legal parentage. Unif. Parentage Act §11 (1973), 9B U.L.A. 445 (2001) (blood tests). See also *Culliton*, supra. As applied in an egg-donation case, however, this principle would require issuance of a birth certificate identifying the genetic mother as the legal mother and a subsequent adoption by the intended mother. Given the legal treatment of AID, does this approach violate equal protection? See Soos v. Superior Ct., 897 P.2d 1356 (Ariz. Ct. App. 1994). As a practical matter, would the state require genetic testing of each child at birth to determine parentage?

b. *New Uniform Parentage Act.* Because of technological advances in genetics and reproductive medicine, the National Conference of Commissioners on Uniform State Laws (now called the Uniform Law Commission) promulgated a new UPA in 2000 and revised it in 2002. This model statute generally treats egg donors as sperm donors, with no legal status, and makes the intended mother the legal mother without government intervention. Unif. Parentage Act §702 (2000, amended 2002), 9B U.L.A. 355 (2001). More broadly, this model always recognizes as the legal mother the woman giving birth, with her husband as the presumed father. Unif. Parentage Act §201(a), 9B U.L.A. 15 (Supp. 2008). See also, e.g., *C.K.G.*, supra (recognizing gestational, intended mother). The Act, however, goes on to provide for "gestational agreements," as follows:

**Section 801. Gestational Agreement Authorized**

>    (a) A prospective gestational mother, her husband if she is married, a donor or the donors, and the intended parents may enter into a written agreement providing that:
>        (1) the prospective gestational mother agrees to pregnancy by means of assisted reproduction;
>        (2) the prospective gestational mother, her husband if she is married, and the donors relinquish all rights and duties as the parents of a child conceived through assisted reproduction; and
>        (3) the intended parents become the parents of the child.
>    (b) The man and the woman who are the intended parents must both be parties to the gestational agreement.
>    (c) A gestational agreement is enforceable only if validated as provided in Section 803.
>    (d) A gestational agreement does not apply to the birth of a child conceived by means of sexual intercourse.
>    (e) A gestational agreement may provide for payment of consideration.
>    (f) A gestational agreement may not limit the right of the gestational mother to make decisions to safeguard her health or that of the embryos or fetus.

Unif. Parentage Act §801 (2000, amended 2002), 9B U.L.A. 58 (Supp. 2008). Validation of a gestational agreement requires procedures tantamount to a preconception adoption, including a home study and judicial approval, and makes the intended parents the child's legal parents. Unif. Parentage Act §§803, 807 (2000, amended 2002), 9B U.L.A. 60 (Supp. 2008); 9B U.L.A. 368 (2001). The parties can terminate a validated gestational agreement only before the pregnancy begins, or a court can do so for good cause. Unif. Parentage Act §806 (2000, amended 2002), 9B U.L.A. 367 (2001). A gestational agreement without validation is not enforceable, but the intended parents may be liable for support. Unif. Parentage Act §809 (2000, amended 2002), 9B U.L.A. 369 (2001). Eight states have enacted the new UPA (Alabama, Delaware, North Dakota, Oklahoma, Texas, Utah, Washington, and Wyoming), and it is pending in New Mexico. See http://www.nccusl.org/Update/uniformact_factsheets/uniformacts-fs-upa.asp (last visited Oct. 1, 2008). However, only five of the eight address surrogacy (North Dakota, Texas, Utah, Washington, and Wyoming). The American Bar Association's Family Law Section has proposed a model act governing assisted reproduction; while comprehensively addressing the issues, the drafters indicate that this model's provisions are not designed to conflict with or supersede the UPA's treatment of a number of topics, e.g., the status of resulting children and gestational agreements. See American Bar Association Model Act Governing Assisted Reproduction, arts. 6 & 7 (February 2008), available at http://www.abanet.org/family/committees/artmodelact.pdf (legislative notes). See generally Charles P. Kindregan & Steven H. Snyder, Clarifying the Law of ART: The New American Bar Association Model Act Governing Assisted Reproductive Technology, 42 Fam. L.Q. 203 (2008). See generally Amy M. Larkey, Note, Redefining Motherhood: Determining Legal Maternity in Gestational Surrogacy Arrangements, 51 Drake L. Rev. 605 (2003) (surveying approaches and urging enactment of new UPA); Adam P. Plant, Commentary, With a Little Help from My Friends: The Intersection of the Gestational Carrier Surrogacy Agreement, Legislative Inaction, and Medical Advancement, 54 Ala. L. Rev. 639 (2003).

c. *An "interpretive approach."* Professor Marsha Garrison proposes an "interpretive approach" that would apply to children conceived with technological assistance the same legal principles that govern parentage of other children. Marsha Garrison, Law Making for Baby Making: An Interpretive Approach to the Determination of Legal Parentage, 113 Harv. L. Rev. 835 (2000). Under this approach, which relies on analogy and "fairness," the court properly classified *Baby M* as an adoption case because one woman intended to rear the child of another. 113 Harv. L. Rev. at 882, 898. This approach also leads Garrison to conclude that the law should treat semen donors as fathers when unmarried women use AID (because, outside this context, the law always recognizes two parents). Id. at 903-912. Considering the closest analogies, she goes on to recommend that the law treat egg donors as semen donors, recognize the genetic mother in gestational surrogacy cases, and require adoption proceedings in cases like *Buzzanca*, supra. Garrison, supra, at 897-898, 912-920. Do you agree?

d. *Functional approaches.* Some contemporary authorities emphasize conduct and lived familial relationships in determining parentage. E.g., Nancy E. Dowd, From Genes, Marriage and Money to Nurture: Redefining Fatherhood, 10 Cardozo Women's L.J. 132 (2003); E. Gary Spitko, The Constitutional Function of Biological Paternity: Evidence of the Biological Mother's Consent to the Biological Father's Co-Parenting of her Child, 48 Ariz. L. Rev. 97 (2006). See also American Law Institute, Principles of the Law of Family Dissolution §2.03 (2002) (recognizing parents by estoppel and de facto parents). To what extent does intent-based parentage resemble a functional approach? See Richard F. Storrow, Parenthood by Pure Intention: Reproduction and the Functional Approach to Assisted Parentage, 53 Hastings L.J. 597 (2002). Why does the majority emphasize the intent to rear the child in the parties' joint home? Does the *K.M.* majority simply re-examine the parties' original intent in light of their conduct, by which both K.M. and E.G. functioned as the twins' parents? See Melanie B. Jacobs, Applying Intent-Based Parentage Principles to Nonlegal Lesbian Coparents, 25 N. Ill. U. L. Rev. 433 (2005). What does the news story about K.M. add to the analysis?

4. *Default rules and departures.* Most of the rules surveyed above attempt to articulate default rules that determine parentage in the absence of affirmative steps to achieve a different allocation of rights and responsibilities, for example, a termination of parental rights and adoption, steps that entail considerable state intervention. Even with a rule based on intent, however, must the parties take action to memorialize their plans and prevent future challenges?

a. *Adoption.* When should the law make adoption necessary? Why does California require adoption by the intended mother in traditional surrogacy cases while allowing intent to control in gestational surrogacy cases? See, e.g., Janet L. Dolgin, An Emerging Consensus: Reproductive Technology and the Law, 23 Vt. L. Rev. 225 (1998). In recognizing the commissioning couple as the parents in *Buzzanca*, supra, the court expressly rejected an "adoption default" model for most collaborative reproductive arrangements. 72 Cal. Rptr. 2d at 289. On what basis should couples like the Buzzancas be able to avoid adoption procedures in order to become the parents of a child with no genetic nor gestational tie to either of them? Evaluate the approach of the new UPA, supra, which requires, in effect, a preimplantation adoption whenever the intended mother is not the woman giving birth.

The pitfalls of an adoption requirement for the intended parents (as illustrated in *Baby M,* Chapter 6, section A2) have prompted fertility clinics to avoid traditional surrogacy arrangements; even when the intended mother can supply neither ova nor gestational capacity, the preferred approach now combines the use of ova from one woman and the gestational services of another — an arrangement more likely to evoke recognition of the intended parents by default. Unif. Parentage Act (2000, amended 2002), 9B U.L.A. 361 (2001) (prefatory cmt. to Art. 8, before 2002 amendment). See, e.g., *Litowitz*, supra.

b. *Birth certificates.* Default rules also determine the parentage information entered on the child's birth certificate. In some cases, however, the parties have gone to court before the child is born to litigate the content of the anticipated birth certificate. In *Culliton*, supra, a gestational surrogacy case, the genetic and intended parents successfully petitioned to be named as parents on the original birth certificate. In other gestational surrogacy cases, courts have reached a similar result, contrary to the new UPA. E.g., Belsito v. Clark, 644 N.E.2d 760 (Ohio Com. Pleas 1994), *superseded by statute*, Ohio Rev. Code Ann. chap. 3705 (2008), *as recognized* in Nemcek v. Paskey, 849 N.E.2d 108 (Ohio

Com. Pleas 2006) (explaining how statute deprives Probate Court of jurisdiction over birth certificates); Doe v. N.Y. City Bd. of Health, 782 N.Y.S.2d 180 (Sup. Ct. 2004) (ordering two sets of birth certificates, with the first (naming the gestational mother) to be sealed).

c. *Prebirth stipulations and judgments.* Justice Kennard's dissenting opinion in *K.M.* notes the increasingly common California practice of obtaining pre-birth stipulated judgments of parentage for children of assisted reproduction. Same-sex couples have used this procedure more often than others. Howard Fink & June Carbone, Between Private Ordering and Public Fiat: A New Paradigm for Family Law Decision-making, 5 J.L. Fam. Stud. 1, 45 (2003). To what extent does *K.M.* jeopardize this practice? Does a prebirth judgment foreclose a later change of mind? If not, what good is it? If so, what limits should apply? Although obtaining a prebirth judgment represents a departure from default parentage rules, the procedure arguably produces fewer opportunities for judicial disapproval than do conventional adoptions. Fink & Carbone, supra, at 47. (Recall *Lofton*, Chapter 3, section A1b). Should an adoption follow after the child is born? See Fink & Carbone, supra, at 50. See also Steven H. Snyder & Mary Patricia Byrn, The Use of Prebirth Parentage Orders in Surrogacy Proceedings, 39 Fam. L.Q. 633 (2005) (exploring utility of prebirth orders in various states).

d. *Other consequences.* Fixing parental status before or at the time of birth (either through a default rule or a prebirth judgment) can have other important consequences, such as eligibility for authority to consent to the infant's medical care and insurance coverage for neonatal intensive care. See Mid-South Ins. Co. v. Doe, 274 F. Supp. 2d 757 (D.S.C. 2003).

## Depictions in Popular Culture: Baby Mama (2008)

In this comedic portrayal of surrogacy, Kate, a high-powered, unmarried, and fertility-challenged businesswoman (played by Tina Fey) hires a scheming and lower-class Angie (played by Amy Poehler) to carry her fertilized eggs. When Angie moves in with Kate, their different backgrounds and perspectives stand out distinctly—and invite viewers to laugh. The story line presents a number of unexpected twists, but, throughout, the film assumes without questioning that women long for both motherhood and marriage and that the best sort of parenthood rests on biological connection. For less than enthusiastic reviews, see, e.g., Manohla Dargis, Learning on the Job About Birthing Babies, N.Y. Times, Apr. 25, 2008, at E1; Anthony Lane, Switching Places, The New Yorker, Apr. 28, 2008, at 86 (from column on "The Critics: The Current Cinema").

Soon after the release of *Baby Mama*, a journalist published a lengthy account of her own experience of producing a genetic son by means of gestational surrogacy. Alex Kuczynski, Her Body, My Baby, N.Y. Times, Nov. 30, 2008, §MM, at 42. Accompanying photographs highlighted apparent class differences between the two women. See Clark Hoyt, The Privileged and Their Children, N.Y. Times, Dec. 7, 2008, §WK, at 9 (public editor's column). The piece inspired numerous letters, including many critiques of the underlying elitism and the absence of thoughtful exploration of both economic issues and the feelings of the "surrogate." Id.; Letters, Her Body, My Baby, N.Y. Times, Dec. 14, 2008, §MM, at 16.

Given the shortcomings of *Baby Mama* and Kuczynski's account, what aspects of gestational surrogacy would you deem important to include in a portrayal aimed at the general public? Aimed at lawmakers?

5. *Variations.* One emerging technique, a variation on the process sometimes called "cloning," allows the creation of a child using genetic material from two women—an option that might hold particular interest for lesbian couples. See Lee M. Silver, Remaking Eden: How Genetic Engineering and Cloning Will Transform the American Family 206-222 (1998). In the United Kingdom, the 2008 amendments to the Fertilisation and Embryology Act address this possibility, permitting use under certain conditions of eggs and embryos made with such mitochondrial donations. Human Fertilisation and Embryology Act of 2008, ch. 22, §26 (U.K.); Human Fertilisation and Embryology Act 2008: Explanatory Notes 26-27, available at http://www.opsi.gov.uk/acts/acts2008/en/ukpgaen_20080022_en.pdf. However, donating an egg or other genetic material does not make a woman the mother of the resulting child. Human Fertilisation and Embryology Act of 2008, ch. 22, §47 (U.K.).

6. *Emotional aspects.* A recent study shows a range of emotional reactions to the prospect of donating unused frozen embryos to other families. One woman surveyed said "she would worry too much about 'what kind of parents they were with, what kind of life they had.'" See Denise Grady, Parents Torn Over Extra Frozen Embryos from Fertility Procedures, N.Y. Times, Dec. 4, 2008, at A26. For the complex emotions and moral questions faced by woman using donor eggs, including the impact of pervasive "resemblance talk" (concerning whether children resemble their parents), see Peggy Orenstein, Your Gamete, Myself, N.Y. Times, July 15, 2007, §6 (Magazine), at 34.

## 2. "MOTHERLESS" CHILDREN?

IN RE ROBERTO D.B.

923 A.2d 115 (MD. 2007)

Opinion by BELL, C.J. . . .

. . . The case sub judice presents a novel question of law, one of first impression in this Court: must the name of a genetically unrelated gestational host of a fetus, with whom the appellant contracted to carry in vitro fertilized embryos to term, be listed as the mother on the birth certificate, when, as a result, children are born? The Circuit Court for Montgomery County held that it must. We shall reverse. . . .

[The appellant, Roberto d.B., an unmarried male, initiated IVF with donor eggs, producing two embryos. They were implanted in the putative appellee, a woman with whom he contracted to act as a carrier, and she delivered twin children at Holy Cross Hospital in Silver Spring, Maryland.]

The medical records department of a hospital in Maryland is required to submit information regarding births to the Maryland Division of Vital Records ("MDVR"), a part of the Maryland Vital Statistics Administration. Maryland Code (1982, 2005 Repl. Vol., 2006 Supp.) §4-208(a)(4)(iii) of the Health-General Article ("HG"). The MDVR, having received this information, issues the birth certificates. Unless a court order otherwise provides, the hospital will report the gestational carrier as the "mother" of the child to the MDVR. HG §4-208. Holy Cross Hospital followed this procedure.

Neither the appellee nor the appellant, however, wanted the gestational carrier's name to be listed on the birth certificate as the "mother" of the children. It is the appellant's and the appellee's contention that the appellee was merely acting as a gestational carrier for children that were never intended, by either party, to be hers, and to whom she has no genetic relationship. The appellee does not wish to exercise parental rights to, or over, these two children, nor does the appellant desire that she do so. The appellee contends that, under her agreement, she had a reasonable expectation that her role in the lives of these children would terminate upon delivery of the children, and that the faithful performance of her duties under the agreement would not permanently impact her life, nor the lives of her family.

Thus, the appellee joined the appellant's petition to the Circuit Court for Montgomery County, asking it to issue an "accurate" birth certificate, i.e., one that did not list the gestational carrier as the children's mother. In the petition, they asked the court to declare that the appellant was the father of the children, and authorize the hospital to report only the name of the father to the MDVR. [The Circuit Court refused, in an oral ruling that cites two reasons: First, no Maryland case law exists that would give a trial court the power to remove the mother's name from a birth certificate. Second, removing the name of the surrogate from the birth certificate is inconsistent with the "best interests of the child" standard ("BIC"), citing, generally, "health reasons."]

The appellant's primary contention is that the parentage statutes in Maryland, as enforced by the trial court below, do not "afford equal protection of the law to men and women similarly situated." Maryland's Equal Rights Amendment (E.R.A.), Article 46 of the Maryland Declaration of Rights, specifies that "[e]quality of rights under the law shall not be abridged or denied because of sex." The appellant contends that because Maryland's parentage statutes allow a man to deny paternity, and do not, currently, allow a woman to deny maternity, these statutes, unless interpreted differently, are subject to an E.R.A. challenge. . . .

[Under Maryland's paternity law, a] court has the power to declare that an alleged father has no paternal status when no genetic connection is found. The appellant argues that a woman has no equal opportunity to deny maternity based on genetic connection — in essence, that in a paternity action, if no genetic link between a man and a child is established, the man would not be found to be the parent, and the matter would end, but a woman, or a gestational carrier, as in this case, will be forced by the State to be the "legal" mother of the children, despite her lack of genetic connection.

The appellant offers that, under his interpretation of the parentage statutes, the E.R.A. problem is avoided, "because a non-genetic gestational carrier could apply to the court for a parentage order and receive one upon a showing that she was not genetically related to the child and never intended to be its parent."

Maryland law currently accommodates, if not contemplates, a birth certificate on which the mother is not identified. Thus, the trial courts may pass such an order. [The court cites the statute, §4-211 of the Health-General Article, which authorizes the issuance of new birth certificates after an order of parentage.] The appellant contends that, because the statute controlling new birth certificates only addresses "parentage," without limitation to as to which, in the abstract, it does not preclude the courts from issuing an order authorizing a birth certificate that does not list the mother's name.[12] We agree; the only matter remaining is construing the parentage statutes in a way that affords women the same opportunity to deny parentage as men have.

The paternity statute was added to the Family Law Article in 1984 [when today's assisted reproductive technologies did not exist. It] provides an opportunity for genetically unlinked males to avoid parentage, while genetically unlinked females do not have the same option. This Court has [applied strict scrutiny to find] that any action by the State, without a substantial basis, that imposes a burden on, or grants a benefit to one sex, and not to the other, violates the Maryland Equal Rights Amendment. . . . This Court has long held that a statute will be construed to avoid a conflict with the Constitution whenever that course is possible.

The language of the paternity statute need not be rewritten. Interpreting the statute to extend the same rights to women and maternity as it applies — and works quite well — to men and paternity is all that is required. [We thus] hold that it is within a trial court's power to order the MDVR to issue a birth certificate that contains only the father's name.

The Circuit Court opined that "it is not in the best interests of the minor child [to remove the surrogate mother's name from the birth certificate]." The only explanation it provides, however, is as follows:

> There are a lot of public policy reasons why it is not in the best interests of the child not to have the mother's name on the birth certificate.
> There are health reasons why you might want to have, and it would be good to have the mother's name on the birth certificate, and have that information available."

It is clear, however, that, the trial court's explanation aside, the best interests of the child ("BIC") standard [which controls in adoption cases and custody disputes between parents] does not apply to the unusual circumstance in the case sub judice. . . . In the case sub judice, a third party desires to relinquish

---

12. We note that §4-211 (a) (2) (iii) allows for a new birth certificate to be issued when a man is later determined, as a result of a paternity action, to be the father of a child. Under the provisions set forth in this case, a later-determined mother's name could also be added to the certificate.

parental rights, not assert them. There simply is no contest over parental rights. There is no issue of unfitness on the part of the father. Moreover, there is nothing with which to measure the father's ability to be a parent against, in order for a trial court to rule that it is not in the best interests of the child to grant the father the relief he seeks. Accordingly, the implication by the trial court that the BIC standard should be used in the case sub judice is inappropriate, and its use by the trial court was error. . . .

It requires noting that surrogacy contacts, that is, payment of money for a child, are illegal in Maryland [where statutes prohibit the sale of a minor and payment therefore.] Finally, we reiterate that the Division of Vital Records has expressed no objection to the removal of the gestational carrier's name from the birth certificate in response to an order of the Court. . . .

Dissenting opinion by CATHELL, J. . . .

This case illustrates that the process of manufacturing children can lead to unusual situations that would have been virtually inconceivable decades ago when the relevant statutory scheme was enacted. I do not necessarily agree or disagree that the remedy for the present situation created by the majority is appropriate or otherwise. I think it is wrong for the majority to fashion, in the first instance, the public policy it is creating as a remedy. The issues present in this case, going as they do to the very heart of a society, are, in my view, a matter for the Legislative Branch of government and not initially for the courts.

It is important to note what this case is not. It is not about a woman, married or otherwise, wanting to be a mother, who has difficulty in conceiving through sexual intercourse or who does not want to conceive through sexual intercourse or direct artificial insemination, and thus wants to have her egg fertilized outside her body and then implanted back into her womb where she will, hopefully, be able to give natural birth to a child she will raise as the mother. This case has nothing to do with attempts to cope with female fertility problems of any kind. In this case (so far as the record reflects), there is no woman, genetic mother, birth mother, or otherwise, who wants to mother the resulting child or who wants her name on the birth certificate.

This is simply the case, apparently, of a man who wants to be a father and, recognizing that he could not do it by himself, went out and arranged for (perhaps hired) two different women and an assembler to help him manufacture a child—one woman to donate (or sell) the egg (a genetic mother), a technician (apparently paid) to fertilize the egg in a dish,[1] and another woman (the birth mother) to carry the fetus through the gestation period and then to eject the child in what would normally be considered the birthing process. At the end of this manufacturing process, the result is a child who, according to the majority, is to have no mother at birth.

The hospital, having some familiarity with normal birthing processes, understandably perceives what happens to be a birth and places the name of the woman from whence the child has come (at least the child emerged from the birth canal of the woman), on the birth certificate as required by State law. Everybody, (except the child and the hospital) then claims foul because

---

1. The record is unclear as to the source of the sperm.

the law requires the naming of a mother on a birth certificate. Then the majority of this Court joins the clamor and decrees that the child has no mother at birth — a concept thought impossible for tens of thousands of years.

One supposes that under the aegis of what is occurring in this case, that if a source of sperm does not intend to be a father, he could assert that he was not the father, and under the theories of the majority, a child could come into the world with neither a mother nor a father at birth.[3]

. . . What the majority fails to realize in its opinion, is that what a man is doing when he challenges paternity is that he denies his particular involvement in fertilizing an egg and thus he asserts he is not the particular or correct father of the child — a man is not asserting that the child has no father at all. In the present case, what the majority does, is to establish as a matter of public policy that it is possible for there to be a denial of all maternity, i.e., that there is no mother at all at birth, not that a particular woman is not the mother. . . . With the majority's decision today, if a genetic and/or birth mother does not intend to act as a mother during this manufacturing process — they have no responsibility as a mother. . . . If a genetic mother and a birth mother can deny maternity because neither intended to be mothers, men, who at the time of intercourse in many instances do not intend to be fathers either, can certainly present an argument that they are being discriminated against. If genetic and birth mothers can deny all maternity, why cannot genetic fathers and fathers present at birth deny all paternity[?] In so far as the Constitution is concerned, it would make no difference if the child results from accident or intent. One could even logically determine that a person who intends conception to occur (for whatever purpose), as opposed to one who hopes it would not, should have at least some, if not more, of a support burden. . . .

Additionally, the literature relating to families is replete with conclusions respecting the value of having fathers as a part of the process of family life — available from the birth of the child. Certainly there is similar, or even greater, value in having mothers involved in the rearing of children. Until now, I presume that it was not thought necessary to specifically relate such issues to females in that mothers obviously were going to be present at birth. But with this case, according to the majority, there is to be no mother — just a petri dish.

One only has to contemplate what might occur as the child matures, in order to believe that this issue is best left to the representatives of the people. What happens when a child is asked to present a birth certificate at a customs

---

3. With the majority's decision today that the mother from whom the child is delivered is not to be considered the mother (and apparently the donor of the egg is not to be considered the mother), the Court opens up the very real possibility that completely disinterested persons will (or could) commence the manufacture of children. For instance, an entrepreneur could contract with a sperm donor, contract with an egg donor, contract with an assembler, contract with a woman to carry the child through the gestation period, and a child could be manufactured with neither a mother nor a father. The child could then be put up for adoption at a price — and a new business, in the spirit of American ingenuity, is created. That is, of course, if it can be determined who, if anybody or any entity, would have custody of the child. This is, I realize, virtually incomprehensible to reasoned thought — but, why will it not be something that can happen on the way down the "slippery slope" created by the majority?

area in a foreign country (until recently that is all that was required of American citizens in many countries, and remains so in some) and a customs inspector sees that the birth certificate indicates that the person standing in front of him or her states that the person has no mother — or even no father *or* mother? What happens when the child presents such a birth certificate to authorities outside (or inside) this State in an attempt to acquire a passport? What happens when such a certificate is presented in the admission processes of colleges or presented when one wants to enlist in the armed services? How is the child going to be adversely affected throughout its minority when it has no mother from whom support can be obtained — and no mother at all? There are many reasons why the General Assembly might decide that it is in the best interests of children to have a surrogate or donor mother's name on a birth certificate and that, if afterwards she could establish that she should not have the obligations of a mother, she could seek the termination of her status in order to end her legal responsibility. But the Court assumes the policy mantle instead. . . .

Dissenting Opinion by HARRELL, J., which RAKER, J., Joins. . . .

The Majority opinion supplies a judicial gloss to the Maryland statutory scheme [chauvinistically titled "Paternity Proceedings"], ostensibly in order to avoid declaring the statute violative of equal protection principles, a conclusion it indicates it otherwise would reach if forced to confront the challenge frontally. . . .

This case proceeded essentially as what tennis players call a walkover. That is, there was no opponent on the other side of the net; no person or entity to expose or test Appellant's contentions, factual or legal; a situation which the Majority opinion sweeps up and describes simply as "the unusual procedural posture of this case." . . . We believe the interests of the children need to be heard and considered. We would remand the case and direct the trial judge to appoint counsel for the twins and compel Appellant to pay their counsel's legal fees. Only then might a record be made upon which we might be satisfied that we should go where the Majority opinion goes. . . . It should not be left entirely to judicial conjecture and creativity, however, what the universe of those reasons may be. This record begs for further development before we come to grips with the issues decided by the Majority opinion. If Appellant wishes us to lead through uncharted Maryland waters in an area where the Legislature is better suited to consider the competing legal and societal values, but may have been unwilling to do so, he needs to do a better job of persuading us if he wants our vote. . . .

## NOTES AND QUESTIONS

1. *Rationale?* What is the basis of the majority's decision in *Roberto d.B.*? Does the majority apply intent-based parentage, discussed in *K.M.*, supra, to decide that Roberto is the twins' only parent? Or does it use some other test? To what extent does Judge Cathell's dissent correctly distinguish this case from those in which a man successfully denies paternity? Does the state's Equal Rights Amendment (ERA) compel the result? Are men and women "similarly situated" for purposes of the analysis required in parentage cases? See also

Soos v. Superior Ct., 897 P.2d 1356 (Ariz. Ct. App. 1994) (holding that women must have rights, equal to men, to rebut the presumption of parentage). But cf. Amy G. v. M.W., 47 Cal. Rptr. 3d 297 (Ct. App. 2006) (declining to apply the presumption of legitimacy to biological father's wife, despite equal protection arguments). What problems, if any, do you discern in the approach of Dantzig v. Biron, 2008 WL 187532 (Ohio Ct. App. 2008), which holds that the genetic mother is a necessary party in an action to establish paternity of children born to a gestational surrogate using donated eggs?

2. *Same-sex marriage.* What implications does the skepticism of Maryland courts for sex-based classifications have for laws excluding same-sex couples from marriage? What rationale might explain why Maryland's highest court, after deciding *Roberto d.B.*, would conclude that the prohibition on same-sex marriage does not violate the state E.R.A.? Conaway v. Deane, 932 A.2d 571 (Md. 2007). See id. at 680-681 (Battaglia, J., dissenting) (invoking *Roberto d.B.* to contend that a law limiting marriage to male-female couples requires strict scrutiny). In which context are differences between males and females more salient and arguably justified—in reproduction or marriage? Why?

3. *The motherhood mystique.* If women can choose to be the sole parent of a child born by donor insemination, see Chapter 6, section B1, does equal protection require a legal avenue for men to achieve the same family status? Why is the idea of a child without a mother more unsettling than the idea of a child without a father? See also J.F. v. D.B., 879 N.E.2d 740, 743 (Ohio 2007) (Cupp, J., dissenting) (gestational surrogacy contract violates public policy because "it would be necessary to legally declare that the children do not have a mother"). What does "mother" mean in the era of assisted reproduction? The *Roberto d.B.* majority found it unnecessary to address this assertion made by appellant:

> [I]n this case, the gestational carrier who actually gave birth to the children is not genetically related to the children in any way, but might be considered the birth mother. And the person who is, in fact, genetically related to the children, and might be considered the mother of the children under a genetic definition of the term, is not listed anywhere. So, who actually belongs on the birth certificate as mother depends entirely on the definition accorded to the term.

923 A.2d at 125 n.14. How would you define "mother"? To what extent does a functional test for parentage distinguish gestation, which only women can perform, from the genetic contributions, which men and women alike can make? Does an emphasis on gestation reinforce stereotypical gender roles and constitute sex discrimination? Cf. Jennifer Hendricks, Essentially a Mother, 13 Wm. & Mary J. Women & L. 429 (2007).

Is motherhood important because the law has made it so? Note, historically, the legally determinative role played the status of a child's mother, from the presumption of legitimacy (see Chapter 1, section B1a) to the antebellum rule that made the offspring of slave mothers the property of the master. See Camille A. Nelson, American Husbandry: Legal Norms Impacting the Production of (Re)productivity, 19 Yale J.L. & Feminism 1, 17-20 (2007).

4. *Gay male couples.* What does *Roberto d.B.* mean for gay male couples? Does it pave the way for a default rule, requiring no judicial intervention, that

would list two fathers on a birth certificate, just as cases based on a presumption of legitimacy applied to lesbian couples produce a default rule naming two mothers at the time of birth? See Susan Frelich Appleton, Presuming Women: Revisiting the Presumption of Legitimacy in the Same-Sex Couples Era, 86 B.U. L. Rev. 227 (2006); Jessica Hawkins, My Two Dads: Challenging Gender Stereotypes in Applying California's Recent Supreme Court Cases to Gay Couples, 41 Fam. L.Q. 623 (2007). Anecdotal evidence indicates that many surrogates prefer to work with male couples. See, e.g., Ginia Bellafante, Surrogate Mothers' New Niche: Bearing Babies for Gay Couples, N.Y. Times, May 27, 2005, at A1. What reasons might explain this preference? For a critique of the new Uniform Parentage Act's treatment of children born to same-sex couples by assisted reproduction, see Mary Patricia Byrn, From Right to Wrong: A Critique of the 2000 Uniform Parentage Act, 16 UCLA Women's L.J. 163 (2007).

5. *Gestational surrogacy arrangements.* To what extent do gestational surrogacy arrangements avoid the problems, whether based in law or policy, presented by "traditional surrogacy arrangements," exemplified in *Baby M*, Chapter 6, section A2? As noted, the practice of assisted reproduction now splits gestational and genetic contributions in surrogacy arrangements, as illustrated in *Roberto d.B.*, in order to prevent outcomes such as that in *Baby M.* Unif. Parentage Act (2000, amended 2002), 9B U.L.A. 361 (2001) (prefatory cmt. to Art. 8 before 2002 amendments).

A majority of the Ohio supreme court has determined that gestational surrogacy contracts do not violate public policy, thus embracing an intent-based approach and upholding an agreement against a gestational surrogate seeking to assert parental rights, including custody, over triplets conceived using donor eggs. J.F. v. D.B., 879 N.E.2d 740 (Ohio 2007). The court observed:

> A written contract defining the rights and obligations of the parties seems an appropriate way to enter into [a] surrogacy agreement. If the parties understand their contract rights, requiring them to honor the contract they entered into is manifestly right and just.

Id. at 741. According to the dissenting opinion, agreements among unrelated persons for the creation of a child for payment violate public policy, enforcement requires a legal declaration that the children have no mother, and the ruling will make Ohio "an interstate, and perhaps international, marketplace for gestational surrogacy," given the more restrictive approaches in other jurisdictions. Id. at 744 (Cupp, J., dissenting). See also J.F. v. D.B., 941 A.2d 718 (Pa. Super. Ct. 2008) (child support dispute growing out of same contract); Robert E. Rains, What the Erie "Surrogate Triplets" Can Teach State Legislatures About the Need to Enact Article 8 of the Uniform Parentage Act (2000), 56 Clev. St. L. Rev. 1 (2008) (recounting additional details of the controversy).

6. *"Manufacturing process" versus "embryo adoption."* Judge Cathell, dissenting, likens the process employed by Roberto to a "manufacturing process" and distinguishes the arrangement here from a situation in which a woman, married or not, turns to assisted reproduction. What's the difference? How

would Judge Cathell categorize the arrangement in In re Marriage of Buzzanca, 72 Cal. Rptr. 2d 280 (Ct. App. 1998), in which the intended parents' commissioned a surrogate to gestate donated genetic material (and the court recognized the intended parents as the child's legal parents)?

Professor Elizabeth Bartholet uses the term "technological adoptions" for arrangements in which the intended parents have no genetic relationship to the expected child. Elizabeth Bartholet, Family Bonds: Adoption and the Politics of Parenting 219 (1999). Abortion opponents use the term "embryo adoption" for what others call "embryo donation." E.g., Sarah Blustain, Embryo Adoption, N.Y. Times, Dec. 11, 2005, §6 (Magazine), at 67. How does the terminology affect our understanding of adoption, with its traditional emphasis on child welfare? Should the law encourage or discourage such advances? Congress has authorized funding to promote the practice. See Paula J. Manning, Baby Needs a New Set of Rules: Using Adoption Doctrine to Regulate Embryo Donation, 5 Geo. J. Gender & L. 677, 678 (2004). Professor Garrison would recommend adoption procedures in such cases. Marsha Garrison, Law Making for Baby Making: An Interpretive Approach to the Determination of Legal Parentage, 113 Harv. L. Rev. 835, 917-920 (2000) (noted supra section C1). Would additional restrictions on the use of such reproductive technologies prompt more adoptions of already-born children awaiting placements? On the other hand, "why do infertile couples alone and not all persons who reproduce have the obligation to adopt kids in need of parents"? John A. Robertson, Children of Choice: Freedom and the New Reproductive Technologies 277 (1993).

7. *Race and class.* In Johnson v. Calvert, 851 P.2d 776 (Cal. 1993) (discussed in K.M. v. E.G., supra), the gestational surrogate was part African-American; the genetic, intended mother was Filipina; and the genetic, intended father was white. Janet L. Dolgin, Just a Gene: Judicial Assumptions About Parenthood, 40 UCLA L. Rev. 637, 687 (1993). To what extent did the race of the parties influence the court's decision to recognize the intended parents as the legal parents? See April L. Cherry, Nurturing in the Service of White Culture: Racial Subordination, Gestational Surrogacy, and the Ideology of Motherhood, 10 Tex. J. Women & L. 83 (2001). Will gestational surrogacy produce a new class of poor and minority women who provide care for the children of wealthy whites — prenatally? See, e.g., Dorothy E. Roberts, Spiritual and Menial Housework, 9 Yale J.L. & Feminism 51 (1997); Angie Godwin McEwen, Note, So You're Having Another Woman's Baby: Economics and Exploitation in Gestational Surrogacy, 32 Vand. J. Transnat'l L. 271 (1999).

To what extent does a preference for white babies explain why the infertile might choose "embryo adoption" over conventional adoption? Alternatively, does the use of the term "adoption" in this new context reinforce adoption's stigma by suggesting "there is something deeply suspect" about parenting someone else's child? Bartholet, supra, at 69. Cf. Matter of Doe, 793 N.Y.S.2d 878 (Sur. Ct. 2005) (applying adoption exclusion in settlor's trust to his daughter's twins, born to gestational surrogate with donor ova). See generally Susan Frelich Appleton, Adoption in the Age of Reproductive Technology, 2004 U. Chi. Legal F. 393, 438-442; Katheryn D. Katz, Snowflake Adoptions and Orphan Embryos: The Legal Implications of Embryo

Donations, 18 Wis. Women's L.J. 179 (2003); Charles P. Kindregan & Maureen McBrien, Embryo Donation: Unresolved Legal Issues in the Transfer of Surplus Cryopreserved Embryos, 49 Vill. L. Rev. 169 (2004). For additional legislative proposals, see Becky A. Ray, Comment, Embryo Adoptions: Thawing Inactive Legislatures with a Proposed Uniform Law, 28 S. Ill. U. L.J. 423 (2004). In contrast to adoption, does the use of donated genetic material raise the specter of eugenics? What sort of regulation might respond to this concern? See, e.g. Diane B. Paul, On Drawing Lessons from the History of Eugenics, in Reprogenetics: Law, Policy, and Ethical Issues 3 (Lori P. Knowles & Gregory E. Kaebnick, eds. 2007).

8. *Payment for gestational services.* In addition to permitting participants to avoid the conclusion in *Baby M* that a "traditional surrogate" is the child's mother, do paid gestational surrogacy arrangements also avoid the application of baby-selling prohibitions? What are the intended parents purchasing from a gestational surrogate? What is the value of gestational services? Does the *amount* of payment influence the perception of surrogacy as exploitation versus well-earned employment compensation? What do you think of the approach followed by some attorneys who advise their clients working as gestational surrogates to treat the payments as child support, which does not constitute taxable income under the Internal Revenue Code, I.R.C. §71(c) (2008).

Suppose a paid gestational surrogate works for an employer covered by the Family and Medical Leave Act, Family and Medical Leave Act, 29 U.S.C. §§2601-2654 (2008), so that she would otherwise be entitled to twelve weeks of leave and a return to her job (either because of her own incapacity during pregnancy and delivery or in order to care for the child after birth). Does the fact that she has contracted to serve as a paid gestational surrogate change the employer's obligations under the law? Should it?

If a gestational surrogate decides to keep the children, must she reimburse the commissioning individual or couple for her fee and other expenses? See J.F. v. D.B., 848 N.E.2d 873 (Ohio Ct. App. 2006) (upholding contract and requiring reimbursement), *aff'd in part, rev'd in part, & remanded,* 879 N.E.2d 740 (Ohio 2007) (holding contract does not violate public policy, but remanding on issues of breach and assessment of damages). Whose medical insurance policy should cover the health care expenses of the gestational surrogate during pregnancy and at delivery? See Florida Health Science Ctr., Inc. v. Rock, 2006 WL 3201873 (M.D. Fla. 2006).

9. *Limitations.*

a. *Egg selling.* What limits would you recommend on payment for egg donation? Many college newspapers publish advertisements for young, white donors, with high SAT scores. See Kenneth Baum, Golden Eggs: Towards the Rational Regulation of Oocyte Donation, 2001 BYU L. Rev. 107; Julia D. Mahoney, The Market for Human Tissue, 86 Va. L. Rev. 163 (2000). See generally Sarah Terman, Note & Comment, Marketing Motherhood: Rights and Responsibilities of Egg Donors in Assisted Reproductive Technology Agreements, 3 Nw. J.L. & Soc. Pol'y 167 (2008). Some fertility clinics have oocyte sharing programs, allowing patients to receive treatment for reduced fees in exchange for donating some of their eggs to other patients. What is the proper way to balance autonomy, protection from exploitation, and fair compensation for hormonal therapy and surgery that entail some risks? See The Ethics Committee of the American Society for Reproductive Medicine, Financial Compensation of Oocyte Donors, 88 Fertility & Sterility 305 (2007) (more than $5,000 requires justification, more than $10,000 is inappropriate, and sharing programs need clear and fair policies), available at http://www.asrm.org/Media/Ethics/financial_incentives.pdf.

With respect to rules allowing or prohibiting payments, should the law treat sperm, eggs, and embryos alike? Why? See generally Martha M. Ertman, What's Wrong with a Parenthood Market? A New and Improved Theory of Commodification, 82 N.C. L. Rev. 1, 14-16 (2003). While conceding an existing commerce in sperm and eggs, the President's Council on Bioethics has called for interim legislation prohibiting the purchase and sale of human embryos. Why? See The President's Council on Bioethics, Reproduction and Responsibility: The Regulation of New Biotechnologies 226-227 (2004).

What reasons might support payments for genetic material? See Naomi R. Cahn, Test Tube Families: Why the Fertility Market Needs Legal Regulation 161 (2009). For an extended profile of a law student-egg donor, see Rebecca Mead, Eggs for Sale, The New Yorker, Aug. 9, 1999, at 56.

b. *Screening.* Should the state screen intended parents who use assisted reproduction, as adoption law requires? What limits ought to govern? Should the law condition surrogacy on the intended mother's infertility? See Robin Fretwell Wilson, Uncovering the Rationale for Requiring Infertility in Surrogacy Arrangements, 29 Am. J.L. & Med. 337 (2003). Should social factors, such as marital status, play a role? May embryo donors themselves screen the recipients? See Mark W. Premo-Hopkins, Comment, Between Organs and Adoption: Why Pre-Embryo Donors Should Not Be Allowed to Discriminate Against Recipients, 2006 U. Chi. Legal F. 441.

c. *Age.* In response to pregnancies achieved by postmenopausal women using donor eggs, France enacted legislation restricting infertility procedures to living heterosexual couples of childbearing age. Sherri A. Jayson, Comment, "Loving Infertile Couple Seeks Woman Age 18-31 to Help Have Baby. $6,500 Plus Expenses and a Gift": Should We Regulate the Use of Assisted Reproductive Technologies by Older Women?, 11 Alb. L.J. Sci. & Tech. 287, 325-327 (2001). See also Terry Wilkinson, Fertility Law Divides Italians, L.A. Times, June 11, 2005, at A3 (attributing support for Italy's new restrictions, in part, to past "granny births"). Would similar legislation in the United States survive constitutional challenge? Does "old" parenthood pose harm to children? Parents? Society? Should similar restrictions apply to alternative insemination to deter old fatherhood? Such questions followed reports of the birth of a daughter to a 63-year-old California woman, who used a donor egg. See Gina Kolata, Childbirth at 63 Says What About Life?, N.Y. Times, Apr. 27, 1997, §1, at 20.

10. *Other countries.* Surrogacy was legalized in Israel in 1996 with the passage of the Surrogate Motherhood Agreements Law, 1996 S.H. 1577. By March 2004, 78 children had been born there by surrogacy, and no birth mothers had attempted to breach the agreement. The legislation permits only gestational surrogacy in which the surrogate has no genetic connection

to the child. A governmental committee must approve all surrogate agreements. Many of the legal requirements for surrogacy are based on religious ("halachic") considerations: the surrogate must be unmarried, a nonrelative of the commissioning parents, and a member of the same religion as the intended mother; the sperm must be that of the intended father (although egg donation is permitted). In addition, all parties must be adults and residents of Israel. Government protocols specify that surrogates must not undergo more than seven implantation attempts during an 18-month period; prohibit surrogacy by birth mothers who are older than 40, who have more than 5 previous births, and who have undergone 2 previous caesarean sections; the intended mother must be age 48 or younger, and the intended father must be 59 or younger. The intended mother must document her infertility or her inability to carry a child to term. Payments are permitted to cover actual costs, compensation for inactivity, suffering, lost income, or temporary loss of earning ability, or any other reasonable compensation. See D. Kelly Weisberg, The Birth of Surrogacy in Israel 197-200 (2005).

The law in the United Kingdom generally recognizes the woman carrying the pregnancy as the mother, but authorizes a court order treating the "applicants" as a child's parents. Applicants must be a couple — either married, civil partners, or a pair "who are living as partners in an enduring family relationship and are not within prohibited degrees" for intimate relationships; further, the child must be conceived with the gametes of one of the applicants. Single persons remain ineligible for parental orders. Human Fertilisation and Embryology Act of 2008, ch. 22, §§33, 54 (U.K.); Human Fertilisation and Embryology Act 2008: Explanatory Notes 32, available at http://www.opsi.gov.uk/acts/acts2008/en/ukpgaen_20080022_en.pdf. For other international perspectives on surrogacy, see Surrogate Motherhood: International Perspectives (Rachel Cook & Shelley Day Sclater eds., 2003); Vanessa S. Browne-Barbour, Bartering for Babies: Are Preconception Agreements in the Best Interests of Children?, 26 Whittier L. Rev. 429, 460-467 (2004).

## PROBLEMS

1. Robert and his wife, Denise, arranged to have a Denise bear a child conceived from embryos created for them with Robert's sperm and eggs from an anonymous donor. Clinic doctors transferred some of the embryos not only to Denise but also to Susan, an unmarried woman who arranged to become a single mother with an embryo from anonymous donors. Denise gave birth to a girl and Susan a boy — genetic siblings. After the clinic disclosed the error, Robert and Denise sue for parental rights to the boy while Susan asserts that she is his sole legal parent. Whom should the court recognize as the parents? Why? Can intent-based parentage resolve this dispute? Should the court give both families some access to the child? See Robert B. v. Susan B., 135 Cal. Rptr. 2d 785 (Ct. App. 2003); Marjorie M. Shultz, Taking Account of ARTs in Determining Parenthood: A Troubling Dispute in California, 19 Wash. U. J.L. & Pol'y 77 (2005).

If the mix-up had resulted in one woman giving birth to twin boys, one of whom was genetically hers and her husband's and the other the genetic child of a second married couple, would your answers change? Suppose the error were disclosed before the twins' birth. Suppose the second couple's own efforts to have a child had failed—so the twin in question was their only chance for offspring. Suppose the first couple and their genetic son are Caucasian and the second couple and the second twin are African-American. See Perry-Rogers v. Fasano, 715 N.Y.S.2d 19 (App. Div. 2000); Leslie Bender, Genes, Parents, and Assisted Reproductive Technologies: ARTs, Mistakes, Sex, Race, & Law, 12 Colum. J. Gender & L. 1 (2003). Suppose the mix-up in either case resulted not from negligence but from the clinic's deliberate misuse of genetic material, malfeasance that came to light several years after the children were born. See Prato-Morrison v. Doe, 126 Cal. Rptr. 2d 509 (Ct. App. 2002); Alice M. Noble-Allgire, Switched at the Fertility Clinic: Determining Maternal Rights When a Child Is Born from Stolen or Misdelivered Genetic Material, 64 Mo. L. Rev. 517 (1999). See Women Whose Eggs Were Stolen at UC Irvine Paid 23m So Far, S.F. Chron., June 26, 2007, at B6 (reporting settlements in *Prato-Morrison*, litigation stemming from the birth of about a dozen children from stolen genetic material).

2. Jim and Tom, a gay couple, live in a state that has neither same-sex marriage nor legally recognized domestic partnerships but has enacted the new UPA, as amended in 2002. They locate a woman willing to serve as a commercial surrogate for them. The court refuses to grant the necessary pre-conception adoption, however, because the legislation specifically refers to "[t]he man and the woman who are the intended parents." Unif. Parentage Act §801(b) (2000, amended 2002), 9B U.L.A. 58 (Supp. 2008). On what basis can Jim and Tom challenge this restriction? Will they succeed? How would their challenge fare if they were attacking instead the 2000 version of the UPA, which specified that the intended parents must be a married couple? Unif. Parentage Act §801(b) (2000), 9B U.L.A. 362 (2001). See Brooke Dianah Rodgers-Miller, Adam and Steve and Eve: Why Sexuality Segregation in Assisted Reproduction in Virginia Is No Longer Acceptable, 11 Wm. & Mary J. Women & L. 293 (2005). In each scenario, how would the recognition of same-sex marriage or domestic partnerships change the result? See generally Marla J. Hollandsworth, Gay Men Creating Families Through Surro-Gay Arrangements: A Paradigm for Reproductive Freedom, 3 Am. U. J. Gender & L. 183 (1995); Ann MacLean Massie, Restricting Surrogacy to Married Couples: A Constitutional Problem? The Married-Parent Requirement in the Uniform Status of Children of Assisted Conception Act, 18 Hastings Const. L.Q. 487 (1991). See also Byrn, supra.

3. Ruth and Rob have discovered that he is infertile. They wish to have a child, but they find abhorrent the thought of using a third party's genetic material, as donor insemination would require. Assume that the directors of a research laboratory have told them that it might be possible to create an embryo from genetic material provided by Ruth alone. Their state, however, is one of several banning human reproductive cloning. E.g., Cal. Health & Safety Code §24185 (2008); R.I. Gen. Laws §23-16.4-2 (2008). What constitutional challenges can they raise against the state ban? Do their reasons for pursuing cloning matter? Will their challenge succeed? See Lori B. Andrews, Is There a Right to Clone? Constitutional Challenges to Bans on Human Cloning,

in The Reproductive Rights Reader: Law, Medicine, and the Construction of Motherhood 320 (Nancy Ehrenreich ed., 2008); Jessica Lin Lewis, Predicting the Judicial Response to an Asserted Right to Reproductive Cloning, 29 J. Legal Med. 523 (2008); Cass R. Sunstein, Is There a Constitutional Right to Clone?, 53 Hastings L.J. 987 (2002) (part of symposium "Conceiving a Code for Creation: The Legal Debate Surrounding Human Cloning"). See also Yuriko Mary Shikai, Don't Be Swept Away by Mass Hysteria: The Benefits of Human Reproductive Cloning and its Future, 33 Sw. U. L. Rev. 259 (2004); Evelyne Shuster, Human Cloning: Category, Dignity, and the Role of Bioethics, 17 Bioethics 518 (2003). See generally Kerry Lynn Macintosh, Illegal Beings: Human Clones and the Law (2005); Bonnie Steinbock, Reproductive Cloning: Another Look, 2006 U. Chi. Legal F. 87 (reviewing debate and concluding that the only real problems are safety based—a situation that might change). Would two women partners, seeking to combine their genetic material using a variation on cloning techniques have a stronger or weaker constitutional case against the cloning ban than Ruth and Rob?

## Depictions in Popular Culture: Kazuo Ishiguro, Never Let Me Go (2005)

In this haunting dystopian novel Kathy H., the narrator, reminisces in rich detail about her pleasant-enough years at Hailsham, a British boarding school that seems to lack the opportunities and facilities that surely would be available at an institution reputed to be the best, as Hailsham is. Yet everyone seems to accept not only the absence of the privileges one would expect but also other apparent absences. Why do Kathy and her classmates never mention their parents or other family members? How do they know they will never have children? And what does it mean to become, after leaving Hailsham, a "carer" and then a "donor"? While depicting familiar experiences of childhood, Ishiguro subtly communicates that something here is eerily unfamiliar. Slowly, the reader begins to decipher the role of Kathy and her friends in a world in which therapeutic cloning has become an established practice, offering valuable medical treatment to some— but not all—segments of the population.

One reviewer asks whether, in selecting the theme of cloning, Ishiguro is "issuing a warning about the ethics of reproductive science." Sarah Kerr, When They Were Orphans, N.Y. Times, Apr. 17, 2005, §7, at 16 (book review). She answers her own question as follows:

I suspect Ishiguro's intention is both more personal and more literary. The theme of cloning lets him push to the limit ideas he's nurtured in earlier fiction about memory and the human self. . . .

So the dare Ishiguro has taken on might be this: to capture what is unmistakably human, what survives and insists on subtly expressing itself after you subtract the big stuff—the specific baggage, the parents, orientation toward a culture, a past and possible futures—that shapes people into individuals. . . . At times uncomfortably, for a work that aims to give us a distilled and persevering human essence, we can sense the controlling care with which Ishiguro invents and organizes [Kathy's] memories. Yet if the novel feels a bit too distant to move us to outright heartbreak, it delivers images of odd beauty and a mounting existential distress that hangs around long after we read it.

Id. To the extent the reviewer is correct about Ishiguro's objectives and accomplishments, the novel might still have some relevance to "the ethics of reproductive science." How would you articulate this relevance? Are therapeutic and reproductive cloning distinguishable as a matter of ethics? As a matter of law? What legal implications does the novel have?

# CHAPTER 8

# ASSISTED REPRODUCTION ACROSS STATE AND NATIONAL BOUNDARIES

Divergent approaches to determining the parentage of children born of ARTs and regulatory variations governing ARTs practice show that the law remains in a state of flux. Such differences also invite participants to travel to the most hospitable regime—whether in this country or abroad—in turn raising questions of choice of law, jurisdiction, and enforcement.

## A. PARENTAGE DETERMINATIONS AND THE CONFLICT OF LAWS

### MILLER-JENKINS v. MILLER-JENKINS

661 S.E.2d 822 (Va. 2008)

Opinion by Justice BARBARA MILANO KEENANA

In this appeal, we consider whether the Court of Appeals erred in directing a circuit court to register a custody and visitation order rendered by a Vermont court, based on the Court of Appeals' previous holding in the same custody and visitation dispute that the federal Parental Kidnapping Prevention Act, 28 U.S.C. §1738A (2000 & Supp. V 2005), requires that the courts of this Commonwealth give full faith and credit to the Vermont order.

In 2000, Lisa Miller-Jenkins (Lisa) and Janet Miller-Jenkins (Janet) entered into a civil union (the civil union) in Vermont that was permitted under Vermont law. Lisa and Janet decided that Lisa would bear a child, and in April 2002, after successful artificial insemination, Lisa gave birth to IMJ in Virginia. Lisa, Janet, and IMJ lived together in Virginia until July 2002, when they moved to Vermont, where they lived until September 2003. At that time, Lisa and IMJ returned permanently to Virginia over Janet's objection.

In November 2003, Lisa filed a petition in a Vermont family court (the Vermont court), seeking to dissolve the civil union and to gain custody of

327

IMJ. The Vermont court dissolved the civil union and entered a custody and visitation order (the Vermont custody order) granting temporary custody of IMJ to Lisa and temporary visitation rights to Janet. After initially allowing Janet to visit IMJ in June, Lisa thereafter refused to permit Janet to have contact with IMJ as required by the terms of the Vermont custody order.

On July 1, 2004, Lisa filed a petition in the Frederick County Circuit Court [in Virginia] (the circuit court), asking the circuit court to determine that Lisa was IMJ's "sole parent" and seeking sole custody of IMJ. On July 7, 2004, Janet filed a motion in the Vermont court seeking enforcement of the Vermont custody order and a determination that Lisa was in contempt of that court for her failure to abide by the terms of the Vermont custody order. On July 19, 2004, the Vermont court entered an order holding that the Vermont court had continuing jurisdiction over all custody matters in the case, and that the Vermont court would not defer to an order entered by a court in another state purporting to resolve the issue of custody.

In August 2004, the circuit court entered an order temporarily awarding sole custody of IMJ to Lisa and ordered that IMJ not be removed from Virginia (the Virginia custody order). Because the Vermont custody order included a provision granting Janet scheduled visitation with IMJ in Vermont, the Virginia custody order was in direct conflict with the Vermont custody order. In September 2004, the Vermont court issued an order holding Lisa in contempt for violating the terms of the Vermont custody order.

In October 2004, the circuit court concluded that it had jurisdiction over the custody dispute and entered an order awarding sole custody to Lisa, holding that Janet did not have any parental rights, and that Lisa was IMJ's "sole" parent. In November 2004, the Vermont court issued a contrary order holding that Lisa and Janet were both "parents" of IMJ.

[On appeal by Janet, in] November 2006, the Court of Appeals reversed the circuit court's judgment entering the Virginia custody order, holding that the circuit court did not have jurisdiction to enter the order because the dispute was a "custody and visitation determination" subject to the provisions of the Parental Kidnapping Prevention Act, 28 U.S.C. §1738A (2000 & Supp. V 2005) (the PKPA), which accorded Vermont sole jurisdiction over the custody and visitation dispute. [Miller-Jenkins v. Miller-Jenkins, 637 S.E.2d 330, 337-338 (Va. Ct. App. 2006).] The Court of Appeals concluded that the provisions of the Defense of Marriage Act, 28 U.S.C. §1738C (2000 & Supp. V 2005) (the DOMA), did not alter the applicability of the PKPA to the custody and visitation dispute, and that the PKPA preempted all state law to the contrary, including Code §20-45.3 ([Virginia's] Marriage Affirmation Act).

The Court of Appeals further held in the first Virginia appeal that Vermont law governed the parties' dispute, and that the courts of Virginia were bound by Vermont's interpretation of its own law. Accordingly, based on its holding that Vermont had sole jurisdiction over the case, the Court of Appeals declined to address the issue whether the civil union would have been recognized under Virginia law. Following the Court of Appeals' entry of judgment in the first Virginia appeal, Lisa filed a petition for appeal to this Court. We dismissed Lisa's petition because she failed to file a notice of appeal.

[Janet successfully registered the Vermont custody order in the juvenile and domestic relations court in Virginia; Lisa appealed to the circuit court, which reversed. Janet appealed to the Court of Appeals, which reversed] and reinstated the registration of the Vermont custody order, holding that this result was mandated by the Court of Appeals' decision in the first Virginia appeal. Lisa appeals from the Court of Appeals' judgment.

Addressing the merits of her appeal, Lisa argues that the Court of Appeals erred in concluding that the PKPA requires that Virginia courts give full faith and credit to the Vermont custody order. Lisa maintains that the DOMA, not the PKPA, is applicable in determining whether Virginia must accord full faith and credit to Vermont's child custody orders, and that the Court of Appeals erred in holding that the PKPA preempts the Marriage Affirmation Act and in not addressing whether the PKPA also preempts Article I, §15-A of the Constitution of Virginia (the Virginia Marriage Amendment). Lisa also contends, among other things, that both the Court of Appeals' judgment and the Vermont judgment violated her fundamental parental rights.

Janet argues, however, that this Court should not reach the merits of Lisa's appeal. Janet contends that Lisa's claims are barred by the "law of the case" doctrine because all the issues presented in this appeal were resolved by the Court of Appeals' decision in the first Virginia appeal, which Lisa failed to timely appeal to this Court. Janet maintains that the first Virginia appeal and the present appeal are the same "case," because the present appeal involves the same parties and the same issue of custody and visitation. [The court decides in favor of Janet on this point.]

Our conclusion is not altered by Lisa's argument that the "law of the case" doctrine is inapplicable to the present appeal because this appeal is not the same "case" as the first Virginia appeal. Although Lisa and Janet separately filed the cases from which the two appeals arose, both cases involved these same parties and sought adjudication of the same issue, custody and visitation regarding IMJ. The two Virginia appeals were part of the "same litigation" seeking to resolve the single question which custody order, the Vermont custody order or the circuit court's order, would govern the parties' custody and visitation dispute.

Finally, we observe that the Court of Appeals' holding in the first Virginia appeal is binding under the "law of the case" doctrine only with respect to the parties and the issues in the case before us. Thus, based on our holding that the Court of Appeals' decision in the first Virginia appeal is the "law of the case," we do not reach the merits of the underlying issues presented in this appeal. [Affirmed.]

---

The principal case represents the culmination of a series of opinions issued by courts in Vermont and Virginia. The United States Supreme Court has repeatedly declined to hear the case, denying certiorari to rulings in Vermont and Virginia, including the principal case, 127 S. Ct. 2130 (2007); 128 S. Ct. 1127 (2008); 129 S. Ct. 306 (2008); and 129 S. Ct. 726 (2008). The following excerpt offers one view of the litigation before the opinion in the principal case was issued:

---

### APRIL WITT, ABOUT ISABELLA

Washington Post, Feb. 4, 2007, at W14

. . . As with other couples who have split, [the truths of Janet and Lisa] have diverged; through the lens of loss, each views their time together differently. Unlike most warring couples, however, the once hopeful and happy Miller-Jenkinses are at the center of a high-stakes, ideologically charged legal dispute waged across several courtrooms in two states. On one side are lawyers who are leading gay-rights activists; on the other are legal combatants for a conservative Christian foundation associated with Jerry Falwell.

These lawyers are sifting through every detail of the Miller-Jenkinses' lives — from how Isabella was conceived to who burped the baby. They are not fighting over the mundane detritus of love lost: Who gets the house? Who gets stuck with the old car? Who is on the hook for braces should Isabella require them? They are debating questions so profound that the answers have the power to affect legions of families gay and straight: Who is a parent? Who has the legal rights of a parent?

In the *Miller-Jenkins* case, those questions have been raised in Vermont, where state statutes explicitly recognize parental rights for same-sex couples in civil unions, and in Virginia, where they don't. That discrepancy has left Isabella — and a growing number of children like her nationwide — on the legal battlefield of what one judge in the case called civil war. . . .

[After Lisa moved from Vermont to Virginia with Isabella in 2003,] Lisa began attending a conservative Christian church. "All those years of going to church, going to Christian schools, all that started to come back to me," Lisa said. She began to wonder, she said, if she really was gay or merely sexually confused as a result of childhood trauma. . . . Lisa was determined to "leave the lifestyle," she said. "It wasn't a struggle," she recalled. "I felt peace." . . .

In early 2004, seven weeks after Lisa asked the court to dissolve their union, Janet filed a counterclaim seeking custody of Isabella for herself and visitation for Lisa. She felt like Isabella was as much her daughter as she was Lisa's, she said. . . .

Lisa didn't doubt that Janet and Isabella loved each other, and that it was in Isabella's best interests for them to see each other regularly, she later testified. She just didn't think that Janet was a legal parent with rights equal to hers. "To me, it was more like Isabella and Janet had a deep friendship," rather than a mother-daughter bond, Lisa said. Janet scoffed: "Friends don't pay child support for other people's kids."

[Lisa's first attorney, Linda Reis, notified the trial judge in Vermont, William Cohen] that they planned to argue that Janet was not Isabella's legal parent. . . . After a few months, Lisa, frustrated by the case's slow pace, decided to change lawyers. [Eventually, she hired Deborah Lashman, a Vermont law firm's expert in civil union law.]

Lashman is a central figure in the history of legal rights for gay parents in Vermont. [She had pioneered second-parent adoption in Vermont.] Lashman later became an outspoken board member of the Vermont Freedom to Marry Task Force, which supports same-sex marriage.

Lisa didn't know any of that when she hired Lashman, she later said. She maxed out new credit cards and borrowed money from her father to send Lashman the $3,000 retainer she requested. [Thirty minutes before the next court hearing, she met Lashman for the first time.] Lisa's new lawyer "told me that she felt that this was a custody case and that we needed to proceed as such," Lisa later testified. "I said, 'No. I don't even feel that she's a parent, so why should she even have visitation or custody.' She said, 'The judge isn't going to go for that,' and I needed . . . to come up with some kind of [visitation] schedule. I said, 'No, I don't agree with it.' And she said, 'You have to get used to the fact that Janet is a parent.' And I said, 'No, I don't.' And then we were called into the courtroom."

According to a transcript of the hearing, Judge Cohen began by saying, "The last time we were in court, when Ms. Reis was representing the plaintiff, there was an issue at that time involving, I believe it was parentage and civil unions and who the parent would be. I understand that there's been a change in tactics, or a change in course, I guess, is a better word."

"Well, I have a different interpretation of the law than Ms. Reis," Lashman told the judge. "My reading of Vermont law is . . . both these folks are legal parents of Isabella."

"Presumed," the judge said.

"Presumed because she was born during the course of the civil union," Lashman said.

"Right," the judge said.

"So I don't think that's an issue at this point," Lashman said.

"That was an issue she raised," the judge noted. "Your client's waiving that issue now?"

"She is, your honor," Lashman said.

Lashman later said in an interview that Lisa knowingly waived her right that day to contest that Janet was [Isabella's] mom. Lisa, however, disputes that [saying that she was nervous and confused and Lashman declined to discuss the matter with her. Later,] Lisa's attorney told her that if she was going to insist that Janet was not Isabella's parent, then Lashman was going to withdraw from the case. Lisa insisted. Lashman withdrew. . . .

Lisa and Janet's breakup had exposed a fundamental flaw in Vermont law, [Lisa's next attorney, Judy Barone] suggested. Vermont's civil union statute made it a rebuttable presumption that Janet was Isabella's parent, yet spelled out no specific grounds for rebuttal. Other Vermont statutes, which predated the civil union law, detailed two routes to establishing legal parental rights: having a biological connection to a child, or adopting. Janet would not meet either of those standards, Barone said. "I think this case is really about the standard in Vermont that we have to be able to establish parentage," Barone told the judge. "What can be more basic and important?" . . .

[On July 1, 2004, Virginia's Marriage Affirmation Act became law.] The new law prohibited civil unions or other contracts "between persons of the same sex purporting to bestow the privileges or obligations of marriage." Furthermore, the law said, same-sex unions performed in other states "shall be void in all respects in Virginia, and any contractual rights created thereby shall be void and unenforceable." . . .

"I believe that no matter what this court does here," Barone told [Judge Cohen in court], "in the long run, it will not be enforceable against Virginia residents, because Virginia has a statute that says that any matter involving civil unions . . . will not be given any credence in the state of Virginia." . . . [Barone called Lashman to testify.]

"Do you agree with me," Barone asked Lashman, that under Vermont law the concept that Janet is Isabella's parent is "a rebuttable presumption?"

"Yes," Lashman said.

"But did you tell her about the rebuttal that she could have to that presumption under the statute?" Barone asked. [Lashman said they did not have that conversation, that she explained to Lisa why Janet was a parent under Vermont's law treating civil unions just like marriages, and that Lisa agreed to waive any argument that Janet was not a parent.]

[Despite losing in the Vermont proceedings, Lisa continued to resist the visitation ordered for Janet.] "I don't see Janet as a parent, first and foremost," Lisa said. "Secondly, I don't want to expose Isabella to Janet's lifestyle. It goes against all my beliefs. I am raising Isabella to pattern herself after Christ. That's my job as a Christian mom. Homosexuality is a sin.

"I didn't give visitation, and God's protected me for two years," Lisa said. "He's protected Isabella, more importantly."

Just a few days earlier, Cohen had held a contempt hearing in Vermont at which he fined Lisa $25 for each day she refused to let Janet see Isabella. The fines were retroactive and mounting. At that point, Lisa owed Janet more than $9,000. Lisa, who, having closed her home-based day-care center and who now earns a modest annual salary teaching at a preschool, already owed legal bills nearing $100,000 and had no way to pay. She said she wasn't worried. . . .

## NOTES AND QUESTIONS

1. *Custody, parentage, and adoption.* The court in the principal case, like the Vermont court before it, treats the litigation as a dispute about child custody and visitation. Thus, it finds controlling the special statutes governing child custody cases, the Uniform Child Custody Jurisdiction Act (UCCJA) and the Parental Kidnapping Prevention Act (PKPA) (examined in Chapter 5, section A). These statutes reflect the fact-intensive nature of custody and visitation adjudications and the modifiability of such decrees. Do you agree that the crux of the litigation in *Miller-Jenkins* is a custody/visitation dispute?

What of Lisa's argument that Janet is not a legal parent at all to Isabella and thus is not a candidate for any parental prerogatives? Did any of the courts address this argument on the merits?

To what extent does Lisa's waiver of the issue, as elaborated in the *Washington Post* story, satisfactorily explain the judicial focus on custody, rather than parentage? And did the court in the principal case refuse to consider the parentage issue only because Lisa failed to file a timely appeal of the first decision of the Virginia court of appeals?

2. *Criteria for parentage: jurisdictional implications.* Recall also the emerging view that the rationale for the UCCJA and PKPA does not apply to adoption cases, which typically do not undertake a comparative assessment of the child's situation and which constitute once-and-for-all decisions, not subject to subsequent modification. Accordingly, the Uniform Adoption Act, not the Uniform Child Custody Jurisdiction and Enforcement Act (discussed in Chapter 5, section A), purport to govern adoption cases.

If, in fact, *Miller-Jenkins* concerns a dispute about who is Isabella's parent, what jurisdictional rules govern? Does the answer depend upon whether the parentage rule in question rests on a single event or datum, such as birth during a civil union or DNA testing, or on more functional criteria, such as parent-like behavior or other conduct that might make one a parent by estoppel or a de facto parent? Why? According to the *Washington Post* story, Lisa's attorney viewed Isabella's birth during the civil union as determinative. The opinion of the Vermont Supreme Court, however, considers such factors as the parties' expectations and intent, Janet's active participation in prenatal care and Isabella's birth, and Janet's performance of a parental role as well as Lisa's explicit treatment of her as a parent. Miller-Jenkins v. Miller-Jenkins, 912 A.2d 951, 970 (Vt. 2006).

3. *A rebuttable presumption?* Suppose that Lisa's attorney had been able to pursue the issue of rebuttal of the presumption of parentage based on the couple's civil union. What sort of evidence would suffice to rebut the presumption? For heterosexual married couples, some courts are increasingly relying on genetic evidence. See Chapter 1, section B1. What would this approach mean for same-sex couples, like Janet and Lisa? See Susan Frelich Appleton, Presuming Women: Revisiting the Presumption of Legitimacy in the Same-Sex Couples Era, 86 B.U. L. Rev. 227, 290-293 (2006).

4. *Finality and full faith and credit.* Do the differences between a custody dispute (as the case was actually decided in Vermont) and a parentage dispute (which Lisa claimed she wanted to litigate in Vermont) have implications for the finality of the outcome of the Vermont proceedings? How would the application of Virginia's Marriage Affirmation Act or the federal Defense of Marriage Act have played out if the Vermont courts had ruled against Lisa on parentage, rather than on custody? Suppose Lisa had prevailed in her arguments in Vermont that Janet has no parental status at all. See Chapter 5, section B. For another case relying on the PKPA to defer to the first forum's adjudication of parentage for a same-sex former partner and to hold that adjudication entitled to full faith and credit, see A.K. v. N.B., 2008 WL 2154098 (Ala. Civ. App. 2008). Cf. Huss v. Huss, 888 N.E.2d 1238 (Ind. 2008) (holding

that pending divorce and custody case in one court precludes another from deciding paternity).

## B. "THE REGULATORY MAP" AND "REPRODUCTIVE TOURISM"[1]

EVANS V. UNITED KINGDOM

(App. no. 6339/05), 1 FLR 1990 (Eur. Ct. H.R. Grand Chamber 2007)

[The applicant and her partner, J, began treatment for IVF at a clinic in Bath, in England. Preliminary tests revealed pre-cancerous tumors that would require the removal of the applicant's ovaries. Ova could be extracted first, but preservation of unfertilized ova for future use has a much lower rate of success than the preservation of fertilized ova. Accordingly, the applicant's eggs were extracted and were used to create with J's sperm six embryos, which were frozen for future use. Both parties were informed that either could withdraw consent for the use of the embryos at any time. Shortly thereafter, surgeons removed the applicant's ovaries. While the embryos were in storage, the couple's relationship broke down, and J notified the clinic of his lack of further consent for the embryos' use, thus obligating the clinic to destroy them under British law, the Human Fertilisation and Embryology Act of 1990 (1990 Act). The applicant sought an injunction requiring J to restore his consent to the embryos' use and storage and a declaration that he could not withdraw his consent. She also sought a declaration that the relevant provisions of the 1990 Act breached her rights under articles (art) 8, 12 and 14 of the Human Rights Act of 1998, and she pleaded that the embryos were entitled to protection under arts 2 and 8 of the Human Rights Act. After a five-day trial, the judge dismissed the applicant's claims. The court of appeal dismissed her appeal, and the House of Lords also refused her leave to appeal. The case then went to a seven-court Chamber of the European Court of Human Rights and ultimately reached that court's Grand Chamber, with 17 judges. The majority of the Grand Chamber reviewed British law and also the law, inter alia, of the Member States of the Council of Europe:]

39. On the basis of the material available to the Court, . . . it would appear that IVF treatment is regulated by primary or secondary legislation in Austria, Azerbaijan, Bulgaria, Croatia, Denmark, Estonia, France, Georgia, Germany, Greece, Hungary, Iceland, Italy, Latvia, the Netherlands, Norway, the Russian Federation, Slovenia, Spain, Sweden, Switzerland, Turkey, Ukraine and the United Kingdom; while in Belgium, the Czech Republic, Finland, Ireland, Malta, Lithuania, Poland, Serbia and Slovakia such treatment is governed by clinical practice, professional guidelines, royal or administrative decree or general constitutional principles.

---

[1] The quoted phrases come from Debora Spar, Perspective: Reproductive Tourism and the Regulatory Map, 352 New Eng. J. Med. 531 (2005).

40. The storage of embryos, for varying lengths of time, appears to be permitted in all the above States where IVF is regulated by primary or secondary legislation, except Germany and Switzerland, where in one cycle of treatment no more than three embryos may be created which are, in principle, to be implanted together immediately, and Italy, where the law permits the freezing of embryos only on exceptional, unforeseen medical grounds.

41. In Denmark, France, Greece, the Netherlands and Switzerland, the right of either party freely to withdraw his or her consent at any stage up to the moment of implantation of the embryo in the woman is expressly provided for in primary legislation. It appears that, as a matter of law or practice, in Belgium, Finland and Iceland there is a similar freedom for either gamete provider to withdraw consent before implantation.

42. A number of countries have, however, regulated the consent issue differently. In Hungary, for example, in the absence of a specific contrary agreement by the couple, the woman is entitled to proceed with the treatment notwithstanding the death of her partner or the divorce of the couple. In Austria and Estonia the man's consent can be revoked only up to the point of fertilisation, beyond which it is the woman alone who decides if and when to proceed. In Spain, the man's right to revoke his consent is recognised only where he is married to and living with the woman. In Germany and Italy, neither party can normally withdraw consent after the eggs have been fertilised. In Iceland, the embryos must be destroyed if the gamete providers separate or divorce before the expiry of the maximum storage period. . . .

[Relevant international texts, such as the Council of Europe Convention on Human Rights and Biomedicine and the Universal Declaration on Bioethics and Human Rights, emphasize the need for consent.]

## The Law

### I. Alleged violation of art 2 of the convention

53. In her original application and in her observations before the Chamber, the applicant complained that the provisions of English law requiring the embryos to be destroyed once J withdrew his consent to their continued storage violated the embryos' right to life, contrary to art 2 of the Convention, which reads as follows: "1. Everyone's right to life shall be protected by law. . . ."

54. In its judgment of 7 March 2006, the Chamber recalled that in Vo v France [2004] ECHR 53924/00 at para 82, the Grand Chamber had held that, in the absence of any European consensus on the scientific and legal definition of the beginning of life, the issue of when the right to life begins comes within the margin of appreciation which the Court generally considers that States should enjoy in this sphere. Under English law, as was made clear by the domestic courts in the present applicant's case, an embryo does not have independent rights or interests and cannot claim — or have claimed on its behalf — a right to life under art 2. There had not, accordingly, been a violation of that provision. . . .

56. The Grand Chamber, for the reasons given by the Chamber, finds that the embryos created by the applicant and J do not have a right to life within the

meaning of art 2, and that there has not, therefore, been a violation of that provision.

## II. Alleged violation of art 8 of the convention

57. The applicant contended that the provisions of [Schedule] 3 to the 1990 Act, which permitted J to withdraw his consent after the fertilisation of her eggs with his sperm, violated her rights to respect for private and family life under art 8 of the Convention, which states:

> "1. Everyone has the right to respect for his private and family life. . . .
> 2. There shall be no interference by a public authority with the exercise of this right except such as is in accordance with the law and is necessary in a democratic society in the interests of national security, public safety or the economic well-being of the country, for the prevention of disorder or crime, for the protection of health or morals, or for the protection of the rights and freedoms of others."

## A. The Chamber Judgment

58. In its judgment of 7 March 2006 the Chamber held, in summary, that art 8 was applicable, since the notion of "private life" incorporated the right to respect for both the decisions to become and not to become a parent. The question which arose under art 8 was "whether there exists a positive obligation on the State to ensure that a woman who has embarked on treatment for the specific purpose of giving birth to a genetically related child should be permitted to proceed to implantation of the embryo notwithstanding the withdrawal of consent by her former partner, the male gamete provider."

59. Given that there was no international or European consensus with regard to the regulation of IVF treatment, the use of embryos created by such treatment, or the point at which consent to the use of genetic material provided as part of IVF treatment might be withdrawn; and since the use of IVF treatment gave rise to sensitive moral and ethical issues against a background of fast-moving medical and scientific developments, the margin of appreciation to be afforded to the respondent State must be a wide one.

60. The 1990 Act was the culmination of an exceptionally detailed examination of the social, ethical and legal implications of developments in the field of human fertilisation and embryology. Its policy was to ensure continuing consent from the commencement of treatment to the point of implantation in the woman. While the pressing nature of the applicant's medical condition required that she and J reach a decision about the fertilisation of her eggs without as much time for reflection and advice as might ordinarily be desired, it was undisputed that it was explained to them both that either was free to withdraw consent at any time before the resulting embryo was implanted in the applicant's uterus. [S]trong policy considerations underlay the decision of the legislature to favour a clear or "bright-line" rule which would serve both to produce legal certainty and to maintain public confidence in the law in a sensitive field. Like the national courts, the Chamber did not find, therefore, that the absence of a power to override a genetic parent's withdrawal of

consent, even in the exceptional circumstances of the applicant's case, was such as to upset the fair balance required by art 8 or to exceed the wide margin of appreciation afforded to the State. . . .

[The applicant argues that the woman's role in IVF is much more extensive and "emotionally involving" than the male's and that a woman in her position would have no way to secure her future prospects of bearing a child if the man can unilaterally withdraw his consent.]

### B. The Court's Assessment
#### 1. The nature of the rights at issue under art 8

71. It is not disputed between the parties that art 8 is applicable and that the case concerns the applicant's right to respect for her private life. The Grand Chamber agrees with the Chamber that "private life," which is a broad term encompassing, inter alia, aspects of an individual's physical and social identity including the right to personal autonomy, personal development and to establish and develop relationships with other human beings and the outside world, incorporates the right to respect for both the decisions to become and not to become a parent.

72. It must be noted, however, that the applicant does not complain that she is in any way prevented from becoming a mother in a social, legal, or even physical sense, since there is no rule of domestic law or practice to stop her from adopting a child or even giving birth to a child originally created in vitro from donated gametes. The applicant's complaint is, more precisely, that the consent provisions of the 1990 Act prevent her from using the embryos she and J created together, and thus, given her particular circumstances, from ever having a child to whom she is genetically related. The Grand Chamber considers that this more limited issue, concerning the right to respect for the decision to become a parent in the genetic sense, also falls within the scope of art 8.

73. The dilemma central to the present case is that it involves a conflict between the art 8 rights of two private individuals: the applicant and J. Moreover, each person's interest is entirely irreconcilable with the other's, since if the applicant is permitted to use the embryos, J will be forced to become a father, whereas if J's refusal or withdrawal of consent is upheld, the applicant will be denied the opportunity of becoming a genetic parent. . . .

74. In addition, the Grand Chamber, like the Chamber, accepts the Government's submission that the case does not involve simply a conflict between individuals; the legislation in question also served a number of wider, public interests, in upholding the principle of the primacy of consent and promoting legal clarity and certainty, for example. . . .

#### 3. The margin of appreciation

77. A number of factors must be taken into account when determining the breadth of the margin of appreciation to be enjoyed by the State in any case under art 8. Where a particularly important facet of an individual's existence or identity is at stake, the margin allowed to the State will be restricted [citations

omitted]. Where, however, there is no consensus within the Member States of the Council of Europe, either as to the relative importance of the interest at stake or as to the best means of protecting it, particularly where the case raises sensitive moral or ethical issues, the margin will be wider [citations omitted]. There will also usually be a wide margin if the State is required to strike a balance between competing private and public interests or Convention rights [citations omitted].

78. The issues raised by the present case are undoubtedly of a morally and ethically delicate nature. . . .

79. In addition, while the Court is mindful of the applicant's submission to treat the comparative law data with caution, it is at least clear, and the applicant does not contend otherwise, that there is no uniform European approach in this field. . . . While the United Kingdom is not alone in permitting storage of embryos and in providing both gamete providers with the power freely and effectively to withdraw consent up until the moment of implantation, different rules and practices are applied elsewhere in Europe. It cannot be said that there is any consensus as to the stage in IVF treatment when the gamete providers' consent becomes irrevocable.

80. While the applicant contends that her greater physical and emotional expenditure during the IVF process, and her subsequent infertility, entail that her art 8 rights should take precedence over J's, it does not appear to the Court that there is any clear consensus on this point either. . . .

81. In conclusion, therefore, since the use of IVF treatment gives rise to sensitive moral and ethical issues against a background of fast-moving medical and scientific developments, and since the questions raised by the case touch on areas where there is no clear common ground amongst the Member States, the Court considers that the margin of appreciation to be afforded to the respondent State must be a wide one.

82. The Grand Chamber, like the Chamber, considers that the above margin must in principle extend both to the State's decision whether or not to enact legislation governing the use of IVF treatment and, once having intervened, to the detailed rules it lays down in order to achieve a balance between the competing public and private interests.

### 4. Compliance with art 8

83. It remains for the Court to determine whether, in the special circumstances of the case, the application of a law which permitted J effectively to withdraw or withhold his consent to the implantation in the applicant's uterus of the embryos created jointly by them struck a fair balance between the competing interests. . . .

90. As regards the balance struck between the conflicting art 8 rights of the parties to the IVF treatment, the Grand Chamber, in common with every other court which has examined this case, has great sympathy for the applicant, who clearly desires a genetically related child above all else. However, given the above considerations, including the lack of any European consensus on this point, it does not consider that the applicant's right to respect for the decision to become a parent in the genetic sense should be accorded greater weight than

J's right to respect for his decision not to have a genetically-related child with her.

91. The Court accepts that it would have been possible for Parliament to regulate the situation differently. However, as the Chamber observed, the central question under art 8 is not whether different rules might have been adopted by the legislature, but whether, in striking the balance at the point at which it did, Parliament exceeded the margin of appreciation afforded to it under that article.

92. The Grand Chamber considers that, given the lack of European consensus on this point, the fact that the domestic rules were clear and brought to the attention of the applicant and that they struck a fair balance between the competing interests, there has been no violation of art 8 of the Convention.

### III. Alleged violation of art 14 of the convention taken in conjunction with art 8

93. In her application and in the proceedings before the Chamber, the applicant complained of discrimination contrary to art 14 taken in conjunction with art 8, reasoning that a woman who was able to conceive without assistance was subject to no control or influence over how the embryos developed from the moment of fertilisation, whereas a woman such as herself who could conceive only with IVF was, under the 1990 Act, subject to the will of the sperm donor. . . .

95. The Grand Chamber agrees with the Chamber and the parties that it is not required to decide in the present case whether the applicant could properly complain of a difference of treatment as compared to another woman in an analogous position, because the reasons given for finding that there was no violation of art 8 also afford a reasonable and objective justification under art 14.

96. Consequently, there has been no violation of art 14 of the Convention.

### For These Reasons, The Court

1. Holds, unanimously, that there has been no violation of art 2 of the Convention;

2. Holds, by thirteen votes to four, that there has been no violation of art 8 of the Convention;

3. Holds, by thirteen votes to four, that there has been no violation of art 14 of the Convention, taken in conjunction with art 8.

[In a joint opinion, the four dissenting judges explained that they would find a violation of article 8 because the interference with the applicant's right to respect for the decision to become a genetically related parent was not necessary or proportionate, under the special circumstances of the case. Invoking for purposes of comparison an infertile man, they would also find a violation of article 14 because the law treats men and women the same even though a "woman is in a different situation as concerns the birth of a child, including where the legislation allows for artificial fertilisation methods."]

HODAS v. MORIN

814 N.E.2d 320 (Mass. 2004)

MARSHALL, C.J.

Does a Probate and Family Court judge have authority pursuant to G. L. c. 215, §6, to issue prebirth judgments of parentage and to order the issuance of a prebirth record of birth, see Culliton v. Beth Israel Deaconess Med. Ctr., 756 N.E.2d 1133 (Mass. 2001), where neither the genetic parents nor the gestational carrier with whom they contracted to bear a child reside in Massachusetts, but where the contract specifies that the birth occur at a Massachusetts hospital? . . . We conclude that, in the circumstances here, the plaintiffs are entitled to the relief they seek: judgments of paternity and maternity and a prebirth order establishing their legal parentage.

1. *Facts.* The plaintiffs, who are married, reside in Connecticut. The gestational carrier and her husband, both nominal defendants, reside in New York. The hospital, the other nominal defendant, is a licensed Massachusetts hospital whose statutory duties include, among others, reporting information concerning births at the hospital to the city or town clerk where the birth occurred.

In April, 2003, the plaintiffs, the gestational carrier, and the gestational carrier's husband entered into a fifteen-page "Contract Between a Genetic Father, a Genetic Mother, a Gestational Carrier and Her Husband" (gestational carrier agreement). . . . Among other things, the gestational carrier agreement provided that any child resulting from the agreement would be delivered at the hospital, if at all possible, and that in any event the gestational carrier would "take all reasonable steps to give birth to any child carried pursuant to this Agreement at a Hospital located in the State of Massachusetts." It is undisputed that the parties chose Massachusetts as the site of the birth in part to facilitate obtaining a prebirth order. [Plaintiffs' counsel further represented that the gestational carrier's insurance would not cover a delivery at a Connecticut hospital.] The parties' preference for Massachusetts was further expressed in the following choice of law provision:

> "The Gestational Carrier and [her] husband agree that they are entering into this Agreement with the intention that in accordance with the laws of the State of Massachusetts, they will take whatever steps are necessary to have the Genetic Father and the Genetic Mother named as the natural, legal and genetic parents, to have the Genetic Father and the Genetic Mother named as the father and mother, respectively, of [the] child on the child's birth certificate, and to permit the Genetic Father and the Genetic Mother to obtain physical custody of any child born as the result of this Agreement. . . . The parties further agree that this Agreement shall be governed by Massachusetts law."

Approximately six months after the parties entered into the gestational carrier agreement, the gestational carrier was successfully implanted with an embryo produced from the male plaintiff's sperm and the female plaintiff's egg. The implantation took place in Connecticut. The gestational carrier received at least some prenatal care at the hospital. At oral argument on

June 30, 2004, counsel informed the court that an induced delivery was planned at the hospital the following week.

2. *Jurisdiction.* [The court decides that the Probate Court has jurisdiction to grant the relief requested.] [W]e held in Culliton v. Beth Israel Deaconess Med. Ctr., 756 N.E.2d 1133 (Mass. 2001), a Probate Court judge has [statutory] authority to consider a request for a prebirth order where, as here, "(a) the plaintiffs are the sole genetic sources of the [child]; (b) the gestational carrier agrees with the orders sought; (c) no one, including the hospital, has contested the complaint or petition; and (d) by filing the complaint and stipulation for judgment the plaintiffs agree that they have waived any contradictory provisions in the [gestational carrier] contract (assuming those provisions could be enforced in the first place)." That the gestational carrier, her husband, and the plaintiffs all reside outside of Massachusetts does not bar the Probate Court's subject matter jurisdiction . . . , because the equity statute poses no residency requirement.[6]

Second, personal jurisdiction is also proper. The Probate Court, of course, has personal jurisdiction over the hospital, a Massachusetts corporation. Indeed, it is doubtful that any other State could grant the plaintiffs the injunction they seek requiring the hospital to report certain information about the child's parentage to Massachusetts officials. The Probate Court's personal jurisdiction over the gestational carrier and her husband derives from their stipulation for entry of judgment in favor of the plaintiffs. . . .

3. *Choice of law.* The driving issue in this case, rather, concerns choice of law. The interested couples come from different States; the chosen hospital from yet a third. None of the individual parties resides in the Commonwealth, yet they have contracted that Massachusetts law govern the gestational carrier agreement and, by extension, the petition for judgments of parentage and for a prebirth order. We must consider whether to respect their choice.

The gestational carrier agreement implicates the policies of multiple States in important questions of individual safety, health, and general welfare. Complicating matters is the fact that the laws of Connecticut, New York, and Massachusetts, the three States that potentially could govern the agreement, are not in accord. In Connecticut, where the genetic parents reside, gestational carrier agreements are not expressly prohibited by, and perhaps may be contemplated by, the recently amended statute governing the issuance of birth certificates. See Conn. Gen. Stat. c. 93, §7-48a, 2004 Conn. Legis Serv. P.A. 04-255 (West 2004) ("On and after January 1, 2002, each birth certificate shall contain the name of the birth mother, except by the order of a court of competent jurisdiction . . ."). The gestational carrier resides in New York, a State that has expressed a strong public policy against all gestational carrier agreements. See N.Y. Dom. Rel. Law §122 (McKinney 1999) ("Surrogate parenting contracts are hereby declared contrary to the public policy of this state, and are

---

6. No statutory directive limits the court's jurisdiction in actions relating to gestational agreements to Massachusetts residents. Cf. Uniform Parentage Act §802, 9B U.L.A. 363 (Master ed. 2001 & 2004 Supp.) ("A proceeding to validate a gestational agreement may not be maintained unless: the [gestational carrier] or the intended parents have been residents of this State for at least 90 days") and comment (noting that the ninety-day residency requirement is to "discourage forum shopping"). Moreover, the statutory scheme for the recording of births in Massachusetts makes no distinction between resident and nonresident parents. . . .

void and unenforceable").[8] Massachusetts, as we have noted, recognizes gestational carrier agreements in some circumstances. See Culliton v. Beth Israel Deaconess Med. Ctr., supra; R.R. v. M.H., 689 N.E.2d 790 (Mass. 1998).

In light of these differing State policies and the parties' declared intent to follow Massachusetts law, we look to our established "functional" choice of law principles and to the Restatement (Second) of Conflict of Laws, with which those principles generally are in accord. . . . The Restatement . . . presumes that the law the parties have chosen applies,[10] unless "(a) the chosen state has no substantial relationship to the parties or the transaction and there is no other reasonable basis for the parties' choice, or (b) application of the law of the chosen state would be contrary to a fundamental policy of a state which has a materially greater interest than the chosen state" and is the State whose law would apply under §188 of the Restatement "in the absence of an effective choice of law by the parties." Restatement (Second) of Conflict of Laws, supra at §187 (2).

Under the two-tiered analysis of §187 (2), we readily conclude that Massachusetts has a "substantial relationship" to the transaction. See §187 (2) (a). That substantial relationship is anchored in the parties' negotiated agreement for the birth to occur at a Massachusetts hospital and for a Massachusetts birth certificate to issue, and bolstered by the gestational carrier's receipt of prenatal care at a Massachusetts hospital in anticipation of delivery at that hospital. See §187 comment f, supra at 566-567 (place of partial performance considered to be sufficient to establish a reasonable basis for the parties' choice of law).

Turning to the second prong of §187 (2), it is a close question whether applying the parties' choice of law would be "contrary to a fundamental policy" of another State with a "materially greater interest." See §187 (2) (b). Certainly the interests of New York and Connecticut are material and significant, for the contracting parties reside in these States. Nevertheless, the interests of New York and Connecticut may be at cross purposes here. New York, the home of the gestational carrier and her husband, expressly prohibits gestational carrier agreements in order to protect women against exploitation as gestational carriers and to protect the gestational carrier's potential parental rights. See N.Y. Dom. Rel. Law §122.[11] New York has thus expressed a "fundamental policy" on a matter in which it has a great interest. Connecticut, the plaintiffs' home State, is

---

8. Under New York law, a surrogate parenting contract includes an agreement where "a woman agrees . . . to be impregnated with an embryo that is the product of an ovum fertilized with the sperm of a man who is not her husband." N. Y. Dom. Rel. Law §121 (4) (McKinney 1999).

10. R.R. v. M.H., 689 N.E.2d 790 (Mass. 1998), is not to the contrary. That case concerned a surrogacy agreement where the genetic mother (not married to the father) carried the child, was required to consent to the father's custody of the child prior to birth, and was to be paid $10,000 for being a gestational carrier. The gestational carrier was a Massachusetts resident, the child was born in Massachusetts, and the genetic father and his wife were residents of Rhode Island. Although the gestational carrier contract provided that "Rhode Island Law shall govern the interpretation of this agreement," we applied Massachusetts law to invalidate the contract as contrary to Massachusetts public policy as expressed through G. L. c. 210, §11A.

11. Massachusetts also seeks to prevent the exploitation of women by prohibiting gestational carrier agreements that compensate the gestational carrier beyond pregnancy-related expenses. Such agreements "raise the concern that, under financial pressure, a woman will permit her body to be used and her child to be given away." R.R. v. M.H., supra.

silent on the question of gestational carrier agreements, but in any event does not expressly prohibit the plaintiffs from entering into such an arrangement. Massachusetts also has interests here, including interests in "establishing the rights and responsibilities of parents [of children born in Massachusetts] as soon as is practically possible" and "furnishing a measure of stability and protection to children born through such gestational surrogacy arrangements."[12] Culliton v. Beth Israel Deaconess Med. Ctr., supra.

However, even if we were to decide that New York had a "materially greater interest" than both Connecticut and Massachusetts, New York's policy would not operate to overrule the parties' choice of law unless New York would have been the applicable law in the absence of any articulated choice by the parties. [Given uncertainties about the place of contracting and the place of negotiation and Massachusetts's role as the planned place of performance,] whatever New York's interest in protecting the gestational carrier and her husband, it is doubtful that the principles of §188 would result in application of New York law to this particular contact. . . .

We conclude, then, that the [probate] judge should have applied the parties' choice of law, the law of Massachusetts, to resolve the plaintiffs' complaint. Although the judge in her decision prudently raised the issue of forum shopping in declining to consider the complaint, we are satisfied that, in the circumstances of this case, the parties' choice of law, is one we should respect. We are also satisfied that our established conflict of laws analysis will work to prevent misuse of our courts and our laws. . . .

## NOTES AND QUESTIONS ON *EVANS* AND *HODAS*

1. *Regulatory variation.* As *Evans* demonstrates, European nations have taken different approaches to the question of "precommitment strategies versus contemporaneous consent" (explored in Chapter 7, section B). The United Kingdom's detailed statutory approach contrasts with what one finds in most of the United States: judicial resolution as courts face disputes or silence on the issue. The British statute indirectly controls individual conduct in fertility treatment "by exercising direct control over the clinics providing that treatment." Katharine Wright, Competing Interests in Reproduction: The Case of Natallie Evans, 19 King's L.J. 135 (2008).

Parliament enacted the Human Fertilisation and Embryology Act, which has now been amended several times, after the careful study of surrogacy, IVF, and related issues by a commission. See Department of Health & Social Security, Report of the Committee of Inquiry into Human Fertilisation and Embryology (Chairman: Dame Mary Warnock DBE) (Presented to Parliament by Command of Her Majesty, July 1984). *Evans* applied the 1990 version. In this country, a handful of states, e.g., New Jersey and New York, convened commissions to advise on appropriate legislative responses to the issues presented by ARTs. See, e.g., Robert Hanley, Jersey Panel Backs Limits on Unpaid

---

12. While it is true that Massachusetts interests are contingent on the actual birth of a child in the Commonwealth, any order of a Massachusetts court concerning Massachusetts birth records of course will have minimal, if any, significance if the birth occurs outside the Commonwealth. No party argues otherwise.

Surrogacy Pacts, N.Y. Times, Mar. 12, 1989, §1, at 38; Lawrence K. Altman, Health Panel Seeks Sweeping Changes in Fertility Therapy, N.Y. Times, Apr. 29, 1998, at A1. The President's Council on Bioethics has weighed in as well, publishing detailed reports. See, e.g., The President's Council on Bioethics, Reproduction and Responsibility: The Regulation of New Biotechnologies (2004). Although the Uniform Parentage Act and the American Bar Association's proposed model statute provide templates, many states still have not addressed such questions at all. See Unif. Parentage Act (2000, revised 2002), 9B U.L.A. 295 (2001) & 9B U.L.A. 4 (Supp. 2008); American Bar Association Model Act Governing Assisted Reproduction §504 (February 2008), available at http://www.abanet.org/family/committees/artmodelact.pdf.

2. *Conflict of laws issues.* The varied responses to surrogacy and other ARTs among states and foreign countries may draw individuals to the most permissive jurisdictions. Such forum shopping will result in legal questions parallel to those posed at one time or another by out-of-state abortions, so-called "marriage evasion," migratory divorce, and interstate (and international) child custody battles. See Unif. Parentage Act (2000, amended 2002), 9B U.L.A. 57-58 (Supp. 2008) (Prefatory Comment to Art. 8, "Gestational Agreement"). Can residents of states with restrictive laws evade them elsewhere? How should the restrictive states respond? See Susan Frelich Appleton, Surrogacy Arrangements and the Conflict of Laws, 1990 Wis. L. Rev. 399; Anastasia Grammaticaki-Alexiou, Artificial Reproduction Technologies and Conflict of Laws: An Initial Approach, 60 La. L. Rev. 1113 (2000). What good is a law like New York's antisurrogacy statute, in light of *Hodas*?

In disagreeing with a majority of the Ohio supreme court, which ruled that gestational surrogacy arrangements do not violate public policy, one dissenting judge wrote that Ohio will become "an interstate, and perhaps international, marketplace for gestational surrogacy," given the more restrictive approaches in other jurisdictions. J.F. v. D.B., 879 N.E.2d 740, 744 (Ohio 2007) (Cupp, J., dissenting). Is that necessarily a consequence that a state would want to avoid? See Amelia Gentelman, India Nurtures Business of Surrogate Motherhood, N.Y. Times, Mar. 10, 2008, at A9.

Must a state recognize the information on the birth certificate issued by another state? If a woman goes to a permissive state and becomes pregnant there with a donated embryo, how can her home state, even if more restrictive, enforce its laws? Should residency required? For whom? Within the United States, does the constitutional right to travel protect the freedom of those who would participate in assisted reproduction in other states? See generally, e.g., Saenz v. Roe, 526 U.S. 489 (1999).

Birth certificates may determine the child's citizenship. In In re I.L.P., 2009 WL 130279 (Pa. Super. Ct. 2009), a genetic and intended father, a citizen of Taiwan, and his domestic partner, a U.S. citizen, sought to have the gestational carrier's name removed from the birth certificate of twins she bore for the couple, using donor eggs, in Pennsylvania. The couple wanted the twins to have dual Taiwanese-U.S. citizenship. Without negating the parental rights of the carrier, however, the twins' citizenship would follow hers (U.S.), according to the rules followed by the Taiwanese government. The trial court denied the request to change the birth certificate; the superior court remanded with a strong recommendation to reconsider that decision. Why?

3. *Public policy and failed surrogacy agreements.* Would New York's express antisurrogacy policy have received more weight in *Hodas* if all the interested parties did not agree? For example, if the gestational carrier decided not to relinquish the child, would New York's public policy become more important in the resulting dispute? Should it? On what basis does *Hodas* distinguish R.R. v. M.H., discussed in footnote 10? Is it pertinent that *R.R.* concerned an agreement that the "surrogate" refused to perform? (The court held the contract void and unenforceable.)

In In re Paternity and Custody of Baby Boy A., 2007 WL 4304448 (Minn. Ct. App. 2007), a New York man, P.G.M., and his niece, J.M.A., who lived in Minnesota, entered a gestational surrogacy agreement with a clause stating that Illinois law would control. The two subsequently traveled to Illinois, where clinic technicians fertilized an anonymously donated egg with P.G.M.'s sperm and placed the fertilized egg in J.M.A. J.M.A. stayed with P.G.M. in New York for two months during the pregnancy, when their relationship deteriorated and J.M.A. demanded money. After J.M.A. returned to Minnesota and gave birth there, she refused to relinquish the child to P.G.M., who filed a paternity action in Minnesota. Following the choice of law clause and applying Illinois law, which recognizes surrogacy agreements that meet specified conditions, the Minnesota court held the contract enforceable. The court rejected J.M.A.'s argument that the contract violated Minnesota's public policy because Minnesota has no statute or case law prohibiting gestational surrogacy (nor does it have authority expressly supporting it). Should J.M.A. have invoked New York's public policy instead?

4. *A unitary standard?*

a. *The United States.* What are the advantages and disadvantages of the variation among legal approaches? Do ARTs pose problems particularly well suited to local responses? Problems whose solution must emerge from the "'laboratory' of the States" such that experimentation constitutes a valuable asset in the development of the law? See Cruzan v. Director, Missouri Dept. of Health, 497 U.S. 261, 292 (1990) (O'Connor, J., concurring). Alternatively, do ARTs call for a more uniform standard? For example, within the United States, should the federal government establish uniformity, as in the PKPA, 28 U.S.C. §1738A (2008)? See, e.g., Katherine Drabiak et al., Ethics, Law, and Commercial Surrogacy: A Call for Uniformity, 35 J.L. Med. & Ethics 300 (2007). Or, should uniformity emerge through constitutional adjudication, as it did for abortion in Roe v. Wade, 410 U.S. 113 (1973)? Note that any clash between a state's law and a national standard (whether imposed by federal statute or constitutional provision) constitutes a conflict of laws issue.

b. *The European Union.* Just as in the United States where a federal law or a constitutional ruling can trump a state's approach to ARTs (thus imposing a unitary standard), parallel questions arise in the European Union. See Elizabeth Ferrari Morris, Development: Reproductive Tourism and the Role of the European Union, 8 Chi. J. Int'l L. 701 (2008). Illustrating such questions, *Evans* explores whether specific provisions in the Convention for the Protection of Human Rights and Fundamental Freedoms, drawn up by the Council of

Europe and made effective in the United Kingdom by the Human Rights Act of 1998, require departing from the rules spelled out in the United Kingdom's Human Fertilisation and Embryology Act of 1990. To what extent does article 8's "right to respect for . . . private and family life" resemble the constitutional rights to privacy, reproductive autonomy, and family autonomy recognized in the United States? (See Chapter 1, section B2 & Chapter 7, section A.) To what extent does article 14's protection against discrimination resemble the Fourteenth Amendment's Equal Protection Clause? What is the basis of the alleged discrimination in *Evans*: females versus males, those with fertility problems versus those who can reproduce without assistance, or prospective parents who procreate versus those who adopt? See Anne Donchin, Toward a Gender-Sensitive Assisted Reproduction Policy, 23 Bioethics 28 (2009); Wright, supra, at 148-150.

Do you find the *Evans* majority's approach persuasive? Why? To what extent does the "margin of appreciation" invoked in *Evans* reflect a good middle ground, allowing deference to a country or state's own approach, while still leaving room for imposition of an outer limit? For an analysis of *Evans*, including summaries of the decisions of the four different courts, which all ruled against Evans, see Wright, supra.

In a well-publicized earlier controversy in the United Kingdom, at the request of a woman, physicians extracted sperm from her husband while he was comatose and just before he died. Later, she sued the Human Fertilisation and Embryology Authority, which refused to let her use the semen because her late husband had not consented to such use. Although she unsuccessfully argued that she should be able to proceed without consent in the United Kingdom, she also argued that she should be allowed to export the semen to another nation in the European Community (EC), pursuant to §§59-60 of the EC Treaty, provisions which protect the rights of EC citizens to receive treatment in another member state. The British court directed the Authority to reconsider its position in light of these provisions, and the Authority then granted permission to export the semen for treatment in a Belgian fertility clinic, enabling the widow to give birth to two sons. See R. v. Human Fertilisation and Embryology Authority, ex parte Blood, [1997] 2 All E.R. 687 (Ct. of Appeal, Civ. Div.); Jeremy Laurance, Woman Gives Birth to Husband's Baby 30 Months After His Death, The Independent (London), Oct. 4, 2004, News section, at 19 (updating this case and reviewing new case). Should the use of the frozen semen be governed by the United Kingdom's strict requirements or Belgium's more permissive approach?

5. *Subsequent amendments.* The 2008 amendments to the Human Fertilisation and Embryology Act extend the limit on storage of embryos to ten years. Human Fertilisation and Embryology Act of 2008, ch. 22, §15 (U.K.). See Human Fertilisation and Embryology Act 2008: Explanatory Notes 21, available at http://www.opsi.gov.uk/acts/acts2008/en/ukpgaen_20080022_en.pdf. Further, according to explanatory comments, some of the provisions have an intended geographic scope: "[Under section 33 of the amended Act, it] will remain the case that the woman who carries a child following assisted reproduction (*anywhere in the world*) is the child's mother, unless the child is subsequently adopted or parenthood is transferred through a parental order." Id. at 28 (emphasis added). How effective is such language? Would

a Massachusetts court deciding a case like *Hodas* involving a British "gestational carrier" necessarily follow this rule if it conflicted with the procedure for determining parentage prebirth in Massachusetts? See also id]. at 38 (explaining provision for recognition in Northern Ireland of mother's partner as a parent upon entry into domestic partnership in her domicile).

6. *An international market.* Worldwide, 8 to 12 percent of couples experience some infertility. Marcia C. Inhorn, Global Infertility and the Globalization of New Reproductive Technologies: Illustrations from Egypt, 56 Soc. Sci. & Med. 1837, 1839 (2003). Further, significant differences among both regulatory approaches and costs have prompted the rise of worldwide "reproductive tourism." See, e.g., Felicia R. Lee, Driven by Costs, Fertility Clients Head Overseas, N.Y. Times, Jan. 25, 2005, at A1; Debora Spar, Perspective: Reproductive Tourism and the Regulatory Map, 352 New Eng. J. Med. 531 (2005). See also Lynn D. Wardle, Global Perspective on Procreation and Parentage by Assisted Reproduction, 35 Cap. U. L. Rev. 413, 435 (2006) (canvassing laws pertinent to gay and lesbian families and noting the practice of "fertility tourism"). What are the advantages of this development? The disadvantages? What would you recommend among the possible regulatory approaches for the "baby business," a term used to refer to the market for children, via adoption and assisted reproduction, by Debora Spar (formerly a member of the faculty at Harvard Business School and now the President of Barnard College)? Consider the following possibilities that she lists:

DEBORA L. SPAR, THE BABY BUSINESS: HOW MONEY, SCIENCE, AND POLITICS DRIVE THE COMMERCE OF CONCEPTION (2006)

217-221

### The Luxury Model

One possibility would be to treat the acquisition of children like the purchase of fine jewelry. Children are precious, one could argue just like jewels, and acquiring them entails a certain degree of luxury. . . . We could ensure that property rights are well-defined and the legal environment ensures the enforcement of baby-making contracts. We could posit, for example, that the presumption of parenthood rests with the intended parents. . . . And then we could extend this framework to include all forms of assisted reproduction, from IVF to surrogacy, sperm donation and adoption.

Few observers would want to classify any of these transactions as constructing a luxury market. But they effectively function, and could well be regulated, along those lines. Under this approach, access to the market would not be a cause for public concern, nor would equity among the various participants. This is exactly what one would expect in a high-priced luxury market.

### The Cocaine Model

Alternatively, we could think of regulating reproduction as we regulate cocaine or heroin. In other words, we could decide that both assisted reproduction and adoption constitute unnatural interventions in the course of human affairs. We could therefore decide to ban them or push whatever transactions might still occur into an explicitly black market. . . .

## The Kidney Model

A third option would be to treat babies, and the components of babies, the way we treat kidneys. In the United States, as in most industrialized nations, it is explicitly illegal to sell a kidney, a liver, or a heart. Indeed, under the terms of the National Organ Transplant Act (NOTA), it is illegal for any person to "acquire, receive, or otherwise transfer any human organ for valuable consideration." People can donate their organs posthumously. They can even donate kidneys while they're still alive. But they cannot sell their organs, because doing so would constitute a federal crime.

There are several advantages to this kind of regulatory model. First, by removing the organ trade from any vestiges of the commercial market, it eliminates any concerns over commodification of the "sale of human flesh." . . . Second, this regime still allows for organ exchange. . . . A final virtue of the organ donor model is its tilt toward order and safety. Organs are not exchanged in any open market; instead, the transaction is mediated by the nonprofit National Organ Procurement and Transplantation Network in the United States, and by similar organizations abroad. . . .

## The Hip Replacement Model

. . . Hips (like fertility treatments) are expensive, and the need for their replacement is distributed more or less randomly: some people have perfectly fine hips that work for the duration of their lives, but others do not. When hips deteriorate, replacements are rarely critical, because people can live without them. Yet forgoing replacement hips would arguably place those who need them at a distinct and tragic disadvantage: like those who suffer from infertility, they would be forced, through no fault of their own, to live a distinctly less pleasant life. If we left hip replacements to the free market, therefore, the pain of bad hips would be distributed along economic lines. . . .

In most of the industrialized world, however, we have chosen to treat hips quite differently. [W]e treat their provision as some form of a social good. . . . In Europe and Canada, provision comes generally through a state-sponsored system of national health care. In the United States, it comes through a combination of private insurance and government programs such as Medicaid and Medicare. The results in both cases are largely the same: after enduring waits, completing paperwork, and clearing administrative hurdles, most people who need replacement hips get them for free. . . .

### Depictions in Popular Culture: Renée van Oostveen, Have Womb, Will Travel (2008)

This self-indulgent account consists mainly of email exchanges between Renée and Alon in Israel and the gestational surrogate from

Montana, Jennefer, whom they meet on a website. The arrangement takes them to Kiev in the Ukraine for eggs and the embryo transfer. The reader becomes acquainted with all the details—medical, legal, and emotional—that the participants must navigate. Ultimately, after the twins arrive in Montana, as planned, with Renée and Alon by Jennefer's side, the new family departs for Israel.

This book reveals the simultaneous relevance and irrelevance of state and national boundaries in the ARTs era. Although Renée and Alon must comply with various legal requirements imposed by the different jurisdictions connected to their arrangement (so that, for example, they can get passports for the twins for the trip to Israel), the existence of such boundaries appears as a just one of many inconvenient details in this truly transnational effort to create a family. For another international effort to overcome fertility problems that ultimately reach a resolution locally, see Peggy Orenstein, Waiting for Daisy: A Tale of Two Continents, Three Religions, Five Infertility Doctors, an Oscar, an Atomic Bomb, a Romantic Night, and One Woman's Quest to Become a Mother (2007). While the author's unwavering drive to have children pervades *Have Womb*, by contrast *Waiting for Daisy* includes much self-reflection—from a feminist perspective—about the whether to become a parent and at what cost.

## PROBLEMS

1. Samantha, an unmarried attorney, asked her friend Daryl if he would provide semen so that she could conceive a child by artificial insemination. Daryl agreed, Samantha conceived and gave birth to twins, and then a disagreement erupted. Daryl sought recognition as the twins' father, with all parental rights and responsibilities. He sues in Kansas on behalf of himself and the children after Samantha refused to include him in the children's lives. Daryl contends that Samantha assured him he would be the child's father and that he need not put that understanding in writing. The parties do not dispute the following: Both Samantha and Daryl lived in Kansas, but they could not find a local physician who would inseminate an unmarried woman. As a result, the insemination took place in Missouri. Samantha gave birth to the twins in Kansas. Kansas has a statute that says a man who provides semen for artificial insemination is "not the birth father" absent a written agreement with the woman. Missouri has no such statute. The parties never entered any written agreement.

What result and why in Daryl's suit in Kansas? Could Daryl have sued in Missouri? Should he have done so? Why? See In re K.M.H., 169 P.3d 1025, 1030 (Kan. 2007), *cert. denied sub nom.* Hendrix v. Harrington, 129 S. Ct. 36 (2008) (discussed in Chapter 6, section B1).

2. Helen, at her home in England, placed an ad on the internet that she wanted to serve as a "gestational surrogate." Charles and Martha flew Helen to California, where they live and where Helen signed a detailed contract. At a

nearby fertility clinic, technicians placed in Helen three donor eggs fertilized with Charles's sperm. After Helen returned to England and discovered that she was pregnant with twins, Charles and Martha insisted that she use "selective reduction" so that she would give birth to only one baby, pursuant to an explicit term in the contract. Helen refuses; Charles and Martha insist that they want one of the children, but they will not accept two; and Helen (now back in California) thinks they should get neither baby and that she should find other prospective parents for the twins. The parties also disagree over whether such prospective parents should be responsible for Helen's fee and the costs of the IVF and donor eggs. Assume that in England, "surrogates" have full legal rights to the children whom they bear for the first six months; California follows, with some variations, an "intent test" (discussed in Chapter 7, section C1). In California, Helen seeks to relinquish her rights and any belonging to Charles and Martha so that the twins will be available for adoption by others. What result and why? Can the issues be resolved before Helen gives birth or only afterwards? See Chris Taylor, One Baby Too Many; With Twins on the Way, a Surrogate Mom Says She Has Been Abandoned by the Would-Be Parents, Time Magazine, Aug. 27, 2001, at 55.

3. Shannon, a nurse who works in the high-risk obstetrics and delivery department of a major metropolitan hospital, has decided that she wants to serve as a gestational surrogate. She states that her own children, ages seven and nine, and her work have persuaded her of the value of helping adults who cannot procreate without assistance. Her husband supports her interest. She submits an application to a surrogacy "matchmaker" whom she finds online, and after a couple, intended parents who live in another state, select Shannon, the matchmaker — who is a licensed attorney — mails her a contract and encourages Shannon to review the contract with her own attorney before any medical procedures take place. (The couple has several frozen embryos, made from donor eggs and the husband's semen.)

Shannon has made an appointment with you, her local attorney, to review the contract, which you have not yet seen. She has already informed you that, although the contract states that the birth and delivery of the child will take place in the intended parents' home state (which uses intent to determine parentage and issues prebirth judgments of parentage), she wants to deliver in her home state, at the hospital where she works and trusts the obstetrical facilities and staff. Her home state, however, has no statute governing surrogacy and no appellate judicial opinions on the subject. In preparing to meet with Shannon and review the contract, what specific issues will you put on your "check list" to make certain that the contract covers in a way that will avoid possible problems for your client? How would you counsel her more generally about her plan to become a gestational surrogate? See generally Kelly A. Anderson, Certainty in an Uncertain World: The Ethics of Drafting Surrogacy Contracts, 21 Geo. J. Legal Ethics 615 (2008).

# *TABLE OF CASES*

*Italics indicate principal cases.*

# INDEX

Page numbers followed by "n" indicate notes.